Self and Social Regulation

Self and Social Regulation

Social Interaction and the Development of Social Understanding and Executive Functions

EDITED BY

Bryan W. Sokol

Ulrich Müller

Jeremy I. M. Carpendale

Arlene R. Young

Grace Iarocci

OXFORD

UNIVERSITY PRESS

2010

OXFORD
UNIVERSITY PRESS

Oxford University Press, Inc., publishes works that further
Oxford University's objective of excellence
in research, scholarship, and education.

Oxford New York
Auckland Cape Town Dar es Salaam Hong Kong Karachi
Kuala Lumpur Madrid Melbourne Mexico City Nairobi
New Delhi Shanghai Taipei Toronto

With offices in
Argentina Austria Brazil Chile Czech Republic France Greece
Guatemala Hungary Italy Japan Poland Portugal Singapore
South Korea Switzerland Thailand Turkey Ukraine Vietnam

Published by Oxford University Press, Inc.
198 Madison Avenue, New York, New York 10016
www.oup.com

Oxford is a registered trademark of Oxford University Press

Library of Congress Cataloging-in-Publication Data
Self and social regulation : social interaction and the development of
social understanding and executive functions / edited by
Bryan W. Sokol ... [et al.].
p. cm.
ISBN 978-0-19-532769-4
1. Social perception in children.   2. Social interaction in children.
3. Cognition in children.   I. Sokol, Bryan W.
BF723.S6S43 2010
155.4—dc22
2009016325

1 3 5 7 9 8 6 4 2
Printed in the United States of America
on acid-free paper

PREFACE

The impetus for this volume grew out of the many rich ideas that were shared between participants of a small conference at Simon Fraser University, Canada, in the fall of 2004. The three interwoven themes of the conference were children's developing executive functions, social understanding, and social interaction. Much like the intellectual excitement experienced at the conference, the recent surge of scholarly interest in these topics, particularly in developmental quarters, has been hard to contain. The contributions to this volume represent our efforts to pull together (in one contained book) the exciting work that was presented at the conference and continues, well beyond the conference program, in the field today. Trying to narrow down the broad research literatures dealing with these topics, however, has not been easy—even agreeing on a title for the volume proved to be a challenge. The rationale behind choosing the complementary notions of self and social regulation was based on our collective desire, as editors, to capture the narrower "conceptual space" where executive functions, social understanding, and social interaction could be understood to relate to one another. In particular, we needed conceptual categories that could shoulder the heavy load of bridging the more "cognitive" (and neuro-physiological) emphases reflected in the contemporary executive functioning literature with the more "social" interests seen in the "theories-of-mind" tradition, or, what we call here, "social understanding." Recognizing that success at such conceptual reorienting would require more than simply changing our vocabulary, we also decided to offer critical commentary throughout the volume to help readers understand the challenges that contributors to the field now face, particularly regarding the complex role that social interactions play in children's socio-cognitive growth. As an added benefit to this commentary strategy, we felt that our editorial remarks would help simulate the conversational structure and scholarly debate that characterized much of the conference proceedings (and, perhaps, even some of the excitement!). As editors, then, we have intentionally steered away from simply summarizing the content of the book chapters, a task that careful readers naturally do for themselves. Instead, our main goal is to engage our audience—just as presenters at the conference did—by generating critical questions about the topics discussed here and where, we would argue, the field could productively direct its research energies next. If we have been successful at any part of this venture, it is because we have had a lot of help along the way. We owe debts of gratitude to the many volume contributors who, by sharing their rich insights and thoughtful research, have made the task of engaging our readership much easier. Graduate students were also heavily involved throughout this project. We thank them for keeping all of us on our toes! This volume would never have been assembled without the generous advice and encouragement of Catharine Carlin and her colleagues at Oxford University Press. We especially, though, thank them for their patience! Finally, we want to acknowledge the Human Early Learning Partnership (HELP), the Consortium for the Advancement of Child Health (CACH), and Simon Fraser University's Department of Psychology for their generous financial support and guidance in organizing a very successful conference.

CONTENTS

CONTRIBUTORS

James Allen
Department of Psychology
University of Victoria
Victoria, Canada

Dagmar Bernstein
Department of Psychology
Simon Fraser University
Burnaby, Canada

Maximilian B. Bibok
Department of Psychology
Simon Fraser University
Burnaby, Canada

Jacob A. Burack
Department of Educational Psychology
McGill University
Rivieres-des-Prairies Hospital
Montreal, Canada

Gustavo Carlo
Department of Psychology
University of Nebraska-Lincoln
Lincoln, Nebraska

Jeremy I. M. Carpendale
Department of Psychology
Simon Fraser University
Burnaby, Canada

Emma Climie
Department of Psychology
University of Calgary
Calgary, Canada

Tammy Dawkins
Department of Educational Psychology
McGill University
Montreal, Canada

Anthony Steven Dick
Human Neuroscience Laboratory
University of Chicago
Chicago, Illinois

Rosie Ensor
Centre for Family Research
University of Cambridge
Cambridge, United Kingdom

Laura Failows
Department of Psychology
Simon Fraser University
Burnaby, Canada

Charles Fernyhough
Department of Psychology
Durham University
Durham, United Kingdom

Emma Flynn
Department of Psychology
Durham University
Durham, United Kingdom

Mary Gauvain
Department of Psychology
University of California at Riverside
Riverside, California

Gerald F. Giesbrecht
Department of Pediatrics
University of Calgary
Calgary, Canada

Thomas Giritzer
Department of Psychology
University of Salzburg
Salzburg, Austria

Melanie Glenwright
Department of Psychology
University of Manitoba
Manitoba, Canada

Rebecca Goodvin
Department of Psychology
Western Washington University
Bellingham, Washington

Suzanne Hala
Department of Psychology
University of Calgary
Calgary, Canada

Stuart I. Hammond
Department of Psychology
Simon Fraser University
Burnaby, Canada

Maureen Hoskyn
Faculty of Education
Simon Fraser University
Burnaby, Canada

Marianne Hrabok
Department of Psychology
University of Victoria
Victoria, Canada

Snjezana Huerta
Department of Psychology
Arizona State University
Tempe, Arizona

Claire Hughes
Centre for Family Research
University of Cambridge
Cambridge, United Kingdom

Mariëtte Huizinga
Department of Social and Behavioral
  Sciences
University of Amsterdam
Amsterdam, The Netherlands

Grace Iarocci
Department of Psychology
Simon Fraser University
Burnaby, Canada

Kimberly A. Kerns
Department of Psychology
University of Victoria
Victoria, Canada

Daniela Kloo
Department of Psychology
University of Salzburg
Salzburg, Austria

George P. Knight
Department of Psychology
Arizona State University
Tempe, Arizona

Susan H. Landry
Children's Learning Institute
University of Texas-Houston Health
    Science Center
Houston, Texas

Charlie Lewis
Department of Psychology
Lancaster University
Lancaster, United Kingdom

Katerina Maridaki-Kassotaki
Department of Home Economics of
    Ecology
Harokopion University
Athens, Greece

Jack Martin
Department of Psychology
Simon Fraser University
Burnaby, Canada

Meredith McGinley
Department of Psychology
University of Nebraska-Lincoln
Lincoln, Nebraska

Michael R. Miller
Department of Psychology
University of Victoria
Victoria, Canada

Chris Moore
Department of Psychology
Dalhousie University
Halifax, Canada

Louis J. Moses
Department of Psychology
University of Oregon
Eugene, Oregon

Ulrich Müller
Department of Psychology
University of Victoria
Victoria, Canada

Willis F. Overton
Department of Psychology
Temple University
Philadelphia, Pennsylvania

Susan M. Perez
Department of Psychology
University of North Florida
Jacksonville, Florida

Josef Perner
Department of Psychology
University of Salzburg
Salzburg, Austria

Penny Pexman
Department of Psychology
University of Calgary
Calgary, Canada

Scott C. Roesch
Department of Psychology
San Diego State University
San Diego, California

Kristin Rostad
Department of Psychology
University of Calgary
Calgary, Canada

Natalie Russo
Department of Psychology
City College of New York
New York City, New York

Karen E. Smith
Department of Neurology
University of Texas Medical Branch
Galveston, Texas

Bryan W. Sokol
Department of Psychology
Saint Louis University
St. Louis, Missouri

Deniz Tahiroglu
Department of Psychology
University of Oregon
Eugene, Oregon

John Towse
Department of Psychology
Lancaster University
Lancaster, United Kingdom

Arlene R. Young
Department of Psychology
Simon Fraser University
Burnaby, Canada

PART I

Theoretical Perspectives on Self and Social Regulation

STUART I. HAMMOND, MAXIMILIAN B. BIBOK,
AND JEREMY I. M. CARPENDALE

There is growing convergence in research on the development of children's problem-solving skills (i.e., cognitive development) and their ability to understand the minds of others (i.e., social cognitive development). Furthermore, recent research suggests that children's social experiences may directly influence both their cognitive and social cognitive development. Research on social cognitive development, often referred to as "theory of mind," has focused on the development of preschoolers' understanding that people may hold beliefs that can be false. Research on the development of children's problem-solving skills has conceptualized such abilities in terms of executive functions (EFs): "the psychological processes involved in the conscious control of thought and action" (Zelazo & Müller, 2002, p. 445). The finding that children's development in these two domains tends to be highly correlated has resulted in much theoretical discussion regarding the nature of this relation. In addition, there is now considerable evidence that various aspects of children's social experience are predictive of their cognitive and social cognitive development, in particular, their false belief understanding. Beyond the relations between (a) social understanding and EFs, and (b) social interaction and social understanding, a third relation suggests itself in a potential link between (c) EFs and social interaction. Although much of the research on EF is grounded in neuropsychological accounts asserting that development results from neural maturation, recent research is beginning to suggest that social interaction may also play a causal role in the development of EFs. It is this newly emerging relation in research, between social interaction and the two domains of cognitive and social cognitive development, which is the motivation for the current volume. This first part focuses on theoretical issues concerning these topics, including how best to define and conceptualize EFs and social understanding, and understand their relation and development, as well as attempt to square conceptual issues with emerging research.

The thesis that social interaction and the development of EFs may be indissociable is consistent with arguments raised in different ways by the authors of the chapters in the first part of the book. Dick and Overton analyze the concept of EF from the perspective of split and relational meta-theories. They argue that split meta-theories stipulate an a priori conceptual separation between mind and body when attempting to understand human functioning, and that one side of the "split" is privileged. In the context of understanding the development of EFs, research programs conceptually situated within such split meta-theories emphasize the brain as the causal factor of sole importance. In other words, the psychological processes involved in the control of thought and action are assumed to have their developmental origin primarily within neurological functioning. Dick and Overton, in contrast, argue against such reductionism, and the temptation to see the development of EFs as primarily the result of biological maturation and neurological factors. They argue instead in favor of a *relational* position, in which they conceive of EFs as emerging from the interplay of biological, cultural, and social factors that are inherently nonreducible to one another. If social factors are to be given equal treatment as biological factors in accounts of EFs, then EFs cannot be defined solely as the product of brain maturation.

The analysis of definitions of EFs is continued by Martin and Failows who argue that what theoretically underlies neurological accounts of EFs is a commitment to *psychologism*: the reduction of actions and behaviors to mental (or neural) processes. The development of action is assumed to originate solely in the mind/brain and the influence of other factors, such as society, is a priori dismissed as inconsequential. Both Dick and Overton, and Martin and Failows, see relational approaches as an alternative to reductionism. These chapters represent a promising start to conceptualizing the role of social experience in EFs and social understanding. At the same time, they should not be understood as proposing an alternate configuration of split meta-theory, whereby society dominates the individual. Their approaches are holistic, rather than reductionistic, and would admit a role for not only brain processes, but also for conscious thought, and society in developmental accounts of EF. This approach is to look at EFs from the perspective of the person acting in the world: action is indelibly biological, psychological, and social. That is, when viewed from a relational perspective, EFs are adaptive behaviors performed by individuals with respect to their environments, and these behaviors are determined by biological, psychological, and social factors.

Fernyhough contributes to the argument advanced by many of the authors of the chapters in this part, in that he argues that EFs (at least those EFs mediated by language) originate in social interaction. Fernyhough's view of EFs offers a concrete illustration of the relational approach. Drawing on the work of Luria and Vygotsky, Fernyhough points out that the idea of EFs was originally formulated in terms of a relational theory. Luria, a pioneer of EF research, was adamant that "higher mental functions are complex, organized functional systems that are social in origin" (Luria, 1966, p. 34). Fernyhough takes this position in his discussion of the genesis of higher mental functions from rudimentary forms of prelinguistic capacities (elementary functions), which implies a biological foundation for EFs. Fernyhough reiterates problems with reductionism, suggesting instead that EFs occur through relations of brain, person, and society in activity. EFs, according to Fernyhough, are mediated by both neural activity and thought-as-language in a sociocultural context. One outcome of this view is that conceptual barriers between what traditionally has been perceived of as two separate psychological abilities, EF and social understanding, are dissolved. The same developmental processes mediate both abilities, though both are oriented toward different aspects of the social environment. EFs are higher thought processes directed toward objects and rules, whereas social understanding is directed toward people. A consequence of this view, as Fernyhough anticipates, is that the developmental trajectory of the developing brain may be a function of the social and physical environments in which a person interacts with persons and objects.

Lewis, Carpendale, Towse, and Maridaki-Kassotaki analyze the links between EFs and social understanding by first reconsidering whether these abilities represent separable, coherent domains, in which children's abilities are stable and measurable. They point out variability in children's performance across both series of tasks, as well as slight changes in task procedures and forms of interaction with the experimenter. This evidence suggests that EFs and social understanding are interdependent and develop gradually within the same processes of children's interaction with their physical and social world.

Burack, Russo, and Dawkins also further discuss such variability in action involving EFs. They use sports as an example in order to illustrate the variable use of EFs in real life, so as to help shift our attention from the simple attainment of EFs (i.e., as tested in the lab) to the variable use of such skills across differing situations. In real-world situations social and emotional dynamics alter our ability to solve problems. Our ability to follow, and manage, rules is a function of these dynamics. If we think of EFs as rule-following, we must consider the nature of rules and rule-following. The sociologist Durkheim also thought that social life was structured by rules, and argued that rules originated in society, external to the individual. Yet, Durkheim encountered a problem: "[s]ince each rule is a general prescription, it cannot be applied exactly and mechanically in identical ways in each particular circumstance. It is up to the person to see how it applies in a given situation" (Durkheim, 1961, p. 23). Durkheim encountered, and never really solved, the need to reconcile the social origin of rules with their conscious application. Piaget argued that Durkheim's conception of rules was authoritarian as it held that rules were external to the individual, therefore necessitating a source of authority to enforce individual's compliance with such rules. For Durkheim, "what there is in the conception of rules beyond the notion of regularity [is] *the idea of authority*" (Durkheim, 1961, p. 29). In contrast, Piaget stressed an alternate, democratic approach to social rules (Vidal, 1998). Piaget found that children form rules (e.g., for a game of marbles) in particular forms of social interaction, and that children can negotiate these rules, reinterpret them, and change them (Piaget, 1932/1965). These rules are renegotiated (though perhaps parts of them are conserved across interactions) in every interaction. Burack et al.'s approach to EF could be understood in either light, with individuals attempting to follow rules created by others (Durkheimian), or negotiating rules in interaction (Piagetian).

An outcome of the views of EF proposed by the authors in this part, when considered collectively, is that the developmental trajectory of the developing brain may be a function of the social and physical environments in which a person interacts with persons and objects. Hrabok and Kerns take a neurological perspective on EF, exploring the relations between behavior and brain structures, and review research on the localization of functions related to self-regulation. In their view, no clear distinction can be found within the brain between strictly cognitive and strictly social areas. In particular, the extent of neurological plasticity observed in recent research suggests that brain development is a dynamic interactive process, with bidirectional relations between experience and neurological development. That is, brain systems are shaped by children's social experience and such neurological systems may also make further forms of social interaction possible. This bidirectional influence among causal factors necessitates that the development of persons' cognitive and social cognitive abilities be recognized as having both biological and social dimensions. Luria, Vygotsky, and Piaget recognized that the importance of social interaction requires that developmental psychology be viewed as both "a branch of sociology, concerned with the study of the socialization of the individual [and] at the same time as a branch of psychology itself" (Piaget, 1995, p. 36).

Hoskyn reviews the working memory component of EFs from both constructive perspectives and information-processing perspectives, and argues that from either perspective working memory is acknowledged as important for processes involved in interacting with others. Furthermore, parental scaffolding may support the development of children's working memory by breaking actions into appropriate sized chunks, as well as by offering cues and prompts to provide motivation. Within such scaffolded interactions, children are enabled to develop strategies to control their attention and improve their working memory. Given the chapters by Dick and Overton, and Martin and Failows, questions arise regarding Hoskyn's review of the literature on working memory: (a) to what extent does such work reflect a split approach, and (b) to what extent does it imply psychologism? In contrast, scaffolding demonstrates a relational approach where processing occurs within social interaction.

If the origin of EFs is not to be sought solely within the individual, what conceptualization would best serve to integrate both social and biological factors without reduction to the other? What the chapters in this part illustrate is a dynamic relation between EFs and social factors and their systematic interconnectedness. Perhaps, then, instead of conceptualizing EFs as developing, which places emphasis on EFs, per se, EFs should be seen to be the outcome or consequence of a developing system jointly composed of individuals and their environments. That is, EFs, as adaptations to social environments, cannot be reduced to either biological or social factors, but represent an abstraction of children's behavioral adaptations to social environments. It may be more theoretically profitable, therefore, to view EFs as behavioral rather than psychological or biological in nature, as suggested by both Dick and Overton, and Martin and Failows.

By thinking of cognitive development in the light of concepts drawn from evolutionary theory of variation and selection, EFs can be defined as responses to the social environment. Thus, the social environment defines the behavioral functional abilities that definitionally are called EFs, but does not constitute EFs ontologically—they are not interiorized interactions. Such an evolutionary perspective (in an ontogenetic, not phylogenetic, sense) would find support in the arguments by both Martin and Failows, and Dick and Overton, that EFs are above all else, descriptions of the behavior of person within their sociocultural and sociohistorical contexts. That is, EFs, or persons' activities that are criterial for the ascription of EFs, manifest themselves in persons' activities. Such activities, however, must be accompanied by both neurological and psychological changes, as discussed by Hrabok and Kerns; this does not entail, as Dick and Overton point out, that such neurological and psychological changes will correspond to those abilities in a one-to-one relationship. As a result, the development of children's EFs through social interaction is in large part evolutionary from the point of view of the psychological system under development and the responses it produces. This view, in turn, is consistent with both Dick and Overton and Martin and Failows that rather than viewing psychological development from the meta-theoretical perspective of a Cartesian split between mind and world, that emphasis be placed instead on interactional systems.

REFERENCES

Durkheim, E. (1961). *Moral education* (E. K. Wilson & H. Schnurer, Trans.). New York: Free Press. (Original work published 1925)

Luria, A. R. (1966). *Higher cortical functions in man*. New York: Basic Books.

Piaget, J. (1965). *The moral judgment of the child*. New York: The Free Press. (Original work published 1932)

Piaget, J. (1995). *Sociological studies* (L. Smith, Trans.). New York: Routledge. (Original work published1965)

Vidal, F. (1998). Immanence, affectivité et démocratie dans *Le jugement moral chez l'enfant* [Immanence, affectivity and democracy in *The moral judgment of the child*]. *Bulletin de Psychologie, 51*, 585–597.

Zelazo, P. D., & Müller, U. (2002). Executive function in typical and atypical development. In U. Goswami (Ed.), *Blackwell handbook of childhood cognitive development* (pp. 445–469). Malden, MA: Blackwell Publishers.

1

Executive Function: Description and Explanation

ANTHONY STEVEN DICK AND WILLIS F. OVERTON

The concept of "executive function," which has broadly referred to the psychological processes involved in the conscious control of action and thought (Anderson, 1998; Zelazo & Müller, 2002), has come to occupy a central place in the study of cognition and cognitive development. However, while adequate as an initial working definition, this understanding is vague and imprecise. At this point in its history "executive function" requires some conceptual analysis and clarification if it is to continue to operate as a fruitful framework for empirical research projects. While virtually every paper published on the topic of executive function presents some form of definition, both historical and contemporary attempts to detail a precise understanding of the concept have been seriously flawed by its vagueness and the ambiguity that this vagueness fosters. This ambiguity arises primarily through the fact that proposed definitions conflate several alternative possible uses of the concept. Specifically, the use of the concept as a description has been conflated with its use as an explanation, and its use as an explanation has conflated several levels of explanation, especially biological and psychological levels. In many cases this conflating of uses is not recognized, although there are exceptions (e.g., for exceptions, see Rabbitt, 1997; Stuss, 1992; Welsh, Pennington, & Grossier, 1991; Zelazo, Carter, Reznick, & Frye, 1997). The ambiguity generated by these conflations ultimately impacts the empirical methods, findings, and conclusions of research on executive function. Our initial task then is to more precisely clarify and disentangle the nature of these conflating meanings.

Explanation begins with description, which operates at the behavioral level of analysis. Here, inquiry focuses on details of cognitive task performance.

Behavioral descriptions are obviously necessary, but their primary function is to serve as vehicles for making inferences about underlying structures and processes. Confusion begins when behavioral descriptions fuse with psychological explanations. Thus, for example, common executive function measures such as the Stroop task (Stroop, 1935) and the Wisconsin Card Sort Test (WCST; Berg, 1948) often are presented as explanatory "measures of cognitive flexibility" without evidence for such flexibility beyond performance on the task itself. This practice is most commonly found in approaches that define executive function as a list of component functions (see, e.g., Bennetto & Pennington, 2003; Levin et al., 1991; Lezak, 1995; Pennington & Ozonoff, 1996; Shute & Huertas, 1990; Stuss & Benson, 1986; Tranel, Anderson, & Benton, 1994).

Legitimate psychological explanations of cognitive phenomena are found not at the behavioral but at the psychological level of analysis. At this latter level, the focus is on inferences drawn concerning the mental organization, structures, or processes that account for the conscious control of action and thought. Behavioral description constitutes the ground from which these inferences are drawn, but behavioral descriptions are themselves not explanations. The movement from description to explanation occurs when structures or processes are inferred and these inferences yield differential predictions that move significantly beyond currently observed behaviors.

Biology represents a second level of analysis that generates explanations. Here, the focus is on biological correlates of task performance. The biological approach is generally undertaken with the assumption that these correlates represent necessary or necessary and sufficient conditions for the mental structures. This level becomes reductionistic, and reductionism becomes problematic, when psychological events are understood *as nothing but* neurological events (Miller, 1996; Searle, 1992), or when biological explanations are presented as replacements for psychological explanations (Miller & Keller, 2000). In the executive function literature, executive function defined as the functions of the prefrontal cortex illustrates a reductionism when these functions are presented as necessary and sufficient causal conditions for task performance. Establishing the neurophysiological organization necessary for cognitive functioning is an essential part of the explanatory process, but a necessary biological condition, in and of itself, provides little information about the psychological meaning of the constructs under investigation (for similar discussions, see Pennington & Ozonoff, 1996; Stuss, Eskes, & Foster, 1994; Tranel et al., 1994).

The present essay critically examines several contemporary approaches to the development of executive function as they operate as behavioral descriptions and as biological or psychological explanations. Here, we explore executive function from a relational perspective (Overton, 2006) emphasizing that description and multiple explanatory levels of analysis are fundamental features of a complete understanding and explanation of this field of enquiry. Within a relational approach, analyses at different levels of explanation are complementary. Thus, any complete explanation may entail all levels—including, for example, a level not discussed further in this paper, the cultural level—but no level represents a competing alternative to other levels.

Within this relational context, we will examine contemporary research on executive function. We will highlight the conceptual confusions that operate in this arena, and we will offer clarifications that will hopefully be helpful in advancing scientific knowledge. In the following, we first outline a general relational approach to research questions. Within this context we then explore the advantages that accrue to executive function research by clearly identifying the operation of complementary levels of analysis. And we conclude with suggestions uniting the levels into an integrated system of explanation.

Split and Relational Metatheories

Metatheoretical assumptions are a constitutive feature of any field of enquiry. These often silent background assumptions form the defining context within which theoretical and methodological concepts are formulated. Accordingly, metatheory determines the meaningfulness/acceptability or meaninglessness/nonacceptability of any substantive scientific concept. This effect includes the formulation of descriptive and explanatory concepts that guide the research agenda. Two broad metatheoretical approaches have been termed the "split" and the "relational" (Overton, 2003, 2006). Split and relational metatheories order the world in different ways; split metatheory orders the world as aggregates of additive elements, while relational metatheory orders the world as systems of dynamic changing part-whole relations.

SPLIT METATHEORY

This perspective originated in the Cartesian thesis that subject and object (mind and body) constitute two pure and, hence, independent forms—thus being split from each other—and the further thesis that beyond the flux of the manifest world of appearance could be found a rock bottom base or "foundation" of reality, hence a "foundationalism." The consequence of these theses is that the world becomes dichotomized, with one member of the dichotomous pair being elevated to a privileged position while the other is marginalized and treated as mere appearance (e.g., the antinomies such as subject-object, mind-body, and nature-nurture). This is, in fact, the framework for a reductionistic approach to enquiry, whereby the concepts of one domain are defined in terms of another domain so that the meaning of one domain is completely captured by the other, with the result that the reduced term becomes unnecessary (i.e., mere appearance; Miller & Keller, 2000). Of central relevance to definitions of executive function are attempts to reduce psychological definitions to biological definitions—that is, to redefine psychological definitions of executive function in terms of the functions of specific brain regions. This reductionism is often implicit, as when investigators use terms such as "underlie" to describe the relation between biology and psychology. The implication here is that the biological explanation is foundationally more basic.

RELATIONAL METATHEORY

This perspective rejects the Cartesian theses of pure forms, splitting, and rock bottom foundations. A relational perspective casts all explanations, including the biological and the psychological, as a set of differentiated but indissociable complementarities. The challenge for relational metatheory is to demonstrate how such seemingly disparate explanatory frames can, in fact, be integrated as indissociable complementarities, while at the same time maintaining their individual identities.

The relational approach is above all else a commitment to *holism*. As distinct from elements (pure forms) and the addition of elements into aggregates of the split metatheory, the relational approach represents the basic units of analysis as parts of a dynamic functioning system. Part-whole analyses rather than atomistic reductionism constitute the broad methodological center of this metatheory. The identity of any event or object of enquiry is the consequent of the relational context or system of parts in which it is embedded (for an extended discussion, see Overton, 2006; Overton & Ennis, 2006). Each part of the system both defines and is defined by the others and by its relation to the whole. Given this commitment to holism there are three subsidiary principles that constitute the operational methodology of relationism.

1. *The identity of opposites*: While we generally picture the world according to the Aristotelean law of identity (A cannot equal not A), within a relational perspective a first moment of analysis entails changing orientation and picturing the world according to a dialectical logic in which the law of identity is replaced with an identity of opposites (A equals not A). Within this moment of analysis pure forms cease to operate, and categories flow into each other. The most

vivid examples of how this moment of analysis functions come from various perceptual "illusions." For example, in the famous sketch by M.C. Escher titled "Drawing Hands" the sketch of a left and a right hand assume a relational posture according to which each is simultaneously drawing and being drawn by the other. Each hand is identical with the other in the sense of each drawing and each being drawn (identity). At the same time each hand preserves its own identity in the sense of there being a left and a right hand (opposites).

Within the framework of this principle, traditional polar opposites (e.g., mind-body, subject-object, and nature-nurture) are transformed into indissociable complementarities, and questions of causality are simultaneously transformed into reciprocal interpenetrating determinates. The most immediate implication here for present purposes is that, to paraphrase John Searle (1992), the fact that a behavior is biologically determined does not imply that it is not psychologically determined, and, the fact that it is psychologically determined does not imply that it is not biologically determined. The relational principle of the identity of opposites establishes the metatheoretical position that biology and psyche, like culture and psyche, operate in a truly *interpenetrating* manner, and not as a conventional interaction of elements of each.

2. *The opposites of identity.* Suspending the law of identity establishes the interpenetration of causal forces across various explanatory levels—biological, cultural, psychological. However, reasserting this law in a second moment of analysis is necessary both to avoid a complete relativism and to establish relatively stable bases or *standpoints* for inquiry. This is the moment at which precision and clear distinctions become figure over the dialectical background. At this moment the focus switches back to the oppositional quality of the relational pair; the identity fades to background, the opposite or differentiating qualities become figure. Despite the identity of the two, there are differences; the left hand of the Escher sketch *is* the left hand and *not* the right, and one may examine the whole from either the standpoint of the left hand or the standpoint of the right. Each standpoint will present a different, but interrelated, perspective on the same whole. Another example is that of two people standing at opposite sides of a room. Each has a view of the whole room, but each sees the room differently as well. Truth lies in the coordination of their perspective and not in denying one or the other view. In a similar fashion, despite their identities, biological explanation is biological explanation and not psychological, and one may examine executive function from either the biological explanatory standpoint or the psychological explanatory standpoint without privileging either. Adequate explanation resides in the coordination of these explanations, not in the reduction of one to the other.

3. *The synthesis of wholes.* This principle is fundamentally a reminder that for any relational pair there is invariably a third member that serves to coordinate the two. Thus, for example, when biological and psychological explanations are understood relationally, it is the social world or culture that joins these two. It is only in the context of culture that we have biological and psychological explanation. In a similar fashion cultural explanation and psychological explanation are coordinated by biology, while the psychological perspective coordinates biological and cultural explanations. The impact of this principle is recognition that the complete explanation of any phenomenon, including executive function, entails the coordination of multiple perspectives—or here "levels" of analysis—and not the reduction of the many to a single standpoint. In the following we consider executive function in the context of three standpoints—the behavioral, the biological, and the psychological.

Approaches to Defining Executive Function: Behavioral Description

With the principles of a relational metatheory as background, we can now examine common approaches to defining executive function and attempt to differentiate and order behavioral description and explanation on the one hand and psychological explanation and biological explanation on the other. Our first step, then, will be to elaborate the issue of the conflation of description and explanation, by exploring descriptive definitions of executive function.

A common definition of executive function entails a list of higher-order component functions required to control and coordinate performance on complex problem-solving tasks. For example, in a recent review, Bennetto and Pennington (2003) describe executive function as a range of skills including organization, planning, working memory, inhibiting inappropriate responses, and switching flexibly from one task or strategy to another. Similarly, Pennington and Ozonoff (1996) offer the functions of set shifting or cognitive flexibility, planning, working memory, contextual memory, inhibition, and fluency. Other functions that appear in such lists include anticipation, goal establishment, performance monitoring, set maintenance and evaluation, impulse control, and judgment and decision-making (Levin et al., 1991; Lezak, 1993, 1995; Shute & Huertas, 1990; Stuss & Benson, 1986; Tranel et al., 1994).

It is only rarely acknowledged that many of these "functions" (e.g., planning, inhibition, decision-making, etc.) are, in fact, descriptions of behavioral outcomes and not explanations. For example, consider a recent explanation of the 3-year-old's difficulty on problem-solving tasks involving conditions of conflict. Often in these tasks, children perseverate (i.e., get stuck) on an irrelevant task rule or method of responding. As an explanation for this perseveration, Diamond, Kirkham, and colleagues (Diamond & Kirkham, 2005; Kirkham, Cruess, & Diamond, 2003) point to the child's problem with "Attentional Inertia." That is, the authors argue that "children of 3 years have difficulty inhibiting their focus on the first aspect of a stimulus … that was relevant for their behavior …" (Kirkham et al., 2003, p. 451). This essentially describes the problem (i.e., young children have difficulty shifting), but it is not clear how this could serve to predict performance on other tasks involving conflict, or how the older child or adult is able to overcome this "Attentional Inertia." A development of the ability to inhibit has been presented as an explanation (Kirkham et al., 2003), but this suffers from many of the same problems. That is, the behavioral outcome—the older child or adult's inhibition, or suppression, of the irrelevant aspect of the task—is presented as an explanation for success. This explanation, though, is viciously circular and unfalsifiable. One is hard pressed to imagine a situation that could possibly refute the stated explanation that the young child fails to inhibit because they lack the ability to inhibit.

In addition to the list component "inhibition," many other list components masquerade as explanatory concepts. In exploring executive function, investigators have attempted to distill components by grouping tasks that prima facie make similar cognitive demands. They have then used statistical tools, such as factor or principal components analysis, in an attempt to isolate latent variables. Arguably, the use (or rather misuse) of these statistical tools has exacerbated the tendency to map behavioral descriptions to explanations. The primary mistake that many investigators make lies in the assumption that the isolation and labeling of latent variables, in and of itself, provides an explanation (for a similar criticism, see Zelazo & Müller, 2002).

A brief review of this approach illustrates the problem. In one developmental study, Welsh and colleagues (1991) examined associations among a number of common executive function tasks, including the Wisconsin Card Sort Test (WCST; Berg, 1948) and two versions of the Tower of Hanoi (ToH; Simon, 1975). A principal components analysis revealed three dissociable factors across eight tasks. Most studies that have used factor analysis to assess executive function are consistent with Welsh and colleagues and report multiple components (e.g., Brookshire, Levin, Song, & Zhang, 2004; Carlson & Moses, 2001; Hughes, 1998; Levin et al., 1991, 1996; Mariani & Barkley, 1997; Miyake et al., 2000; Pennington, 1997; Shute & Huertes, 1990; Welsh et al., 1991).

Observation of more than one factor implies a differentiation of cognitive components (Greve, Ingram, & Bianchini, 1998), supporting the intuitive differences among these tasks and the idea of dissociable, separable functions.

However, two problems significantly handicap the ability of the latent variable approach as a method of providing explanatory concepts. First, when multiple factors are reported, there is inconsistency in the number of reported components, and in the way in which tasks load on multiple factors. Many studies find three-factor models (Levin et al., 1991; Miyake et al., 2000; Patton, Stanford, & Barratt, 1995; Pennington, 1997; Spinella, 2005; Welsh et al., 1991), but some analyses return four-factor (Mariani & Barkley, 1997; Shute & Huertes, 1990) and five-factor models (Amieva, Phillips, & Della Sala, 2003; Brookshire et al., 2004; Levin et al., 1996; Pineda & Merchan, 2003).

Two clear sources of the differences in the number of reported factors are the selection of tasks with which to measure executive function, and the selection of the population that performs the tasks (e.g., normal vs. clinical vs. children vs. elderly). The use of different tasks should be expected to result in different factor structures, and differing populations surely add variation. However, although many of these studies use similar tasks and sample from the same populations, the same tasks have loaded on different factors across studies. For example, the WCST and Tower tasks have loaded on the same (Brookshire et al., 2004) and separate factors (e.g., Levin et al., 1991, 1996; Welsh et al., 1991). To be fair, these tasks likely require multiple cognitive functions (e.g., the WCST; Barcelo & Knight, 2002). In addition, as executive functions are higher-level control functions, tasks designed to assess them are often confounded with what would seem on the face of it to be nonexecutive processes, which makes them susceptible to a high degree of task impurity (Friedman et al., 2006). It is thus often difficult to determine whether a task or set of tasks assesses a single executive component, or the interaction of several subcomponents. In defining executive processes, we must also consider how cognitive processes that might be considered nonexecutive (e.g., long-term memory) interact with executive processes.

If we were to solve these problems, a second obstacle, that of interpretation of the statistical output, still severely handicaps the latent variables approach. Despite considerable investigation, there has been no clear agreement about how to understand the factors discovered via these analyses. Even if we consider only factor studies that have used the WCST, we find that this task has loaded on factors diversely labeled Impulse Control (Welsh et al., 1991), Shifting (Miyake et al., 2000; Pennington, 1997), Perseveration/Disinhibition (Levin et al., 1991), Conceptual Productivity (Levin et al., 1996), Problem Solving (Brookshire et al., 2004), Organization and Flexibility (Pineda & Merchan, 2003), and Executive Memory (Burgess, Alderman, Evans, Emslie, & Wilson, 1998). Scoring of the WCST itself results in multiple outcome variables, such as perseverative errors, categories achieved, and maintenance of set. These subscores of the WCST have loaded on both a single factor (Bowden et al., 1998) and separate factors (Greve, Stickle, Love, Bianchini, & Stanford, 2005; Kizilbash & Donders, 1999). Inconsistency here reveals some of the difficulties with this approach to understanding executive function.

The problems of making psychological interpretations based on the analysis of latent variables are not new. Consider, for example, the debate surrounding the meaning of the "Big-Five" latent personality variables in the personality psychology literature (Block, 1995a, 1995b). A fundamental criticism that arises in this literature is the fact that "factor analysis by itself cannot be empowered to make paramount and controlling decisions regarding the concepts to be used in the field ..." (Block, 1995a, p. 209). The lesson to be learned in the executive function literature is this: we might be comfortable with asserting that latent variable analyses have broadly supported the understanding of executive function as a set of separable, but still associated, components (Friedman & Miyake, 2004; Miyake et al., 2000; Stuss & Alexander, 2000; Teuber, 1972), but latent variable analyses tell us nothing about the nature of these components. To assume that latent variable analyses directly generate psychological explanations is to conflate levels of analysis.

The conflation of description and explanation is an ever present danger to any list approach to the definition of executive function. Although lists facilitate the focusing of research questions and grouping of seemingly similar experimental tasks, their utility is limited to the taxonomy of task demands. Rabbitt (1997) has articulated the conclusions of several investigators (Parkin, 1998; Pennington & Ozonoff, 1996; Reitan & Wolfson, 1994; Stuss et al., 1994; Tranel et al., 1994) that executive function lists are handicapped by their descriptive, rather than explanatory, nature.

> When these criteria are listed together it becomes clear that they all describe the *outcomes*, but not the *functional aetiology* of the cognitive activities that we hope to understand. They are consensus descriptions ... Such descriptions are intuitively appealing, and even illuminate our subjective experience, but are untrustworthy guides as to how to investigate function. (Rabbitt, 1997, p. 7)

Lists fail as explanation because they entail behavioral descriptions of the outcomes of cognitive processes, not the processes themselves. It is likely that many list components (e.g., planning, inhibition, and cognitive flexibility) represent emergent functions of interactions among specialized psychological and/or biological subsystems (Robbins, 1996). That said, a list approach is a useful point of departure, but does not, in and of itself, constitute explanation.

EXPLANATION

If component lists function as descriptive summary statements, what constitutes the movement from this arena to the arena of explanation? Here a brief conceptual orientation to the changing nature of scientific explanation is needed. From the metatheoretical split position, which framed an earlier neo-positivistic methodology, scientific explanation was narrowly identified with issues of contingent causality (i.e., a search for causal antecedents and only causal antecedents). These causal antecedents were classically defined as efficient and material causes and/or necessary and sufficient antecedent conditions of the phenomenon of enquiry. With the demise of neo-positivism and the rise of an increasingly relational methodology (Overton, 2006), the articulation of dynamic patterns, systems, or processes that underlie the phenomenon of enquiry has come to be recognized as a feature of any scientific explanation that is as fundamental as, and logically prior to, the discovery of contingent causes (Bunge, 1962, 2004; Cartwright, 1980; Hanson, 1958; Kitcher, 1981; Laudan, 1996; Overton & Reese, 1981; Putnam, 1983; Toulmin, 1953).

Hanson (1958) describes the relational quality of this approach to explanation in a discussion of Galileo's approach to the law of falling bodies.

> He [Galileo] seeks not a descriptive formula; nor does he seek to predict observations of freely falling bodies. He already has a formula ... He seeks more: an *explanation* of these data. They must be intelligibly systematized ... He has no confidence in observations which cannot be explained theoretically. Galileo was not seeking the cause of the acceleration; that was Descartes' program. Galileo wished only to understand. His law of constant acceleration (1632) is not a causal law. (p. 37)

Pattern or system explanation entails the discovery and specification of both *formal* (i.e., the dynamic form or organization of a phenomenon) and *final* (the direction of change of the phenomenon across time) patterns that systematize the phenomenon of interest. Each of these pattern explanations constitutes a principle of intelligibility (Randall, 1960; Taylor, 1995), rather than a cause. That is, each establishes the (immediate and temporal) meaning of the object of study and offers an intelligible context within which further empirical investigation proceeds. Formal principles establish order, constancy, and coherence of an activity at particular points in time, while final principles do the same across temporal sequences. This distinction is especially important for developmental theories as final principles are explanations of why development occurs (i.e., movement toward a specified end), and formal principles are explanations of what develops.

A further contrast between dynamic pattern explanation and casual explanation is that pattern principles are arrived at and assessed through an abductive or retroductive process, while causal determinants are inductive in origin. In fact, causal explanation can proceed only within the intelligible context provided by pattern explanation. Examples of both formal and final pattern explanations can be found in the natural sciences (e.g., the structure of the atom, the structure of DNA, and the structure of the universe), and in the biological and psychological sciences (e.g., the biological structure of consciousness: Edelman & Tononi, 2000; reasoning and decision-making: Damasio, 1994; conceptual and cognitive development: Case, 1985; Piaget, 1952; Werner, 1957, 1958). In these and all other pattern explanations a model (system) is initially proposed to account for the activity of interest. The model is empirically assessed through observations of the fit between the model and data sets that extend beyond that data set that formed the basis for the original pattern inferences. To the extent that the novel data sets are consistent with the model, the pattern explanation is supported. Extending the scope (novel data sets) as well as assessing the precision of the model strengthens the claims of the model as a rich, powerful, and valid explanation. Failure to observe a fit between model and data sets weakens support for the model and may lead to its modification or abandonment.

With this orientation to explanation in contemporary scientific thinking as background we may now turn to the explanation of executive function at both the biological and psychological levels of analysis. Before making this turn, however, we need to note that with the introduction of pattern or system explanation a sharp dividing line between description and explanation begins to fade. If pattern explanations are inferences designed to give meaning to the phenomena under investigation, would not component lists be both descriptive and explanatory? It is difficult here to not give "descriptions" some explanatory value. On the other hand, list descriptions of executive function are so close to common sense intuitions, so devoid of the attributions of process, and so lacking in any potential explanatory power that it is best to again note that they are better considered a point of departure for explanation, rather than explanation itself.

Explanatory Approaches to Executive Function

BIOLOGICAL EXPLANATIONS

Following from the assumption of a split metatheory, the refusal to acknowledge pattern explanation as a legitimate explanatory form strongly impacts on the analysis of executive function at both the psychological and the biological levels of explanation. When biology is the standpoint of enquiry a restriction of explanation to contingent causality promotes the tendency to identify descriptive components with specific brain locations. This strategy opens two issues: (a) a *reductionism* issue discussed earlier with respect to split metatheory (here the issue concerns the relation of biological explanation to psychological explanation) and (b) a *localization* issue, which is an issue of understanding function at the biological level itself. Reductionism enters when the suggestion is raised that biological explanation can ultimately replace or substitute for psychological explanation. Localization arises with the suggestion that specific brain regions will ultimately explain the behavior associated with descriptive component features of executive function.

Both reductionism and brain localization emerge from the split metatheoretical assumption of wholes as additive aggregates that are ultimately decomposable into foundational fixed elements, and the further assumption that movement and change of these elements are fully explained physical forces termed causes. The suggestion that discrete anatomical regions of the prefrontal cortex (e.g., dorsolateral prefrontal cortex) constitute necessary and sufficient causes—and hence a complete explanation—of performance on executive function tasks illustrates the commitment to an explanatory approach that encompasses both reductionism and to localization. Here the psychological level of analysis is treated as a set of behaviors to be explained by the biological and psychological explanations, if they are acknowledged at all, function as derivative summary statements for an underlying biological foundation. In the executive function literature, this reductionism is often implicit. For instance, the term "prefrontal task" has come to be synonymous with tasks that assess executive cognitive functions, and it is common for executive functions to be relabeled and defined as prefrontal functions (e.g., Daigneault, Braun, & Whitaker, 1992; Roberts, Hager, & Heron, 1994; for similar criticisms, see Stuss, 1992). But executive function should not be defined solely in terms of the functions of the prefrontal cortex—these terms are not interchangeable (Robbins, 1996). Rather, the emerging view is that, while the prefrontal cortex plays a central role, the integrity of other brain regions is necessary for intact executive function (Anderson, 1998; McIntosh, 1999).

Localization itself implies that (a) specific brain regions function largely independently of other brain regions (i.e., the brain is an additive aggregate of elements), and (b) functions formulated from behavioral descriptions (e.g., inhibition, planning, working memory, etc.) find their causal nexus within these particular brain regions. Empirical data are far from supportive of localization for higher-order functions such as executive function. For example, lesion findings (Bechara, Damasio, Damasio, & Anderson, 1994; Milner, 1963;

Shallice, 1982; Stuss et al., 2000) are often cited to support a picture of local-ization, but replication has been inconsistent (Anderson, Damasio, Jones, & Tranel, 1991; Corcoran & Upton, 1993; Grafman, Jonas, & Salazar, 1990; Reitan & Wolfson, 1995; Teuber, Battersby, & Bender, 1951; van den Broek, Bradshaw, & Szabadi, 1993). In some studies, patients with frontal damage have actually performed better than those without frontal damage (Corcoran & Upton, 1993; Teuber et al., 1951; van den Broek et al., 1993), and patients with dam-age outside the prefrontal cortex also show executive deficits (Axelrod et al., 1996; van den Broek et al., 1993; for reviews, see Demakis, 2003, 2004; Reitan & Wolfson, 1994).

As stated earlier, the relational alternative to reductionism, and localization as well, begins with holism. Holism encourages a view of the psychological organism and brain as interpenetrating part systems of the embodied agent actively engaged in the world. These part systems, like other part systems of the embodied agent, are dynamic and self-organizing in character, and not decomposable into foundational elements. Explanation is not found in inde-pendent causes, but in formulating models that account for system function-ing at each level of analysis, further exploring the systemic relations among levels and, within this context searching for specificity of conditions. At the biological level, the brain is a self-organizing system that functions in the context of the psychological and other biological (e.g., body) systems. From this assumptive perspective it would be expected that neural organization of complex cognitive functions would be best characterized in terms of a broad distribution of function at multiple neural levels rather than a physiologically elementaristic notion of localization of function (Damasio & Damasio, 1989). Thus, as Fuster (2001, p. 319) suggests from this perspective, "any hypothetical modularity of the prefrontal cortex … [would be] functionally meaningless if taken out of wide-ranging networks that extend far beyond the confines of any given prefrontal area."

Empirical support for this view is growing, with more recent work in the neurosciences supporting a model of the brain as a self-organizing system characterized by a broad distribution of function at multiple neural levels. Several imaging studies (e.g., PET and fMRI) find that more posterior areas, such as posterior parietal cortex, are also an important component of a dis-tributed executive system (D'Esposito et al., 1998; Smith & Jonides, 1999; Sohn, Ursu, Anderson, Stenger, & Carter, 2000; see Carpenter, Just, & Reichle, 2000). These imaging findings are consistent with findings from research with non-human primates, indicating that executive function requires the coordinated participation of multiple brain regions (Fuster, 1997; Goldman-Rakic, 1987). Such a holistic understanding of a distributed neurological system for execu-tive function is, in fact, familiar to many investigators who work primarily in

the neurosciences. Luria (1966) is particularly explicit about such an understanding of neurological functions defining them specifically as functional
systems, which are both dynamic and situated at multiple levels of the nervous
system.

Other investigators in the neurosciences are approaching biological investigations from the perspective that brain representations are complex and
distributed at multiple levels, and rejecting traditional notions of structure
and function, where there is a clear one-to-one mapping between them (e.g.,
Carpenter & Just, 1999; Carpenter et al., 2000; McIntosh, 1999; Mesulam, 1998;
Stuss, 1992). Poeppel and Hickok (2004) have synthesized such a biological
systems understanding of biological function into a kind of mantra to guide
empirical investigations: "if we must work locally, we should … at least think
globally" (p. 2). Investigation of executive function at the biological level should
take seriously this principle of holism, and concede both the anatomical and
functional heterogeneity of the prefrontal region, and its role within a distributed neurological system that includes both cortical and subcortical regions
of the brain, as well as sensory-somatic systems of the body proper. It is only
in this context, and in the establishment of systemic regulative principles, that
these biological approaches constitute sufficient explanations.

PSYCHOLOGICAL EXPLANATIONS

In turning to a review of psychological explanations of executive function we
must face important conceptual distinctions. Just as the biological and psychological explanations constitute a relational whole, which can be analyzed
only as the opposites of identity, psychological explanation itself is composed of several relational levels. In the broadest terms psychological explanation is distinguished by a personal and a subpersonal level (Elton, 2000;
Bruun & Langlais, 2003; Dennett, 1986; Müller & Carpendale, 2001; Russell,
1999). The personal level is the phenomenological level, and it is constituted
by genuine psychological concepts (e.g., acts, thoughts, feelings, desires, and
wishes) that have intentional qualities, are open to interpretation, and are
available to consciousness (Shanon, 1993); or in other words, have psychological meaning.

The subpersonal level entails the articulation of mechanisms. Here, however it must be understood that "mechanism" does not necessarily commit one
to a mechanistic metatheory. The fact of the matter is that "mechanism" can be
identified both as a "method" ("the agency or means by which an effect is produced or a purpose is accomplished" [mechanism; dictionary.com]), and as a
set of contingent causes or functional input–output relations. This distinction

is important because it suggests that there are at least two sublevels of the subpersonal. The first sublevel, call it the subpersonal *system* level, again brings us back to the earlier discussed idea of pattern explanation, for here the agency or means by which an intention or end is accomplished consists of some noncausal pattern or system. Thus, "action systems," "dynamic systems," "self-organizing systems," "mental structures," as well as more narrowly defined "schemes," "operations," "attachment behavioral system," and "self system" are all examples of the lexicon employed at this subpersonal system level. The second sublevel, call it the subpersonal *functional* level, engages terms such as "input," "output," "computation," "information processing," "antecedent cause," and "network." Some have incorporated biological explanation into the taxonomy of subpersonal levels of explanation (e.g., Müller & Carpendale, 2001). However, as discussed earlier conflating psychological and biological explanations should be avoided, and as a consequence we will not include the biological among these subpersonal levels.

The distinctions among these various levels, including the biological, are of course, easier to make in theory than in practice. For example, it is quite possible that an approach calling itself "dynamic systems"—the subpersonal system level—in fact, on analysis, relies heavily on input–output explanations—the subpersonal functional level. Despite such ambiguities, and others that may arise, beginning analysis with unambiguous conceptual distinctions permits further clarification of these ambiguities, while avoiding conceptual clarification simply ensures confusion. We reiterate that, although it deserves much greater discussion and analysis than is possible here, a relational metatheory argues for the interdependence without reductionism of all of these psychological levels, and the same interdependency between the biological and psychological levels. But, again, it serves analysis best to be clear conceptually at the beginning and move from there to the hard work of articulating the nature of the interdependencies as opposed to beginning and ending with the confusion of vagueness and imprecision.

With the personal–subpersonal levels distinctions in hand we move to a review of several explanations of executive function at reside primarily at the psychological level. As noted earlier, a good deal of what is offered as psychological explanation is, in fact, little more than observational generalization and description. There are, however, a number of exemplars of work that do offer legitimate psychological explanations of executive function. We will examine these and relate them to other levels of explanation, such as the biological. In this section, we largely restrict our discussion to recent developmental explanations.

In an effort to avoid what has been termed the "homunculus" problem in executive function, various developmental theories have incorporated a system-level psychological explanation. The homunculus problem arises when functions that should be considered as the output of an organized system as a whole are instead construed as the output of a smaller component of that system. For example, consider approaches that view executive control as an aspect or component of working memory, an approach that has gained popularity in both the developmental (Baddeley & Hitch, 2000; Case, 1985; Demetriou, Christou, Spanoudis, & Platsidou, 2002; Gordon & Olson, 1998; Pascual-Leone, 2000) and adult literatures (for a recent review of the adult literature, see Miyake & Shah, 1999). In such cases, the executive component of the working memory system is often poorly specified. Instead, there is an appeal to a global administrative component of executive control, such as the "central executive" of Baddeley and Hitch (Baddeley & Hitch, 1974), the Supervisory Attentional System of Norman and Shallice (1986), Pascual-Leone's "mental attention" (Pascual-Leone & Baillargeon, 1994), Case's "total processing space" (Case, 1985), or the "Working Hypercognition" of Demetriou and colleagues (2002). This executive component is taken to perform most of the functions that are logically necessary for the other aspects of the model to be effective (e.g., to direct attention, to plan, or to suppress prepotent or irrelevant responses), but there is little specification of how they are implemented.

In these global conceptualizations, the theoretical construct of executive function is taken out of the context of the system itself—it is presented as a static component or a set of processes that act on information from the system, but largely in isolation from the system. As a result, appeals to such components have been criticized for invoking a homunculus to explain how these functions are carried out (Parkin, 1998). This problem is avoided by situating executive function within a broader psychological organization (i.e., a system-level explanation). Russell (1999, p. 253) is unequivocal about how to conceptualize executive function within the broader psychological system: "the knowing system—the system of concepts and reasoning ... cannot be understood apart from the functioning of [the] executive system."

This understanding is gaining increasing support in the developmental literature on executive function. Prominent are accounts that are offered under the umbrella of dynamic systems, connectionism, and complexity. However, even at this global system-level, explanations differ markedly in a number of respects. Some theoretical perspectives incorporate personal level concepts of mental representation, and specify cognitive structure or organization at the subpersonal systems level (e.g., complexity theories). Others marginalize mental concepts, or eschew them as altogether unnecessary (e.g., some flavors of connectionism or dynamic systems), and instead focus their efforts at the subpersonal functional level of analysis.

Our discussion of the similarities and differences among contemporary theories of executive function development is best considered within the context of the tasks that are typically used to assess the predictions derived from the theories. One task that has received extensive attention in the executive function literature is Piaget's A-not-B task (Piaget, 1954). In the canonical version of the A-not-B task, the infant watches as an object is hidden in one of two hiding places. A few seconds later, the infant is allowed to reach for and retrieve the object, and after a few retrievals at the first location (A), the object is moved, in full view of the infant, to a second location (B). Despite witnessing the movement of the object to the B location, with standard delays between hiding and searching younger infants perseverate and continue to reach to the A location (i.e., they commit the A-not-B error) until about 10–12 months (for a review, see Wellman, Cross, and Bartsch, 1986).

Piaget's original explanation for this phenomenon was situated at both the personal and subpersonal level of psychological explanation. At the personal level, Piaget pointed to the immaturity of the object concept (i.e., the understanding that objects can continue to exist when they are out of sight) to explain the younger infant's poor performance. Explanation of the child's acquisition of the object concept was, on the other hand, at the level of the subpersonal systems, namely those of assimilatory cognitive structures. To clarify, the notion of object-permanence meets all the criteria for being at the personal level (e.g., it is available to consciousness), but explanation of object permanence in terms of "operations" and the integration of operations is at the subpersonal systems level. An action is at the personal level, but action systems are at the subpersonal systems level. An act may be explained in terms of intentionality, all acts entail a goal, but assimilation is a part of an operational system and this is the subpersonal systems level.

Two recent explanations that attempt to explain executive function at a global system level can be understood at both a personal and a subpersonal systems level. Originating from a complexity perspective, the two theories, relational complexity and cognitive complexity, explain children's development in problem solving in terms of the nature of the organization of representations that the child is able to process. The personal level notion of representation used in this sense generally refers to something that stands for something else and is available to consciousness (e.g., the word "dog" refers to a dog; a "rule" specifies antecedent consequent relations; a "cognitive map" reflects spatial relations in the environment; see Bermudez, 2000). An important conceptual distinction is raised, however, when complexity theories attempt to explain developments in executive function by referring to changes in the structure of representational systems. When the form or organization of a system of representations is the focus of explanation, this explanation is now formulated at a subpersonal level, specifically the subpersonal systems level. This should not, however, be construed to imply that the subpersonal systems explanation replaces the personal level explanation; rather, subpersonal and personal level explanations are relational and nonautonomous. Useful and indispensable explanations occur on both sides of the table, but this does not mean that these differences warrant the demarcation of completely autonomous domains of explanation (Bermudez, 2000).

In the context of the A-not-B task, the two broadly compatible complexity theories (relational complexity and cognitive complexity) explain task difficulty by pointing to the number of individual representations that must be integrated into a single cognitive representation to solve the problem. Thus, the younger infant has trouble because she/he cannot consider the relation between the two hiding locations and integrate these into a single representation to guide action (relational complexity; Halford, Wilson, & Philips, 1998), or coordinate representations in a conscious representational system in order to overcome a response-based system activated by motor output (cognitive complexity; Marcovitch & Zelazo, 1999). Both theories also extend to executive function development in the preschool period and later childhood, arguing that the number of representations that can be integrated into a single representation increases with age, allowing for more successful problem solving on more complex tasks (Andrews, Halford, Bunch, Bowden, & Jones, 2003; Frye, Zelazo, & Palfai, 1995; Halford et al., 1998).

In the above examples, the concept of "representation" was incorporated as a personal level explanation. However, the notion of representation can be ambiguous (Markman & Dietrich, 2000), sometimes being used as above, but sometimes being defined at the subpersonal level, as for example, in connectionist and dynamic systems models. The notion of representation in connectionist and dynamic systems models is categorically different from the more traditional notion used in most cognitive theories (Fodor & Pylyshyn, 1988). For example, in connectionist models, representation is defined broadly as "patterns of activation across a pool of neuron-like processing units" (Elman et al., 1996, p. 25). Activation patterns on a layer of the network might be offered as "representing" categories because the modeler can understand that these patterns are stable patterns in relation to outputs of the network, but this is clearly not a personal level "representation" directly relevant to the child's conscious understanding of the world (Smith & Samuelson, 2003). Representations in this example are thus not viewed as the "standard symbolic variety" (van Gelder, 1995; i.e., internal models of external conditions). Consequently, this understanding of "representations" is situated at the subpersonal, not the personal level of explanation (Keijzer, 2002).

Examples of approaches in the executive function literature that understand representation at the subpersonal level are Thelen and colleagues' dynamic systems model (Thelen, Schöner, Scheier, & Smith, 2001; Thelen & Smith, 1994) and the connectionist model presented by Munakata and colleagues (Morton & Munakata, 2002; Munakata, 1998). These approaches have rejected personal level symbolic representational systems. Despite the phrase "dynamic systems" in one of these approaches, both have favored bottom-up or emergentist explanations that concentrate on causal mechanisms (i.e., subpersonal functional level). For example, the dynamic systems explanation of the A-not-B error views perseveration as an emergent outcome of the interaction of dynamic processes, specifically of online visually guided reaching processes, and memory processes that encode the history of the child's behavior. Development here is modeled by changes in parameters that contribute to the model (e.g., changes in the motor planning process). For this model, structure is *outside the organism*; behavior is the focus, and there is no emphasis on mental organization of the organism (Thelen & Bates, 2003). Although this model has aspects of a pattern explanation in that it is dynamic and emergent, its rejection of explanation in terms of mental organization, and subsequent emphasis on causal connections and input–output relations, situates the explanation at the subpersonal functional level of analysis.

Munakata and colleagues' connectionist model (Morton & Munakata, 2002; Munakata, 1998) is also at the subpersonal functional level; the emphasis is on modeling information-processing mechanisms and causal relations among units in a connectionist network. The model specifies two components, active and latent representations, which compete to determine behavior, and developmental improvement is understood as reflecting the ability of the active representation to compete with and overcome the latent representation (Morton & Munakata, 2002; Munakata, 1998). Here again, the term "representation" is not offered at the personal level; this form of representation has no direct meaning for the child.

Although these dynamic systems and connectionist examples offer psychological subpersonal explanations, this fact does not preclude the possibility of personal level explanations within the same models. That is, the use of, for example, subpersonal functional explanations does not suggest a necessary incompatibility between these and other levels of explanation of the same phenomenon. Incompatibility occurs only when reductionism is an auxiliary hypothesis in the model or when the different explanations make different predictions or specify different models. Thus, Thelen and Bates (2003) may be correct when they argue that nothing in a dynamic systems framework precludes the analysis of mental representation at the personal level, and Müller and Carpendale (2001) may similarly be correct when they argue that

Piaget's account and the dynamic systems account of the A-not-B error may be seen as compatible explanations pitched at different levels of explanation. Several models in the literature have in fact integrated explanatory concepts across levels. These include van Geert's (1994) and Bidell and Fischer's (2000) models that incorporate a relational developmental systems perspective with personal level aspects of mental structure, and models presented from a complexity perspective by Zelazo and colleagues (Müller, Dick, Gela, Overton, & Zelazo, 2006; Zelazo, Müller, Frye, & Marcovitch, 2003) that have analyzed component cognitive mechanisms (e.g., inhibition and working memory) to supplement the analysis of mental organization. From our relational perspective, the psychological levels of analysis, along with the biological level, all represent potential standpoints from which to converge on a broad, but precise understanding of executive function without engaging in the zero sum game of reductionism.

Conclusions

In the present chapter, we have argued that definitions of executive function suffer from a vagueness and ambiguity that impacts on empirical methods, findings, and conceptual conclusions of research in this area. Part of this confusion grows from the fact that many researchers fail to explicitly acknowledge that the construct of executive function can be explored from different standpoints. Further, researchers fail to acknowledge that descriptions as summary statements do not constitute explanations. We have argued that the rejection of a split metatheory in favor of a relational metatheory represents a necessary step in clarifying the executive function construct. Recast within a relational metatheory, description and explanation are at the same time distinguished to clarify each individual concept, and integrated to form a framework for empirical and theoretical investigation. A relational metatheory also frames the explanatory standpoint, where pattern and causal explanation form complementary relations. Similarly, biological and psychological explanations are taken as legitimate standpoints from which to investigate executive function, but also represent integrated explanatory constructs within a relational matrix. Within this relational metatheory, the commitment to the principle of holism understands basic units of analysis as parts of a dynamic functioning system. From such an understanding, pattern or system-level explanation is a necessity at both the psychological and biological levels of analysis. At the psychological level, recognition and distinction of both personal and subpersonal level explanation allows for an increasing conceptual clarity in the field of executive function research.

REFERENCES

Amieva, H., Phillips, L., & Della Sala, S. (2003). Behavioral dysexecutive symptoms in normal aging. *Brain and Cognition, 53*, 129–132.

Anderson, S. W., Damasio, H., Jones, R. D., & Tranel, D. (1991). Wisconsin Card Sorting Test performance as a measure of frontal lobe damage. *Journal of Clinical and Experimental Neuropsychology, 13*, 909–922.

Anderson, V. (1998). Assessing executive functions in children: Biological, psychological, and developmental considerations. *Neuropsychological Rehabilitation, 8*, 319–349.

Andrews, G., Halford, G. S., Bunch, K. M., Bowden, D., & Jones, T. (2003). Theory of mind and relational complexity. *Child Development, 74*, 1476–1499.

Axelrod, B. N., Goldman, R. S., Heaton, R. K., Curtiss, G., Thompson, L. L., Chelune, G. J., et al. (1996). Discriminability of the Wisconsin Card Sorting Test using the standardization sample. *Journal of Clinical and Experimental Neuropsychology, 18*, 338–342.

Baddeley, A. D., & Hitch, G. J. (1974). Working memory. In G. A. Bower (Ed.), *Recent advances in learning and motivation* (Vol. 8, pp. 47–90). New York: Academic Press.

Baddeley, A. D., & Hitch, G. J. (2000). Development of working memory: Should the Pascuel-Leone and the Baddeley and Hitch models be merged? *Journal of Experimental Child Psychology, 77*, 128–137.

Barcelo, F., & Knight, R. T. (2002). Both random and perseverative errors underlie WCST deficits in prefrontal changes. *Neuropsychologia, 40*, 349–356.

Bechara, A., Damasio, A. R., Damasio, H., & Anderson, S. W. (1994). Insensitivity to future consequences following damage to human prefrontal cortex. *Cognition, 50*, 7–15.

Bennetto, L., & Pennington, B. F. (2003). Executive functioning in normal and abnormal development. In S. Segalowitz & I. Rapin, *Handbook of neuropsychology*, 2nd ed., Part II: Child Neuropsychology (Vol. 8, pp. 785–802). Amsterdam: Elsevier.

Berg, E. A. (1948). A simple objective treatment for measuring flexibility in thinking. *Journal of General Psychology, 39*, 15–22.

Bermudez, J. L. (2000). Personal and sub-personal: A difference without a distinction. *Philosophical Explorations, 3*, 63–82.

Bidell, T. R., & Fischer, K. W. (2000). The role of cognitive structure in the development of behavioral control: A dynamic skills approach. In W. J. Perrig & A. Grob (Eds.), *Control of human behavior, mental processes, and consciousness: Essays in honor of the 60th birthday of August Flammer* (pp. 183–201). Mahwah, NJ: Lawrence Erlbaum Associates.

Block, J. (1995a). A contrarian view of the five-factor approach to personality description. *Psychological Bulletin, 117*, 187–215.

Block, J. (1995b). Going beyond the five-factors given: Rejoinder to Costa and McCrae (1995) and Goldberg and Saucier (1995). *Psychological Bulletin, 117*, 226–229.

Bowden, S. C., Fowler, K. S., Bell, R. C., Whelan, G., Clifford, C. C., Ritter, A. J., et al. (1998). The reliability and internal validity of the Wisconsin Card Sorting Test. *Neuropsychological Rehabilitation, 8,* 243–254.

Brookshire, B., Levin, H. S., Song, J. X., & Zhang, L. (2004). Components of executive function in typically developing and head-injured children. *Developmental Neuropsychology, 25,* 61–83.

Bruun, H., & Langlais, R. (2003). On the embodied nature of action. *Acta Sociologica, 46,* 31–49.

Bunge, M. (1962). *Causality: The place of the causal principle in modern science.* New York: World Publishing.

Bunge, M. (2004). How does it work? The search for explanatory mechanisms. *Philosophy of the Social Sciences, 34,* 182–210.

Burgess, P. W., Alderman, N., Evans, J., Emslie, H., & Wilson, B. A. (1998). The ecological validity of tests of executive function. *Journal of the International Neuropsychological Society, 4,* 547–558.

Carlson, S. M., & Moses, L. J. (2001). Individual differences in inhibitory control and children's theory of mind. *Child Development, 72,* 1032–1053.

Carpenter, P. A., & Just, M. A. (1999). Modeling the mind: Very-high-field functional magnetic resonance imaging activation during cognition. *Topics in Magnetic Resonance Imaging, 10,* 16–36.

Carpenter, P. A., Just, M. A., & Reichle, E. D. (2000). Working memory and executive function: Evidence from neuroimaging. *Current Opinion in Neurobiology, 10,* 195–199.

Cartwright, N. (1980). The reality of causes in a world of instrumental laws. *PSA: Proceedings of the Biennial Meeting of the Philosophy of Science Association, 2,* 38–48.

Case, R. (1985). *Intellectual development: Birth to adulthood.* New York: Academic Press.

Corcoran, R., & Upton, D. (1993). A role for the hippocampus in card sorting? *Cortex, 29,* 293–304.

Daigneault, S., Braun, C. M. J., & Whitaker, H. A. (1992). Early effects of normal aging on perseverative and non-perseverative prefrontal measures. *Developmental Neuropsychology, 8,* 99–114.

Damasio, A. R. (1994). *Descarte's error: Emotion, reason, and the human brain.* New York: G. P. Putnam.

Damasio, H., & Damasio, A. R. (1989). *Lesion analysis in neuropsychology.* New York: Oxford University Press.

Demakis, G. J. (2003). A meta-analytic review of the sensitivity of the Wisconsin Card Sorting Test to frontal and lateralized frontal brain damage. *Neuropsychology, 17,* 255–264.

Demakis, G. J. (2004). Frontal lobe damage and tests of executive processing: A meta-analysis of the Category Test, Stroop Test, and Trail-Making Test. *Journal of Clinical and Experimental Neuropsychology, 26,* 441–450.

Demetriou, A., Christou, C., Spanoudis, G., & Platsidou, M. (2002). The development of mental processing: Efficiency, working memory, and thinking. *Monographs of the Society for Research in Child Development, 67,* Serial No. 268.

Dennett, D. (1986). *Content and consciousness*. London: Routledge.

D'Esposito, M., Aguirre, G. K., Zarahn, E., Ballard, D., Shin, R. K., & Lease, J. (1998). Functional MRI studies of spatial and nonspatial working memory. *Cognitive Brain Research, 7*, 1–13.

Diamond, A., & Kirkham, N. (2005). Not quite as grown-up as we like to think: Parallels between cognition in childhood and adulthood. *Psychological Science, 16*, 291–297.

Edelman, G., & Tononi, G. (2000). *A universe of consciousness: How matter becomes imagination*. New York: Basic Books.

Elton, M. (2000). The personal/sub-personal distinction: An introduction. *Philosophical Explorations, 3*, 2–5.

Elman, J. L., Bates, E. A., Johnson, M. H., Karmiloff-Smith, A., Parisi, D., & Plunkett, K. (1996). *Rethinking innateness*. Cambridge, MA: MIT Press.

Fodor, J., & Pylyshyn, Z. W. (1988). Connectionism and cognitive architecture: A critical analysis. *Cognition, 28*, 3–71.

Friedman, N. P., & Miyake, A. (2004). The relations among inhibition and interference control functions: A latent-variable analysis. *Journal of Experimental Psychology: General, 133*, 101–135.

Friedman, N. P., Miyake, A., Corley, R. P., Young, S. E., DeFries, J. C., & Hewitt, J. K. (2006). Not all executive functions are related to intelligence. *Psychological Science, 17*, 172–179.

Frye, D., Zelazo, P. D., & Palfai, T. (1995). Theory of mind and rule-based reasoning. *Cognitive Development, 10*, 483–527.

Fuster, J. M. (1997). *The prefrontal cortex* (3rd ed.). New York: Raven Press.

Fuster, J. M. (2001). The prefrontal cortex—An update: Time is of the essence. *Neuron, 30*, 319–333.

Goldman-Rakic, P. S. (1987). Circuitry of the pre-frontal cortex and the regulation of behavior by representational knowledge. In F. Plum & V. Mountcastle (Eds.), *Handbook of physiology* (Vol. 5, pp. 373–417). Bethesda, MD: American Physiological Society.

Gordon, A. C. L., & Olson, D. R. (1998). The relation between acquisition of a theory of mind and the capacity to hold in mind. *Journal of Experimental Child Psychology, 68*, 70–83.

Grafman, J., Jonas, B., & Salazar, A. (1990). Wisconsin Card Sorting Test performance based on location and size of neuroanatomical lesion in Vietnam veterans with penetrating head injury. *Perceptual and Motor Skills, 71*, 1120–1122.

Greve, K. W., Ingram, F., & Bianchini, K. J. (1998). Latent structure of the Wisconsin Card Sorting Test in a clinical sample. *Archives of Clinical Neuropsychology, 13*, 597–609.

Greve, K. W., Stickle, T. R., Love, J. M., Bianchini, K. J., & Stanford, M. S. (2005). Latent structure of the Wisconsin Card Sorting Test: A confirmatory factor analytic study. *Archives of Clinical Neuropsychology, 20*, 355–364.

Halford, G. S., Wilson, W. H., & Phillips, S. (1998). Processing capacity defined by relational complexity: Implications for comparative, developmental, and cognitive psychology. *Behavioral and Brain Sciences, 21*, 803–865.

Hanson, N. R. (1958). *Patterns of discovery*. London and New York: Cambridge University Press.

Hughes, C. (1998). Executive function in preschoolers: Links with theory of mind and verbal ability. *British Journal of Developmental Psychology, 16*, 233–253.

Keijzer, F. (2002). Representation in dynamical and embodied cognition. *Cognitive Systems Research, 3*, 275–288.

Kirkham, N. Z., Cruess, L., & Diamond, A. (2003). Helping children apply their knowledge to their behavior on a dimension-switching task. *Developmental Science, 6*, 449–476.

Kitcher, P. (1981). Explanatory unification. *Philosophy of Science, 48*, 507–531.

Kizilbash, A., & Donders, J. (1999). Latent structure of the Wisconsin Card Sorting Test after pediatric traumatic head injury. *Child Neuropsychology, 5*, 224–229.

Laudan, L. (1996). *Beyond positivism and relativism: Theory, method, and evidence*. Boulder, CO: Westview Press.

Levin, H. S., Culhane, K. A., Hartmann, J., Evankovich, K., Mattson, A. J., Harward, H., et al. (1991). Developmental changes in performance on tests of purported frontal lobe functioning. *Developmental Neuropsychology, 7*, 377–395.

Levin, H. S., Fletcher, J. M., Kufera, J. A., Harward, H., Lilly, M. A., Mendelsohn, D., et al. (1996). Dimensions of cognition measured by the Tower of London and other cognitive tasks in head-injured children and adolescents. *Developmental Neuropsychology, 12*, 17–34.

Lezak, M. D. (1993). Newer contributions to the neuropsychological assessment of executive functions. *Journal of Head Trauma Rehabilitation, 8*, 24–31.

Lezak, M. D. (1995). *Neuropsychological assessment* (3rd ed.). Oxford, UK: Oxford University Press.

Luria, A. R. (1966). *Higher cortical functions in man*. New York: Basic Books.

Marcovitch, S., & Zelazo, P. D. (1999). The A-not-B error: Results from a logistic meta-analysis. *Child Development, 70*, 1297–1313.

Mariani, M., & Barkley, R. A. (1997). Neuropsychological and academic functioning in preschool boys with attention deficit hyperactivity disorder. *Developmental Neuropsychology, 13*, 111–129.

Markman, A. B., & Dietrich, E. (2000). In defense of representation. *Cognitive Psychology, 40*, 138–171.

McIntosh, A. R. (1999). Mapping cognition to the brain through neural interactions. *Memory, 7*, 523–548.

Mechanism. (n.d.). Dictionary.com Unabridged (v1.0.1). Retrieved August 9, 2009, from Dictionary.com website: http://dictionary.reference.com/browse/mechanism.

Mesulam, M.-M. (1998). From sensation to cognition. *Brain, 121*, 1013–1052.

Miller, G. A. (1996). Presidential address: How we think about cognition, emotion, and biology in psychopathology. *Psychophysiology, 33*, 615–628.

Miller, G. A., & Keller, J. (2000). Psychology and neuroscience: Making peace. *Current Directions in Psychological Science, 9*, 212–215.

Milner, B. (1963). Effects of different brain lesions on card sorting: The role of the frontal lobes. *Archives of Neurology, 9*, 90–100.

Miyake, A., Friedman, N. P., Emerson, M. J., Witzki, A. H., Howerter, A, & Wager, T. D. (2000). The unity and diversity of executive functions and their contributions to complex "frontal lobe" tasks: A latent variable analysis. *Cognitive Psychology, 41*, 49–100.

Miyake, A., & Shah, P. (1999). *Models of working memory: Mechanisms of active maintenance and executive control.* Cambridge; New York: Cambridge University Press.

Morton, J. B., & Munakata, Y. (2002). Active versus latent representations: A neural network model of perseveration, dissociation, and decalage. *Developmental Psychobiology, 40*, 255–265.

Müller, U., & Carpendale, J. I. M. (2001). Objectivity, intentionality, and levels of explanation. *Behavioral and Brain Sciences, 24*, 55–56.

Müller, U., Dick, A. S., Gela, K., Overton, W. F., & Zelazo, P. D. (2006). The role of negative priming in preschoolers' flexible rule use on the Dimensional Change Card Sort Task. *Child Development, 77*, 395–412.

Munakata, Y. (1998). Infant perseveration and implications for object permanence theories: A PDP model of the AB task. *Developmental Science, 1*, 161–211.

Norman, D. A., & Shallice, T. (1986). Attention to action: Willed and automatic control of behavior. In R. J. Davidson, G. E. Schwartz, & D. Shapiro (Eds.), *Consciousness and self-regulation* (Vol. 4, pp. 1–18). New York: Plenum Press.

Overton, W. F. (2003). Development across the life span: Philosophy, concepts, theory. In I. B. Weiner (Ed. in Chief), R. M. Lerner, M. A. Easterbrooks, & J. Mistry (Eds.), *Comprehensive handbook of psychology: Developmental psychology* (Vol. 6, pp. 13–42). New York: Wiley.

Overton, W. F. (2006). Developmental psychology: Philosophy, concepts, methodology. In W. Damon (Series Ed.) and R. M. Lerner (Vol. Ed.), *Handbook of child psychology: Vol. 1. Theoretical models of human development* (6th ed., pp. 18–88). New York: Wiley.

Overton, W. F., & Ennis, M. D. (2006). Cognitive-developmental and behavior-analytic theories: Evolving into complementarity. *Human Development, 49*, 143–172.

Overton, W. F., & Reese, H. W. (1981). Conceptual prerequisites for an understanding of stability-change and continuity-discontinuity. *International Journal of Behavioral Development, 4*, 99–123.

Parkin, A. J. (1998). The central executive does not exist. *Journal of the International Neuropsychological Society, 4*, 518–522.

Pascual-Leone, J. (2000). Reflections on working memory: Are the two models complementary? *Journal of Experimental Child Psychology, 77*, 138–154.

Pascual-Leone, J., & Baillargeon, R. (1994). Developmental measurement of mental attention. *International Journal of Behavioral Development, 17*, 161–200.

Patton, J. H., Stanford, M. S., & Barratt, E. S. (1995). Factor structure of the Barratt Impulsiveness Scale. *Journal of Clinical Psychology, 51*, 768–774.

Pennington, B. F. (1997). Dimensions of executive functions in normal and abnormal development. In N. A. Krasnegor, G. R. Lyon, & P. S. Goldman-Rakic (Eds.), *Development of the prefrontal cortex: Evolution, neurobiology, and behavior* (pp. 265–281). Baltimore: Paul H. Brookes Publishing Co., Inc.

Pennington, B. F., & Ozonoff, S. (1996). Executive functions and developmental psychopathology. *Journal of Child Psychology and Psychiatry, 37,* 51–87.

Piaget, J. (1952). *The origins of intelligence in children.* New York: W. W. Norton & Company.

Piaget, J. (1954). *The construction of reality in the child.* London: Routledge.

Pineda, D. A., & Merchan, V. (2003). Executive function in young Colombian adults. *International Journal of Neuroscience, 113,* 397–410.

Poeppel, D., & Hickok, G. (2004). Towards a new functional anatomy of language. *Cognition, 92,* 1–12.

Putnam, H. (1983). *Realism and reason: Philosophical papers* (Vol. 3). New York: Cambridge University Press.

Rabbitt, P. (1997). Introduction: Methodologies and models in the study of executive function. In P. Rabbitt (Ed.), *Methodology of frontal and executive function* (pp. 1–35). New York: Psychology Press.

Randall, J. H. (1960). *Aristotle.* New York: Columbia University Press.

Reitan, R. M., & Wolfson, D. (1994). A selective and critical review of neuropsychological deficits and the frontal lobes. *Neuropsychology Review, 4,* 161–198.

Reitan, R. M., & Wolfson, D. (1995). Category test and trail making test as measures of frontal lobe functions. *The Clinical Neuropsychologist, 9,* 50–56.

Robbins, T. W. (1996). Dissociating executive functions of the prefrontal cortex. *Philosophical Transactions of the Royal Society of London Series B-Biological Sciences, 351,* 1463–1470.

Roberts, R. J., Hager, L. D., & Heron, C. (1994). Prefrontal cognitive processes: Working memory and inhibition in the antisaccade task. *Journal of Experimental Psychology: General, 123,* 374–393.

Russell, J. (1999). Cognitive development as an executive process—in part: A homeopathic dose of Piaget. *Developmental Science, 2,* 247–295.

Searle, J. R. (1992). *The rediscovery of the mind.* Cambridge, MA: MIT Press.

Shallice, T. (1982). Specific impairments in planning. *Philosophical Transactions of the Royal Society of London Series B-Biological Sciences, 298,* 199–209.

Shanon, B. (1993). *The representational and the presentational: An essay on cognition and the study of mind.* New York: Harvester Wheatsheaf.

Shute, G. E., & Huertes, V. (1990). Developmental variability in frontal lobe function. *Developmental Neuropsychology, 6,* 1–11.

Simon, H. A. (1975). The functional equivalence of problem solving skills. *Cognitive Psychology, 7,* 268–288.

Smith, E. E., & Jonides, J. (1999). Storage and executive processes in the frontal lobes. *Science, 283,* 1657–1661.

Smith, L. B., & Samuelson, L. K. (2003). Different is good: Connectionism and dynamic systems theory are complementary emergentist approaches to development. *Developmental Science, 6,* 434–439.

Sohn, M., Ursu, S., Anderson, J. R., Stenger, V. A., & Carter, C. S. (2000). The role of prefrontal cortex and posterior parietal cortex in task switching. *Proceedings of the National Academy of Sciences, 97,* 13448–13453.

Spinella, M. (2005). Self-rated executive function: Development of the executive function index. *International Journal of Neuroscience, 115*, 649–667.

Stroop, J. R. (1935). Studies of interference in serial verbal reactions. *Journal of Experimental Psychology, 18*, 643–662.

Stuss, D. T. (1992). Biological and psychological development of executive functions. *Brain and Cognition, 20*, 8–23.

Stuss, D. T., & Alexander, M. P. (2000). Executive functions and the frontal lobes: A conceptual view. *Psychological Research, 63*, 289–298.

Stuss, D. T., & Benson, D. F. (1986). *The frontal lobes.* New York: Raven.

Stuss, D. T., Eskes, G. A.., & Foster, J. K. (1994). Experimental neuropsychological studies of frontal lobe functions. In F. Boller & J. Grafman (Eds.), *Handbook of neuropsychology* (Vol. 9, pp. 149–185). Amsterdam: Elsevier.

Stuss, D. T., Levine, B., Alexander, M. P., Hong, J., Palumbo, C., Hamer, L., et al. (2000). Wisconsin Card Sorting Test performance in patients with focal frontal and posterior brain damage: Effects of lesion location and test structure on separable cognitive processes. *Neuropsychologia, 38*, 388–402.

Taylor, C. (1995). *Philosophical arguments.* Cambridge, MA: Harvard University Press.

Teuber, H. L. (1972). Unity and diversity of frontal lobe functions. *Acta Neurobiologiae Experimentalis, 32*, 615–656.

Teuber, H.-L., Battersby, W. S., & Bender, M. B. (1951). Performance of complex visual tasks after cerebral lesions. *Journal of Nervous and Mental Disease, 114*, 413–429.

Thelen, E., & Bates, E. (2003). Connectionism and dynamic systems: Are they really different? *Developmental Science, 6*, 378–391.

Thelen, E., Schöner, G., Scheier, C., & Smith, L. B. (2001). The dynamics of embodiment: A field theory of infant perseverative reaching. *Behavioral and Brain Science, 24*, 1–86.

Thelen, E., & Smith, L. (1994). *A dynamic systems approach to the development of cognition and action.* Cambridge, MA: MIT Press.

Toulmin, S. (1953). *The philosophy of science.* New York: Harper and Row.

Tranel, D., Anderson, S. W., & Benton, A. (1994). Development of the concept of "executive function" and its relationship to the frontal lobes. In F. Boller & J. Grafman (Eds.), *Handbook of Neuropsychology* (Vol. 9, pp. 125–148). Amsterdam: Elsevier.

van den Broek, M. D., Bradshaw, C. M., & Szabadi, E. (1993). Utility of the Modified Wisconsin Card Sorting Test in neuropsychological assessment. *British Journal of Clinical Psychology, 32*, 333–343.

van Geert, P. (1994). *Dynamic systems of development: Change between complexity and chaos.* New York: Prentice-Hall.

van Gelder, T. (1995). What might cognition be if not computation? *Journal of Philosophy, 91*, 345–381.

Wellman, H. M., Cross, D., & Bartsch, K. (1986). Infant search and object permanence: A meta-analysis of the A-not-B error. *Monographs of the Society for Research in Child Development, 54*(214).

Welsh, M. C., Pennington, B. F., & Grossier, D. B. (1991). A normative-developmental study of executive function: A window on prefrontal function in children. *Developmental Neuropsychology, 7,* 119–230.

Werner, H. (1957). The concept of development from a comparative and organismic point of view. In D. B. Harris (Ed.), *The concept of development: An issue in the study of human behavior* (pp. 125–148). Minneapolis, MN: University of Minnesota Press.

Werner, H. (1958). *Comparative psychology of mental development.* New York: International Universities Press.

Zelazo, P. D., Carter, A., Reznick, J. S., & Frye, D. (1997). Early development of executive function: A problem-solving framework. *Review of General Psychology, 1,* 198–226.

Zelazo, P. D., & Müller, U. (2002). Executive function in typical and atypical development. In U. Goswami (Ed.), *Handbook of childhood cognitive development* (pp. 445–469). Oxford, England: Blackwell Publishing.

Zelazo, P. D., Müller, U., Frye, D., & Marcovitch, S. (2003). The development of executive function in early childhood. *Monographs of the Society for Research in Child Development, 68*(3), Serial No. 274.

2

Executive Function: Theoretical Concerns

JACK MARTIN AND LAURA FAILOWS

I n recent years, research interest in the area of executive function (EF) has burgeoned. In particular, much theoretical and empirical work has centered on the role of EF in developmental disorders and the relation between EF and children's developing conceptions of mental life or theory of mind. Despite its recent popularity, however, theorists and researchers concerned with EF face several significant theoretical challenges. Many of these stem from the fact that there is no universally accepted, consistent definition of EF or its various components. Moreover, different investigators focus on different executive components and subscribe to different conceptions of how these various parts relate to executive functioning as a whole. They also use different tasks, problems, and methods in their studies of EF and its components. In addition to these definitional, conceptual, and methodological challenges, a critical examination of this area of research reveals pervasive, although mostly unstated, assumptions that call out for explication and examination. Some of these assumptions posit various inner psychological and neurological entities and mechanisms (structures, processes, and skills) as underlying a variety of functional actions on various tasks and problems. Others appear to reduce important aspects of personhood, and attribute the worldly activities of persons, to the operations of these hypothesized inner mechanisms. Important theoretical questions concern the ontological status of the inner processes assumed, and whether or not such reductions can be sustained.

We begin with a survey of definitions, methods, and conceptions that currently resist integration. We move on to tackle broader issues of psychologism, reductionism, and mechanism as these might apply to theory and research on EF. We then conclude by suggesting that theories of EF would do well to privilege descriptions of the functional activities of children in particular task environments and contexts over postulations of inner psychological and neurological, explanatory mechanisms, at least until some of the challenges we discuss have been clarified and resolved.

Definitions, Methods, and Conceptions

A brief survey of definitions of EF and methods that have been employed in EF research provides a concrete sense of the subject matter that concerns researchers in this area of contemporary developmental psychology. It also serves to introduce the conceptual frameworks currently employed in major programs of inquiry.

DEFINITIONS

It is widely acknowledged that EF is poorly defined (Brocki & Bohlin, 2004; Lehto, Juujarvi, Kooistra, & Pulkkinen, 2003; Zelazo & Müller, 2002). At a general level, EF has been variously described as "the psychological processes involved in the conscious control of thought and action" (Zelazo & Müller, 2002, p. 445), "an umbrella term for all of the complex set of cognitive processes that underlie flexible goal-directed responses to novel or difficult situations" (Hughes & Graham, 2002, p. 131), or simply as "self-control" (Perner, Lang, & Kloo, 2002). Although noteworthy differences can be found at this general level of description, there is, for the most part, convergence on the idea that EF involves controlling one's actions.

At the more particular level of how such control is achieved, however, a much different story is evident. Here, the specific cognitive processes or components that are said to constitute EF seem almost to depend on the subjective preferences of individual investigators. For instance, Tranel, Anderson, and Benton (1994, as cited in Zelazo & Müller, 2002), after reviewing lists of posited components, describe EF as being made up of planning, decision-making, judgment, and self-perception. Brocki and Bohlin (2004), on the other hand, describe EF as inhibition, planning, strategy development, persistence, and flexibility of action, while Hughes (1998) claims that EF is constituted by planning, inhibitory control, attentional flexibility, and working memory. Eslinger (1996) reported 33 different EFs that were provided by experts in the area, few of which came close to achieving consensus amongst those surveyed (also see, Beveridge, Jarrold, & Pettit, 2002). Clearly, there is no currently agreed taxonomy of EFs, although some of the most commonly proposed EFs include planning, self-monitoring, verbal self-regulation, and change of mental set.

METHODS

Further complicating this lack of consensus is the fact that the tasks designed to assess EF are numerous, varied, and widely criticized for their lack of construct validity (Brocki & Bohlin, 2004; Miyake, Friedman, Emerson, Witzki, & Kowerter, 2000), low test-retest reliability (Miyake et al., 2000),[1] lack of discriminant validity (Hughes, 2002a), and task impurity (i.e., any EF in action will implicate other, nonrelevant, cognitive processes, both executive and nonexecutive—Brocki & Bohlin, 2004; Miyake et al., 2000). Consequently, it is not uncommon to find that tasks claimed by one investigator to be classic measures of one EF are argued by another to measure something entirely different. For example, the Tower of Hanoi task is described as a "pure" measure of planning by Zelazo and Müller (2002), while Miyake et al. (2000) argue that it is more accurately a measure of inhibition.[2]

The long list of tasks used by EF researchers to measure EF and its various components includes the *Day-Night Stroop Task* (Gerstadt, Hong, & Diamond, 1994), the *Dimensional Change Card Sort* (Frye, Zelazo, & Palfai, 1995), the *Go-NoGo Task* (Luria, 1966), the *Handgame* (Hughes, 1998), the *Tower of London* (Shallice, 1982, based on the Tower of Hanoi), the *Windows Task* (Russell, Mauthner, Sarpe, & Tidswell, 1991), and the *Wisconsin Card Sorting Test* (based on Grant & Berg, 1948), although many others also exist. Several of these tasks obviously require respondents to inhibit a well-practiced response in favor of a less-practiced response (e.g., in the *Day-Night Stroop Task*, children are asked to say "day" when shown a line drawing of the moon and stars, and "night" when shown a line drawing of the sun). However, in many cases, alternative interpretations and analyses of such tasks and their associated response requirements also are possible (e.g., that the *Day-Night Stroop Task* requires children to attend to the line drawings, while simultaneously holding the instructions that are to guide their responses in working memory).

Other tasks, such as the *Dimensional Change Card Sort* and the *Wisconsin Card Sorting Test*, require children to sort cards that differ on various dimensions (color, shape, etc.) depending on sorting rules and feedback supplied by researchers. Interpretations of the psychological requirements of such tasks also vary, with some investigators emphasizing inhibitory skills and capabilities, others privileging working memory capabilities, and still others offering accounts that focus on interactions between inhibition, working memory, and other EF components, or postulating the execution of more complex series of problem-solving skills like problem representation, planning, execution, and evaluation (e.g., Zelazo, Carter, Reznick, & Frye, 1997). Still other EF tasks, such as the *Windows Task*, have encouraged an even wider array of interpretations that, in addition to running the usual gamut of explanations due to inhibition, working memory, flexibility, and problem solving, have expanded to include links between EF and neuropsychological research on the prefrontal cortex (PFC) and its development, and Theory of Mind (ToM) research that frequently employ the same and similar tasks (for a recent review and discussion, see Carpendale & Lewis, 2006, chapter 5).

In an attempt to achieve greater clarity concerning the psychological factors that might be interpreted as underlying EF, factor analyses of data derived from children's responses to various EF tasks recently have been undertaken (see Zelazo & Müller, 2002, for a summary and discussion of earlier factor analytic studies of EF in children). However, here again, a range of different interpretations and conclusions reigns. Lehto et al. state that "conceptual confusion about the true nature of EF tasks," as well as differences in the types of factor analysis employed, make comparing the results of different factor studies difficult (2003, p. 75). Brocki and Bohlin (2004) report the results of three separate factor analyses with 3–12-year-olds: the main EF factors in these studies were fluency, hypothesis testing/impulse control, and planning. They cite Barkley, Edwards, Laneri, and Fletcher (2001) whose analysis of data from adolescents with Attention Deficit Disorder and Oppositional Deficit Disorder led them to conclude that inattention, working memory, and inhibition were the main factors of EF. Brocki and Bohlin's (2004) own analysis (with 6–13-year-olds) revealed three independent factors which they named disinhibition (capturing the concept of inhibiting prepotent responses as well as inhibition that does not require withholding a response), speed/arousal (reflecting what Barkley referred to as inattention, which involves self-regulation of speed, arousal, and motivation), and working memory/fluency (which is claimed to be similar to Barkley's working memory). Finally, Lehto and colleagues' (2003) investigation of the dimensions of EF with 8–13-year-olds revealed three factors that they interpreted as overlapping with the ones previously discussed: inhibition, working memory, and planning. This last study was an attempt to replicate the findings of Miyake et al. (2000), an analysis in which similar, but differently named main factors (shifting, updating, and inhibition) were interpreted to be the basic EFs in adults.

Despite a few potentially promising links and overlaps across different studies, it is important to remember that factor analysis, even in its more confirmatory guises, is an empirically heavy-handed means of attempting to facilitate conceptual and theoretical advance in any area of psychological research. As Brocki and Bohlin (2004) note, in such analyses, results are very much dependent on the particular mix of tasks employed as data sources, the interpretation of factors and factor loadings by particular investigators, and the makeup and age range of the samples. Consequently, the results of different factor analytic studies are notoriously difficult to compare. Moreover, interpretations of the results of such analyses are underdetermined by the data that enter into them, and necessarily reflect the conceptualizations of researchers, which constitute yet another area of disagreement in EF inquiry.

CONCEPTIONS

"Narrowing" Accounts

While the dominant view in the field is to regard EF as a multidimensional construct (Lehto et al., 2003), constituted by a number of functions (Zelazo & Müller, 2002), a common alternative is to emphasize just one aspect of EF as its defining feature. Theories based on this idea attempt to simplify EF, and as such can be referred to as "narrowing" accounts. Despite their focus on different aspects of EF, all narrowing accounts share the motivation of simplification. Barkley (1997), for example, claims that *inhibition* is central to EF functioning, while Roberts and Pennington (1996) treat the *interaction* between inhibition and working memory as central (Brocki & Bohlin, 2004). In Russell's (1999) theory, inhibition and working memory are also thought to form the core of EF, but they are viewed as isolated, independent processes (Lehto et al., 2003). Such narrowing accounts frequently refer to the EF components that they highlight as "skills" (Carpendale & Lewis, 2006, p. 122), implying that they might be improved with practice and experience. Not surprisingly, because of their relative parsimony, narrowing accounts often are characterized as inadequate for capturing the complexity of EF (e.g., Zelazo & Müller, 2002).

A second alternative conceptualization shares the motivation to simplify, and thus also can be seen as a narrowing account. However, on this conceptualization, instead of focusing on particular components of EF, EF as a whole is conceptualized as a single entity (Duncan, Burgess, & Emslie, 1995; Duncan, Emslie, Williams, Johnson, & Freer, 1996), or as a "higher-order cognitive mechanism or ability" (Zelazo & Müller, 2002, p. 446). EF tasks, much like general intelligence measures, require multiple cognitive processes to operate together in novel ways to meet the demands of particular situations. This has led some researchers to conclude that EF may be equivalent to "g" (as noted in Beveridge et al., 2002; Hughes, 2002a). Theoretical analogy and some evidence of cognitive congruence (cognitive task performance that is positively correlated with performance on other tasks) lend support to this view (Hughes & Graham, 2002). Lehto et al. (2003) however, report low correlations among executive tasks, and claim that this is an established finding. Moreover, their factor analytic results do not fit the unitary model posited by the "g" hypothesis. In a somewhat different vein, Hughes and Graham (2002) cite findings from participants with brain lesions, whose EF performance is more highly correlated across tasks than would be expected by cognitive congruence alone. Finally, Zelazo and Müller (2002) claim that treating EF as a general ability "essentially invokes a homunculus" and fails to consider adequately relations among various aspects of EF and possible mechanisms by means of which EF is accomplished (p. 446).

Problem-Solving Account

Zelazo et al. (1997) and Zelazo and Müller (2002) promote a different approach to conceptualizing EF. Their conceptualization views EF as a function, a behavioral construct defined in terms of its problem-solving outcomes. To characterize EF as a function, its hierarchical structure must be described and its subfunctions delineated and organized around the common outcome of problem solving (Zelazo & Müller, 2002). In this model, "functionally distinct phases of PS [problem solving] can be organized around the constant outcome of solving a problem, and we can attempt to show how these phases contribute to that outcome" (p. 447). The first stage is problem representation, followed by planning, execution (intending/rule use), and ending with evaluation (error detection/correction). According to Zelazo and Müller, the problem-solving framework avoids a homuncular conception of EF, describes the interaction of different executive processes as they come together to fulfill the higher order function, and informs the selection of well-defined measures.

"Widening" Accounts

A fourth common approach to EF has been called the "componential approach" by Ozonoff and Strayer (1997) and the "fractionation of EF" by

Hughes and Graham (2002). In contrast to narrowing accounts, this approach "widens" EF through its focus on multiple components, which may or may not be related to each other. Research based on this approach seeks to identify EF components and investigate relations among them. This approach has been presented as a means of avoiding common methodological difficulties, such as using the same task to measure different EFs or assuming that different versions of similar tasks draw on the same processes (Beveridge et al., 2002). It is also claimed that such componential analysis is a necessary requirement for adequately interpreting the results of EF tasks (Hughes & Graham, 2002). Beveridge et al.'s study (with 6- and 8-year-olds) combined the componential approach and within-task manipulation. Their goal was to reveal the relation between inhibition and working memory. They note that in order to show that dissociable subcomponents of EF exist, it is necessary not only to show that varying one component within a task affects performance, but also to show that "within the same task two or more sub-components can be varied so as to produce performance effects that show independence of each other" (Beveridge et al., 2002, p. 109). Their hypothesis was informed by the work of Roberts and Pennington (1996), who argue, like Schmeichel and Baumeister (2004), that individuals have a limited capacity for executive control. Different EF processes or components are seen to tap into the same pool of executive resources (Beveridge et al., 2002). According to this view, a working memory by inhibition interaction would imply that "a unitary, capacity-limited executive system is tapped by both of these processes" (Beveridge et al., 2002, p. 110). The expected interaction, however, was not found. Such findings are consistent with the view that working memory and inhibition are independent processes.

Hughes (2002a) reports evidence gathered from employing a componential approach with children. In the studies she cites, the *independence* of EF components (primarily inhibition and working memory) is emphasized. All in all, although posited relationships among various EF components vary considerably and evidence for particular relations often conflicts or is unavailable, the componential view seems to be the most popular way of conceptualizing EF. Nonetheless, the independence versus the interdependence of various EF components, such as working memory and inhibition, remains far from decided.

"Distributed" Accounts

A fifth way to view EF builds upon the idea of separate EF components or processes, and also may be considered to be a "widening" account. However, instead of seeing EF as a true "executive" function, overseeing and controlling various cognitive, reasoning, or functional components, the "distributed" view understands EF to be located within and spread across all of the components, processes, or skills that combine to constitute it. One potentially important consequence of opting for a distributed conception of EF concerns the possible role of social factors in EF. In the componential view, EF typically is composed mostly of various internal, cognitive processes or skills. The distributed view, on the other hand, may be more amenable to the possibility of, and even might encourage a focus on, the external distribution of EF in the social, interpersonal world (Carpendale & Lewis, 2006).

There is increasing evidence that EF is influenced by social interaction. Carpendale and Lewis (2006) note that Luria, one of the first to promote the term EF, held that cognition results from social interaction. From such a perspective, EF is assumed to be embedded in the social context and mediated by communication (see Zelazo & Jacques, 1996). Consequently, some recent research has examined social, interpersonal factors and processes in EF task environments. For example, the *Windows Task*, a common measure of inhibition, requires a child to point to an empty box instead of a baited box containing a prize, so as to deceive the experimenter. Despite the negative feedback of not obtaining the prize for themselves if they point to the baited box, the standard finding is that (even on trials in which transparent windows on the sides of the containers allow the children clearly to see the prize or its absence) 3-year-olds repeatedly fail the task by pointing to the baited container (Russell et al., 1991). Hala and Russell (2001) and Russell, Hala, and Hill (2003) devised manipulations of the standard windows task, which involved various amounts and kinds of social interaction. A version of the task that replaced deception with collaboration, and a version in which the child used a pointing hand to cue an experimenter, both resulted in improved executive performance.[3] In another study, Hala (2004) provided children with an "ally" with whom they could collaborate to achieve enhanced executive control. Still other studies reveal that children who are told that the experimenter has heard that they are good at a particular executive skill will subsequently perform better on tasks of delay of gratification (Toner, Moore, & Emmons, 1980), inhibition, and set shifting (Lewis, Harrison, & Warburton, in progress, as cited in Carpendale & Lewis, 2006) than those told that the experimenter has heard that they had many friends. Links between number of siblings and EF (Cole & Mitchell, 2000), language and EF (Ferneyhough & Fradley, 2005), parenting and EF (Landry, Miller-Loncar, Smith, & Swank, 2002), labeling and EF (Müller, Zelazo, Hood, Lenone, & Rohrer, 2004), and SES and EF (Noble, Norman, & Farah, 2005) highlight the role of social context and processes in EF.[4] In the distributed view, EF is understood as distributed both internally (in and across various internal, cognitive or reasoning components and skills) and externally (within social contexts and interactions).

"Unity in Diversity" Account

The sixth and final conception of EF considered herein can be seen as a sort of hybrid between the narrowing and the widening accounts. This view, known as the "unity in diversity" view, can be credited to Miyake and his colleagues (2000), who, noting many of the difficulties that confront EF research, argue that correlational, exploratory factor analyses are of limited usefulness for revealing the organization of EF. They introduce latent variable analysis as overcoming some of the problems they perceive, and as more useful to the further theoretical development of EF. Three EFs were chosen for examination: *Shifting* between tasks or mental sets, *Updating* and monitoring of working memory representations, and *Inhibition* of dominant or prepotent responses. The goals of the study were to assess the degree to which the three target EFs were unitary or separable, and if at least somewhat distinguishable, to outline their relative contributions to EF tasks. The results of the confirmatory factor analysis revealed that the three EFs, while not completely independent, were clearly distinguishable. At the same time, they shared some underlying commonality. Thus, these three EFs were interpreted by Miyake et al. (2000) as both separable and related, showing both unity and diversity.

Suggestions as to what the source of the commonality might be included a shared reliance on either working memory or inhibition. Lehto et al. (2003) used the same model to investigate whether EFs might be similarly organized in children. As mentioned earlier, they obtained three similar factors. More importantly with respect to conceptualizing EF, their data fit Miyake et al.'s model of "separate but interrelated" EFs better than either a model in which the different EFs were treated as independent, or a unitary model (Lehto et al., 2003, p. 73). Miyake et al. (2000) also note that there may be additional EFs to add to the three factors they reported, and that it may be possible to further decompose the three reported EFs into more basic processes.

Finally, it is worth noting that the taxonomy of conceptions of EF offered here should not be assumed to be either exhaustive or definitive. Other conceptualizations and conceptual schemes certainly are possible, as are different or multiple placements of particular works within the taxonomic categories proposed. For example, Zelazo and Müller's (2002) functional, problem-solving account of EF also contains some elements similar to the unity in diversity and distributed conceptualization discussed previously. In their functional, problem-solving model, separate cognitive, behavioral processes, or EFs are located both internally and in the social context, and combine to serve a common function defined in terms of a common outcome (problem solving). Clearly, the concepts of separateness and relatedness could thus be argued to characterize their approach as well.

Theoretical Incoherence, Psychologism, Mechanism, and Reductionism

Having selectively reviewed some of the most frequently encountered definitions and conceptions of EF, and discussed briefly some of the methods employed in research on EF, we now turn to an examination of theoretical concerns that attend the current state of inquiry in this important area of contemporary developmental psychology. In so doing, we shift our focus from some of the details of particular programs of inquiry to more general conceptual and assumptive issues that characterize the broader ideational frameworks within which particular programs of inquiry are embedded. This shift from particulars to more general theoretical issues takes a decidedly critical turn, as possible problems and challenges associated with definitional and conceptual incoherence, psychologism, mechanism, and reductionism are identified and discussed.

THE POSSIBILITY OF THEORETICAL INCOHERENCE

As already hinted, the wide variety of definitions and conceptions of EF risks theoretical incoherence. This is particularly true when EF is defined and considered in ways that appear difficult to integrate, and perhaps even stand in mutually contradictive relations to each other. Definitions of EF that stipulate it as self-control, flexible goal-directed responding, or problem solving might conceivably be made to mesh with definitions that describe EF as constituted by various component processes, operations, and skills operating at functional and underlying psychological levels. Further, some combination of such macroscopic and componential definitions might not be inconsistent with suggestions that the general and specific operations referred to might be correlated with particular kinds and areas of brain activity (especially in the PFC). However, any such integration would require much more theoretical articulation than has been achieved thus far in this area of inquiry. In fact, not unlike several other areas of contemporary psychological investigation, theoretical work in EF that is concerned with the definition, conceptualization, and clarification of terms and claims has taken a back seat to empirical inquiry that has made use of existing tasks, measures, and methods without explicit theorizing that connects the components of these tasks and methods to the theoretical entities they purport to inform, require, or demonstrate.

Nonetheless, of perhaps even more immediate concern are definitions and conceptualizations that appear to be diametrically opposed in part or in whole. For example, despite complex possibilities such as "unity in diversity," it is not strictly possible for something (in this case, EF) to be both "A" and "not A" simultaneously. Consequently, EF must be either multidimensional or not, and if not, the single defining dimension must be the same across different accounts. Further, although EF might be correlated with, or constituted by, processes at different levels (i.e., behavioral/functional, psychological/ cognitive/emotional, and neurophysiological), it ought not be defined simultaneously as higher-order cognitive mechanisms or abilities, problem-solving behaviors, and neurophysiological PFC activity, at least in the absence of a clear over-arching conceptualization and definition. Further, problem-solving behaviors may be enabled and supported by underlying psychological and neurophysiological processes and activities, but they ought not be identified with these purported underlying operations, just as a game of baseball ought not be identified with baseball players, their equipment, their behavioral and cognitive strategies, and the functioning of their brains. To do otherwise is to risk theoretical incoherence.

THE DANGERS OF PSYCHOLOGISM

Psychologism is the philosophical doctrine asserting that logical and rational entities and processes can be reduced to or explained by underlying mental states or activities. Important psychological distinctions such as that between performance and competence depend on the doctrine of psychologism, and so do many conceptualizations of EF. Consider, for example, the emphases on inner, mental, psychological, or neuropsychological states in many descriptions of executive functioning. "The term 'executive function' refers to a complex cognitive construct that encompasses the set of processes that underlie flexible goal-directed behaviour (e.g., planning, inhibitory control, attentional flexibility, working memory)" (Hughes, 2002b). "The construct of EF is intended to capture the psychological abilities whose impairment is presumed to underlie these manifest deficits" (Zelazo & Müller, 2002). "However the neural and cognitive processes which underpin performance in executive function (EF) tasks have yet to be fully specified" (Beveridge et al., 2002, p. 107; also see Rabbitt, 1997).

The kind of psychologism that is so clearly evident in these quotations does several things that may not be immediately obvious. First, it *reduces* complex psychological and behavioral processes such as planning, attending, and inhibiting primarily to mental (cognitive) and neural (brain) states or processes. What is misleading about such a reduction is that activities such as planning typically go well beyond a planner's thoughts about what she might do. Planning frequently includes making lists of possible alternative courses of action and their advantages and disadvantages, consulting relevant schedules and timetables, preparing itineraries, and so forth. Notice that when considered in this way, planning certainly includes thinking (and requisite/relevant cerebral events and processes), but is not reduced to the mental life of the planner in isolation from the worldly activity in which the planner engages. In contrast, psychologism *understands* activities of persons (such as planning, attending, and inhibiting) in terms of underlying mental and neural states and processes somewhat cut off from the worldly engagement of active persons. Moreover, psychologism *locates the causes* or origins of activities such as planning, attending, and inhibiting in inner mental and neural states and processes—as opposed, for example, to understanding such activities as constituted within recreational, familial, and sociocultural events and practices, such as vacations, weddings, business trips, and so on.

In effect, what psychologism does is to trap our definitions, conceptualizations, and explanations of EF *inside* our bodies and brains. When this occurs, the focus of psychological theorizing and inquiry shifts from the activity of persons in a biophysical and sociocultural world, which includes materials and practices shared with others, to the inner psychological and neurological processes (mental representation, information processing, and PFC activation) of individuals. When we fall prey to the "inner trap" of psychologism, we forget, as Carpendale and Lewis (2006, p. 131) remind us that "the theoretician who promoted the term executive function, Alexander Luria (1961) ... was attempting to set executive skills within a social framework in which the child acquires cultural symbols."

As many developmental theorists (e.g., Bickhard, 2004; Chapman, 1991; Gauvain, 2001a, 2001b; Hobson, 2002; Martin, 2003; Mead, 1934; Tomasello, 1999; Vygotsky, 1978) have recognized, the sources of consciousness, meaning, mind, and self-understanding lie in interactivity with others within historical, cultural practices and forms of life. Indeed, the very conception of psychological development itself requires that we do not cut ourselves off from the world by adopting strong versions of psychologism. First, if we only have access to the world through our mental representations and neural configurations, there is no way that we can detect errors in such representations and configurations. Consequently, we are left with no way to explain the readily observable, progressive refinements in our actions and capabilities that so much of the literature in developmental psychology so clearly documents. Second, if we understand our minds and selves (including our executive functioning) solely or primarily as inner, mental, and neural processes and states, we are tempted to explain the origins of our representations and configurations by adopting a rather extreme form of "innate-ness." For, if we are cut off radically from the world and others, to the extent that all of our perceptions, conceptions, and actions always must be filtered through our internal systems of representation and configuration, the temptation is to understand all of our conceptual structures (in either full-blown or "seeded" form) as given by our biophysical makeup. After all, if such internal structures have functional primacy, it seems likely that they also should have developmental primacy. Such "innate-ism" poses seemingly intractable theoretical problems concerning which representations and configurations might be derived from which more basic ones, and what structural relations pertain amongst them (Edelman, 1987).

Fortunately, there is no need to adopt strong forms of psychologism that court developmental nihilism by isolating our mental life and functioning from our ongoing activity within historically and socioculturally evolved systems of interactivity and shared practice. It is in our worldly activity, not in our underlying mental and neural functioning, that the meaning and significance required to fuel our goal-directed functioning may be located. When psychologism blinds us to this essential fact of human development, we are deprived of the raw materials of mental life, EF included. That persons employ psychological structures and processes is not to be denied. The point is that such structures and processes require, emerge and unfold within, and never are separated entirely from our ongoing worldly activity.

MECHANISM AND REDUCTIONISM

In addition to those matters discussed earlier, several additional, pernicious consequences for developmental theory flow from psychologism. Some of these consequences are made even more dire by a further reduction of psychological activity such as executive functioning to neurological configurations and processes alone. In order to appreciate the way in which psychologism provides a platform for strong forms of neurophysiological mechanism and reductionism, it is necessary to reflect briefly on the *homunculus* problem. As noted by Zelazo and Müller (2002, p. 446), defining EF as a higher-order cognitive mechanism, ability, or module (e.g., Baddeley, 1996; Denckla & Reiss, 1997; Norman & Shallice, 1986) "essentially invokes a homunculus" that offers only the illusion of explanation. This is so because any mental mechanism that explains and constitutes EF must itself be explained and constituted. Otherwise, all that has been accomplished is to add another, and possibly unnecessary, hypothetical level or layer of complexity to our conceptualization of EF. Unless we know how to specify and explain the cognitive mechanism invoked, we succeed only in complicating matters when we insist that executive functioning consists of a cognitive mechanism that *underlies* "planning, decision-making, judgment, and self-perception" (Zelazo & Müller, 2002, p. 446). Our reading of much of the literature on executive functioning failed to produce any convincing specification and explanation for any cognitive mechanism of this kind.

Some may quarrel with this conclusion and claim that conceptualizations of EF as a series of components of problem solving or decision-making (such as Zelazo et al.'s, 1997, list of problem representation, planning, execution, and evaluation) avoid the homunculus problem because such accounts do not invoke an over-arching executive module or mechanism. However, in our view there are only two ways in which componential, widening and distributed accounts might be thought to succeed in dispensing with a homunculus. The first of these, which we regard as unviable, involves a further reduction of psychological components to nothing more than their neurological bases. [Indeed, in psychology in general, psychologism frequently leads to reductive neurologism for precisely such reasons—cf. Martin, Sugarman, & Thompson, 2003.] Unfortunately, this way of avoiding the homunculus problem invokes a strongly reductionistic account of components of executive functioning such as problem representation and planning. Such accounts strip component executive skills and abilities of the kinds of significance and meaning required for an adequate conceptualization and explanation of the kind of goal-directed activity that EF purports to be about. After all, relevant states and processes, including those in the PFC, although obviously necessary for the executive functioning of persons, do not by themselves envision, pursue, plan, and act in relation to tasks such as the *Tower of London* or the *Wisconsin Card Sorting Test*, let alone the multitude of tasks that confront us as we navigate our daily lives. Neural activity in the orbitofrontal cortex (OFC) or the dorsolateral prefrontal cortex (DL-PFC) is associated with but do not constitute EF or any of its possible components. Consequently, any attempt to avoid the homunculus problem by neurophysiological reduction must be seen as inadequate in that we have no way of explaining how the neural patterns and properties invoked constitute or explain what needs to be explained. Moreover, the absence of such an explanation probably is not simply a function of our currently inadequate state of knowledge about such matters. For, as mentioned earlier, any viable explanation of EF and similar complex human social–psychological processes necessarily must attend to human activity in historical and sociocultural context. History, culture, and society cannot be reduced to the psychology or the neurology of individual human beings alone.

In our view, the only viable way to understand EF without courting an inner homunculus (and this is the second way in which componential, widening, and distributed accounts of EF might work) is to treat EF as the activity of embodied persons in sociocultural context. As Bennett and Hacker (2003) recently have argued, the problems encountered and courted by both psychologism and neurologism all flow from *the mereological fallacy*. This fallacy consists in our ascription of psychological attributes to anything less than the person as a whole. Thus, the problems of psychologism, mechanism, and reductionism that attend so much theorizing concerning executive functioning may be seen to flow from the tendency of many researchers in this area of inquiry to ascribe to inner, mental, and neural "parts of persons" capabilities and attributes that logically can be applied only to persons as a whole.

By parsing the worldly activity of developing persons into information processing, schematic, memorial, and neural structures and processes, we create hypothetical models of self-regulation and executive functioning of highly debatable ontological status. As already pointed out, it is highly unlikely that the executive functioning of persons can be considered to reside in inner psychological and neural entities alone. Psychologism and neurologism of this kind only can explain executive functioning if it is assumed that the executive (the person or self) equates to the postulated inner structures and functions. But, it is persons, not parts of persons, such as brains or cognitive processes and structures, who think and act in the world. It makes no sense, grammatically or logically, to talk as if self-regulatory mechanisms or EFs set goals, plan, remember, inhibit, and evaluate. Such predicates are sensibly applied only to persons active within a world of relational, linguistic interactivity governed by sociocultural conventions concerning what is meaningful, significant, and proper. To say that depersonalized, inner, psychological, or neural systems have goals, plans, and reactions is to forget that these hypothesized parts of persons cannot function in these ways. It is persons who have goals, plans, and reactions not their brains or their central nervous systems, however necessary these may be to the existence and execution of persons' goals, plans, and reactions (Bennett & Hacker, 2003). It follows that only persons and their worldly activities are the proper focus for psychological inquiry into matters of self-regulation and EF.

In saying all of this, we do not want to imply that we view all work on EF to be irretrievably committed to what we regard as problems and fallacies of psychologism, mechanism, and reductionism. As mentioned previously, in our discussion of distributed conceptions of EF, we applaud work in this area of inquiry that has highlighted the important role of social context and processes. For example, the work of Zelazo and his colleagues (e.g., Zelazo & Jacques, 1996; Zelazo & Müller, 2002) strives to position both psychological and neuropsychological components and processes of EF within the sociocultural activity of embodied persons. Nonetheless, our reading of much of the literature on EF reveals what we regard as a worrying tendency to emphasize and privilege mental, neuropsychological components and processes over the more holistic functioning of persons within sociocultural contexts and practices of problem solving and goal-directed, strategic activity.

Conclusions

Lying behind the definitional, conceptual, and theoretical difficulties discussed herein is the specter of ontological and related epistemological confusion—the possibility that because we do not know what EF is, we do not know what we are talking about when we theorize about it. Given the various matters that have been discussed and illustrated, it seems clear that the ontological status of EF is both uncertain (differences in definitions and conceptions) and arguably confused (difficulties occasioned by tendencies to psychologism, mechanism, and reductionism).

Nonetheless, there also is considerable evidence that many of the difficulties and possible confusions discussed here are well known to leading researchers in the area of EF—witness the various quotations indicative of such recognition that have formed an important part of the preceding text. More recently, there also have been a number of promising proposals to balance and integrate the focus of EF research on psychological and neural processes with a focus on the nature and analysis of the various tasks employed in this research, and the social contexts that surround these tasks. For example, several contributors to a special issue of *Infant and Child Development* suggest that "what is also needed is a closer examination of the task requirements" (Colvert, Custance, & Swettenham, 2002, p. 1999), a recommendation that obviously has influenced some of the empirical work reported in that same issue (e.g., Beveridge et al., 2002). And, of course, as mentioned previously, the possibility of a distinctively social turn in research on EF is well documented in Carpendale and Lewis (2006). Moreover, it is possible to interpret functional approaches to EF such as that proposed by Zelazo and Müller (2002) as emphasizing demonstrable action capabilities across different problem-solving contexts and tasks, thus downplaying hints of psychologism and neurologism that occasionally seem to creep into such accounts.

At the same time, it must be said that, at least to date, there does not appear to be a wide-spread appetite for the endorsement of more holistic conceptions of EF and self-regulation among EF researchers in general. The difficulty here may be a reluctance to move away from forms of psychological theorizing that privilege inner mechanisms, structures, and processes, given the central place of such theoretical forms in the scientific and disciplinary practices of psychologists. However, even here, there are encouraging signs of more integrative forms of theorizing that seek to understand personal capabilities like executive functioning as nested and emergent within sociogenetic and socio-cultural frameworks (e.g., Bickhard, 2004; Martin, 2003; Mascolo, Fischer, & Neimeyer, 1999; Tomasello, 1999). If such approaches were adopted in EF research, EF might eventually be transmogrified into a set of functionally related capabilities that persons use to navigate various problem situations and tasks, the origins of which are found in the worldly activity of developing persons in interaction with others. Such a focus would not deny the inner experiences and functioning of persons, but would recognize the necessarily social origins of their experience and functioning, and stop well short of identifying any such inner experiences and functions with the problem solving, task activities to be explained. Theories of EF then could be developed that would be more thoroughly grounded in detailed descriptions of the functional activities of individuals in particular task environments and contexts. Such detailed descriptions and related analyses of actions and interactions within and across focal tasks and contexts would take theoretical preference over inner, psychological and neurological, explanatory mechanisms of dubious ontological status. The intentions, beliefs, reasoning, and strategic reactions of children as developing psychological persons would not be ignored or denied. However, it would be clearly recognized that such psychological attributes are emergent attributes of developing persons in the worldly contexts in which they exist and act with others.

NOTES

1. Low test-retest reliability might be expected, if it is assumed that EF only is engaged in novel task environments (see Hughes & Graham, 2002).
2. It is conceivable that this particular difference in interpretation might reflect a difference in the level of analysis selected—that is, whether researchers' interest is in the overall solution to the problem, or in what might be regarded as a critical subcomponent or key requisite that enables appropriate problem solving to proceed and unfold.
3. However, so too did a less social, automated version of the windows task.

4. Also see the chapter by Landry and Smith in the current volume for a summary of social (including linguistic and parental) influences on the development of self-regulation and EF.

REFERENCES

Baddeley, A. (1996). Exploring the central executive [Special issue: Working memory]. *Quarterly Journal of Experimental Psychology: Human Experimental Psychology, 49A*, 5–28.

Barkley, R. A. (1997). Behavioral inhibition, sustained attention, and executive functions. *Psychological Bulletin, 121*, 65–94.

Barkley, R. A., Edwards, G., Laneri, M., & Fletcher, K. (2001). Executive functioning, temporal discounting, and sense of time in adolescents with attention deficit hyperactivity disorder (ADHD) and oppositional defiant disorder (ODD). *Journal of Abnormal Child Psychology, 29*, 541–556.

Bennett, M. R., & Hacker, P. M. S. (2003). *Philosophical foundations of neuroscience.* Oxford, England: Blackwell Publishing.

Beveridge, M., Jarrold, C., & Pettit, E. (2002). An experimental approach to executive fingerprinting in young children. *Infant and Child Development, 11*, 107–123.

Bickhard, M. H. (2004). The social ontology of persons. In J. I. M. Carpendale & U. Muller (Eds.), *Social interaction and the development of knowledge* (pp. 111–132). Mahwah, NJ: Lawrence Erlbaum Associates.

Brocki, K.C., & Bohlin, G. (2004). Executive functions in children aged 6 to 13: A dimensional and developmental study. *Developmental Neuropsychology, 26*, 571–593.

Carpendale, J., & Lewis, C. (2006). *How children develop social understanding.* Oxford, UK: Blackwell Publishing.

Chapman, M. (1991). The epistemic triangle: Operative and communicative components of cognitive competence. In M. Chandler (Ed.), *Criteria for competence: Controversies in the conceptualization and assessment of children's abilities* (pp. 209–228). Hillsdale, NJ: Lawrence Erlbaum Associates.

Cole, K., & Mitchell, P. (2000). Siblings in the development of executive control and a theory of mind. *British Journal of Developmental Psychology, 18*, 279–295.

Colvert, E., Custance, D., & Swettenham, J. (2002). Rule-based reasoning and theory of mind in autism: A commentary on the work of Zelazo, Jacques, Burack and Frye. *Infant and Child Development, 11*, 197–200.

Denckla, M. B., & Reiss, A. L. (1997). Prefrontal-subcortical circuits in developmental disorders. In N. A. Krasnegor, G. R. Lyon, & P. S. Goldman-Rakic (Eds.), *Development of the prefrontal cortex: Evolution, neurobiology, and behavior* (pp. 283–293). Baltimore: Paul H. Brookes Publishing Co., Inc.

Duncan, J., Burgess, P., & Emslie, H. (1995). Fluid intelligence after frontal lobe lesions. *Neuropsychologia, 33*, 261–268.

Duncan, J., Emslie, H., Williams, P., Johnson, R., & Freer, C. (1996). Intelligence and the frontal lobe: The organization of goal-directed behavior. *Cognitive Psychology, 30*, 257–303.

Edelman, G. (1987). *Neural Darwinism*. New York: Basic Books.

Eslinger, P. (1996). Conceptualizing, describing, and measuring components of executive functioning: A summary. In G. R. Lyon & N. A. Krasnegor (Eds.), *Attention, memory, and executive function* (pp. 367–396). Baltimore: Paul H. Brookes Publishing Co., Inc.

Fernyhough, C., & Fradley, E. (2005). Private speech on an executive task: Relations with task difficulty and task performance. *Cognitive Development, 20*, 103–120.

Frye, D., Zelazo, P. D., & Palfai, T. (1995). Theory of mind and rule-based reasoning. *Cognitive Development, 10*, 483–527.

Gauvain, M. (2001a). Cultural tools, social interaction and the development of thinking [Special issue: Cultural minds]. *Human Development, 44(2–3)*, 126–143.

Gauvain, M. (2001b). *The social context of cognitive development*. New York: Guilford Press.

Gerstadt, C. L., Hong, Y. J., & Diamond, A. (1994). The relationship between cognition and action: Performance of children 3 1/2–7 years old on a Stroop-like day-night test. *Cognition, 53*, 129–153.

Grant, D. A., & Berg, E. A. (1948). A behavioral analysis of degree of reinforcement and ease of shifting to new responses in a Weigl-type card-sorting problem. *Journal of Experimental Psychology, 38*, 404–411.

Hala, S. (2004, September). *The role of collaboration in enhancing executive control for 3-year-olds in the windows task*. Presented at the Consortium for the Advancement of Child Health: Executive Functioning and Social Interaction, Vancouver, Canada.

Hala, S., & Russell, J. (2001). Executive control within strategic deception: A window on early cognitive development? *Journal of Experimental Child Psychology, 80*, 112–141.

Hobson, P. (2002). *The cradle of thought*. Hampshire, England: Macmillan Education Ltd.

Hughes, C. (1998). Executive function in preschoolers: Links with theory of mind and verbal ability. *British Journal of Developmental Psychology, 16*, 233–253.

Hughes, C. (2002a). Executive functions and development: Emerging themes. *Infant and Child Development, 11*, 201–209.

Hughes, C. (2002b). Executive functions and development: Why the interest? *Infant and Child Development, 11*, 69–71.

Hughes, C., & Graham, A. (2002). Measuring executive functions in childhood: Problems and solutions? *Child and Adolescent Mental Health, 7(3)*, 131–142.

Landry, S. H., Miller-Loncar, C. L., Smith, K. E., & Swank, P. R. (2002). The role of early parenting in children's development of executive processes. *Developmental Neuropsychology, 21*, 15–41.

Lehto, J. E., Juujarvi, P., Kooistra, L., & Pulkkinen, L. (2003). Dimensions of executive functioning: Evidence from children. *British Journal of Developmental Psychology, 21,* 59–80.

Luria, A. R. (1961). *The role of speech in the regulation of normal and abnormal behavior.* New York: Liveright.

Luria, A. R. (1966). *Higher cortical functions in man* (2nd ed.). New York: Basic Books. (Original work published 1962).

Martin, J. (2003). Emergent persons. *New Ideas in Psychology, 21,* 85–99.

Martin, J., Sugarman, J., & Thompson, J. (2003). *Psychology and the question of agency.* Albany, NY: State University of New York Press.

Mascolo, M. F., Fischer, K. W., & Neimeyer, R. A. (1999). The dynamic codevelopment of intentionality, self, and social relations. In J. Brandtstädter & R. M. Lerner (Eds.), *Action & self-development: Theory and research through the life span* (pp. 133–166). Thousand Oaks, CA: Sage Publications.

Mead, G. H. (1934). *Mind, self, and society: From the standpoint of a social behaviorist.* Chicago: University of Chicago.

Miyake, A., Friedman, N. P., Emerson, M. J., Witzki, A. H., & Kowerter, A. (2000). The unity and diversity of executive functions and their contributions to complex "frontal lobe" tasks: A latent variable analysis. *Cognitive Psychology, 41,* 49–100.

Müller, U., Zelazo, P. D., Hood, S., Leone, T., & Rohrer, L. (2004). Interference control in a new rule-use task: Age-related changes, labeling, and attention. *Child Development, 75,* 1594–1609.

Noble, K. G., Norman, M. F., & Farah, M. J. (2005). Neurocognitive correlates of socioeconomic status in kindergarten children. *Developmental Science, 8,* 74–87.

Norman, D. A., & Shallice, T. (1986). Attention to action: Willed and automatic control of behavior. In R. J. Davidson, G. E. Schwartz, & D. Shapiro (Eds.), *Consciousness and self regulation* (Vol. 4, pp. 4–18). New York: Plenum.

Ozonoff, S., & Strayer, D. L. (1997). Inhibitory function in nonretarded children with autism. *Journal of Autism and Developmental Disorders, 27,* 59–77.

Perner, J., Lang, B., & Kloo, D. (2002). Theory of mind and self-control: More than a common problem of inhibition. *Child Development, 73,* 752–767.

Rabbitt, P. (1997). *Methodology of frontal and executive function.* Hove, East Sussex, UK: Psychology Press.

Roberts, R. J., & Pennington, B. F. (1996). An interactive framework for examining prefrontal cognitive processes. *Developmental Neuropsychology, 12,* 105–126.

Russell, J. (1999). Cognitive development as an executive process—in part: A homeopathic dose of Piaget. *Developmental Science, 2,* 247–295.

Russell, J., Hala, S., & Hill, E. (2003). The automated windows task: The performance of preschool children, children with autism, and children with moderate learning difficulties. *Cognitive Development, 18,* 111–137.

Russell, J., Mauthner, N., Sharpe, S., & Tidswell, T. (1991). The "windows task" as a measure of strategic deception in preschoolers and autistic subjects. *British Journal of Developmental Psychology, 9,* 331–349.

Schmeichel, B. J., & Baumeister, R. F. (2004). Self-regulatory strength. In R. F. Baumeister & K. D. Vohs (Eds.), *Handbook of self-regulation: Research, theory, and applications* (pp. 84–98). New York: Guilford Press.

Shallice, T. (1982). Specific impairments of planning. In D. E. Broadbent & L. Weiskrantz (Eds.), *The neuropsychology of cognitive function* (pp. 199–209). London: The Royal Society.

Tomasello, M. (1999). *The cultural origins of human cognition.* Cambridge, MA: Harvard University Press.

Toner, I. J., Moore, L. P., & Emmons, B. A. (1980). The effect of being labeled on subsequent self-control in children. *Child Development, 51,* 618–621.

Tranel, D., Anderson, S. W., & Benton, A. (1994). Development of the concept of "executive function" and its relationship to the frontal lobes. In F. Boller & J. Grafman (Eds.), *Handbook of Neuropsychology* (Vol. 9, pp. 125–148). Amsterdam: Elsevier.

Vygotsky, L. (1978). *Mind in society: The development of higher psychological processes.* Cambridge, MA: Harvard University Press.

Zelazo, P. D., Carter, A., Reznick, J. S., & Frye, D. (1997). Early development of executive function: A problem-solving framework. *Review of General Psychology, 1,* 198–226.

Zelazo, P. D., & Jacques, S. (1996). Children's rule use: Representation, reflection and cognitive control. *Annals of Child Development, 12,* 119–176.

Zelazo, P. D., & Müller, U. (2002). Executive function in typical and atypical development. In U. Goswami (Ed.), *Blackwell handbook of childhood cognitive development* (pp. 445–469). Malden, MA: Blackwell Publishers.

3

Vygotsky, Luria, and the Social Brain

CHARLES FERNYHOUGH

In order to explain the highly complex forms of human consciousness one must go beyond the human organism. One must seek the origins of conscious activity and "categorical" behavior not in the recesses of the human brain or in the depths of the spirit, but in the external conditions of life. Above all, this means that one must seek these origins in the external processes of social life, in the social and historical forms of human existence.

– Luria (1981, p. 25)

The question of how children acquire the capacity to regulate their own cognition and behavior has given rise to an impressive body of recent research. As the contributions to this volume show, researchers in the fields of developmental psychology, developmental cognitive neuroscience, cognitive psychology, and cognitive neuropsychology have contributed in various ways to our understanding of executive functioning (EF), defined as the ability to control, inhibit, and monitor one's own physical and mental activity (Russell, 1996). EF has been suggested to be important for meeting various challenges encountered by children in their cognitive (Carlson, Mandell, & Williams, 2004) and social (Blair, 2002; Shoda, Mischel, & Peake, 1990) lives, while EF deficits have been implicated in developmental disorders such as ADHD (Barkley, 1997) and autism spectrum disorders (Happé, Booth, Charlton, & Hughes, 2006; Hill, 2004; Pennington & Ozonoff, 1996). A tendency to regard EF as a unitary construct, stemming partly from evidence for

EF deficits following lesions to the prefrontal cortex (Baddeley, 1986; Luria, 1966/1980; Shallice, 1988), has yielded in recent years to a view of EF as consisting of a group of independent subprocesses specialized for functions such as planning (Shallice & Burgess, 1991) and task coordination (e.g., Baddeley, Logie, Bressi, Della Sala, & Spinnler, 1986; Miyake et al., 2000).

For the most part these findings have been interpreted within a view of EF which sees it as being driven by the maturation of the prefrontal cortex in the first five or so years of life (e.g., Luria, 1973). Among the evidence cited in support of this view are findings that lesions to the prefrontal cortex are behaviorally silent in young children (Eslinger, Biddle, & Grattan, 1997; Golden, 1981; although see Zelazo & Müller, 2002, for a review of contrasting views). Although the idea that EF is localized exclusively in the frontal lobes has been questioned in recent years (Zelazo & Müller, 2002), the assumption that children's executive capacities are developmentally regulated by cortical maturation remains deep-rooted (Diamond, 2002; Diamond, Prevor, Callender, & Druin, 1997; Welsh, Pennington, Ozonoff, Rouse, & McCabe, 1990). The value of seeking neurological specificity in tracing the rich array of functions that contribute to EF is demonstrated in the recent separation of "hot" from "cool" EF, each associated with particular patterns of localization in the brain (Zelazo & Müller, 2002).

This view of EF development as being driven by cortical maturation is most commonly associated with the Soviet neuropsychologist, A. R. Luria (e.g., 1966/1980, 1973). Luria's status as a founding father of modern neuropsychology (Mecacci, 2005) has occasionally served to obscure the breadth of his thinking about causality in human development. In particular, researchers in the field of EF have sometimes neglected Luria's importance as a proponent of a sociocultural approach to development, within which the causes behind EF development are sought as much outside as within the brain. In this chapter, I propose that close attention to Luria's background in the historical–cultural approach, which was emerging in Soviet psychology at the time of his entry into the field (Luria, 1979), can be of value in our attempts to disentangle the developmental interrelations among social interaction, social understanding, and EF. In the first section, I briefly review evidence for the developmental linkage between EF and social understanding. In the second section, I examine the potential value of a Vygotskian interfunctional approach to explaining these developmental relations. In the final section, I consider these relations in light of Luria's coconstructivist approach to neurodevelopment which allowed for bidirectional causal influences between biology and social environment.

Executive Functioning and Social Understanding

Among Luria's many accomplishments as a psychologist and neurologist was his recognition of the importance of a class of psychological functions involved in planning, monitoring, and inhibiting thought and action. Luria's functional analysis involved individuating these capacities according to what they accomplish in terms of cognitive and behavioral outcomes, rather than treating them as explanatory constructs in their own right (Müller, Jacques, Brocki, & Zelazo, 2009). In turn, this functional approach allowed Luria to frame hypotheses about EF development independently of considerations about their neurological underpinning. The subtlety of Luria's thinking about neurological functions, particularly his emphasis on the necessity of examining the functioning of cognitive subsystems in the context of the roles they play in larger functional systems, has often been obscured by the "modularizing" tendencies that characterize much contemporary work in this area (Zelazo, Carter, Reznick, & Frye, 1997).

Indeed, Luria explicitly rejected the idea that a psychological function can be equated with "a direct property of a particular, highly specialized group of cells of an organ" (Luria, 1966/1980, p. 21). To the extent that a function can be localized in the brain at all, it is as "a network of complex dynamic structures or combination centers, consisting of mosaics of distant points of the nervous system, united in a common task" (Luria, 1966/1980, p. 21). Luria attributed the inspiration for his antimodular view of the localization of functions to Vygotsky's (e.g., 1934/1965) views on the need to reconsider existing principles of brain localization in doing justice to the complexity of functional systems (Luria, 1965).[1] Arguing that any specific higher cognitive function "is a product of an integral activity of a very differentiated, hierarchically constructed complex of separate zones ... of the brain" (Vygotsky, 1934/1965, p. 383), Vygotsky set out three main tenets underlying the functional systems approach: the assumption of dynamic and developing interfunctional relations, the assumption of the hierarchical organization of mental functions such that complex functional systems are built up through the integration of more primitive functions, and the assumption that psychological activity is rendered meaningful by its reflection of external reality. For present purposes, three key implications of this approach can be identified: (1) the need for new principles for localization of psychological functions in the brain which take account of how elementary functions are combined into dynamic, integrated functional systems; (2) the need for a new attitude to the significance of damage to different cortical areas at different points in development; and (3) the need for an interfunctional[2] approach to higher mental functions such as EF. These implications of the functional systems approach for our understanding of EF and other cognitive processes are considered further in the second and third sections of this chapter.

Contemporary accounts of EF development have paid only scant attention to Luria's construal of EF as a functional system depending on the interaction of hierarchically organized subsystems whose neurological foci may be spread out across the brain (Luria, 1966/1980). As Zelazo et al. (1997) note, appealing to "narrowly localized, modular mechanisms" (p. 219) has the effect of shifting the burden of explanation from the broader context of an organism's behavior to unobservable mechanisms. Those working within the cognitivist tradition, however, have frequently approached EF in terms of a unitary capacity. One influential group of theories has conceived of EF development as being driven by children's growing capacities to inhibit inappropriate behavior (e.g., Carlson & Moses, 2001). A second group of theories has proposed that working memory changes play a primary causal role in determining how well children are able to use multiple sources of information in planning and monitoring action (e.g., Case, 1995). A third group of accounts, often referred to as complexity accounts (e.g., Zelazo, Müller, Frye, & Marcovitch, 2003), has attributed EF development to children's increasing mastery of hierarchical rule structures, possibly articulated in inner speech. In contrast to competing inhibition and memory accounts, Zelazo and colleagues' view of EF as a functional system involving the integration of language with other cognitive functions is distinctive among cognitivist accounts in its adherence to Luria's functional systems approach to EF.

A thorough evaluation of the relative merits of these different cognitivist approaches is beyond the scope of this chapter. For present purposes, it is sufficient to note two main areas of challenge for such accounts of EF development: the problem of explaining the control of behavior in terms of processes arising from within the organism, and the related challenge of situating EF development within a social and cultural context.

The first of these challenges relates to the venerable problem of how to account for volitional behavior in terms of chains of mechanistic psychological processes. Accounting for a voluntary act in terms of the causal power of a mental event C raises a problem of recursion, whereby one is bound to propose a further mental event C' to explain what caused the causal event C, and so on (Akins & Dennett, 1986). Without such a mechanistic explanation, one is left with the unsatisfactory alternatives of dualism and reductive behaviorism (Luria, 1981, chap. 6) or, in Vygotsky's words, "waver[ing] between the poles of extreme materialism and extreme spiritualism" (Vygotsky, 1960). The same point is made in a slightly different way by Zelazo and Müller (2002), who note that the tendency to hypostasize neurological foci or "centers" to explain a psychological function involves attributing homuncular abilities which fail to provide adequate explanations of complex psychological phenomena such as conscious volition.

The second challenge facing cognitivist accounts of EF is the related one of explaining how the emerging executive functions might be shaped by the social context within which they are developing. Vygotsky's proposed solution to the "historical crisis" in psychology (Vygotsky, 1997), or the problem of providing nonreductivist scientific explanations which go beyond the mere description of complex psychological phenomena, was to seek the origins of such behavior in realms beyond the biological organism. Specifically, Vygotsky's interfunctional approach (see Note 2) allowed him to show how social and cultural factors may become organizing forces in behavior. In contrast, cognitivist accounts typically view EF development as potentially impacting upon social behavior, but not being developmentally shaped by them. The value of an interfunctional approach in this respect is considered further in the second section of this chapter.

The challenges of providing nonreductive mechanistic explanations that do justice to the social context of ontogenesis have recently been brought into focus in the case of another important aspect of cognitive development in the preschool years. Those capacities brought together under the umbrella terms *theory of mind* and *social understanding* (SU; Carpendale & Lewis, 2004) have so far proved resistant to narrowly modular accounts of their development, while also proving highly sensitive to individual differences in social experience. These parallels between the cases of EF and SU have constituted one reason for the growth of interest in the developmental relations between these two important areas of development. A further reason has been the difficulty in establishing the direction of causation in any relation of influence. Among the important questions that have been considered here are as follows: (1) whether a certain level of SU is a prerequisite for establishing the self-control of behavior (e.g., Perner, 1998); (2) whether a certain level of EF is necessary for making judgments about the mental states of others (e.g., Russell, 1996); and (3) whether individual differences in EF can continue to shape children's social interactions once EF has developed (Hughes, 1998).

A thorough overview of the empirical evidence for the relation between EF and SU is beyond the scope of this chapter. Attempts to account for these relations have typically focused on the issue of the direction of causation, specifically whether SU is dependent on EF or vice versa (see Perner, Lang, & Kloo, 2002, for an evaluation of these two main alternatives; see also Kloo et al., this volume). My assumption in what follows is that our understanding of the EF–SU relation will be enhanced by a direction of attention away from issues of causal direction toward a focus on the benefits of an interfunctional approach to both of these general classes of psychological process. At the same time, it is acknowledged that the specifics of the developmental relation between these two areas of cognition are far from established, and that future research will continue to elucidate the complex ways in which particular executive abilities relate to the various capacities brought under the umbrella of SU.

An obvious alternative to a simple unidirectional causal model in explaining the relation between two variables is to postulate a third factor which determines change in both primary variables. In the section that follows, I will suggest that a relevant third factor in this case may be children's linguistically mediated social experience. The proposed reconceptualization of the EF–SU relation will, however, go beyond a simple third-factor model, and will instead involve taking an interfunctional approach to both EF and SU development, where each capacity is seen as being built from a partly overlapping set of subsystems. In so doing, I shall advocate a view of both capacities as being constituted of functional systems developmentally structured by social experience.

Interfunctional Approaches to EF and SU

The benefits of taking a functional systems approach to the EF–SU relation are apparent on a close examination of Vygotsky's and Luria's ideas about psychological functions and their neuroanatomical localization. Luria (1966/1980) defined one useful sense of the term psychological function as "an organism's complex adaptive activity, directed toward the performance of some physiological or psychological task" (p. 22). Luria went on to argue that this sense of a psychological function is best understood as a functional system comprising "a complex dynamic 'constellation' of connections, situated at different levels of the nervous system, that, in the performance of the adaptive task, may be changed with the task itself remaining unchanged" (Luria, 1966/1980). This systemic view of the cooperation of highly differentiated, interchangeable constituent components allows for change in the profile of the subsystems employed in achieving a fixed task from one occasion to another. For example, the same gross motor action can be performed using different combinations of components of the musculature. Functional systems can thus be characterized as "complex in composition, plastic in the variability of their elements, and possessing the property of dynamic autoregulation" (Luria, 1966/1980, p. 23).

As befitted his interest in neurology, Luria's primary focus in adopting a functional systems approach was to explore its implications for the localization (see Note 1) of psychological functions within the human nervous system. Although the issue of localization was one that also exercised Vygotsky (e.g., 1934/1965), his primary interest as a developmental psychologist was in determining how different psychological functions with, crucially, different trajectories of development come to interact in the formation of functional systems. For this reason, my focus in this section is on the implications of Vygotsky's ideas about interfunctionality (see Note 2) for our understanding of the EF–SU relation, with the issue of localization returned to in the final part of this chapter.

One assumption that needs to be clearly articulated here is that the capacities involved in EF and SU are examples of *higher mental functions* (Vygotsky, 1930–1935/1978). In Vygotsky's theory, the higher mental functions are accessible to consciousness, under voluntary control, and mediated by cultural artifacts such as signs. They are thereby distinguished from the *elementary mental functions*, which are unconscious, involuntary, and unmediated. The two classes of psychological functions develop along two distinct lines of development, the cultural and the biological, respectively. In contrast to the elementary mental functions, which are biologically specified, entirely driven by environmental stimulation, and represent a natural endowment shared with some nonhuman animals, the higher mental functions have their origin in social interactions.

Viewing EF and SU as examples of higher mental functions (Fernyhough, 1996, 2008) entails several important implications for understanding the ontogenetic relations between these two variables. First, it means that a functional systems approach to these variables is particularly appropriate, with the implication that a satisfactory account of how they interrelate developmentally will require attention to the components that interact in forming a functional system. Indeed, the existence of "plastic, changeable interfunctional relations" (Vygotsky, 1934/1965, p. 382) was a central assumption of Vygotsky's systemic approach. Elsewhere, Vygotsky (1934/1987, chap. 1) argued that the failure to adopt an interfunctional approach when studying complex psychological phenomena was as misguided as would be the attempt to understand chemical compounds in terms of the properties of their constituent elements.

A second important implication is that EF and SU should be considered as higher mental functions whose origins lie in social activity. As noted earlier, Vygotsky's proposed solution to the perceived crisis in psychology lay in the search for causal influences on thought and behavior in the world beyond the biological individual, particularly in the social world. An interfunctional approach to EF and SU thus avoids the problem typical of cognitivist accounts of seeking the ultimate causes of behavior within the individual.

A third implication is that, as functional systems, EF and SU will be underpinned by shifting agglomerations of interchangeable cognitive elements, the relations among which will have different significances depending on the point in development at which they are observed. In Luria's (1966/1980) words, "at successive stages of their development the structure of the higher mental functions does not remain constant but [those functions] perform the same task by means of different, regularly interchanging systems of connections" (p. 34). A corollary of this is that the significance of damage to functional systems through brain injury will depend on the stage of development at which the damage occurs (Vygotsky, 1934/1965).

Further implications of the functional systems approach for cortical development are considered in the final section. In the remainder of this section, I consider how the interfunctional approach can be applied specifically to the cases of EF and SU, and what benefits result from this alternative to typical cognitivist interpretations of these phenomena.

AN INTERFUNCTIONAL APPROACH TO EF DEVELOPMENT

Adherents to the sociocultural approach have typically framed the problem of EF ontogenesis in terms of children's developing self-regulation of thought and behavior. Vygotsky (e.g., 1934/1987) argued that self-regulation reaches a major milestone when biologically specified forms of thinking are reformulated by the internalization of semiotically mediated activities (primarily linguistic activities) that are initially distributed or shared between individuals. Specifically, children gain enhanced control over their own behavior when words which were previously used to regulate the behavior of others, or which others have used to regulate the child's behavior, become employed in regulating the behavior of the self. In terms of the Vygotskian–Lurian approach described earlier, mediated EF forms a functional system in which prelinguistic capacities for monitoring, planning, and inhibition of behavior begin to relate interfunctionally with the language capacity.

In Vygotsky's view, the revolution that follows from children's beginning use of semiotic systems in mediating their cognition represents the intertwining of preintellectual and prelinguistic strands of cognition, or the fusing of the natural and cultural lines of development (Vygotsky, 1930–1935/1978). The development of self-regulation thus involves "the creation or use of artificial stimuli which become the immediate causes of behavior" (Vygotsky, 1930–1935/1978, p. 39), which occurs through the progressive internalization of verbal interactions with others. One important implication of this view is that the causes of behavior should be sought in processes that occur outside the limits of the individual organism. In addition, the capacities brought under the umbrella of EF will be mediated by signs, primarily words and utterances in natural language (Luria, 1932).

Empirical studies have generally supported Vygotsky's claims about the development of verbal self-regulation through social interaction (see e.g., Winsler, Fernyhough, & Montero, 2009). Although Vygotsky did not specify in detail what forms of monitoring, planning, and inhibition precede the self-regulatory use of language, it is clear that prelinguistic infants have some rudimentary abilities in this respect. For example, success on the A-not-B object search task requires some level of inhibition of a previously successful action (Diamond, 1991). In Vygotsky's view, the advent of verbal self-regulation transforms these elementary executive capacities through their incorporation into new functional systems. For example, researchers such as Wertsch and Stone (1985) have presented evidence for the progressive transfer of strategic responsibility from adult to child in dyadic problem-solving contexts, such that children become able to regulate their own problem-solving activity using the internalized dialogue previously shared with more expert collaborators. Empirical research on the social origins of self-regulation thus answers Vygotsky's call for the search for the origins of volitional behavior to be made outside the realm of the individual. In Luria's (1981) words, "we must go beyond the limits of the individual organism and examine how volitional processes are formed for the child in his/her concrete contacts with adults … [T]he source of the volitional act is the child's communication with adults." (p. 89).

The strongest support for Vygotsky's ideas about verbal self-regulation has emerged from research into children's self-directed speech. In his early observations of children's language, Piaget (1923/1959) described a type of speech which appeared to have no communicative function and which he took to reflect the young child's egocentrism. Vygotsky (1934/1987) took issue with this interpretation, claiming that such noncommunicative speech (now commonly known as private speech) in fact played an important role in the development of self-regulation. Private speech was seen to constitute a distinctive stage in the process whereby mediated interpersonal activity is internalized to form inner speech or verbal thought.

The empirical predictions which follow from this view of children's noncommunicative speech have received support from a number of empirical studies (for reviews, see Berk, 1992; Winsler, 2004). Consistent with Vygotsky's (1934/1987) claims about the progressive internalization of this form of language activity, private speech has been shown to follow an inverted U-shaped developmental trajectory, emerging in the early preschool years and subsequently dropping away in later childhood (Kohlberg, Yaeger, & Hjertholm, 1968; Winsler & Naglieri, 2003). In addition, support has been found for Vygotskian predictions about the relation between private speech and task difficulty, particularly the suggestion that private speech levels will peak when the task is pitched at a level appropriate to the child's current level of competence (Frauenglass & Diaz, 1985).

Vygotsky's claims about the importance of verbal self-regulation for EF development entail that children's use of such speech should relate to their performance on those cognitive tasks in which verbal self-regulation is used. In support of this prediction, private speech researchers have documented positive relations between this form of speech and both concurrent (Winsler, Diaz, McCarthy, Atencio, & Adams Chabay, 1999) and future (Behrend, Rosengren, & Perlmutter, 1992; Bivens & Berk, 1990) task performance. Two recent studies have focused particularly on children's verbal self-regulation while solving puzzles of a classic EF task, the Tower of London (Shallice, 1982). Fernyhough and Fradley (2005) made videotape recordings of 46 children aged 5 and 6 as they attempted progressively more difficult Tower of London puzzles. Children's speech was subsequently coded for the use of noncommunicative utterances with an apparently self-regulatory function. Children's rate of production of such utterances was positively related to their concurrent performance on the EF task. Similar findings were reported by Al-Namlah, Fernyhough, and Meins (2006), who observed Tower of London puzzle-solving in a sample of 121 children aged 4–8 from samples recruited in the United Kingdom and Saudi Arabia. Support for Vygotsky's views on the developmental significance of private speech is thus provided by data from classic EF tasks as well as the nonexecutive tasks typically used in private speech research (such as the semantic task used by Frauenglass & Diaz, 1985).

The functional systems approach thus provides a framework for making sense of emerging evidence for social influences on EF development. If mediated EF is derived from social interaction, as Vygotsky's theory holds, then it should be possible to observe influences of social interactional experience on private speech and EF development. With regard to social influences on private speech development, Al-Namlah et al. (2006) found some limited support for predictions that children's private speech would relate to their culturally specific experience of reciprocal social interaction with adults. In an earlier study, Berk and Garvin (1984) investigated private speech use in a rural Appalachian culture previously characterized as involving low levels of reciprocal adult–child interaction. As predicted, the development of private speech in this sample appeared delayed relative to what would be predicted in a typical American sample. Furthermore, these documented social influences on private speech development have been observed to relate to the cognitive facilitatory effects of this form of speech. In their study of 40 preschoolers engaged in a selective attention task, Winsler, Diaz, and Montero (1997) found that children's production of private speech related to their previous experience of tutoring interactions in which an experimenter scaffolded the child's task performance. Following scaffolding, children who used private speech were more successful on the task than those who did not.

Turning to EF as typically operationalized within the cognitivist tradition, social influences on EF have not to date been the focus of concerted research attention. One exception is a longitudinal study by Landry, Miller-Loncar, Smith, and Swank (2002; see also Landry & Smith, this volume) which showed an association between parental scaffolding of children's task performance at age 3 and EF measures obtained at age 6, a relation that was mediated by children's language scores at age 4. Landry et al.'s careful longitudinal analysis did not, however, include measures of verbal self-regulation, meaning that it is impossible to establish from their findings whether the benefit in EF performance associated with scaffolding was mediated by private speech (Müller et al., 2009).

A functional systems approach to EF, according to which progress from elementary to more advanced forms of EF is determined by developing interfunctional relations between rudimentary executive capacities and language, is further supported by findings of strong relations between children's verbal ability and EF performance (Carlson et al., 2004; Hughes & Ensor, 2005; Perner et al., 2002; although see Müller et al., 2009, for discussion of conflicting findings). Further evidence for the value of the approach comes from findings of a facilitatory effect of overt labeling of stimuli in EF tasks (for a review, see Müller et al., 2009). For example, young preschoolers who spontaneously used labeling in an attentional control task (requiring the selection of a colored card to receive a differently colored candy) showed enhanced performance compared to their nonlabeling peers (Müller, Zelazo, Hood, Leone, & Rohrer, 2004; Experiment 1). A subsequent experiment in which children in one condition were explicitly instructed to label the stimuli also showed a facilitatory effect of labeling (Müller et al., 2004; Experiment 2).

In evaluating the significance of these findings, it is worth noting that the Lurian tradition of research into verbal self-regulation, within which these labeling studies have been conducted, differs in important ways from the empirical approach adopted by Vygotsky. Luria's empirical approach (e.g., 1981, chap. 6) relied on observations of children's responses to explicit invitations by an adult experimenter to use labeling and other verbal regulatory stimuli in performing EF tasks. In contrast, researchers within the Vygotskian empirical tradition have been primarily concerned with children's spontaneous self-directed speech, as generated in a broader range of cognitive contexts than EF tasks. As Berk (1992) has observed, this difference in emphasis means that caution should be exercised in integrating data derived from the two research programs, as the two kinds of speech may not have the same functional or developmental significance. Despite these differences in empirical and methodological approaches, both theorists were in agreement that language performs an important function in EF. In Luria's (1981) words, "[i]t is because of language that humans can delve into the essence of things, transcend the limits of direct impression, organize their purposeful behavior, unravel complex connections and relationships which are not accessible to direct perception, and transmit information accumulated over generations to other persons" (p. 199).

In summary, a Vygotskian–Lurian functional systems approach to EF development makes the following important claims. First, the forms of EF which appear in the preschool period are examples of the semiotically mediated higher mental functions. In contrast, forms of EF which appear in infancy are shared with some nonhuman animals and form part of the natural, rather than the cultural, line of development. These more primitive forms of EF are not semiotically mediated and do not derive from social interaction, but form the basis for the development of mediated EF when they begin to be incorporated into new functional systems through internalization and the emergence of semiotic mediation. Second, EF develops in the context of interpersonal exchanges where more expert partners allow children to participate in activities which they will only later master for themselves (Wertsch, 1985). Third, the Vygotskian–Lurian approach implies that EF will preserve certain characteristics of the social interaction from which it derives, particularly its dialogic nature (Fernyhough, 1996, 2008; Wertsch, 1980).

AN INTERFUNCTIONAL APPROACH TO SU DEVELOPMENT

An interfunctional approach to EF can thus provide a powerful framework for making sense of how language can transform existing, biologically specified EF capacities in the creation of new functional systems. As noted earlier, another important cognitive capacity which may benefit from an interfunctional approach is children's understanding of other people as mental agents. Researchers in this field have faced a challenge in recent years in accounting for the very strong evidence for an involvement of language in children's developing theory of mind or SU[3] (see e.g., Astington & Baird, 2005). For example, several studies have shown SU task performance to be strongly correlated with language ability (Cutting & Dunn, 1999; de Villiers, 2000; Jenkins & Astington, 1996). Among the properties of linguistic discourse that have been proposed to facilitate SU development are conversational pragmatics (e.g., Harris, 1999), lexical semantics (e.g., Peterson & Siegal, 2000), and complementation syntax (e.g., de Villiers & de Villiers, 2000). SU development therefore appears to bear some similarity to EF development in its sensitivity to social experience and environmental, specifically linguistic, input.

This apparent commonality between EF and SU suggests that it may be possible to account for these findings in terms of language interacting interfunctionally with more rudimentary abilities in transforming elementary forms of SU (such as intentional-agent understanding) into higher, characteristically human forms. Elsewhere (Fernyhough, 2008) I have proposed that progress in SU development depends on the development of such interfunctional relations between rudimentary forms of social cognition and preexisting and parallel-developing cognitive abilities, specifically language (or other semiotic mediational systems). Drawing on the Dialogic Thinking (DT) model of cognitive development (Fernyhough, 1996, 2004a, 2004b, 2005, 2006, 2008, 2009), I have proposed that the internalization of mediated interpersonal activity described by Vygotsky found children's capacity to operate with the internalized, semiotically mediated perspectives of others. This claim is in turn based on the assumption that the mediated higher mental functions retain the dialogic character of the social activity from which they are derived (Fernyhough, 1996).

Several testable predictions follow from this view of SU development. One is that SU development should be sensitive to experience of mediated social exchanges in which alternative perspectives on reality are presented (Fernyhough, 2008). The Vygotskian approach to SU development thus provides a useful framework for interpreting data-relating individual differences in SU development to social-environmental variables such as mental-state causal talk (Dunn, Brown, Slomkowski, Tesla, & Youngblade, 1991), family size (Lewis, Freeman, Kyriakidou, Maridaki-Kassotaki, & Berridge, 1996), attachment security (Meins, Fernyhough, Russell, & Clark-Carter, 1998), and mind-mindedness (Meins et al., 2002, 2003). A second prediction is that progress in SU development should go hand-in-hand with a shift to semiotic mediation in other cognitive domains. Some preliminary data in support of this prediction are reported by Fernyhough and Meins (2009), who obtained measures of self-regulatory private speech and theory-of-mind task performance in three separate cross-sectional studies (mean ages 49, 56, and 71 months). Correlations between these variables were computed with partialling for age and verbal ability. As predicted, private speech and SU performance were significantly positively related in the youngest sample, while the sign of the correlation shifted to negative in the oldest sample, in line with the assumption that children who were still using overt private speech at this point were relatively delayed in the process of internalization.

Viewing both EF and SU as mediated higher mental functions thus presents an alternative way of conceptualizing the developmental relations between these variables. Rather than attempting to account for the relation in terms of a strong executive component to SU tasks, or conversely an SU load on standard EF tasks, a combined interfunctional approach to EF and SU would see the development of both capacities as being driven by the internalization of dialogic, mediated interpersonal activity (Fernyhough, 1996, 2008, 2009). That said, it also seems likely that EF and SU will be differentially sensitive to the varieties of social experience that children encounter, and that any social-environmental effects will vary in their influence depending on the age at which they occur. Indeed, it is axiomatic for the Vygotskian–Lurian functional systems approach that there will be shifting patterns of relations across age between the components of such systems (Vygotsky, 1934/1965). What the functional systems approach offers to future research in this area is the possibility of making sense of these differing patterns of interfunctional relations across the course of development.

The Social Brain

I have proposed that conceiving of EF and SU as functional systems may have important benefits for our developing understanding of these psychological processes. First, such an approach will pay dividends for our theorizing about how more rudimentary forms of these capacities are augmented by developmental advances in other cognitive domains. Second, a conception of EF and SU as systems that rely crucially on semiotic mediation (predominantly through language) can shed new light on the observed developmental relations between these variables.

In the final section of this chapter, I suggest that the functional systems approach confers a third important advantage, specifically for our understanding of the neuroanatomical localization of EF and SU. One reason for rejecting a view of SU as a modular capacity is the lack of any compelling evidence that it is underpinned by a unitary neuroanatomical substrate (e.g., Apperly, Samson, & Humphreys, 2005). As Vygotsky and Luria showed, a functional systems approach requires us to rethink the question of how the complex systems that underlie apparently discrete psychological functions are localized in the brain. Among the most important implications are (1) that the functional systems underlying EF and SU will comprise neuroanatomical components whose patterns of interrelation will alter throughout the course of development; (2) that patterns of localization in the adult brain will, for this reason, not necessarily provide an accurate model of how these functions are neurologically subserved in the developing brain; (3) that cortical development will involve bidirectional transactions between biological and social causes; and (4) that the cortical areas that subserve these functions will be differently organized to those areas not associated with mediated functional systems. I now consider each of these points in turn.

With regard to the changing interrelations between systemic components throughout development, one way of thinking about Luria's contribution in this respect is as a method of applying Vygotsky's ideas about functional systems to the problem of localization of functions within the brain (Wertsch, 1981). Recognizing that Vygotsky's insights about functional systems had allowed the transformation of psychology into "a science of *the social formation of natural phenomena*" (Luria, 1965, p. 389, original emphasis), Luria turned his attention to the problem of how to conceptualize the "material structure" of these phenomena. Luria proposed that Vygotsky's psychological concept of a functional system (which could be described without necessary reference to its neuroanatomical substrate) could be translated into the neurological concept of a "functional organ" (a concept derived from Leont'ev, 1981), the creation of which, "under the influence of social conditions" (Luria, 1966/1980, p. 33), created "a new means of unlimited development of the brain" (Luria, 1965, p. 391). In other words, new trajectories of brain development are made possible by the interaction of social and neurological causes in the creation of functional systems.

The result of this process, according to Luria, is the development of "a system of highly differentiated zones of the cortex working together, accomplishing new tasks by means of new 'inter-areal' relations" (Luria, 1965, p. 391). Furthermore, the psychological significance of these inter-areal connections will change throughout the course of development, meaning that only a "chronogenetic" (Vygotsky, 1934/1965), or time-sensitive, approach to the neurological instantiation of these systems would provide an accurate picture of their structure. From a modern cognitive developmental neuroscience perspective, therefore, the challenge for EF and SU investigators is to specify which cortical regions work together at different stages of development in providing the neuroanatomical substrate for these functional systems.

A second implication that follows from the functional systems approach is that evidence for the localization of EF and SU in the adult brain will not necessarily provide a reliable guide to how these functions are instantiated during the course of development. Evidence that EF and SU dysfunction co-occur in some developmental and adult disorders, while showing patterns of double dissociation in others, has been held to support the view that these capacities are subserved by distinct but anatomically proximate neural areas (e.g., Saxe, Carey, & Kanwisher, 2004). Evidence from imaging studies of adults that the medial prefrontal cortex is heavily involved in reasoning about intentions (Frith & Frith, 2003) may thus be of only limited value in understanding the neurological underpinnings of SU in adolescence and earlier (Blakemore & Choudhury, 2006). Furthermore, Vygotsky's (1934/1965; Luria, 1965) arguments about the changing developmental significance of brain lesions are particularly relevant to attempts to bring neuroanatomical and neuroimaging evidence to bear on findings of EF and SU dysfunction in developmental disorders such as autism. A functional systems approach to these capacities would therefore seem to fit well with the growing recognition that evidence for modularity in adults cannot necessarily be taken to imply similar modularity in children and adolescents, and that the study of any particular psychological impairment in development will not necessarily provide clues to the neurological route to that impairment (Karmiloff-Smith, Scerif, & Ansari, 2003; Thomas & Karmiloff-Smith, 2002).

A third important implication for cognitive developmental neuroscientific approaches to EF and SU is that cortical development will be susceptible to bidirectional causal influences between the biological and social worlds (Fernyhough, 2006). As noted earlier, Luria's position is particularly interesting in this respect. On the one hand, he is commonly credited with the idea that EF development is constrained by maturation of the prefrontal cortex. On the other hand, his writings on functional systems clearly indicate a role for social causation in brain development. Elsewhere (Fernyhough, 2006) I have proposed that Luria's position can be construed as a coconstructivist (Lindenberger, 2004) approach to development, in which the social influences the biological potentially as strongly as the biological influences the social.[4] With regard to the application of Luria's ideas to EF and SU development, the challenge is to specify how the mediation of cognition by cultural artifacts such as words in natural language allows the brain to "programme and reprogramme itself" (Mecacci, 2005, p. 820) in the course of development.

The fourth implication is that these principles will apply to specific parts of the cortex, the organization of which shows fundamental differences with that of the brains of nonhuman animals (Mecacci, 2005). Consistent with his belief that Vygotsky's ideas had provided a solution to a fundamental problem in psychology, Luria argued that the implications of the functional systems approach for brain development could only be described in terms of a new principle of brain organization, in which social causes had their effects through the establishment of "extra-cerebral connections" (Vygotsky, 1960) between the brain and cultural artifacts such as signs. In Luria's words, "[s]ocial history ties those knots which form definite cortical zones in new relations with each other, and if the use of language … evokes new functional relations …, then this is a product of historical development, depending on 'extra-cerebral ties' and new 'functional organs' formed in the cortex" (Luria, 1965, p. 391).

This organizational principle was held to apply exclusively to areas in the frontal and parietal lobes, regions attributed with particular importance in the emergence of the higher mental functions (Vygotsky, 1934/1965). Vygotsky's reference to these regions as "specifically-human" (Vygotsky, 1934/1965, p. 382) was not meant to deny the existence of these anatomical areas in other animals, but rather to underline the fact that it is these areas which, through the tying of extra-cerebral connections, acquire functions that are specific to human psychology. As noted, the prefrontal cortex is the area commonly associated with EF in studies of brain lesions (Luria, 1973). Lesions to the prefrontal cortex typically leave motor patterns, including speech production, intact, while specifically impairing patients' ability to benefit from the self-regulatory function of speech, such as the use of a self-directed verbal command in inhibiting behavior (Luria, 1981, chap. 7). Rather than being necessary for the production of speech per se, the prefrontal cortex appears to play an important role in the interfunctional integration necessary for verbal self-regulation. To put it another way, when the neurological substrate of the functional system is damaged, the "extra-cerebral ties" which organize these forms of behavior are cut as well.

Conclusion

My aim in this chapter has been to show how close attention to Vygotsky's and Luria's writings on functional systems can pay dividends for our understanding of the developmental relations between EF and SU. Rather than becoming excessively concerned with establishing the direction of causation between these two variables, future researchers may benefit from a view of development in both of these areas as being driven by the cognitive changes that result from a general transition toward semiotic mediation in the preschool years. In the process, it can be hoped that the view of these psychological functions as monolithic, indivisible entities will continue to lose ground to conceptions of both as complexes of constituent subsystems which demonstrate subtly patterned, dynamic interrelations throughout development.

NOTES

1. It is important to emphasize that "localization," in the sense employed by Vygotsky (1934/1965), does not entail modularization. Vygotsky was concerned to trace the complex distribution of psychological functions within the brain, and warned explicitly against the assumption that functions could be traced to unitary anatomical loci.

2. Central to Vygotsky's enterprise was the acknowledgment of the importance of "interfunctional relationships" (1934/1987, pp. 43–44), by which he meant the changing developmental relations between cognitive functions such as thinking and language. The significance of psychological interfunctionality for EF and SU development is considered further in the next section.

3. Given the theory-laden nature of the term "theory of mind," I prefer the term social understanding (SU; Carpendale & Lewis, 2004). Although the use of both umbrella terms might be thought to obscure important theoretical, empirical, and methodological subtleties, I shall treat them as interchangeable.

4. Broadly speaking, this position is congruent with emerging views of brain development as shaped and constrained in important ways by experience (e.g., Johnson, 2001; Mareschal et al., 2007).

REFERENCES

Akins, K. A., & Dennett, D. C. (1986). Who may I say is calling? *Behavioral and Brain Sciences, 9*, 517.

Al-Namlah, A. S., Fernyhough, C., & Meins, E. (2006). Sociocultural influences on the development of verbal mediation: Private speech and phonological recoding in Saudi Arabian and British samples. *Developmental Psychology, 42*, 117–131.

Apperly, I. A., Samson, D., & Humphreys, G. W. (2005). Domain-specificity and theory of mind: Evaluating neuropsychological evidence. *Trends in Cognitive Sciences, 9*, 572–576.

Astington, J. W., & Baird, J. A. (2005). *Why language matters for theory of mind.* Oxford, UK: Oxford University Press.

Baddeley, A., Logie, R., Bressi, S., Della Sala, S., & Spinnler, H. (1986). Dementia and working memory. *Quarterly Journal of Experimental Psychology Section A: Human Experimental Psychology, 38*, 603–618.

Baddeley, A. D. (1986). *Working memory.* Oxford, UK: Oxford University Press.

Barkley, R. A. (1997). Behavioral inhibition, sustained attention, and executive functions: Constructing a unifying theory of ADHD. *Psychological Bulletin, 121*, 65–94.

Behrend, D. A., Rosengren, K. S., & Perlmutter, M. (1992). The relation between private speech and parental interactive style. In R. M. Diaz & L. E. Berk (Eds.), *Private speech: From social interaction to self-regulation* (pp. 85–100). Hillsdale, NJ: Lawrence Erlbaum Associates.

Berk, L. E. (1992). Children's private speech: An overview of theory and the status of research. In R. M. Diaz & L. E. Berk (Eds.), *Private speech: From social interaction to self-regulation* (pp. 17–53). Hillsdale, NJ: Lawrence Erlbaum Associates.

Berk, L. E., & Garvin, R. A. (1984). Development of private speech among low-income Appalachian children. *Developmental Psychology, 20*, 271–286.

Bivens, J. A., & Berk, L. E. (1990). A longitudinal study of the development of elementary school children's private speech. *Merrill-Palmer Quarterly, 36*, 443–463.

Blair, C. (2002). School readiness: Integrating cognition and emotion in a neuro-biological conceptualization of children's functioning at school entry. *American Psychologist, 57,* 111–127.

Blakemore, S-J., & Choudhury, S. (2006). Development of the adolescent brain: Implications for executive function and social cognition. *Journal of Child Psychology and Psychiatry, 47,* 296–312.

Carlson, S. M., Mandell, D. J., & Williams, L. (2004). Executive function and theory of mind: Stability and prediction from age 2 to 3. *Developmental Psychology, 40,* 1105–1122.

Carlson, S. M., & Moses, L. J. (2001). Individual differences in inhibitory control and theory of mind. *Child Development, 72,* 1032–1053.

Carpendale, J. I. M., & Lewis, C. (2004). Constructing an understanding of mind: The development of children's social understanding within social interaction. *Behavioral and Brain Sciences, 27,* 79–151.

Case, R. (1995). Capacity-based explanations of working memory growth: A brief history and reevaluation. In F. E. Weinert & W. Schneider (Eds.), *Memory performance and competencies: Issues in growth and development.* Mahwah, NJ: Lawrence Erlbaum Associates.

Cutting, A. L., & Dunn, J. (1999). Theory of mind, emotion understanding, language, and family background: Individual differences and interrelations. *Child Development, 70,* 853–865.

de Villiers, J. (2000). Language and theory of mind: What are the developmental relationships? In S. Baron-Cohen, H. Tager-Flusberg, & D. J. Cohen (Eds.), *Understanding other minds: Perspectives from autism and developmental cognitive neuroscience.* Oxford, UK: Oxford University Press.

de Villiers, J. G., & de Villiers, P. A. (2000). Linguistic determinism and the understanding of false beliefs. In P. Mitchell & K. J. Riggs (Eds.), *Children's reasoning and the mind* (pp. 191–228). Hove, UK: Psychology Press.

Diamond, A. (1991). Neuropsychological insights into the meaning of object concept development. In S. Carey & R. Gelman (Eds.), *The epigenesis of mind: Essays on biology and cognition* (pp. 67–110). Hillsdale, NJ: Lawrence Erlbaum Associates.

Diamond, A. (2002). Normal development of prefrontal cortex from birth to young adulthood: Cognitive functions, anatomy, and biochemistry. In D. T. Stuss & R. T. Knight (Eds.), *Principles of frontal lobe function* (pp. 466–503). London, UK: Oxford University Press.

Diamond, A., Prevor, M. B., Callender, G., & Druin, D. P. (1997). Prefrontal cortex cognitive deficits in children treated early and continuously for PKU. *Monographs of the Society for Research in Child Development, 62*(4), Serial no. 252.

Dunn, J., Brown, J., Slomkowski, C., Tesla, C., & Youngblade, L. M. (1991). Young children's understanding of other people's feelings and beliefs: Individual differences and their antecedents. *Child Development, 62,* 1352–1366.

Eslinger, P. J., Biddle, K. R., & Grattan, L. M. (1997). Cognitive and social development in children with prefrontal cortex lesions. In G. R. Lyon & N. A. Krasnegor

(Eds.), *Attention, memory, and executive function* (pp. 295–335). Baltimore: Paul H. Brookes Publishing Co., Inc.

Fernyhough, C. (1996). The dialogic mind: A dialogic approach to the higher mental functions. *New Ideas in Psychology, 14*, 47–62.

Fernyhough, C. (2004a). Alien voices and inner dialogue: Towards a developmental account of auditory verbal hallucinations. *New Ideas in Psychology, 22*, 49–68.

Fernyhough, C. (2004b). More than a context for learning? The epistemic triangle and the dialogic mind (Commentary on Carpendale & Lewis). *Behavioral and Brain Sciences, 27*, 104–105.

Fernyhough, C. (2005). What is internalised? Dialogic cognitive representations and the mediated mind. (Commentary on Tomasello et al.). *Behavioral and Brain Sciences, 28*, 698–699.

Fernyhough, C. (2006). Private speech, executive functioning and theory of mind: A Vygotskian-Lurian synthesis. In I. Montero (Ed.), *Current research trends in private speech: Proceedings of the First International Symposium on self-regulatory functions of language*. Madrid: University Press of Universidad Autónoma of Madrid.

Fernyhough, C. (2008). Getting Vygotskian about theory of mind: Mediation, dialogue, and the development of social understanding. *Developmental Review, 28*, 225–262.

Fernyhough, C. (2009). Dialogic thinking. In A. Winsler, C. Fernyhough, & I. Montero (Eds.), *Private speech, executive functioning, and the development of verbal self-regulation*. Cambridge, UK: Cambridge University Press.

Fernyhough, C., & Fradley, E. (2005). Private speech on an executive task: Relations with task difficulty and task performance. *Cognitive Development, 20*, 103–120.

Fernyhough, C., & Meins, E. (2009). Private speech and theory of mind: Evidence for developing interfunctional relations. In A. Winsler, C. Fernyhough, & I. Montero (Eds.), *Private speech, executive functioning, and the development of verbal self-regulation* (pp. 95–104). Cambridge, UK: Cambridge University Press.

Frauenglass, M. H., & Diaz, R. M. (1985). Self-regulatory functions of children's private speech: A critical analysis of recent challenges to Vygotsky's theory. *Developmental Psychology, 21*, 357–364.

Frith, U., & Frith, C. D. (2003). Development and neurophysiology of mentalizing. *Philosophical Transactions of the Royal Society of London B, 358*(1431), 459–473.

Golden, C. J. (1981). The Luria-Nebraska children's battery: Theory and formulation. In G. W. Hynd & J. E. Obrzut (Eds.), *Neuropsychological assessment and the school-aged child* (pp. 277–302). New York: Grune & Stratton.

Happé, F., Booth, R., Charlton, R., & Hughes, C. (2006). Executive function deficits in autism spectrum disorders and attention-deficit/hyperactivity disorder: Examining profiles across domains and ages. *Brain and Cognition, 61*, 25–39.

Harris, P. L. (1999). Acquiring the art of conversation. In M. Bennett (Ed.), *Developmental psychology: Achievements and prospects* (pp. 89–105). Hove, UK: Psychology Press.

Hill, E. L. (2004). Evaluating the theory of EF deficits in autism. *Developmental Review, 24,* 189–233.

Hughes, C. (1998). Finding your marbles: Does preschoolers' strategic behavior predict later understanding of mind? *Developmental Psychology, 34,* 1326–1339.

Hughes, C., & Ensor, R. (2005). Executive function and theory of mind in 2 year olds: A family affair? *Developmental Neuropsychology, 28,* 645–668.

Jenkins, J. M., & Astington, J. W. (1996). Cognitive factors and family structure associated with theory of mind development in young children. *Developmental Psychology, 32,* 70–78.

Johnson, M. H. (2001). Functional brain development in humans. *Nature Reviews Neuroscience, 2,* 475–483.

Karmiloff-Smith, A., Scerif, G., & Ansari, D. (2003). Double dissociations in developmental disorders? Theoretically misconceived, empirically dubious. *Cortex, 39,* 161–163.

Kohlberg, L., Yaeger, J., & Hjertholm, E. (1968). Private speech: Four studies and a review of theories. *Child Development, 39,* 691–736.

Landry, S. H., Miller-Loncar, C. L., Smith, K. E., & Swank, P. R. (2002). The role of early parenting in children's development of executive processes. *Developmental Neuropsychology, 21,* 15–41.

Leont'ev, A. N. (1981). *Problems of the development of mind.* Moscow: Progress.

Lewis, C., Freeman, N. H., Kyriakidou, C., Maridaki-Kassotaki, K., & Berridge, D. M. (1996). Social influences on false belief access: Specific sibling influences or general apprenticeship? *Child Development, 67,* 2930–2947.

Lindenberger, U. (2004). *Lifespan changes in cognition: A co-constructivist view on mind and brain.* Keynote address at the International Society for the Study of Behavioural Development, Ghent, July 2004.

Luria, A. R. (1932). *The nature of human conflicts, or emotion, conflict and will* (W. Horsley Gantt, Ed. & Trans.). New York: Liveright.

Luria, A. R. (1965). L. S. Vygotsky and the problem of localization of functions. *Neuropsychologia, 3,* 387–392.

Luria, A. R. (1973). *The working brain: An introduction to neuropsychology* (B. Haigh, Trans.). New York: Basic Books.

Luria, A. R. (1979). *The making of mind: A personal account of Soviet psychology* (M. Cole & S. Cole, Eds.). Cambridge, MA: Harvard University Press.

Luria, A. R. (1980). *Higher cortical functions in man* (2nd ed.). New York: Basic Books. (Original work published 1966)

Luria, A. R. (1981). *Language and cognition* (J. V. Wertsch, Ed.). New York: Wiley.

Mareschal, D., Johnson, M. H., Sirois, S., Spratling, M. W., Thomas, M. S. C., & Westermann, G. (Eds.). (2007). *Neuroconstructivism: How the brain constructs cognition* (Vol. 1). Oxford, UK: Oxford University Press.

Mecacci, L. (2005). Luria: A unitary view of human brain and mind. *Cortex, 41,* 816–822.

Meins, E., Fernyhough, C., Russell, J., & Clark-Carter, D. (1998). Security of attachment as a predictor of symbolic and mentalising abilities: A longitudinal study. *Social Development, 7,* 1–24.

Meins, E., Fernyhough, C., Wainwright, R., Clark-Carter, D., Das Gupta, M., Fradley, E., et al. (2003). Pathways to understanding mind: Construct validity and predictive validity of maternal mind-mindedness. *Child Development, 74,* 1194–1211.

Meins, E., Fernyhough, C., Wainwright, R., Das Gupta, M., Fradley, E., & Tuckey, M. (2002). Maternal mind-mindedness and attachment security as predictors of theory of mind understanding. *Child Development, 73,* 1715–1726.

Miyake, A., Friedman, N. P., Emerson, M. J., Witzki, A. H., Howerter, A., & Wager, T. D. (2000). The unity and diversity of executive functions and their contributions to complex "frontal lobe" tasks: A latent variable analysis. *Cognitive Psychology, 41,* 49–100.

Müller, U., Jacques, S., Brocki, K., & Zelazo, P. D. (2009). The executive functions of language in preschool children. In A. Winsler, C. Fernyhough, & I. Montero (Eds.), *Private speech, executive functioning, and the development of verbal self-regulation* (53–68). Cambridge, UK: Cambridge University Press.

Müller, U., Zelazo, P. D., Hood, S., Leone, T., & Rohrer, L. (2004). Interference control in a new rule use task: Age-related changes, labeling, and attention. *Child Development, 75,* 1594–1609.

Pennington, B. F., & Ozonoff, S. (1996). Executive function and developmental psychopathology. *Journal of Child Psychology and Psychiatry, 37,* 51–87.

Perner, J. (1998). The meta-intentional nature of executive functions and theory of mind. In P. Carruthers & J. Boucher (Eds.), *Language and thought* (pp. 270–283). Cambridge, UK: Cambridge University Press.

Perner, J., Lang, B., & Kloo, D. (2002). Theory of mind and self-control: More than a common problem of inhibition. *Child Development, 73,* 752–767.

Peterson, C. C., & Siegal, M. (2000). Insights into theory of mind from deafness and autism. *Mind and Language, 15,* 123–145.

Piaget, J. (1959). *The language and thought of the child.* New York: Meridian Books. (Original work published 1923)

Russell, J. (1996). *Agency: Its role in mental development.* Hove, UK: Lawrence Erlbaum Associates.

Saxe, R., Carey, S., & Kanwisher, N. (2004). Understanding other minds: Linking developmental psychology and functional neuroimaging. *Annual Review of Psychology, 55,* 87–124.

Shallice, T. (1982). Specific impairments in planning. *Philosophical Transactions of the Royal Society of London, B298,* 199–209.

Shallice, T. (1988). *From neuropsychology to mental structure.* Cambridge, MA: Cambridge University Press.

Shallice, T., & Burgess, P. W. (1991). Deficits in strategy application following frontal-lobe damage in man. *Brain, 114,* 727–741.

Shoda, Y., Mischel, W., & Peake, P. K. (1990). Predicting adolescent cognitive and self-regulatory competencies from preschool delay of gratification: Identifying diagnostic conditions. *Developmental Psychology, 26*, 978–986.

Thomas, M., & Karmiloff-Smith, A. (2002). Are developmental disorders like cases of adult brain damage? Implications from connectionist modelling. *Behavioral and Brain Sciences, 25*, 727–788.

Vygotsky, L. S. (1960). *Development of higher psychological functions.* Moscow: Publishing House of the Academy of Pedagogical Sciences.

Vygotsky, L. S. (1965). Psychology and localization of functions. *Neuropsychologia, 3*, 381–386. (Original work published 1934).

Vygotsky, L. S. (1978). *Mind in society: The development of higher mental processes* (M. Cole, V. John-Steiner, S. Scribner, & E. Souberman, Eds. & Trans.). Cambridge, MA: Harvard University Press. (Original work published 1930–1935)

Vygotsky, L. S. (1987). Thinking and speech. N. Minick (Trans.). In R. W. Rieber, & A.S. Carton (Eds.), *The collected works of L. S. Vygotsky, Vol. 1. Problems of general psychology* (pp. 37–285). New York: Plenum. (Original work published 1934)

Vygotsky, L. S. (1997). The historical meaning of the crisis in psychology: A methodological investigation. In R. W. Rieber & J. Wollock (Eds.), R. van der Veer (Trans.), *The collected works of L. S. Vygotsky* (Vol. 3, pp. 233–343). New York: Plenum.

Welsh, M. C., Pennington, B. F., Ozonoff, S., Rouse, B., & McCabe, E. R. B. (1990). Neuropsychology of early-treated phenylketonuria: Specific executive function deficits. *Child Development, 61*, 1697–1713.

Wertsch, J. V. (1980). The significance of dialogue in Vygotsky's account of social, egocentric and inner speech. *Contemporary Educational Psychology, 5*, 150–162.

Wertsch, J. V. (1981). Editor's introduction. In A. R. Luria, *Language and cognition* (J. V. Wertsch, Ed.). Wiley.

Wertsch, J. V. (1985). *Vygotsky and the social formation of mind.* Cambridge, MA: Harvard University Press.

Wertsch, J. V., & Stone, C. A. (1985). The concept of internalization in Vygotsky's account of the genesis of the higher mental functions. In J. V. Wertsch (Ed.), *Culture, communication and cognition: Vygotskian perspectives.* Cambridge, UK: Cambridge University Press.

Winsler, A. (2004). *Still talking to ourselves after all these years: Vygotsky, private speech, and self-regulation.* Invited address given at First International Symposium on Self-Regulatory Functions of Language, Madrid, November 2004.

Winsler, A., Diaz, R. M., McCarthy, E. M., Atencio, D. J., & Adams Chabay, L. (1999). Mother-child interaction, private speech, and task performance in preschool children with behavior problems. *Journal of Child Psychology and Psychiatry, 40*, 891–904.

Winsler, A., Diaz, R. M., & Montero, I. (1997). The role of private speech in the transition from collaborative to independent task performance in young children. *Early Childhood Research Quarterly, 12*, 59–79.

Winsler, A., Fernyhough, C., & Montero, I. (2009). *Private speech, executive functioning, and the development of verbal self-regulation.* Cambridge, UK: Cambridge University Press.

Winsler, A., & Naglieri, J. (2003). Overt and covert verbal problem-solving strategies: Developmental trends in use, awareness, and relations with task performance in children aged 5 to 17. *Child Development, 74,* 659–678.

Zelazo, P. D., Carter, A., Reznick, J. S., & Frye, D. (1997). Early development of executive function: A problem-solving framework. *Review of General Psychology, 1,* 198–226.

Zelazo, P. D., & Müller, U. (2002). Executive function in typical and atypical development. In U. Goswami (Ed.), *Handbook of childhood cognitive development* (pp. 445–469). Oxford, UK: Blackwell Publishing.

Zelazo, P. D., Müller, U., Frye, D., & Marcovitch, S. (2003). The development of executive function in early childhood. *Monographs of the Society for Research in Child Development, 68*(3), Serial No. 274.

4

Epistemic Flow and the Social Making of Minds

CHARLIE LEWIS, JEREMY I. M. CARPENDALE, JOHN TOWSE,
AND KATERINA MARIDAKI-KASSOTAKI

Over the past quarter century two issues have permeated developmental psychology and, indeed, a number of other branches of cognitive science: an understanding of self and others in psychological terms, often referred to as "theory of mind," and the control of action, often labeled "executive functions." In addition, correlations between these two areas of development have been reported and many explanations have been offered for these links. Indeed much of the research on each topic over the past decade has concerned possible links between these two areas of psychological functioning. It is assumed by some that the control of one's actions in the face of misleading lures (as in obeying a false instruction in the game Simon says) forms the basis of our ability to make inferences about the relationship between our own knowledge of the world and others' outdated views. The converse claim is that an understanding that people can have different views on the world provides an important route into being able to control impulsive actions. This debate has touched upon all the issues that are central to this book. In this chapter, we argue that resolving the contrasting views of the relations between social understanding (a term we prefer over "theory of mind"; Carpendale & Lewis, 2006) and executive skills requires thinking about each side of the debate in a way that takes the other two topics in the book, self-regulation and social interaction, into consideration.

Our discussion divides into three sections. In the first, we review recent attempts to compare executive processes in preschoolers with their "theory-of-mind" proficiency. We argue that it is not easy to show how these constructs relate to one another, nor is it clear what each component skill of executive function is composed of. The aim is to show that both social understanding and executive skills are substantiated and develop within the flow of interaction with people and objects, a point neglected in most contemporary debate. The second section draws upon our recent analysis of the notion of social understanding, to suggest that development in both areas of skill needs to be understood in terms of a broader perspective involving social interactions and the acquisition of self-regulation skills. We coin the term "epistemic flow" to convey the dynamic of children's development as they regulate their actions within the unfolding of social interactions concerning the physical and social world. The third and final section describes some of our recent work in order to underline the closeness of these constructs and the role of social interaction in their development. We describe studies showing that both knowledge and the control of responses to events arise in interaction with others and are constantly mediated through such interactions.

How Can We Conceptualize Social Understanding and Executive Function?

It is worth stating at the outset that none of the topics under consideration here is easy to define. For example, the term executive function usually refers to a range of problem-solving skills such as attentional flexibility, working memory, and inhibitory control. In extending this to children, an assumption in some approaches appears to be that these skills simply result from biological maturation and that there are distinct parallels in these processes in adults and children. However, these constructs are derived largely from analyses of test battery data and there are no clear definitions, nor accounts of the origins, functions, and relations between these constituent skills. Similarly, the term "theory of mind" is often used as a catch-all reference to individuals' understanding of themselves and others in psychological terms or sometimes, more specifically, to children's grasp of false beliefs. This belies the fact that there has been a heated debate over the past 30 years about what this term might mean and how it explains children's understanding of the social world (Carpendale & Lewis, 2004, 2006). An attempt to resolve the debates about both constructs in the current volume is timely. We contend that our understanding of each needs to be broadened before we can properly conceptualize it and relate it to the other. Indeed such an exercise leads to the conclusion that the two skills are interdependent, not only upon one another, but also within a framework of other social-cognitive processes.

In this section, we briefly reflect upon two issues that have preoccupied researchers in this area and we use this to articulate a challenge as to whether simple links between the two domains can be made. The first part concerns the problem of evaluating explanations for associations between the two constructs of executive function and "theory of mind," before we have a complete grasp of each, while the second part examines two particular executive function tasks to show how recent work has revealed a need to explore another dimension: the social interactional basis of executive skill.

HOW SHOULD ASSOCIATIONS BETWEEN FALSE BELIEF UNDERSTANDING AND EXECUTIVE FUNCTION SKILLS BE EXPLAINED?

The majority of the debate over the past decade has taken these two constructs as possible influences over the other, but it has been difficult to pin down just what causes what. As mentioned, from one side of the argument Perner, Kain, and Barchfeld (2002; see also Kloo, Perner, & Giritzer, this volume; Lang & Perner, 2002) argue that the key cognitive advance in the later preschool years is caused by better self-insight and self-control resulting from acquiring a representational understanding of mind. Their claim rests in part on the finding that preschoolers' understanding of reflex movements as unintentional was related to success in false-belief and executive function tasks. Such an association may support their claim, but it could also be the case that the three skills they examine have the same underlying complexity and/or require similar reasoning capabilities. In addition, the evidence for a longitudinal association between earlier "theory-of-mind" performance predicting later executive skills has been largely absent from studies. Data supporting the opposite view is also patchy but executive skills have been reported to emerge earlier than false-belief skills in microgenetic research (Flynn, O'Malley, & Wood, 2004). In addition, longitudinal research suggests that some earlier executive function tasks predict some later "theory-of-mind" skills (e.g., Carlson, Mandell, & Williams, 2004; Hughes, 1998). As the balance has been in favor of the causal link in this direction we will explore claims along these lines.

The theoretical links between skills in executive function and social understanding have been notoriously difficult to support. Earlier, simple accounts, like the suggestion that working memory or inhibition underpins "theory of mind" (Davis & Pratt, 1995), have not been supported in other research when other factors, like verbal IQ and chronological age (Carlson, Moses, & Breton, 2002), or other executive skills (Hala, Hug, & Henderson, 2003), were taken into account. The same holds for some studies which attempt to identify a simple link between inhibitory control and false-belief understanding (Keenan, 1999).

These early, and relatively crude, theoretical perspectives have gradually been replaced by models that incorporate combinations of executive skills such as conflict inhibition and working memory (Hala et al., 2003; Carlson & Moses, 2001). Such combinations may support both structural accounts—that these skills have adjacent functions in the prefrontal cortex (Diamond, 1990)—and those suggesting that these skills are functionally related. Partly as a result, a prominent current account (notably Moses & Carlson, 2004; Moses, Carlson, & Sabbagh, 2005; Moses & Sabbagh, 2007) suggests that executive skills *influence* rather than *cause* children's ability to utilize existing skills in "theory-of-mind" understanding—known as the "emergence" account, as it suggests that the acquisition of domain general skills are necessary but not sufficient for false beliefs to be understood.

Whilst these models take a more subtle or nuanced stance with respect to the specification of relationships between mental constructs, our contention is that they require strong assumptions to be made about the validity of the constructs themselves. Yet, there are problems even with such loose interpretations of these constructs. On first inspection it seems as if the emergence account receives clear support, particularly when recent cross-cultural data are taken into account. These show similar relationships between executive skills and social understanding in Europe, Africa, and Latin America (Chasiotis, Kiessling, Winter, & Hofer, 2006), which complement previous research conducted in North America. Evidence for the idea that executive function skills are a necessary prerequisite for social understanding has also been found in Eastern cultures in which children are advanced in executive skills. These show that working memory (Tardif, So, & Kaciroti, 2007) and a set of executive skills appear to be advanced in Chinese children, and yet these skills still are significant predictors of concurrent false-belief understanding (Sabbagh, Xu, Carlson, Moses, & Lee, 2006).

Although the evidence from China appears to support the emergence account (for a slight exception, see Lewis, Huang, & Rooksby, 2006), our recent data from another culture, Korea, does not give such clear support (Oh & Lewis, 2008). Like China, Korea is a Confucian society in which the control of action and strong interpersonal commitments are highly valued attributes. Korean 3-year-olds, for example, typically spend 1 hr of their time at nursery school each day receiving class-based instruction and are encouraged to show self-control, by sitting still and concentrating upon the topic of the lesson (French & Song, 1998).

We report some results from a study whose methods echoed those described earlier. First, we found that Korean children were markedly better on executive function tests than English children. Figure 4.1 illustrates this set of findings with reference to four tests of inhibitory control. Three of these (Luria's hand game and tapping tasks, and the Day-Night test) are well known and test the same control skills as a new Blue-Red task, devised by Seungmi Oh, at approximately the same time as Simpson and Riggs (2005) were developing a similar procedure. In this new task children had to point to a red square when the experimenter said "blue" and a blue square when she or he said "red." Figure 4.1 shows that English preschoolers follow a clear developmental progression from age 3 to their fifth birthdays, but Korean children appear to be almost 2 years ahead on these measures and thus do not show such gains in the fourth and fifth years. Second, correlational analyses did not show links between these executive measures and Korean children's "theory-of-mind" performance. That such patterns were not found in two separate experiments (Oh & Lewis, 2008) raises questions about the strength of the connection between skills in executive function and social understanding across cultures. These data do not completely overturn the Emergence view, as these children's levels of executive control were in place long before false-belief understanding, which followed the expected patterns of success around the child's fourth birthday. However, the length of the lag between Korean children's impressive mastery of inhibitory control and their more modest understanding of false beliefs raises the question of just how necessary is the

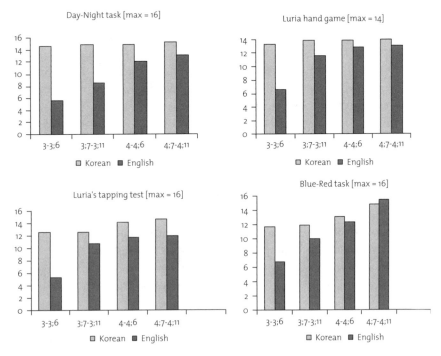

FIGURE 4.1. Performance of English and Korean children on four executive function tests.

relation between the two skills. The data may also suggest that cultural processes are involved in the acquisition of these skills—a point we return to in
the middle section of the chapter.

ANALYSES OF SINGLE TASKS: THE EXAMPLES OF THE DIMENSIONAL CHANGE CARD SORT AND THE WINDOWS TASK

The issues in these areas of development are perhaps deeper than simply
the problematic link between executive function and social understanding. At the level of individual tests, it is hard to discern what they actually
measure. In this analysis, we highlight how such tests are open to multiple interpretations and show how close inspection suggests more complex
understandings of how executive processes work and may relate to social
understanding.

Although most tests of executive skills are administered in batteries without much analysis of the exact constructs tapped by each, the Dimensional
Change Card Sort (DCCS) task perhaps comes closest to a full analysis as
it has received close attention over the past decade (Zelazo, Müller, Frye, &
Marcovitch, 2003). In this task children are required to sort cards, differentiated by color and shape, into one of two trays. The sorting criteria are changed
half way through the task from one dimension to another (from color to shape
or vice versa). Care is taken to ensure that preschoolers are told clearly of the
change in the rules, but 3-year-olds typically continue to sort cards by the
preswitch rules. They even make the perseverative error when there are just
one or two preswitch trials, despite being able to give an appropriate verbal
response to indicate where the card should go (Zelazo, Frye, & Rapus, 1996 [see
also Frye, Zelazo, & Palfai, 1995; Experiment 2]) and despite having the rules
explained to them prior to the sort. Children have thus been characterized
as making "abulic" errors, which is to say that they know the rules but do not
know how to act upon them. The experimental evidence is impressive, particularly because children appear to divide into two groups over a very small
number (ordinarily 5 or 6) of postswitch trials, those who fail most or all and
those who make no errors. This contrasts with most executive tests in which
the data are less dichotomized.

According to Frye and Zelazo, young children's failure on the DCCS task
shows the child's ability to construct higher-order rules that make the two
rule systems (e.g., the shape and color rule sets) accessible to conscious control. This is known as Cognitive Complexity and Control (CCC) theory (see
e.g., Zelazo et al., 2003 for a recent version of this theory). According to CCC
theory, 3-year-olds make their judgments based on simple if-then rules and

are unable to succeed at tasks requiring embedded rules ("If this is the color game, then if red car, then here; but if it is the shape game, then if red car, then here"). Crucial for this analysis is that the DCCS correlates highly with false-belief test performance (e.g., Frye et al., 1995). Frye et al. argue that this is because both tasks contain an if-if-then structure requiring similar embedded rules.

Despite repeated replications of the DCCS procedure, a number of alternatives to the embedded rule account have been proposed. Although these differ from one another, they concentrate on the demands of moving from one task phase to another (e.g., Brace, Morton, & Munakata, 2006; Kirkham, Cruess, & Diamond, 2003; Munakata & Yerys, 2001; Towse, Redbond, Houston-Price, & Cook, 2000). Two examples of these experiments are as follows. Towse et al. (2000) found that if 3-year-olds are given support to ensure that the postswitch rules are explained in the same way as the preswitch rules (i.e., including the use of exemplar stimuli for demonstrating the sorting rules) they showed much greater levels of success. Moreover, erroneous sorting behavior with postswitch rules is accompanied by more ambiguous or erroneous labeling of the test cards. This suggests that the card sort task may be difficult, not because the child has to understand embedded rules, but because the first sorting strategy becomes cognitively salient to him or her. Similarly, Brace et al. (2006) showed that a demonstration of the correct response was more successful than instruction, suggesting that if the required working memory is reduced by scaffolding with a demonstration then children will succeed.

These contrasting interpretations of the DCCS leave the discipline with two problems. First, they challenge the assumption that one can unequivocally establish the construct validity of the task. For critics of the CCC framework, the perseveration by preschoolers may simply result from attentional inertia (Kirkham et al., 2003) or working memory (e.g., Brace et al., 2006), although they leave unclear why children show the abulic errors described earlier. Yet Zelazo et al. (2003; Happaney & Zelazo, 2003) accommodate such results in terms of CCC theory. This impasse makes it hard to take these data further and is related to the second problem.

A second issue is that although one can establish statistical links between set shifting (as indexed by the DCCS) and mental state attribution (as indexed by false belief), the psychological meaning of this remains opaque. Perner, Stummer and Lang, (1999) showed that an understanding of the involuntary nature of the knee-jerk reflex, which does not involve any obvious conditional reasoning requirements, relates not only to the DCCS, but also to false-belief understanding, and a test of inhibitory control. They used such evidence to criticize the use of CCC theory as an account of "theory-of-mind" skills. In addition, Perner (2000) argues that the embedded rules that serve as the rationale for the card-sort task may not necessarily fit the traditional false-belief task, which can be depicted as two if-then conditions. It is not wholly clear whether this critique is valid since the task has been described in both ways, but it serves to underline the problems in trying to relate executive function and "theory of mind" through the comparison of disparate tests which can be open to many interpretations. The issues we have discussed in this subsection reflect a move toward accounts that suggest that both "theory of mind" and executive function are more general and intertwined cognitive skills (Bjorklund, Cormier, & Rosenberg, 2005). The central question concerns how they intertwine.

One way of attempting to understand the relationship between mental state understanding and more general cognitive skills is to use a single research design to assess both together. Despite protracted criticism of a reliance on one procedure, false-belief tasks have been used as *the* measure of social understanding. A weakness in this approach is that it is a one-shot procedure and once tested children cannot be retested, except with new materials and procedures. Although there are moves to broaden the database for examining "theory of mind" (e.g., Wellman & Liu, 2004), this does not help us to harmonize the links with executive skills because it is hard to discern what underlies a correlation between two tests that differ in a number of ways. A better alternative would be to devise single tests which assess both executive skills and social understanding within the same design. One task which to some extent succeeds is the Windows Task (Russell, Mauthner, Sharpe, & Tidswell, 1991), in which children are exposed to 20 trials of a game in which they have to point to a box for the experimenter to open, knowing that they will get the reward if they point to the empty box, not the one containing the reward. Three-year-olds and older children with autism normally select the box baited with the reward over many trials even though, after each, the experimenter receives the reward. Russell et al. suggested that this perseveration (i.e., the act of repeatedly making the same choice, despite continually losing out on the reward) may reflect an inability in younger children and those with autism to inhibit making a reference to the object's actual location.

Like the DCCS, the Windows Task is open to other interpretations. To begin with, the shift between ages 3 and 4 found by Russell et al. has not always been replicated (Moore, Barresi, & Thompson, 1998; Samuels, Brooks, & Frye, 1996). There is also controversy over what the task involves. Simpson, Riggs, and Simon (2004) suggest that children's difficulty with the task is that they have to infer the rule "point to the empty box," and this is not immediately apparent to 3-year-olds. Our interpretation is that by giving the child this explicit rule, Simpson et al. helped the child to suppress the normal expectation to point to where the object is. Indeed we suggest that only a close analysis of a task allows us to infer what it shows about children's understanding. The data from the Windows Task procedure serves as a means of exploring the theoretical issues that are at the core of this chapter, which we turn to now.

From our perspective, more recent findings that demonstrate variability of task performance show the role of social interaction in children's performance on the Windows Task. Analyses of children's performance on the Windows Task have suggested that the inhibitory component is more complex and influenced by the nature of the social interaction between the child and the experimenter. For example, if instead of pointing to the empty box children are required to use a symbolic token like a star or to place a model "pointing hand" 3-year-olds perform significantly better (Hala & Russell, 2001). After only a few trials the majority of the children were at ceiling when using a symbolic token to mark the box that an experimenter should open. For Hala and Russell pointing is a "natural" form of communication and links goal and response, while a "pointer" or a star, is a "nonnatural," symbolic response mode, which distances the child from the actions he or she performs. Three-year-olds' performance also increased greatly in another condition in which they were told that they would play together on a team with an experimenter. Hala and Russell argued that this improved performance was due to distancing through a social means because the decision became a joint action.

Similar results were found in a slightly different task in which children have to point to a set of smaller objects in order to obtain a reward (Carlson, Davis, & Leach, 2005). When the sets to be pointed to are symbolic representations like an elephant and a mouse rather than the objects themselves, children perform more successfully. The use of a symbolic representation for a few trials has the effect of generalizing to a more standard Windows Task (Apperly & Carroll, in press). The use of a symbol to communicate the response seems to allow children to gain more control over their actions, as such symbols distance them from the action. Thus these effects show that executive and social understanding skills are not either present or absent in children—because when developing, they are mediated by the means by which the child communicates her or his response. This fits with Vygotsky's (1978) view of mediation; a zone of proximal or potential development is created when experimenters provide this structure.

To conclude this section, we have briefly reviewed the literature on executive function and social understanding to argue against the predominant belief that these are stable entities that can be easily defined, measured, and then correlated. Rather, preschoolers' skills seem to be open to manipulation in interactions with others. We thus need an alternative approach to understanding these constructs which takes into account some of the core themes in this book.

From Social to Self-Regulation: Epistemic Flow

Implicit in our analysis of the studies in the previous section is the contention that the approaches usually taken to both executive function and "theory of mind" are too individualistic and inflexible. In addition to the variability in task performance that we have just discussed in relation to the child's access to symbolic means of suppressing prepotent responses to cues, there are also clear social correlates of these skills. The different types of social predictors of false-belief understanding are so diverse that we have reviewed these at length (Carpendale & Lewis, 2006, chaps. 6 and 7). Factors that have been shown to be positively related to tests of social understanding (usually false-belief understanding) include security of attachment, family SES, aspects of parent–child talk, and having older siblings, whereas deafness and blindness tend to be negatively related to social understanding. The literature on the social correlates with executive performance is less uniform but only a little digging reveals that performance is varied in children in different social groups that echo those differences between cultures reported in the previous section. For example, executive functions were found to be associated with parental scaffolding (Landry, Miller-Loncar, Smith, & Swank, 2002) and socioeconomic status (e.g., Ardila, Roselli, Matute, & Guajardo, 2005; Noble, McCandliss, & Farah, 2007). Furthermore, Gerstadt, Hong, and Diamond's (1994) first study on the Day-Night task showed more successful performance in children in day care than those raised exclusively at home. Such differences suggest that the demands of out of home care in Western cultures exert an influence on preschoolers' control.

Yet the social and symbolic correlates of "executive function" skills have received less attention than one might expect given the historical backdrop of research from Luria and Vygotsky (Zelazo et al., 2003; Zelazo & Jacques, 1997). The literature on self-regulation (e.g., Landry & Smith, this volume; Sokol & Müller, 2007) attempts to explore these issues more centrally. This area of research charts the move from "externally to internally regulated behaviour" (Rothbart & Derryberry, 1981, p. 562). The phrase is sometimes used to refer to a broader area of children's developing competence, including emotional self-regulation (i.e., "the ability to manage levels of arousal and irritability," Karreman, van Tuijl, van Aken, & Dekovi, 2006, p. 561). It can also be conceptualized as involving autonomy or agency (Grolnick & Farkas, 2002); that is, the ability to resist simply responding to the immediate environment but instead to make choices. The term self-regulation is rooted within a relational framework. For example, Kopp (1982) analyzed the role of social interactional factors in the development of internalized and controlled behavior. According to this view, in the second year of life, toddlers become aware of the demands on social control that are negotiated with their care-givers, particularly their parents. Self-regulation thus gradually develops within relationships, and attachments in particular, as shown in a recent meta-analysis (Karreman et al., 2006).

This socially embedded view of self-regulation has an earlier pedigree (Luria, 1961). Luria's (1981, p. 7) work took a social approach in which "the ontogenesis of voluntary action begins with the practical act that the child performs in response to the command of the adult. Clearly this hypothesis is basic to modern psychology. It views complex ontogenetic processes not as resulting from biological development, but from social forms of human activity." Much of Luria's work is focused on the role of speech in self-regulatory behavior, which received critical attention in the 1960s and 1970s (e.g., Miller, Shelton, & Flavell, 1970). Luria's work itself draws on an older and broader literature (especially Vygotsky, 1978; but see also Mead, 1934) attempting a broader description of intelligent behavior.

We coin the term epistemic flow as a label for the processes that Vygotsky (1978) described. There are two strands in Vygotsky's argument that we need to be aware of. The first concerns the nature of cognitive processes themselves. Vygotsky argued that the intelligent behavior characteristic of humans requires the ability to select from alternative actions; this involves the development of a distance from an immediate reaction to the world—the prepotent responses made by other animals and evident when humans fail to inhibit actions. At the centre of his theory was the idea, derived from Engels, that language and social interaction necessarily allow us to establish new links between and within each of our cognitive functions. The role of speech in cognitive processing has been well rehearsed, but Vygotsky's focus included the development of all higher-level cognitive processes, including planning, memory and inhibitory control (Vygotsky, 1978, especially pp. 27–31 and 47–51; see Frawley, 1997, chap. 3 for a discussion). In these processes the shift from lower- to higher-mental functions is mediated by symbolic systems such as language, and this transforms the nature of perceptual experience.

Vygotsky (1978, p. 28) stated that "unlike the ape, which Köhler tells us is 'the slave of its own visual field,' children acquire an independence with respect to their concrete surroundings." That is, children develop the ability to direct their own attention, rather than being tied to responding to what they see. "Once children learn how to use the planning function of their language effectively, their psychological field changes radically" (p. 28). Vygotsky wrote about a change in children's planning ability but this also results in a change in inhibition. As the child develops the capacity to consider more possible courses of action she is no longer a slave of her own visual field, and she can select from among options rather than impulsively and slavishly responding to the environment. We could describe the development of this intelligent behavior in terms of executive function skills such as planning, flexibility, and inhibition. But is the development of a skill at inhibition independent of content? Or is it that the development of more options in that context results in intelligent behavior that we could describe in terms of inhibition (i.e., in a way inhibition is a by-product)?

Vygotsky used examples of simple operations, like tying a knot in one's handkerchief, to pinpoint their influence in constructing higher levels of thinking. Executive skills, like memory, could be divided into two types. First, there is a nonmediated form, or "natural memory," and, second, there are memory processes that are deemed to be operations that are mediated by signs. The pivotal feature of these higher-order functions is that they are generated by the individual's engagement with environmentally generated stimuli and as such they change or refract these stimuli. The process of transformation is captured by the term "flow" in which the child's skill is constantly changing as the structure of the situation changes to separate him or her from the lure of the immediate environment. The result is a fluid set of symbolic associations.

For Vygotsky interaction with others allows individuals to perform actions, initially beyond their individual capabilities, and they gradually come to master these skills. Vygotsky's work was largely dedicated to opposing the associationist ideas of classical conditioning. This led him to formulate a model which does not simply reduce to stimulus–response (S–R) connections, caused by reward, punishment, and extinction. Rather, the mediated sign systems that we described earlier are channeled through cultural–historical processes. In *Mind and Society*, for example, Vygotsky (1978, p. 40) described symbolic mediation as having the effect that "the direct impulse to react is inhibited" and this opens the mind to create new means of self-control. These are inherently social in their orientation and they are centrally involved in self-regulation and executive control:

> this type of organization is basic to all psychological processes.... The intermediate link in this formula is not simply a method of improving the previously existing operation, nor is it a mere additional link in an S–R chain. Because this auxiliary stimulus possesses the specific function of reverse action, it transfers the psychological operation to higher and qualitatively new forms and permits humans, by the aid of

extrinsic stimuli, *to control their behaviour from the outside.* The use of signs leads humans to a specific structure of behaviour that breaks away from biological development and creates new forms of a cultur- ally-based psychological process. (Vygotsky, 1978, p. 40, emphasis in original)

This view of executive control has a resonance with our social construc- tivist account of how social understanding develops within interaction and language (Carpendale & Lewis, 2004, 2006). In this approach, we integrate the work of Vygotsky with the earlier and later writings of Piaget and the later work of Wittgenstein. This link between Piaget and Vygotsky has been theo- rized in terms of an "epistemic triangle" (Chapman, 1991), in which the child's grasp of any "object of knowledge" is always mediated by her or his interac- tions with a real or hypothetical interlocutor. This occurs with more skilled members of one's culture, but such an interlocutor becomes internalized in the same way that speech becomes internalized in Vygotsky's view of how the use of signs leads to higher forms of thinking. We have analyzed at length how such processes allow infants to develop social understanding (see Carpendale & Lewis, 2006; Carpendale, Lewis, Müller, & Racine, 2005) and will only sum- marize our argument here.

Within the constructivist framework, language, self-regulation, and social understanding develop in the natural course of the individual's daily activity and communicative exchanges. Language is built on prior forms of interaction in which attention is coordinated with others, referred to as joint attention (Mead, 1934; Tomasello, 2003). We reject a code model of language, according to which meaning is a matter of decoding words. Instead, language is used to direct others' attention within situations of shared understanding. Mind related words do not refer to hidden inner mental entities that cause behavior, but rather they redescribe human activity. Children's social under- standing develops further by learning to use words referring to the psycho- logical world. Such understanding becomes increasingly complex and flexible as the child's use of terms broaden to different contexts. Let us examine one example.

We have argued that joint attention allows infants to start using words within interactions grounded in shared understanding. For example, a word like "look" could be added to interactions in which the attention of another is being directed with a pointing gesture. With further develop- ment, such a word can be used to convey many possible meanings within typical exchanges. It could mean "Pay attention" or "Wow," or something completely different dependent on the circumstances. At around their first birthdays, children learn how to make and respond to such pointing gestures, and they often seem insistent in experimental procedures where the interlocutor purposely pays attention to an irrelevant object (a piece of card rather than the exciting toy beyond it but out of the adult's field of vision; Liszkowski, Carpenter, Striano, & Tomasello, 2006; Tomasello, Carpenter, & Liszkowski, 2007). Only within the immediacy and complexity of interactional exchanges can children come to use and understand the use of different gestures. With this shared understanding of such situations, children can begin to use words such as "look." This indicates that children's use of symbols has social origins.

Children's ability to understand such words referring to others' attention is important for their understanding of false-belief situations. Being able to understand the word "look" in the (in)famous false-belief test ["Where will Maxi look for his chocolate?"] is the product of a complex history of learning how to converse about people in psychological terms. This is quite an accomplishment, but is only a landmark in a long journey. Later understandings of the term are much more sophisticated. You might say "You look great" because you know that you are expected to make a positive comment on the success of a purchase, not because you have information about how well your partner's visual system is working, or because you like what she is wearing! More complex social understanding is built on language or symbolic associations, in the way Vygotsky describes the development of higher mental functions. Thus, from this perspective, learning about the psychological aspects of human activity occurs in a piecemeal manner. Children achieve competence in elementary forms of interaction with others in contexts of shared understanding and gradually learn the various uses of particular words in such situations. Such talk focuses upon what each participant in the interaction is doing, but necessarily makes explicit (e.g., some uses of "think") or implicit (as in the example of "look") reference to attention and knowledge. Thus, to learn such words involves an ability to interact with other people. Some of these skills are universal, while others may be open to cultural variation (Vinden, 1996, 1999).

In summary, in the first two sections we have argued that the two areas of psychological functioning, executive function and "theory of mind," may not be radically separate spheres. We concur with Vygotsky that all mental processes concern the development of skills that are socially and symbolically mediated. Social understanding is based on children's experience of interactions and conversations concerning attention, knowledge, emotions, and intentions. This account makes the assumption that an understanding of false beliefs involves a complexity of interacting processes that can be separated into two dimensions. First, it involves an understanding of the use of terms like "look" and "think" in different contexts. Second, it involves the self-regulation skills that permit the child to detach her- or himself from an impulsive reaction to the immediate present.

Woven together, the skills in both areas (executive function and social understanding) are equivalent to those described by Vygotsky (1978) specifically referring to executive function, in terms of planning, memory, and inhibition. If it is the case that an understanding of beliefs involves these executive skills, then this would explain the close relationships between the two sets of skills in experimental work. Evidence indicating just how closely they are related comes from Kloo and Perner's (2003) training study, which has been replicated in full in our laboratory (Short, 2007). In these studies, it was found that training a child either on a task of attentional flexibility (the DCCS task) or on false-belief tasks leads to improvements not only in the trained skill but also on tests of the other skill. Such findings are hard to explain in terms of the causal theories discussed in the first section (that executive skills underpin social understanding or the reverse). Given that the two sets of skills appear to be interrelated, we need an explanation that takes this link into account. We turn now to the third section of the chapter in which we explore the dynamics of epistemic flow further to explore this interrelationship.

Epistemic Flow in Self-Regulation and Children's Social Understanding

In this final section we flesh out some empirical examples in order to justify the need for an alternative direction for contemporary thinking, based on the theoretical approach to self-regulation, social cognition, and executive function, described in the previous section. We return here to the idea of an epistemic triangle as a useful basis for theorizing how children construct an understanding of these skills. In order to reconcile the "social" and "cognitive" aspects of development, the triangle consists of three sides—the interactions between the child and the object of knowledge, between a child and a real or hypothetical interlocutor, and between the interlocutor and the object of knowledge. As we stated earlier, an "object of knowledge" can refer to any aspect of the physical or social world that the individual can gain knowledge about through her or his engagement. This can be at a simpler perceptual level or such knowledge might be meditated via simple or more complex symbolic processes.

Our model builds upon Vygotsky's claims suggestion that the development of higher-level cognitive functions is dependent on social interaction and the gradual distancing of the self in the process of developing symbolic understanding of events. A complete, but technically difficult, analysis would show how the triangle as a whole functions as a dynamic system. However, here we examine some of the ways in which we can analyze the three components of this system.

1. THE SELF IN DYNAMIC INTERACTION WITH OBJECTS OF KNOWLEDGE

One key feature of both "theory of mind" and executive function is that they are dynamic skills. Our abilities to inhibit prepotent responses, use rules flexibly and recall information that is relevant to particular circumstantial needs, are supported in some situations but not in others. It is hard to measure "theory of mind" in such a way, although there are possibilities for doing this with the repeated trials of Call and Tomasello's (1999) "nonverbal" false-belief task. Tests of executive skills can assess dynamic change in participants' engagement in events, in that performance over series of, usually demanding, trials can be examined. This provides excellent opportunities to model these dynamics and yet, strangely, attempts to provide detailed analyses of such dynamics are limited even in research on adults (e.g., Tatler & Hutton, 2007; Ward & Allport, 1997).

How can we examine executive skills as continuous processes? Duncan, Emslie, Williams, Johnson, and Freer (1996) have brought the relevance of task and goal focus to the foreground of cognitive theorizing, and to do so they have developed a paradigm that does lend itself to a consideration of dynamic changes over trials. Ignoring a task cue, despite showing every indication of knowing what to do with the cue in the abstract, was referred to as goal neglect observed in daily activities of frontal patients, as well as in an experimental environment that involved conducting a speeded monitoring task with a number of sub-elements. Duncan et al. designed a task that involved a written instruction to watch one of two places to the left or the right of the prompt on a computer screen. The command "Watch Left" provided a cue to name letters on the left and ignore digits in a fast sequence on the right side of the screen. Participants were instructed that they should also respond to a plus or a minus sign by monitoring the left or right stimulus streams, respectively. Duncan et al. also found that this goal neglect (toward the second cue) was resolved over blocks of trials; between each block, participants were reminded of all the task rules. Thus, while goal neglect occurred more frequently among individuals with low "g" scores on IQ tests, among the elderly and among frontal-lobe patients, it was neither inevitable nor permanent.

How does Duncan et al.'s (1996) paradigm generalize to preschoolers? There is abundant anecdotal evidence that children struggle with prospective actions (when such and such happens, do X). Thus we (Towse, Lewis, & Knowles, 2007) adapted Duncan et al.'s goal neglect paradigm to examine the nature of children's performance in response to changing cues as in the first- and second-side-instruction, described earlier. To make Duncan et al.'s procedure age appropriate, we developed the Selective Image Naming Task (SINT). We reduced the number of stimuli and turned the activity into a game in which the child had to help a teddy bear find food in one of two locations: one of two differently colored houses on the left or right of the screen. We simplified sequence presentation so as to involve only response items (rather than include also items to be ignored) since pilot work showed that children found the partial response configuration very difficult. Nevertheless, the core of the adult procedure was preserved with simultaneous screen events presented to children, and centrally presented cues appeared that directed participants to attend to one or the other location.

We explored two issues. In a first session, we examined children's ability to identify food items in the target house and, following one of two cues, to switch on some trials to naming the food in a second house. Initially, the first-side-instruction was always an arrow and the second-side-instruction was a red or blue colored square, to indicate which house the child should attend to. The sequence of main events is presented in Figure 4.2. The second issue in a follow-up experiment concerned whether children's abilities to switch sides in response to the second-side-instruction was influenced by the nature of the cue alerting them to do so. Duncan et al. had speculated that the imperative/abstract nature of a cue affected the success of goal focus in adults, and the recovery from instances of neglect. They had found that participants coped better with an additional dot probe instruction associated with a more compatible response (relating to the spatial height of the dot position) than the symbolic second-side-instruction.

There is good reason to believe that the SINT task assesses a number of skills that unfold over the course of the test session. Some task failures were observed in response to the first-side-instruction, when children either named the food items in both houses or failed to name any item. Other task failures occurred in response to the cue to switch to the other house. Analysis demonstrated that fulfilling the requirements of the early and late cues reflected different processes, in that they were differentially related to commonly used tests of set shifting (i.e., the DCCS task and the Blue-Red inhibition task described earlier). We found that responses to the first-side-instruction were associated with a measure of conflict inhibition, while the second-side-instruction correlated with set shifting as measured by the DCCS. Figure 4.3 shows that these

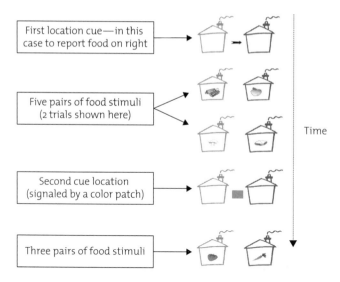

First location cue—in this case to report food on right

Five pairs of food stimuli (2 trials shown here)

Second cue location (signaled by a color patch)

Three pairs of food stimuli

Time

FIGURE 4.2. The sequence of events in the Selective Image Naming Task.

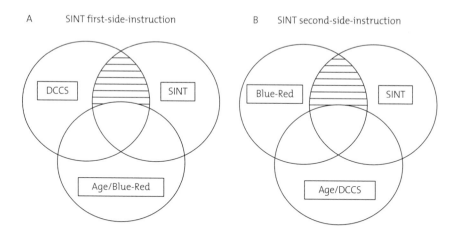

A   SINT first-side-instruction

DCCS   SINT

Age/Blue-Red

B   SINT second-side-instruction

Blue-Red   SINT

Age/DCCS

FIGURE 4.3. The interrelationships between task and subject variables in Towse, Lewis, and Knowles (2007). (a) Focusing on the shaded intersection area, which represents the association between SINT and DCCS independent of age and Blue-Red performance, there was a significant correlation with SINT success following the second-side-instruction but not the first-side-instruction (r = 0.45 and r = 0.24, respectively). (b) Focusing on the shaded intersection area, which represents the association between SINT and the Blue-Red task independent of age and DCCS performance, there was a nonsignificant correlation with SINT success following the second-side-instruction but a significant correlation with performance following the first-side-instruction (r = 0.16 and r = 0.67, respectively).

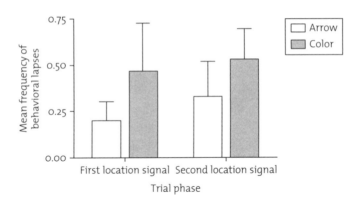

FIGURE 4.4. Effects of cue type and order on children's goal neglect, including standard error bars, from Towse, Lewis, and Knowles (2007).

relationships held even after other factors were partialled out, suggesting that set shifting and inhibition may be dissociated and are not grounded in the same construct (as has been suggested by Zelazo & Jacques, 1996).

Convergent with the outcomes from Hala and Russell's (2001) Windows Task study described in the first section of the chapter, we also established that the type of cue made a difference to task compliance. Children made more errors in response to a color signal than an arrow following the second-side-instruction, irrespective of order of presentation (see Figure 4.4). This difference suggests that children's propensity to make executive shifts is guided by the strength of an exogenous cue. Whether the arrow has greater symbolic detachment from the immediate stimulus, is a stronger impetus to direct attention, or the extent to which these alternatives are discriminable has yet to be explored. Nonetheless, the findings suggest that the role of symbolic mediation is important in influencing children's self-regulation. It also serves to reinforce the relevance of studying executive skills as continuous and changing processes rather than assuming that they are fixed and stable abilities that are present or absent. Indeed, the aim of this example has been to reemphasize the point that executive skills are dynamic—performance is dependent on a subtle interaction between the individual's interactions with procedures and the demands that are made by the different phases of the SINT for brief periods of time.[1] Moreover, there is almost certainly a waxing and waning in the severity of executive demands imposed by any task within and between trials, yet unfortunately this is often ignored for the sake of interpretive expediency (see, e.g., the Day-Night task, first and second half; Gerstadt et al., 1994). We suggest that trying to capture this fluidity of executive processes and social interactions will ultimately be more compelling and productive than treating them as easily defined and uniform constructs captured in single paradigms.

2. INTERACTIONS WITH INTERLOCUTORS, SOCIAL UNDERSTANDING, AND EXECUTIVE SKILLS

We have emphasized earlier the number of studies which show that social factors and language correlate strongly with children's performance on tests of social understanding, like false-belief tasks (see Carpendale & Lewis, 2006). This research served as the platform for our claim that an understanding of "theory of mind" must be embedded in an alternative theoretical framework (Carpendale & Lewis, 2004). However, "theory theorists" have argued that these social factors can be accommodated within their perspectives (e.g., Bartsch & Estes, 2004; Ruffman, 2004), in that social stimulation might simply provide experiences in which the child can develop and test new theoretical perspectives on the social world. The theory-theory perspective, however, implies that children develop a theory that applies across situations. We will review evidence that is inconsistent with this claim and instead suggest that children's understanding of their social world is acquired in a more patchwork manner, linked to particular situations and words. We discuss two sets of studies, which we feel add to the debate about social factors in the development of self-regulation. The first suggests that social experience, executive skills, and mental state understanding can be explored in intervention studies. The aim is to suggest that training within and between these areas of cognitive performance reveal much about the relationship between the child's social experience of social interactions, and their social and cognitive development.

Research in the mid-1990s showed that preschoolers can be trained to pass false-belief tests (e.g., Appleton & Reddy, 1996; Slaughter & Gopnik, 1996). In Appleton and Reddy's (1996) study preschoolers watched a video clip in which someone's belief becomes false. Children were asked questions (e.g., "Why did the first child look [in the original place] for the object?" [p. 281]), and this "conversational training" resulted in 78% of the training group becoming successful on a further false-belief test, compared with 4% of a control group. Appleton and Reddy's findings suggest that only brief exposure to questioning about false-belief situations leads to the development of skills that transfer to related tasks. Similar findings emerged in a study in which brief training in the understanding of the structure of sentences involving sentential complements led to improvements in false-belief understanding (Hale & Tager-Flusberg, 2003).

As Hale and Tager-Flusberg point out, it is not clear whether children learn about false beliefs through decomposing the syntax of sentences which have a similar structure to those referring to beliefs or whether they gain semantic information about the nature of mental state terms. There have been many suggestions about the role of language in the development of mental state understanding (Astington & Baird, 2005). These extend from the child's understanding of the syntax of sentences, like those involving beliefs, which necessarily take complements (e.g., "He believed that [the chocolate was in the cupboard]") (de Villiers, 2005), to general issues concerning the role of conversation in providing the child with different perspectives (e.g., Harris, 1996). Perhaps the most complete study to date involves a comparison between four different training conditions examining the relative effects of sentential complements, discourse about perspectives, or both, compared to a control condition. In this study, Lohmann and Tomasello (2003) found that three sessions of training with either type of intervention led to improvements compared to the control group, but that the greatest improvement was in the condition combining both types of training, suggesting that both the structure of language and its communicative intent are involved in children acquiring the ability to talk about and understand themselves and others in psychological terms.

We have argued that language works through directing others' attention within situations of shared understanding, not as a means for transmitting meaning encoded in words. Words related to mind such as "look," "think," and "intend" refer to human activity and children learn such words in the process of coming to understand human activity in increasingly complex situations of shared understanding. This ability is then a means for communicating with others and answering questions such as those on false-belief tests, as well as a tool for reflection.

If social interaction is central to the development of social understanding, does it also influence the development of executive function? Some of the ideas in Vygotsky's and Luria's writings filtered into research in the 1970s but since then have been neglected in recent literature on executive function (for an exception see Fernyhough, this volume; Müller, Liebermann, Frye, & Zelazo, 2008; Zelazo & Jacques, 1997). The aim is to show that the interaction between the child and the experimenter has a direct bearing upon the former's executive performance. For example, in a series of studies by Ignatius Toner (Ritchie & Toner, 1984; Toner, Moore, & Emmons, 1980; Toner & Smith, 1977) children were told either that the experimenter had heard that they were good at a delay inhibition task (a task-relevant remark) or that they had a lot of friends in the preschool (a task-irrelevant remark). The children then performed a delay inhibition task in which the child was told that the experimenter would keep adding chocolates to a pile until the child decided to eat one. One chocolate was added every 30 s, and the task finished as soon as the child touched the chocolate. Toner found that in the task-relevant remark group children waited significantly longer, even when the remark about their self-control was made by a second experimenter on the way to the testing area, and the experimenter who administered the test was unaware of which group the child had been allocated to.

We (Charlie Lewis, Amy Harrison, and Kathryn Warburton) have replicated this study and found that in the task-relevant remark condition children waited on an average until 415 s had elapsed while the mean for the task-irrelevant remark condition was 283 s over the 500 s testing period. We also examined children's performance on conflict-inhibition tasks and found stronger effects of a task-relevant remark leading to greater control in conflict-inhibition tasks, like the DCCS and Luria's Hand Game. Plus we found that if children performed a delay task on one day and a conflict-inhibition task the next day that the performance-enhancing effect of the task-relevant remark was found for each task, but the effect from one test did not carry over to the other test performed the next day.

The studies reported in this section lead to complementary conclusions. The training studies on false-belief understanding add to the study of Kloo and Perner (2003) that we discussed earlier. We feel that such brief training cannot really be attributed to a shift in children's supposed overarching "theories." Rather, we suggest that structured interactions can lead to a change in children's understanding of particular types of interaction, perhaps restricted to the situation of false-belief experiment itself. The research on social influences on executive functions appears to show that training need not be specific at least in terms of the children's performance on some executive tasks. Children's responses seemed to be subtly influenced by general social demands or motivational cues just before testing. Taken together, both areas of research not only remind us of the complexities of experimentation with children, but also how children's performance is influenced by the interactions they have with others.

3. COMPLETING THE TRIANGLE: INTERACTIONS BETWEEN "OTHERS" AND OBJECTS OF KNOWLEDGE

We return here to the main points of the second section of the chapter. We argued that we can draw two highly related conclusions from Vygotsky's theory: (1) social processes play a role in the development of an individual's skills, and (2) symbols are involved in the development of higher mental functions, such as those now referred to as executive functions. The links between these processes were depicted by Vygotsky (1978), and Chapman's (1991) interpretation of Piaget, as triangular structures (cf. others e.g., Ferrari, 2007), in which the social and the cognitive are brought together. If these conclusions are to be supported, then we should be able to see their effects in research in the two domains under consideration. Although most research avoids these broad issues we draw upon two pieces of research that we feel support the perspective which we have offered. The first examines influences of social interactions on an executive skill and social understanding, while the second concerns the role of language in children's success on false-belief tasks.

In one study, Peskin and Ardino (2003) explored the links between children's abilities to perform two types of everyday activity—keeping a secret about a "birthday gift" for one of the experimenters, and the ability to play hide-and-seek—and the two most standard two false-belief tasks, unexpected transfer and the deceptive box tasks. They found a correlation between each of these everyday skills and one of the latter tasks in a series of multivariate analyses. Children's skills at hide-and-seek predicted their performance on the unexpected transfer test, as both require an understanding of the movements of objects in space. At the same time, their ability to keep the gift secret predicted deceptive box test results. Both of these involve the child's knowledge of the contents of a container, although the former is supposed to be a measure of delay inhibition (i.e., executive skill), whereas the latter is taken to be one of the key assessments of false-belief understanding. For our purposes these findings serve to show the interrelatedness of these constructs and the experiment as a whole suggests that the child constructs knowledge of social activity in a piecemeal manner based on her or his everyday experiences such as hiding and keeping secrets rather than as a global set of rules applying to beliefs.

In the second study we return to the issue of children's developing social understanding in relation to language development and, once again, the word "look." We have already mentioned some of the competing views about the role of language in social cognition (Astington & Baird, 2005). Research on early language development suggests that learning words requires an appreciation of speakers' intentions concerning what they are referring to (Baldwin, 1993; Tomasello, 2003). Indeed, some even suggest that this requires a "theory of mind" in the first place (Bloom, 2000), although the nature of this suggestion is not fully specified and could not be referring to false-belief understanding, so it must be in reference to earlier forms of social understanding in infancy such as the ability to coordinate attention with others, as discussed earlier.

Here we describe some research on false-belief understanding in order to show more local influences of language use on social understanding. Our work on Greek children's grasp of false belief was inspired in part because their language has two terms that can be used synonymously to mean "look," the key term in one version of the unexpected transfer test (Maridaki-Kassotaki, Lewis, & Freeman, 2003). Although largely synonymous, the two words are subtly different. "Psahno" refers to the act of locating an object, whereas "kitazo" refers to the act of looking—as in an exclamation. With the complement "na vro" both words mean to "look for." So, an instruction "Look for your glasses" with kitazo would refer to the other's act of seeing and the search strategy, whereas with psahno it would specify the fact that the glasses should be found. A parental questionnaire revealed that 93% said they would use the latter term to state "Where will Maxi look for his chocolate?" in the classic test of false belief. However, two experiments revealed a very different set of findings concerning children's understanding: with psahno even 5-year-olds were *below* chance on standard false-belief tasks, whereas 3- to 4-year-olds were significantly *above* chance when kitazo was used.

These data show the close link between particular word use and social understanding. Our approach to interpreting this evidence is that we expect children to learn these different words in slightly different contexts or routines of activity and that one may be more helpful in directing their attention in the right way. With the complement "na vro," kitazo is about the act of looking or gazing; it refers to someone in the process of looking and is used in such contexts. It may make the false-belief task easier because it directs 3-year-olds to the looking behavior of the protagonist. Young children may understand it in the sense of the process of looking or searching for the object and thus as referring to the first place looked, which would result in them passing the test. In the same context, the word psahno, on the other hand, puts pressure on the child to locate the object, and thus might be understood in the sense of where will the chocolate be found. If children understand it in this way they may tend to say where the chocolate actually is and thus fail the test. If these words do have these different senses then young children might be directed to different aspects of what will happen when Maxi wants his chocolate, that is, what he will do first versus where he will eventually find it. That is, children learn such words in particular situations, and thus they differ in facilitating the child's understanding of the false-belief question. Evidence like this suggests that children do not simply develop theories or rules that apply to beliefs in general. Rather, children come to understand words about the psychological world (i.e., referring to people's actions, knowledge, intentions, etc.) within particular situations.

Conclusion

We now sum up our argument and relate it to the theme of the book, exploring the links between executive functions and social understanding, and the ways in which development in both areas may be based on social interaction. We have suggested that claims about how executive functions and social understanding are related rest on a prior assumption that these are two separate, coherent domains and children have stable, measurable abilities in these areas. Examining relevant research indicates variability in a number of ways. At the level of the analysis of particular tasks and what is required to solve them, the examples of the DCCS and the Windows Task revealed that executive functions are not easily defined and measured. Children's performance on many of these tasks varies across the series of trials presented to children, and their performance is influenced by slight changes in task procedures, and also by the nature of their social interaction with the adult experimenters. This suggests that rather than being stable, fixed abilities, executive functions appear to emerge in the flow of children's interaction with the physical and social world. It may be more productive to study executive function and social understanding as processes rather than treating them as easily defined and uniform constructs captured in single tasks. We have referred to the fluid nature of young children's emerging knowledge within their interaction with the physical and social world as "epistemic flow."

This view of the nature of executive functions and social understanding has implications for our understanding of development in these areas. The extensive links between social interaction and social cognitive development are now well known. Although there is less research on the influence of social interaction on the development of executive functions, evidence is now accumulating (Landry & Smith, this volume) and the research we have reviewed on cross-cultural differences suggests that children's history of social experience does play a role in the development of executive functions. According to our alternative approach to social cognitive development, social understanding develops within social interaction as children learn to talk about situations of shared understanding. We suggest that executive function and social understanding may be interdependent and emerge through the same processes within social interaction.

NOTE

1. We are currently working on two approaches to this problem. In the first (CL, Peter Diggle, Andrea Towse & Ivonne Solis-Trapala) we modifying statistical procedures used in other areas of the biomedical and social sciences for exploring even finer shifts in functioning—the transitions between binary trials across long sequences. In the second we are using microgenetic approaches to explore the dynamics of task performance (Cheshire et al., 2007). Our work on goal neglect serves to suggest why a dynamic approach is needed.

REFERENCES

Apperly, I. A., & Carroll, D. (in press). How do symbols affect 3- to 4-year-olds' executive function? Evidence from a reverse-contingency task. *Psychological Science*. University of Birmingham.

Appleton M., & Reddy, V. (1996). Teaching three-year-olds to pass false belief tests: A conversational approach. *Social Development, 5*, 275–291.

Ardila, A., Roselli, M., Matute, E., & Guajardo, S. (2005). The influence of parents' educational level on the development of executive functions. *Developmental Neuropsychology, 28*, 539–560.

Astington, J. W., & Baird, J. A. (Eds.). (2005). Why language matters for theory of mind. New York: Oxford University Press.

Baldwin, D. A. (1993). Early referential understanding: Infants' ability to recognize referential acts for what they are. *Developmental Psychology, 29*, 832–843.

Bartsch, K., & Estes, D. (2004). Articulating the role of experience in mental state understanding: A challenge for theory-theory and other theories. *Behavioral and Brain Sciences, 27*, 99–100.

Bjorklund, D. F., Cormier, C. A., & Rosenberg, J. S. (2005). The evolution of theory of mind: Big brains, social complexity, and inhibition. In W. Schneider, R. Schulmann-Hengsteler, & B. Sodian (Eds.), *Young children's cognitive development*. Mahwah, NJ: Lawrence Erlbaum Associates.

Bloom, P. (2000). *How children learn the meanings of words*. Cambridge MA: MIT Press.

Brace, J. J., Morton, J. B., & Munakata, Y. (2006). When actions speak louder than words: Improving children's flexibility in a card-sorting task. *Psychological Science, 17*, 665–669.

Call, J., & Tomasello, M. (1999). A nonverbal theory of mind test: The performance of children and apes. *Child Development, 70*, 381–395.

Carlson, S. M., Davis, A. C., & Leach, J. G. (2005). Less is more: Executive function and symbolic representation in preschool children. *Psychological Science, 16*, 609–616.

Carlson, S. M., Mandell, D. J., & Williams, L. (2004). Executive function and theory of mind: Stability and prediction from ages 2 to 3. *Developmental Psychology, 40*, 1105–1122.

Carlson, S. M., & Moses, L. J. (2001). Individual differences in inhibitory control and children's theory of mind. *Child Development, 72*, 1032–1053.

Carlson, S. M., Moses, L. J., & Breton, C. (2002). How specific is the relation between executive function and theory of mind? Contribution of inhibitory control and working memory. *Infant and Child Development, 11*, 73–92.

Carpendale, J. I. M., & Lewis, C. (2004). Constructing an understanding of mind: The development of children's social understanding within social interaction. *Behavioral and Brain Sciences, 27*, 79–96.

Carpendale, J. I. M., & Lewis, C. (2006). *How children develop social understanding*. Oxford, UK: Blackwell Publishing.

Carpendale, J. I. M., Lewis, C., Müller, U., & Racine, T. P. (2005). Constructing perspectives in the social making of minds. *Interaction Studies, 6*, 341–358.

Chapman, M. (1991). The epistemic triangle: Operative and communicative components of cognitive development. In M. Chandler & M. Chapman (Eds.), *Criteria for competence: Controversies in the conceptualization and assessment of children's abilities* (pp. 209–228). Hillsdale, NJ: Lawrence Erlbaum Associates.

Chasiotis, A., Kiessling, F., Winter, V., & Hofer, J. (2006). Sensory motor inhibition as a prerequisite for theory of mind: A comparison of clinical and normal preschoolers differing in sensory motor abilities. *International Journal of Behavioral Development, 30*, 178–190.

Cheshire, A., Muldoon K. P., Francis, B., Lewis, C., & Ball, L. (2007). Can we take microgenetic data seriously without modelling change? *Infant and Child Development, 16*, 119–134.

Davis, H. L., & Pratt, C. (1995). The development of theory of mind: The working memory explanation. *Australian Journal of Psychology, 47*, 25–31.

de Villiers, J. G. (2005). Can language acquisition give children a point of view? In J. W. Astington & J. A. Baird (Eds.), *Why language matters for theory of mind* (pp. 186–219). New York: Oxford University Press.

Diamond, A. (1990). The development and neural bases of memory functions as indexed by the AB and delayed response tasks in human infants and infant monkeys. *Annals of the New York Academy of Sciences, 608*, 267–317.

Duncan, J., Emslie, H., Williams, P., Johnson, R., & Freer, C. (1996). Intelligence and the frontal lobe: The organisation of goal directed behavior. *Cognitive Psychology, 30*, 257–303.

Ferrari, M. (2007). Examining triangle metaphors: Utility in developmental theory and scientific application. *Human Development, 50*, 234–240.

Flynn, E., O'Malley, C., & Wood, D. (2004). A longitudinal, microgenetic study of the emergence of false belief understanding and inhibition skills. *Developmental Science, 7*, 103–115.

Frawley, W. (1997). *Vygotsky and cognitive science: Language and the unification of the social and computational mind.* Cambridge, MA: Harvard University Press.

French, L., & Song, M. (1998). Developmentally appropriate teacher-directed approaches: Images from Korean kindergartens. *Journal of Curriculum Studies, 30*, 409–430.

Frye, D., Zelazo, P. D., & Palfai, T. (1995). Inference and action in early causal reasoning. *Cognitive Development, 10*, 120–131.

Gerstadt, C. L., Hong, Y. J., & Diamond, A. (1994). The relationship between cognition and action—performance of children 3 1/2–7 years old on a stroop-like day-night test. *Cognition, 53*, 129–153.

Grolnick, W. S., & Farkas, M. (2002). Parenting and the development of children's self-regulation. In M. H. Bornstein (Ed.), *Handbook of parenting* (Vol. 5: Practical issues in parenting) (pp. 89–110). Mahwah, NJ: Lawrence Erlbaum Associates.

Hala, S., Hug, S., & Henderson, A. (2003). Executive function and false belief understanding in preschool children: Two tasks are harder than one. *Journal of Cognition and Development, 4*, 275–298.

Hala, S., & Russell, J. (2001). Executive control within strategic deception: A window on early cognitive development? *Journal of Experimental Child Psychology, 80*, 112–141.

Hale, C. M., & Tager-Flusberg, H. (2003). The influence of language on theory of mind: A training study. *Developmental Science, 6*, 346–359.

Happaney, K., & Zelazo, P. D. (2003). Inhibition as a problem in the psychology of behavior. *Developmental Science, 6*, 468–470.

Harris, P. L. (1996). Desires, beliefs, and language. In P. Carruthers & P. K. Smith (Eds.), *Theories of theories of mind* (pp. 200–220). Cambridge: Cambridge University Press.

Hughes, C. (1998). Executive function in preschoolers: Links with theory of mind and verbal ability. *British Journal of Developmental Psychology, 16*, 233–253.

Karreman, A., van Tuijl, C., van Aken, M. A. G., & Dekovi, M. (2006). Parenting and self regulation: A meta-analysis. *Infant and Child Development, 15*, 561–579.

Keenan, T. (1999). Working memory, "holding in mind," and the child's acquisition of a theory of mind. In J. W. Astington (Ed.), *Minds in the making: Essays in honor of David R. Olson*. Oxford, UK: Blackwell Publishing.

Kirkham, N. Z., Cruess, L., & Diamond, A. (2003). Helping children apply their knowledge to their behavior on a dimension-switching task. *Developmental Science, 6*, 449–467.

Kloo, D., & Perner, J. (2003). Training transfer between card sorting and false belief understanding: Helping children apply conflicting descriptions. *Child Development, 74*, 1823–1839.

Kopp, C. (1982). Antecedents of self-regulation: A developmental perspective. *Developmental Psychology, 18*, 199–214.

Landry, S. H., Miller-Loncar, C. L., Smith, K. E., & Swank, P. R. (2002). The role of early parenting in children's development of executive processes. *Developmental Neuropsychology, 21*, 15–41.

Lang, B., & Perner, J. (2002). Understanding intention and false belief and the development of self control. *British Journal of Developmental Psychology, 20*, 67–76.

Lewis, C., Huang, Z., & Rooksby, M. (2006). Chinese preschoolers' false belief understanding: Is social knowledge underpinned by parental styles, social interactions or executive functions? *Psychologia, 49*, 252–266.

Liszkowski, U., Carpenter, M., Striano, T., & Tomasello, M. (2006). Twelve- and 18-month-olds point to provide information for others. *Journal of Cognition and Development, 7*, 173–187.

Lohmann, H., & Tomasello, M. (2003). The role of language in the development of false belief understanding: A training study. *Child Development, 74*, 1130–1144.

Luria, A. R. (1961). *The role of speech in the regulation of normal and abnormal behavior*. New York: Pergamon.

Luria, A. R. (1981). *Language and cognition*. Chichester: Wiley.

Maridaki-Kassotaki, K., Lewis, C., & Freeman, N. H. (2003). Lexical choice can lead to problems: What false-belief tests tell us about Greek alternative verbs of agency. *Journal of Child Language, 29*, 145–164.

Mead, G. H. (1934). *Mind, self, and society.* Chicago: University of Chicago Press.

Miller, S. A., Shelton, J., & Flavell, J. H. (1970). A test of Luria's hypotheses concerning the development of self-regulation. *Child Development, 41*, 651–665.

Moore, C., Barresi, J., & Thompson, C. (1998). The cognitive basis of future-oriented prosocial behavior. *Social Development, 7*, 198–218.

Moses, L. J., & Carlson, S. M. (2004). Self-regulation and children's theories of mind. In C. Lightfoot, C. Lalonde, & M. Chandler (Eds.), *Changing conceptions of psychological life* (pp. 127–146). Mahwah, NJ: Lawrence Erlbaum Associates.

Moses, L., Carlson, S., & Sabbagh, M. (2005). On the specificity of the relation between executive function and theories of mind. In W. Schneider, R. Schulmann-Hengsteler, & R. Sodian (Eds.), *Young children's cognitive development* (pp. 131–145). Mahwah, NJ: Lawrence Erlbaum Associates.

Moses, L. J., & Sabbagh, M. A. (2007). Interactions between domain general and domain specific processes in the development of children's theories of mind. In M. J. Roberts (Ed.), *Integrating the mind: Domain general versus domain specific processes in higher cognition* (pp. 375–391). Hove, East Sussex, UK: Psychology Press.

Müller, U., Liebermann, D., Frye, D., & Zelazo, P. D. (2008). Executive function, school readiness, and school achievement. In S. K. Thurman & K. A. Fiorello (Eds.), *Applied Cognitive Research in K-3 Classrooms.* London: Routledge.

Munakata, Y., & Yerys, B. E. (2001). All together now: When dissociations between knowledge and action disappear. *Psychological Science, 12*, 335–337.

Noble, K. G., McCandliss, B. D., & Farah, M. J. (2007). Socioeconomic gradients predict individual differences in neurocognitive abilities. *Developmental Science, 10*, 464–480.

Oh, S., & Lewis, C. (2008). Korean preschoolers' advanced inhibitory control and its relation to other executive skills and mental state understanding. *Child Development, 70*, 80–99.

Perner, J. (2000). About+belief+counterfactual. In P. Mitchell & K. Riggs (Eds.), *Children's reasoning and the mind* (pp. 367–401). Hove, East Sussex, UK: Psychology Press.

Perner, J., Kain, W., & Barchfeld, P. (2002). Executive control and higher-order theory of mind in children at risk of ADHD. *Infant and Child Development, 11*, 141–158.

Perner, J., Stummer, S., & Lang, B. (1999). Executive functions and theory of mind: Cognitive complexity or functional dependence? In P. D. Zelazo, J. W. Astington, & D. R. Olson (Eds.), *Developing theories of intention: Social understanding and self-control* (pp. 133–152). Mahwah, NJ: Lawrence Erlbaum Associates.

Peskin, J., & Ardino, V. (2003). Representing the mental world in children's social behavior: Playing hide-and-seek and keeping a secret. *Social Development, 12*, 496–512.

Ritchie, F. K., & Toner, I. J. (1984). Direct labeling, tester expectancy and delay mainte-nance behaviour in Scottish preschool children. *International Journal of Behavioral Development, 7,* 333–341.

Rothbart, M., & Derryberry, D. (1981). Development of individual differences in tem-perament. In M. Lamb & A. Brown (Eds.), *Advances in Developmental Psychology* (Vol. 1, pp. 37–86)). Hillsdale, NJ: Lawrence Erlbaum Associates.

Ruffman, T. (2004). Children's understanding of mind: Constructivist but theory-like. *Behavioral and Brain Sciences, 27,* 120–121.

Russell, J., Mauthner, N., Sharpe, S., & Tidswell, T. (1991). The windows task as a mea-sure of strategic deception in preschoolers and autistic subjects. *British Journal of Developmental Psychology, 9,* 331–349.

Sabbagh, M., Xu, F., Carlson, S. M., Moses, L. J., & Lee, K. (2006). The development of executive functioning and theory of mind: A comparison of Chinese and US preschoolers. *Psychological Science, 17,* 74–81.

Samuels, M. C., Brooks, P. J., & Frye, D. (1996). Strategic game playing through the Windows Task. *British Journal of Developmental Psychology, 14,* 159–172.

Short, B. (2007). The effect of training and the transfer of skills between false belief, card sorting and inhibitory control tasks: Is one method of training superior? Unpublished MSc theses, Department of Psychology, Lancaster University, UK.

Simpson, A., & Riggs, K. J. (2005). Inhibitory and working memory demands of the day-night task in children. *British Journal of Developmental Psychology, 23,* 471–486.

Simpson, A., Riggs, K. J., & Simon, M. (2004). What makes the windows task diffi-cult for young children: Rule inference or rule use? *Journal of Experimental Child Psychology, 87,* 155–170.

Slaughter, V., & Gopnik, A. (1996). Conceptual coherence in the child's theory of mind: Training children to understand belief. *Child Development, 67,* 2967–2988.

Sokol, B. W., & Müller, U. (Eds.). (2007). The development of self-regulation: Toward the integration of cognition and emotion (Special issue). *Cognitive Development, 22,* 401–567.

Tardif, T., So, C. W-C., & Kaciroti, N. (2007). Language and false belief: Evidence for general, not specific effects in Cantonese-speaking preschoolers. *Developmental Psychology, 43,* 318–340.

Tatler, B. W., & Hutton, S. B. (2007). Trial by trial effects in the antisaccade task. *Experimental Brain Research, 179,* 387–396.

Tomasello, M. (2003). *Constructing a language: A usage-based theory of language acquisition.* Cambridge, MA: Harvard University Press.

Tomasello, M., Carpenter, M., & Liszkowski, U. (2007). A new look at infant pointing. *Child Development, 78,* 705–722.

Toner, I. J., Moore, L. P., & Emmons, B. A. (1980). Effect of being labelled on subsequent self-control in children. *Child Development, 51,* 618–621.

Toner, I. J., & Smith, R. A. (1977). Age and overt verbalisation in delay-maintenance behavior in children. *Journal of Experimental Child Psychology, 24,* 123–128.

Towse, J., Lewis, C., & Knowles, M. (2007). When knowledge is not enough; the phenomenon of goal neglect in preschool children. *Journal of Experimental Child Psychology, 96*, 320–332.

Towse, J. N., Redbond, J., Houston-Price, C. M. T., & Cook, S. (2000). Understanding the dimensional change card sort Perspectives from task success and failure. *Cognitive Development, 15*, 347–365.

Vinden, P. G. (1996). Junin Quechua children's understanding of mind. *Child Development, 67*, 1701–1716.

Vinden, P. G. (1999). Children's understanding of mind and emotion: A multi-cultural comparison. *Cognition and Emotion, 13*, 19–48.

Vygotsky, L. S. (1978). *Mind in society: The development of higher psychological processes.* Cambridge, MA: Harvard University Press.

Ward, G., & Allport, A. (1997). Planning and problem-solving using the 5-disc Tower of London task. *Quarterly Journal of Experimental Psychology, 50*, 49–70.

Wellman, H. M., & Liu, D. (2004). Scaling of theory of mind tasks. *Child Development, 75*, 523–541.

Zelazo, P. D., Frye, D., & Rapus, T. (1996). An age-related dissociation between knowing rules and using them. *Cognitive Development, 11*, 37–63.

Zelazo, P. D., & Jacques, S. (1997). Children's rule use: Representation, reflection and cognitive control. *Annals of Child Development, 12*, 119–176.

Zelazo, P. D., Müller, U., Frye, D., & Marcovitch, S. (2003). The development of executive function in early childhood. *Monographs of the Society for Research in Child Development, 68*, Serial No. 274.

5

Developments and Regressions in Rule Use: The Case of Zinedine Zidane

JACOB A. BURACK, NATALIE RUSSO, TAMMY DAWKINS,
AND MARIËTTE HUIZINGA

In the closely contested championship match of the 2006 World Cup of football (soccer to North Americans), Zinedine Zidane head-butted the Italian defender Marco Matarazzi in the chest and was ejected from the playing field. Although the head butt did not directly decide the outcome of the match, the most watched sports event in history, experts and fans alike generally consider it to be the seminal moment. A recurrent refrain across the postmatch analyses was that Zidane's action was particularly shocking and unexpected because he was an experienced player who had often thrived on such an international stage and seemed to perform his best when the pressure to succeed was the greatest. Virtually every fan of the sport anticipated that Zidane would be the player whose decisions would most optimize his team's chances of victory. Yet in a matter of seconds, he planned and carried out a relatively violent and self-defeating act. Why? Even if as Matarazzi later reported, he had uttered something particularly uncomplimentary about Zidane's sister, the parameters or rules of the situation in which Zidane found himself, and that had provided him the context for so many conquests over his distinguished career, would supersede his momentary anger. Surely, this was not the first instance in his career in which unpleasantries were directed his way during a match. So why did, or how could, Zidane violate a rule that was so ingrained?

This question serves as a beginning point for this chapter in which we provide a developmental framework for understanding rules, their uses, and their roles in different contexts. We especially consider the circumstances under which rules are violated, even when, as in the case with Zidane and soccer, the rules are fully understood and well-learned through practice. These ideas are addressed in the context of two specific types of rules that are essential to successful performance in sports competitions. One rule is the type that frames the conditions of the contest (i.e., "context-specific rules") as in the case of the rule that Zidane violated. The second rule is the type that is self-imposed in order to optimize performance (i.e., "guideline-for-success rules"), as in the case of a team's adoption of a specific strategic style of play designed for a given opponent. Even the most elite competitions involving world-class athletes include frequent instances when both the expert and casual viewers criticize players' actions in specific situations. Often, the questionable action or decision is so apparent to any knowledgeable spectator, that the prevailing thought is why and how a world-class competitor could make such an obvious blunder in a situation when better alternatives are evident to virtually everyone else, including those who are far less expert in the sport.

Relevant theories of cognitive control and complexity (e.g., Frye, Zelazo, & Burack, 1999; Zelazo & Muller, 2002a, 2002b; Zelazo, Muller, Frye, & Marcovitch, 2003) are considered against a backdrop of classic developmental principles, including progression from action to thought, from concrete to abstract, from rigid to flexible, and of microgenetic regression to ontogenetically prior states that are invoked in specific situations (Sroufe & Rutter, 1984; Werner, 1957). According to this classic developmental framework, stressful situations can lead to the abandonment of more reflective and optimal strategies and toward a dependence on earlier, and less advantageous, action modes of behavior that are ingrained in the repertoire of functioning (Zigler & Glick, 1986). Consistent with the distinction between decontextualized "cool" executive function and the contextually dependent "hot" EF (Sokol & Muller, 2007; Zelazo & Cunningham, 2007), the emphasis is shifted from the simple attainment of a specific function at a certain age to the ability to implement these functions across a variety of complex and stressful real-life scenarios (Carlson, 2003). The success of the latter task will be considered with regard to issues of development, training, and context. Although the examples will be from the world of sports, the issues are relevant to virtually all everyday pursuits, such as education, work, and parenting, as success in each is largely contingent on the abilities to recall and utilize the most adaptive behavioral rules despite the complexity and demands of the environment that might precipitate less optimal behaviors.

DIFFERENT TYPES OF RULES AND THEIR IMPLICATIONS

Zidane's action would be inappropriate under most circumstances, but it violated one or more specific rules of soccer. "Context-specific" rules provide the regulations and framework for a given situation or competition, that may or may not be relevant in other settings. They might be thought of in terms of the regulations of a game, as they are the cornerstones for fair competition based on a common understanding of the parameters of participation. The other, or second, type of rules can be considered "guidelines for success" as they are imposed in order to optimize performance in a specific situation. They are generally associated with strategies and styles of play that are invoked by an individual or team as essential to performance in the game, match, or event.

Context-Specific Rules

Context-specific rules are highly prescribed and essential guidelines for adaptation in a specific situation, but may be inconsistent and even meaningless with regard to everyday living outside of the specific context. The most obvious case might be the sport of boxing in which the competitors are allowed to punch each other in ways that would be unacceptable and even criminal outside the ring, and yet may be disqualified for excessively holding an opponent in a way that limits the amount of physical damage that can be inflicted. In ice hockey, the extent of a penalty seems to be inversely related to the societal standards for the severity of an action. A player may be penalized for 10 min or even an entire game for uttering disrespectful comment to an opponent or to an official, but only 5 min for engaging in a fist fight, and 2 min for slashing an opponent with a lethal weapon (a stick). Other context-specific rules have little reference to life outside the confines of the particular setting. For example, offside is a penalty that is recognized across a variety of sports such as soccer, American football, and ice hockey. These violations are enforced with the intention of limiting positional advantage of one team over another, but are meaningless without the specific framework of the sport.

Although the rules of each sport are generally well delineated, the athletes' relations to them are more complex. The "black and white" descriptions in the rule book are treated as "gray areas" in real-life competition and the officials' interpretation and implementation of the rules generally determine the extent to which they are observed. This type of ambiguity is evident in the context of rules found across various team sports that prescribe the extent to which the defending team can impede the progress of the team that is attempting to score and the penalties that are imposed for the cases when these rules are violated. The implicit understanding is that the competitors will generally "push the limits" of the rules to the extent that will be allowed by the officials whose discretion will determine whether and when a competitor should be penalized. In this scenario, the players' actions in relation to respecting the rule are guided by various factors including the specific situation, the team's overarching strategy, the difficulty of their task, their need or willingness to push the limit of the rule, their understanding of the officials' interpretation of the rule and anticipated level of tolerance when the rule is impinged. Thus, the competitors' relationship with the rules and the violation of them in a specific moment in time entails a complex decision-making processing with implicit higher-order processing such as the evaluation of the circumstances in the match or game, an assessment of others' interpretations, and the cost-benefit analysis of various actions.

The difficulty in making these choices in the context of a competition is generally exacerbated by the minimal timeframe and the complex and stressful environments in which they must be made. Teams will often employ an overarching defensive strategy that will include some plan about the extent to which they are willing to be penalized in order to thwart the offensive efforts of the opposition in general. Although this may provide guidelines for the players' actions in relation to the rules, within the context of the competition, each participant ultimately needs to make individual moment-to-moment decisions in constantly changing, novel situations. These decisions pertain both to specific actions that might or might not be penalized, but also for the actions that lead to the likelihood of being in a situation in which a rule might need to be violated. We suggest that the notion that individuals with more practice and experience should be more likely to make decisions that are both consistent with team strategy and advantageous for the team is consistent with developmental theory. These benefits can be seen as resulting from a greater opportunity for the individual to act on, assimilate, and accommodate the rules that represent the most adaptive response to a situation.

Guideline for Success Rules

Some "guideline for success" rules are universally taught to enhance skill level at every stage of competition for a specific sport or sometimes even across sports. For example, in sports in which forward progress is made by controlling a puck with a stick as in field or ice hockey, by dribbling a ball with one's feet as in soccer, or by dribbling a ball by bouncing it as in basketball or team handball, athletes are taught to keep their head up in order to avoid attempts at impedance by opposing players and to enhance the opportunities to pass the ball or puck to teammates. Although this type of individual guideline is not sufficient to ensure success, it is commonly accepted as necessary for optimal performance. Thus, it is emphasized by coaches and commonly practiced by competitive athletes.

Other "guideline for success" rules are team-oriented and strategic. One common example across many team sports is that athletes are taught to make short passes and to avoid throwing (basketball, American football), kicking (soccer), or shooting (ice hockey) a cross-field, cross-court, or cross-ice pass within the defensive zone when being pressured by the other team, as the pass might easily be intercepted and provide an easy scoring opportunity for the opposing team. Of course, adherence to the rule is not simple as the defending team might try to force that type of pass by eliminating the opposing team's other options. Other strategic rules are unique to a specific competitor or team as the choice of styles and strategies vary across coaching philosophies and in relation to the athletes' abilities. For example, in the movie "Hoosiers" about a high school boys' basketball team that won the Indiana state championship in the 1950s, the coach (played by Gene Hackman) institutes a rule that the players are only allowed to attempt a shot at the basket after a certain number of passes had been completed. As in the case of the more individual-relevant guidelines for success, both universal and team specific team-oriented strategies are discussed and practiced. Ideally, in the context of team sports, the practice sessions are intended to ensure that all the members of a team will collaborate to implement the strategic plan in a cohesive way and that, regardless of the situation, will allow the individuals and the team as a whole to adhere to the plan of action.

The implication of the guidelines for success is that adherence to these specified rules will lead to victory. Inherently, the primary impediment to achieving this positive outcome is that competition entails one or more opponents, and each individual competitor or team is intent on implementing their own strategy or game plan while impeding that of the other. Thus, the strategy, which inevitably works in the abstract without a hitch, must be modified, often considerably, within the context of the competition. One outcome of this type of competitive scenario is that the parameters of rules or guidelines can change during a match or game. Thus, in one example, a team with more talented offensive players might try to capitalize on its superior skill level by trying to maximize scoring opportunities even if it also allows the opponents more offensive opportunities at the outset of the competition. Conversely, a less talented offensive team might attempt to implement a more cautious plan in which the opponent's talent advantage is mitigated. However, if the more talented team is winning near the end of the game or match then their initial strategy of aggressively offensive play might be changed to a more conservative one in an attempt to preserve their lead by minimizing the opponents' opportunities to score. Conversely, if the team that initially utilized a more cautious strategy is losing near the end of the competition, they might adopt a more adventurous strategy in order to create more scoring opportunities for themselves. And, yet even in these cases, the commitment to one approach or another must often be modulated in light of the context and situation. In the midst of a comeback attempt, excessive aggressiveness or lack of caution may lead to costly mistakes that end any hope of success, while extreme caution while leading a game may lead to tentative play that allows the opponents an opportunity to take control of the game.

Within the context of a sporting event then, the need to decide on an action is mitigated by prelearned rules that are based in strategy, but that may be constantly modified in relation to a specific context and that may be in conflict with one or more other rules. The difficulty in choosing the optimal tactic in a sports situation, or other domains of life, is that the decision entails several options that may be incompatible with each other, and must often be made under duress, often with little time for conscious processing. Although every competition involves decisions with regard to strategy and action both during a competition and in the preparation for it, the nature of these decisions can vary considerably. For example, prior to and during a competition, macro-decisions are made about tactics and strategies, whereas during the competition, micro-decisions are often necessary and the ability to consistently make the best decisions is often central to success. In virtually all competitions, the participants must continually make decisions in rapid succession. In some cases, these decisions can be made simply and in strict adherence to the prepared and practiced guidelines, but in others, the nature of the competition and efforts of the opponent necessitate some improvisation.

As with the case of the context-specific rules, decisions regarding strategies need to be made in fractions of a second from among the numerous options. The player must consider various factors, including the positioning and movements of both teammates and the opposition, the anticipation of subsequent movements and positioning, the team strategies, the score, the time remaining in the match, the confidence in his or her own ability to carry out any or all of the options, the confidence in his or her teammates, the degree of concern about the abilities of the opponents, and the condition of the surface and surroundings. And every move or decision by the player affects those of the others in this ongoing transactional context. Thus, success in the situation is dependent on the ability to access and to implement the prescribed guidelines rapidly in a changing, complex, and even stressful environment. This entails access to appropriate rules that need to be well learned and ingrained, and yet are flexible enough to be adapted optimally to different environments and situations.

DEVELOPMENTAL CONSIDERATIONS IN UNDERSTANDING RULE USE

To understand the link between experience and success, we suggest a developmental framework in which behavior, and specifically, the use of rules, becomes increasingly more efficient and adaptable with development. Our notion of optimal rule use as highly ingrained and flexible is based on the premise of general constructivist notions of development that the behavioral, the social, the emotional, and the cognitive repertoire becomes both increasingly fine-tuned and more flexible with time. According to Werner (1957), this occurs within the context of an orthogenetic principle in which development proceeds from states of relative globality to increasing differentiation and integration, and in which perception proceeds from a focus on a whole to an analytic focus on parts, and eventually to a synthesis. However, these types of developmental progressions cannot be seen as part of an absolutely stable system, in which some "predestined" highest level of functioning is attained and development then stagnates.

Even performance that is perfect with regard to the choice of the correct, or most adaptive, responses does not mean that the task is mastered (Diamond & Kirkham, 2005). The more salient issue then becomes the increased efficiency and accessibility of the optimal behaviors across situations. These higher level forms of mastery can be attained with practice that is not just learning of one or more behaviors, but that allows for the increased flexibility to maintain and adapt optimal behaviors, regardless of the demands of the context. However, as Werner notes, development is not relentlessly progressive, and often entails some regression. In some cases, the regression is intrinsic to later development. In other cases, it reflects a retreat from a skill that is already developed, although possibly not entirely entrenched in the individual's repertoire, to a lower developmental, and likely less adaptive, response that is called upon in a very specific situation.

DEVELOPMENTAL SYNTHESIS

The advantage of developmental integration or synthesis for rule use was highlighted by Huizinga and van der Molen (2007) who identified different developmental trajectories for set-switching and set-maintenance processes on the Wisconsin Card Sorting Task (WCST) among 7, 11, 15, and 21-year-olds. Set-switching abilities are associated with efficiently switching to the new sorting rule on the basis of feedback, and are indexed inversely to perseverative errors that represent the failure to switch to another sorting rule after receiving negative feedback on the previous trial (see also Heaton, Chelune, Talley, Kay, & Curtis, 1993) and efficient errors that reflect switches to the wrong sorting rule in the second trial of an otherwise clear series requiring a new sorting rule. Set-maintenance processes require the preservation of the current sorting rule despite the presence of potentially distracting irrelevant aspects of the stimuli, and are indexed inversely to distraction errors as when the sorting rule is missed continuously, or when a single isolated error occurs in an otherwise series of correct rule use. The set-switching abilities reached young-adult levels by 11 years, whereas set-maintenance abilities continued to develop until adolescence.

Consistent with the orthogenetic principle, development across the two abilities seemed to be more integrated later in childhood and early adulthood. A principle components analysis revealed that set-switching and set-maintenance abilities loaded on two factors for the 7-year-olds but not for the older children and adults. Thus, the abilities to flexibly switch to a new sorting principle and to maintain set appear to influence performance independently in 7-year-olds, but appear to be more integrally related in the older groups. This is consistent with developmental evidence that the ability to maintain set is associated with an increased ability to keep information on-line in working memory (Barceló & Knight, 2002; Case, 1992; Crone, Ridderinkhof, Worm, Somsen, & Van der Molen, 2004), and with the notion of an enhanced efficiency of executive function, that might reflect increasingly less diffuse and more focal prefrontal cortex activation (e.g., Amso & Casey, 2006; Casey, Tottenham, Liston, & Durston, 2005).

DEVELOPMENT AS AN ONGOING PROCESS: PERFECTION DOES NOT IMPLY MASTERY

Zelazo and colleagues (for a summary, see Zelazo et al., 2003) demonstrated a developmental trajectory in planning abilities in which children can initially learn rules, but are only later able to switch between conflicting rules. In the Dimension Change Card Sort (DCCS) task that entails sorting test cards that match target cards on two incompatible dimensions, such as color and shape, children as young as 3 years of age are able to use a given rule to sort test cards (e.g., color or shape), but are unable to switch and sort cards by the second dimension (e.g., shape or color) after a few trials with the first rule. Even when the children are told the rules and can verbalize it, they are unable to apply them to the task at hand. By the age of 5, however, children are consistently able to apply multiple rule sets and switch flexibly between them.

In the case of the DCCS task or any relevant task, switching between rules in accordance with the demands of the task is generally considered as evidence that this ability has been mastered. Yet, perfectly accurate performance might not signify that the highest developmental level has been attained. Diamond and Kirkham (2005) highlighted this point with a timed version of the DCCS task when they showed that 18–22 year olds who were perfectly capable of sorting by two incompatible rules took longer to sort by a second rule dimension than by the first rule dimension. This exemplifies the notion of a developmental trajectory that traverses, but also distinguishes among the acquisition of knowledge of rules, the ability to implement them, the ability to flexibly switch among them to access the most adaptive ones.

These distinctions are also evident in other timed or untimed experimental contexts in which level of performance continues to improve even in situations in which the use of rules appears to be perfect on a standard procedure. These situations might involve stimuli that are increasingly degraded or complex so that relevant decisions about them are ambiguous, or environments that are dynamic in that sense that decisions occur within the context of competing tasks. The amorphous parameters of optimal performance suggest that the notion of a "mastery" of the use of one or more rules is illusory within the contexts of changing and more challenging situations or expectations. Yet, continued improvement in performance can be expected. Within a Wernerian perspective, this improvement can be associated with ontogenetic development that involves general development as exposure to situations in which the rule can be used and adapted.

THE DEVELOPMENTAL ROLE OF EXPERIENCE IN RULE USE

In sports, the notion of ontogenetic developmental progression entails experience with the sport in general as well as with both the context-specific and guidelines-for-success type of rules. Experience in sports can be attained in different ways. It is often most simply considered with regard to the number of seasons or years of involvement in the sport, but experience can also be construed with regard to the amount of time at a specific level of competition or exposure to certain situations. For example, Zidane was considered an experienced player both because of the longevity of his career and because he played at the highest levels of competition. He played at a professional level for well more than a decade, often participated in the highest level of competition with his club team in European team championship tournaments and as a member of the French national team in European and World Cup tournaments, and was a member of several championship teams. Experience can also be gained over a shorter period of time by repeated exposure to both the rules that need to be applied and to the contexts in which they are applied. This type of experience is typically referred to as practice, although the implications of this term are different for a developmental framework than for the behaviorist ones that are traditionally associated with it. In this context, practice is effective because it provides a process for the rules to become more ingrained within the athlete's general cognitive schemas, thereby allowing its use to be more flexibly applied and preventing against regressions to earlier, and less adaptive, strategies.

These roles of sporting experience and practice come equipped with their own clichéd mantras and accepted wisdoms. Mistakes made by younger, or less experienced, participants are inevitably attributed to youth or inexperience—the "rookie mistake." In contrast, experience is generally considered an essential safeguard against committing mistakes that could prove costly, and cases of success by younger, less experienced participants are generally attributed to an overwhelming talent level or energy that could not be overcome by the benefits of prior experience. Thus, coaches' and managers' choices of the members of elite sports squads are often determined by some consideration of the tradeoff between level of talent regardless of the age of the player and the reliability and leadership that are considered more characteristic of veteran players. Similarly, prior exposure to so-called pressure situations such as the defining moments near the culmination of some game, match, or event that are directly associated with victory or loss, and previous appearances in meaningful events, matches, and tournaments are both considered to be positive predictors of success. Extensive and repeated practice is considered one way to enhance abilities to perform but, more important, to instill a higher and more optimal level of decision-making.

Experience as a Marker of Development

The notion of experience as a predictor of the more optimal utilization of rules and of success is commensurate both with theories associated with the traditional developmental theories of Jean Piaget (1970) and Heinz Werner (1948) and with findings based on empirical studies of the development of executive function (Diamond, 2006; Huizenga, Smeding, Grasman, & Schmand, 2007) and rule use (Zelazo et al., 2003). Across traditional developmental theories, development is viewed as an active process of continuous but meaningful change that usually involves some complex relation among an individual, his or her cognition, and the environment.

According to Piaget (1970), cognitive development in children is virtually entirely dependent on the children's actions on the environment—increasingly higher levels of understanding emerge as the children need to assimilate and accommodate evidence from the outside world that they uncover during their explorations. As this process only occurs with concepts that are meaningful to the individual's current understanding in situations in which the current level of understanding is challenged, the transitions from lower to higher developmental stages of cognition occur as a result of the ongoing experiential relation between the active, the seeking, and the exploring child and the relevant aspects of the environment that they continuously evaluate and act upon. Werner's (1957) model of development also involves ongoing and complex interactions between the individual and the environment. He contends that the level of cognitive and perceptual functioning and performance on related tasks is dependent on a combination of internal factors, such as developmental level and experience, external factors, such as the complexity of the stimuli, and the relation among them. The role of developmental level can be viewed within the context of the orthogenetic principle in which development occurs from a state of relative diffuse globality to increasing differentiation and hierarchic integration.

The developmental progression depicted in the orthogenetic principle is useful both as a broad framework for understanding developmental progression in general and for conceptualizing the emergence of concurrently developing systems within the complex entity of the evolving organism. The universality of this framework is highlighted by the similarity across ontogenetic and microgenetic processes of development, both of which fit with the orthogenetic principle. For example, Werner (1957) compared patterns of developmental progression responses to Rorschach cards for microgenetic changes in differences in time of exposure to the stimuli and ontogenetic exchanges as indicated by developmental level of the participants. Although the microgenetic changes were associated with external manipulation of the presentation of the stimuli and ontogenesis with the differences in internal representations, the developmental changes reflect a similar course of responses from globally diffuse to more defined and integrated. According to Werner, "the activity patterns, percepts, thoughts are not merely products but processes that, whether, they take seconds, or hours, or days, unfold in terms of a developmental sequence" (pp. 141–143). This framework can be used to understand similarly enhancing effects on performance of both experience and practice.

The theoretical link between experience and success is consistent with the notion of the increasing efficiency and adaptability to use rules, as exposure and practice in using a rule (e.g., rule A) that leads to a generalized improvement in the ability to use different rules (e.g., rules B or C). In one example, Dowsett and Livesey (2000) found that 3-year-old children were unable to withhold responding to a target in a go/no-go task, despite being able to verbally state the rules for action and no-action. Subsequently, half of the children were assigned to a "practice" task condition that was similar in terms of rule structure and cognitive requirements to the go/no-go task, whereas the other half received no practice. Upon retest, the children in the practice session were able to perform the task, while the group of children in the no-practice group did not improve.

In this context, the notion of level, or the process, of development can be seen in relation to an individual's increasing level of understanding and experience with their environment, their ability to generalize from one situation to another, reflect on potential alternative responses, and then implement the action that is most appropriate to the situation at hand. For example, the rookie or newcomer to a team who initially only knows a few of the team's strategic choices and must resort to them, eventually learns other choices and is increasingly able to implement them successfully even when the context is not the same as the one in which the rule was originally taught. In this scenario, the knowledge of any rule becomes more precise and accessible through experience, while becoming increasingly integrated within complex repertoires of functioning that are hierarchically organized to allow for increased flexibility and adaptive utility within specific situations.

THE DEVELOPMENTAL IMPLICATIONS OF REGRESSION

Conceptual frameworks and scientific evidence that support a direct link between experience and optimal rule use also need to be informative about cases, such as Zidane's head butt, in which this pattern is not evident. As Zidane's action highlights that even an experienced athlete may violate a well-learned rule in a situation with little subtlety, the likelihood of examples of less-than-optimal decision-making would be expected to be seen among athletes at different levels across situations with varying levels of complexity and nuance. However, the Zidane incident led to the initial question about why or how a well-learned rule would be violated in a situation in which the violation is associated with some meaningfully deleterious outcome. What leads to discrepancies between the understanding of a rule and the rules implementation across situations? Within a developmental framework (see Werner, 1957; Zigler & Glick, 1986), this rule violation can be seen as a regression in which behavior, or performance, is elicited at a level lower than that of the developmental level attained by the individual. The focus then is on the consistency of the deployment of cognitive thought in relation to the individual's developmental level and the situations in which regressions occur.

Developmental regression does not need to be seen as a step backward in development, but rather is better conceptualized within the context of the flexibility of functioning, that entails the ability to adjust a response to a particular situation. In this framework, regression is viewed as an integral aspect of developmental progression. In relation to rule violations, in times of stress, early modes of functioning may become manifest because a more recently acquired behavioral repertoire should be more susceptible to disruption and give way to earlier, more ingrained forms of responding. In this scenario, the violation of a rule may indicate a disconnection between understanding the rule and the ability to follow it because some aspect of the environment led to a dissociation between what one knows and how one behaves. The basic concept is that earlier structures or modes of operation are not gone but rather become restructured, incorporated within, and ultimately subordinate to new, higher structures. Accordingly, a variety of developmental levels of functioning are available for every individual, with greater flexibility and more choices later in development.

Werner's Views on Regression

The notion that developmental regression does not mean a permanent loss of current skill level parallels Werner's orthogenetic principle and his idea of regression. Werner focused on an individuals' adaptability in terms of their ability to navigate back and forth between developmental structures, depending on the situation. To Werner, more "primitive" developmental states are characterized by relative fusion between an organism and its environment. Ontogenetically, the infant's interactions with the environment rely on sensory systems and processes. This lack of organism–environment differentiation leads to behavioral responses to the environment that are reflexive, immediate, and not modulated by higher perceptual or conceptual processing. Zigler and colleagues (e.g., Zigler & Glick, 1986; Zigler & Phillips, 1962) proposed that behavior responses that include impulsive, aggressive, and action-orientation reflect rather lower developmental levels. Such responses reflect a fusion between the organism and its environment and are therefore regarded as more primitive since they do not require higher cognitive processing. Indeed the very behaviors that characterize such responses belie cognitive reflection and impulse control.

Werner (1957) noted that with development, earlier forms of behavior become hierarchically integrated within more complex forms. Therefore, Werner's presumption that action is developmentally prior to thought gives credence to the possibility that even experts, under periods of extreme stress, may revert back to ingrained action patterns and neglect their ability to think through a decision. This in no way implies that this individual "expert" is now stuck in this developmentally prior state, or suffers from some regression that permanently alters the ways in which they interact with the environment. Rather, due to the extreme circumstances, less mature developmental stages of responding were utilized, but the more adaptive modes of functioning can be returned to in more typical situations. Within this framework, higher developmental levels are always more adaptive as the increased flexibility allows for the implementation of the most adaptive rule.

Werner argues that an individual's overall cognition or level of operation will be dependent on both internal and external factors, such as experience and complexity of the situation. Thus, stress can be thought of as a type of complexity, which renders the person unable to react in a developmentally appropriate manner due to the nature of the situation they are facing. Knowing the rules does not necessarily entail that the individual will use the rule—at least not under all circumstances.

Geisbrecht, Muller, and Miller's (this volume) discussion of psychological distancing provides a useful framework within which Werner's views of regression can be applied. The development of a cognition of self versus action and of self versus the outside world is thought to be a necessary condition for the development of successful emotion regulation. When emotional regulation is effective, the individual prepotent responses can be inhibited during stressful situations, in order that to allow for effective evaluation and optimal responses. However, when it is less effective in highly stressful situations, the relevant executive function, or impulse control, are overridden and less adaptive forms of behavior are elicited.

This Wernererian notion of regression is supported by evidence from development, neurobiology, and neuropsychology. For example, patients with compromised LatPFC function are often described as *overly reliant* on well-learned rules that they have difficulty overriding in favor of weaker, but more contextually appropriate rules, even when they are able to verbalize what the appropriate rule is (see, e.g., Braver & Barch, 2002; Cohen & Servan-Schreiber, 1992; Miller & Cohen, 2001; Shallice & Burgess, 1991). Similarly, the growth of knowledge among children can sometimes develop faster than the ability to control behavior (Zelazo, Frye, & Rapus, 1996), as evidenced by 3-year-old children who are unable to withhold their responding in go-nogo tasks despite being able to verbally state the rules for action and no-action (Dowsett & Livesey, 2000), and who fail card sorting tasks although they indicate accurate knowledge of the rules (Diamond & Kirkham, 2005).

Stress and Developmental Regression

Both the Zidane incident and the common sports folk theory that experience is crucial in the most meaningful contests also highlight that developmental regressions in decision-making may be affected by emotional states, such as those associated with high stress. Whereas vigilant decision-making involves the rational search for alternative choices before a decision is made (Janis, 1982), hypervigilance overwhelms the then system and brings about an incomplete search for alternative choices. In turn, this leads to hasty decision-making and action that may often result in regret. This link between stress and less than adaptive behaviors has been demonstrated with various indices and in different contexts. In an example with biological measures, Blair and Razza (2007) examined the relationship between performance on executive function tasks and levels of cortisol, a corticosteroid hormone produced in response to stressful situations, in a group of children between the ages of 4 and 5 years during performance on peg tapping, a measure of inhibition, and the Flexible Item Selection Task (FIST), a measure of cognitive flexibility. They found elevated levels of cortisol were associated with more impulsivity on the peg tapping task and an impaired ability to shift sets on the FIST task, implying that as stress increased children relied more on action and less on conscious control of cognition.

The deleterious effects of stress on optimal decision-making and performance are not limited to children. Even the performance of experts, or persons trained specifically to handle acute stress can be adversely affected. This was exemplified by Morgan, Doran, Steffian, Hazlett, and Southwick (2006) who tested 200 special operations soldiers on the Rey Ostereith Complex Figure (ROCF) task, that entails the reproduction of a standardized complex figure under immediate copying or recall conditions before, during, or after training at Survival School in which soldiers are taught how to survive imprisonment as a Prisoner of War. The performance of the soldiers in the stress group was significantly worse, and was characterized by a different strategy from those who used by those who did not experience stress whereas those in the pre- and post-stress group began by drawing the global elements of the figure, those in the stress group began by drawing local elements of the picture, a pattern of drawing that is seen in children until about the age of 9 (Waber & Holmes, 1985, 1986).

Conclusion

Zidane's head butt was used here to illustrate the dissociations between knowing rules and using them. In the literature on development, the ability to flexibly use rules is generally considered to be fully developed by the age of 5 years. However, outside of the experimental setting, the ability to act on the rules and make optimal choices is often dependent on the individual's experience with the rule and on the external context. Zidane clearly knew that head-butting the opponent was not the correct action, but his fateful decision may have been effected by the excitement of his final professional appearance on the world stage and the insult provided by Matarazzi. The man who was chosen as captain to serve as an example for the younger, less-experienced players, would be expected to act appropriately. Although we probably can never understand the thought processes of any individual, Werner's orthogenetic principle of development and the notion of regression provides a framework for understanding Zidane's impulsive behavior, as it allows that even well-ingrained rules can be overwhelmed by lower developmental behaviors in certain circumstances. In this context, the notion of the development of rule learning and use is more nuanced than the simple attainment of the understanding or even the ability to of a rule in certain situations, but entails the adaptability to implement the optimal choice of rules even in particularly challenging and stressful situations, such as the World Cup final.

ACKNOWLEDGMENTS

The authors are grateful to David Evans, Tamara Fitch, and Philip D. Zelazo for their insightful comments on earlier drafts of this chapter, and to Alexandra D'Arrisso, Heidi Flores, and other members of the McGill Youth Study Team for their help in various aspects of the publication process. We hope that we did not offend Zinedine Zidane.

REFERENCES

Amso, D., & Casey, B. J. (2006). Beyond what develops when: Neuroimaging may inform how cognition changes with development. *Current Directions in Psychological Science, 15,* 24–29.

Blair, C., & Razza, R. P. (2007). Relating effortful control, executive function, and false belief understanding to emerging math and literacy ability in kindergarten. *Child Development, 78,* 647–663.

Braver, T. S., & Barch, D. M. (2002). A theory of cognitive control, aging cognition, and neuromodulation. *Neuroscience Biobehavioral Review, 26,* 809–817.

Carlson, S. M. (2003). Executive function in context: Development, measurement, theory, and experience. *Monographs of the Society for Research in Child Development, 68*(3), 138–151.

Case, R. (1992). The role of the frontal lobes in the regulation of cognitive development. *Brain and Cognition, 20,* 51–73.

Casey, B. J., Tottenham, N., Listen, C., & Durston, S. (2005). Imaging the developing brain: What have we learned about cognitive development? *Trends in Cognitive Sciences, 9,* 104–110.

Cohen, J. D., & Servin-Schreiber, D. (1992). Context, cortex, and dopamine: A connectionist approach to behavior and biology in schizophrenia. *Psychology Review, 99,* 45–77.

Crone, E. A., Ridderinkhof, K. R., Worm, M., Somsen, R. J. M., & Van der Molen, M. W. (2004). Switching between spatial stimulus-response mappings: A developmental study of cognitive flexibility. *Developmental Science, 7,* 443–455.

Diamond, A. (2006). Bootstrapping conceptual deduction using physical connection: Rethinking frontal cortex. *Trends in Cognitive Sciences, 10,* 212–218.

Diamond, A., & Kirkham, N. (2005). Not quite as grown-up as we like to think: Parallels between cognition in childhood and adulthood. *Psychological Science, 16,* 291–297.

Dowsett, S. M., & Livesey, D. J. (2000). The development of inhibitory control in preschool children: Effects of "executive skills" training. *Developmental Psychobiology, 36,* 161–174.

Frye, D., Zelazo, P. D., & Burack, J. A. (1999). Cognitive complexity and control: Implications for theory of mind in typical and atypical populations. *Current Directions in Psychological Science, 7,* 116–121.

Heaton, R. K., Chelune, G. J., Talley, J. L., Kay, G. G., & Curtis, G. (1993). *Wisconsin Card Sorting Test Manual, revised and expanded.* Psychological Assessment Resources, Odessa, FL.

Huizenga, H. M., Smeding, H., Grasmana, R. P. P. P., & Schmand, B. (2007). Multivariate normative comparisons. *Neuropsychologia, 45,* 2534–2542.

Huizinga, M., & van der Molen, M. W. (2007). Age-group differences in set-switching and set-maintenance on the Wisconsin Card Sorting Task. *Developmental Neuropsychology, 31,* 193–215.

Janis, I. L. (1982). *Groupthink* (2nd ed.). Boston: Houghton Mifflin.

Miller, E. K., & Cohen, J. D. (2001). An integrative theory of prefrontal cortex function. *Annual Review of Neuroscience, 24,* 167–202.

Morgan, C. A. III, Doran, A., Steffian, G., Hazlett, G., & Southwick, S. M. (2006). Stress-induced deficits in working memory and visuo-constructive abilities in Special Operations soldiers. *Biological Psychiatry, 60,* 722–729.

Piaget, J. (1970). Piaget's theory. In P. H. Mussen & W. Kessen (Eds.), *Handbook of child psychology: Vol. 1, History, theory, and methods.* New York: Wiley.

Shallice, T., & Burgess, P. W. (1991). Deficits in strategy application following frontal lobe damage in man. *Brain, 114*, 727–741.

Sokol, B. W., & Muller, U. (2007). Editorial: The development of self-regulation: Toward the integration of cognition and emotion. *Cognitive Development, 22*, 401–405.

Sroufe, L. A., & Rutter, M. (1984). The domain of developmental psychopathology. *Child Development, 55*, 17–29.

Waber, D. P., & Holmes, J. M. (1985). Assessing children's copy productions of the Rey-Osterreith complex figure. *Journal of Clinical and Experimental Neuropsychology, 7*, 264–280.

Waber, D. P., & Holmes, J. M. (1986). Assessing children's memory productions of the Rey-Osterrieth Complex Figure. *Journal of Clinical and Experimental Neuropsychology, 8*, 563–580.

Werner, H. (1948). *Comparative psychology of mental development.* New York: Houghton-Mifflin.

Werner, H. (1957). The concept of development from a comparative and organismic point of view. In D. Harris (Ed.), *The concept of development: An issue in the study of human behavior.* Minneapolis, MN: University of Minnesota Press. New York: International Universities Press.

Zelazo, P. D., & Cunnigham, W. A. (2007). Executive function: Mechanism underlying emotion regulation. In J. J. Gross (Ed.), *The development of emotion regulation* (pp. 135–158). New York: Guilford.

Zelazo, P. D., Frye, D., & Rapus, T. (1996). An age-related dissociation between knowing rules and using them. *Cognitive Development, 11*, 37–63.

Zelazo, P. D., & Mueller, U. (2002a). The balance beam in the balance: Reflections on rules, relational complexity, and developmental processes. *Journal of Experimental Child Psychology, 81*, 458–465.

Zelazo, P. D., & Mueller, U. (2002b). Executive functions in typical and atypical development. In U. Goswami (Ed.), *Handbook of childhood cognitive development* (pp. 445–469). Oxford, UK: Blackwell Publishing.

Zelazo, P. D., Mueller, U., Frye, D., & Marcovitch, S. (2003). The development of executive function in early childhood. *Monographs of the Society for Research in Child Development, 68*, Serial No. 274.

Zigler, E., & Glick, M. (1986). *A developmental approach to adult pxychopathology.* New York: Free Press.

Zigler, E., & Philips, L. (1962). Social competence and the process-reactive distinction in psychopathology. *Journal of Abnormal Social Psychology, 65*, 215–222.

6

The Development of Self-Regulation: A Neuropsychological Perspective

MARIANNE HRABOK AND KIMBERLY A. KERNS

S elf-regulation is, broadly speaking, a system for the control and modification of one's behavior, cognition, and emotion. Self-regulation is vital for autonomous and adaptive psychological and social functioning. From a neuropsychological perspective, self-regulation is considered to be highly dependent on the frontal lobes of the brain, as evidenced by the significant difficulty in self-regulation often observed following frontal lobe injury or disease. Within the field of neuropsychology, abilities subserved by the frontal lobes of the brain are broadly labeled "executive functions" (EF). Indeed, EF have been considered by some to be synonymous with self-regulation, when viewed from a neuropsychological perspective (Banfield, Wyland, Macrae, Munte, & Heatherton, 2004).

The aim of this chapter is to discuss self-regulation from a neuropsychological perspective. Neuropsychology broadly concerns the relationships between behavior and brain structure and function. Developmental neuropsychology also addresses the development of brain systems and functions, and the behavioral correlates of that development. Information about the brain systems related to behavior in adults is gleaned from studies of people who have sustained damage to different areas of the brain or through the use of imaging techniques that look at the activity of the brain while individuals are engaged in various cognitive or behavioral tasks.

In children it is more difficult to infer the function of different brain regions, as focal injury is less common, and because brain functions develop over time. For the purposes of this chapter, we will first address some of the definitional and conceptual issues relevant to EF from a neuropsychological perspective. This will be followed by a discussion of functions of regions of the prefrontal cortex (PFC) believed to be important for self-regulation, based primarily on lesion studies in adults. Following this, a model of self-regulation as it relates to attentional networks in the brain developed by Posner and his colleagues (e.g., Posner & Rothbart, 1994, 1998, 2007) will be described. Next, there are sections on EF as it relates to self-regulations, the development of self-regulation, neuroplasticity, and the role of learning. The chapter concludes with discussion of limitations of neuropsychological research regarding self-regulation, discussion of potential enhancement of self-regulation in children, and areas important for future research.

CONCEPTUALIZATION AND ASSESSMENT OF EF

As noted earlier, from a neuropsychological perspective, self-regulation and the modification of behavior in response to the external and internal environment are considered to be subserved by various EF. The construct of EF is complex, and both the definition and measurement of these higher-level functions pose a number of methodological concerns (e.g., Burgess, 1997). In spite of these concerns, the exploration of EF and of the role of frontal cortices that subserve these functions has generated a great deal of research that has enhanced our understanding of the capacity of humans to think flexibly, plan ahead, and control their behavior in order to achieve goals. Perhaps due to their complexity and prominent role in behavior, there have been a wide range of theories that have offered different conceptualizations of the functional role of frontal brain structures in EF (e.g., Fuster, 1999; Knight & Stuss, 2002; Norman & Shallice, 1986; Roberts & Pennington, 1996). Consistent across these conceptualizations is EF as higher-order capacities that exert control over lower-order processes.

A great deal of knowledge regarding the control of behavior has been gained through careful investigation of individuals who have suffered trauma or injury to the frontal lobes of the brain, as this kind of injury often results in major disturbances in behavior, thinking, and social interaction. Individuals with frontal brain injury are typically described as impulsive, easily distracted, inflexible in their thinking, and lacking in "social graces." Inspite of detailed reports describing such cognitive and behavioral alterations following frontal brain injury, our ability to utilize psychometric measures to assess and quantify such changes has often been met with limited success. Indeed, some individuals with significant behavioral dysregulation may perform adequately on most standardized neuropsychological testing. Walsh (1978), a keen observer of behavioral sequelae of brain injury, clearly captured that difficulty in the following quote:

> The first thing to say about the frontal lobes is that there is an old controversy among psychologists (and others) as to whether or not they are, as some people claim, man's crowning glory or not. There have been strong arguments on both sides. The most convincing argument against the paramount role of the frontal lobes seems to lie in the fact that both have been removed in patients without any apparently disastrous effects on standardised tests .... This seemed to indicate to some that the frontal lobes had no particular value, to others is suggested that this sort of psychological testing had no particular value—I am inclined to the second point of view. (Walsh, 1978, p. 23, as cited in McDonald, 2007)

In general, neuropsychological assessment of EF has focused on problem-solving and planning abilities, and on the ability to regulate one's performance on prescribed tasks. EF are known to be particularly important for performing novel tasks, and the assessment of EF has been made more difficult by the fact that humans are exceptionally adaptive. As a result, behaviors quickly become relatively automatized within a particular task and thus may be less dependent on EF. It is not until there is some need for a change in plan or a modification of the approach to a situation or to solving a problem, or there is some inherent conflict in correct responding from a more prepotent response, that executive control is required and accessed. Indeed, the very process of "standardized" testing typically provides sufficient structure and information about the correct approach to task completion that the need for executive control is reduced. It has been noted that individuals who demonstrate problems with EF seem most unable to deal with complex real-life situations that require the ability to plan and organize multiple goal-directed behaviors in situations that are relatively open-ended (Duncan, Burgess, & Emslie, 1995; Goldstein, Bernard, & Fenwick, 1993; Shallice & Burgess, 1991). Assessment of these "real-world" behaviors has been difficult to quantify with valid and reliable neuropsychological measures.

The focus of most assessment of EF has also largely neglected the "social" and "emotional" aspects of EF. Such changes are typically asked about in interviews with significant others, but are rarely quantified. However, current theories of EF have begun to emphasize a distinction between aspects of self-regulation dependent on varying levels of affective or emotional valence. As such, there is a growing interest in the interactions between cognitive and affective processes and their relationship to self-regulation.

In beginning to bridge these domains, Zelazo and Müller (2002) described a distinction between "hot" and "cool" self-regulatory processes. The so-called "cool" regulatory processes are involved in planning and problem-solving behavior, the areas that traditional neuropsychological measures have attempted to capture. In contrast, "hot" regulatory processes are hypothesized to be involved in affective and motivational processing (Metcalfe & Mischel, 1999; Zelazo & Müller, 2002) and in interpersonal and social tasks (McDonald, 2007; Stuss & Anderson, 2004; Stuss, Gallup, & Alexander, 2001; Stuss & Levine, 2002). These emotionally related regulatory processes have been the focus of fewer investigations, and even less is known about the behavioral regulation when both "hot" and "cool" systems are required.

FUNCTIONS OF THE PREFRONTAL CORTEX

Inspite of significant limitations in assessing the full range of EF, there has been considerable knowledge gained regarding the brain systems involved in self-regulation and the internally generated control of behavior. It is generally agreed that the prefrontal cortex (PFC) is involved in problem-solving, planning, inhibitory control, working memory, and the execution of goal-directed and intentional behavior. Three regions of the PFC have been viewed as differentially important in EF, including the dorsolateral prefrontal cortex (DLPFC), the orbitofrontal cortex (OFC), and the medial PFC (particularly the anterior cingulate cortex, ACC). These regions are most accurately understood as functioning within circuits. Particularly relevant for their role in self-regulation of behavior, each region has connections with motor (particularly striatal) systems of the brain (Bradshaw, 2001).

Functions Associated with Dorsolateral Prefrontal Cortex

Abilities such as problem-solving, planning (Tranel, Anderson, & Benton, 1994), cognitive flexibility, and working memory (Fuster, 1999; Roberts & Pennington, 1996) have all been linked to the DLPFC through lesion and neuroimaging studies. DLPFC is an area that is highly connected with other areas within the brain (including posterior areas of the cortex). The DLPFC-striatal circuit originates in the DLPFC and projects to structures of the basal ganglia (e.g., dorsolateral head of caudate, dorsolateral globus pallidus) and thalamus (ventral anterior and dorsomedial thalamic nuclei), before returning to the DLPFC.

In adults, lesions to this area typically result in impairments in planning, attention, temporal coding (Dimitrov et al., 1999), initiation, inhibition (Turner & Levine, 2004), cognitive fluency, and maintaining or shifting set (Bradshaw, 2001). The functions of the DLPFC are significant for supporting self-regulation because of their role in integrating information about sensation, movement, and long-term memory from visual and parietal cortices, as well as supporting "working memory" whereby information can be temporarily stored for setting up action plans and a preparatory set for action (Bradshaw, 2001). In the Zelazo and Müller (2002) model, the DLPFC would be associated with "cool" EF.

There are a number of "cool" EF measures currently used with young children (see Carlson, 2005; Zelazo & Müller, 2002). Many of these tasks involve inhibition and working memory. Inhibition tasks include those that require suppression of an automatic response in favor of a less automatic response, such as "Stroop" tasks or "Simon says" type tasks (Archibald & Kerns, 1999; Carlson, 2005). Working memory tasks involve holding information in mind for a short period of time. Tasks used with preschoolers have commonly emphasized spatial working memory (e.g., Espy, Kaufmann, Glisky, & McDiarmid, 2001; Luciana & Nelson, 2002; Sonuga-Barke, Dalen, Daley, & Remington, 2002).

A considerable amount of research has shown that there are major advances in what would be considered EF during infancy, as measured by tasks such as the "A-Not-B" and "Delayed Response" tasks (Diamond, 2002), and that the preschool period is a time of significant development of EF, particularly in the areas of inhibition and working memory (Carlson, 2005; Diamond, 2002). Advances in inhibition and working memory have also been linked to the development of other complex cognitive abilities within the domain of EF, including problem-solving (Senn, Espy, & Kaufmann, 2004) and aspects of theory of mind (Carlson, Moses, & Breton, 2002; Carlson, Moses, & Claxton, 2004).

Functions Associated with the Orbitofrontal Cortex

In contrast to the DLPFC, the OFC has strong ties with lower-level brain systems, most notably the limbic system. The lateral OFC-striatal circuit originates in the lateral OFC and projects to structures of the basal ganglia (e.g., ventromedial caudate nucleus, dorsomedial globus pallidus) and thalamus (ventral anterior and medial dorsal thalamic nuclei), before returning to the lateral OFC.

This system is considered to be, in functional terms, highly reward-sensitive and involved in appraisal of the motivational significance of stimuli

(Hongwanishkul, Happaney, Lee, & Zelazo, 2005; Zelazo & Müller, 2002). Connections with limbic regions make this an important system for "hot" EF. For example, the OFC processes the reward value of a stimulus and plays a role in the reinforcement of behavior. This includes, for example, specific somato-sensory information (e.g., texture of food), abstract reinforcers (e.g., money), and approach (reward-related) and avoidance (punishment-related) behavior (Rolls, 2004).

In adults, damage to the OFC is manifest behaviorally through emotional and behavioral disinhibition and impulsivity. Impairments in these functions are often seen as underlying and contributing to apparent difficulties with appropriate social behavior and social judgment (Damasio, 1994), with the case of "Phineas Gage" (Macmillan, 1996) being the most classic example.

The OFC is believed to be important in self-regulation because it is involved in processing information pertaining to the behavioral significance of stimuli (e.g., recognition of reinforcing stimuli, stimulus-response learning, and pro-cessing changes in reinforcement contingencies), by integrating information from sensory association cortices, the limbic system, and subcortical regions involved in autonomic behavior (Bradshaw, 2001).

As noted, affective-motivational self-regulation, presumably under the control of the OFC, has been considered to be reflective of "hot" aspects of cognition (Metcalfe & Mischel, 1999; Zelazo & Müller, 2002). These aspects of EF have been less extensively studied than "cool" EF in both adults and chil-dren (Hongwanishkul et al., 2005; McDonald, 2007; Zelazo & Müller, 2002). Recently, this dimension of self-regulation has begun to be examined in chil-dren through tasks such as the "Children's Gambling" task (Kerr & Zelazo, 2004), the "Less is More" task (Carlson, Davis, & Leach, 2005), and variants of "Delay of Gratification" measures (Prencipe & Zelazo, 2005). These tasks require children to forego a salient reward in favor of a more advantageous, but less immediate option. Although investigation of affective-motivational self-regulation during the preschool period is relatively scarce, research has shown that developmental advances occur during this time (Kerr & Zelazo, 2004; Prencipe & Zelazo, 2005).

Functions of Medial Aspects of the Prefrontal Cortices

Medial aspects of the PFC (such as the ACC) are also reciprocally connected with the limbic system. The ACC-striatal circuit originates in the ACC and projects to the basal ganglia and associated structures (e.g., nucleus accum-bens, olfactory tubercle, ventromedial caudate and putamen, rostrolateral glo-bus pallidus) and thalamus (dorsomedial thalamic nuclei), before returning to the ACC. On the basis of a review of empirical research, Bush, Luu, and Posner (2000) subdivided the ACC into two different regions that subserve different functions. The first region is the dorsal region of the ACC. This region has mainly cognitive functions and is activated by tasks that involve aspects such as stimulus-response selection with competing information (e.g., Stroop, divided attention, working memory tasks). The second region is the rostral-ventral region of the ACC which, in contrast to the dorsal region, appears more involved in assessing emotional and motivational information and regulating affective responses.

In adults, damage to the ACC leads to disturbances in drive and motivation (e.g., apathy, reduced initiative, akinetic mutism). The ACC has heterogeneous subdivisions and connections and has been associated with motivation, spontaneous initiation of action, early phases of learning, regulation of autonomic functions, and executive control. Less is known about the development of the ACC than the other prefrontal regions, but its development is thought to be protracted (Conel, 1939–1967, as cited by Bush et al., 2000).

Research has also shown that in adults, the ACC is particularly involved in conflict resolution and in performance and error monitoring (Holroyd & Coles, 2002). Performance monitoring is essential for dynamic decision-making processes. In goal-directed action selection and reward-based learning, performance and error monitoring serve as critical functions in judging whether a response is appropriate for a goal, and whether it will be rewarded. Logan (1985) suggested that error monitoring is one of the executive control processes that provides "top-down" adjustment of elementary mental operations. Holroyd, Yeung, Coles, and Cohen (2005) proposed a mechanism whereby error detection is imbedded in reinforcement learning. Specifically, they proposed that the ACC and basal ganglia serve crucial functions in the detection of errors, by identifying internal or external environmental cues which signal a positive or negative outcome of a response, and by recognizing "particular stimuli-response combinations." The result of error detection serves to guide the individual in learning appropriate mappings and allows for the adjustment of behavior to changing feedback.

Integrative Functions of DLPFC, OFC, and ACC in Self-Regulation

In terms of self-regulation, it is important to consider that there are significant connections between regions of PFC, which are also reciprocally connected with the limbic system. When viewed in a larger context, it is apparent why the PFC is integral in self-regulation. Deecke and Lange (1996, as cited by Bradshaw, 2001) identify three strategic questions addressed by frontostriatal circuits. The first is "what to do," hypothesized to be mediated by the functions of lateral OFC in determining behavioral significance of stimuli (e.g., reward value). The second is "how to do it," which is mediated by DLPFC and lateral premotor areas in terms of integrating goals with the most recent sensory information and both cognitive and motor planning. The third is "when to do it," hypothesized to be mediated by the ACC (motivation) and supplementary motor areas (timing and intentionality).

Developmentally, the planning and problem-solving aspects of the DLPFC, the reward sensitivity and appraisal functions of the OFC, and the motivational and attentional functions of the medial PFC contribute in important ways to the progression of self-regulation from being more externally controlled in the young child to being increasingly internally driven as the child matures. The development of skills associated with these areas likely provides the child with the necessary ability to interpret and evaluate past and present experiences, to develop behavioral self-regulation, and to support the ability to engage in successful goal-oriented behavior.

SELF-REGULATION AND ATTENTION

As noted previously, much of the neuropsychological research investigating self-regulation has been done in adults, primarily through lesion studies of individuals with damage to specific neural areas, and more recently, from neuroimaging of individuals as they are participating in tasks that require varying levels of self-regulation. Alternatively, Posner and colleagues have utilized constructs from cognitive neuroscience to speculate on the neural systems subserving self-regulation and the development of these systems. These researchers (Posner & Rothbart, 1991, 1994, 1998, 2000, 2007; Rueda, Posner, & Rothbart, 2005) discuss the role of attention, specifically the control of attention, as being the functional basis of self-regulation. Posner and Petersen (1990) view attention as a hierarchical construct, with different functions and neural systems associated with various subtypes of attention. Indeed, Posner and Rothbart's framework for the development of these attentional control systems illustrates how research from cognitive neuroscience (i.e., the neural bases of attention) can be successfully integrated with findings from developmental psychology to explore the underlying neural basis and developmental sequence of self-regulation.

Much of Posner and his colleagues' work is based on the ideas of Luria. For example, Luria (1973) posited the existence of two attention systems. The first is an involuntary type of attention that predominates during the first few months of life, when the infant is attracted by biologically salient stimuli.

A second, higher-order attention system was proposed to be under voluntary control and to undergo a lengthy formation, intertwined with social influences. Luria suggested that this second attention system stabilizes during the preschool period.

Posner and colleagues have expanded on these ideas, incorporating findings from contemporary studies of attention in a theoretical framework which focuses on the link between attention and self-regulation (Posner & Rothbart, 1991, 1994, 1998, 2000, 2007; Rueda et al., 2005). They hypothesized the existence of three integrated attention networks that are responsible for volitional control of behavior and self-regulation.

The most basic system is that involved in the maintenance of the alert state, and this network is hypothesized to include areas of the midbrain (locus coeruleus) and aspects of the frontal and parietal cortex. This attention system seems to develop first and is modulated by norepinephrine (Posner & Rothbart, 2007). The second network to develop is the orienting network which is involved in orienting to sensory stimuli. Key brain regions hypothesized to be involved in this network include the temporal parietal junction, and the superior parietal lobe and frontal eye fields, as well as aspects of the superior colliculus and pulvinar. This network is primarily modulated by acetylcholine and is thought to be involved in the control of distress (Posner & Rothbart, 1998). The highest level of the hierarchy is the executive attention network. The executive network has been found to be active in tasks involving selection, conflict, and error detection, which are functions similar to those found in other models of cognitive control (e.g., Norman & Shallice, 1986). This network, thought to be the last to develop, is hypothesized to be primarily modulated by dopamine and involves brain regions including anterior cingulate, lateral PFC, and basal ganglia.

An important aspect of Posner and Rothbart's framework is Posner and Petersen's (1990) conceptualization of attention, as well as Ruff and Rothbart's (1996) framework for understanding the development of the orienting and executive attention networks in early childhood. As noted, the first, and developmentally earliest system, is the vigilance network which functions to maintain an alert state. Vigilance, a basic form of attention, enables the child to be alert to incoming stimuli while exploring the environment, and supports other cognitive and perceptual functions. To investigate this form of attention Posner (1978) has used "warned reaction time" tasks. These paradigms generally involve serial presentation of a warning and a reaction signal to which the participant is required to respond as quickly as possible (Murphy-Berman & Wright, 1987).

On the basis of a decrease in errors of omission and response time on this reaction time task between 3.5 and 4.5 years of age, as well as decreases in instances of looking away during tasks demanding different degrees of attention, Ruff and Rothbart postulate that it is at this time that the vigilance network advances (Akshoomoff, 2002) or comes under the child's internal verbal control. Morrison (1982) found that 8 year olds and adults alerted more quickly and sustained alertness better than 5 year olds, suggesting that vigilance develops relatively early and is at adult levels at some time between ages 5 and 8. In the framework put forth by Ruff and Rothbart (1996), vigilance is established early and does not occupy a prominent role in the regulation of behavior. It is essentially supportive of the higher level orienting and executive attention networks.

The second network to develop is the orienting system (Ruff & Rothbart, 1996) and its characteristic processes including engaging, disengaging, and shifting attention (Posner & Petersen, 1990), which for the child is essential in selecting information from available sensory stimuli. The flow of information in this network is "bottom-up," suggesting that it is an exogenous, stimulus-driven control process. Cognitive function inherent to this system has been assessed through use of a spatial orienting task designed by Posner and Cohen (1984). In this task, a location cue is presented (on one of two sides of the screen), followed by a target. "Valid cues" appear in the same location as the target, while "invalid cues" appear opposite to the location of the actual target. Response times are faster for validly cued trials than invalidly cued trials, suggesting that the orienting system directs attentional resources based on "cue" information received prior to the actual target.

The heavy involvement of subcortical structures in this network has led researchers to postulate that this attention system also emerges and develops early in life (Posner, Rothbart, Thomas-Thrapp, & Gerardi, 1998). As a consequence, much research has been conducted on the development of the orienting system in infancy, leading to the conclusion that attraction to biological importance, operant contingency, signal value, novelty, intensity, and unpredictability dominate in the first year of life (Ruff & Rothbart, 1996).

Evidence for the early functioning of this network can be seen in a newborn, whose attention is gained by patterns and objects with large features and high contrast. The tendency for attention to be directed to these stimuli is so powerful that infants have trouble disengaging their look once a salient stimulus has been presented (Stechler & Latz, 1966, as cited by Ruff & Rothbart, 1996). This network develops further at 2–3 months, when an infant begins to have more specific preferences (such as faces or bulls eyes; Ruff & Turkewitz, 1975, 1979), and is better able to disengage attention (Johnson, Posner, & Rothbart, 1991). The refinement of this system continues, as the ventral (involved in form and object representation) and dorsal (involved in representation of object location and motion) visual streams develop and exploratory activity increases in frequency (Gibson, 1988).

The period of 9 to18 months represents a transition period, during which attention becomes increasingly controlled by the "executive attention" system as opposed to the lower attention networks. Ruff and Rothbart (1996) postulate that as this occurs, behavior gradually becomes controlled by internally generated plans rather than attributes of the environment, thus making attention a more endogenous (goal-directed) than exogenous (stimulus directed) process.

The executive attention system is the most sophisticated attentional network. Operations associated with this network include target and error detection, conflict resolution, inhibition, and goal-directed behavior (Bush et al., 2000). In 1978, Posner conceptualized this network as "conscious attention," and attributed to it the functions of inhibition (higher level systems inhibiting lower systems from acting), translation (coordination of activities of subsystems by a central system), and generalization (flexible application of patterns of behavior). Later, Posner and DiGirolamo (1998) utilized Norman and Shallice's (1986) model of attention, and suggested that functions associated with the executive attention network include planning/decision-making, error correction, novel responses, particularly under conditions deemed difficult or dangerous, and/or when it is necessary to overcome habitual responses. These are also functions that have been associated with the ACC (e.g., Colebatch, Cunningham, Deiber, Frackowiak, & Passingham, 1991, as cited by Posner & DiGirolamo, 1998). This system would subserve both "hot" and "cool" aspects of EF. The functions associated with the executive attention network may allow for a resolution of conflict among thoughts, feelings, and behavior (Posner & Rothbart, 2004).

The executive attention network is the last of the attentional networks to develop, emerging near the end of the first year of life and evidencing important transitions at 18 months and then again at 4 years (Ruff & Rothbart, 1996), developmental time periods when EF also undergoes significant advancements (Diamond, 2002; Welsh & Pennington, 1988). Ruff and Rothbart view focused attention as reflective of the development of the executive attention network, and suggest that it is the child's internal goal-directed behavior that propels his/her ability to focus attention. The higher-order nature of executive attention and the functions associated with the ACC have led to the hypothesis that attention plays a role in higher-order behavioral functions, including self-regulation (Posner & Rothbart, 2000).

Part of the foundation of Posner and colleagues theory of the relation between attention and self-regulation is derived from research on the interaction between environmental and social forces and the orienting system. For example, distressed infants were able to be soothed by orienting to interesting auditory and visual events (Harman & Rothbart, 1992, as cited by Posner & Rothbart, 1994). With development, the executive attention network takes over the role of the orienting system in exerting influence over self-regulatory processes (Posner & Rothbart, 2000).

As the child becomes older, the development of executive attention (conflict resolution, error monitoring, inhibition, and goal-directed behavior), combined with social forces that act as the bridge between involuntary attention and higher forms of attention (Luria, 1973), assumes a level of control above that of the orienting network (Harman & Fox, 1997). With development, this system operates more influentially in self-regulation.

As discussed previously, most research and theory has historically focused on "cool" EF, despite the importance of understanding the development of "hot" EF. Recently, however, some research has focused on these relations, as discussed in the following section.

STUDIES EXAMINING SELF-REGULATION AND EXECUTIVE FUNCTIONS

Several studies have examined the relationship between cognitive aspects of EF and self-regulation (Berger, Jones, Rothbart, & Posner, 2000; Davis, Bruce, & Gunnar, 2002; Gerardi-Caulton, 2000; Hongwanishkul et al., 2005; Wolfe & Bell, 2003). Some of these studies have assessed EF through cognitive measures of inhibition (such as spatial conflict: Gerardi-Caulton, 2000; Go/No Go: Davis et al., 2002; Stroop tasks: Wolfe & Bell, 2003). Others have addressed self-regulation in naturalistic contexts, primarily through delay of gratification measures (such as food delay from Vaughn, Kopp, & Krakow, 1984; Vaughn, Kopp, Krakow, Johnson, & Schwartz, 1986; Gift Task from Davis et al., 2002; Bow Task from Wolfe & Bell, 2003) and parental questionnaires of temperament and regulation (Children's Behavior Questionnaire [CBQ]; Rothbart, Ahadi, Hershey, & Fisher, 2001). The results of these studies generally suggest that there are significant links between cognitive inhibition and self-regulation.

Hrabok, Kerns, and Müller (2006) extended this area of research by examining the relations between executive attention (inhibition and working memory) and self-regulation in a sample of 4–5 four-year-olds. Measures of inhibition included a "Go/No-Go" task and a "Motor Conflict" task, both of which required the child to inhibit an automatic or "prepotent" response in favor of a less automatic but required response. Measures of working memory included a "Self-Ordered Pointing" task and a "Delayed Alternation/ Nonalternation" task, in which the child was required to hold information in mind over a short period of time. Measures of self-regulation included the CBQ, a parental report measure of temperament and self-regulation, and the "Snap Game."

The "Snap Game" is a rigged competitive game that has been used as a means of directly observing self-regulated and disruptive behavior (Hughes, Cutting, & Dunn, 2001; Hughes et al., 2002). In this game, the researcher sits in front of two children and simultaneously deals both children a pair of cards. If the child receives a matching pair, the child is allowed to move a magnetic counter one place along a playing board. The children are told that the first to reach the end of the board with their counter wins the game. Although the cards are rigged so that each child receives a winning streak (10 deals) and a losing streak (10 deals), the game ends in a tie, and each child is given a prize. The following behaviors were coded during the game: positive comments about the self (e.g., gloating, such as "ha, ha, I'm going to be the winner!"), negative comments about the other player (e.g., insults, such as "you're not very good at this"), complaints (e.g., "it's not fair!"), whining/sad appeals (e.g., "can't I win now?"), cheating (child saying "Snap" when their cards do not match, and attempts to move their counter), controlling behavior (e.g., "give me a 'Snap' now!" or physical aggression), and minor disruptive acts (e.g., making distracting sounds during the game).

Interestingly, the children who demonstrated more negative comments, cheating, or appeals were also found to perform significantly worse on inhibition measures than children who were not elevated on these behaviors. This provides some further support for the relation between inhibition and self-regulation, particularly in a naturalistic, social context.

THE DEVELOPMENT OF SELF-REGULATION: MODELS AND NEURAL BASES

The influence of the development of PFC circuits, Posner and Rothbart's framework, and research conducted on the relations between EF and self-regulation provide insight into how development of brain regions affects self-regulation. In contrast to theory and research in the neuropsychological literature, the development of affective dimensions of self-regulation has been a central theme in a variety of developmental theories, including psychoanalytic, behavioral, sociocultural, and cognitive-developmental theories (Bronson, 2000; Flavell, Miller, & Miller, 2002). Despite the difference in perspective, this literature is congruent and complementary to the neuropsychological perspective.

The development of self-regulation progresses from very rudimentary to more sophisticated processes early in development (Kopp, 1982, 1989). Infants, in their earliest months of life, have limited ability to regulate their emotional states. Regulation strategies consist primarily of avoidance of unpleasant stimuli (e.g., turning their heads away), and crying, to signal discomfort (Kopp, 1982). Posner and Rothbart (2007) note that, when infants are under three months of age, caregivers generally soothe them by holding and rocking them, but by around three months of age, infants begin to be able to respond to distraction, to diminish their distress. Ruff and Rothbart (1996) identify landmark periods in the first year of life with regard to control of distress and orienting to objects. They hypothesize that changes in this ability to regulate behavior are related to the development of areas of the brain responsible for attentional selection.

As reviewed earlier, Posner and colleagues hypothesize that the increase in the infant's ability to focus attention during the first year of life results in the ability to self-regulate more efficiently. By the end of the first year, the infant begins to be able to engage in self-distraction, such as by shifting away from unpleasant stimuli and focusing attention on more positive stimuli (Posner & Rothbart, 1994). Development of this self-reorienting, as a form of self-regulation is proposed to be related to the changes in anatomy and circuitry of attentional networks (Posner & Rothbart, 2000).

By 12 months of age, the infant has advanced in many cognitive, emotional, social, and physical domains of functioning. Advances in motor coordination enable the infant to engage in sequences of motor behavior that allow approach to or avoidance of stimuli in a more direct manner. Advances in working memory at this age are hypothesized to support the infant's ability to retrieve schemata and compare current situations with previous situations, allowing for behavior to appear increasingly goal-directed and intentional (Kagan & Herschkowitz, 2005).

During the second year, the child becomes increasingly self-directed, again supported by improvements in motor functioning, EF, and language skill, which enable the child to respond not only to the influence of caregivers (Kopp, 1982), but increasingly to internalized self-control (Kochanska, Coy, & Murray, 2001). Improvements in EF and language continue in the preschool years, enabling the child to use verbal mediation as well as other supporting strategies for emotional regulation (e.g., self-distraction and use of private speech). In general, over the course of early development, intentionality, and goal-directed behavior become more developed with less reliance on external sources of regulation or control. The development of self-regulation is reflected in the child's ability to deploy attention flexibly, and to control impulses and emotions, which have important ramifications for social behavior and problem-solving. This broad level of analysis of the development of self-regulation is critical, but it is also important to examine the mechanisms that may underlie these developments. These influences will be discussed in terms of neural plasticity and Hebbian learning, and the potential role of these mechanisms in social learning.

The Role of Neural Plasticity in the Development of Self-Regulation

Neural plasticity refers to the ability of neural circuits to undergo changes in function or organization due to previous activity or experience. A child can be provided with any number of social or environmental experiences, but in order for these experiences to impact brain functioning, the brain must be amenable to change. Therefore, plasticity is of great interest in neuropsychology, specifically in the contexts of neurodevelopment and rehabilitation. Plasticity is a key to understanding the development of self-regulation, as it is through this process that the brain is directly impacted by experience via what is termed "Hebbian learning." According to Hebb (1949, as cited by Posner & Rothbart, 2004), Hebbian learning occurs when presynaptic and postsynaptic neurons are activated at the same time, and the connectivity between these neurons is enhanced. The more this activation occurs, the stronger the association between these neurons. Likewise, if two neurons or groups of neurons have been disconnected by a lesion (by injury or damage), they may become reconnected if they are activated at the same time. In Hebb's terminology, neurons that "fire together, wire together," allowing for modification in brain connectivity.

An extension of the proposed mechanisms of plasticity is the idea of "interactive specialization" (Johnson, 2000; Johnson et al., 2005). According to this theory, brain development is not modularly specific, but is a highly dynamic process. This is in contrast to the idea that the brain is innately endowed with encapsulated information processing devices ("modules") that are simply activated or deactivated due to maturational processes. Early in development different regions are activated somewhat nonspecifically. From these nonspecific activations, experience-specific circuitry emerges for specific functions. By way of example, Johnson and colleagues (2005) posit that a region may initially be activated by a number of different visual stimuli, but eventually will become specialized for a particular kind of visual stimuli, for example, a brain region becomes specialized for processing human faces. This idea is important because it emphasizes the bidirectional role of experience and brain development as well as the high degree of connectivity between brain regions.

There are qualitatively different ways of fostering "Hebbian learning" and connections between neural circuits. For example, Robertson and Murre (1999) describe two approaches to promoting this type of learning in a rehabilitation context. One is through the use of a "bottom-up" approach, in which the therapist facilitates externally generated "cued inputs" (that may be perceptual or motor) in order to specifically foster connections. An example of this approach is extensive repetitions of specific finger movements in dystonic or hemiplegic limb, in an attempt to consistently activate the same "neural network" and promote stronger connectivity. A second way of enhancing connections is a "top-down" approach, whereby anterior attentional systems are recruited for the enhanced activation of more posterior neural circuits of the brain. In this approach, mental attention to a task is crucial. An example of this comes from animal research, which has shown that activity-dependent reorganization in sensory and motor maps requires active attention to the relevant stimuli. Likewise in rehabilitation with patients who demonstrated unilateral neglect, training in the use of a "self-instructional" procedure has been shown to improve the ability to sustain attention to the neglected side and reduce the symptoms of unilateral neglect (Robertson, Tegnér, Tham, Lo, & Nimmo-Smith, 1995).

THE ROLE OF LEARNING IN THE DEVELOPMENT OF SELF-REGULATION

These proposed approaches to enhancing connectivity raise interesting questions about the role of learning in self-regulation. Hofer (1994, as cited by Calkins, 2004) has suggested that early in life, a mother provides regulation at multiple sensory levels (e.g., olfactory, oral, tactile). An example of this is soothing a baby through gentle rocking or singing. These would be examples of bottom-up stimulation, and may be especially important in infancy. In contrast, top-down stimulation, such as when a child attempts a task and uses private speech (e.g., self-talk) to monitor his/her performance (e.g., Broderick, 2001; Fernyhough & Fradley, 2005), may play a greater role later in development. This also suggests that certain types of regulation (e.g., state regulation resulting from soothing sensory input, such as an embrace, when a child is in an elevated state of distress) may always be more amenable to bottom-up stimulation, whereas other types of regulation may require top-down stimulation (e.g., the child's ability to implement a strategy during a delay of gratification task).

Initially, infants rely heavily on external sources for self-regulation and thus the caregiver exerts a significant influence early in life (Bowlby, 1969/1982).

Caregivers clearly provide a major source of influence on the development and learning of self-regulation. "Scaffolding" is an element of parent–child interaction that has received attention in the neuropsychological literature and has been hypothesized as supporting the development of EF (Landry, Miller-Loncar, Smith, & Swank, 2002). It refers to the process of an adult guiding a child's behavior in ways that support his/her current level of development, but also encourages progression to a more advanced stage (termed "zone of proximal development"; Vygotsky, 1978).

As noted, an infant's behaviors are mostly externally regulated by caregivers. Development of frontal cortex, supported by caregivers' early efforts in soothing the infant, may help to train the ability to regulate emotion (Posner & Rothbart, 2007). Luria (1973) suggested that attention is important in social situations and interactions. Caregivers scaffold their infant's ability to attend by orienting the child to new or relevant stimuli while ignoring irrelevant or distracting stimuli. Pollak (2005) noted that aspects of attention (a form of top-down regulation) and social functioning are linked in social situations. A child must attend to internal information (e.g., level of comfort, distress, etc.), contextual information (e.g., who is present in the environment), and social cues from others in determining the most appropriate course of action.

Maternal behavior, and particularly what has been termed "maternal scaffolding," has been shown to be instrumental in children's development. Over the preschool years, the imparting of and drawing attention to rules by mothers has been found to progress from rules concerning basic safety, to more complex rules concerning interpersonal behavior and socialization to cultural norms and standards (Gralinski & Kopp, 1993).

Findji (1993) found that the quality and amount of maternal scaffolding (e.g., drawing an infant's attention to objects and thus regulating the infant's distress) is related to attentional abilities at 5 months of age. Using a longitudinal design, Landry and colleagues (2002) investigated maternal scaffolding in children who were 3, 4, and 6 years of age. They found that maternal scaffolding at 3 years of age (e.g., using language to label and guide behavior, providing support and labeling of actions as children engage in cognitive tasks) directly influenced language and nonverbal problem solving at age 4. At age 6, the EF of children in this sample were directly influenced by their language capacities, suggesting that language skills are a critical in executive control of behavior. It is hypothesized that both "hot" affective and "cool" cognitive dimensions of self-regulation, which were discussed earlier, have similar developmental timetables, exert similar control influences over lower processes, and are aided by similar strategies such as private or internalized speech (Broderick, 2001; Fernyhough & Fradley, 2005). They are also heavily influenced by parent–child interactions and the attachment relationship (Calkins, 2004; Landry, Miller-Loncar, & Smith, 2002).

The importance of "internalized" or "private" speech in executive control and regulation of behavior has been highlighted by Barkley (1997) in his theory of EF. Barkley notes that children with Attention-Deficit/Hyperactivity Disorder (ADHD) are slower to develop internalized speech and have less internalized speech than typically developing children. Children with ADHD also have considerable difficulty with aspects of EF and self-regulation. Barkley proposes internalized speech is one of the major developmental components of EF and that it follows the development of working memory (1997). Barkley proposes that following the development of internalized speech, children are able to make use of increasingly complex rules, and the child's internalization of these rules and use of "private speech" translates into improved self-control and regulation and increasingly internalized control of behavior.

Conclusions, Implications, and Future Directions

In summary, neuropsychological theory and research has important contributions for understanding self-regulation through the conceptualization and investigation of EF. Despite the significant advances in these areas, many questions for future research remain. As suggested by Johnson et al. (2005), it cannot be assumed that a brain region involved in an operation in adults is the same brain region involved in children when they perform the same or a similar task (see also Bunge, Dudukovic, Thomason, Vaidya, & Gabrieli, 2002). Thus, an important area of future research is to investigate the trajectory of brain regions involved in the same process over infancy and childhood (e.g., how do the functions of the DLPFC, OFC, and ACC change from infancy to childhood), develop new measures of important EF constructs and minimizing the need to make "downward extensions" from adult research to research with children. This is especially true with respect to a complex process such as self-regulation, which clearly involves multiple regions and circuits and appears to be highly influenced and interdependent with evolving social and contextual variables.

The PFC, with its high level of connectivity, is crucial in integrating arousal, stored knowledge and conceptual information, and strategies to manage this information. A number of researchers have proposed models accounting for connections among various cognitive, affective, and behavioral units, including Mischel and Ayduk's (2004) concept of Cognitive-Affective Processing System and Stuss and Anderson's (2004) model of consciousness. The level of integration among information in the tertiary zones of the PFC illustrates that there is a high degree of transformation that occurs with incoming information.

A process as complex as self-regulation is likely to be highly constructive, which may in part explain why there is a high degree of variability both across individuals and within individuals in different contexts. An important area for future research will be to examine relations between circuitry involving regions of the PFC and forms of self-regulation. Answering such questions as whether enhancing this circuitry can lead to improvements in self-regulation could have significant clinical importance. For example, recent work by Rueda and colleagues (2005) has begun investigating the impact of improving the attentional system through training at a young age. Understanding whether such interventions could result in not only improved attentional abilities but also improved performance on measures of self-regulation (e.g., delay of gratification, disappointment paradigms, parent-reported measures of self-regulation) could have significant impact, especially for populations of children with difficulties in this area. Finally, determining whether specific environmental influences can alter the trajectory of developmental executive dysfunction could be critical for children with a number of developmental disorders.

As discussed, scaffolding has been shown to be related to the development of EF. To date we still lack a clear understanding of the brain mechanisms, as well as the specific social influences that function to support the development of these crucial abilities. Extending our knowledge of the developmental trajectory of the various brain systems, their degree of vulnerability and dependency on social and environmental influences are of considerable importance. In addition, a further understanding of the brain mechanisms whereby private language and internalized speech impact executive control systems is also crucial. While it is clear that internalized speech is related to one's ability to regulate their behavior, there are no specific theories about how this system develops and operates. Posner and Rothbart (2007) note that in great apes and humans the ACC has evolved considerably, and that in higher primates this structure includes unique cells found mainly in Layer V (Nimchinsky et al., 1999, as cited by Posner & Rothbart, 2007). While the purpose of these cells is as yet unknown, their proximity to vocalization areas in primates may provide a link between emotional, language, and motor areas, perhaps laying the groundwork for the regulation of emotion and behavior through internalized language.

Self-regulation is an exceedingly difficult object of study. As with EF, self-regulation cannot be traced to a single brain system, and is instead the product of multiple neural systems. As suggested by Pollak (2005), the construct of attention is a good example of a complex process that has been successfully decomposed into component parts and studied at behavioral and neural levels.

It is important that this be done with even more multifaceted functions, such as various aspects of self-regulation, with investigations again at the behavioral, neuronal, and relational levels of study. These types of analysis will be critical in answering the most pressing questions involving the relationships of brain systems to self-regulation. During the act of self-regulating, what brain regions and mechanisms are involved? Do these mechanisms differ as a function of the emotional significance of the activity? When the PFC is active, what specific processes are engaged that enable a child to learn to correctly know what, how, and when to engage in socially relevant goal directed behavior? Investigation of strategy use (e.g., self talk/internal speech) along with neuroimaging may help in answering these questions.

Finally, the concept of self-regulation is also in need of greater definitional clarity. Although there is considerable interest in self-regulation emerging in a wide range of disciplines, difficulty integrating the findings from various fields of study can result from multiple definitions of self-regulation, and lead to confusion and loss of information in translation among disciplines. It is likely that researchers with diverse backgrounds and areas of interest will continue to view self-regulation from a perspective that is consistent with their discipline. However, a dimensional or hierarchical model of self-regulation that encompasses a variety of conceptualizations of self-regulation, and at the same time captures the multifaceted nature of self-regulation, could be useful to furthering our understanding of the development of this crucial ability.

REFERENCES

Akshoomoff, N. (2002). Selective attention and active engagement in young children. *Developmental Neuropsychology, 22,* 625–642.

Archibald, S. J., & Kerns, K. A. (1999). Identification and description of new tests of executive functioning in children. *Child Neuropsychology, 5,* 115–129.

Banfield, J. F., Wyland, C. L., Macrae, C. N., Munte, T. F., & Heatherton, T. F. (2004). The cognitive neuroscience of self-regulation. In R. F. Baumeister & K. D. Vohs (Eds.), *Handbook of self-regulation: Research, theory, and applications* (pp. 62–83). New York: Guilford Press.

Barkley, R. A. (1997). *ADHD and the nature of self-control.* New York: Guilford Press.

Berger, A., Jones, L., Rothbart, M. K., & Posner, M. I. (2000). Computerized games to study the development of attention in childhood. *Behavior Research Methods, Instruments, & Computers, 32,* 297–303.

Bowlby, J. (1982). *Attachment and loss: Vol. 1. Attachment.* New York: Basic Books. (Original work 1969)

Bradshaw, J. L. (2001). *Developmental disorders of the frontostriatal system: Neuropsychological, neuropsychiatric, and evolutionary perspectives*. Philadelphia, PA: Psychology Press.

Broderick, N. Y. (2001). An investigation of the relation between private speech and emotion regulation in preschool-age children. *Dissertations Abstracts International, 61*, 11B.

Bronson, M. B. (2000). Recognizing and supporting the development of self-regulation in young children. *Young Children, 55*, 32–37.

Bunge, S. A., Dudukovic, N. M., Thomason, M. E., Vaidya, C. J., & Gabrieli, J. D. E. (2002). Immature frontal lobe contributions to cognitive control in children: Evidence from fMRI. *Neuron, 33*, 301–311.

Burgess, P. W. (1997). Theory and methodology in executive function research. In P. Rabbitt (Ed.), *Methodology of frontal and executive function* (pp. 81–116). East Sussex, UK: Psychology Press.

Bush, G., Luu, P., & Posner, M. I. (2000). Cognitive and emotional influences in anterior cingulate cortex. *Trends in Cognitive Sciences, 4*, 215–222.

Calkins, S. D. (2004). Early attachment processes and the development of emotional self-regulation. In R. F. Baumeister & K. D. Vohs (Eds.), *Handbook of self-regulation: Research, theory, and applications* (pp. 324–339). New York: Guilford Press.

Carlson, S. M. (2005). Developmentally sensitive measures of executive function in preschool children. *Developmental Neuropsychology, 28*, 595–616.

Carlson, S. M., Davis, A. C., & Leach, J. G. (2005). Less is more: Executive function and symbolic representation in preschool children. *Psychological Science, 16*, 609–616.

Carlson, S. M., Moses, L. J., & Breton, C. (2002). How specific is the relation between executive function and theory of mind? Contributions of inhibitory control and working memory. *Infant and Child Development, 11*, 73–92.

Carlson, S. M., Moses, L. J., & Claxton, L. J. (2004). Individual differences in executive functioning and theory of mind: An investigation of inhibitory control and planning ability. *Journal of Experimental Child Psychology, 87*, 299–319.

Damasio, A. R. (1994). *Descartes' error: Emotion, reason, and the human brain*. New York: Putnam.

Davis, E. P., Bruce, J., & Gunnar, M. R. (2002). The anterior attention network: Associations with temperament and neuroendocrine activity in 6-year-old children. *Developmental Psychobiology, 40*, 43–56.

Diamond, A. (2002). Normal development of prefrontal cortex from birth to young adulthood: Cognitive functions, anatomy, and biochemistry. In D. T. Stuss & R. T. Knight (Eds.), *Principles of frontal lobe function* (pp. 466–503). Toronto: Oxford University Press.

Dimitrov, M., Granetz, J., Peterson, M., Hollnagel, C., Alexander, G., & Grafman, J. (1999). Associative learning impairments in patients with frontal lobe damage. *Brain and Cognition, 41*, 213–230.

Duncan, J., Burgess, P., & Emslie, H. (1995). Fluid intelligence after frontal lobe lesions. *Neuropsychologia, 33*, 261–268.

Espy, K. A., Kaufmann, P. M., Glisky, M. L., & McDiarmid, M. D. (2001). New procedures to assess executive functions in preschool children. *The Clinical Neuropsychologist, 15,* 46–58.

Fernyhough, C., & Fradley, E. (2005). Private speech on an executive task: Relations with task difficulty and task performance. *Cognitive Development, 20,* 103–120.

Findji, F. (1993). Attentional abilities and maternal scaffolding in the first year of life. *International Journal of Psychology, 28,* 681–692.

Flavell, J. H., Miller, P. H., & Miller, S. A. (2002). *Cognitive development.* Englewood Cliffs, NJ: Prentice-Hall.

Fuster, J. M. (1999). Cognitive functions of the frontal lobes. In B. L. Miller & J. L. Cummings (Eds.), *The human frontal lobes* (pp. 187–195). New York: Guilford Press.

Gerardi-Caulton, G. (2000). Sensitivity to spatial conflict and the development of self-regulation in children 24–36 months of age. *Developmental Science, 3,* 397–404.

Gibson, E. J. (1988). Exploratory behavior in the development of perceiving, acting, and the acquiring of knowledge. *Annual Review of Psychology, 39,* 1–41.

Goldstein, L. H., Bernard, S., & Fenwick, P. B. (1993). Unilateral frontal lobectomy can produce strategy application disorder. *Journal of Neurology, Neurosurgery & Psychiatry, 56,* 274–276.

Gralinski, J. H., & Kopp, C. B. (1993). Everyday rules for behavior: Mother's requests to young children. *Developmental Psychology, 29,* 573–584.

Harman, C., & Fox, N. A. (1997). Frontal and attentional mechanisms regulating distress experience and expression during infancy. In N. A. Krasnegor & L. G. Reid (Eds.), *Development of the prefrontal cortex: Evolution, neurobiology, and behavior* (pp. 191–208). Sydney: Brookes.

Holroyd, C. B., & Coles, M. G. H. (2002). The neural basis of human error processing: Reinforcement learning, dopamine, and the error-related negativity. *Psychological Review, 109,* 679–709.

Holroyd, C. B., Yeung, N., Coles, M. G. H., & Cohen, J. D. (2005). A mechanism for error detection in speeded response time tasks. *Journal of Experimental Psychology: General, 134,* 163–191.

Hongwanishkul, D., Happaney, K. R., Lee, W., & Zelazo, P. D. (2005). Hot and cool executive function: Age-related changes and individual differences. *Developmental Neuropsychology, 28,* 617–644.

Hrabok, M., Kerns, K. A., & Müller, U. (2006). The vigilance, orienting and executive networks in 4-year-old children. *Child Neuropsychology, 13,* 408–421.

Hughes, C., Cutting, A. L., & Dunn, J. (2001). Acting nasty in the face of failure? Longitudinal observations of "hard-to-manage" children playing a rigged competitive game with a friend. *Journal of Abnormal Child Psychology, 29,* 403–416.

Hughes, C., Oksanen, H., Taylor, A., Jackson, J., Murray, L., Caspi, A., et al. (2002). "I'm gonna beat you!" SNAP!: An observational paradigm for assessing young children's disruptive behaviour in competitive play. *Journal of Child Psychology and Psychiatry, 43,* 507–516.

Johnson, M. H. (2000). Functional brain development in infants: Elements of an inter-active specialization framework. *Child Development, 71,* 75–81.

Johnson, M. H., Griffin, R., Csibra, G., Halit, H., Farroni, T., DeHaan, M., et al. (2005). The emergence of the social brain network: Evidence from typical and atypical development. *Development and Psychopathology, 17,* 599–619.

Johnson, M. H., Posner, M. I., & Rothbart, M. K. (1991). Components of visual orient-ing in early infancy: Contingency learning, anticipatory looking, and disengaging. *Journal of Cognitive Neuroscience, 3,* 335–344.

Kagan, J., & Herschkowitz, N. (2005). *A young mind in a growing brain.* London: Lawrence Erlbaum Associates.

Kerr, A., & Zelazo, P. D. (2004). Development of "hot" executive function: The chil-dren's gambling task. *Brain and Cognition, 55,* 148–157.

Knight, R. T., & Stuss, D. T. (2002). Prefrontal cortex: The present and the future. In D. Stuss & R. Knight (Eds.), *Principles of frontal lobe function* (pp. 573–597). Toronto: Oxford University Press.

Kochanska, G., Coy, K. C., & Murray, K. T. (2001). The development of self-regulation in the first four years of life. *Child Development, 72,* 1091–1111.

Kopp, C. B. (1982). Antecedents of self-regulation: A developmental perspective. *Developmental Psychology, 18,* 199–214.

Kopp, C. B. (1989). Regulation of distress and negative emotions: A developmental view. *Developmental Psychology, 25,* 343–354.

Landry, S. H., Miller-Loncar, C. L., Smith, K. E., & Swank, P. R. (2002). The role of parenting in, children's development of executive processes. *Developmental Neuropsychology, 21,* 15–41.

Logan, G. D. (1985). Executive control of thought and action. *Acta Psychologia, 60,* 193–210.

Luciana, M., & Nelson, C. A. (2002). Assessment of neuropsychological function through use of the Cambridge neuropsychological testing automated battery: Performance in 4- to 12-year-old children. *Developmental Neuropsychology, 22,* 595–624.

Luria, A. R. (1973). *The working brain: An introduction to neuropsychology.* New York: Basic Books.

Macmillan, M. (1996). Phineas gage: A case for all reasons. In C. Code, C.-W. Wallesch, J. Yves, & A. R. Lecours (Eds.), *Classic cases in neuropsychology* (pp. 243–262). Oxford: Lawrence Erlbaum Associates.

McDonald, S. (2007). The social, emotional and cultural life of the orbitofrontal cor-tex. *Brain Impairment, 8,* 41–51.

Metcalfe, J., & Mischel, W. (1999). A hot/cool system analysis of delay of gratification: Dynamics of willpower. *Psychological Review, 106,* 3–19.

Mischel, W., & Ayduk, O. (2004). Willpower in a cognitive-affective processing sys-tem: The dynamics of delay of gratification. In R. F. Baumeister & K. D. Vohs (Eds.), *Handbook of self-regulation: Research, theory, and applications* (pp. 99–129). London: Guilford Press.

Morrison, F. J. (1982). The development of alertness. *Journal of Experimental and Child Psychology, 34,* 187–199.

Murphy-Berman, V., & Wright, G. (1987). Measures of attention. *Perceptual and Motor Skills, 64,* 1139–1143.

Norman, D. A., & Shallice, T. (1986). Attention to action: Willed and automatic control of behavior. In R. J. Davidson, G. E. Schwartz, & D. Shapiro (Eds.), *Consciousness and self-regulation* (Vol. 4; pp. 1–18). New York: Plenum.

Pollak, S. D. (2005). Early adversity and mechanisms of plasticity: Integrating affective neuroscience with developmental approaches to psychopathology. *Development and Psychopathology, 17,* 735–752.

Posner, M. I. (1978). *Chronometric explorations of mind.* Hillsdale, NJ: Lawrence Erlbaum Associates.

Posner, M. I., & Cohen, Y. (1984). Components of visual orienting. In H. Bouma & D. G. Bowhuis (Eds.), *Attention and performance X* (pp. 531–556). Hillsdale, NJ: Lawrence Erlbaum Associates.

Posner, M. I., & DiGirolamo, G. J. (1998). Executive attention: Conflict, target detection, and cognitive control. In R. Parasuraman (Ed.), *The attentive brain* (pp. 221–256). Cambridge, MA: The MIT Press.

Posner, M. I., & Petersen, S. E. (1990). The attention system of the human brain. *Annual Review of Neuroscience, 13,* 25–42.

Posner, M. I., & Rothbart, M. K. (1991). Attentional mechanisms and conscious experience. In A. D. Milner & M. D. Rugg (Eds.), *The neuropsychology of consciousness* (pp. 91–111). San Diego: Academic.

Posner, M. I., & Rothbart, M. K. (1994). Attention regulation: From mechanism to culture. In P. Bartelson, P. Elen, & G. d'Ydewalle (Eds.), *International perspectives on psychological science: Leading themes* (pp. 41–54). Hillsdale, NJ: Lawrence Erlbaum Associates.

Posner, M. I., & Rothbart, M. K. (1998). Attention, self-regulation, and consciousness. *Philosophical Transactions of the Royal Society of London, 353,* 1915–1927.

Posner, M. I., & Rothbart, M. K. (2000). Developing mechanisms of self-regulation. *Development and Psychopathology, 12,* 427–441.

Posner, M. I., & Rothbart, M. K. (2004). Hebb's neural networks support the integration of psychological science. *Canadian Psychology, 45,* 265–278.

Posner, M. I., & Rothbart, M. K. (2007). *Educating the human brain.* Washington, DC: American Psychological Association.

Posner, M. I., Rothbart, M. K., Thomas-Thrapp, L., & Gerardi, G. (1998). The development of orienting to locations and objects. *In R. D.* Wright (Ed.), *Visual attention* (pp. 269–288). London: Oxford University Press.

Prencipe, A., & Zelazo, P. D. (2005). Development of affective decision-making for self and other: Evidence for the integration of first- and third-person perspectives. *Psychological Science, 16,* 501–505.

Roberts, R. J., & Pennington, B. F. (1996). An interactive framework for examining prefrontal cognitive processes. *Developmental Neuropsychology, 12,* 105–126.

Robertson, I. H., & Murre, J. M. J. (1999). Rehabilitation of brain damage: Brain plasticity and principles of guided recovery. *Psychological Bulletin, 125*, 544–575.

Robertson, I. H., Tegnér, R., Tham, K., Lo, A., & Nimmo-Smith, I. (1995). Sustained attention training for unilateral neglect: Theoretical and rehabilitation implications. *Journal of Clinical and Experimental Neuropsychology, 17*, 416–430.

Rolls, E. T. (2004). The functions of the orbitofrontal cortex. *Brain and Cognition, 55*, 11–29.

Rothbart, M. K., Ahadi, S. A., Hershey, K. L., & Fisher, P. (2001). Investigations of temperament at three to seven years: The Children's Behavior Questionnaire. *Child Development, 72*, 1394–1408.

Rueda, M. R., Posner, M. I., & Rothbart, M. K. (2005). The development of executive attention: Contributions to the emergence of self-regulation. *Developmental Neuropsychology, 28*, 573–594.

Ruff, H., & Rothbart, M. K. (1996). *Attention in early development: Themes and variations.* New York: Oxford University Press.

Ruff, H., & Turkewitz, G. (1975). Developmental changes in the effectiveness of stimulus intensity on infant visual attention. *Developmental Psychology, 28*, 851–861.

Ruff, H., & Turkewitz, G. (1979). The changing role of stimulus intensity in infants' visual attention. *Perceptual and Motor Skills, 48*, 815–826.

Senn, T. E., Espy, K. A., & Kaufmann, P. M. (2004). Using path analysis to understand executive function organization in preschool children. *Developmental Neuropsychology, 26*, 445–464.

Shallice, T., & Burgess, P. (1991). Deficits in strategy application following frontal lobe damage in man. *Brain, 114*, 727–741.

Sonuga-Barke, D. J. S., Dalen, L., Daley, D., & Remington, B. (2002). Are planning, working memory, and inhibition associated with individual differences in preschool ADHD symptoms? *Developmental Neuropsychology, 21*, 255–272.

Stuss, D. T., & Anderson, V. (2004). The frontal lobes and theory of mind: Developmental concepts from adult focal lesion research. *Brain and Cognition, 55*, 69–83.

Stuss, D. T., Gallup, G. G., & Alexander, M. P. (2001). The frontal lobes are necessary for "theory of mind." *Brain, 124*, 279–286.

Stuss, D. T., & Levine, B. (2002). Adult clinical neuropsychology: Lessons from studies of the frontal lobes. *Annual Review of Psychology, 53*, 401–433.

Tranel, D., Anderson, S. W., & Benton, A. (1994). Development of the concept of "executive function" and its relation to the frontal lobes. In F. Boller & J. Grafman (Eds.), *Handbook of neuropsychology, 9*, Elsevier Science Amsterdam, pp. 125–148.

Turner, G. R., & Levine, B. (2004). Disorders of executive functioning and self-awareness. In J. Ponsford (Ed.), *Cognitive and behavioural rehabilitation: From neurobiology to clinical practice* (pp. 224–268). New York: Guilford Press.

Vaughn, B. E., Kopp, C. B., & Krakow, J. B. (1984). The emergence and consolidation of self-control from eighteen to thirty months of age: Normative trends and individual differences. *Child Development, 55*, 990–1004.

Vaughn, B. E., Kopp, C. B., Krakow, J. B., Johnson, K., & Schwartz, S. S. (1986). Process analyses of the behavior of very young children in delay tasks. *Developmental Psychology, 22,* 752–759.

Vygotsky, L. S. (1978). *Mind in society: The development of higher psychological processes.* Cambridge, MA: Harvard University Press.

Walsh, K. W. (1978). *Frontal lobe problems.* Paper presented at the 1976 Brain Impairment Workshop, Melbourne, Australia.

Welsh, M. C., & Pennington, B. F. (1988). Assessing frontal lobe functioning in children: Views from developmental psychology. *Developmental Neuropsychology, 4,* 199–230.

Wolfe, C. D., & Bell, M. A. (2003). Working memory and inhibitory control in early childhood: Contributions from physiology, temperament, and language. *Developmental Psychobiology, 44,* 68–83.

Zelazo, P. D., & Müller, U. (2002). Executive function in typical and atypical development. In U. Goswami (Ed.), *Blackwell handbook of childhood cognitive development* (pp. 445–469). Malden, MA: Blackwell Publishers.

7

Working Memory in Infancy and Early Childhood: What Develops?

MAUREEN HOSKYN

Working memory is theoretically conceived as a limited, attentional capacity that temporarily stores and manipulates information in the face of distraction and/or attention shifts (Baddeley & Logie, 1999; Just & Carpenter, 1992; Turner & Engle, 1989). The ability to selectively attend to information that is important, while simultaneously inhibiting interfering information is thought to mediate a wide range of activities that require reasoning, planning, and action in children (Savage, Cornish, Manly, & Hollis, 2006) and adults (Engle, 2002; Just & Carpenter, 1992; Turner & Engle, 1989; Vos, Gunter, Kolk, & Gijsbertus, 2001). A number of studies have documented the developmental growth in working memory that occurs over late childhood and adolescence (Gathercole, Pickering, Ambridge, & Wearing, 2004; Gathercole, Tiffany, Briscoe, Thorn, & ALSPAC team, 2005; Kail, 1997; Kail & Park, 1994; Swanson, 1999) as well as the capacity constraints of adults in cognitive decline (Hoskyn & Swanson, 2003; Swanson, 1999). Further, research shows that the expression of disabilities associated with learning (Gathercole & Alloway, 2006; Swanson & Ashbaker, 2000), language (Gathercole et al., 2004), and attention (Budson & Price, 2005) is linked to capacity constraints in working memory. Clinical studies of the behavioral sequelae following damage to prefrontal cortex of the brain among individuals with disorders such as aphasia, Huntington's, and Alzheimer's disease (Budson & Price, 2005) also show impaired working memory.

More recently, attention has been focused on gathering understandings about the emergence of working memory early in ontology along with its corresponding neural structure. Also, a frequently overlooked, but important consideration for developmental theorists is that age-related changes in working memory capacity coincide in time with children's developing understandings of language and its use in social activity (Heimann et al., 2006). This path of inquiry is gaining importance as an increasing number of studies show that near the latter part of the first year of life, infants begin to use language as a symbolic resource to communicate with others about objects and/or events in their social worlds (Bates, Camaioni, & Volterra; 1975; Liszkowski, Carpenter, Henning, Striano, & Tomasello, 2004; Meltzoff, 1995; Woodward, 1998; Woodward & Sommerville, 2000). By the age of 4 years, most children engage in communicative exchanges in which they not only position sounds, gestures, objects, events, and intentional actions of agents, but also the mental states of others (Frith & Frith, 1999). The ability to keep multiple types of information in mind while simultaneously activating new information to meet intentional goals is thought to be a function of working memory. Moreover, broadly stated, working memory affords infants and young children rich experiences during social communication. The interactivity that takes place during these social events is critical for furthering children's understandings about the linguistic tools of their culture (Tomasello, 2003), for developing social understandings (Carpendale & Lewis, 2004), and for facilitating social competence (Keller, 2003).

To forge links between children's working memory and language, discussion in this chapter relies almost exclusively on usage-based theories of language acquisition (e.g., Bates, 1976; Tomasello, 2003). Such theories are mutually reinforcing of a strand of thought in philosophy that is concerned with action-oriented approaches to language and language use, identified with such authors as Wittgenstein (Wittgenstein & Waismann, 2003), Austin (1962), and Searle (1998). In this view, infants and young children accomplish things with their gestures and early vocalizations: they describe, question, request, and so on, and the function of such communication is to facilitate social contact and influence others. At 9–12 months of age, infants begin to follow the eye gaze of their caregivers, use adults as social reference points, and interact with objects as they have seen adults do (Tomasello, 2003). By the time they reach their first birthday, most infants produce their first words, evidence that they have begun to internalize and use the linguistic symbols in their language. In the words of Tomasello (2003): "when a child learns the conventional use of linguistic symbols, what she is learning are the ways her forebears in the culture found it useful to share and manipulate the attention of others in the past" (p. 13). A multitude of linguistic symbols and constructions that "embody attentional construals" are fine tuned through social experience to represent granularity (e.g., *animals—dog; fish—salmon*), perspective (e.g., *chase-flee*, *give-take, acquire-develop*), and function (*mother, woman, doctor, Canadian*). However, attention to the semantic features of a linguistic symbol is but one aspect of the language learning process; for a child also learns what Tomasello describes as the "human perspective" embodied in the symbol—the way that a situation is attentionally construed by the individuals who use the symbol. To effectively communicate using prelinguistic (i.e., gesture) or linguistic symbols (i.e., words, sentences) in human communication to meet intentional goals, children must attend to symbol-use when in interactions with others and adapt their use to changing communicative circumstances. This activity is cognitively and linguistically complex because social phenomena can be represented in different ways, depending on the perspective and motivation of the speaker. It is within this dynamically changing, flexible communicative architecture that young children actively engage in a kind of social cognition that allows them to share and to manipulate the intentional and mental states of others in increasingly complex ways (Carpenter, Akhtar, & Tomasello, 1998; Tomasello, 1999, 2003).

Working memory is thought to prepare infants and young children for participation in these complex, social endeavors by allowing for multiple sources of information or knowledge states to be simultaneously activated and discriminately used to meet personal goals. Conversely, although the research base is far from complete, there is sound theoretical justification for the proposition that children's communicative transactions with adults in social activity leads to capacity increases in working memory. A main objective of this chapter is to critically examine theories and empirical research on these points, with the overarching view that working memory both influences and is influenced by the communication of infants and young children with others in their social worlds.

The Construct of Working Memory

One problem faced by researchers interested in learning about working memory early in the human lifespan is that a widely accepted definition of the construct does not exist. Theoretical descriptions of working memory are for the most part, derived from either constructivist or information-processing paradigms, and, although these interpretations share points of similarity, the philosophical traditions upon which each rests differ significantly (see De Ribaupierre & Bailleux, 2000, for a comprehensive review; Kemps, De Rammelaere, & Desmet, 2000). Briefly, constructivist theories such as Pascual-Leone's theory of silent operators posit that working memory contains both activated knowledge (or schemes) from long-term memory and an attentional control mechanism that is responsible for integrating knowledge within and among these varied states. In contrast, information-processing models view working memory as an interrelated cognitive system which allows for the processing of incoming information as well as the storage of the temporary products of processing (De Ribaupierre & Bailleux, 2000). Information-processing models have historically described the working memory system that underlies performance on general reasoning tasks as a multicomponent, modular system (e.g., Baddeley & Hitch's [1974] model of working memory); however, recently a number of single component, unitary models of working memory have been proposed in the literature (e.g., MacDonald & Christiansen, 2002). A complete discussion and critique of constructivist versus multicomponent or unitary information-processing views of working memory is well beyond the scope of this chapter. What is important to this discussion is the relative emphasis that each perspective places on the mental representations (or schemes) that constitute the contents of working memory and on the executive (or attentional control mechanism) that serves to coordinate the operations within a working memory system. It is these core processes that either individually or in combination, appear to be important in developmental change in working memory capacity, for social pragmatic theories of early childhood language acquisition (i.e., Tomasello, 2003) and to the emergence of self-control, theory of mind (Carlson, Moses, & Breton, 2002), emotion regulation, and planning in toddlers and preschool aged children (Rothbart, Posner, & Kieras, 2006; Rueda, Posner, & Rothbart, 2005).

Constructivist Theories of Working Memory Development

Influenced heavily by neo-Piagetian schema theory and by Hegel's laws of dialectics, Pascual-Leone (1987, 1989) proposed the "field of working memory" to represent the combination of figurative, operative, and executive schemes that become activated during effortful processing (Pascual-Leone & Ijaz, 1989). Figurative knowing refers to the construction of symbols that imitate a world of objects and events. Silent operators activate these figurative schemes within a subset of working memory that Pascual-Leone called the "field of attention." They are content-free and carry no specialized information: the *M-operator* refers to the capacity for mental energy and the means by which task-relevant schemes are attended to and activated during problem solving; the *I-operator* is responsible for inhibiting activation of task-irrelevant schemes; and the *F-operator* is important to the management of attention and represents the capacity to produce a single, unified whole, despite having multiple structures involved in performance of a cognitive task. A fourth process, the *E-operator*, is a set of executive schemes and structures that allocate resources required for planning of mental actions and monitoring nonexecutive attentional processes affiliated with the *M-operator* and the *I-operator*.

A mathematical model was developed by Pascual-Leone to explain age-related increases in the number schemes activated by the *M-operator* within the field of attention. Total capacity for mental energy is symbolized as $(e + k)$, where *e* refers to space to store information necessary for the performance of tasks across cognitive domains and *k* refers to space allocated to the processing information specific to the task at hand. The value of *e* is thought to be epigenetic and largely invariant; whereas *k* is flexible and increases systematically and "lawfully" during cognitive development. These increments in units of activation of task-relevant schemes (represented mathematically as $k +1$, $k +2, ..., k +7$) correspond with successive Piagetian stages that occur every second year between the ages of 3 and 16. Therefore, as children's attentional capacity increases, more schemes and structures become activated during processing, and children are able to participate in increasingly complex cognitive and social activities. To test this mathematical model, Pascual-Leone and his colleagues conducted numerous experiments in which the demands of a task on attention were systematically varied and predictions about performance were made based on the age of the children in the sample. Typically, an experiment involved a span task that required processing of numerical or spatial information. In one such study (Case, 1972), children were shown a series of digits in temporal order with some digits missing in the array (e.g., 3, 8, and 12). The children were then instructed to find the place for one of the missing numbers (e.g., 10). After repeated practice, the task was modified, and the digits were shown to the children one at a time, and children were asked to indicate where the last digit should appear in the sequence. As in most working memory span tasks, this measure required children to (a) selectively attend to and process a series of similar operations, (b) store the partial products of this processing under conditions where interfering information was present, and (c) elicit a response that provided information in temporal order (Case, 1995). By asking that the child recall both the numbers as well as the sequence in which they were presented, the task clearly involved dual processing. In general, the findings were supportive of Pascual-Leone's model: a maturational increase in span of 1–3 units was found between the developmental period between 4 and 7 years, a deceleration in units processed occurred from the age of 8 years until an asymptotic performance was reached at 10 years, which coincides with Piaget's formal operational stage of cognitive development. Case and his colleagues (Case, 1985; Case, Kurland, & Goldberg, 1982) later refined Pascual-Leone's theory and posited that the size of working memory capacity is invariant over time; however, as children grow older and construction of representational schemes becomes efficient and automatized, the demand on processing becomes less, which in turn frees up more capacity for the storage of the partial products of processing. From this perspective, processing demands within working memory capacity are determined by complexity of the task at hand and are modality-specific. It follows, therefore, that working memory supports the construction of representational schemes of both actions and the use of symbols to communicate about these actions.

Bates (1976) argues that for older infants or young children to communicate about the figurative knowledge available to them in these representational schemes, the content must first be objectified into symbolic communicative schemes. When an older infant or child prepares such communicative schemes, knowledge is grouped into a propositional array of one or more schemes. A proposition is defined here as "a relation predicated of one or more arguments" (p. 79). At first glance, this definition suggests that on the surface, a one-word utterance made by an infant is likely not propositional. However, Bates suggests that a single word used in social context may convey combinatorial meanings that together represent more than suggested explicitly by the form of the single word (e.g., /kUki/ spoken by a toddler maybe representative of "I want a cookie" or "I see a cookie" or "Give me the cookie"). To formulate words or sentences to be used in social communication, a selected portion or "chunk" of a propositional array is then "transferred" to be operated on and turned into a single or a concatenation of sounds that constitute a word or combination of words. Bates proposes that the number of words produced in a spoken utterance is a function of developmental constraints in this "chunk-and-transfer capacity" (p. 94), and although not directly stated, this capacity appears to be synonymous with the bounds of the field of working memory described in Pascual-Leone's theory of silent operators.

Recent findings from studies of infant development show that the prerequisite cognitive skills necessary to constitute the figurative contents of working memory are met at a much earlier age than initially described in Pascual-Leone's quantitative model. By the age of 6 months, most infants show deferred imitation (Collie & Hayne, 1999; Herbert, Gross, & Hayne, 2006), a cognitive ability that in classic developmental theory is not thought to emerge until the end of stage 5 of the sensorimotor stage, when infants are approximately 18 months of age (Piaget, 1962). Deferred imitation in this sense refers to an infant's ability to construct and maintain a mental representation of an action over time and then imitate the action based on recall (Bauer & Kleinknecht, 2002). It differs from other forms of imitation learning that focus either on objects or on goals involved with objects such as local enhancement (Spence, 1937, as cited in Want & Harris, 2002), emulation, (Tomasello, 1998), or goal emulation

(Whiten & Ham, 1992). Infants who display deferred imitation recognize both the goal of the person they observe and the actions that successfully meet the person's goal (Tomasello, 1998); most important, they are able to use this knowledge to meet their own similar goals. In its most simple form, deferred imitation occurs when an infant observes a straightforward intentional action of an adult (e.g., pulling two parts of a toy apart) and then recreates this action sequence to meet the same goal. This interaction is qualitatively different from the face-to-face dyadic mimicry that occurs in early infancy because the infant and the adult share a mutual understanding of a specific goal state (Meltzoff, 1995) and because the interaction involves the use of prelinguistic symbols (i.e., gestures) to communicate this goal state to one another. Studies show that younger infants require more exposure to targets on deferred imitation tasks and are less accurate in their imitation of intentional actions than older infants; however, by the age of 9 months, infants are able to maintain two separate object representations in mind while tracking their respective locations (Kaldy & Leslie, 2003, 2005), and by the age of 11 months, most infants are able to recall and reproduce multistep action sequences up to a month after watching an adult perform them (for a review, see Bauer & Kleinknecht, 2002).

One explanation of developmental change in infant performance on deferred imitation tasks emphasizes that with maturity, infants are better able to form figurative schemes of the actions they observe within working memory. A second view holds that an increase in infant attentional capacity, rather than symbolic capacity, within working memory mediates recall of cause-effect action sequences. Bauer (1992; as reanalyzed in Bauer & Kleinknect, 2002) increased demands on infant attention on a traditional deferred imitation task by inserting a source of distraction into the action sequence; further, the intensity of attentional demands on each trial was controlled through a number of action sequences to be recalled. On a two-step causal sequence with a single action inserted as a distraction (e.g., placing a horse on a table, brushing its mane, and rocking it), most infants at 20 months of age (60%) responded consistently on two trials by either emulating the cause-effect portion of the sequence (i.e., ignoring the irrelevant action of brushing the horse's mane) or by either imitating the sequence in its entirety (i.e., including brushing of the horse's mane). With increased demands of a three-step sequence (with an interfering action), the majority of infants (60%) emulated the cause-effect sequence on the first trial and imitated the entire sequence of actions on the second trial. Strategy use became less stable as demands on attention were increased, leading Bauer to conclude that the infant's capacity to meet the attentional demands of the task accounted for variation in infant performance. Notably, when attentional demands were increased further and exceeded working memory capacity, infants tended to recall the entire action sequence rather than only the cause-effect sequence. Working memory in this sense may be adaptive, for two routes were possible to meet the infant's intentional aims of making the horse rock (i.e., either performing all three steps in the action sequence or performing only two steps by placing the horse on the table and then making it rock); however, infants with larger working memory capacities may inhibit, or cognitively suppress, goal-irrelevant information (i.e., the interfering, second step) and produce a more parsimonious response.

Findings from studies of children's development during the preschool years also shed light on the potential role of working memory and/or inhibitory control during controlled action. Research that probes the nature of young children's performance on conflict tasks based on the rule use paradigm (Zelazo & Jacques, 1996) is illustrative. Such tasks require that children attend to, apply, and switch rules to control action (e.g., see Diamond, Kirkham, & Amso, 2002; Gerstadt, Hong, & Diamond, 1994; Hanauer & Brooks, 2005; Müller, Zelazo, Hood, Leone, & Rohrer, 2004). On the standard version of the Dimensional Change Card Sort (DCCS) task (Frye, Zelazo, & Palfai, 1995; Zelazo, 2006; Zelazo, Müeller, Frye, & Marcovitch, 2003), children are shown two target cards, such as a blue flower and a yellow car, and asked to match a series of cards (i.e., yellow flowers and blue cars) to the targets on a single dimension (i.e., shape). Three-year-olds typically perform well on this task, but when asked to switch the rule for sorting to the alternative dimension (i.e., color), children's response accuracy declines (Frye et al., 1995; Moriguchi & Itakhura, 2005; Zelazo, 2006). Typically, 3-year-old children perseverate and use the preswitch rule previously applied to sort the cards. However, when children are questioned about the rules for sorting, they demonstrate knowledge of both the preswitch (e.g., shape) and current (e.g., color) rules (Zelazo, 2006). Even when they are provided additional feedback about the errors they make, young children continue to sort erroneously by the dimension relevant to the preswitch rule (Yerys & Munakata, 2006). By the age of 4 or 5 years, most children resist the prepotent response to sort on the dimension relevant to the preswitch rule and sort cards by applying the current rule accurately (Carlson & Moses, 2001; Diamond et al., 2002).

There are several theoretical interpretations of these findings. For example, according to cognitive complexity and control-revised (CCC-r) theory (Zelazo, 2006; Zelazo & Frye, 1997), the rules that guide controlled action are represented and structured hierarchically. At 2 1/2 years of age, most children sort by a single rule, and often put all the cards in a sorting box according to a single dimension (e.g., either color or shape) even before the rule has changed (Kirkham, Cruess, & Diamond, 2003). By the age of 3 years, children appear able to hold two independent rules (i.e., if, then-) in mind (i.e., "If it is yellow, then it goes in this box, and if it is blue, then it goes in this other box" or "if it is a car, then it goes in this box, and if it is a flower, then it goes in this other box.") for when they are questioned about where the cards should go, they point to the correct sorting box. Perseveration arises in part, from children's inability to consciously reflect upon and construct the more complex, embedded rule structures (i.e., if, if, then-) that are necessary to resolve conflict among incompatible lower order rules (i.e., "If it is the shape game and if the shape is a flower, then it goes here but if it is the color game and if the flower is blue, then it goes there"). Another source of perseveration errors is thought to be related to the process of negative priming, whereby ignoring the rule that is irrelevant for sorting during the preswitch phase leads to difficulty sorting by the rule at postswitch (Müller, Dick, Gela, Overton, & Zelazo, 2007). That is, when children first sort by shape, they suppress attention to the dimension of color, and this leads to difficulty activating attention to color rule at postswitch.

Alternatively, attentional inertia theory (Diamond, Carslon, & Beck, 2005; Kirkham et al., 2003; Rennie, Bull, & Diamond, 2004) posits that perseveration errors of younger children on the DCCS task results from a pull to continue attending to the dimension that was relevant in the preswitch rule and an inability to inhibit this attentional pull at postswitch, when this dimension becomes irrelevant to task performance. Rennie et al. (2004) argue that because children perform well when asked to sort cards separately on either dimension (without switching), it is the switching component, or the conflict part of the DCCS task that is problematic for younger children. During this phase, children must view the DCCS task from a different perspective and to think about the same item by focusing attention to its color rather than its shape. The attentional pull to the dimension that was relevant in the preswitch rule is referred to as "attentional inertia" (Kirkham et al., 2003). The relevant rule for postswitch DCCS task performance is activated in working memory; however, inhibitory control of attention is critical to allow for the disengagement from a mindset (a way of thinking about the initial stimulus) that is no longer relevant (Kirkham et al., 2003). In this sense, working memory and inhibitory control are dissociable forms of executive control (Kirkham & Diamond, 2003). However, the relations between working memory, representational knowledge, attention and/or inhibitory control in young children are not well understood.

Working memory may play a more important role in explaining children's performance on the DCCS task than either CCT-r or attentional inertia theory seems to suggest (Cepeda & Munakata, 2007). Perseveration errors on conflict tasks could theoretically result when working memory capacity is insufficient to allow for the activation of representations relevant to the current rule and for the simultaneous inhibition of irrelevant representations contained in previously rewarded, preswitch rule (Case, 1995; Goldman-Rakic, 1987; O'Reilly, Braver, & Cohen, 1999). This explanation is generally compatible with attentional inertia theory for conflict in attentional control is assumed to be the source of children's perseveration errors; however, both forms of attentional control (i.e., increased attention to features in the relevant dimension and the inhibition of attention to the features of the irrelevant dimension) are assumed to exist within working memory (Hasher & Zacks, 1988).

An alternative view holds that working memory and inhibitory control are not dissociable forms of executive function and that processing of information within a unitary working memory system accounts for perseveration errors on the DCCS task (Yerys & Munakata, 2006). In this graded working memory account, information is represented and recalled in two forms: as active or latent memories (Munakata, 2004). Latent memories consist of latent information gathered and strengthened by repeated experience (i.e., such as by sorting on the preswitch rule) and active memories involve the maintenance of information with little experiential support (i.e., *sorting by the new rule in the postswitch phase*). Active and latent memories are not all-or-none but rather vary continuously in their strength (Morton & Munakata, 2002), and when latent memories, or habits, are stronger than active representations held in working memory, perseveration occurs (Yerys & Munakata, 2006). Conversely, when the active representations are stronger, the outcome is inhibition (Morton & Munakata, 2002). Working memory covaries with inhibitory control for the tension between processing of active and latent memories gives rise to both conditions. Connectionist accounts such as the graded working memory model have been theoretically and empirically linked to neural processing within the brain; however, discussion of neural network models resumes later in the chapter, when information-processing accounts of working memory are presented in more detail.

Findings from studies of children's performance on deferred imitation and conflict tasks also provide indirect evidence to suggest that the development of working memory capacity in early childhood influences and is influenced by participation in social activity. For example, variation in performance outcomes due to slight changes in the stimulus materials (Kirkham & Diamond, 2003) or in labeling procedures (Müller et al., 2004) during the presentation of DCCS task suggests that children's social environments may be shaped in ways that facilitate creation of stable knowledge representations within working memory and/or improve children's control of attention.

For example, adult scaffolding of children's cognition during social activity (Vygotsky, 1978) clearly has potential to optimize attention to and processing of the figurative contents of working memory. Adult scaffolding has potential to support cognition by regulating children's interest and engagement

(Perlmutter, Behrend, Kuo, & Muller, 1989); drawing children's attention to task-relevant actions (Landry, Miller-Loncar, Smith, & Swank, 2002) while ignoring task-irrelevant actions; bracketing observed actions into age-appropriate, manageable chunks for processing within working memory; and/or providing extra resources in the form of strategies, prompts, and cues that optimize memory performance (Flavell, 1994). Further, adults who respond to children's communicative attempts by using semantically contingent language reduce ambiguities and provide redundancy, both of which increase the saliency of the linguistic symbols to be represented in working memory and used by children in communicative exchanges about the actions they observe (Girolametto, Hoaken, Weitzman, & van Lieshout, 2000; Yoder, Warren, McCathern, & Leew, 1998).

Scaffolding as exemplified here is generally consistent with the description provided by Wood, Bruner, and Ross (1976) because adults respond to young children in ways that facilitate children's engagement; however, adult scaffolding also serves to expand children's use of strategies to communicate with others in social activity. Children's participation in these rich communicative transactions, rather than the end state or outcome of the exchange is the process that potentially explains developmental plasticity in working memory capacity. During these transactions, children develop strategies to support attention to intentions, goal states and actions that, in turn, formulate the contents of working memory during social communication. Capacity increments in children's working memory therefore theoretically result from a number of sources that include improvements in strategy use, formation of stable representational knowledge, increases rates of fluency of processing these representations, or improvements in attentional control to goal-relevant stimuli.

Theoretically, children's experiences communicating with adults in social activity strengthens the quality of internal representations of actions and their use of linguistic symbols within these actions. For example, Tomasello (1999, 2003) argues that for infants or young children to learn about a linguistic symbol (e.g., word) and to use it reliably in social communication with others, they must first use this symbol with an adult in the same way that the symbol was used toward the infant.

This act of "role reversal imitation" is described by Tomasello as follows:

> This is clearly a process of imitative learning in which the child aligns herself with the adult in terms of both the goal and the means for attaining that goal; it is just that in this case the child must not only substitute herself for the adult as actor (which occurs in all types of cultural learning) but also substitute the adult for herself as the target of the intentional

act (that is, she must substitute the adult's attentional state as goal for her own attentional state as goal). (p. 27)

Accordingly, when the aim of the infant parallels that of the adult, the infant substitutes herself in place of the adult who is observed and then re-creates the cause-effect sequence in working memory.

Recoding the actions of the adult with the role of self as an agent and an observer is necessary for internalization to occur (Ratner, Foley, & Gimpert, 2002). Evidence of the association between internalization of observed and performed actions is found in physiological studies of brain activity in both human and nonhuman primates, where it is reported that components of the neural system that underlies these processes overlap. The implication is that observing and constructing a mental representation automatically activates the same neural substrate used to execute that action (Kilner & Frith, 2008). Interest in this interpretation has grown since the discovery of mirror neurons and the mirror neuron system, first observed in the macaque monkey in the premotor area and later in the posterior parietal cortices (Rizzolatti & Craighero, 2004).

Mirror neurons fire equally during observation and production of an action sequence, a finding that has led many researchers to suggest that mirror neurons are critical for understanding actions of others (for a review, see Rizzolatti & Craighero, 2004). However, the precise role of mirror neurons in understanding of action sequences is a matter of some debate (Iacoboni, 2005; Jacob & Jeannerod, 2005). Most recently, a number of researchers contend that actions have to be understood at many levels: an intention level; a goal-level which represents the actions required to satisfy one's intentions; a motor signal level that physiologically allows an action to be executed; and a kinematic level, which accounts for the movement in time and space. Further, understanding intentions in others in novel situations or in situations that are difficult to interpret may recruit neural activity in higher cortical regions outside of the mirror system (i.e., the superior temporal sulcus [STS], the posterior STS, and the anterior frontal areas), whereas the goal and the kinematics of the action involve activity in lower cortical regions associated with the mirror system (for a review, see Kilner & Frith, 2008).

To tease apart the components of a working memory system that may link to the mirror, or other neural systems, researchers typically turn to information-processing models. In contrast to constructivist theories of working memory that emphasize that developmental change in capacity is attributable to developmental growth in children's ability to attend to and/or formulate figurative schemes, information-processing models of working memory focus on the components of processing within the working memory system that underlie age and/or individual differences in performance on complex reasoning tasks.

Information-Processing Models of Working Memory

Within the information-processing literature, Baddeley and Hitch's (1974) tri-component model has been extensively used to investigate the nature of age- and/or individual differences in a working memory system. The model includes a central executive that interacts with two ancillary systems, the phonological loop, and the visual-spatial sketchpad. The phonological loop temporarily stores and maintains the products of phonological processing through articulation; the visual sketch pad accesses and temporarily stores visual-spatial information that is necessary to formulate mental representations. Both systems are under control of the central executive, a supervisory attentional resource which coordinates activities within a general cognitive system and also allocates resources to the two subsystems (Baddeley, 1986; Baddeley & Loggie, 1999). Baddeley's (2000, 2003) most recent version of model includes an episodic buffer that is responsible for the integration of information from several sources (including long-term memory, the phonological loop, and the visual-spatial sketchpad) through conscious awareness.

One issue that has been historically controversial is whether processing within the phonological loop and the visual-spatial sketchpad is synonymous with short-term memory; a passive, temporary storage buffer, the capacity of which is measured by simple memory span tasks and mediated by efficiency of practiced strategies, such as rehearsal and chunking (Kail, 1997). Despite a long history of debate, recent studies of adults (Cantor, Engle, & Hamilton, 1992), school-aged children (Conway et al., 2005; Swanson & Ashbaker, 2000), and preschoolers (Hoskyn & Tzoneva, 2008) suggest that processing in the phonological loop and/or visual-spatial sketchpad is at least in part, independent of short-term memory. Further, employment of mnemonic strategies (i.e., rehearsal and chunking) that support retention of information in short-term memory support, but are not sufficient, to account for processing of phonological or visual-spatial information in working memory.

Baddeley's model has been used extensively in studies that investigate age and individual differences in overall working memory capacity. In a cross-sectional study of 700 children, aged 4–17 years, Gathercole et al. (2004) showed a linear increase in capacity for each component of the model from the age of 4 years to early adolescence; further from the age of 6 years onward, the structure of working memory system was considered to be continuous with the adult model. In a subsequent study, Gathercole and her colleagues (2005) report findings that suggest that the trajectory of development of spontaneous articulatory rehearsal is highly volatile for children between the ages of 4 and 7 years; therefore, the authors conclude that younger children draw on the visual-spatial sketchpad to formulate visual representations of visual inputs that are subsequently recoded into phonological forms. The idea that visual working memory develops earlier than verbal working memory is also supported by Vuontela et al. (2003), who found that the visual-spatial component of working memory appeared to reach functional maturity earlier than audio-spatial working memory in children aged 6–13 years.

Alternatively, Hoskyn and Tzoneva (2008) report that increases in a general working memory executive system, as well as improvements in processing associated with the phonological loop and visual-spatial sketchpad together explained developmental variations in children aged 3–7 years. Further, development of a working memory executive explained unique variance in children's performance on emergent literacy tasks beyond that attributable to processing in the phonological loop and/or the visual-spatial sketchpad. Taken together, the study findings suggest that the working memory system that underlies social activities (in this case, literacy practices) becomes increasingly specialized in children as they grow older; however, among very young children, the system appears to be relatively undefined, and when the memory demands are high, children activate a working memory executive as well as lower-level cognitive systems to support task performance. Findings reported in this research are generally consistent with a *general capacity model*, in which age differences in working memory capacity are associated with increases in the central executive that serves to allocate resources, to focus, to divide, and to shift and control attention.

In this view, the executive shares resources with lower level component systems; however, the flow of information is unidirectional, top-down, from the executive to the subcomponent systems that, for the most-part, operate independently of the executive. Thus, for older children, the executive resource pool is larger and is not depleted to the same extent as the pool of resources available to younger children. Further, a working memory system is thought to develop separately from children's ability to encode or process task-specific information. Infants and younger children have smaller working memory capacities than older children; however, these differences are attributable to incremental change in a working memory executive that facilitates performance across a wide range of cognitive tasks (Swanson, 1999; Swanson & Ashbaker, 2000).

On the other hand, a *processing efficiency* view generally parallels the ideas of Case (1985) and predicts that age-related constraints in working memory capacity are a function of the efficiency and speed with which children of different ages retrieve phonological information from long-term memory and rehearse speech-based information in the phonological loop (Roodenrys, Hulme, & Brown, 1993). Evidence that affirms the role of the phonological loop is found in studies where linguistic manipulations such as articulatory suppression, word length, and phonological similarity, interrupt processing associated with the phonological loop (for a review, see Baddeley, 2003). As processing demands increase (i.e., among young children who are less proficient in retrieval of phonological codes), fewer resources are available in working memory for the storage of partial products of processing. More specifically, subvocal, speech-based information in the phonological loop is maintained through articulatory rehearsal; therefore, as articulation rate increases, more resources become available for the storage of the temporary products of the rehearsal process (Hitch & Towse, 1995), and retention of phonological information improves (Kail & Park, 1994). Inefficiencies in phonological retrieval as measured by performance on articulation speed tasks have the potential to create a bottleneck that demands resources and restricts the flow of information upward through the system, which in turn, accounts for age differences in overall working memory capacity. For example, Kail (1997) reports that for children aged 6–10 years, articulation speed and phonological awareness accounts for more age-related variation in performance on phonological working memory span measures than the reverse. Simply put, it is the efficiency with which children process phonological information that accounts for linear growth in working memory capacity.

Resource-sharing models such as the one described by Baddeley and his colleagues have been challenged on a number of grounds, the most critical of which suggests that a domain free ability to control attention underlies performance on working memory span tasks, irrespective of the specific domain the measure is designed to tap (for a review, see Barrett, Tugade, & Engle, 2004). In response, a number of unitary, computational models in which working memory functions as a general attentional resource to activate mental representations stored in long-term memory (Cantor & Engle, 1993) have been proposed. In the next section, an overview of assumptions that are foundational to these models is presented.

Unitary Models of Working Memory

Originating with the ideas of Hume and Locke, empiricist principles of associationism underlie these connectionist models. From this perspective, the mind connects things that are experienced together and generalizes to new objects and events according to their similarity to known ones with comparable sensible qualities (MacDonald, 2003). A distributed system of processing units or connections function in the same way that neural networks operate in the brain to solve information-processing problems (Christiansen & Chater, 2001). Each unit or "activation node" (i.e., neuron) receives information from the environment and sends excitatory or inhibitory messages to other nodes by pathways (i.e., the dendrites and the axons that make up the neural pathways that connect neurons in the brain). Nodes, like neurons, receive input from other activated nodes across pathways of varying strength. These connection weights are stored and continuously readjusted based on experience. Mental representations that are functional become strengthened with repeated use; whereas those that are functionally marginal, rare, or have errors, disappear.

Common to all connectionist models is the idea that critical information becomes encoded economically. Thus, learning in this neural net is not simply additive, but includes processes of subtraction and reorganization. Distinctions between components within a working memory system become blurred for the interactions in a connectionist model are probabilistic and contextual. In contrast to constructivist and/or multicomponent information-processing theories that describe working memory as an encapsulated, fixed capacity system, connectionist accounts assume that the bounds of working memory extend across a neural net. When age-related deficiencies or breaks in the system occur, the total amount of activation remains stable; however, resources may be reallocated to different areas to compensate for the limitations in the system. Age-related increments in the working memory executive are therefore considered to be a function of the total amount of activation available in a neural net.

The earliest manifestation of the neural correlates associated with the core executive processes of a working memory system is found in studies that link a response on an "A-not-B" task to emerging prefrontal cortical activity (Pushina, Orekhova, & Stroganova, 2005; Reznick, Morrow, Goldman, & Snyder, 2004). In this task, an infant is shown a preferred toy that is repeatedly hidden in one of several locations (position "A"). After a delay of a few seconds, a distraction is provided and the infant searches for the toy. When the toy is hidden in a new location "B" in full view, the infant typically responds by reaching for the toy in the position where it was first hidden and makes an "A-not-B" error. As discussed previously in the chapter, the ability to flexibly adapt to a changing environment is an essential component of human cognition. Infants as young as 5.5 months are successful on "A-not-B" tasks, provided that they are searching for a person instead of an object and they respond using eye gaze instead of reaching (Reznick et al., 2004). At 12 months, infants are able to manage increasingly longer delays from the time that an object is hidden and the search begins without making an "A-not-B" error (Diamond, 1991). Working memory theoretically supports task performance by providing a flexible workspace for the temporary storage of expected information (i.e., the location of the toy at the first location) and ongoing information (i.e., the location of the toy in the second location), as well as for the processing of expected events (i.e., procedural information necessary to obtain the toy) and for the control over interfering influences (i.e., the interference mechanism).

In a study of infant performance on an A-not-B task, Stredron, Sahni, and Munakata (2005) tested whether a single-mechanism, connectionist model is adequate to explain outcomes when interference is present (i.e., working memory demands are high) and when the task has no memory demands. The A-not-B task in both conditions required that infants pull one of two cloths to reach a toy; the cloths were placed in a parallel arrangement in front of the infant. A toy was placed *on* the cloth to the *left* and placed *behind* the cloth to the *right* for a number of repeated trials. After the infant pulled the cloth to the left and successfully grasped the toy, the arrangement was reversed: the toy was placed on the right cloth and behind the left cloth. Infants at 9 months of age perseverated in their responses, and continued to pull the cloth to the left, although they were no longer successful at obtaining the toy. Eleven-month-old infants succeeded on this task. On the second version of the task, the solution to the task was visible at all times because the toy was attached to the cloth on which it was placed. In this version, memory demands were minimal for the infant simply had to pull the cloth with the toy attached to reach the toy; 7-month-old infants perseverated in their responses and 9-month-old infants succeeded.

The model created by Stredon, Sahni, and Munakata (2005) to explain infant performance consists of separate input layers that represented information about the left and right side of the environment and whether the toy is placed on or attached to the cloth. The model also includes hidden, prefrontal cortex and output layers. The relative strengths of connections between these layers are modeled using a Hebbian learning rule, and inhibitory connections within layers were modeled as competition between representations. By increasing the connection weights within these networks, the model associates attention to relevant information in the environment with overcoming the pull of pre-potent responses. The fit of models under both conditions was comparable; therefore, the authors argue that the same neural mechanism in the prefrontal cortex that supports development of working memory for nonvisible solutions also supports attention to visible solutions (i.e., that have no memory demands), and that perseveration in the absence of working memory demands does not require a separate explanatory mechanism.

Connectionist models have only recently been tested using data from neuroimaging studies; therefore, their validity remains somewhat controversial in the field. Assuming a one-to-one correspondence between neurons in a neural net and the mental representations that they encode is clearly an oversimplification of the workings of the brain (Bishop, 2000); further, because information is stored economically, the complexity of the social environment in which mental representations are constructed is ignored. For example, intentionality in connectionist models is construed broadly as a result of competition between controlled and automatic processes that are triggered by environmental stimuli (Bargh & Ferguson, 2000) and that is monitored by the executive in working memory (Barrett et al., 2004). Modeling the working memory system that underlies children's language or social interaction is well beyond the scope of current connectionist approaches. Nevertheless, connectionist models have been helpful to illustrate how attentional control, automaticity, and neural connectivity in working memory are inextricably linked and how experience can potentially influence the functionality of this working memory system.

Neuroimaging Studies of Working Memory

A number of studies using various neuroimaging techniques affirm that similar regions of the brain appear to be activated during performance of working memory tasks for school-aged children and adults (Klingberg, Forssberg, & Westerberg, 2002; Munakata, 2004; Nelson et al., 2000). Specifically, the prefrontal cortex appears to become involved during the delay part of a delayed performance task; which suggests the prefrontal region is important for stable memory without interference in both children (Bell, 2001; Bell & Fox, 1992; Diamond, 1991) and adults (Leung, Gore, & Goldman-Rakic, 2005). Two explanations of activation in the prefrontal cortex during performance on working memory tasks have been proposed. One group of models posits that the prefrontal cortex is divided into two areas that are specialized to the contents of working memory: the ventrolateral prefrontal regions (BA 45/47) are activated on tasks that require object working memory (i.e., the "what" of a visual task), and the dorsolateral regions (BA 46/9) are activated when spatial working memory is recruited (i.e., the "where" of a visually guided action; Goldman-Rakic, 1987; Wilson, O'Scalaidhe, & Goldman-Rakic, 1993). Another group of models posits that the prefrontal region is important for stimulus selection and a wide range of brain activities that are not specific to content (Mecklinger, Bosch, Gruenwald, Bentin, & von Cramon, 2000; Stredon et al., 2005). Research that directly compares brain activity in the prefrontal cortex in children with that of adults is limited; however, there is some evidence that white matter maturation in the frontal lobe regions is associated with working memory development (for a review, see Klingberg, 2006).

Although brain activity in the prefrontal regions is associated with performance on working memory tasks among school-aged children and adults, the frontal regions in infants and very young children have traditionally been considered too immature to support performance on memory tasks (Bell, 2001). However, Kaldy and Sigala (2004) provide some preliminary evidence using behavioral measures that suggests the ventrolateral and dorsolateral brain regions may be integrated in infants by 6.5 months for one object and by the age of 9 months for two objects. Further, studies that use physiological measures of brain activity report that as infants near their first birthday, an increase in glucose metabolism is observed in the frontal regions. Moreover, EEG activity in these same regions increases during performance on working memory tasks (Nelson, 1995). Bell and Wolfe (2007) measured EEG activity in a sample of 53 infants at 8 months of age while performing a passive A-not-B task. For 43 of these infants, EEG recordings were taken again at the age 4.5 years of age as they performed the Day-Night Stroop task. Findings from EEG power and coherence analyses showed that during infancy, brain activity is widespread; however, as children mature this cortical functioning becomes more localized in the frontal regions.

Taken together, these findings suggest that working memory may be available to support children's learning and development much earlier than originally conceived. Although the application of such findings from brain research to social settings, particularly educational settings, has intuitive appeal to caregivers and early childhood educators, there are several reasons to be cautious in this approach. Unfortunately, despite a clear gap between findings from basic science and their direct application, a plethora of commercial programs and packages based on the construct of "brain-based learning" are available for use in preschool contexts. Use of these programs and materials is usually justified by the publishers through the use of prevailing "neuromyths," information that is presented inaccurately as scientific fact (for a review, see Goswami, 2006).

One neuromyth is that intervention-related increases in brain activity found in the prefrontal regions (i.e., associated with working memory) has sufficient stability to affect reasoning across a broad range of working memory tasks. Whether the neural systems associated with working memory in humans are plastic for children of all ages is unknown (Olesen, Westerberg, & Klingberg, 2004). Further, most of the work that has attempted to alter neural activity associated with working memory has been conducted in studies with nonhuman primates. For example, Rainer and Miller (2002) trained macaques with increasingly more difficult delayed response tasks over several weeks; task difficulty was controlled by gradually degrading the salience of the computer-generated, visual stimulus. Findings showed that repeated practice of the tasks led to changes in the receptive neuronal characteristics in the regions near the principal sulcus in the prefrontal cortex. Among human adults, experimental evidence exists to suggest that increased activity in the prefrontal and parietal regions occurs after repeated practice on computerized, working memory tasks over a 5-week-period (Olesen et al., 2004). However, what is often overlooked in the interpretation of such findings is that any form of repeated practice will be reflected in changes in brain activity; the question is whether the observed increases in neural circuitry associated on computer-generated tasks translates to meaningful changes in the working memory system that underlies children's engagement in activities encountered in their social lives.

A study conducted by Rueda and her colleagues (Rueda, Rothbart, McCandliss, Saccamanno, & Posner, 2005) on the effects of training of working memory and attention in preschoolers is illustrative of this issue. The training exercises used in the study were modeled after those used to train rhesus macaques for space travel to improve stimulus discrimination, anticipation, and conflict resolution. On one working memory task, children were asked to pick the larger of two arrays of digits presented on a computer screen; interference was included by using smaller digits in the larger array. On another computerized working memory task, children manipulated a cat character in a game of tag with a duck. The duck presented challenges for the cat, such as diving into a pond, only to resurface some distance away. For the child who was controlling the cat to tag the duck, the place where the duck was about to surface was anticipated using information gained observing previous dives. Difficulty of the task was manipulated by controlling the delay between the duck's disappearance and resurfacing, and by varying the time between the entry into the pool and the resurfacing of the duck. A conflict task was administered in each session before and after training to assess children's ability to switch attention (without perseverating). Subtests on an intelligence test were also administered before intervention and 5 days after intervention. Control children did not receive matched computer training; rather, they watched videos for five sessions in the research laboratory. Even when compared to a no-treatment control, the effects of the training on children's control of attention were not statistically detectable. Performance of the 4-year-old children on measures of nonverbal intelligence test improved after training (Ravens Matrices and Kauffman nonverbal IQ); however, since the tests were administered only 5 days apart, these gains in performance were likely attributable to item familiarity and a practice effect. Subsequent EEG data showed that the training changed brain activity of the 6-year-olds in the anterior cingulate in a way that matched that of adults; for 4-year-olds, the effect was marginal. On the basis of these results, the authors argue that "training improves executive attention in a way that also generalizes to aspects of intelligence" (Posner & Rothbart, 2005, p. 101). This claim may be premature in light of the study's methodological limitations. Moreover, it seems unlikely that the effects of repeated practice on narrowly conceived, static computerized task will generalize to the more broadly construed, fluid reasoning required during more complex forms of social activity.

Having stated these limitations, basic research on the plasticity of the biological processes may shed light on the optimal times when children's early experience mediates change in a working memory system. Also, although the application of brain research on working memory to preschool education has yet to be empirically validated, there are important reasons to continue with this avenue of research. Neuroimaging techniques may help to resolve inconsistencies in behavioral research findings, such as determining the source of individual differences in performance of preschool academic or social activities that reportedly require working memory. Another important goal for future research will be to clarify how children's interactions with their caregivers, teachers, and peers influence and are influenced by development of the neural systems that underlie expansion of working memory capacity.

Conclusion

In summary, whether viewed from a constructivist or an information processing perspective, working memory is defined as a capacity to attend to mental representations stored in long-term memory, to inhibit irrelevant information, and to either prereflexively or reflexively monitor the products of processing. Coordination of these core executive processes are thought to contribute to planning, inductive reasoning, and flexible, strategic problem-solving, all of which support young children as they attempt to read the intentions of others and/or to achieve future-oriented goals during social communication (Welsh, Friedman, & Spieker, 2006). Scaffolding of infant or child participation within social communication may moderate constraints in working memory capacity by bracketing actions into manageable chunks, by providing resources in the form of cues and prompts to aid the creation of stable mental representations, and by creating interest and enthusiasm. Through collaborative and supported communication, children are provided with opportunities to become proficient in strategies to support attention to the intentions, goal states, and actions of others that they eventually internalize and transform to become their own. These improvements in children's ability to attend to and formulate figurative schemes in working memory (i.e., a constructivist interpretation), or improvements in general processing within the working memory executive system (i.e., an information-processing interpretation) are theoretically associated with plasticity in working memory capacity. Whether performance gains on narrowly defined, computerized working memory tasks after repeated practice are stable over time or whether this improved performance generalizes to new tasks in diverse social settings has not been determined; further research is needed to define the validity of links between working memory tasks and real world social activities. Further, basic research involving neuroimaging techniques has considerable potential to clarify the times in children's development when the working memory system is most stable, or most plastic and open to change.

REFERENCES

Austin, J. L. (1962). *How to do things with words.* Oxford, UK: The Clarendon Press.

Baddeley, A. D. (1986). *Working memory.* Oxford, UK: The Clarendon Press.

Baddeley, A. D. (2000). The episodic buffer: A new component of working memory? *Trends in Cognitive Sciences, 4,* 417–422.

Baddeley, A. D. (2003). Working memory: Looking back and looking forward. *Nature Reviews, 4*(10), 829–839.

Baddeley, A. D., & Hitch, G. J. (1974).Working Memory. In G. A. Bower (Ed.), *Recent advances in learning and motivation* (pp. 47–89). New York: Academic Press.

Baddeley, A. D., & Logie, R. H. (1999). The multiple-component model. In A. Miyake & P. Shah (Eds.), *Models of working memory: Mechanisms of active maintenance and executive control* (pp. 28–61). Cambridge, England: Cambridge University Press.

Barrett, L. F., Tugade, M. M., & Engle, R. W. (2004). Individual differences in working memory capacity and dual-process theories of the mind. *Psychological Bulletin, 130*(4), 553–573.

Bargh, J. A., & Ferguson, M. J. (2000). Beyond behaviorism: On the automaticity of higher mental processes. *Psychological Bulletin, 126,* 925–945.

Bates, E. (1976). *Language, thought, and culture: The acquisition of pragmatics.* New York: Academic Press.

Bates, E., Camaioni, L., & Volterra, V. (1975). The acquisition of performatives prior to speech. *Merrill-Palmer Quarterly, 21,* 205–224.

Bauer, P. J. (1992). Holding it all together: How enabling relations facilitate young children's event recall. *Cognitive Development, 7,* 1–28.

Bauer, P. J., & Kleinknecht, E. E. (2002). To "ape" or to emulate? Young children's use of both strategies in a single study. *Developmental Science, 5*(1), 18–20.

Bell, M. (2001). Brain electrical activity associated with cognitive processing during a looking version of the A not B task. *Infancy, 2,* 311–330.

Bell, M., & Fox, N. A. (1992). The relations between frontal brain electrical activity and cognitive development during infancy. *Child Development, 63*, 1142–1163.

Bell, M., & Wolfe, C. D. (2007). Changes in brain functioning from infancy to early childhood: Evidence from EEG power and coherence during working memory tasks. *Developmental Neuropsychology, 31*(1), 21–38.

Bishop, D. V. M. (2000). How does the brain learn language? Insights from the study of children with and without language impairment. *Developmental Medicine and Child Neurology, 42*, 133–142.

Budson, A. E., & Price, B. H. (2005). Memory dysfunction. *The New England Journal of Medicine, 352*(7), 692–699.

Cantor, J., & Engle, R. W. (1993). Working memory capacity as long-term memory and verbal abilities: How do they relate? *Intelligence, 15*, 229–246.

Cantor, J., Engle, R. W., & Hamilton, G. (1992). Short-term memory, working memory and verbal abilities: How do they relate? *Intelligence, 15*, 229–246.

Carslon, S. M., & Moses, L. (2001). Individual differences in children's inhibitory control and theory of mind. *Child Development, 72*, 1032–1053.

Carlson, S. M., Moses, L., & Breton, C. (2002). How specific is the relation between executive function and theory of mind? Contributions of inhibitory control and working memory. *Infant and Child Development, 11*, 73–92.

Carpendale, J., & Lewis, C. (2004). Constructing an understanding of mind: The development of children's social understanding within social interaction. *Behavioral and Brain Sciences, 27*, 79–151.

Carpenter, M., Akhtar, N., & Tomasello, M. (1998). Fourteen- through 18-month-old infants differentially imitate intentional and accidental actions. *Infant Behavior and Development, 21*(2), 315–330.

Case, R. (1972). Validation of a neo-Piagetian capacity construct. *Journal of Experimental Child Psychology, 14*, 287–302.

Case, R. (1985). *Intellectual development: Birth to adulthood.* New York: Academic Press.

Case, R. (1995). Capacity-based explanations of working memory growth: A brief history and reevaluation. In F. E. Weinert & W. Schneider (Eds.), *Memory performances and competencies: Issues in growth and development* (pp. 23–44). Mahwah, NJ: Lawrence Erlbaum Associates.

Case, R., Kurland, D. M., & Goldberg, J. (1982). Operational efficiency and the growth of short-term memory span. *Journal of Experimental Child Psychology, 33*, 386–404.

Cepeda, N. J., & Munakata, Y. (2007). Why do children perseverate when they seem to know better: Graded working memory, or directed inhibition? *Psychonomic Bulletin & Review, 14*(6), 1058–1065.

Christiansen, M. H., & Chater, N. (2001). Connectionist psycholinguistics: Capturing the empirical data. *Trends in Cognitive Sciences, 5*, 82–88.

Collie, R., & Hayne, H. (1999). Deferred imitation by 6- and 9-month-old infants: More evidence for declarative memory. *Developmental Psychobiology, 35*(2), 83–90.

Conway, A. R., Kane, M. J., Bunting, M. F., Hambrick, D. Z., Wilhelm, O., & Engle, R. W. (2005). Working memory span tasks: A methodological review and user's guide. *Psychonomic Bulletin & Review, 12*(5), 769–786.

De Ribaupierre, A., & Bailleux, C. (2000). The development of working memory: Further note on the comparability of two models of working memory. *Journal of Experimental Child Psychology, 77*, 110–127.

Diamond, A. (1991). Neuropsychological insights into the meaning of object concept development. In S. Carey & R. Gelman (Eds.), *The epigenesis of mind: Essays on biology and cognition* (pp. 67–110). Hillsdale, NJ: Lawrence Erlbaum Associates.

Diamond, A., Carlson, S., & Beck, D. (2005). Preschool children's performance in task switching on the Dimensional Change Card Sort task: Separating the dimensions aids the ability to switch. *Developmental Neuropsychology, 28*(2), 689–729.

Diamond, A., Kirkham, N., & Amso, D. (2002). Conditions under which young children can hold two rules in mind and inhibit a prepotent response. *Developmental Psychology, 38*, 352–362.

Engle, R. (2002). Working memory capacity as executive function. *Current Directions in Psychological Science, 11*, 19–23.

Flavell, J. H. (1994). Cognitive development: Past, present and future. In R. E. Ross, P. A. Ornstein, J. J. Rieser, & C. Zahn-Waxler (Eds.), *A century of developmental psychology* (pp. 569–587). Washington, DC: American Psychological Association.

Frith, C. D., & Frith, U. (1999). Interacting minds—A biological basis. *Science, 286*, 1692–1695.

Frye, D., Zelazo, P. D., & Palfai, T. (1995). Theory of mind and rule-based reasoning. *Cognitive Development, 10*, 483–527.

Gathercole, S. E., & Alloway, T. P. (2006). Practitioner review: Short-term and working memory impairments in neurodevelopmental disorders: Diagnosis and remedial support. *Journal of Child Psychology and Psychiatry, 47*(1), 4–15.

Gathercole, S. E., Pickering, S. J., Ambridge, B., & Wearing, H. (2004). The structure of working memory from 4 to 15 years of age. *Developmental Psychology, 40*(2), 177–190.

Gathercole, S. E., Tiffany, C., Briscoe, J., Thorn, A., & ALSPAC team. (2005). Developmental consequences of poor phonological short-term memory function in childhood: a longitudinal study. *Journal of Child Psychology and Psychiatry, 46*(6), 598–611.

Gerstadt, C. I., Hong, Y. J., & Diamond, A. (1994). The relationship between cognition and action: Performance of children 3 ½ –7 years old on a Stroop-like daylight test. *Cognition, 53*, 129–153.

Girolametto, L., Hoaken, L., Weitzman, E., & van Lieshout, R. (2000). Patterns of adult-child linguistic interaction in integrated day care groups. *Language, Speech, and Hearing Services in the Schools, 31*, 155–158.

Goldman-Rakic, P. S. (1987). Circuitry of primate prefrontal cortex and regulation of behaviour by representational memory. In F. Plum (Ed.), *Handbook of physiology, the nervous system, higher functions of the brain* (Vol. 5, pp. 373–417). Bethesda, MD: American Physiological Society.

Goswami, U. (2006). Neuroscience and education: From research to practice? *Nature Reviews Neuroscience,7*(5), 2–7.

Hanauer, J. B., & Brooks, P. J. (2005). Contributions of response set and semantic relatedness to cross-modal Stroop-like picture-word interference in children and adults. *Journal of Experimental Child Psychology, 90,* 21–47.

Hasher, L., & Zacks, R. (1988). Working memory, comprehension, and aging: A review and a new view. In G. H. Bower (Ed.), *The psychology of learning and motivation* (Vol. 22, pp. 193–226). New York: Academic Press.

Heimann, M., Strid, K., Smith, L., Tjus, T., Ulvund, S. E., & Meltzoff, A. N. (2006). Exploring the relation between memory, gestural communication, and the emergence of language in infancy: A longitudinal study. *Infant and Child Development, 15,* 233–249.

Herbert, J., Gross, J., & Hayne, H. (2006). Age-related changes in deferred imitation between 6 and 9 months of age. *Infant Behavior & Development, 29*(1), 136–139.

Hitch, G. J., & Towse, J. N. (1995). Working memory: What develops? In W. Schneider & F. E. Weinert (Eds.), *Memory performance and competencies* (pp. 3–21). Hillsdale, NJ: Lawrence Erlbaum Associates.

Hoskyn, M. J., & Tzoneva, I. (2008). Relations between working memory and emergent writing among preschool-aged children. *Exceptionality Education Canada.18*(1), *33–58*

Hoskyn, M. J., & Swanson, H. L. (2003). The relationship between working memory and writing in older and younger adults. *Reading and Writing: An Interdisciplinary Journal, 16*(8), 759–784.

Iacoboni, M. (2005). Neural mechanisms of imitation. *Current Opinion in Neurobiology, 15,* 632–637.

Jacob, P., & Jeannerod, M. (2005). The motor theory of social cognition: A critique. *Trends Cognitive Science, 9,* 21–25.

Just, M., & Carpenter, P. A. (1992). A capacity theory of comprehension differences in working memory. *Psychological Review, 99,* 122–149.

Kail, R. (1997). Phonological skill and articulation time independently contribute to the development of memory span. *Journal of Experimental Child Psychology, 67,* 57–68.

Kail, R., & Park, Y. (1994). Processing time, articulation time, and memory span. *Journal of Experimental Child Psychology, 57,* 281–291.

Kaldy, Z., & Leslie, A. M. (2003). Identification of objects in 9-month-old infants: Integrating "what" and "where" information. *Developmental Science, 6,* 360–373.

Kaldy, Z., & Leslie, A. M. (2005). A memory span of one? Object identification in 6.5-month-old infants. *Cognition, 97,* 153–177.

Kaldy, Z., & Sigala, N. (2004). The neural mechanisms of object working memory: What is where in the infant brain? *Neuroscience and Biobehavioral Reviews, 28,* 113–121.

Keller, H. (2003). Socialization for competence. *Human Development, 46*, 288–311.

Kemps, E., De Rammelaere, S., & Desmet, T. (2000). The development of working memory: Exploring the complimentarity of two models. *Journal of Experimental Child Psychology, 77*, 89–109.

Kilner, J. M., & Frith, C. D. (2008). Action observation: Inferring intention without mirror neurons. *Current Biology, 18*(1), R32–R33.

Kirkham, N. Z., Cruess, L., & Diamond, A. (2003). Helping children apply their knowledge to their behavior on a dimension-switching task. *Developmental Science, 6*, 449–467.

Kirkham, N. Z., & Diamond, A. (2003). Sorting between theories of perseveration: Performance in conflict tasks requires memory, attention, and inhibition. *Developmental Science, 6*, 474–476.

Klingberg, T. (2006). Development of a superior frontal-interparietal network for visuo-spatial working memory. *Neuropsychologia, 44*, 2171–2177.

Klingberg, T., Forssberg, H., & Westerberg, H. (2002). Increased brain activity in frontal and parietal cortex underlies the development of visuospatial working memory capacity during childhood. *Journal of Cognitive Neuroscience, 14*(1), 1–10.

Landry, S. H., Miller-Loncar, C. L., Smith, K. E., & Swank, P. R. (2002). The role of early parenting on children's development of executive processes. *Developmental Neuropsychology, 21*(1), 15–41.

Leung, H. C., Gore, J. C., & Goldman-Rakic, P. S. (2005). Differential anterior prefrontal activation during the recognition stage of a spatial working memory task. *Cerebral Cortex, 15*(11), 1742–1749.

Liszkowski, U., Carpenter, M., Henning, A., Striano, T., & Tomasello, M. (2004). Twelve-month-olds point to share attention and interest. *Developmental Science, 7*(3), 297–307.

MacDonald, M. C., & Christiansen, M. H. (2002). Reassessing working memory: Comment on Just and Carpenter (1992) and Waters and Kaplan (1996). *Psychological Review, 109*(1), 35–54.

MacDonald, P. (2003). *History of the concept of mind: Speculations about soul, mind and spirit from Homer to Hume*. Burlington, VT: Ashgate.

Mecklinger, A., Bosch, V., Gruenwald, C., Bentin, S., & von Cramon, D. Y. (2000). What have klingon letters and faces have in common? An fMRI study on content-specific working memory systems. *Human Brain Mapping, 11*, 146–161.

Meltzoff, A. N. (1995). Understanding the intentions of others: Re-enactment of intended acts by 18-month-old children. *Developmental Psychology, 31*, 838–850.

Moriguchi, Y., & Itakhura, S. (2005). Effect of conflicting and no conflicting cues on a rule-switching task. *Psychological Reports, 96*, 1049–1056.

Morton, J. B., & Munakata, Y. (2002). Active versus latent representations: A neural network model of perseveration and dissociation in early childhood. *Developmental Psychobiology, 40*, 255–265.

Müller, U., Dick, A. S., Gela, K., Overton, W. F., & Zelazo, P. D. (2007). The role of negative priming in preschoolers' flexible rule use on the Dimensional Change Card Sort task. *Child Development, 77*(2), 395–412.

Müller, U., Zelazo, P. D., Hood, S., Leone, T., & Rohrer, L. (2004). Interference control in a new rule use task: Age-related changes, labeling, and attention. *Child Development, 75*(5), 1594–1609.

Munakata, Y. (2004). Computational cognitive neuroscience of early memory development. *Developmental Review, 24,* 133–153.

Nelson, C. A. (1995). The ontogeny of human memory: A cognitive neuroscience perspective. *Developmental Psychology, 31*(5), 723–738.

Nelson, C. A., Monk, C. S., Lin, J., Carver, L. J., Thomas, K. M., & Truwit, C. L. (2000). Functional neuroanatomy of spatial working memory in children. *Developmental Psychology, 36,* 109–116.

Olesen, P. J., Westerberg, H., & Klingberg, T. (2004). Increased prefrontal and parietal activity after training of working memory. *Nature Neuroscience, 7*(1), 75–79.

O'Reilly, R. C., Braver, T. S., & Cohen, J. D. (1999). A biologically based computational model of working memory. In A. Miyake & P. Shah (Eds.), *Models of working memory: Mechanisms of active maintenance and executive control* (pp. 375–411). New York: Cambridge University Press.

Pascual-Leone, J. (1987). Organismic processes for neo-Piagetian theories: A dialectical causal account of cognitive development. *International Journal of Psychology, 22,* 531–570.

Pascual-Leone, J. (1989). An organismic process model of Witkin's field-dependence-independence. In T. Globerson & T. Zelniker (Eds.), *Cognitive style and cognitive development* (pp. 36–70). Norwood, NJ: Ablex.

Pascual-Leone, J., & Ijaz, I. (1989). Mental capacity testing as a form of intellectual-developmental assessment. In R. J. Samuda, S. L. Kong, J. Cummins, J. Pascual-Leone, & J. Lewis (Eds.), *Assessment and placement of minority students* (pp. 143–171). Toronto: C. J. Hogrefe.

Perlmutter, M., Behrend, S. D., Kuo, F., & Muller, A. (1989). Social influences on children's problem solving. *Developmental Psychology, 25,* 744–754.

Piaget, J. (1962). *Play, dreams, and imitation in childhood.* New York: Norton.

Posner, M. I., & Rothbart, M. K. (2005). Influencing brain networks: Implications for education. *Trends in Cognitive Sciences, 9*(3), 99–103.

Pushina, N. N., Orekhova, E. V., & Stroganova, T. A. (2005). Age-related and individual differences in the performance of a delayed response task (the A-not-B task) in infant twins aged 7–12 months. *Neuroscience and Behavioral Physiology, 35*(5), 481–491.

Rainer, G., & Miller, E. K. (2002). Timecourse of object-related neural activity in the primate prefrontal cortex during a short-term memory task. *European Journal of Neuroscience, 15*(7), 1244–1254.

Ratner, H. H., Foley, M. A., & Gimpert, N. (2002). The role of collaborative planning in children's source-monitoring errors and learning. *Journal of Experimental Child Psychology, 81,* 44–73.

Rennie, D., Bull, R., & Diamond, A. (2004). Executive functioning in preschoolers: Reducing the inhibitory demands of the Dimensional Change Card Sort task. *Developmental Neuropsychology, 26*(1), 423–443.

Reznick, J. S., Morrow, J. D., Goldman, B. D., & Snyder, J. (2004). The onset of working memory in infants. *Infancy, 6*(1), 145–154.

Rizzolatti, G., & Craighero, L. (2004). The mirror-neuron system. *Annual Review of Neuroscience, 27,* 169–192.

Roodenrys, S., Hulme, C., & Brown, G. (1993). The development of short term memory span: Separable effects of speech rate and long-term memory. *Journal of Experimental Child Psychology, 56,* 431–442.

Rothbart, M. K., Posner, M. I., & Kieras, J. (2006). Temperament, attention and the development of self-regulation. In K. McCartney & D. Phillips (Eds.), *Handbook of early childhood development* (pp. 167–187). New York: Blackwell Publishing.

Rueda, M. R., Posner, M. I., & Rothbart, M. (2005). The development of executive attention: Contributions to the emergence of self-regulation. *Developmental Neuropsychology, 28*(2), 573–594.

Rueda, M. R., Rothbart, M. R., McCandliss, B., Saccamanno, L., & Posner, M. (2005). Training, maturation and genetic influences on the development of executive attention. *Proceedings of the National Academy of Sciences of the USA, 102*(4), 14931–14936.

Savage, R., Cornish, K., Manly, T., & Hollis, C. (2006). Cognitive processes in children's reading and attention: The role of working memory, divided attention and response inhibition. *British Journal of Psychology, 97,* 365–385.

Searle, J. (1998). *Mind, language, and society: Philosophy in the real world.* New York: Basic Books.

Spence, K. W. (1937). Experimental studies of learning and higher mental processes in infra-human primates. *Psychological Bulletin, 34,* 806–850.

Stredon, J. M., Sahni, S. D., & Munakata, Y. (2005). Common mechanisms for working memory and attention: The case of perseveration with visible solutions. *Journal of Cognitive Neuroscience, 17*(4), 623–631.

Swanson, H. L. (1999). What develops in working memory? A lifespan perspective. *Developmental Psychology, 35*(4), 986–1000.

Swanson, H. L., & Ashbaker M. H. (2000). Working memory, short term memory, speech rate, word recognition, and reading comprehension in learning disabled readers: Does the executive system have a role? *Intelligence, 28*(1), 1–30.

Tomasello, M. (1998). Emulation learning and cultural learning. *Behavioural and Brain Sciences, 21,* 703–704.

Tomasello, M. (1999). *The cultural origins of human cognition.* Cambridge, MA: Harvard University Press.

Tomasello, M. (2003). *Constructing a language: A usage-based theory of language acquisition.* Cambridge, MA: Harvard University Press.

Turner, M. L., & Engle, R. W. (1989). Is working memory capacity task dependent? *Journal of Memory and Language, 28,* 127–154.

Vos, S. H., Gunter, T. C., Kolk, H. J., & Mulder, G.. (2001). Working memory constraints on syntactic processing: An electrophysiological investigation. *Psychophysiology, 38,* 41–63.

Vuontela, V., Steenari, M., Carlson, S., Koivisto, J., Fjallberge, M., & Aronen, E. T. (2003). Audiospatial and visuospatial working memory in 6–13 year old school children. *Learning and Memory, 10,* 74–81.

Vygotsky, L. (1978). Mind in society: The development of higher psychological processes. In M. Cole (Ed.). Cambridge, MA: Harvard University Press.

Want, S. C., & Harris, P. L. (2002). How do children ape? Applying concepts from the study of non-human primates to the developmental study of "imitation" in children. *Developmental Science, 5*(1), 1–41.

Welsh, M. C., Friedman, S., & Spieker, S. J. (2006). Executive functions in developing children: Current conceptualizations and questions for the future. In K. McCartney & D. Phillips (Eds.), *Handbook of Early Childhood Development* (pp. 167–187). New York: Blackwell Publishing.

Whiten, A., & Ham, R. (1992). On the nature and evolution of imitation in the animal kingdom: Reappraisal of a century of research. *Advances in the Study of Behaviour, 21,* 239–283.

Wilson, F. A. W., O'Scalaidhe, S. P., & Goldman-Rakic, P. S. (1993). Dissociation of object and spatial processing domains in primate prefrontal cortex. *Science, 260,* 1955–1958.

Wittgenstein, L., & Waismann, F. (2003). *The voices of Wittgenstein.* England: Routledge.

Wood, D., Bruner, J., & Ross, G. (1976). The role of tutoring in problem-solving. *Journal of Child Psychology and Psychiatry, 17,* 89–100.

Woodward, A. (1998). Infants selectively encode the goal object of an actor's reach. *Cognition, 69,* 1–34.

Woodward, A., & Sommerville, J. A. (2000). Twelve-month-old infants interpret action in context. *Psychological Science, 11*(1), 73–77.

Yerys, B. E., & Munakata, Y. (2006). When labels hurt but novelty helps: Children's perseveraton and flexibility in a card-sorting task. *Child Development, 77*(6), 1589–1607.

Yoder, P. J., Warren, S. F., McCathern, R., & Leew, S. (1998). Does adult responsivity to child behaviour facilitate communicative development? In A. Wetherby, S. Warren, & J. Reichle (Eds.), *Transitions in prelinguistic communication* (Vol. 7, pp. 39–58). Baltimore: Paul H. Brookes.

Zelazo, P. D. (2006). Implications of a 3-year-olds' successful performance on a no conflict version of the Dimensional Change Card Sort. *Psychological Reports, 98,* 858–860.

Zelazo, P. D., & Frye, D. (1997). Cognitive complexity and control: A theory of development of deliberate reasoning and intentional action. In M. Stamenov (Ed.), *Language, structure, and access to consciousness* (pp. 113–153). Philadelphia, PA: Benjamins.

Zelazo, P. D., Frye, D., & Rapus, T. (1996). An age-related dissociation between knowing rules and using them. *Cognitive Development, 11,* 37–63.

Zelazo, P. D., & Jacques, S. (1996). Children's rule-use: Representation, reflection, and control. *Annals of Child Development, 12,* 119–176.

Zelazo, P. D., & Jacques, S. (1996). Children's rule use: Representation, reflection, and cognitive control. In R. Vasta (Ed.), *Annals of child development* (pp. 119–176). London: Jessica Kingsley.

Zelazo, P. D., Müeller, U., Frye, D., & Marcovitch, S. (2003). The development of executive function in early childhood. *Monographs of the Society for Research in Child Development, 68*, 1–137.

PART II

Social Understanding and Self-Regulation: From Perspective-Taking to Theory of Mind and Back

BRYAN W. SOKOL, JAMES ALLEN, SNJEZANA HUERTA,
AND ULRICH MÜLLER

Although the theme of social understanding, in one form or another, runs through every chapter of this volume, the particular contributions to the present part illustrate the diverse directions that research in this area may take. The term social understanding, itself, grows out of mounting concern (Carpendale & Lewis, 2004) that developmental research, particularly in the theories-of-mind literature, takes an overly narrow approach to investigating the ways that children experience, reflect upon, and grow within their social worlds. The wide scope of research questions addressed in this part serves, in many ways, as a response to this concern. The topics range from more central aspects of social understanding, at least traditionally speaking, such as theory of mind (e.g., Moses & Tahiroglu, this volume), to more marginal, but clearly still related, topics of executive functioning (e.g., Kloo, Perner, & Giritzer, this volume), selfhood (e.g., Moore, this volume), and the relations between perspective taking and prosocial behavior (e.g., Carlo, Knight, McGinley, Goodvin, & Roesch, this volume).

As important as such diversity and breadth may be, the contributions here also represent something of an irony, at least for anyone acquainted with the historical circumstances surrounding the emergence of the contemporary theories-of-mind enterprise. In the late 1970s and mid-1980s, when theories-of-mind research had captured the collective imagination of developmental psychology (e.g., Astington, Harris, & Olson, 1988; Premack & Woodruff, 1978; Wimmer & Perner, 1983), the then-dominant approach to the study of children's social-cognition was closely tied to Piagetian notions of perspective taking. Then—much like now—dissatisfaction with the narrowness of the dominant approach, particularly Piaget's heavy cognitivist and structuralist assumptions, was on the rise. The theory-of-mind framework, with its eclectic theoretical orientation (e.g., drawing from comparative psychology, analytic philosophy, and cognitive science, to name just a few), presented an attractive alternative—one that quickly eclipsed anything having to do with perspective taking. Over the next two decades, however, the pioneering conceptual and methodological innovations that initially characterized the theory-of-mind landscape grew ever more sparse, until eventually only one nubbin of an idea remained—children's false belief understanding, or the so-called litmus test (Wellman, 1990) for possessing a theory of mind. The enduring quality of this idea is evident even in the present chapters, despite prevailing sentiments that false belief understanding amounts to just one socio-cognitive milestone on a much longer developmental journey. Nevertheless, and here the present irony is compounded, not only do contributors to the present section enlist broad notions of social understanding to combat any potential charges of narrowness, they do so by often turning (or, perhaps better, "returning") to the more timeworn matters of perspective taking.

Although perspective taking has held a variety of definitions (for further discussion, see Martin, Sokol, & Elfers, 2008), it is generally understood to characterize how individuals coordinate and integrate their own understanding of a situation in relation to others'. Developmentally speaking, such understanding may include prereflective forms of coordinated intersubjective activity (again, see Martin et al., 2008), but, more typically, it is framed as a psychological, or reflective, "ability to 'put oneself in the place of' another person and to make inferences concerning the [other] ...." (Light, 1979, pp. 9–10). The present set of chapters makes use of perspective taking in this reflective, or mentalistic, sense, especially to capture the cognitive processes involved in children's theory-of-mind abilities. Moses and Tahiroglu remark, for instance, that theory of mind boils down to "the ability to appreciate the *perspectives* of others" (p. 2; emphasis added), just as Moore indicates that successful false belief understanding involves "recognizing the relation between ... *two perspectives*" (p. 22; emphasis added). Similarly, in proposing their "redescription hypothesis," Kloo et al. argue that the relation between executive functions and theory of mind revolves around children's ability to "understand that one and the same thing can be described differently under *different perspectives*" (p. 3; emphasis added). Perhaps all of this suggests the obvious, as Carlo et al. comment, "that theory of mind and perspective taking are conceptually linked" (p. 2). Still, the question of precisely "*how* they are linked" remains open. In the following discussion, we will see that there are several ways to elaborate on such a conceptual linkage. Before we come to this, however, it is important to draw out another common thread from these contributions.

The chapters in this part each, in their own way, attempt to identify and analyze the basic constituent parts of social experience and social understanding. In doing so, they reveal a heavy "cognitivist" orientation—or "psychologized" tendency (see Hammond, Bibok, & Carpendale's commentary for further discussion)—to breaking down individuals' social worlds. To be fair, however, such cognitivism is more a by-product of formalizing the features of social understanding than a reductionistic attempt to privilege only the "cognitive half" of social-cognition. In fact, the prospect that the whole of children's social understanding might converge on a single cognitive mechanism is all but ruled out in these chapters. This is seen most clearly in the chapters exploring how changes in children's theory-of-mind abilities are functionally related to executive functioning skills (i.e., Kloo et al.; Moses & Tahiroglu). Although empirical support for the relation between theory of mind and executive functioning is well established, several theoretical possibilities remain as to how this relation may be explained (for discussion, see Frye, 1999; Perner & Lang, 1999). The chapter by Moses and Tahiroglu, in particular, discusses four theoretical possibilities: (1) a theory of mind may be instrumental in the development of executive functioning; (2) executive functions may make possible the expression of a previously developed theory of mind; (3) executive functions may be necessary for the emergence of a theory of mind; and (4) theory of mind and executive functions may both draw from the same underlying, domain-general, cognitive structure, such as the ability to reason with hierarchically embedded rules (Kloo et al. also discuss options 1 and 4 from this list), that is necessary for the development of each. Given that evidence for these various theoretical possibilities is mixed, Moses and Tahiroglu conclude that none of them can be completely ruled out. Ultimately, they suggest that a complete understanding of the relations between theory of mind and executive functioning may include aspects from all four.

The richness and complexity of the relations between theory of mind and executive functioning shares many of the same features that Carlo et al. draw out in their analysis of perspective taking and prosocial behavior. In fact, Carlo et al. use a similar analytic strategy in breaking down each of these multidimensional phenomena into their more basic parts, and then, reexamining the relations between them. Specifically, they argue that perspective taking consists of three main types: (1) social-cognitive perspective taking, or understanding another's thoughts and intentions; (2) affective perspective taking, or understanding the emotional state of another; and (3) perceptual-spatial perspective taking, or the ability to understand another's visual point of view. They go on to suggest that prosocial behavior must also be viewed through a similar multidimensional lens and argue that greater care should be taken in how aspects of perspective taking are potentially matched with different prosocial behaviors. As Carlo (2006) has suggested elsewhere, "the differentiation of prosocial behaviours is needed to ... better explain prior inconsistent empirical relations between prosocial behaviours and theoretically relevant correlates" (p. 555; for a similar argument, see Lalonde & Chandler, 1995). Building on these claims, Carlo et al. provide an important critique of Underwood and Moore's (1982) now classic meta-analysis showing only a very modest correlation between perspective taking and prosocial behavior. They argue, in particular, that Underwood and Moore's (1982) findings may be the result of a lack of task specificity between different measures of perspective taking and prosocial behavior. In their own follow-up meta-analysis, Carlo et al. attempt to match these measures according to three broad dimensions: (1) the level of emotionality, (2) the physical similarities of the other person, and (3) the level of assessment (global or specific). Consistent with their task specificity hypothesis, they find that the magnitude of the relationship between perspective taking and prosocial behavior is greater when measures are appropriately matched. Moreover, they find that the relation between them is strongest during middle childhood and early adolescence.

Researchers exploring other aspects of social understanding would do well to heed Carlo et al.'s concerns about task specificity, particularly given the variability of results that characterize the relation between theory of mind and executive functioning. Kloo et al. seemed to be especially attuned to this issue when, citing Towse, Redbond, Houston-Price, and Cook (2000, pp. 348–349), they note that executive functions "is a term so broad as to lose meaning." To address this concern, researchers have begun to approach executive functions using finer-grained analytic strategies. Some, for instance, have begun to distinguish between "hot" and "cool" levels of emotionality in executive functioning tasks (e.g., Zelazo & Müller, 2002; Zelazo, Qu, & Müller, 2005), noting that certain measures of executive functions differentially tap motivational-affective (hot) and cognitive-representational (cool) control centers of the brain. Others, like Kloo et al., have tried to show how some of the more diverse aspects of executive functioning might be consolidated (Lehto, Juujärvi, Kooistra, & Pulkkinen, 2003; Miyake, Friedman, Emerson, Witzki, & Howerter, 2000). In this regard, Kloo et al. describe how object based set shifting, or the ability to switch between different ways of thinking about objects, may involve at least two other executive functioning skills: (1) understanding how the same object may be described differently from different perspectives, and (2) inhibiting previous ways of describing an object in order to generate new descriptions. The study that they present explores both skills and ultimately concludes that neither alone is sufficient to explain the development of set shifting.

A clear account of set shifting abilities, or what is sometimes referred to as representational flexibility, is further complicated by the fact that at least two different forms can be identified. That is, insofar as set shifting may occur sequentially or simultaneously, two different processes of coordinating representational content may be involved. Drawing on Perner, Stummer, Sprung, and Doherty's (2002) theory of perspective, these two processes have been called: "*switching perspectives* (taking different perspectives at different times) and *confronting perspectives* (representing two perspectives simultaneously; understanding that there are different perspectives)" (p. 1466). The former process of switching perspectives is implicated in many rule use tasks that are used to assess executive functioning in preschool children. For example, in a variant of the common childhood game "Simon Says" called the Bear-Dragon task, children are instructed to execute an action when one puppet (the Bear) utters a command and to refrain from the action when commanded by the other puppet (the Dragon). To be successful at this task, children need only to sequentially switch from one representation of the situation (e.g., Bear) to a different representation (e.g., Dragon), and regulate their behavior accordingly. On the other hand, in standard measures of false belief understanding, such as the classic "Maxi" task, two perspectives are brought into conflict with one another (e.g., the privileged perspective of the participant and the inaccurate perspective of Maxi, the story protagonist). To be successful at this task, children must simultaneously coordinate, and, as Perner et al. (2002) describe, "integrate in a single representation" (p. 1466), the two divergent perspectives each party holds.

Future-oriented decision-making, particularly of the kind that Moore describes in his chapter, also involves simultaneously coordinating and successfully integrating two perspectives, although, in this case, the perspectives are situated across time. That is, future-oriented decision-making involves the awareness of two temporal modes by which an imagined future event is made present by being represented as an event that will be perceived in the future (Marbach, 1993). This complex organization of consciousness indicates that individuals recognize a temporal dimension to their existence, or what Moore calls a temporally extended self (see also Bieri, 1986; Fraisse, 1958/1963; Straus, 1958/1966). The temporal structure is manifest in the ability to locate experiences within a personal history, which, in turn, is based on an understanding that an individual's temporal relation toward the events in the world is continuously changing. In other words, we must be able to differentiate between and coordinate two temporal perspectives: events that we represent as present or future now will later be experienced as present (or remembered as past), and events we represent as past now once were experienced as present. We must establish what Stern (1934/1938) calls *mnemic continuity*: "I am the *same one* who *now* remembers what I *then* experienced" (p. 250)—a competence that requires the understanding of perspective and perspective difference. For this reason, Moore argues that children's future-oriented decision-making skills, notions of a temporally extended self, theory-of-mind ability, and executive functioning should all be related. Not only do his research findings support this claim, but Moore also shows that children typically begin to master the coordination of these skills around 4 years of age.

Moore's conclusions regarding 4-year-olds' consolidation of several key cognitive abilities, much like Carlo et al.'s findings concerning the age-graded changes in the magnitude of the relation between perspective taking and prosocial behavior, draws attention to the importance of understanding perspective taking within a developmental framework. Not only might perspective taking be differentiated according to different kinds of physical, conceptual, or affective content, as researchers like Carlo et al. suggest, but, as a more general process, perspective taking may also be seen as holding different forms—or even undergoing structural changes—across time. Returning to the historical ironies that initiated this discussion, it is worth noting that developmental accounts of perspective taking are anything but novel. The structural transformations of perspective taking have been well documented by Piaget (e.g., Piaget & Inhelder, 1948/1963; see also, Kesselring, 1993) and even extended and formalized in Selman's (1980) widely circulated developmental theory. In fact, some of the details of Selman's model of perspective taking are especially relevant to situating Perner et al.'s (2002) processes of perspective switching and confronting into a developmental framework. Specifically, perspective switching fits well with Selman's (1980) description of Level 1, or what he calls, "Social Informational, Differentiated, and Subjective," perspective taking. At this level, young children recognize that others may hold different perspectives from their own, and, given that the coordination demands are relatively modest, they demonstrate an ability to *sequentially* move back and forth between perspectives. Children at this level, however, are not yet able to *simultaneously* coordinate and integrate two perspectives. Such simultaneity, instead, characterizes Level 2 of Selman's model, or what he calls, "Self-Reflective, Second-person, and Reciprocal" perspective taking. At this level, children are capable of independently managing two conflicting perspectives at the same time, or, as Perner et al. describe, to engage in perspective confronting. Importantly, Level 2 perspective taking also ushers in a new understanding of self whereby individuals may reflexively treat themselves as objects of their own thought, in a way much like Moore's discussion of a temporally extended self.

The historical connections and remarks provided here are not motivated by a desire to return to the "grand theories" of the past. Rather, they grow out of concern that many of the current perspectives on children's social understanding need to be better integrated with past work in this area. Moving toward such integration should not only help the field steer itself in more productive ways, but also help to avoid retracing the steps that have led to overly narrow conceptions of children's social lives and development. The contributions to this part all highlight the value of expanding the ways that researchers approach the development of social understanding. We should try to follow their lead.

REFERENCES

Astington, J. W., Harris, P. L., & Olson, D. R. (Eds.). (1988). *Developing theories of mind.* New York: Cambridge University Press.

Bieri, P. (1986). Zeiterfahrung und Personalität [Temporal experience and personhood]. In H. Burger (Ed.), *Zeit, Natur und Mensch* (pp. 261–281). Berlin: Arno Spitz Verlag.

Carlo, G. (2006). Care-based and altruistically based morality. In M. Killen & J. G. Smetana (Eds.), *Handbook of moral development* (pp. 551–579). Mahwah, NJ: Lawrence Erlbaum Associates.

Carpendale, J. I. M., & Lewis, C. (2004). Constructing an understanding of mind: The development of children's social understanding within social interaction. *Behavioral and Brain Sciences, 27,* 79–96.

Fraisse, P. (1963). *The psychology of time.* New York: Harper & Row. (Original work published 1958)

Frye, D. (1999). The development of intention. The relation between executive function to theory of mind. In P. D. Zelazo, J. W. Astington, & D. R. Olson (Eds.), *Developing theories of intention* (pp. 119–132). Mahwah, NJ: Lawrence Erlbaum Associates.

Kesselring, T. (1993). Egocentrism and equilibration. Is there an intrinsic logic in mental development? In D. Maurice & J. Montagero (Eds.), *Equilibrium and equilibration* (pp. 63–78). Geneva: Foundation Archives of Jean Piaget.

Lalonde, C. E., & Chandler, M. J. (1995). False belief understanding goes to school: On the social-emotional consequences of coming early or late to a first theory of mind. *Cognition and Emotion, 9,* 167–185.

Lehto, J. E., Juujärvi, P., Kooistra, L., & Pulkkinen, L. (2003). Dimensions of executive functioning: Evidence from children. *The British Journal of Developmental Psychology, 21,* 59–80.

Light, P. (1979). *The development of social sensitivity: A study of social aspects of role-taking in young children.* Cambridge, England: Cambridge University Press.

Marbach, E. (1993). *Mental representation and consciousness.* Dordrecht: Kluwer Academic Publishers.

Martin, J., Sokol, B. W., & Elfers, T. (2008). Taking and coordinating perspectives: From pre-reflective interactivity, through reflective intersubjectivity, to meta-reflective sociality. *Human Development, 51,* 294–317.

Miyake, A., Friedman, N. P., Emerson, M. J., Witzki, A. H., & Howerter, A. (2000). The unity and diversity of executive functions and their contributions to complex "frontal lobe" tasks: A latent variable analysis. *Cognitive Psychology, 41*, 49–100.

Perner, J., & Lang, B. (1999). Development of theory of mind and executive control. *Trends in Cognitive Sciences, 3*, 337–344.

Perner, J., Stummer, S., Sprung, M., & Doherty, M. (2002). Theory of mind finds its Piagetian perspective: Why alternative naming comes with understanding belief. *Cognitive Development, 17*, 1451–1472.

Piaget, J., & Inhelder, B. (1963). *The child's conception of space* (F. J. Langdon & J. L. Lunzer, Trans.). London: Routledge & Kegan Paul. (Original work published 1948)

Premack, D., & Woodruff, G. (1978). Does the chimpanzee have a theory of mind? *Behavioral and Brain Sciences, 4*, 515–526.

Selman, R. L. (1980). *The growth of interpersonal understanding: Developmental and clinical analyses.* New York: Academic Press.

Stern, W. (1938). *General psychology from the personalistic standpoint.* New York: Macmillan. (Original work published 1934)

Straus, E. W. (1966). Remembering and infantile amnesia. In E. W. Straus (Ed.), *Phenomenological psychology* (pp. 59–74). New York: Basic Books. (Original work published 1958)

Towse, J. N., Redbond, J., Houston-Price, C. M. T., & Cook, S. (2000). Understanding the dimensional change card sort. Perspectives from task success and failure. *Cognitive Development, 15*, 347–365.

Underwood, B., & Moore, B. (1982). Perspective-taking and altruism. *Psychological Bulletin, 91*, 143–173.

Wellman, H. M. (1990). *The child's theory of mind.* Cambridge, MA: MIT Press.

Wimmer, H., & Perner, J. (1983). Beliefs about beliefs: Representation and constraining function of wrong beliefs in young children's understanding of deception. *Cognition, 13*, 103–128.

Zelazo, P. D., & Müller, U. (2002). Executive function in typical and atypical development. In U. Goswami (Ed.), *Handbook of childhood cognitive development* (pp. 445–469). Oxford, England: Blackwell Publishing.

Zelazo, P. D., Qu, L., & Müller, U. (2005). Hot and cool aspects of executive functioning: Relations in early development. In W. Schneider, R. Schumann-Hengsteler, & B. Sodian (Eds.), *Young children's cognitive development: Interrelationships among executive functioning, working memory, verbal ability, and theory of mind* (pp. 71–93). Mahwah, NJ: Lawrence Erlbaum Associates.

8

Object-Based Set-Shifting in Preschoolers: Relations to Theory of Mind

DANIELA KLOO, JOSEF PERNER, AND THOMAS GIRITZER

This chapter focuses on children's ability to shift between different ways of thinking about an object, which is termed *object-based set-shifting*. First, we outline crucial developments in social cognition (theory of mind) and executive functions in the preschool years. At around age 4, children master the false belief task and the Dimensional Change Card Sorting (DCCS) task, the latter being a measure of object-based set-shifting. Then, we describe studies showing that these developmental advances are related. We present the "redescription" hypothesis as an explanation for the relationship between the false belief task and the DCCS task: at age 4, children understand that one and the same thing can be described differently under different perspectives, a cornerstone for object-based set-shifting. We then describe an experiment, which explores the nature of object-based set-shifting. The results suggest that both executive abilities (inhibitory control) and conceptual abilities (redescription understanding) play a role in the development of object-based set-shifting. Finally, we discuss various theories aiming to explain the general developmental link between theory of mind and executive functions.

Executive Functions

The umbrella term "executive functions" refers to higher cortical functions, which enable the conscious control of thought and action and are assumed to be carried out by the prefrontal cortex (e.g., Welsh, Pennington, & Groisser,

1991). However, it does not refer to elementary cognitive processes, like sensation, perception, or motor activation. One problem is that executive function "is a term so broad as to lose meaning" (Towse, Redbond, Houston-Price, & Cook, 2000, p. 348–349). Its definition is "provisional and under-specified" (Pennington & Ozonoff, 1996, p. 55). The following anecdote from a conference illustrates the absence of a universal definition of executive functions: "An informal survey was taken of what behaviors were indicated by the term *executive function*. The 10 respondents in the working group on executive function generated 33 terms" (Eslinger, 1996, p. 380). That is, executive functions encompass a rather heterogeneous collection of behaviors and skills, and are therefore difficult to define. Among other things, the umbrella term executive function is likely to include planning, working memory, interference control, regulation of attention, inhibition of inappropriate actions, and set-shifting.

Set-shifting clearly is an important aspect of human cognition: The ability to shift cognitive sets is necessary for flexibility in thought and action, which is, for example, required for switching between different tasks. There is a great amount of research on set-shifting in adults. In recent years, task-set shifting paradigms have been the focus of intense research (for a recent review, see Monsell, 2003). In these paradigms, subjects are required to shift between different tasks. For example, they have to switch between discriminating the color, size, or form of an object (Mayr, 2001). Switching to a new task is usually associated with switching costs, that is, with an increase of reaction time. A number of imaging studies have shown that switching of attentional sets is associated with increased activity in dorsolateral and ventrolateral prefrontal cortex (e.g., Berman et al., 1995; Dove, Pollmann, Schubert, Wiggins, & von Cramon, 2000; Meyer et al., 1998; Nagahama et al., 2001; Sohn, Ursu, Anderson, Stenger, & Carter, 2000).

Probably one of the most frequently used tests of the ability to shift cognitive set is the Wisconsin Card Sorting Test (WCST; Grant & Berg, 1948). In this test, participants are shown stimulus cards that differ on various dimensions (color, number, and shape), and are shown individual cards that match different stimulus cards on different dimensions. Participants must determine the rule according to which each card must be sorted, and the experimenter informs the participants after each card whether the sorting is right or wrong. After a certain number of consecutive correct responses, the rule is changed without warning or comment from the experimenter. Now, participants are required to sort by a different dimension than the one that was just reinforced. Patients with frontal lesions (e.g., Shallice, 1988; Stuss et al., 2000) but also individuals with autism (for a review, see Pennington & Ozonoff, 1996) have difficulty in this test. They tend to perseverate in sorting according to the previously used (but no longer correct) dimension despite constant negative feedback.

There is now a growing body of research on set-shifting in children (e.g., Cepeda, Kramer, & Gonzalez de Sather, 2001; Crone, Bunge, van der Molen, & Ridderinkhof, 2006; Ellefson, Shapiro, & Chater, 2006; Kray, Eber, & Lindenberger, 2004) showing that with age children's ability to switch between different tasks increases. Because of its inductive nature, the WCST is not appropriate for studying set-shifting in children younger than 6 years. In preschool children, a modification of the WCST, the DCCS task (Zelazo, Müller, Frye, & Marcovitch, 2003) is frequently used as a measure of set-shifting. In contrast to the inductive nature of the WCST, the DCCS is a deductive task. In this card-sorting task, children are explicitly told the rules by which to sort test cards. These test cards showing pictures that vary in two dimensions (e.g., red pears and blue apples) must be sorted first according to one dimension (e.g., color) and then according to another dimension (e.g., shape) into two boxes each marked with a target card (red apple or blue pear). Each test card matches one target card on one dimension and the other target card on the other dimension. In the preswitch phase, children are told a pair of rules, for example, the color rules: they are asked to sort all the blue ones into the box portraying something blue and to sort all the red ones into the box displaying something red. Typically, 3-year-olds have no problems when sorting the cards according to the first dimension. However, they usually have severe difficulties when, after a series of trials, the sorting rules change: Now, in the postswitch phase, the cards should be sorted according to a new dimension, for example, according to shape. It is not until the age of about 4 years that children continue to sort correctly during the postswitch phase. Most 3-year-olds perseverate and continue to sort according to the first dimension. Typically, they have problems irrespective of whether sorting starts with color or shape (e.g., Zelazo, Frye, & Rapus, 1996).

Theory of Mind

Another important aspect of human cognition is the ability to impute mental states to oneself and to others, and to predict other people's behavior on the basis of their mental states, which has been termed "Theory of Mind" (ToM; Premack & Woodruff, 1978). In our everyday life, we often want to know why people did what they did, and we wonder what they are going to do next. That is, everyday we try to predict, explain, and interpret human behavior. In order to do this, we refer to a person's mental states, such as beliefs, desires, thoughts, emotions, intentions, doubts, ideas, and so on.

Core concepts of the so-called theory of mind are beliefs, desires, and intentions. People do things because they *desire* something and *believe* some act will achieve it. Therefore, behavior is the product of belief and desire. For adults, it is clear that our assumptions about reality do not necessarily match the real world; but we know, regardless of whether our beliefs are true or not, our beliefs direct our actions. In contrast, it is not until the age of about 4 years that children explicitly understand that one can be mistaken about the world and that actions can be based on this false belief.

A widely used measure designed to tap these changes in theory of mind understanding around 4 years is the unexpected transfer *false belief* task (Wimmer & Perner, 1983). In the standard version, children are told a story about an unexpected transfer. For example, Maxi puts chocolate in the desk and goes away. While he is away, his mother takes a bit of chocolate for cooking and then puts it in a drawer and goes out. Then Maxi comes back. Now children are asked: "Where will Maxi look for the chocolate?" Three-year-olds often answer wrongly, "In the drawer," where the object actually is. In contrast most children older than 4, and a clear majority of 5-year-olds answer correctly: "He will look in the desk." In order to answer correctly, children must understand that Maxi will act on the basis of his false belief rather than on the basis of reality. Older children are also able to explain Maxi's false belief based action (e.g., "because he thought it was in there"). They understand that Maxi's false belief, rather than reality, guides his behavior.

A variation of this unexpected transfer task is the "Smarties task" (Gopnik & Astington, 1988; Hogrefe, Wimmer, & Perner, 1986). In this task, the experimenter shows the children a familiar container (e.g., a "Smarties" box) and asks, "What do you think is inside it?" They are then shown that the box actually contains, for example, a pencil. Then, the pencil is put back into the box, and the box is closed again. The child is then asked, "What did you think was in here?" Typically, most 3-year-olds answer with the actual content of the box and reply, "a pencil." In contrast, most 4-year-olds correctly report their own earlier false belief, "Smarties."

Three-year-olds have difficulties not only with false belief tasks, but also with so-called Level 2 perspective-taking tasks. They have problems to understand that, even though two persons see one and the same stimulus, it may present different visual appearances to the two if their viewing circumstances differ (e.g., they view it from different positions).

To assess Level 2 visual perspective-taking, Flavell, Everett, Croft, and Flavell (1981) placed, for example, a picture of a turtle horizontally on a table between the child and the experimenter. Children were asked how the turtle was viewed by themselves and by the experimenter. Even 3-year-old children were capable of reporting whether they saw the turtle as "standing on its feet" or "lying on its back" (when the picture was turned around). However, 3-year-olds could not indicate in which of these two orientations the turtle appeared to the experimenter.

Typically, children pass these kinds of tasks at around 4 years of age. Wellman, Cross, and Watson (2001) found a consistent developmental pattern in their recent meta-analysis of 178 separate false belief studies: Children younger than about 42 months of age performed below chance, whereas children older than about 47 months of age performed above chance. This indicates that at around 4 years, children become able to understand their own and other's mental states and to attribute false beliefs to themselves and to others.

That is, at around 4 years, crucial changes occur in theory-of-mind development. Children understand that one entity (e.g., the identity of an object or a certain situation) can be described differently under different perspectives. They become able to attribute false beliefs to other persons in the false belief task, and they recognize that the same thing may present different visual appearances to two people if they view it from different positions in the visual perspective-taking task.

Theory of Mind and Executive Functions

As outlined earlier, a host of studies shows that at around 4 years of age important developmental changes occur. Children improve markedly on theory-of-mind tasks (like the false belief task) as well as on executive function tests (like the DCCS task). There is increasing evidence that this parallel development is not merely coincidental. Several recent studies have found positive correlations between developmental advances in theory of mind and executive function in preschool children in the age range of 3–5 years (e.g., Carlson & Moses, 2001; Carlson, Moses, & Breton, 2002; Carlson, Moses, & Claxton, 2004; Davis & Pratt, 1995; Frye, Zelazo, & Palfai, 1995; Gordon & Olson, 1998; Hala, Hug, & Henderson, 2003; Hughes, 1998a, 1998b; Perner, Lang, & Kloo, 2002; Russell, Mauthner, Sharpe, & Tidswell, 1991).

For example, Hala et al. (2003) reported correlations between false belief tasks and a battery of two inhibitory tasks (the day-night task and Luria's tapping task). These relations remained significant once age and verbal mental age were controlled for. Carlson et al. (2002) administered task batteries measuring inhibitory control, working memory, and theory of mind to preschool children. They found that performance on inhibitory control tasks in which an inappropriate response needed to be suppressed while a conflicting response was activated (conflict tasks) significantly predicted performance on false belief tasks over and above working memory, verbal and performance intelligence, a simple delay task, and age.[1] In a similar vein, Carlson et al. (2004)

showed that conflict tasks, but not planning tasks, are significantly related to theory of mind after controlling for age and receptive vocabulary. In summary, this suggests that theory-of-mind development is specifically linked to one type of executive task, namely, inhibitory tasks involving some kind of conflict.

Further evidence for a relationship between theory of mind and executive control also comes from studies in non-western cultures and clinical populations. Sabbagh, Xu, Carlson, Moses, and Lee (2006) found a similar robust correlation between theory of mind and executive control tasks in Chinese preschoolers, which remained significant when controlling for age, sex, and verbal ability. And, children with autism are impaired in both theory of mind and executive function, and these deficits appear to be associated (Ozonoff, Pennington, & Rogers, 1991, Zelazo, Jacques, Burack, & Frye, 2002).

Theory of Mind and Object-Based Set-Shifting

Apart from the general relation between theory of mind and executive control, a specific relation between various theory-of-mind measures and one of the most commonly used executive measures in preschool children, the DCCS task, has been repeatedly demonstrated even with age and verbal intelligence partialled out. Frye et al. (1995) found correlations between theory-of-mind tasks (e.g., false belief and appearance-reality tasks) and rule use tasks like the DCCS task with age partialled out. Perner et al. (2002) reported correlations between the DCCS task and both false belief prediction tasks and false belief explanation tasks with age and verbal intelligence partialled out (Exp. 1). Furthermore, they showed that the correlation between false belief understanding and performance on the DCCS task is not due to the ability to inhibit interfering response tendencies as measured by the no-go trials in a go/no-go task (Exp. 2), suggesting that the relation between theory of mind and DCCS performance is not due to response inhibition requirements. Carlson and Moses (2001) found correlations between various theory-of-mind tasks and the DCCS task. However, when age, gender, and verbal ability were partialled out, only performance on the deceptive box task was significantly correlated with DCCS performance.

Perhaps the strongest evidence for a relation between the false belief task and the DCCS task comes from a training study by Kloo and Perner (2003) showing transfer of training between the false belief task and the DCCS task. In this study, there were three different training groups. A false belief group was trained on stories about false statements and false beliefs. A card sorting group was given training on the DCCS task. And a control group received one of two different control trainings (relative clause or number conservation training).

Children ranging in age from 36 to 50 months were pretested on a false belief task, the card sorting task, and a control task. All children who failed at least one of the two test questions of the false belief task—a prediction test question and an explanation test question—or sorted more than one card (out of five) incorrectly in the postswitch phase of the DCCS were included in the study. They were randomly allocated to one of the training groups matched for pretest performance. Each child participated in two training sessions, each lasting about 15 min, within approximately 1 week of each other.

The posttest was conducted about 1 week after training. Children were given a false belief task, a card sorting task, and a control task using the same format as at pretest, but different material. The posttest showed that generalization worked both ways: The false belief training led to a significant rise in card sorting performance. And the card sorting training significantly increased children's performance on the false belief task (see Figure 8.1).

As it is the case with many complex executive measures such as the WCST, the precise nature of the cognitive processes implicated in performance on the DCCS is still unclear. However, in order to gain a better insight into the relationship between theory of mind and executive functions, the source of

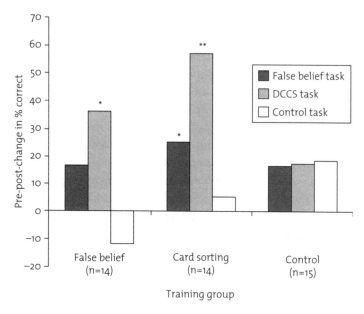

FIGURE 8.1. Mean pre-post-change in percent correct for each task in the three training groups.

preschool children's difficulty with the executive measures typically used has to be specified.

As regards the DCCS task, Kloo and Perner (2005; see also Kloo & Perner, 2003; Perner & Lang, 2002) have put forward the "redescription hypothesis" in order to explain children's sorting problems. This hypothesis states that the younger children fail the DCCS task because they do not understand that one and the same object can be described differently under different perspectives. Therefore, children have difficulty redescribing the objects on the cards in the standard DCCS from, say, "a red thing" (when sorting by color) to "an apple" (when sorting by shape).

More specifically, it is argued that in the DCCS task, the use of target cards may induce children to encode the sorting rules as the general rule "put each test card to the corresponding target." In order to put this rule into effect, children have to treat objects, for example, a red apple either as "a red thing" (in the color game) or as "an apple" (in the fruit game) but not both—or else they would not know which box was the "corresponding target" (due to the fact that each test card matches one target card on one dimension and the other target card on the other dimension). However, when the postswitch phase starts, the objects on the cards have to be redescribed according to the other dimension. But 3-year-old children may not understand that redescription is possible and, therefore, may show perseverative sorting behavior in the postswitch phase. In fact, there is independent evidence that young children below the age of about 4 years have difficulty explicitly acknowledging that things can be redescribed (e.g., that something can be described as a *rabbit* and as a *bunny*; Doherty & Perner, 1998; see also Perner, Stummer, Sprung, & Doherty, 2002).

Empirical support for the explanation that the DCCS task requires an understanding that one and the same thing can be described differently comes from two recent studies. Kloo and Perner (2005) as well as Diamond, Carlson, and Beck (2005) showed that one crucial factor for children's difficulties on the DCCS task is the integration of both sorting dimensions within one and the same object. In both studies, separating the two dimensions (color and shape) as properties of a single object (Diamond et al.: by displaying black shapes on colored backgrounds; Kloo & Perner: by displaying colorless line drawings of familiar objects next to colored circles; see Figure 8.2) improved performance considerably. That is, if the need to describe one object in two different ways at the same time and place is removed by allocating the two dimensions onto different objects children perform better.

These studies indicate that in the DCCS task the central difficulty for 3-year-old children lies in shifting between different ways of thinking about one and the same object. In the following, we will refer to this as *object-based set-shifting*.

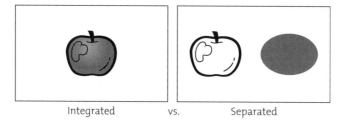

FIGURE 8.2. Exemplary integrated vs. separated cards used by Kloo and Perner (2005).

Exploring the Nature of Object-Based Set-Shifting—What Develops?

Though there is strong evidence that object-based set-shifting becomes possible at about 4 years (and possibly lies at the heart of the relationship between theory of mind and DCCS performance) there are two different theoretical positions about how object-based set-shifting develops. Diamond et al. (2005) favor some kind of an expression account (in that they assume that insufficient executive abilities impede the expression of existing conceptual knowledge), whereas Kloo and Perner (2005) assume a fundamental conceptual development around age 4.

Diamond et al. (2005) argue that in the standard DCCS young preschoolers remain stuck in thinking about the objects according to the objects' initially—in the preswitch phase—relevant attribute. To switch, the old way of thinking about the objects must be inhibited. That is, children's inflexibility on the DCCS task is due to insufficient inhibitory control. In contrast, Kloo and Perner (2005) argue that their inflexibility is due to insufficient conceptual ability. The younger children do not understand that one and the same thing can be described differently under different perspectives.

To investigate this issue, a correlational study was undertaken. Children were given a DCCS task, four (to obtain a more reliable measure) unexpected transfer false belief tasks, and the day-night task (Gerstadt, Hong, & Diamond, 1994). The false belief test requires an understanding that one and the same thing, in this case, a situation, can be described differently under different perspectives—to understand false belief, one has to understand that someone else can have a description of the real world that differs from one's own description. In contrast, the day-night task requires inhibitory control. In the day-night task, children are instructed to say "day" when shown a picture of the moon and stars, and to say "night" when shown a picture of the sun. That is, children must inhibit the natural response tendency to say what the pictures really show. Young children often have problems doing this and say "day" to the sun picture and "night" to the moon picture. One might object that the day-night task also involves redescription; the picture of the sun must be redescribed as "night." However, this kind of "redescription" is not assumed to be difficult for 3-year-old children, because they do not have to understand that one thing (the sun) can be described differently and *correctly* under different perspectives. Supposedly, children fairly well know that the picture of the sun does not depict a night-time scene and play a "say the opposite" game.

In contrast, recent evidence (Simpson & Riggs, 2005) indicates that response set is the major factor for the difficulty of the day-night task: The names of the stimuli ("day" and "night") and the responses (say "night" or "day") are from the same response set. And children have difficulty inhibiting the conflicting, prepotent responses triggered by the stimuli. "The child is planning to make one of two responses and the wrong one is triggered by the stimulus" (Simpson & Riggs, 2005, p. 369).

If a conceptual change—the ability to reconceptualize objects—is critical for object-based set-shifting (Kloo & Perner, 2003, 2005), then the false belief test—but not the day-night task—should explain a significant and unique (independent from the day-night task) amount of the variance of the DCCS. In contrast, if improvements in inhibitory control are critical, then the day-night task—but not the false belief task—should explain a significant and unique (independent from the false belief task) amount of the variance of the DCCS task.

A study by Peskin and Ardino (2003) has already shown that these three tasks are significantly intercorrelated (DCCS and unexpected transfer false belief: $r = 0.50$, $p < 0.001$; DCCS and day-night: $r = 0.28$, $p < 0.05$; unexpected transfer false belief and day-night: $r = 0.35$, $p < 0.01$). However, the uniquely shared variances between DCCS and day-night as well as between DCCS and unexpected transfer false belief have not been examined.

METHOD

Participants

A total of 58 children were recruited from four nursery schools in Upper Austria. Twelve of the initial 58 children were excluded because they were unable to complete both sessions or to understand the task instructions. The final sample comprised 46 children (21 girls and 25 boys). Most participants were Caucasian and came from a middle-class background, although data about race and socioeconomic status were not systematically collected. Their ages ranged from 3,5 to 4,11 years ($M = 4,2$ years, $SD = 5.28$ months). The sample comprised 18 three-year-olds (8 girls, 10 boys; $M = 3,8$ years, range = 3,5–3,11 years, $SD = 1.79$ months) and 28 four-year-olds (13 girls, 15 boys; $M = 4,6$ years, range = 4,1–4,11 years, $SD = 2.88$ months).

Design

Each child was tested individually in two sessions, which occurred approximately 1 week apart. Each session lasted about 25 min. Half of the children were given an unexpected transfer false belief task, the DCCS task, and a second false belief task in the first session, and a third false belief task, an alternative-naming task (used for exploratory purposes in a different research project), a fourth false belief task, and the day-night task (Gerstadt et al., 1994) in the second session. The other half received the reverse ordering. In the DCCS task, the direction of shift (from color to shape or from shape to color) was counterbalanced.

Procedure and Materials

CARD SORTING We used a set of cards (10.5 × 7.5 cm) consisting of two target cards (a blue fish and a red bird) and 12 test cards (6 red fish and 6 blue birds). The two target cards were each affixed to a (22 × 15 × 15 cm) box, where they remained throughout the task. The test cards had to be posted into one of these boxes through a slit on top. There were two phases: a preswitch phase and a postswitch phase. The procedure followed the standard version of the DCCS (Zelazo et al., 1996).

First, the experimenter pointed at the two target cards and explained the two dimensions (shape and color). Then, he said, "Now we are playing a game, the animal game. In this game, all the fish go into the box with a fish on it (point), but all the birds go into the box with a bird on it (point)." The experimenter then sorted one test card of each kind (one fish and one bird) into each box to demonstrate what the child was required to do. Then, the children were asked to sort five cards on their own. On each trial, the experimenter randomly selected a test card (with the constraint that the same type of card was not given more than twice in a row), labeled the card by the relevant dimension only (e.g., "Here is a fish."), and asked the children to post the card appropriately with the supporting question, "Where does this go in the animal game?" On each trial, children were told whether they had sorted the card correctly.

When the children had completed five preswitch trials, the postswitch phase began. Children were told, "Okay, now we are going to play a new game, the color game. The color game is different: All the red ones go into the box with a red thing on it (point), but all the blue ones go into the box with a blue thing on it (point)." Again, children had to sort five cards according to the new rules. Children were given no direct feedback. However, every time a card had been sorted incorrectly, the experimenter repeated the postswitch rules.

FALSE BELIEF TASKS   Four unexpected transfer false belief tasks modeled after Wimmer and Perner (1983) were administered. Two stories were acted out with Playmobil figures in a three-dimensional model scenario (30 × 22 × 22 cm). One story was about a dog looking for his unexpectedly transferred bone. The other story was about a girl looking for a bird who had unexpectedly moved to a new location. The other two tasks consisted of picture stories, one about a girl looking for her chocolate bar that was unexpectedly transferred and one about a boy looking for his rabbit who had unexpectedly moved to another location. Each task included a prediction and an explanation test question.

First, children had to *predict* the protagonist's action based on her or his false belief. In the case of no response, the experimenter provided the answer alternatives (the two locations) in a forced-choice format. In each case, the child was then shown a picture illustrating the protagonist's erroneous search in the empty location and was asked to *explain* this action (e.g., "Why then does Laura go to the desk to get her chocolate?"). Laura's goal ("to get her chocolate") was included into the question to prevent children from explaining the action in terms of Laura's desire "to get her chocolate."

The memory of critical story events was checked by four control questions (e.g.): (1) "Where is the chocolate now?", (2) "Where did Laura put the chocolate at the beginning?", (3) "How did the chocolate get there (pointing)?", and (4) "Could Laura see this?"

Day-Night Task

In this Stroop-like task following Gerstadt et al. (1994), children were instructed to say "day" when shown a card depicting a yellow moon and stars against a black background and to say "night" when shown a card depicting a large yellow sun against a white background. Each card was 9.5 × 13 cm.

On the practice trials, the experimenter showed a card depicting the moon and stars, and instructed children to say "day" to that card. Then, he showed a card depicting the sun and instructed children to say "night" to that card. Children were also quizzed on what response to give to each card. Up to 12 practice trials were conducted to ensure that children understood the instructions. If the child made an error within a block of two trials, the experimenter repeated the rules. After four consecutive correct responses or after a maximum of 12 practice trials testing began.

On the test trials, children received 24 test trials (12 "day" cards and 12 "night" cards) in a fixed random order. No feedback was given. In the case of four consecutive correct responses in the practice phase, these trials were counted as test trials, and, consequently, only 20 test trials were administered.

RESULTS

First, we report children's performance on the various tasks. Then, we look at the relation between DCCS, false belief, and day-night performance.

Card Sorting

In both phases of this task, a score between 0 and 5 could be obtained representing the number of correct sorts. During the preswitch phase, children were almost perfect. Only one child sorted one card incorrectly. In the postswitch phase, most children sorted either mostly correctly (four or five correct) or mostly incorrectly (none or one correct). Twelve children had none correct, 2 children had three correct, and 32 children had four or five correct. Performance was not influenced by the order of dimensions (color or shape first), $t(44) = 0.28, p > 0.70$.

Day-Night Task

In the practice phase, the number of errors was recorded. Fifteen children made no error, 13 children made one error, and 18 children made two to six errors. In the test phase, the number of correct responses was recorded. Four children had none to 10 correct, 27 children had 11 to 20 correct, and 15 children had 21 to 24 correct.

False Belief Tasks

On the prediction and explanation task, children received a score between 0 and 4 based on the four test questions. On the explanation tasks, children's answers to the open question were classified in the following categories: (a) mental state, for example, "He thought it was in there"; (b) relevant story facts, for example, "He had been away"; (c) desire answers, for example, "because he wants the ball"; (d) wrong location answers, for example, "because the ball isn't in here"; (e) irrelevant statements, for example, "Why?"; and (f) no answer or "Don't know" answer. For further analysis answers of categories (a) and (b) were classified as "correct answers" indicating an understanding of belief. Answers of the remaining categories were classified as "incorrect answers" failing to show such understanding (Wimmer & Mayringer, 1998).

On the four prediction tasks, 6 children had none correct, 3 children had one correct, 5 children had two correct, 10 children had three correct, and 22 children had all four correct. On the four explanation tasks, 14 children had none correct, 4 children had one correct, 3 children had two correct, 7 children had three correct, and 18 children had all four correct. Performance on the prediction tasks was significantly related to performance on the explanation tasks ($r = 0.42$, $p < 0.01$), providing a justification for a false belief score (ranging from 0 to 8) based on all eight test questions.

All scores were transformed into values between 0 and 1 indicating the proportion of correct answers.

Relations among Tasks

Table 8.1 shows the mean percent correct and standard deviations for each task as well as correlations (including partial correlations controlling for age) for all tasks. As can be seen, replicating Peskin and Ardino (2003), all three tasks are significantly intercorrelated. With age partialled out, the relation between DCCS performance and the other two tasks remains significant but the correlation between day-night and false belief performance falls below significance.

A preliminary multiple regression analysis with DCCS performance as the dependent variable and age as independent variable showed that age does not explain a significant amount of variance of DCCS performance, $R^2 = 0.04$, $F_{inc}(1, 44) = 1.90$, $p > 0.05$, so age was dropped from subsequent analyses. In contrast, taken together, the false belief score and the day-night score explain a significant amount of DCCS variance, $R^2 = 0.345$, $F_{inc}(2, 43) = 11.34$, $p < 0.001$. We calculated semipartial correlations in order to obtain the unique contribution of each task. This yielded 15.8% ($p < 0.01$) explained nonshared variance for the day-night task and 7.3% ($p < 0.05$) explained nonshared variance for the false belief task. Consequently, the explained shared variance for all three tasks amounts to 11.4%.

TABLE 8.1. Basic Statistics and Correlations (Controlling for Age) for All Tasks.

| Variables | Mean% (SD) | Variables | | |
		FB	DCCS	Day-night
Age	—	45**	0.20	0.22
FB	63.6 (33.1)	—	0.43**	0.34*
DCCS	69.1 (42.7)	[0.39**]	—	0.52**
Day-night	68.1 (24.5)	[0.28]	[0.50**]	—

Note: * $p \leq 0.05$, ** $p < 0.01$.

Discussion

In summary, this experiment showed that both the day-night task (15.8%) and the false belief test (7.3%) independently explain significant amounts of variance of the DCCS task. This suggests that both inhibitory control and conceptual ability (an understanding that one thing can be described differently under different perspectives) play a role in the DCCS task. Furthermore, all three tasks share 11.4% of variance.

What conclusions can we draw from this? A preliminary explanation is that the unique common denominator between the DCCS task and the false belief task may be conceptual ability (namely an understanding that one thing can be described differently under different perspectives). And the unique common denominator underlying the DCCS task and the day-night task may be children's ability to use rules to guide their behavior ("All the red ones go into the box with a red thing on it"; "If you see this card, then you have to say 'day'"). Concerning the shared variance for all three tasks, a possible explanation (see Carlson et al., 2004; Diamond et al., 2005) is that all tasks involve the same executive abilities, namely, working memory and inhibition. In all these tasks, children have to hold two things in mind (two perspectives, descriptions or rules) and to inhibit focusing on what is most salient (one's own perspective or the most salient description). For example, Diamond et al. (2005, p. 713) argued that the day-night task requires "remembering to say *day* when shown a night-time scene and to say *night* when shown a daytime scene and inhibiting saying what the pictures really represent."

That is, neither conceptual change accounts nor expression accounts may be able to explain the development of object-based set-shifting on their own. In contrast, both on the DCCS task and on the false belief task, there may be an interaction between conceptual understanding and inhibitory control plus working memory. First, one has to *understand* that there can be two different descriptions of the same thing.

But to *express* this understanding inhibitory control plus working memory are necessary in order to hold both descriptions in mind and to inhibit the more salient description. Due to the expression component object-based set-shifting always requires cognitive effort—even in adults as Diamond and Kirkham (2005) have shown. However, first, we argue, conceptual understanding has to develop.

Alternatively, working memory and inhibition may be necessary in order to develop and express conceptual understanding. "Acquiring and expressing mental state concepts requires both working memory and inhibitory skill. Effective social cognition is not possible unless one is able to hold in mind relevant perspectives (working memory) and to suppress irrelevant ones (inhibition)" (Moses & Carlson, 2004, p. 135).

Growing experimental evidence has demonstrated the fundamental importance of objects in cognition and attention. For example, visual attention cannot only be space-based, as traditionally assumed (e.g., Eriksen & Yeh, 1985; Posner, 1980), but it can also be object-based (e.g., Scholl, 2001; Soto & Blanco, 2004). Future research will have to explore the role of objects for set-shifting. Further studies are needed to disentangle the cognitive processes implicated in object-based set-shifting and to explain the emergence of object-based set shifting competence at around 4 years of age.

General Discussion

Apart from the specific relationship between the DCCS task and the false belief task, various theories have been put forward in order to explain the general developmental relationship between theory of mind and executive functions. These theories can broadly be divided into two categories: expression accounts (see also Moses, 2001; Moses & Carlson, 2004) and functional dependency accounts. *Expression accounts* (e.g., Carlson, Moses, & Hix, 1998; Hughes & Russell, 1993; Russell et al., 1991) assume that typical theory-of-mind tasks require inhibitory control, because, for example, in the false belief task children need to inhibit their knowledge of the true state of affairs in order to predict the protagonist's false belief based action. And these inhibitory requirements prevent children from expressing their already developed belief understanding. In contrast, other authors propose a *functional dependency* between the development of executive control and theory of mind: Either theory of mind may be a prerequisite for executive functions (e.g., Perner, 1991; Wimmer, 1989), or executive control may be a necessary requirement for building a theory of mind (e.g., Russell, 1996, 1999).

EXPRESSION ACCOUNTS

Proponents of expression accounts (e.g., Carlson et al., 1998; Hughes & Russell, 1993; Russell et al., 1991) stated that typical theory-of-mind tasks contain executive components and, therefore, correlate with executive tasks. Indeed, Russell et al. (1991) found that success on the false belief task was associated with the ability to suppress the tendency of pointing to a baited box in the windows task. In this task, children had to play a game against an experimenter for chocolate. The chocolate was placed in one of two boxes with windows that faced the children. Therefore, the chocolate was clearly visible to the children but not to the experimenter. It was explained that pointing to the empty box would be successful in winning the chocolate: If the experimenter went to the empty box, the child won the chocolate. A substantial portion of 3-year-old children not only pointed to the baited box on the first test trial but also continued to point to the baited box throughout 20 trials. Russell et al. concluded that the false belief task and the windows task are associated because both require children to inhibit reference to a salient object or location.

More specific empirical support for this position was provided by studies showing that children perform better on such strategic deception tasks when the inhibitory demands are reduced by using novel methods of deception (Carlson et al., 1998; Hala & Russell, 2001). In these easier tasks, children were given the opportunity to point an arrow to the empty location (Carlson et al., 1998) or to manipulate a cardboard hand in order to direct the opponent (Hala & Russell, 2001). These researchers argued that pointing to where things really are may be a prepotent response for young children, whereas there is no prepotent response tendency for using an arrow to point.

Other authors also argue that children have to inhibit salient reality in order to answer correctly in the false belief task. Mitchell (1996) hypothesized that young children make realist errors in the false belief task because their attention is dominated by current reality. Some support for this hypothesis comes, for example, from a study by Mitchell and Lacohée (1991). In their "posting" version of the Smarties task, children were asked to select and then post a picture of what they thought was in the box at the moment they first saw it. It was found that making the belief content visible enhanced performance (but see Robinson, Riggs, & Samuel, 1996; Zelazo & Boseovski, 2001, for failures to replicate this effect).

However, at least one clear prediction from this theory (Russell et al., 1991, p. 342) for the false belief task has been disconfirmed, namely, that the explanation version of the false belief task, which does not share the alleged executive problem, should be easier than the prediction version. In the explanation version of the false belief task, children watch the protagonist look in the empty location before they are asked to explain the protagonist's erroneous action. Children are asked an open "why"-question (e.g., "Why then does Maxi go to the desk to get his chocolate?"), which is unlikely to elicit a prepotent wrong answer strategy. Furthermore, the physical realization of the protagonist's wrong search (children watch the protagonist move to the wrong place) provides the needed reality counterpart to his false belief and, therefore, should reduce distraction by the actual location of the critical object. Thus, it is hard to see an executive problem of suppressing a prepotent response in the explanation task. However, the explanation version, when controlling for correct guesses, is not easier than the prediction version (Wimmer & Mayringer, 1998) and correlates with executive tasks as strongly as the prediction version (Hughes, 1998a; Perner et al., 2002; for an elaborate discussion of this issue, see Perner et al., 2002).

Moreover, children show an implicit understanding of false beliefs (indicated by looking at the correct location and spontaneous helping actions) before they can answer correctly to the test question (Clements & Perner, 1994; Garnham & Perner, 2001). And one would not expect that the pull of reality would be more easily overcome in such an implicit, spontaneous action than in a considered verbal statement.

Further evidence against an expression account comes from Sabbagh et al. (2006). They found that Chinese preschoolers outperformed U.S. preschoolers on executive functioning tasks. But this advanced level of executive control did not result in a similar advantage on theory-of-mind measures.[2] In summary, this suggests that the observed relationship between theory of mind and executive function is not just due to executive demands in theory-of-mind tasks.

FUNCTIONAL DEPENDENCY ACCOUNTS

Theory of Mind as a Prerequisite for Executive Control

Perner (1991) and Wimmer (1989) suggested that improved understanding of one's mind leads to greater self-control as the child develops; that is, theory of mind is seen as a prerequisite for executive functions. In a similar fashion, Carruthers (1996) argues that the observed executive function deficits of individuals with autism are a consequence of their theory-of-mind impairment.

Some evidence against this position was provided by Hughes (1998b; for similar results, see also Carlson, Mandell, & Williams, 2004; Flynn, O'Malley, & Wood, 2004). In her longitudinal study, early executive function performance at ages 3–4 predicted children's understanding of mind a year later, even when effects of age and verbal ability were removed. However, early theory-of-mind performance did not predict later executive function performance. Furthermore, two single case studies, one of a child with autism (Baron-Cohen & Robertson, 1995) and one of a man with frontotemporal dementia (Lough, Gregory, & Hodges, 2001), demonstrated theory-of-mind deficits in the absence of impaired executive performance suggesting that theory-of-mind understanding cannot be a prerequisite for executive control.

Executive Control as a Prerequisite for a Theory of Mind

Other authors argue that executive control is necessary for developing a theory of mind. Russell (1996, 1997, 1999) argues that self-control is a prerequisite for building a theory of mind because theory of mind must be grounded upon a first-person experience of agency. In his view, the exercise of agency is a *necessary condition* for a conception of our own and others' minds. Agency is defined as "the ability to alter perceptual inputs at will" (Russell, 1999, p. 250). However, as Russell (1999, p. 257) points out "this is not to say that endogenous changes in executive control *cause* a theory of mind to be acquired, but rather that the acquisition of a theory of mind cannot develop adequately without these endogenous changes taking place." In a similar vein, Hughes (1998b, p. 1327) hypothesizes that "early goal-directed action may ... provide the grounding for introspective awareness of mental states."

Some evidence against this position comes from a study by Perner, Kain, and Barchfeld (2002). They compared preschool children "at risk of" Attention Deficit Hyperactivity Disorder (ADHD) with an age-matched control group: The group at risk of ADHD showed impaired performance relative to the control group on several executive tasks but no impairment at all on advanced theory-of-mind tasks (e.g., the understanding of second-order beliefs). Similarly, Charman, Carroll, and Sturge (2001) found no differences between 22 boys with a diagnosis of ADHD (6–10 years old) and 22 typically developing controls on advanced theory-of-mind measures. However, significant differences emerged on one of two executive tasks: the group with ADHD produced more commission errors on a go/no-go task than the control group. There were no significant differences between the two groups on a planning task (Tower of Hanoi). These findings of an executive deficit but no equally clear deficit in theory of mind seem to suggest that executive competence cannot be a prerequisite for acquiring a theory of mind.

However, this conclusion may be premature, because children with ADHD are not equally impaired on all aspects of executive functioning. There are quite consistent impairments in motor inhibition. But performance on a classic set-shifting paradigm, the WCST, is less consistently impaired (Pennington & Ozonoff, 1996). That leaves open the door for the explanation that one specific executive function, namely, shifting cognitive sets is necessary for developing a theory of mind. Interestingly, persons with autism, who are typically impaired on theory-of-mind tasks, are particularly impaired on set-shifting measures like the WCST or extra-dimensional shift tasks, but not so on classic tests of inhibition like the Stroop task (for a recent review, see Hill, 2004). Such an interpretation would also fit the results obtained by Charman et al. (2001), who found impaired inhibition in boys with ADHD but no deficit on advanced theory-of-mind measures.

ACKNOWLEDGMENTS

This study is part of a research project financed by the Austrian Science Fund (FWF project T251-G04).

NOTES

1. One might object that Davis and Pratt (1995) as well as Gordon and Olson (1998) found a relationship between theory of mind and working memory, but, in contrast to Carlson et al. (2002) these authors did not control for performance on inhibitory control tasks.
2. This also speaks against the suggestion that theory of mind—at least as measured by theory of mind tests—is a prerequisite for executive control. However, theory of mind in self-application (understanding how one's own mind works) may well be a prerequisite for executive functions.

REFERENCES

Baron-Cohen, S., & Robertson, M. (1995). Children with either autism, gilles de la tourette syndrome or both: Mapping cognition to specific syndromes. *Neurocase, 1,* 101–104.

Berman, K. F., Ostrem, J. L., Randolph, C., Gold, J., Goldberg, T. E., Coppola, R., et al. (1995). Physiological activation of a cortical network during performance of the Wisconsin Card Sorting Test: A positron emission tomography study. *Neuropsychologia, 33,* 1027–1046.

Carlson, S. M., Mandell, D. J., & Williams, L. (2004). Executive function and theory of mind: Stability and prediction from age 2 to 3. *Developmental Psychology, 40,* 1105–1122.

Carlson, S. M., & Moses, L. J. (2001). Individual differences in inhibitory control and children's theory of mind. *Child Development, 72,* 1032–1053.

Carlson, S. M., Moses, L. J., & Breton, C. (2002). How specific is the relation between executive function and theory of mind? Contributions of inhibitory control and working memory. *Infant and Child Development, 11,* 73–92.

Carlson, S. M., Moses, L. J., & Claxton, L. J. (2004). Individual differences in executive functioning and theory of mind: An investigation of inhibitory control and planning ability. *Journal of Experimental Child Psychology, 87,* 299–319.

Carlson, S. M., Moses, L. J., & Hix, H. R. (1998). The role of inhibitory processes in young children's difficulties with deception and false belief. *Child Development, 69,* 672–691.

Carruthers, P. (1996). Autism as mind-blindness: An elaboration and partial defence. In P. Carruthers & P. K. Smith (Eds.), *Theories of theories of mind* (pp. 257–273). Cambridge, UK: Cambridge University Press.

Cepeda, N. J., Kramer, A. F., & Gonzalez de Sather, J. C. M. (2001). Changes in executive control across the life span: Examination of task-switching performance. *Developmental Psychology, 37,* 715–730.

Charman, T., Carroll, F., & Sturge, C. (2001). Theory of mind, executive function and social competence in boys with ADHD. *Emotional and Behavioural Difficulties, 6,* 31–49.

Clements, W. A., & Perner, J. (1994). Implicit understanding of belief. *Cognitive Development, 9,* 377–397.

Crone, E. A., Bunge, S. A., van der Molen, M. W., & Ridderinkhof, K. R. (2006). Switching between tasks and responses: a developmental study. *Developmental Science, 9,* 278–287.

Davis, H. L., & Pratt, C. (1995). The development of children's theory of mind: The working memory explanation (Special Issue: Cognitive development). *Australian Journal of Psychology, 47,* 25–31.

Diamond, A., Carlson, S. M., & Beck, D. M. (2005). Preschool children's performance in task switching on the Dimensional Change Card Sort task: Separating the dimensions aids the ability to switch. *Developmental Neuropsychology, 28*(2), 689–729.

Diamond, A., & Kirkham, N. (2005). Not quite as grown-up as we like to think: Parallels between cognition in childhood and adulthood. *Psychological Science, 16,* 291–297.

Doherty, M., & Perner, J. (1998). Metalinguistic awareness and theory of mind: Just two words for the same thing? *Cognitive Development, 13,* 279–305.

Dove, A., Pollmann, S., Schubert, T., Wiggins, C. J., & von Cramon, D. Y. (2000). Prefrontal cortex activation in task switching: An event-related fMRI study. *Cognitive Brain Research, 9,* 103–109.

Ellefson, M. R., Shapiro, L. R., & Chater, N. (2006). Asymmetrical switch costs in children. *Cognitive Development, 21,* 108–130.

Eslinger, P. J. (1996). Conceptualizing, describing, and measuring components of executive function. In G. R. Lyon & N. A. Krasnegor (Eds.), *Attention, memory, and executive function* (pp. 367–395). Baltimore, MD: Paul H. Brookes Publishing.

Eriksen, C. W., & Yeh, Y. Y. (1985). Allocation of attention in the visual field. *Journal of Experimental Psychology: Human Perception and Performance, 11,* 583–597.

Flavell, J. H., Everett, B. A., Croft, K., & Flavell, E. (1981). Young children's knowledge about visual perception: Further evidence for the Level 1–Level 2 distinction. *Developmental Psychology, 17,* 99–103.

Flynn, E., O'Malley, C., & Wood, D. (2004). A longitudinal, microgenetic study of the emergence of false belief understanding and inhibition skills. *Developmental Science, 7,* 103–115.

Frye, D., Zelazo, P. D., & Palfai, T. (1995). Theory of mind and rule-based reasoning. *Cognitive Development, 10,* 483–527.

Garnham, W. A., & Perner, J. (2001). Actions really do speak louder than words—but only implicitly: Young children's understanding of false belief in action. *British Journal of Developmental Psychology, 19,* 413–432.

Gerstadt, C. L., Hong, Y. J., & Diamond, A. (1994). The relationship between cognition and action: Performance of children 3½–7 years old on a Stroop-like day-night test. *Cognition, 53,* 129–153.

Gopnik, A., & Astington, J. W. (1988). Children's understanding of representational change and its relation to the understanding of false belief and the appearance-reality distinction. *Child Development, 59,* 26–37.

Gordon, A. C. L., & Olson, D. R. (1998). The relation between acquisition of a theory of mind and the capacity to hold in mind. *Journal of Experimental Child Psychology, 68,* 70–83.

Grant, D. A., & Berg, E. A. (1948). A behavioural analysis of degree of reinforcement and ease of shifting to new responses in a Weigl-type card sorting problem. *Journal of Experimental Psychology, 38,* 404–411.

Hala, S., Hug, S., & Henderson, A. (2003). Executive function and false-belief understanding in preschool children: Two tasks are harder than one. *Journal of Cognition and Development, 4,* 275–298.

Hala, S., & Russell, J. (2001). Executive control with strategic deception: A window on early cognitive development? *Journal of Experimental Child Psychology, 80,* 112–141.

Hill, E. L. (2004). Executive dysfunction in autism. *Trends in Cognitive Sciences, 8,* 26–32.

Hogrefe, J., Wimmer, H., & Perner, J. (1986). Ignorance versus false belief: A developmental lag in attribution of epistemic states. *Child Development, 57,* 567–582.

Hughes, C. (1998a). Executive functions in preschoolers: Links with theory of mind and verbal ability. *British Journal of Developmental Psychology, 16,* 233–253.

Hughes, C. (1998b). Finding your marbles: Does preschoolers' strategic behaviour predict later understanding of mind? *Developmental Psychology, 34,* 1326–1339.

Hughes, C., & Russell, J. (1993). Autistic children's difficulty with mental disengagement from an object: Its implication for theories of autism. *Developmental Psychology, 29,* 498–510.

Kloo, D., & Perner, J. (2003). Training transfer between card sorting and false belief understanding: Helping children apply conflicting descriptions. *Child Development, 74,* 1823–1839.

Kloo, D., & Perner, J. (2005). Disentangling dimensions in the dimensional change card sorting task. *Developmental Science, 8,* 44–56.

Kray, J., Eber, J., & Lindenberger, U. (2004). Age differences in executive functioning across the lifespan: The role of verbalization in task preparation. *Acta Psychologica, 115,* 143–165.

Lough, S., Gregory, C., & Hodges, J. R. (2001). Dissociation of social cognition and executive function in frontal variant frontotemporal dementia. *Neurocase, 7,* 123–130.

Mayr, U. (2001). Age differences in the selection of mental sets: The role of inhibition, stimulus ambiguity, and response-set overlap. *Psychology and Aging, 16,* 96–109.

Meyer, D. E., Evans, J. E., Lauber, E. J., Gmeindl, L., Rubinstein, J., Junck, L., et al. (1998). *The role of dorsolateral prefrontal cortex for executive cognitive processes in task switching.* Poster presented at the meeting of the Cognitive Neuroscience Society, San Francisco, CA.

Mitchell, P. (1996). *Acquiring a conception of mind: A review of psychological research and theory.* Hove, UK: Psychology Press.

Mitchell, P., & Lacohée, H. (1991). Children's early understanding of false belief. *Cognition, 39,* 107–127.

Monsell, S. (2003). Task switching. *Trends in Cognitive Sciences, 7,* 134–140.

Moses, L. J. (2001). Executive accounts of theory-of-mind development. *Child Development, 72,* 688–690.

Moses, L. J., & Carlson, S. M. (2004). Self-regulation and children's theories of mind. In C. Lightfoot, C. Lalonde, & M. J. Chandler (Eds.), *Changing conceptions of psychological life* (pp. 127–146). Mahwah, NJ: Lawrence Erlbaum Associates.

Nagahama, Y., Okada, T., Katsumi, Y., Hayashi, T., Yamauchi, H., Oyanagi, C., et al. (2001). Dissociable mechanisms of attentional control within the human prefrontal cortex. *Cerebral Cortex, 11,* 85–92.

Ozonoff, S., Pennington, B. F., & Rogers, S. J. (1991). Executive function deficits in high-functioning autistic individuals: Relationships to theory of mind. *Journal of Child Psychology and Psychiatry, 32,* 1081–1105.

Pennington, B. F., & Ozonoff, S. (1996). Executive functions and developmental psychopathology. *Journal of Child Psychology and Psychiatry, 37,* 51–87.

Perner, J. (1991). *Understanding the representational mind.* Cambridge, MA: MIT Press.

Perner, J., Kain, W., & Barchfeld, P. (2002). Executive control and higher-order theory of mind in children at risk of ADHD. *Infant and Child Development, 11,* 141–158.

Perner, J., & Lang, B. (2002). What causes 3-year-olds' difficulty on the dimensional change card sorting task? *Infant and Child Development, 11,* 93–105.

Perner, J., Lang, B., & Kloo, D. (2002). Theory of mind and self-control: More than a common problem of inhibition. *Child Development, 73,* 752–767.

Perner, J., Stummer, S., Sprung, M., & Doherty, M. (2002). Theory of mind finds its Piagetian perspective: Why alternative naming comes with understanding belief. *Cognitive Development, 17,* 1451–1472.

Peskin, J., & Ardino, V. (2003). Representing the mental world in children's social behavior: Playing hide-and-seek and keeping a secret. *Social Development, 12,* 496–512.

Posner, M. I. (1980). Orienting in attention. *Quarterly Journal of Experimental Psychology, 32,* 3–25.

Premack, D., & Woodruff, G. (1978). Does the chimpanzee have a theory of mind? *Behavioral and Brain Sciences, 1,* 515–526.

Robinson, E. J., Riggs, K. J., & Samuel, J. (1996). Children's memory for drawings based on a false belief. *Developmental Psychology, 32,* 1056–1064.

Russell, J. (1996). *Agency. Its role in mental development.* Hove, UK: Lawrence Erlbaum Associates.

Russell, J. (1997). How executive disorders can bring about an inadequate "theory of mind." In J. Russell (Ed.), *Autism as an executive disorder* (pp. 256–299). Oxford: Oxford University Press.

Russell, J. (1999). Cognitive development as an executive process—in part: A homeopathic dose of Piaget. *Developmental Science, 2,* 247–270.

Russell, J., Mauthner, N., Sharpe, S., & Tidswell, T. (1991). The "windows task" as a measure of strategic deception in preschoolers and autistic subjects. *British Journal of Developmental Psychology, 9,* 331–349.

Sabbagh, M. A., Xu, F., Carlson, S. M., Moses, L. J., & Lee, K. (2006). The development of executive functioning and theory of mind: A comparison of Chinese and U.S. Preschoolers. *Psychological Science, 17,* 74–81.

Scholl, B. J. (2001). Objects and attention: The state of the art. *Cognition, 80,* 1–46.

Shallice, T. (1988). *From neuropsychology to mental structure.* Cambridge: Cambridge University Press.

Simpson, A., & Riggs, K. J. (2005). Factors responsible for performance on the day-night task: Response set or semantics? *Developmental Science, 8,* 360–371.

Sohn, M. H., Ursu, S., Anderson, J. R., Stenger, V. A., & Carter, C. S. (2000). The role of prefrontal cortex and posterior parietal cortex in task switching. *Proceedings of the National Academy of Sciences, 97,* 13448–13453.

Soto, D., & Blanco, M. J. (2004). Spatial attention and object-based attention: A comparison within a single task. *Vision Research, 44,* 69–81.

Stuss, D. T., Levine, B., Alexander, M. P., Hong, J., Palumbo, C., Hamer, L., et al. (2000). Wisconsin Card Sorting Test performance in patients with focal frontal and posterior brain damage: Effects of lesion location and test structure on separable cognitive processes. *Neuropsychologia, 38,* 388–402.

Towse, J. N., Redbond, J., Houston-Price, C. M. T., & Cook, S. (2000). Understanding the dimensional change card sort. Perspectives from task success and failure. *Cognitive Development, 15,* 347–365.

Wellman, H. M., Cross, D., & Watson, J. (2001). Meta-analysis of theory-of-mind development: The truth about false belief. *Child Development, 72,* 655–684.

Welsh, M. C., Pennington, B. F., & Groisser, D. B. (1991). A normative-developmental study of executive function: A window on prefrontal function in children. *Developmental Neuropsychology, 7,* 131–149.

Wimmer, H. (1989). Common-Sense Mentalismus und Emotion. Einige entwicklungspsychologische Implikationen. In E. Roth (Hrsg.), *Denken und Fühlen* (pp. 56–66). Berlin: Springer.

Wimmer, H., & Mayringer, H. (1998). False belief understanding in young children: Explanations do not develop before predictions. *International Journal of Behavioral Development, 22*(2), 403–422.

Wimmer, H., & Perner, J. (1983). Beliefs about beliefs: Representation and constraining function of wrong beliefs in young children's understanding of deception. *Cognition, 13,* 103–128.

Zelazo, P. D., & Boseovski, J. J. (2001). Video reminders in a representational change task: Memory for cues but not beliefs or statements. *Journal of Experimental Child Psychology, 78,* 107–129.

Zelazo, P. D., Frye, D., & Rapus, T. (1996). An age-related dissociation between knowing rules and using them. *Cognitive Development, 11,* 37–63.

Zelazo, P. D., Jacques, S., Burack, J. A., & Frye, D. (2002). The relation between theory of mind and rule use: Evidence from persons with autism-spectrum disorders. *Infant and Child Development, 11,* 171–195.

Zelazo, P. D., Müller, U., Frye, D., & Marcovitch, S. (2003). The development of executive function in early childhood. *Monographs of the Society for Research in Child Development, 68*(3), Serial No. 274.

9

Clarifying the Relation between Executive Function and Children's Theories of Mind

LOUIS J. MOSES AND DENIZ TAHIROGLU

Two defining achievements in human ontogeny are the ability to appreciate the perspectives of others and the ability to regulate one's thoughts and actions appropriately. The first of these developmental achievements is often described as the acquisition of a "theory of mind" (ToM). It is a domain-specific ability that is critical to adaptive functioning in the social world. Without the capacity to understand the beliefs, intentions, and emotions of others social interaction would be limited, superficial, and doomed to flounder (Baron-Cohen, Tager-Flusberg, & Cohen, 1993). The second achievement is often described as executive functioning (EF), and includes such skills as inhibitory control, set-shifting, working memory, and planning (Hughes, 1998a). It is a domain-general ability that is essential for functioning in virtually any situation requiring cognitive flexibility. Without some capacity to adjust thought and action as a function of the demands of the external world, life would surely be fruitless and probably rather short as well.

Intriguingly, evidence is mounting that these two fundamental abilities (EF and ToM) are in some way bound together in development (Schneider, Schumann-Hengsteler, & Sodian, 2005). Marked advances take place in both in the preschool years (Harris, 2006; Zelazo & Müller, 2002), and both are deficient in atypical populations such as autism (Pellicano, 2007). More telling is the fact that during the preschool years individual differences in one ability predict individual differences in the other. Children who have good perspective-taking skills tend to have good self-regulatory skills as well, and vice versa. An increasing number of studies have found moderate to strong correlations between EF and ToM (e.g., Carlson & Moses, 2001; Frye, Zelazo, & Palfai, 1995; Hala, Hug, & Henderson, 2003; Hughes, 1998a; Perner, Lang, & Kloo, 2002). Moreover, these relations typically persist when extraneous variables such as age, verbal ability, and general cognitive ability are held constant (Carlson & Moses, 2001; Carlson, Moses, & Breton, 2002; Carlson, Moses, & Claxton, 2004).

In one of the most extensive examinations of this issue, Carlson and Moses (2001) gave children batteries of EF and ToM tasks over two sessions. The ToM tasks included measures of false belief understanding, the appearance-reality distinction, and deceptive ability. The executive tasks were of two general types. Conflict tasks imposed a conflict between a dominant response and a subdominant response. For example, in the Bear/Dragon task (Kochanska, Murray, Jacques, Koenig, & Vandegeest, 1996) children are required to perform actions commanded by a bear puppet but to refrain from performing actions commanded by a dragon puppet. In the Dimensional Change Card Sort (DCCS) task (Zelazo & Frye, 1997) children first sort cards according to one rule (e.g., by shape) and then are asked to sort them according to a conflicting rule (e.g., by color). In contrast, Delay tasks simply require children to suppress responding altogether for a period of time. For example, in the Gift Delay task (Kochanska et al., 1996) children are asked to turn away from an experimenter for 60 seconds while she noisily wraps a gift for them.

Carlson and Moses (2001) found a strong correlation between the two batteries that persisted when age, sex, and verbal ability were controlled. Moreover, the relation remained significant when they further controlled for other relevant factors such as family size, symbolic understanding, and ability to solve tasks that were structurally similar to the ToM tasks but that did not require mental state understanding. The relation between EF and ToM is clearly sizeable, robust, and not a spurious by-product of a range of other relevant factors.

In this chapter we aim to shed further light on the nature of the EF–ToM relation. What is the underlying basis of the relation? What aspects of EF and what aspects of ToM are implicated in the relation? Is the relation merely a product of task-specific performance factors or does it reflect more fundamental processes in conceptual development? Does the causal relation run from EF to ToM or vice versa, or is some other factor causal to both? In what follows we first describe some possible answers to these questions, and then assess the extent to which existing data from experimental, training, correlational, and cross-cultural studies can help decide among the various possibilities.

Explaining the Relation between Executive Function and Theory of Mind

There are at least four ways in which EF and ToM might be developmentally linked (for a similar taxonomy, see Perner & Lang, 1999). A first possibility is that EF and ToM are related in virtue of some common underlying cognitive capacity (e.g., Andrews, Halford, Bunch, Bowden, & Jones, 2003; Frye et al., 1995). For example, Frye, Zelazo, and colleagues (Frye et al., 1995; Frye, Zelazo, & Burack, 1998) have argued that the ability to reason with hierarchically embedded rules is essential for many ToM tasks as well as many EF tasks. In this view, both task types require children to use a higher order rule to select the condition (or perspective, in the case of ToM) from which to reason. For example, the DCCS task mentioned earlier involves a hierarchical rule structure comprising (1) setting conditions (e.g., "if" sorting by color), (2) antecedent conditions (e.g., "and if" a certain color is presented on a card), and (3) consequent actions (e.g., "then" place the card in a specified location). Frye, Zelazo, and colleagues argue that just as young children have difficulty switching setting conditions in the DCCS, so too do they have analogous difficulty switching perspectives in ToM tasks.

A second possibility is that advances in ToM might be instrumental in generating advances in EF (Perner & Lang, 1999; Perner et al., 2002). For example, it may be that some conception of mental states is necessary in order to monitor or control those states. More specifically, Perner and his colleagues have argued that the metarepresentational capacities central to ToM may be required for certain executive abilities such as inhibitory control. In order to control their actions effectively, children need to represent their action goals as well as the impediments to those goals such as prior learning or habitual response tendencies.

A third possibility is that EF might be implicated in the *expression* of preexisting ToM concepts (Carlson, Moses, & Hix, 1998; Russell, Mauthner, Sharpe, & Tidswell, 1991). For example, with respect to the classic false belief task (Wimmer & Perner, 1983), a child might already possess a conception of false belief but nevertheless fail the task because of executive difficulties. In the false belief task children themselves know where an object is located but a story protagonist does not. The protagonist has a false belief concerning the whereabouts of the object in virtue of being absent while the object was moved. Children are asked where the protagonist will look for the object. However, even if children have some appreciation of false belief, they might incorrectly answer this question. Specifically, they may lack the inhibitory control required to suppress their own salient knowledge of where the object is, and so be unable to recover the protagonist's belief concerning the object's whereabouts. In short, they would have a performance deficit as opposed to a conceptual deficit.

A fourth and final possibility is that EF might be necessary for the very *emergence* of ToM concepts (Moses, 2001; Russell, 1996). For example, a certain level of inhibitory control and working memory may be necessary for children even to entertain the possibility that there might be more than one perspective on a given situation. Without such executive capacity children would be unable to distance themselves from the immediate perceptual flux, and so could never develop abstract concepts like perspective or belief. Rather than having a performance deficit, children might suffer from a conceptual deficit caused, at least in part, by insufficient executive capacity. We turn now to a discussion of how the empirical evidence bears on these four possibilities.

Empirical Investigations of the EF–ToM Relation

EXPERIMENTAL STUDIES

A reasonable place to start in exploring the EF–ToM relation would be to manipulate the executive demands of ToM tasks. If performance improves when these demands are reduced, then that would support the executive expression account described earlier. In a meta-analysis of false belief studies, Wellman and his colleagues identified a number of factors that affect performance (Wellman, Cross, & Watson, 2001). These factors were (a) the salience of the protagonist's mental state, (b) the presence of a deceptive motive, (c) active involvement by the child in moving the object to the new location, and (d) the presence of the target object at the time the test question is asked. All these manipulations can, in retrospect, be viewed as executive in nature in that they shift the salience balance between the true state of affairs and the protagonist's mental state. The first three factors serve to focus the child's attention on the mental state of the protagonist (a) or the events that directly affect that state (b and c); the last factor decreases the salience of the actual state of affairs (d).

In addition, a few studies have more explicitly set out to manipulate executive demands of ToM tasks. For example, Leslie and Polizzi (1998) found that by increasing the executive demands of the false belief task even older preschoolers began to fail. Two other studies examining children's deceptive ability have attempted to reduce executive task demands. Deceptive ability is often tested by giving children the opportunity to point to an empty container in order to deceive an opponent about the location of an object (Russell et al., 1991). Younger preschoolers tend to point to the container in which the object is actually located rather than to the empty location. Moreover, they continue to make this error over repeated trials even when they have seen their competitor easily find the object (Russell et al.). Carlson et al. (1998) argued, however, that requiring children to deceive by pointing may introduce heavy executive demands into the task. Veridical pointing is a highly practiced and well reinforced response for children (e.g., in looking at picture books with parents or caregivers). It may be very difficult for them to set aside this habit in order to point deceptively. This hypothesis was supported in several experiments in which children were given the opportunity to deceive using novel methods (e.g., indicating a location with the aid of a sticker or a game board arrow). Children's performance was significantly better under these conditions than in a standard pointing condition (for very similar results, see Hala & Russell, 2001).

These findings are clearly supportive of the executive expression hypothesis outlined earlier. They suggest that by reducing the executive demands of ToM tasks children become able to express already present ToM knowledge. Nonetheless, the manipulations identified in the Wellman et al. (2001) meta-analysis do not move the performance of children below the age of 3 ½ to above chance levels. Similarly, in the experiments on deceptive pointing, performance was not above chance on every trial, most critically the first trial. Better performance on later trials is thus open to a lower-level learning interpretation, as opposed to an explanation framed in terms of already present conceptual knowledge. Thus, to the extent that the EF–ToM relation is a by-product of executive expression, EF would seem to play a relatively limited role in ToM development. That is, executive difficulties may well affect children's performance but these difficulties could not be the major source of younger children's difficulties with false belief or deception.

TRAINING STUDIES

Training studies represent a uniquely informative way in which to examine the EF–ToM relation, especially with respect to causal direction. If EF plays the causal role in this relation, then training on EF might be expected to enhance ToM. Conversely, if ToM is causal, then training on ToM might enhance EF. To our knowledge, only one study of this type has been carried out with typically developing children. Kloo and Perner (2003) trained children either on EF tasks or ToM tasks (specifically false belief), both trainings emphasizing redescription of objects. They found that EF training led not only to better EF performance, but also to better ToM performance as well. ToM training also led to enhanced EF performance but, surprisingly, ToM training failed to enhance ToM performance.

This last finding calls into question what the "ToM" training was actually training. It may be that although the intention was to train ToM in this study, executive skills were inadvertently trained. That might explain why EF, but not ToM, improved at posttest. Moreover, even if ToM had been successfully trained, that would not rule out that improvements were generated by executive aspects of the training. Indeed, it is difficult to see how something like false belief could be trained without also training executive skills. Training a child to understand false belief inevitably involves helping him or her to recognize the conflict between the protagonist's mental state and the true state of affairs, and to shift attention away from the true state of affairs when questioned about belief.

In that regard, an examination of studies in which children have been successfully trained on ToM shows that training typically focused on notions like redescription, dual representation, and perspective shifting (Appleton & Reddy, 1996; Hale & Tager-Flusberg, 2003; Lohmann & Tomasello, 2003; Slaughter & Gopnik, 1996). All of these trainings can be thought of as involving executive and conceptual components. For instance, in Lohmann and Tomasello's training study, children were trained to recognize the deceptive aspect of the objects (e.g., an object X, looking like Y) and to shift their perspective from salient reality (e.g., "I know that it is really X.") to mental representation of objects (e.g., "Somebody who has not interacted with this object before would think that it is Y."). Training focused on flexibly deploying attention in this way is inherently executive.

In summary, there is good evidence that EF training enhances ToM (Kloo & Perner, 2003). The evidence is much more ambiguous, however, with respect to any causal role ToM might play with respect to EF.

CORRELATIONAL STUDIES

Correlational studies also have the potential to shed light on the EF–ToM relation. We mentioned earlier that Carlson and Moses (2001) gave children both conflict and delay EF tasks. Interestingly, although the relation with ToM was present for both conflict and delay EF tasks, it was considerably stronger for conflict tasks. This difference has been now replicated a number of times (Carlson et al., 2002, 2004; Hala et al., 2003). One difference between conflict and delay tasks is that, although both require inhibitory control, only conflict tasks impose substantial working-memory demands. For example, in a task such as Gift Delay children are required to inhibit turning around for a specified period of time, but the memory demands are minimal: Children only need to remember not to turn around. In contrast, in a conflict task like the Bear/Dragon task children are required to hold in mind two rules (what to do in response to the Bear and what to do in response to the Dragon) while inhibiting a dominant response (responding to all commands). This hypothesis concerning the varying working-memory demands of these tasks was borne out empirically in a subsequent study (Carlson et al., 2002) in which only conflict tasks correlated significantly with working-memory tasks (e.g., backward digit and word span tasks, and a dual counting and labeling task). Hala et al. (2003) found similar effects with other working-memory tasks (the Day-Night stroop control task and the six boxes scramble task). These findings might suggest the hypothesis that EF relates to ToM *only* in virtue of common working-memory requirements. In that respect, working-memory tasks have been found to correlate with ToM performance (Davis & Pratt, 1996; Gordon & Olson, 1998; Keenan, 1998). However, these tasks tend to correlate less with ToM than do tasks that impose heavy demands on *both* inhibition and working memory (Carlson et al., 2002; Hala et al., 2003). The fact that EF tasks with these joint demands correlate more highly with ToM than do tasks that place a heavy burden mainly on inhibition or mainly on working memory makes sense given the structure of ToM tasks. In many ToM tasks both inhibition and working memory appear to be required for successful performance. For example, in the false belief task children must hold in mind two perspectives (their own and that of the protagonist) while inhibiting the dominant perspective (their own).

One apparent exception to the pattern just described comes from a recent study by Mutter, Alcorn, and Welsh (2006). These authors found that working memory was a stronger predictor of false belief understanding than was inhibition. Two points are worth noting with respect to this study. One is that Mutter et al.'s inhibition measure—perseveration in a visual search task—did not involve a substantial working-memory component and, in that respect, was analogous to a delay inhibition task. The other is that, as Mutter et al. point out, the working-memory measure (the "Mr. Circui" task) involved a substantial inhibitory component (the need to avoid perseverating on previously correct responses), as well as a working-memory component. To the extent that this characterization of Mutter et al.'s tasks is correct, their findings can be accommodated within the proposal described earlier emphasizing the joint role of working memory and inhibition in ToM reasoning.

Mutter et al.'s study also highlights a more general interpretive issue. In the literature on EF, tasks are commonly labeled as inhibitory tasks, working-memory tasks, planning tasks, or tasks assessing other aspects of EF. However, we rarely have pure measures of cognitive processes. EF tasks almost always tap, not only more basic cognitive processes in addition to EF, but also more than one component of EF. Hence, caution is required in drawing inferences concerning theoretical constructs like working memory or inhibition from the imperfect empirical indicators used to assess those constructs.

The studies just discussed attempted to isolate which aspects of EF are critical to the EF–ToM relation. Other correlational studies have focused on specifying which aspects of ToM are most strongly associated with EF. In one such study Moses, Carlson, Claxton, and Stieglitz (2009) explored how EF relates to belief, desire, and pretense understanding. In doing so, Moses et al. tried to match tasks measuring each kind of mental state understanding as closely as possible in terms of their structural characteristics. For example, they used tasks developed by Lillard and Flavell (1992) in which children heard stories about a protagonist who either thought, wanted, or pretended that X was the case. Children then discovered that Y was the case and then were simply asked to restate what the protagonist thought, wanted, or pretended. Moses et al. found that EF was strongly related to performance on belief tasks, weakly to performance on desire tasks, and not at all to performance on pretense tasks. They hypothesized that the executive requirements for reasoning about beliefs are stronger because, unlike the other mental states, beliefs are supposed to reflect the true state of affairs. Contrast this with pretense, for example, where the whole point is to create an interesting counterfactual situation. The salience of the true state of affairs may thus be substantially greater in the context of belief reasoning, and hence more difficult to suppress.

This pattern of findings is problematic for the view that the EF–ToM relation arises because of some common, underlying cognitive requirement, such as the need to reason with embedded rules. The tasks measuring belief, desire, and pretense understanding were designed to be as equivalent as possible in terms of their formal structure, including the underlying rule structure. All three task types would appear to require similar reasoning from different setting and antecedent conditions, and yet very different correlations with EF emerged. Similarly, Sabbagh, Moses, and Shiverick (2006) found that EF correlates strongly with performance on false belief tasks but only weakly with performance on so-called false photo tasks (see Müller, Zelazo, & Imresik, 2005, for similar findings). False photo tasks (Zaitchik, 1990) are designed to be structurally similar to false belief tasks: a photo becomes "false" when the scene it captures changes just as a belief becomes false when the situation it represents changes. Children can then be asked about the content of the out of date photo, just as they can be asked about the out of date belief. The underlying rule structure of the false photo task would seem to be the same as that of the false belief task (although for a different view, see Müller et al., 2005), and yet the correlations with EF are markedly different. Sabbagh et al. (2006) argue that the executive demands of photo tasks are minimal because, unlike beliefs, photos are not intended to accurately represent the true state of affairs. Rather they should merely represent the state of affairs at the time at which they were taken. Hence, the true state of affairs should be considerably more potent in the case of beliefs than in the case of photos.

In another correlational study, Moses et al. (2009) found that EF is associated just as strongly with ToM tasks that do *not* impose heavy executive demands as it is with those that do impose such demands. A task of the former kind is the "think-know" task (Moore, Pure, & Furrow, 1990), in which children need to follow the advice either of someone who claims to *know* an object is in location A or of someone who merely *thinks* the object is in location B. After hearing these conflicting statements, children are asked to find the object. Older preschoolers wisely look in location A, presumably recognizing that knowledge implies certainty whereas believing does not. Younger preschoolers, however, have great difficulty with the task. That said, there is apparently no prepotent response bias in the task as would be expected if there were substantial inhibitory demands present. Rather children's performance across trials is more or less random. Yet Moses et al. found that performance on this task correlates just as highly with EF as does performance on the false belief task (which is characterized by a strongly prepotent response option—the actual location of the desired object).

These findings and others like them (e.g., Perner et al., 2002) pose a problem for executive expression accounts. Such performance accounts predict that if executive demands are minimized then children should perform well. Moreover, if a task has minimal executive demands, it should not correlate with EF. Yet younger children perform poorly on tasks like the "think-know" task, and correlations with EF are substantial for such tasks. In contrast, the findings can be accommodated within an executive emergence account. On this account, executive skill is important for the acquisition of mental state concepts and hence EF should relate to any task requiring possession of those concepts, irrespective of online executive demands. The findings are also problematic for the view that relations between ToM and EF arise from some common underlying cognitive requirement, such as the need to reason with embedded rules. The think-know task would appear to have a very simple rule structure: If an individual knows that X is the case his or her statements about X can be trusted, whereas if an individual merely thinks that X is the case his or her statements about X may not be reliable. Despite this relatively simple rule structure, correlations with EF are still obtained.

Some correlational studies also have a bearing on the issue of causal direction. Specifically, in longitudinal research one can determine whether EF or ToM at time 1 more strongly predicts EF or ToM at time 2. Findings from three longitudinal studies suggest that EF may be causal with respect to ToM rather than vice versa. Specifically, Hughes (1998b) found that the correlation between EF at 3 years and ToM at 4 years was considerably stronger than that between ToM at 3 years and EF at 4 years. Carlson, Mandell, and Williams (2004) found much the same pattern predicting from age 2 to age 3, as did Hughes and Ensor (2007) predicting from age 2 to age 4. Similarly, microgenetic studies in which EF and ToM are measured at multiple time-points over shorter periods (Flynn, 2007; Flynn, O'Malley, & Wood, 2004) suggest that EF emerges earlier than ToM. These various findings clearly favor the view that EF is causal with respect to ToM, rather than the reverse.

The microgenetic research is also problematic for the EF expression view. As with training studies, expression accounts predict that once EF is in place, ToM abilities should immediately be revealed. However, Flynn (2007) found that local fluctuations in EF performance were only inconsistently related to local fluctuations in ToM performance.

CROSS-CULTURAL STUDIES

Exploring whether similar relations between EF and ToM are present in diverse cultures can also illuminate the nature of the EF–ToM relation. If the relation is present in some cultures but not in others, then that would clearly rule out the hypotheses that EF is *necessary* for ToM or vice versa. To this point only a small number of cross-cultural studies have been conducted, but all have found significant relations between EF and ToM. For example, Sabbagh and his colleagues found that the relation was just as strong in mainland China as it is in North America (Sabbagh, Xu, Carlson, Moses, & Lee, 2006). Oh and Lewis (2008) found that aspects of EF were related to ToM in Korean children, although not quite as strongly as in a British sample. Finally, Chasiotis and colleagues found that the EF–ToM relation was significant over and above the effects of culture in samples of children from Germany, Cameroon, and Costa Rica (Chasiotis, Kiessling, Hofer, & Campos, 2006).

The Sabbagh et al. (2006) study also provided a test of the executive expression and emergence hypotheses. Exploring the EF–ToM relation in China was of theoretical interest because Chinese parents encourage self-control in children at an early age. Therefore, it was possible that Chinese children would be advanced on EF relative to North American children. The interesting question then would be whether they were also advanced on ToM. If the expression hypothesis is correct, they should be: in the absence of executive deficits, ToM concepts should be revealed. In contrast, if the emergence hypothesis is correct, there is no clear prediction: on that hypothesis EF is necessary but not sufficient for ToM, so advanced ToM might or might not be seen. In testing these hypotheses, Sabbagh et al. found that Chinese children were indeed advanced on EF relative to their North American counterparts. However, no discernible advantage was found with respect to ToM. This pattern of results is inconsistent with the expression hypothesis but can be accommodated within the emergence hypothesis.

The Sabbagh et al. (2006) findings are also problematic with respect to the hypothesis that ToM plays a causal role with respect to EF. The Chinese children appeared to have a surfeit of executive ability yet they had achieved that in the absence of much ToM ability. The fact that they did so would seem to indicate that ToM is not necessary for advances in EF although, of course, it might still play a facilitative role.

Evaluating the Explanations

At the outset of this chapter we described four possible explanations of the EF–ToM relation: explanations framed in terms of (a) common cognitive requirements, (b) a causal role for ToM, (c) executive expression, and (d) executive emergence. How do these explanations fare in light of the empirical data obtained from the varied methodological approaches just discussed? In closing we offer an overall assessment of each potential explanation.

First, the view that the EF–ToM relation arises because of common cognitive requirements for these skills is difficult to rule out entirely. However, the fact that EF–ToM relations persist when many other relevant factors, such as verbal skill and general cognitive ability are held constant speaks against at least some versions of this account. Some aspects of the data also pose problems for the more specific hypothesis that reasoning with embedded rules is the basis for the EF–ToM relation (Frye et al., 1995). That account has difficulty explaining (a) why EF relates to ToM tasks having what appear to be different rule structures (e.g., the false belief task and the "think-know" task) and (b) why EF relates very differently to matched tasks having what appear to be very similar rule structures (e.g., false belief, unfulfilled desire, pretense, and false photo tasks). These latter tasks were designed to be as equivalent as possible in terms of their formal structure and yet very different correlations with EF emerged. We believe that other accounts of this type face similar difficulties (e.g., Andrews et al., 2003).

Support for the view that advances in ToM generate advances in EF is mixed. In its favor the account can explain why EF correlates with ToM tasks with few executive demands. That is because the account posits that ToM concepts (as opposed to performance on the tasks that measure those concepts) are necessary for advances in EF. Consequently, children who have concepts of thinking and knowing (those assessed in the "think-know" task) should perform better on EF tasks than those who do not possess the concepts. The bearing of the training data on the account is more difficult to assess. The difficulty, as noted earlier, is that although ToM training generated improved EF it surprisingly did not generate enhanced ToM (Kloo & Perner, 2003). Hence, it remains unclear whether training in ToM, per se, was responsible for the observed EF advances. Moreover, the ToM causal account has difficulty explaining (a) the positive effects of executive manipulations, (b) the longitudinal and microgenetic data suggesting that early EF more strongly predicts later ToM than early ToM predicts later EF, and (c) the finding that EF advances in Chinese children are apparently generated in the absence of corresponding ToM advances.

The executive expression account also receives mixed support. On the positive side, executive manipulations do sometimes generate improved ToM performance, especially in older preschoolers. Moreover, the fact that training on EF enhances ToM (Kloo & Perner, 2003) is precisely what would be expected if the expression hypothesis is correct. If children already possess ToM concepts but perform poorly because of task-related executive obstacles, then their performance should improve if either the obstacles are removed or they are taught how to surmount these obstacles. That said, executive manipulations do not greatly affect the performance of younger preschoolers, suggesting that conceptual difficulties may also be operating. In addition, the expression hypothesis has difficulty explaining why EF relates to performance on ToM tasks with few manifest executive demands, and it also has difficulty accounting for the fact that Chinese children are advanced in EF but not in ToM. Finally, the inconsistent microgenetic relations between short-term fluctuations in EF and short-term fluctuations in ToM are not easily accommodated within an expression framework. At the very least, then, problems with expression could neither fully explain EF–ToM relations nor be the major rate-limiting factor in the development of children's ToM.

In our view the executive emergence account is best supported by the data. The emergence account predicts that EF will correlate even with ToM tasks that impose minimal executive demands, and it can accommodate the longitudinal, microgenetic, and cross-cultural data. Of course, the account cannot explain why executive manipulations affect task performance. Similarly, the training data are to some extent problematic for the emergence view. In principle, it is possible that children might very quickly acquire ToM concepts after successful EF training. That said, it is perhaps more plausible that EF training makes possible the uncovering of already present ToM concepts rather than the sudden emergence of those concepts. Clearly, even if emergence factors underlie the lion's share of the EF–ToM relation, difficulties with EF expression may also play at least some role.

Conclusion

The relation between EF and ToM is complex and multifaceted. EF and ToM are both heterogeneous constructs, making it difficult to pinpoint the precise nature of the relation. Our review of the evidence provides varying levels of support for each of the explanatory accounts we considered. Indeed, it may well be the case that the central factors highlighted by these accounts all contribute to some extent to the EF–ToM relation. That is, domain general cognitive processes such as reasoning with embedded rules may contribute to the development of both EF and ToM, and hence to their relation. In addition, while we find it doubtful that advances in ToM could lead to the acquisition of EF skills, it would not be at all surprising if ToM played some facilitative role in the subsequent development of those skills. An appreciation of mental states should be helpful in monitoring and controlling thoughts and the actions that stem from thoughts. Finally, executive skills are at the very least necessary for successful performance on ToM tasks, suggesting that executive expression likely plays some role in the EF–ToM relation. That said, we would argue that the evidence best supports the view that advances in EF are necessary for the emergence of ToM skills.

To the extent that EF is importantly implicated in the emergence of mental state concepts, the nature of that process remains to be more fully specified. As we have indicated, one possibility is that the reflective capacity made possible by advancing executive skills allows children to step back from immediate perceptual constraints to consider the existence of unobservable factors such as perspectives, representations, and beliefs. However, it is quite possible that the process is less direct. As many of the contributions to this volume make abundantly clear, social factors are closely intertwined with both EF and ToM development. The role of such factors in the EF–ToM relation must therefore be taken seriously. As Hughes (1998b) has argued, for example, advances in EF may generate more and better opportunities for social interaction. It may be these opportunities, rather than EF per se, that make possible advances in ToM. That said, the reverse could also be true. Social interaction might be a breeding ground for the development of EF which, in turn, might foster advances in ToM. Finally, we need to consider the more radical notion that social processes are responsible for advances in *both* EF and ToM. That is, there might be no relation (direct or indirect) between EF and ToM: advances in these abilities might be independently generated by social factors. However, although social processes are likely to be importantly implicated in the development of EF and ToM, we are skeptical that an account framed solely in terms of such processes can accommodate the range of findings we have discussed (e.g., the facts that EF relates to some ToM concepts but not others, that training EF generates improvements in ToM, and that early EF predicts later ToM but not vice versa). Still, it is clear that the role social factors play in children's developing executive skills and mental state reasoning will need to be carefully scrutinized in future research.

REFERENCES

Andrews, G., Halford, G. S., Bunch, K. M., Bowden, D, & Jones, T. (2003). Theory of mind and relational complexity. *Child Development, 74,* 1476–1499.

Appleton, M., & Reddy, V. (1996). Teaching 3-year-olds to pass false belief tests: A conversational approach. *Social Development, 5,* 275–291.

Baron-Cohen, S., Tager-Flusberg, H., & Cohen, D. (Eds.) (1993). *Understanding Other Minds: Perspectives From Autism.* Oxford: Oxford University Press.

Carlson, S. M., Mandell, D. J., & Williams, L. (2004). Executive function and theory of mind: Stability and prediction from age 2 to 3 years. *Developmental Psychology, 40,* 1105–1122.

Carlson, S. M., & Moses, L. J. (2001). Individual differences in inhibitory control and children's theory of mind. *Child Development, 72,* 1032–1053.

Carlson, S. M., Moses, L. J., & Breton, C. (2002). How specific is the relation between executive function and theory of mind? Contributions of inhibitory control and working memory. *Infant and Child Development, 11,* 73–92.

Carlson, S. M., Moses, L. J., & Claxton, L. J. (2004). Executive function and theory of mind: The role of inhibitory control and planning ability. *Journal of Experimental Child Psychology, 87,* 299–319.

Carlson, S. M., Moses, L. J., & Hix, H. R. (1998). The role of inhibitory control in young children's difficulties with deception and false belief. *Child Development, 69,* 672–691.

Chasiotis, A., Kiessling, F., Hofer, J., & Campos, D. (2006). Theory of mind and inhibitory control in three cultures: Conflict inhibition predicts false belief understanding in Germany, Costa Rica and Cameroon. *International Journal of Behavioral Development, 30,* 249–260.

Davis, H. L., & Pratt, C. (1996). The development of children's theory of mind: The working memory explanation. *Australian Journal of Psychology, 47,* 25–31.

Flynn, E. (2007). The role of inhibitory control in false belief understanding. *Infant and Child Development, 16,* 53–69.

Flynn, E., O'Malley, C., & Wood, D. (2004). A longitudinal, microgenetic study of the emergence of false belief understanding and inhibition skills. *Developmental Science, 7,* 103–115.

Frye, D., Zelazo, P.D., & Burack, J. (1998). I. Cognitive complexity and control: Implications for theory of mind in typical and atypical development. *Current Directions in Psychological Science, 7,* 116–121.

Frye, D., Zelazo, P. D., & Palfai, T. (1995). Theory of mind and rule-based reasoning. *Cognitive Development, 10,* 483–527.

Gordon, A. C. L., & Olson, D.R. (1998). The relation between acquisition of a theory of mind and the capacity to hold in mind. *Journal of Experimental Child Psychology, 68*, 70–83.

Hala, S., Hug, S., & Henderson, A. (2003). Executive functioning and false belief understanding in preschool children: Two tasks are harder than one. *Journal of Cognition and Development, 4*, 275–298.

Hala, S., & Russell, J. (2001). Executive control within strategic deception: A window on early cognitive development? *Journal of Experimental Child Psychology, 80*, 112–141.

Hale, M., & Tager-Flusberg, H. (2003). The influence of language on theory of mind: A training study. *Developmental Science, 6*, 346–359.

Harris, P. L. (2006). Social cognition. In D. Kuhn & R. S. Siegler (Vol. Eds.), *Handbook of child development Vol. 2: Cognition, perception and language* (pp. 811–858). Hoboken, NJ: John Wiley & Sons.

Hughes, C. (1998a). Executive function in preschoolers: Links with theory of mind and verbal ability. *British Journal of Developmental Psychology, 16*, 233–253.

Hughes, C. (1998b). Finding your marbles: Does preschoolers' strategic behavior predict later understanding of mind? *Developmental Psychology, 34*, 1326–1339.

Hughes, C., & Ensor, R. (2007). Executive function and theory of mind: Predictive relations from ages 2- to 4-years. *Developmental Psychology, 43*, 1447–1459.

Keenan, T. (1998). Memory span as a predictor of false belief understanding. *New Zealand Journal of Psychology, 27*, 36–43.

Kloo, D., & Perner, J. (2003). Training transfer between card sorting and false belief understanding: Helping children apply conflicting descriptions. *Child Development, 74*, 1823–1839.

Kochanska, G., Murray, K., Jacques, T. Y., Koenig, A. L., & Vandegeest, K. A. (1996). Inhibitory control in young children and its role in emerging internalization. *Child Development, 67*, 490–507.

Leslie, A. M., & Polizzi, P. (1998). Inhibitory processing in the false belief task: Two conjectures. *Developmental Science, 1*, 247–253.

Lillard, A. S., & Flavell, J. H. (1992). Young children's understanding of different mental verbs. *Developmental Psychology, 28*, 626–634.

Lohmann, H., & Tomasello, M. (2003). The role of language in the development of false belief understanding: A training study. *Child Development, 74*, 1130–1144.

Moore, C., Pure, K., & Furrow, D. (1990). Children's understanding of the modal expression of certainty and uncertainty and its relation to the development of a representational theory of mind. *Child Development, 61*, 722–730.

Moses, L. J. (2001). Executive accounts of theory of mind development. *Child Development, 72*, 688–690.

Moses, L. J., Carlson, S. M., Claxton, L. J., & Stieglitz, S. (2009). Inhibitory control and children's theories of mind: The sequence and generality problems. Manuscript under review, University of Oregon.

Müller, U., Zelazo, P. D., & Imrisek, S. (2005). Understanding false belief and executive function: How specific is the relation? *Cognitive Development, 20*, 173–189.

Mutter, B., Alcorn, M. B., & Welsh, M. (2006). Theory of mind and executive function: Working-memory capacity and inhibitory control as predictors of false-belief task performance. *Perceptual and Motor Skills, 102*, 819–835.

Oh, S., & Lewis, C. (2008). Korean preschoolers' advanced inhibitory control and its relation to other executive skills and mental state understanding. *Child Development, 79*, 80–99.

Pellicano, E. (2007). Links between theory of mind and executive function in young children with autism: Clues to developmental primacy. *Developmental Psychology, 43*, 974–990.

Perner, J., & Lang, B. (1999). Development of theory of mind and executive control. *Trends in Cognitive Sciences, 3*, 337–344.

Perner, J., Lang, B., & Kloo, D. (2002). Theory of mind and self control: More than a common problem of inhibition. *Child Development, 73*, 752–767.

Russell, J. (1996). *Agency: Its role in mental development.* Hove, UK: Lawrence Erlbaum Associates.

Russell, J., Mauthner, N., Sharpe, S., & Tidswell, T. (1991). The "windows task" as a measure of strategic deception in preschoolers and autistic subjects. *British Journal of Developmental Psychology, 9*, 331–349.

Sabbagh, M. A., Moses, L. J., & Shiverick, S. M. (2006). Executive functioning and preschoolers' understanding of false beliefs, false photographs and false signs. *Child Development, 77*, 1034–1049.

Sabbagh, M. A., Xu, F., Carlson, S. M., Moses, L. J., & Lee, K. (2006). The development of executive functioning and theory of mind: A comparison of Chinese and U.S. preschoolers. *Psychological Science, 17*, 74–81.

Schneider, W., Schumann-Hengsteler, R., & Sodian, B. (Eds.). (2005). *Young children's cognitive development: Interrelationships among executive functioning, working memory, verbal ability, and theory of mind.* Mahwah, NJ: Lawrence Erlbaum Associates.

Slaughter, V., & Gopnik, A. (1996). Conceptual coherence in the child's theory of mind: Training children to understand belief. *Child Development, 67*, 2967–2988.

Wellman, H. M., Cross, D., & Watson, J. (2001). Meta-analysis of theory of mind development: The truth about false belief. *Child Development, 72*, 655–684.

Wimmer, H., & Perner, J. (1983). Beliefs about beliefs: Representation and constraining function of wrong beliefs in young children's understanding of deception. *Cognition, 13*, 103–128.

Zaitchik, D. (1990). When representations conflict with reality: The preschooler's problem with false beliefs and "false" photographs. *Cognition, 35*, 41–68.

Zelazo, P. D., & Frye, D. (1997). Cognitive complexity and control: A theory of the development of deliberate reasoning and intentional action. In M. Stamenov (Ed.), *Language structure, discourse, and the access to consciousness* (pp. 113–153). Amsterdam & Philadelphia: John Benjamins.

Zelazo, P. D., & Müller, U. (2002). Executive functions in typical and atypical development. In U. Goswami (Ed.), *Handbook of childhood cognitive development* (pp. 445–469). Oxford, England: Blackwell Publishing.

10

The Developmental Relations between Perspective Taking and Prosocial Behaviors: A Meta-Analytic Examination of the Task-Specificity Hypothesis

GUSTAVO CARLO, GEORGE P. KNIGHT, MEREDITH McGINLEY,
REBECCA GOODVIN, AND SCOTT C. ROESCH

Sharing, comforting, donating, helping, and volunteering are all forms of prosocial behaviors that are deemed desirable to our society. Such behaviors are considered central to understanding the development of moral and social competencies, and, as might be expected, the expression of such behaviors is highly valued by most parents. Developmental scholars have long noted age-related changes in the expression of prosocial behaviors, and researchers have attempted to account for such changes by examining correlates that show similar age-related changes. Scholars have identified two such possible correlates: perspective taking and theory of mind (ToM). Perspective taking refers to understanding the cognitive and affective state of others, and of their social situation (e.g., Carlo, 2006; Eisenberg, Fabes, & Spinrad, 2006; Radke-Yarrow, Zahn-Waxler, & Chapman, 1983; Shantz, 1983). Similarly, ToM can be defined as understanding of mind (e.g., beliefs, thoughts) and emotions (Dunn, 1995; Wellman, 2002).

In the present chapter, we review and critique research linking perspective taking and prosocial behaviors. However, it should be noted that ToM and perspective taking are conceptually linked. Indeed, scholars have noted that ToM research evolved out of the earlier research on perspective taking (Chandler & Carpendale, 1998). The major distinctions between the two approaches are theoretical, age-based, and the use of somewhat different tasks. Theoretically, perspective taking research evolved from Piaget's groundbreaking research on understanding children's shift from egocentrism (self-focused orientation) to sociocentrism. A number of scholars noted inconsistencies in research findings, including findings that suggested that children were less egocentric than previously believed, which led to newer frameworks for studying children's understanding of cognitions and emotions. ToM researchers began to examine children's psychological understanding at younger ages using different tasks (e.g., false belief tasks). This body of research has grown considerably and has proved useful in understanding young children's psychological capabilities, especially before the fourth year of life (for a comprehensive review, see Wellman, 2002). However, despite the emphasis on ToM in recent decades, research on perspective taking has continued. Because of the relatively large existing literature on perspective taking and prosocial behaviors, we focus on perspective taking in the present chapter. Nonetheless, the findings on perspective taking and prosocial behaviors have important implications for research on ToM.

PERSPECTIVE TAKING AND PROSOCIAL BEHAVIORS

There are three common types of perspective taking that scholars have identified (Carlo, 2006; Kurdek, 1978). First, social (or cognitive) perspective taking refers to the understanding of another's thoughts, intentions, and situation. Second, affective perspective taking is defined as the ability to understand the emotional state of another. And third, perceptual (or spatial) perspective taking is the ability to understand the literal visual point of view of another. The notion is that these types of perspective taking are important for individuals to understand another person's needy or distressed situation to help them. Perspective taking also facilitates empathic and sympathy responding such that psychological understanding fosters vicarious emotional responding (Hoffman, 2000). In addition, perspective taking skills are believed to promote higher levels of moral reasoning (Selman, 1980). As a result, researchers have often focused on perspective taking (especially social and affective) as potential candidate antecedents that might account for age differences in prosocial behaviors. Indeed, both perspective taking and prosocial behaviors increase across childhood (Kurdek, 1981; see Radke-Yarrow et al., 1983; Shantz, 1983). Consequently, some investigators attempted to show that age differences in prosocial behaviors are accounted for by age differences in perspective taking.

In an examination of the research on the relations between perspective taking and prosocial behaviors, Underwood and Moore (1982) conducted a meta-analytic review of the literature to discern whether perspective taking was related to prosocial behaviors. Although Underwood and Moore (1982, p. 169) concluded that there is, "an extraordinarily reliable—if only moderately large [overall $r = .28$]—relationship [between perspective taking and altruism]," they also acknowledged that the findings were mixed and that many studies showed weak and nonsignificant relations. Furthermore, they acknowledged certain limitations on their conclusions. First, there was a narrowness of the types of prosocial behaviors studied. According to these researchers, most measures of prosocial behavior were laboratory measures of generosity. Second, there was a failure to sample widely in terms of participants' ages. Most existing studies at that time consisted of examining these relations in preschool to children 14 years of age. And third, they argued for a need to delineate the circumstances under which the relation between perspective taking and prosocial behavior might be unusually strong or weak. The present chapter reports the findings of a meta-analysis designed to address some of these limitations by examining research conducted since the Underwood and Moore (1982) review.

A number of other reviewers of the literature concurred with Underwood and Moore's (1982) findings and pointed out several additional limitations to existing studies of the relations between these constructs (Eisenberg & Miller, 1987; Krebs & Russell, 1981; Kurdek, 1978). According to these scholars, researchers have often utilized perspective taking and prosocial behavior measures without careful consideration of whether the measures of perspective taking assess sociocognitive skills relevant to the specific prosocial behaviors under investigation. For example, assessing a child's understanding of a distressed child's emotions (affective perspective taking) may not inform researchers on the likelihood of helping someone to pick up dropped items. In addition, in response to suggestions (e.g., Ford, 1979; Kurdek, 1978) that some measures of perspective taking and prosocial behaviors are relatively unreliable, some scholars recommended that researchers use aggregate or composite measures. Denham (1986) and Iannotti (1985) found positive relations between composite measures of perspective taking and helping.

The implications of these reviews are that many researchers examining the relations between perspective taking and prosocial behaviors may not have attended closely enough to the different types of perspective taking and the use of measures of these different types of perspective taking in their research. Essentially this suggests that the weaker than expected relations occurred because the underlying cognitive prerequisites of specific prosocial behavior being investigated may not have "matched" the underlying cognitive nature of the perspective taking measures included within specific studies (Eisenberg, 1986; Underwood & Moore, 1982). Hence, the magnitude of the observed relation between perspective taking and prosocial behavior may be greater when the underlying cognitive demands of the two sets of measures are the same or highly similar, and the magnitude of the observed relation may be lesser when there is a fundamental "mismatch" in the cognitive nature of the perspective taking and prosocial behavior measures. For example, helping a needy person in a highly emotionally charged crisis situation is likely to be more highly associated with cognitive or affective perspective taking than spatial perspective taking. That is, if the prosocial behavior opportunity requires recognizing another's situation and emotional state when in a crisis situation, the *cognitive ability* to understand that needy person's situation (cognitive perspective taking) and/or to understand that person's emotional state (affective perspective taking) are likely requisite to behaving prosocially. In contrast, the ability to be aware of that needy person's perception of the physical nature of the immediate surroundings is not likely to foster prosocial behavior.[1]

This *task-specificity hypothesis* is based on information processing and social-cognitive perspectives (Bandura, 1986; Dodge & Crick, 1990; Dweck & Leggett, 1988; Knight, Johnson, Carlo, & Eisenberg, 1994), suggesting the need to examine task-specific cognitive skills that might be associated with specific behavioral outcomes. There are three key elements to the *task-specificity hypothesis*. First, different prosocial behaviors might require different types of perspective taking or other sociocognitive (e.g., ToM) and socioemotive (e.g., sympathy) skills. Second, specific prosocial behaviors might require a specific combination of perspective taking and other sociocognitive and socioemotive skills. And third, there is an assumption that, over time, individuals acquire situation-specific scripts or schema that facilitate behavioral responding across similar situations. A task-specific cognitive skills approach has proven useful in several areas of research (e.g., self-efficacy, attribution biases, and aggression) and could prove useful in accounting for the weaker than anticipated relations between perspective taking and prosocial behaviors (as well as the lesser studied relations between ToM and prosocial behaviors; see e.g., Cassidy, Werner, Rourke, Zubernis, & Balaraman, 2003; Findlay, Girardi, & Coplan, 2006; Slaughter, Dennis, & Pritchard, 2002). Figure 10.1 depicts our conceptual model and suggests that several attributes of the actor, the target, and the context may moderate the relations between perspective taking and prosocial behaviors. Furthermore, this model suggests that there is likely a combination of attributes of these three sources that may function in a multiplicative manner to enhance the likelihood of perspective taking (and other sociocognitive and socioemotive skills) leading to prosocial behaviors.

In the current chapter, we present a meta-analytic review of the prior studies to examine the *task-specificity hypothesis*. Similarity in the measures of perspective taking and prosocial behavior was expected to be associated with the relations between these two constructs. That is, the magnitude of the relation between perspective taking and prosocial behaviors was expected to be larger as the attributes in the perspective taking and prosocial behavior tasks are more similar. This is because children who exhibit specific perspective-taking skills will likely apply those skills to prosocial behavior tasks that prime or

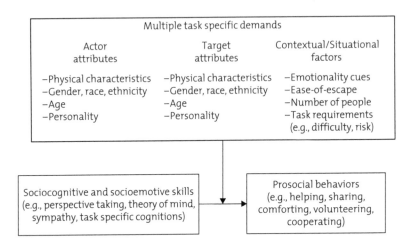

FIGURE 10.1. Conceptual model of the relations between social cognitions and emotions and prosocial behaviors.

activate cognitive, affective, and motivational scripts similar to those needed in the perspective-taking tasks. The closer the match in the situation-specific scripts, the better the predictive power. Those distinctions acknowledge the multidimensional qualities of perspective taking and prosocial behavior. If perspective taking and prosocial behaviors are multidimensional constructs, then it becomes more necessary for future researchers to identify the relevant dimensions (or characteristics) of these constructs that "pull" for the relevant underlying skills or tendencies in the individual.

After careful examination of the specific nature of the most common perspective taking tasks and prosocial behavior measures we identified three dimensions of task characteristics that appeared to be common to these measures and relevant to predicting prosocial behaviors. First, because emotions influence cognitions and prosocial behaviors, similarity in the level of emotionality in the perspective taking and prosocial behavior opportunity was expected to influence the magnitude of the relations between perspective taking and prosocial behavior. That is, when the specific perspective taking and prosocial behavior measures both require an awareness of another's emotional state the association between participants' perspective taking abilities and their prosocial behavior should be enhanced. Furthermore, when both the perspective taking and prosocial behaviors are emotion-laden, one would expect that individual differences in emotion-related processing and expressivity would be manifested in responses to both perspective taking and prosocial behaviors. The extent to which there is a match of emotionality in the tasks should enhance predictive power in the relations between perspective taking and prosocial behaviors.

Second, and partially based on Eisenberg's (1986) suggestion that the physical characteristics of the protagonist in empathy and prosocial behavior situations influence the observer's responses, the relation between perspective taking and prosocial behavior should be enhanced when the target person in the perspective taking and prosocial behavior task are highly similar. Hence, a perspective-taking task that requires an awareness of the difficulty a young child with a broken leg experiences is likely to be more related to a prosocial behavior measure requiring one to help a young child complete an assigned task when that child has some physical limitation than to a measure requiring donations to a generic charity. The similarity of characteristics of the protagonists might facilitate application of situation-specific scripts across these two tasks. Therefore, the strength of the effect size in relations between perspective taking and prosocial behaviors should be influenced by the extent of similarity in the target protagonists of each task.

Finally, on the basis of social cognitive and information-processing theories, it was expected that the magnitude of the relation between perspective taking and prosocial behavior should be enhanced when the level of assessment of these constructs (i.e., a more global assessment vs. a more contextually specific assessment) is highly similar. The more similar the characteristics of specificity in the tasks, the greater the magnitude of effect is expected in the relations between perspective taking and prosocial behaviors. For example, tasks that assess a broad range of prosocial behaviors might require greater task-specific cognitive skills (e.g., higher-order abstraction skills) that facilitate a child's thinking about the spectrum of prosocial behaviors. Therefore, individual differences in cognitive development would be expected to reflect individual differences in responses to these tasks—the extent to which the tasks match in these cognitive prerequisites should be reflected in the expected relations between perspective taking and prosocial behaviors. Furthermore, a close match in the characteristics of the tasks is expected to reflect greater similarity in the scripts relevant to perspective taking and prosocial behavior tasks, which in turn, should foster easier application of those scripts in responding to the tasks.

To examine the task-specificity hypothesis, we conducted a search of the available empirical evidence on the relations between perspective taking and prosocial behavior. Then, for each effect size estimate, independent raters coded the similarity or "match" between the task characteristics of the perspective-taking measure and the prosocial behavior measure. The similarity indices were then included as predictors in weighted, least squares, multiple regression analyses to assess the impact of these predictors on the correlation between perspective taking and prosocial behavior.

THE LITERATURE SEARCH

A literature search was conducted using PsycInfo database, Psychological Abstracts, the Social Sciences Citation Index, and an ancestral search from previous review articles. Only studies published in journals from 1970 to 2002 were utilized. Descriptors included role-taking, perspective taking, social cognitions, sociocognitive skills, empathy, sympathy, moral cognitions, morality, prosocial behaviors, volunteering, altruism, social competence, sharing, donating, comforting, and helping. Studies from existing reviews of the literature (Eisenberg, 1986; Krebs & Russell, 1981; Kurdek, 1978; Underwood & Moore, 1982) were also included.

Studies were excluded if (a) the researchers manipulated perspective taking or prosocial behaviors without providing adequate information to calculate effect sizes within a control condition, (b) there was inadequate information to calculate an overall effect size (a number of studies did not have sufficient information to calculate some effect sizes, see Table 10.1), or (c) the sample was not from the United States. Forty-seven studies, with the potential to produce 264 effect sizes, met these criteria. Of the 264 possible effect sizes, only 167 were reported. Studies included in the analyses are indicated with an asterisk in the Reference section.

THE CODING OF STUDY CHARACTERISTICS

Two undergraduate students independently coded the similarity between the perspective taking and prosocial behavior indices on the physical characteristics of the protagonists (referred to as the target similarity), the level of emotionality in the perspective taking and prosocial behavior tasks (referred to as the emotional similarity), and the level of situational specificity (e.g., whether the study utilized a trait-like or situation-specific index; referred to as the specificity similarity) on a five-point scale from very dissimilar (1) to very similar (5). The coders read only the method section of the articles unless the article did not provide a thorough description of the perspective-taking measure. In this latter case the coders read a more detailed description of the measures from an earlier published study (usually the original publication of the measure). Interrater reliability as indexed by a correlation coefficient for 75 potential effect sizes (out of the 264 original potential effect sizes) was 0.90, 0.91, and 0.66 for the target, specificity, and emotional similarity rating.

TABLE 10.1. Studies of the Relations between Perspective Taking and Prosocial Behaviors.

Study	Sample	Sample Type	Study Context	Perspective-Taking Measure	Helping Measure	Results
Abrams & Gollin (1980)	8 F, 12 M (2–4 yrs, M = 40.4 mos)	7	2	(a) Perceptual composite [3] (b) Conceptual composite +(a) [1,3] (c) IAT [2]	(1) Observation composite (sharing, helping (physical or verbal assistance), physical affection)	Fall: ra1 = ns, rb1 = ns, rc1 = ns Spring: ra1 = ns, rb1 = ns, rc1 = ns
Ahammer & Murray (1979)	49 F, 48 M (4–5 yrs, M = 54.86 mos)	5	1	(a) IAT [2] (b) Mountain task [3] (c) Cubes task [3] (d) Ball and biscuits task [1]	(1) Helping a peer to get toys (2) Sharing raisins	Pretest: ra1 = ns, ra2 = ns, rb1 = ns, rb2 = ns, rc1 = ns, rc2 = ns, rd1 = ns, rd2 = ns Posttest: ra1 = ns, ra2 = ns, rb1 = ns, rb2 = ns, rc1 = 0.21, rc2 = ns, rd1 = ns, rd2 = ns
Barnett & Thompson (1985)	53 F, 64 M (grades 4 & 5)*	4	1	(a) Feelings task [2]	(1) Teacher ratings	ra1 = ns
Barrett & Yarrow (1977)	40 F, 39 M (5–8 yrs)*	1	2	(a) Inferential ability [1]	(1) Observation (sharing, helping, comforting)	Females: ra1 = 0.06 Males: ra1 = –0.02
Batson, Bolen, Cross, & Neuringer-Benefiel (1986)	Easy escape: 30 F Difficult escape: 30 F (college)*	2	1	(a) IRI [1]	(1) Take place of other in shock experiment (easy and difficult escape)	Easy escape: ra1 = 0.21 Difficult escape: ra1 = 0.26

(Continued)

TABLE 10.1. (Continued)

Study	Sample	Sample Type	Study Context	Perspective-Taking Measure	Helping Measure	Results
Abroms & Gollin (1980)	8 F, 12 M (2–4 yrs, M = 40.4 mos)	7	2	(a) Perceptual composite [3] (b) Conceptual composite +(a) [1,3] (c) IAT [2]	(1) Observation composite (sharing, helping (physical or verbal assistance), physical affection)	Fall: ra1 = *ns*, rb1 = *ns*, rc1 = *ns* Spring: Ra1 = *ns*, Rb1 = *ns*, Rc1 = *ns*
Bender & Carlson (1982)	non-MR: 7 F, 7 M (M = 7.9 yrs) EMR: 9 F, 5 M (M = 9.8 yrs) TMR: 7 F, 7 M (M = 16 yrs)	4, 7	1	(a) Picture task [2] (b) Beads task [2]	(1) Picture task: express helping others or self (2) Helping pick up beads (spontaneous) (3) Help with beads (verbally expressed)	*BG chi squares:* Non-MR: Chia1 = *ns*, Chib2 = *ns*, Chib3 = 10.4 Educ MR: Chia1 = *ns*, Chib2 = *ns*, Chib3 = *ns* Trainable MR: Chia1 = *ns*, Chib2 = *ns*, Chib3 = *ns*
Bengtsson & Johnson (1992)	30 F, 30 M (10–12 yrs, M = 130 mos)	6	1	(a) Inner experience [2] (b) One-sided empathic reasoning [2] (c) Extended empathic reasoning [2]	(1) Teacher ratings	ra1 = 0.25 rb1 = −0.48 rc1 = 0.60
Blotner & Bearison (1984)	120 M (4–11 yrs, M = 7.88 yrs)	7	1	(a) Cognitive perspective coordination [1]	(1) Sharing candy with hypothetical boy (2) Helping hypothetical boy on artistic task	ra1 = 0.19 ra2 = 0.19

Study	Sample	Grade		Empathy measure	Prosocial measure	Mann-Whitney U-tests:
Buckley, Siegel, & Ness (1979)	18 F, 23 M (3–9 yrs)*	4,5	1	(a) Sesame Street task [3] (b) IAT [2]	(1) Helped pick up puzzle parts or sharing of cookie	za1 = 2.17 [+] zb1 = 2.45 [+]
Burleson (1984)	72 F, 72 M [137 used] (grades 1–12)*	4	1	(a) Social perspectives task [2]	(1) Verbal comforting (hypothetical situation)	ra1 = 0.82
Carlo, Knight, Eisenberg, & Rotenberg (1991)	39 F, 50 M (preschool-grade 2, M = 81.1 mos)	5,4	1	(a) Apple-dog story [1] (b) Affective attributions[2] (c) Affective reasoning [2]	(1) Turning a crank to help another child get toys	**Congruent cues** (N = 44) ra1 = −0.17 rb1 = 0.28 rc1 = 0.01 — **Incongruent cues** (N = 45) Ra1 = 0.10 Rb1 = −0.17 Rc1 = 0.34
Chapman, Zahn-Waxler, Cooperman, & Iannotti (1987)	30 F, 30 M (preschool-grade 6, M = 8.07 yrs)	4, 5	1	Story task: (a) empathy [2] (b) Altruism [1] (c) Guilt [2] (d) Aggression [2] (e) Denial [1] (f) Aggregate ((a + b + c) − (d + e)) [1,2]	(1) Kitten distress (2) Adult distress (3) Infant distress (4) Total helping (1 through 3)	ra1 = 0.28 ra2 = 0.10 ra3 = 0.42 ra4 = 0.36 rb1 = 0.33 rb2 = 0.06 rb3 = 0.43 rb4 = 0.33 rc1 = 0.42 rc2 = 0.38 rc3 = 0.36 rc4 = 0.55 rd1 = 0.04 rd2 = 0.05 rd3 = −0.06 rd4 = 0.12 re1 = −0.02 re2 = −0.18 re3 = −0.04 re4 = −0.18 rf1 = 0.43 rf2 = 0.20 rf3 = 0.57 rf4 = 0.52
Davis (1983) Study 1	74 F, 84 M (college)*	2	1	(a) IRI [1]	(1) Intent to volunteer	ra1 = n/a

(Continued)

TABLE 10.1. (Continued)

Study	Sample	Sample Type	Study Context	Perspective-Taking Measure	Helping Measure	Results
Davis (1983) Study 2	186 (gender n/a) (college)*	2	1	(a) IRI [1]	(1) Donation to telethon (2) Volunteering time (3) Other donation	ra1 = 0.06 ra2 = 0.03 ra3 = 0.01
Denham (1986)	11 F, 16 M (2–3 yrs, M = 38.99 mos)	5	3	(a) Composite of affective labeling (faces) and puppet task [2] (b) Cognitive puppet task [1]	(1) Help hurt adult & child who wanted cookie (composite) (2) Observed free play	ra1 = 0.51 ra2 = 0.29 rb1 = 0.26 rb2 = –0.07
Eisenberg, Carlo, Murphy, & Van Court (1995)	C1: 16 F, 16 M (T8: M = 17.6 yrs) C2: 20 F, 14 M (M = 17.8 yrs)	4,2	1	(a) IRI [1]	(1) Self-report [C1, C2] (2) Maternal report [C1] (3) Return questionnaire through mail [C1, C2] (4) Donate money [C2]	ra1 = 0.46 ra2 = 0.45 ra3 = –0.15 ra4 = 0.11
Eisenberg et al. (1999)	C1: 16 F, 16 M (T10: M = 258 mos) (T11: M age = 281 mos)	1	2	(a) IRI [1] (b) Friend-report of IRI [1]	(1) Asked for sharing (2) Spontaneous sharing (3) Asked for helping (4) Spontaneous helping (in preschool)	T10: ra1 = 0.13, ra2 = 0.41, ra3 = 0.23, ra4 = 0.08 T10: rb1 = 0.17, rb2 = 0.19, rb3 = 0.18, rb4 = –0.31 T11: ra1 = –0.01, ra2 = 0.19, ra3 = 0.29, ra4 = 0.29 T11: rb1 = –0.02, rb2 = 0.01, rb3 = 0.46, rb4 = –0.20
Eisenberg et al. (1989)	35 F, 39 M (college)*	2	1	(a) IRI [1]	(1) Agreement to donate hours to help a family	ra1 = 0.28

					T6	T7
Eisenberg, Miller, Shell, McNalley, & Shea (1991)	C1: 16 F, 16 M (T6: M = 13.6 yrs) (T7: M = 15.6 yrs) C2: 20 F, 19 M (T6: M = 13.7 yrs) C3: 17 F, 17 M (T7: M = 15.8 yrs)	4	(a) IRI [1]	1	(1) Self-report of helping [T6 & T7] (2) Return of additional questionnaires by mail [T6 & T7]	ra1 = *ns* ra2 = *ns*	ra1 = 0.57 ra2 = *ns*
Eisenberg-Berg & Lennon (1980)	21 F, 30 M (4–5 yrs, M = 56 mos)	4,5	(a) Social comprehension task [2]	1,3	(1) Asked for sharing (2) Spontaneous sharing (3) Asked for helping (4) Spontaneous helping (5) Spontaneous comforting	Rho correlations: pa1 = 0.27 pa2 = *ns* pa3 = *ns* pa4 = *ns* pa5 = *ns*	
Emler & Rushton (1974)	31 F, 29 M (7–13 yrs, M = 9.3 yrs)	1	(a) Nickel-dime task [1] (b) Apple-dog story [1]	1	(1) Donating to charity	ra1 = n/a rb1 = n/a	
Froming, Allen, & Jensen (1985): Study 2	143 (no gender breakdown) (grades 1–3, M = 7.14 yrs)	4	(a) Apple-dog story [1]	1	(1) Donation of M & Ms to peers	Means (SD) — see below	

Means (SD) for Froming, Allen, & Jensen (1985): Study 2 (T6 column):

	Non-role-takers	Role-takers
Exp. absent	6.62 (4.78)	3.9 (3.58)
Exp. present	5.6 (4.98)	9.13 (6.16)

(Continued)

TABLE 10.1. (Continued)

Study	Sample	Sample Type	Study Context	Perspective-Taking Measure	Helping Measure	Results	
Fultz, Batson, Fortenbach, McCarthy, & Varney (1986): Study 2	32 F (college)*	2	1	(a) IRI [1]	(1) Willingness to spend time with lonely student	ra1 = 0.17	
Hudson, Forman, Brion-Meisels (1982)	9 F, 9 M (grade 2, M = 91.85 mos)	4	1	(a) Composite of: intentions task [1] feelings task [2] thoughts task [1]	Observation teaching grade K task: (1) Comforting (2) Sharing (3) Answers questions (4) Fails to answer questions (5) Answers questions ratio (6) Offers to lend a hand (7) Lends a hand (8) Fails to lend a hand (9) Lends a hand ratio	Between Group t-tests (equal n) $t(16)$a1 = 0.93 $t(16)$a2 = 0.21 $t(16)$a3 = 1.01 $t(16)$a4 = −2.17 $t(16)$a5 = 3.72 $t(16)$a6 = 2.06 $t(16)$a7 = 0.78 $t(16)$a8 = −2.88 $t(16)$a9 = 3.43	
Hurwitz & Gaylord-Ross (1983)	14 F, 16 M (9–10 yrs)*	4	1	(a) Story task [1]	(1) Teaching retarded or non-retarded peer task (coded observation): reinforcing verbalizations	Between Group F (equal n) $F(2, 27)$a1 = 7.35	
Iannotti (1978)	60 M (grade K, M = 71.6 mos; grade 3, M = 109.5 mos)	4	1	(a) Composite of nickel-dime task and social dilemma [1]	(1) Sharing candies or raisins with peer	Grade K ra1 = *ns*	Grade 3 ra1 = 0.48

Iannotti (1985)	21 F, 31 M (4–6 yrs, M = 59 mos)	5	3,1	(a) Penny hiding game [1] (b) Gift choice task [1] (c) Nickel-dime task [1] (d) Situational role-taking [2] (e) Emotional (facial expression) role-taking [2]	Observation of: (1) Sharing (2) Cooperating (3) Helping (4) Observation composite (5) Pick up spilt pencils (6) Sharing candies or raisins with friend (7) Teacher ratings	$ra1 = 0.01$ $ra2 = 0.14$ $ra3 = 0.15$ $ra4 = 0.15$ $ra5 = -0.06$ $ra6 = 0.17$ $ra7 = ns$ $rb1 = -0.01$ $rb2 = 0.13$ $rb3 = -0.16$ $rb4 = 0.03$ $rb5 = 0.04$ $rb6 = -0.32$ $rb7 = 0.34$ $rc1 = 0.15$ $rc2 = -0.23$ $rc3 = -0.13$ $rc4 = -0.13$ $rc5 = -0.01$ $rc6 = 0.06$ $rc7 = ns$ $rd1 = -0.24$ $rd2 = -0.04$ $rd3 = -0.16$ $rd4 = -0.21$ $rd5 = 0.29$ $rd6 = -0.24$ $rd7 = ns$ $re1 = 0.33$ $re2 = 0.10$ $re3 = 0.19$ $re4 = 0.31$ $re5 = -0.19$ $re6 = 0.32$ $re7 = ns$
Jennings, Fitch, & Suwalsky (1987)	51 F, 49 M (3–4 yrs, M = 43 mos)	5	1	(a) Composite of cubes task [3], two-sided card [3], upside-down picture [3], pointed stick [4], gift choice [1], penny hiding game [1], IAT [2]	(1) Observation (helping, sympathy, and generosity with task partner)	$ra1 = 0.23$
Jones (1985)	60 F, 49 M (grade K, 2 & 4, M = 90.1 mos)	4	1	(a) Social dilemmas [1]	Sharing crayon: (1) Number of grants (2) Duration of grants	$ra1 = n/a$ $ra2 = n/a$
Kagan & Knudson (1983)	38 F, 50 M (grade K & 2)*	4	1	(a) Feelings task [2]	(1) Altruism scale (2) Donation task	$ra1 = 0.03$ $ra2 = 0.06$

(Continued)

TABLE 10.1 (Continued)

Study	Sample	Sample Type	Study Context	Perspective-Taking Measure	Helping Measure	Results
Knight, Johnson, Carlo, & Eisenberg (1994)	43 F, 43 M (6–9 yrs, M = 90.8 mos)	1	1	(a) Affective reasoning [2]	(1) Donation of money to hospital burn unit	ra1 = 0.02
Krebs & Sturrup (1974)	12 F, 12 M (grades 2 & 3)*	4	1,2	(a) Nickel-dime task [1]	(1) Observation (offers help, offers support, suggests responsibly) (2) Teacher ratings of altruism	ra1 = 0.46 ra2 = 0.41
Krebs & Sturrup (1982)	11 F, 13 M (7–9 yrs)*	4	1,2	(a) Apple-dog story [1] (b) Nickel-dime task [1]	(1) Observation (2) Teacher ratings	ra1 = 0.47 ra2 = 0.42 rb1 = 0.52 rb2 = 0.57
Kurdek (1978)	50 F, 46 M (6–10 yrs, M = 8.15 yrs)	4	3	(a) Cognitive perspective coordination [1] (b) Nickel-dime task [1] (c) Story task [1] (d) Social dilemmas [1]	(1) Teacher ratings of prosocial/adaptive behavior	ra1 = ns rb1 = ns rc1 = ns rd1 = ns
LeMare & Krebs (1983)	20 F, 20 M (6–12 yrs)*	4	1	(a) Composite of visual and social/cognitive [1 & 3]	Teacher Q-sort ratings: (1) Gives, lends, shares (2) Shares willingly (3) Altruistic (4) Helpful, cooperative	ra1 = −0.53 ra2 = −0.49 ra3 = −0.36 ra4 = −0.29

Meyer, Boster, & Hecht (1988)	152 (gender n/a) (college, M = 21.0 yrs)	2	3	(a) Social/cognitive [1]	(1) Self-report of comforting a peer	ra1 = 0.01
Otten, Penner, & Altabe (1991): Study 1	37 F, 34 M (M = 35.5 yrs)	7	1	(a) IRI [1]	(1) Professional helping (willingness to treat clients) (2) Nonprofessional helping (willingness to be interviewed)	ra1 = ns ra2 = n/a
Otten et al. (1991): Study 2	67 F, 52 M (college, M = 22.99 yrs)	2	1	(a) IRI [1]	(1) Professional helping (imagine subjects professionally trained; willingness to treat client) (2) Nonprofessional helping (help develop advertising against drunk driving)	ra1 = n/a ra2 = n/a
Rubin & Schneider (1973)	28 F, 27 M (7 yrs, M = 89.7 mos)	4	1	(a) Communicative task [1]	(1) Candy donation to poor children (2) Helping young child	ra1 = 0.31 ra2 = 0.44
Rushton & Wiener (1975)	7 yrs: 15 F, 15 M* 11 yrs:15 F, 15 M*	4	1	(a) Board game [1] (b) Cylinders task [3]	(1) Generosity to charity (2) Generosity to friend	ra1 = n/a rb1 = n/a ra2 = n/a rb2 = n/a

TABLE 10.1. (Continued)

Study	Sample	Sample Type	Study Context	Perspective-Taking Measure	Helping Measure	Results
Stiff, Dillard, Somera, Kim, & Sleight (1988): Study 1	171 (gender n/a) (college)*	2	1	(a) Perspective taking [1]	(1) Intent to volunteer for organization	ra1 = 0.05
Stiff et al. (1988): Study 2	126 (gender n/a) (college)*	2	1	(a) Perspective taking [1]	(1) Story vignettes: think of comforting a friend	ra1 = 0.14
Strayer (1980)	4 F, 10 M (4–6 yrs, M = 59 mos)	5	2	(a) Picture task [3] (b) Picture story [2]	(1) Observation (comforting, helping, reinforcements, affect displayed) (2) Penny donation to poor children	Rho correlations: pa1 = 0.50 pa2 = ns pb1 = 0.45 pb2 = ns
Strayer & Roberts (1989)	24 F, 27 M (6–7 yrs, M = 80 mos)	4	1	(a) Picture story task [2]	(1) Teacher Q-sort (2) Class behavior scale	ra1 = ns ra2 = 0.25
Tabor & Shaffer (1981)	60 F, 60 M (grades 1–3)*	4	1	(a) IAT [2] (b) Role-taking [1]	(1) Sharing pennies (2) Help in emergency	Grade 1: ra1 = ns ra2 = ns rb1 = ns rb2 = ns Grade 2: ra1 = ns ra2 = 0.11 rb1 = ns rb2 = ns Grade 3: ra1 = ns ra2 = 0.31 rb1 = ns rb2 = 0.22

Study	Sample			Task	Outcome measure	Within each group:	
Waterman, Sobesky, Silvern, Aoki, & McCaulay (1981)	EP: 35 M (M = 124.1 mos) LD: 31 M (M = 137.9 mos) Normal: 14 M (M = 123.0 mos)	7, 4	1	(a) Nickel-dime task [1] (b) Skit emotions task [2]	(1) Teacher ratings (behavior checklist): antisocial/prosocial subscale	ra1 = n/a ra1 = n/a ra1 = n/a	rb1 = n/a rb1 = n/a rb1 = n/a
Zahn-Waxler, Radke-Yarrow, & Brady-Smith (1977)	55 F, 53 M (3–7 yrs)*	1	3	(a) 4 perceptual tasks [3] (b) 6 conceptual tasks [1] (c) Composite [5]	(1) Helping (spilt materials) (2) Sharing (3) Comforting (4) Composite helping	For each age group: ra1 = ns ra2 = ns ra3 = ns ra4 = ns rb1 = ns rb2 = ns	rb3 = ns rb4 = ns rc1 = ns rc2 = ns rc3 = ns rc4 = ns

Note: M = males; F = females; non-MR = non–mentally retarded; EMR = educable mentally retarded; TMR = trainable mentally retarded; EP = emotional problems; LD = learning disabled; for sample type, 1= general, 2 = college students, 3 = clinical, 4 = school children, 5 = day care/preschool, 6 = not specified, 7 = special sample; for study context, 1 = laboratory, 2 = naturalistic, 3 = classroom; IAT = Interpersonal Affective Test (Borke, 1971); IRI = the Interpersonal Reactivity Inventory (Davis, 1983); mos = months. *ns* and n/a refers to not significant and no effect size (these were not used in the analyses) reported, respectively. Only those studies with a reported calculable, zero-order, effect size were used in the analyses.

FINDINGS

The effect size estimate used in this meta-analysis was the Pearson's correlation coefficient describing the relation between perspective taking and prosocial behavior. Weighted multiple regression analyses (using Fisher's r to z transformations) were conducted to assess the relation of mean age, type of helping behavior, characteristics of the sample, and type of perspective-taking variables on the magnitude of the correlation between perspective taking and prosocial behavior. Table 10.1 presents the effect size estimates as well as brief descriptions of the sample and study, the perspective-taking indices, and the prosocial behavior indices for the 47 published studies between 1970 and 2002. Randomly drawing one correlation coefficient from each study produced a set of independent effect size estimates. The *full sample* consisted of 167 correlations, the *independent sample* consisted of 36 correlations.

DESCRIPTIVE DATA

Independent Sample

Table 10.2 presents the weighted mean (standard deviations) correlation coefficient and the weighted median correlation coefficient for each study characteristic for the independent sample. As can be seen in Table 10.2, relatively larger weighted mean correlation coefficients were evident for studies of comforting helping behaviors, studies with school children, and studies with affective perspective-taking measures. Moreover, the overall weighted mean correlation between perspective taking and prosocial behaviors was 0.22.

Full Sample

Table 10.3 presents the weighted mean (standard deviations) and median correlation for each study characteristic for the full sample. Similar to the findings for the independent sample, relatively larger weighted mean correlations were evident for studies of comforting helping tasks, studies with school children, and studies with affective and visual/spatial perspective-taking measures. The overall weighted mean correlation between perspective taking and prosocial behavior was 0.16.

Table 10.4 presents the relations among the potential moderators of the magnitude of relation between perspective taking and prosocial behavior that were examined: emotional similarity, target similarity, specificity similarity, mean age (in months), type of helping, kind of sample, publication year (before and

TABLE 10.2. Weighted Means, Standard Deviations, and Median Effect Size, 95% Confidence Intervals (CI), and Between- and Within-Homogeneity Tests (Q_B and Q_W)for Study Characteristics of the Independent Sample.

Study Characteristic	n	Weighted Mean	Standard Deviation	Weighted Median	95% CI	Q_B	Q_W
Type of Helping Behavior							
Volunteer	3	0.13	0.10	0.05	0.12–14	105.15	2.68
Donating/sharing	7	0.06	0.13	0.02	0.05–0.07		10.02
Comforting	2	0.90	0.40	1.16	0.84–0.96		30.56
General	23	0.21	0.25	0.21	0.20–0.22		68.94
Kind of Sample							
General and special	4	0.14	0.09	0.19	0.13–0.15	32.00	2.38
College students	6	0.07	0.09	0.01	0.06–0.08		5.08
School children	20	0.35	0.42	0.29	0.32–0.38		169.17
Day care/preschool	5	0.19	0.13	0.21	0.17–0.21		4.65
Type of Perspective Taking							
Social/cognitive	17	0.16	0.21	0.06	0.15–0.17	24.90	53.36
Affective	13	0.37	0.42	0.26	0.27–0.47		119.07
Visual/spatial	2	0.15	0.13	0.21	0.13–0.17		2.04
Composite	3	0.04	0.33	0.23	−0.01–0.09		16.23
Overall	35	0.22	0.32	0.19	0.21–0.23		220.67

after the Underwood & Moore, 1982, review) and type of perspective taking. These relations indicate that the kinds of sample and types of perspective taking varied by age. In addition, the helping index varied by the kind of samples.

Influence of Task Similarity on Magnitude of the Correlations in the Independent Sample

Table 10.5 presents the effects of the task similarity predictors based on weighted hierarchical multiple regression analyses with all predictors centered (see Aiken & West, 1991). In the first step, emotional, specificity, and target similarity ratings were entered as predictors and accounted for approximately 14% of the variance in the effect size estimates. As expected, the positive values of the regression coefficients for emotionality, target, and specificity similarity indicated that the magnitude of the relations between perspective taking and prosocial behaviors were significantly *larger* as the perspective-taking tasks and the prosocial behavior indices were *more similar*. In the second step of the

TABLE 10.3. Weighted Means, Standard Deviations, and Median Effect Size for Study Characteristic of the Full Sample.

Study Characteristic	n	Weighted Mean	Standard Deviation	Weighted Median
Type of Helping Behavior				
Volunteer	8	0.10	0.20	0.05
Donating/sharing	20	0.08	0.16	0.06
Comforting	26	0.33	0.35	0.34
General	77	0.12	0.27	0.14
Kind of Sample				
General and special	8	0.13	0.29	0.19
College students	11	0.07	0.08	0.05
School children	73	0.24	0.34	0.26
Day care/Preschool	39	0.07	0.21	0.10
Type of Perspective Taking				
Social/cognitive	65	0.11	0.20	0.06
Affective	44	0.22	0.34	0.26
Visual/spatial	4	0.22	0.16	0.21
Composite	18	0.14	0.44	0.23
Overall	131	0.16	0.29	0.12

TABLE 10.4. Correlations among the Predictors for the Full Sample.

Variable	2	3	4	5	6	7
1. Age	0.30	−0.13	0.20	0.47**	0.43**	0.31
2. Emotional similarity		−0.11	0.25	0.05	0.16	0.01
3. Target similarity			−0.13	0.12	0.11	0.11
4. Specificity similarity				0.04	0.23	0.10
5. Kind of sample					0.33	0.43*
6. Type of perspective taking						0.29
7. Type of helping						

Note: For continuous by continuous relations, Pearson's correlation coefficients are reported. For nominal by continuous relations, Multiple Rs are reported. For nominal by nominal relations, Cramer's V are reported.

* = $p < 0.05$, two-tailed.

** = $p < 0.01$, two-tailed.

TABLE 10.5. Weighted Multiple Regression Analysis of Task Similarity Predicting the Magnitude of Effect Size of the Relations between Perspective Taking and Prosocial Behaviors for the Independent Sample.

Study Characteristic	Unstandardized Beta	Standardized Beta
Step 1		
Emotional similarity	0.153***	0.297
Target similarity	0.070***	0.252
Specificity similarity	0.039*	0.131
Step 2		
Emotional similarity (E)	0.127***	0.248
Target similarity (T)	0.074***	0.265
Specificity similarity (S)	0.087***	0.296
E × S	0.104***	0.267
E × T	0.095**	0.199
S × T	−0.046*	−0.167
Overall:		
R^2	0.256	
Q_r	54.98702***	
Q_e	159.573***	

Note: All tests were one-tailed.
*$p < 0.05$, **$p < 0.01$, ***$p < 0.001$.

regression analyses, the Emotionality by Target interaction, Emotionality by Specificity interaction, and the Specificity by Target interaction were entered. These three two-way interaction effects were all significant and accounted for an additional 12% of the variance in the effect size estimates (over and above the main effects; see Table 10.5). The three-way interaction was not significant.

Because the emotional similarity ratings only ranged from three to five, only the medium and high emotional similarity slopes were computed (see Figure 10.2). The magnitude of the relations between perspective taking and prosocial behaviors was relatively large ($r = 0.51$) when the characteristics of the perspective-taking tasks and the prosocial behavior tasks were jointly similar on levels of emotionality and specificity (see Figure 10.2, top panel). Figure 10.2 (middle panel) shows that the magnitude of the correlation was relatively large ($r = 0.56$) when both measures were jointly similar in target characteristics and level of emotionality, and was relatively large ($r = 0.41$; see Figure 10.2, bottom panel) when the characteristics of the target and specificity were jointly similar. In each of these interaction effects, the correlation between perspective taking and prosocial behaviors was always largest when the ratings were high on two of similarity dimensions.

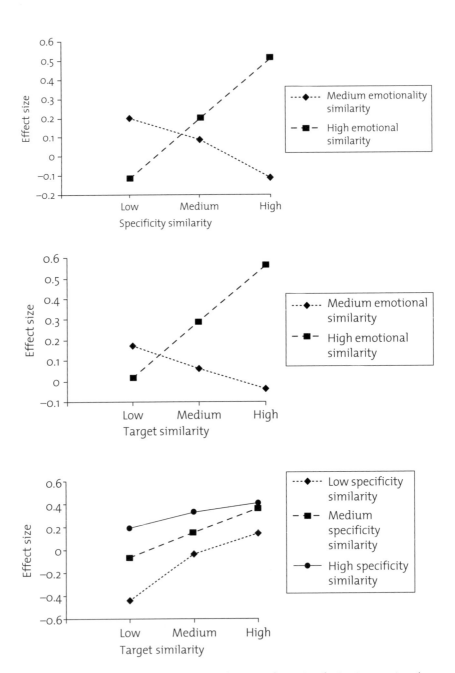

FIGURE 10.2. The Emotional Similarity by Specificity Similarity interaction (top panel), the Emotional Similarity by Target Similarity interaction (middle panel), and the Specificity Similarity by Target Similarity interaction (bottom panel).

Influence of Task Similarity on Magnitude of the Correlation while Controlling for Other Study Characteristics in the Independent Sample

Table 10.6 presents a more conservative examination of the task similarity hypotheses by determining the relations between emotional, specificity, and target similarity ratings and the effect size estimate while controlling for other study characteristics. In the first step, the study characteristics accounted for approximately 63% of the variance in the effect size estimates; mean age of the sample, type of helping, kind of sample, and type of perspective taking were all significant predictors. In the second step, emotional, target, and specificity similarity ratings accounted for a nonsignificant additional 2% of the variance.

TABLE 10.6. Model of the Weighted Multiple Regression Analysis of Study Characteristics Predicting the Magnitude of Effect Size for the Independent Sample.

Step and Study Characteristic	Unstandardized Beta	Standardized Beta
Helping Behavior 1	0.082	0.086
Helping Behavior 2	−0.052	−0.073
Helping Behavior 3	0.597***	0.537
Kind of Sample 1	−0.042	−0.046
Kind of Sample 2	−0.526*	−0.757
Kind of Sample 3	−0.158	−0.249
Mean Age	0.001	0.298
Type of Perspective Taking 1	0.202	0.318
Type of Perspective Taking 2	0.159	0.234
Type of Perspective Taking 3	0.100	0.073
Emotional Similarity (E)	0.092*	0.179
Specificity Similarity (S)	0.050+	0.170
Target Similarity (T)	0.040*	0.142
E × S	0.107*	0.275
E × T	0.027	0.056
S × T	−0.035	−0.130
Overall:		
R^2	0.679	
Q_r	145.721***	
Q_e	68.83906***	

Note: Tests of significance for all vectors were two-tailed except for the similarity vectors which were one-tailed.

$^+p < 0.10$, $^*p < 0.05$, $^{**}p < 0.01$, $^{***}p < 0.001$.

In the final step, type of helping, kind of sample, emotional similarity, target similarity (specificity similarity was marginally significant at the $p < 0.10$ level), and the Emotionality by Specificity interaction were significant predictors of the magnitude of the correlation and accounted for an additional 3.5% of the variance. Positive regression coefficients on the similarity ratings indicated that the magnitude of the relations between perspective taking and prosocial behaviors was significantly *larger* as the characteristics of the perspective-taking tasks and the prosocial behavior indices were *more similar* in terms of the level of emotionality, the target, and level of specificity in the tasks (a marginally significant trend for level of specificity). The significant interaction indicated that the magnitude of effect size was strongest when tasks matched on both emotionality and specificity.

Influence of Task Similarity on Magnitude of the Correlation in the Full Sample

As in the first weighted multiple regression analysis of the independent effect size estimates, an analysis for the full sample of effect sizes was conducted. The main effects of similarity indexes were nonsignificant and accounted for less than 1% of the explained variance in the effect sizes. The Emotionality by Target and the Emotionality by Specificity interaction effects accounted for an additional 6% of the explained variance. The simple slopes tests indicated that the magnitude of the correlation between perspective taking and prosocial behaviors was significantly *larger* as the characteristics of the perspective-taking tasks and the prosocial behavior indices were *more similar*: (a) in level of emotionality and characteristics of the target and (b) in levels of emotionality and specificity. An additional regression analysis was conducted to examine the association of the similarity ratings (including the two-way interactions) with the magnitude of the correlation while statistically controlling for the other study characteristics. The results were interpretably the same as in the previous independent sample analysis (Multiple $R^2 = 0.25$).

Relation between Age and Magnitude of the Correlation in the Full Sample

On the basis of cognitive-developmental theory that suggests there may be restricted variability in perspective-taking skills in early childhood as well as beyond late adolescence, there may be a nonlinear relation between age and the magnitude of the correlation. That is, the restriction of range in perspective-taking scores that is likely to occur among very young children, who are only beginning to develop these skills, and among adults, who have largely developed these skills, could possibly produce attenuation of the magnitude of the relations between perspective taking and prosocial behaviors in these age groups. An analysis with mean age (centered, Aiken & West, 1991) entered in the first step, and the mean age quadratic term entered in the second step, indicated that mean age was not a significant predictor of magnitude of the correlation in the first step (standardized beta = 0.03, Multiple R^2 = 0.001). However, in the second step, the mean age quadratic term was a significant predictor of magnitude of the correlation (standardized beta = −0.45, p < 0.002, R^2 change = 0.07). To examine the nature of the mean age quadratic effect, mean age was broken down into three age groups prescribed by cognitive-developmental theory (because there were few effect sizes (n = 2) reported with 12 to17 year olds, 6 to 11 year olds, and 12 to 17 year olds were combined). The weighted mean correlation among the 3 to 5 year olds was 0.01 (SD = 0.21; n = 40), and was 0.01 (SD = 0.14; n = 14) among the 18 year olds and older. In contrast, the weighted mean correlation between perspective taking and prosocial behavior was 0.22 (SD = 0.34; n = 77) among the studies that involved participants between 6 and 17 years of age. Thus, the mean correlation was near zero in the 3- to 5-year-old age group and the 18-year-old and older age groups, and substantially larger in the six to 17-year-old age group.

Summary and Conclusions

In general, the meta-analysis revealed that the correlation between perspective taking and prosocial behavior was stronger when the level of emotionality, the characteristics of the target, and the level of specificity in the tasks were relatively similar in the perspective taking and prosocial behavior measures. In addition, when the characteristics of perspective taking and prosocial behavior measures were simultaneously similar on two similarity dimensions, the amount of explained variance in magnitude of the correlation between perspective taking and prosocial behavior increased substantially, and to a greater degree than one would expect from a simple additive model. Furthermore, the findings are consistent with the *task-specificity hypothesis* that the weaker than expected relations between perspective taking and prosocial behavior may have been partly the result of a "mismatch" of these task characteristics. The evidence that the attributes of the target and the context are important moderators of the relation between perspective taking and prosocial behavior is consistent with social cognitive and information-processing theories that suggest situation-specific scripts that may be invoked by the characteristics of specific tasks.

The present findings are consistent with prior findings that more detailed conceptual analyses of the perspective taking and prosocial behavior tasks may be needed to more fully understand the relations between perspective taking and prosocial behaviors. For example, Knight et al. (1994) found that an interaction between affective reasoning (an affective perspective-taking index), sympathy, and a task-specific cognitive skill (i.e., understanding of the value and units of money) accounted for a substantially greater proportion of explained variance in donating money among young children than the main effect of affective reasoning. Furthermore, Carlo, Knight, Eisenberg, and Rotenberg (1991) found a significant relation between affective perspective taking and prosocial behavior (helping a child who showed emotional distress) when the cognitive demands of the two tasks matched, but not when there was a mismatch of these cognitive demands (see also Knight, Bohlmeyer, Schneider, & Harris, 1993).

The present modest, overall mean correlation is probably an under–estimate of the true magnitude of the relation between perspective taking and prosocial behavior in real world situations. This is because the perspective-taking requirements of a naturally occurring prosocial behavior are embedded in the situation and there is no disconnect (i.e., there is no mismatch in task demands) between the circumstances in which the sociocognitive/socioemotive demands and prosocial behavior are enlisted. Because research procedures necessitate the assessment of perspective taking separately from the prosocial behavior, the earlier research contexts may have facilitated the use of tasks with dissimilar characteristics, and attenuated the observed magnitude of the relations between perspective taking and prosocial behaviors.

In examining the relation between perspective taking and prosocial behavior, researchers should consider closely matching level of emotionality in the prosocial context to that present in the perspective-taking task context. Children who are adept at understanding the needs of a child who is visibly distressed in a perspective-taking task may be more likely to assist a child in a prosocial behavior task that is emotionally evoking. Researchers could manipulate the facial expressions of the target or manipulate emotional cues in the social context (e.g., facial expressions in a video stimulus task or the background story in picture-story vignette task) to match these characteristics. The physical characteristics of the target in perspective taking and prosocial behavior tasks should also be similar. That is, researchers should consider matching closely the physical characteristics of the target (e.g., age, gender) in both perspective taking and prosocial behavior tasks. Closely matching the range of contexts in both perspective taking and prosocial behavior tasks under which children are required to take another's perspective may also reveal stronger relations between perspective taking and prosocial behaviors. Hence, indices that assess global, trait-like perspective taking should be matched to trait-like indices of prosocial behaviors, and context-specific measures of both perspective taking and prosocial behaviors should be examined. This is important to consider given that social-personality researchers often rely on trait-like perspective-taking tasks (e.g., Davis's, 1983, *Interpersonal Reactivity Index*) but often use situation-specific prosocial behavior tasks (e.g., picking up dropped items).

Our findings clearly indicate that joint consideration of task characteristics can enhance predictive power in the relations between perspective taking and prosocial behaviors. Moreover, consideration of simultaneous task characteristics will serve to enhance the external and ecological validity of the tasks in these studies. For example, if researchers are interested in identifying those likely to help a needy young boy in a crisis situation, it may be most useful to focus on those perspective-taking skills matched to understanding the needs of a young boy (consideration of the target individual) in an emotionally evocative (consideration of the level of emotionality) situation. In this example, because more than one task characteristic is simultaneously considered, researchers are likely to obtain substantial predictive power. Prior studies that utilized perspective-taking indices without careful consideration of the multiple specific characteristics of the task may have tapped into skills other than those intended. If this is the case, then the study of the development of perspective taking and its correlates may necessitate careful task analysis to confirm appropriate comparisons across findings from studies.

However, even when real world prosocial behavior opportunities present themselves, having the requisite sociocognitive and socioemotive skills will not, in and of itself, lead the individual to behave prosocially. That is, having the requisite cognitive skill is likely necessary but not sufficient to produce that prosocial behavior. When the situation presents an opportunity to be prosocial having the requisite sociocognitive and socioemotive skills allows the individual to be more aware of the social nature of the context and the impact of their prosocial behavior on another person. However, there are also likely motivational factors that may lead the individual to either behave prosocially or not. For example, one may recognize that another person is needy and have the sociocognitive and socioemotional skills to recognize how helping that individual will impact that person's emotional state and perceptions of their situation. In this case, the costs of helping that person may be sufficient to prevent helping that needy person. Indeed, the availability of these sociocognitive and socioemotive skills may be essential to behaving in a more socially aware manner but may not fully determine the nature of that social behavior. For example, being capable of affective perspective taking may be essential to acting aggressively in a context in which the sole purpose of that aggression is to make another person feel bad. In this case, affective perspective taking might facilitate a behavior designed to hurt another (see Feshbach, 1987; Sutton, Smith, & Swettenham, 1999).

These findings might help to elucidate broader theoretical models of children's social understanding and their conceptual link to prosocial behaviors. Prior notions of a global construct of perspective taking may have underestimated its multidimensional nature by not considering the multiple specific underlying cognitive subskills that may or may not be substantially interrelated (see Flavell & Miller, 1998). Perspective taking taps into individuals' understanding of others' emotions and their social situations, which is a relatively narrow aspect of the growth of children's social understanding. There may be several domain-specific areas of children's social understanding and the rate of development of understanding in these areas may differ (e.g., Flavell & Miller, 1998). The different rates of development in domain-specific skills related to prosocial behavior may account for individual differences in prosocial behavior. That is, enactment of prosocial behaviors may depend on a number of different domain-specific skills with different rates of development, some or all of which may not be tapped by a particular perspective-taking task. This perspective is also consistent with social cognitive theory (e.g., Bandura, 1986) and social information-processing approaches (e.g., Dodge & Crick, 1990; Knight et al., 1994) in which researchers attempt to account for the specific characteristics and content of social cognition and social behavior tasks rather than proposing global social cognition or behavior constructs.

If perspective taking and prosocial behavior are multidimensional constructs, then this has important assessment implications for researchers studying these constructs. For example, as noted earlier, some authors have suggested forming composites of these indices to obtain more reliable estimates of each construct and to produce a more accurate estimate of the magnitude of the correlation between these constructs. However, there are important limitations to this suggestion. If these different types of perspective-taking skills are assessing different dimensions of a weakly interrelated construct, then forming a composite of these measures may increase measurement error rather than create a more reliable indicator. Only if one forms a composite of several quite similar indices of perspective taking would one produce a more reliable index of that type of perspective taking by increasing the systematic variance in the scores. Similarly, if prosocial behavior measures are related weakly, then forming a composite of these prosocial behavior measures might lead to an increase, rather than decrease, in measurement error, and attenuate the magnitude of the relations between perspective taking and prosocial behavior. Compositing across indices of prosocial behavior that have similar task characteristics would lead to a greater, less attenuated, relation between perspective taking and prosocial behavior because these types of composites are often more reliable (i.e., the composites may have actually reduced the amount of measurement error).

These findings and this perspective also have important theoretical implications for understanding the development of prosocial behavior. If perspective taking and related sociocognitive and socioemotional skills are multidimensional and develop unevenly, and if prosocial behaviors are multidimensional in nature and have somewhat different sociocognitive and socioemotional requisites, relatively modest associations between the sociocognitive and socioemotive skills and prosocial behavior in the research literature should be expected. This would be the case particularly when the specific study does not assess sociocognitive and socioemotive skills that are clearly the same or similar to those requisite given the nature of the prosocial behavior opportunity. Further, even when there is a strong match between the sociocognitive and socioemotive skills assessed and those that are requisite for the prosocial behavior opportunity, as is the case in all real world prosocial behavior opportunities, the necessary but not sufficient nature of these skills makes the enactment of prosocial behavior only probabilistic even when the individual is well skilled in the cognitive demands associated with that prosocial behavior. Finally, these same qualifications may well explain the nature of the relationship between sociocognitive and socioemotive skills and all sorts of social behaviors that have at their core some requisite for recognizing how one's behavior impacts and/or is perceived by another person.

Because of the increased number of studies conducted across different age periods since Underwood and Moore's meta-analytic review, examination of nonlinear age effects on the magnitude of effect size was possible. There was a significant nonlinear relation between age and magnitude of effect size. The relation between perspective taking and prosocial behaviors was greatest among 6 to 17 year olds, and close to zero in the younger and older age groups. Given that the acquisition of perspective-taking skills is a developmentally relevant achievement during middle childhood, one would expect that this is the developmental period at which there is the greatest individual variability in these skills. Further, given this relatively substantial individual variability in perspective-taking abilities, this is the developmental period in which one would expect a stronger relation between perspective taking and prosocial behavior if that perspective taking were a requisite for engaging in that prosocial behavior. In contrast, because most young children may not yet have developed perspective-taking skills, there may be relatively little variability in these skills, and the relations between perspective taking and prosocial behaviors should be weak because of attenuation.

By late adolescence/young adulthood, there should be less variability in these perspective-taking skills because a larger proportion of these individuals have achieved these developmental milestones. This lessened variability should attenuate the relations between perspective taking and prosocial behaviors among these older individuals. However, there may well be some types of prosocial behaviors that require more sophisticated forms of perspective taking, like taking the perspective of multiple individuals or groups simultaneously, or perspective taking in a context that is highly abstract given the individual's own experiences (e.g., understanding the plight of children orphaned by HIV in parts of Africa). Unfortunately, most current measures of perspective taking that have been used with late adolescents and young adults do not assess these more sophisticated forms of perspective taking. Further, very few of the measures of prosocial behavior in the studies of individuals during late adolescence or young adulthood demand these more complex perspective-taking skills. Hence, the weak relations between perspective taking and prosocial behaviors among older individuals may accurately reflect the magnitude of the relation in many less demanding prosocial behavior opportunities but underestimate the magnitude of the relations in some highly complex and abstract prosocial behavior opportunities.

To summarize, the present findings across 167 study effect sizes provide strong supportive evidence for the *task-specificity hypothesis* and is consistent with social cognitive and information-processing theories. As shown previously by Underwood and Moore (1982), there was an overall significant relation between perspective taking and prosocial behaviors suggesting that perspective taking is relevant to understanding such morally important behaviors. However, the present findings extended those prior results by showing that closely matching the characteristics of perspective taking and prosocial behavior tasks enhances the overall magnitude of effect size. Furthermore, the relations between these constructs were found to vary across different age periods. Although the present study focused on perspective taking, the findings have important implications in future studies on the relations between other social cognitions, such as ToM and moral reasoning, that are relevant to understanding prosocial and moral behaviors. Clearly, understanding the developmental relations between social cognitions and moral behaviors will require closer attention to matching the cognitive demands and the characteristics of the tasks.

ACKNOWLEDGMENTS

The authors wish to acknowledge the helpful comments and suggestions by Ross Thompson. The authors appreciated the assistance of data coding and collection by Jeff Melby, Jennifer Wyatt, Billy Aplin, Jacqueline McEwen, and David Stopp. Funding support from the National Science Foundation (BNS 0132302) for this chapter was provided to Gustavo Carlo and George Knight. Correspondence can be addressed to Gustavo Carlo, Department of Psychology, University of Nebraska-Lincoln, 320 Burnett Hall, Lincoln, NE 68588–0308, E-mail: gcarlo1@unl.edu.

NOTE

1. It should be noted that perspective taking might lead to antisocial behaviors (e.g., manipulation, deception) under some circumstances (Feshbach, 1987; Sutton et al., 1999). The notion is that perspective taking, in and of itself, might lead to antisocial outcomes. However, previous research has shown that perspective taking is negatively associated with aggression and externalizing behaviors, that juvenile delinquents score lower on perspective-taking tasks than nondelinquents (Miller & Eisenberg, 1988), and that perspective taking is related positively to empathy and sympathy (Eisenberg & Miller, 1987) and moral reasoning (Tomlinson-Keasey, 1974). Although perspective taking might lead to antisocial behaviors under some circumstances, it appears in general that perspective-taking facilitates prosocial behaviors rather than antisocial behaviors.

REFERENCES

*Abroms, K. I., & Gollin, J. B. (1980). Developmental study of gifted preschool children and measures of psychosocial giftedness. *Exceptional Children, 46,* 334–341.

*Ahammer, I. M., & Murray, J. P. (1979). Kindness in the kindergarten: The relative influence of role playing and prosocial television in facilitating altruism. *International Journal of Behavioral Development, 2,* 133–157.

Aiken, L. S., & West, S. G. (1991). *Multiple regression: Testing and interpreting interactions.* Newbury Park, CA: Sage.

Bandura, A. (1986). *Social foundations of thought and action: A social cognitive theory.* Englewood Cliffs, NJ: Prentice Hall, Inc.

*Barnett, M. A., & Thompson, S. (1985). The role of perspective taking and empathy in children's machiavellianism, prosocial behavior, and motive for helping. *The Journal of Genetic Psychology, 146,* 295–305.

*Barrett, D. E., & Yarrow, M. R. (1977). Prosocial behavior, social inferential ability, and assertiveness in children. *Child Development, 48,* 475–481.

*Batson, C. D., Bolen, M. H., Cross, J. A., & Neuringer-Benefiel, H. E. (1986). Where is the altruism in the altruistic personality? *Journal of Personality and Social Psychology, 50,* 212–220.

*Bender, N. N., & Carlson, J. S. (1982). Prosocial behavior and perspective-taking of mentally retarded and nonretarded children. *American Journal of Mental Deficiency, 86,* 361–366.

*Bengtsson, H., & Johnson, L. (1992). Perspective taking, empathy, and prosocial behavior in late childhood. *Child Study Journal, 22,* 11–22.

*Blotner, R., & Bearison, D. J. (1984). Developmental consistencies in social-moral knowledge: Justice reasoning and altruistic behavior. *Merrill-Palmer Quarterly, 30,* 349–367.

Borke, H. (1971). Interpersonal perception of young children: Egocentrism or empathy? *Developmental Psychology, 5,* 263–269.

*Buckley, N., Siegel, L. S., & Ness, S. (1979). Egocentrism, empathy, and altruistic behavior in young children. *Developmental Psychology, 15,* 329–330.

*Burleson, B. R. (1984). Age, social-cognitive development, and the use of comforting strategies. *Communication Monographs, 51,* 140–153.

Carlo, G. (2006). Care-based and altruistically-based morality. In M. Killen & G. Smetana (Eds.), *Handbook of moral development* (pp. 551–579). Mahwah, NJ: Lawrence Erlbaum Associates.

*Carlo, G., Knight, G. P., Eisenberg, N., & Rotenberg, K. J. (1991). Cognitive processes and prosocial behaviors among children: The role of affective attributions and reconciliations. *Developmental Psychology, 27,* 456–461.

Cassidy, K. W., Werner, R. S., Rourke, M., Zubernis, L. S., & Balaraman, G. (2003). The relationship between psychological understanding and positive social behaviors. *Social Development, 12,* 198–221.

Chandler, M. J., & Carpendale, J. I. M. (1998). Inching toward a mature theory of mind. In M. D. Ferrari & R. J. Sternberg (Eds.), *Self-awareness: Its nature and development* (pp. 148–190). New York: Guilford Press.

*Chapman, M., Zahn-Waxler, C., Cooperman, G., & Iannotti, R. (1987). Empathy and responsibility in the motivation of children's helping. *Developmental Psychology, 23,* 140–145.

*Davis, M. H. (1983). The effects of dispositional empathy on emotional reactions and helping: A multidimensional approach. *Journal of Personality, 51,* 167–184.

*Denham, S. A. (1986). Social cognition, prosocial behavior, and emotion in preschoolers: Contextual validation. *Child Development, 57,* 194–201.

Dodge, K. A., & Crick, N. R. (1990). Social information-processing bases of aggressive behavior in children. *Personality and Social Psychology Bulletin, 16,* 8–22.

Dunn, J. (1995). Children as psychologists: The later correlates of individual differences in understanding of emotions and other minds. *Cognition & Emotion, 9,* 187–201.

Dweck, C. S., & Leggett, E. L. (1988). A social-cognitive approach to motivation and personality. *Psychological Review, 95,* 256–273.

Eisenberg, N. (1986). *Altruistic emotion, cognition and behavior.* Hillsdale, NJ: Lawrence Erlbaum Associates.

*Eisenberg, N., Carlo, G., Murphy, B., & Van Court, P. (1995). Prosocial development in late adolescence: A longitudinal study. *Child Development, 66,* 1179–1197.

Eisenberg, N., Fabes, R. A., & Spinrad, T. L. (2006). Prosocial development. In W. Damon & R. M. Lerner (Series Ed.) & N. Eisenberg (Vol. Ed.), *Handbook of child psychology: Social, emotional, and personality development* (Vol. 3, pp. 646–718). New York: Wiley.

*Eisenberg, N., Guthrie, I. K., Murphy, B. C., Shepard, S. A., Cumberland, A., & Carlo, G. (1999). Consistency and development of prosocial dispositions: A longitudinal study. *Child Development, 70*, 1360–1372.

Eisenberg, N., & Miller, P. A. (1987). The relation of empathy to prosocial and related behaviors. *Psychological Bulletin, 101*, 91–119.

*Eisenberg, N., Miller, P. A., Schaller, M., Fabes, R. A., Fultz, J., Shell, R., et al. (1989). The role of sympathy and altruistic personality traits in helping: A reexamination. *Journal of Personality and Social Psychology, 57*, 41–67.

*Eisenberg, N., Miller, P. A., Shell, R., McNalley, S., & Shea, C. (1991). Prosocial development in adolescence: A longitudinal study. *Developmental Psychology, 27*, 849–857.

*Eisenberg-Berg, N., & Lennon, R. (1980). Altruism and the assessment of empathy in the preschool years. *Child Development, 51*, 552–557.

*Emler, N. P., & Rushton, J. P. (1974). Cognitive-developmental factors in children's generosity. *British Journal of Social & Clinical Psychology, 13*, 277–281.

Feshbach, N. D. (1987). Parental empathy and child adjustment/maladjustment. In N. Eisenberg & J. Strayer (Eds.), *Empathy and its development* (pp. 271–291). New York: Cambridge University Press.

Findlay, L. C., Girardi, A., & Coplan, R. J. (2006). Links between empathy, social behavior, and social understanding in early childhood. *Early Childhood Research Quarterly, 21*, 347–359.

Flavell, J. H., & Miller, P. H. (1998). Social cognition. In W. Damon (Series Ed.) and D. Kuhn & R. S. Siegler (Vol. Eds.), *Handbook of child psychology: Cognition, perception, and language* (Vol. 5, pp. 851–898). New York: Wiley.

Ford, M. (1979). The construct validity of egocentrism. *Psychological Bulletin, 86*, 1169–1188.

*Froming, W. J., Allen, L., & Jensen, R. (1985). Altruism, role-taking, and self-awareness: The acquisition of norms governing altruistic behavior. *Child Development, 56*, 1223–1228.

*Fultz, J., Batson, C. D., Fortenbach, V. A., McCarthy, P. M., & Varney, L. L. (1986). Social evaluation and the empathy-altruism hypothesis. *Journal of Personality and Social Psychology, 50*, 761–769.

Hoffman, M. L. (2000). *Empathy and moral development: Implications for caring and justice.* New York, NY, US: Cambridge University Press.

*Hudson, L. M., Forman, E. A., & Brion-Meisels, S. (1982). Role taking as a predictor of prosocial behavior in cross-age tutors. *Child Development, 53*, 1320–1329.

*Hurwitz, B. D., & Gaylord-Ross, R. J. (1983). Role-taking ability and prosocial behavior between nonretarded and retarded (confederate) peers. *Education and Training of the Mentally Retarded, 18*, 197–203.

*Iannotti, R. J. (1978). Effect of role-taking experiences on role taking, empathy, altruism, and aggression. *Developmental Psychology, 14*, 119–124.

*Iannotti, R. J. (1985). Naturalistic and structured assessments of prosocial behavior in preschool children: The influence of empathy and perspective taking. *Developmental Psychology, 21*, 46–55.

*Jennings, K. D., Fitch, D., & Suwalsky, J. T. D. (1987). Social cognition and social interaction in three-year-olds: Is social cognition truly social? *Child Study Journal, 17*, 1–14.

*Jones, D. C. (1985). Persuasive appeals and responses to appeals among friends and acquaintances. *Child Development, 56*, 757–763.

*Kagan, S., & Knudson, K. A. M. (1983). Differential development of affective role-taking ability and prosocial behavior. *The Journal of Genetic Psychology, 143*, 97–102.

Knight, G. P., Bohlmeyer, E. M., Schneider, H., & Harris, J. D. (1993). Age differences in temporal monitoring and equal sharing in a fixed-duration sharing task. *British Journal of Developmental Psychology, 11*, 143–158.

*Knight, G. P., Johnson, L. G., Carlo, G., & Eisenberg, N. (1994). A multiplicative model of the dispositional antecedents of a prosocial behavior: Predicting more of the people more of the time. *Journal of Personality and Social Psychology, 66*, 178–183.

Krebs, D., & Russell, C. (1981). Role-taking and altruism. In J. P. Rushton & R. M. Sorrentino (Eds.), *Altruism and helping behavior: Social, personality, and developmental perspectives* (pp. 137–165). Hillsdale, NJ: Lawrence Erlbaum Associates.

*Krebs, D., & Sturrup, B. (1982). Role-taking ability and altruistic behavior in elementary school children. *Journal of moral Education, 2*, 94–100.

Kurdek, L. A. (1978). Perspective taking as the cognitive basis of children's moral development: A review of the literature. *Merrill-Palmer Quarterly, 24*, 3–28.

Kurdek, L. A. (1981). Young adults' moral reasoning about prohibitive and prosocial dilemmas. *Journal of Youth and Adolescence, 10*, 263–272.

*LeMare, L., & Krebs, D. (1983). Perspective-taking and styles of (pro) social behavior in elementary school children. *Academic Psychology Bulletin, 5*, 289–298.

*Meyer, D. J., Boster, F. J., & Hecht, M. L. (1988). A model of empathic communication. *Communication Research Reports, 5*, 19–27.

Miller, P. A., & Eisenberg, N. (1988). The relation of empathy to aggressive and externalizing/antisocial behavior. *Psychological Bulletin, 103*, 324–344.

*Otten, C. A., Penner, L. A., & Altabe, M. N. (1991). An examination of therapists' and college students' willingness to help a psychologically distressed person. *Journal of Social and Clinical Psychology, 10*, 102–120.

Radke-Yarrow, M., Zahn-Waxler, C., & Chapman, M. (1983). Children's prosocial dispositions and behavior. In. P. H. Mussen (Ed.), *Carmichael's manual of child psychology* (Vol. 4, pp. 469–546). New York: Wiley.

*Rubin, K. H., & Schneider, F. W. (1973). The relationship between moral judgment, egocentrism, and altruistic behavior. *Child Development, 44*, 661–665.

*Rushton, J. P., & Wiener, J. (1975). Altruism and cognitive development in children. *British Journal of Sociology and Clinical Psychology, 14*, 341–349.

Selman, R. (1980). *The growth of interpersonal understanding.* New York: Academic.

Shantz, C. U. (1983). Social cognition. In P. H. Mussen (Series Ed.) and J. H. Flavell & E. M. Markman (Eds.), *Handbook of child psychology: Vol. 3. Cognitive development.* New York: Wiley.

Slaughter, V., Dennis, M. J., & Pritchard, M. (2002). Theory of mind and peer acceptance in preschool children. *British Journal of Developmental Psychology, 20*, 545–564.

*Stiff, J. B., Dillard, J. P., Somera, L., Kim, H., & Sleight, C. (1988). Empathy, communication, and prosocial behavior. *Communication Monographs, 55,* 198–213.

*Strayer, J. (1980). A naturalistic study of empathic behaviors and their relation to affective states and perspective-taking skills in preschool children. *Child Development, 51,* 815–822.

*Strayer, J., & Roberts, W. (1989). Children's empathy and role taking: Child and parental factors, and relations to prosocial behavior. *Journal of Applied Developmental Psychology, 10,* 227–239.

Sutton, J., Smith, P. K., & Swettenham, J. (1999). Social cognition and bullying: Social inadequacy or skilled manipulation? *British Journal of Developmental Psychology, 17,* 435–450.

Tomlinson-Keasey, C., & Keasey, C. B. (1974). The mediating role of cognitive development in moral judgment. *Child Development, 45,* 291–298.

Underwood, B., & Moore, B. (1982). Perspective-taking and altruism. *Psychological Bulletin, 91,* 143–173.

*Waterman, J. M., Sobesky, W. E., Silvern, L., Aoki, B., & McCaulay, M. (1981). Social perspective-taking and adjustment in emotionally disturbed, learning-disabled, and normal children. *Journal of Abnormal Child Psychology, 9,* 133–148.

Wellman, H. M. (2002). Understanding the psychological world: Developing a theory of mind. In U. Goswami (Ed.), *Blackwell handbook of childhood cognitive development* (pp. 167–187). Malden, MA: Blackwell Publishing.

*Zahn-Waxler, C., Radke-Yarrow, M., & Brady-Smith, J. (1977). Perspective-taking and prosocial behavior. *Developmental Psychology, 13,* 87–88.

11

The Development of Future-Oriented Decision-Making

CHRIS MOORE

Psychologists of a cognitivist persuasion often lose sight of the reality that the function of cognitive performance is the organization of behavior. Despite the considerable body of research that has accumulated in the past 15 years on those related aspects of social cognitive development—theory of mind (ToM) and executive functioning (EF)—remarkably little of it has addressed how the interwoven changes in ToM and EF during the preschool period may impact actual social behavior (but see Astington, 2003). Yet there is a clear assumption evident from the histories of research in both ToM and EF that these cognitive abilities play a role in social behavior.

Modern ToM research has its origins in the proposition that primate intelligence appears rather more sophisticated than that of almost all other organisms (e.g., Humphrey, 1976; Premack & Woodruff, 1978). The idea that primates evolved sophisticated intelligence to cope with the demands of complex social organization was an important stimulant to research on ToM (e.g., Byrne & Whiten, 1988; Whiten, 1991). The evolution of social intelligence from the demands of social organization may be mirrored to some extent in ontogenesis with the development of ToM dependent on participation in social interaction (Carpendale & Lewis, 2004; Moore, 2006). Nevertheless, the bulk of the research on the development of ToM in children has mapped whether children display this or that level of ToM at various ages but not what such levels of ToM enable children to do in their social worlds.

The concept of EF had it origins in part in the neuropsychological tradition whereby different aspects of cognitive functioning were mapped onto different brain regions often by charting losses in function resulting from brain damage. Damage to the frontal lobes appeared to leave many aspects of cognitive functioning intact—that is, perception, language, and problem-solving. It was even suggested at one time that the frontal lobes might be unimportant for human behavior. However both case histories (e.g., Eslinger & Damasio, 1985; Harlow, 1868) and the period of prefrontal brain surgery (see Swayze, 1995) made evident the fact that the frontal regions did indeed play an important role in the organization of behavior—but it was typically a role in the organization of personal and social behavior over the long term. Damage to the frontal lobes often left intact functioning in the immediate here-and-now but resulted in a compromised ability to make future-oriented decisions that would be adaptive over the long term. In the recent spate of research on EF in early development, relatively little of it has addressed how changes in EF may affect children's abilities to organize their behavior beyond the here-and-now.

Having suggested that most of the research on ToM and EF in children has focused on examining developing cognitive performance rather than how such performance impacts social behaviors, it is important to point out that there are some notable exceptions to this focus (e.g., see Astington, 2003; Dunn, 1995; Hughes & Dunn, 1997; Jenkins & Astington, 2000). These studies have largely focused on relations between performance on standard experimental tasks and individual differences in social behavior in relatively naturalistic familial and peer contexts. It is hoped that this volume will serve as a stimulant for further examination of the ways in which social-cognitive development relates to social behavior and thereby provide an important corrective to the field. In this chapter, I review some of our recent work, which has attempted to take a more functional approach to the preschool developments in ToM and EF, in the sense that we have examined how children make practical decisions about the allocation of rewards to self and other and to self at different points in time. Our work differs from most other research that has examined children's social behavior in that we have adopted a laboratory-based experimental approach. Nevertheless, the paradigms that we employ do require children to make action choices rather than just verbally report what they understand about contrived social situations.

A guiding assumption of our approach has been that what sets human cognition apart from that of all other organisms is the ability to imagine and make decisions in regard to noncurrent, most importantly future, situations (Moore & Lemmon, 2001a). In this assumption, our overall view of human cognition is similar to a number of other theorists who have argued for some form of specifically cognitive ability to transcend or distance oneself from the here-and-now (e.g., Geisbrecht, Muller, & Miller, Chapter 14, this volume; Suddendorf & Corballis, 1997; Wheeler, Stuss, & Tulving, 1997). We argue that the cognitive changes characterizing the late preschool period, so beloved by the current generation of cognitive developmentalists, represent a suite of cognitive abilities that enable, for the first time, children to engage in a special form of human reasoning: future-oriented decision-making.

Making prudent decisions about future circumstances clearly requires both ToM and EF. A simple example may demonstrate this best. Imagine you have gone shopping to buy food for tonight's dinner for your family. You only have enough cash to purchase the food you need, but you see an attractive shirt on sale that costs the same amount. You may have a strong immediate desire to buy the shirt but you do not and you move on to finish your grocery shopping. To make such a future-oriented decision, you clearly had to inhibit a response to an immediate desire. Probably part of what enabled that inhibition was the imagination of the future result of indulging the impulse—you and your family would be disappointed later, and they would think you were selfish and uncaring to gratify your own immediate desires. This straightforward example illustrates that many decisions we make require the inhibition of responses to immediate gratification in favor of actions designed to achieve longer term goals, goals which are often set within a social context in which the concerns of others are also at issue.

Theory-of-mind competence, in this example particularly, is required for future-oriented decisions because to make such decisions the actor must be able to represent the future mental states of self and other even when they conflict with current ones. The most commonly used versions of ToM tasks measure children's ability to represent a mental state that does not correspond to the child's own immediate one. For example, the classic displaced object task (Wimmer & Perner, 1983) assesses the participant's ability to represent a story protagonist's belief when it conflicts with the participant's knowledge. EF is clearly also involved in future-oriented decision-making because such decisions intrinsically involve two incompatible possible courses of action, one of which is often prepotent in the sense that it involves a response to immediate, perceptual information, as opposed to a response to information that is only imagined. It is important to note here that overcoming the prepotency or pull of the immediate depends on the development of a concern for others or for oneself in the future. Thus one not only has to be able to imagine noncurrent mental states of self and others, one also has to care about them (Moore & Macgillivray, 2004).

Future-oriented reasoning likely also involves another aspect of developing social cognition. In addition to considering the role of EF and ToM, we have also focused on the role played by the development of self. Of course, children acquire a sense of the objective (or physical) self well before the landmark achievements of the late preschool period (Moore, 2007). By 2 years of age children can recognize themselves in mirrors (e.g., Nielsen, Dissanayake, & Kashima, 2003), can represent their bodily self (e.g., Moore, Mealiea, Garon, & Povinelli, 2007), and can refer linguistically to themselves (Lewis & Ramsay, 2004). As such, 2-year-olds have a clear sense of self as an objective entity existing in a world of objects. And yet there is good evidence that this early sense of self does not carry with it an understanding of the connectedness of the self through time, what has been referred to as the "temporally extended self" (TES; Moore & Lemmon, 2001b). When children are required to consider how the present self is connected to the past self or the future self, it is only later during the fourth year that they begin to show evidence of appreciating that the self exists in relation to a connected series of moments or events in time. Although the self may not yet be understood in an abstract way, independent of its role or participation in particular events, such a self may be considered a narrative self because the child can now tell a story of their own activity, including past, present, and future (Nelson, 2001). Interestingly, this development occurs around the same time as the extensively studied changes in EF and ToM, suggesting that at some level they are related cognitively. We have argued that the ability to make future-oriented decisions also depends on the TES because to make a decision that will benefit oneself in the future at the expense of the present, one has to be able to appreciate that the future self retains an identity with the current self (Moore & Lemmon, 2001a).

In this chapter, we review some of our work, which has examined the links between the social-cognitive developments of ToM, EF, and TES, and children's ability to make decisions that are future oriented. To study future-oriented decision-making we have adopted a trial-based version of delay of gratification. Children receive a series of choices between one (usually smaller) reward available immediately and another (usually larger) reward available later. Traditional delay of gratification research (e.g., Mischel, 1974) has more often used a simple delay task, in which the length of time children can wait for a larger reward is the dependent measure, and the effects of various manipulations on this measure are studied. Although this approach is useful for the study of various influences on inhibition of the prepotent response (i.e., taking the immediately available reward), it is less valuable for studying the combination of cognitive factors in which we are interested. In the trial-based format, we can vary within the task, the relative sizes of the rewards as well as the recipient of the rewards, and this allows some traction on the idea that future-oriented decision-making is often a social enterprise that requires an appreciation of the temporal extension of self.

The Study of Future-Oriented Decision-Making

In our first study on this topic, we (Thompson, Barresi, & Moore, 1997) presented 3- to 5-year-olds with a series of two alternative choices for which the rewards were stickers. Choosing to take the stickers immediately led to the children having the satisfaction of peeling them and putting them in a sticker book. Choosing to take the stickers later meant that satisfaction would be delayed until later in the day. Along with a simply delay of gratification choice for which children could choose between one sticker immediately or two stickers later, children were presented with a variety of choices involving sharing. In two of these choice types, there was no delay involved. To assess sharing without cost, children were asked to choose between one sticker for the self or one sticker for both the self and another person (who was a teenage confederate acting as a play partner). To assess sharing with cost, children were asked to choose between two stickers for self or one sticker each for self and the partner. In a third sharing choice type, children were given a choice between one sticker for self now or one sticker each for the self and the partner later. This latter choice involved the same quantities as the sharing without cost choice but the delay imposed for the sharing option meant that there was now a cost to sharing, albeit it not a material one.

Our results showed clear developmental effects only for the choice types involving a delayed option, with 3-year-olds tending to opt for the immediate rewards and 5-year-olds opting significantly more often to delay. There was no difference in the pattern of performance between the choice type that involved sharing and the choice type that did not. These first results suggested that making future-oriented decisions is difficult for 3-year-olds and this difficulty occurs whether the future benefit would accrue to the self or to others. Interestingly, for the choice types involving sharing without delay, there were no developmental effects. Three-year-olds were as likely as 5-year-olds to opt to share in the here-and-now with the play partner. So 3-year-olds are just as prosocially oriented as older children. Our interpretation of these findings is that younger children are not able to imagine the future in relation to the present, and as a result their action is organized by immediate, not future, concerns. In contrast, older preschoolers of 4 or 5 appear able to imagine their future circumstances even as they conflict with the current situation and make choices that are oriented toward the future.

One interpretive issue that arose in thinking about this developmental pattern is whether the developmental difference here really rests on future orientation. It is possible that younger children are just as able to imagine the future and its connection to the present, they just value immediate rewards more highly. The problem with younger children might, in effect, be a motivational one rather than a cognitive one. To examine this issue, we (Lemmon & Moore, 2007) reasoned that if younger children's difficulties with our future-oriented decision-making task was primarily motivational, then their performance should vary as a function of reward value. However, if younger children's difficulties are primarily cognitive, then they should not be dependent on reward value. To this end we designed two experiments using only choices involving the self in which we varied the reward values that we presented to children from 3 to 4 years of age. In the first experiment, we presented the children with choices in which the immediate reward was always 1 sticker but the delayed reward varied from 2 to 5. The results showed that the size of the future reward made no difference to the younger children—they tended to take the immediate reward no matter what the size of the later reward. So it is unlikely that purely motivational issues are responsible for their failure to exhibit future orientation. In contrast, the 4-year-olds showed a clear effect of reward size—they were significantly more likely to delay with the larger reward sizes than with the smaller reward sizes. This finding is consistent with the claim that older but not younger children are able to imagine the future circumstances in a way that allows the prepotent response to the immediate reward to be inhibited.

In some ways, our second experiment on this issue was more compelling. We reasoned that anyone who could imagine and make decisions with regard to their future concerns, should show some degree of future orientation even when there is no material benefit to delaying. The idea is that if one has a sense of the self in the future then one should aim to apportion or ration available rewards across time so that the concerns of the future self are cared for. In effect, one would not want to end up in a situation in the future in which one had already consumed all the available rewards. To investigate this, we presented 3- and 4-year-olds with our future-oriented decision-making task in which they were presented with trials that varied the available quantity of stickers from one to four but for which the immediate and future options did not differ in amount. For example, children would be asked to choose between two stickers immediately or two stickers later. With such choices there is no quantitative benefit to taking the delayed option and so one might imagine at first gloss that it would make sense to take the immediate option on every trial. However, notice that to do so would mean that the future self would be deprived of all the fun! So, we predicted that older children would still choose to delay on some trials to ration the rewards across time and save some of the fun for their future selves. The results were consistent with this prediction. The 3-year-olds tended to opt to take the stickers immediately and this decision did not differ by reward size. The 4-year-olds were significantly more likely to choose to delay, especially on the trials in which a larger reward was available.

On such trials they approached a temporally neutral stance where they opted to take half the rewards immediately and save half for later.

Together these experiments show that younger children's difficulty in the future-oriented decision-making task is not a problem in motivation. Rather it appears genuinely to be a difficulty with not being able to imagine and act in favor of the concerns of the future self. If so, then an investigation into the social-cognitive and executive aspects of the task seems warranted. In what follows we consider three such aspects: ToM, inhibitory control, and the TES.

Is Future-Oriented Decision-Making Related to Theory of Mind?

So far, we have talked about the need in future-oriented decision-making to consider the "concerns"of the self or of others in the future. The use of the term "concerns" here is meant to cover a range of mental states including desires but also interests. In the literature on children's theories of mind, there is evidence that children are able to think and talk about desires from as early as 2 years of age or even younger (e.g., Repacholi & Gopnik, 1997; Wellman, 1990). However, as noted, the ability to act in favor of the future concerns or desires of self and other appears to require the ability to represent those concerns even when they conflict with the immediate concerns of the here-and-now. This cognitive ability is more similar to that required for passing standard false belief tasks rather than simple desire tasks. In the standard false belief task the child is asked to consider someone else's belief that stands in contrast to what the child knows to be true. So the false belief task is one example of a situation in which the child must consider a mental state that conflicts with his or her own current mental state. Desires may be analyzed in a similar manner. A number of authors have now found that when children are asked to infer other people's desires that conflict with their own current desire they do not perform well until closer to 4 years of age (Cassidy et al., 2005; Gopnik & Slaughter, 1991; Moore et al., 1995).

In two separate experiments, we have assessed children's performance on both future-oriented decision-making and ToM tasks that require the representation of mental states that conflict with the child's current mental state. In our first study (Moore, Barresi, & Thompson, 1998), we tested children on the future-oriented decision-making task with a variety of choice types. Of particular interest, there were two choice types in which a delayed option allowing the sharing of a larger reward between the child and play partner was contrasted with an immediate option in which the child or the other received a smaller reward. Children were also tested on a small battery of ToM tasks that included a conflicting desire task modeled after Gopnik and Slaughter (1991) and false belief tasks. Performance on an aggregate of the ToM tasks was significantly correlated with performance on the delayed sharing trials of the future-oriented decision-making. So children who were able to represent conflicting mental states also tended to choose the delayed option to share stickers with another person.

The sample size in this first study was small (N = 20) with a relatively wide age range (6 months) and no control measures were included, so in later research (Moore & Macgillivray, 2004) we tested a larger number of children (N = 53) all within a month of their fourth birthday as part of a longitudinal study. In this study, we again included a small battery of ToM tasks (false belief and appearance-reality) and various trial types in the future-oriented decision-making task. Children were also tested on the PPVT-III (Dunn & Dunn, 1997) to provide a general verbal intelligence measure. The results showed a significant correlation between the ToM score and children's tendency to choose to make a future-oriented decision in the choice where they could give up an immediate smaller reward for themselves in favor of a larger delayed reward to be shared with their play partner. This result replicated the finding from our earlier study (Moore et al., 1998). It is worth noting that when PPVT-III score was controlled, the correlation between ToM and future-oriented decision-making was no longer significant. Therefore, it appears that future-oriented decision-making involving the interests of both self and others is related developmentally to the ability to represent noncurrent and conflicting mental states. Although this association is not independent of language, it is now well documented that measures of ToM in general are robustly correlated with language (see Astington & Baird, 2004). And language is of course an important means by which distancing from the here-and-now can be achieved (Geisbrecht et al., Chapter 14, this volume; Jacques & Zelazo, 2005).

Is Future-Oriented Decision-Making Related to Executive Function?

We have suggested that future-oriented decision-making requires the ability to imagine the future concerns of the self and others when those concerns differ from immediate ones. However merely being able to imagine noncurrent and conflicting concerns may not automatically allow a decision to be made in favor of those noncurrent concerns. Whenever there is a conflict set up between two sources of information that require incompatible responses, it is usually the case that one source of information and one response are more salient. Current motivational information in relation to immediate perceptual input tends to be more salient than imagined motivational information. Thus, when the choice is between a response to immediate perceptual information (e.g., an immediate desire for stickering) and a response organized in relation to delayed imagined information (e.g., a future desire for stickering), then the immediate response is likely to be prepotent.

Such circumstances are classic EF problems. EF is particularly involved when a response to less salient information is required in the face of a prepotent response to more salient information. Opting to take a reward to satisfy an imagined future desire in the face of a reward that can satisfy an immediate desire requires the ability to keep in mind both the immediate and the future desire, and then inhibit the response to the immediate desire.

Given this analysis of the future-oriented decision-making task, we also decided to examine whether performance on the task would be related to EF ability, in particular to inhibitory control. Our first study (Moore et al., 1998) used the Windows task (Russell, Mauthner, Sharpe, & Tidswell, 1991) as the measure of inhibition. In the Windows task a treat (we used small cookies) is hidden in one of the two boxes over a series of trials. On each trial, the child has to point to one of the boxes for a competitor (a monkey puppet) who then looks in that box. If the competitor finds the treat, he gets to keep it. However, if the competitor does not find the treat, the child gets it. In the initial phase the child does not know in which box the treat is hidden and so is essentially guessing. Once the child has learned the contingency—that the competitor always goes to the box indicated by the child and always keeps the treat if he finds it—the original boxes are replaced by two boxes each with a window facing the child, so that now the child knows which box contains the treat. The session then continues as before. The task for the child is now to gain more treats by pointing to the empty box. Russell and colleagues (1991) showed that this task is very difficult for children younger than about 3.5 years who tend to point to the baited box during the window trials. They fail to benefit from the information about the treat location; indeed it makes their performance worse because they cannot stop themselves pointing to the baited box. Their response is governed by the desire for the treat and they cannot inhibit a response in reaction to that desire (for additional insight into this task, see Hala and colleagues, Chapter 12, this volume).

We tested children from 3 to 4.5 years on both the Windows task and our future-oriented decision-making task, involving choices that included delayed sharing and choices including delay only for the self. Our results showed quite strong and significant relations between future-oriented decision-making and performance on the Windows task. Children who could inhibit pointing to the baited box on the Windows task and thereby win a large number of treats also tended to delay in the future-oriented decision-making task. This correlation was found both for choice types where the delayed reward would be shared with the play partner and for choice types where the future self alone would benefit. It is important to note, however, that significant correlations were only found for the very youngest children, those between 3 and 3.5 years. This is because performance in the Windows task only shows good variability below about 3.5 years. After that children start to perform well and quickly reach ceiling (see Russell et al., 1991).

It is perhaps not surprising that performance on the Windows task is correlated with that on the future-oriented decision-making task. The two tasks have very similar task demands in that a choice must be made between two options over a series of trials. Both tasks appear to require what has been called "conflict inhibition," that is, inhibition of a response to one alternative in a forced choice where the two possible responses are incompatible (see Chapter 9 by Moses & Tahiroglu, this volume). To examine whether inhibitory control alone might be implicated in future-oriented decision-making, in another study we tested children on the decision-making task and a task assessing response inhibition without a conflict component (or "delay inhibition"—Moses & Tahiroglu, Chapter 9, this volume). This study was longitudinal in design, so that children were tested three times—at 3.5, 4, and 4.5 years. At each age children were tested on future-oriented decision-making choices, including delay for self and delayed sharing. They were also tested on a gift delay task, modeled after Kochanska, Murray, Jacques, Koenig, and Vandegeest (1996). The gift delay task was presented at the end of the session. Children were told that they had done a great job in the session and that they were going to get a gift for helping the experimenter. They were then asked to turn and face a blank wall and not peek while the experimenter wrapped their gift. The experimenter proceeded to noisily wrap the gift for 60 seconds during which time the child had to try to stay facing the wall. In this task, there is no conflict between two responses, rather the children have to try to stop themselves from peeking. A number of measures of inhibition were generated including latency to first peek, and type of peek (full head turn around versus surreptitious glance) during the 60 seconds. All of these measures showed significant improvement with age indicating that children's inhibitory skills are changing over this period.

The results from these studies revealed two main interesting findings. First, there were robust associations between future-oriented decision-making for both delay for self and delayed sharing and inhibition even when general verbal intelligence (as measured by the PPVT-III) was controlled. Second, the significant associations were only observed at age 4. There were no significant associations at 3.5 or 4.5 years. These results imply that the development of future-oriented decision-making is linked to delay inhibition during the critical developmental phase when both are becoming part of the children's behavioral repertoires. On the basis of the correlational results from the two studies just outlined, one might conclude that the ability to cope with conflict inhibition situations is developed slightly earlier the ability to cope with delay inhibition, perhaps because the latter depends more on the imagination of a future scenario, rather than an appropriate response to one of two immediate options. However, such an interpretation must remain tentative given the differences in method and sample size across these two studies.

In summary, future-oriented decision-making clearly has an executive component. To make choices in favor of the future concerns of both self and other, children must inhibit the prepotent response to take the immediately available alternative. As such inhibition improves with age, so also does the tendency to make choices in favor of future concerns.

Is Future-Oriented Decision-Making Related to the Temporally Extended Self?

The final facet of social-cognitive development that we have studied in relation to future-oriented decision-making is the TES. Being able to represent the future concerns of self and others, and being able to inhibit a prepotent response can still only get one so far. In addition, one has to recognize a temporal and causal connection between the present and future person, and identify with the person whose future concerns one imagines (Moore & Lemmon, 2001a). Although this principle applies to others as well as the self, it is most thoroughgoing in the case of the self. Why would one make a decision in favor of an imagined future person if one did not recognize that that person has the same identity as the self now and that the choices one makes now will affect that person in the future? The idea that anyone may not appreciate this common sense notion may seem far-fetched; however, there is in fact good evidence that young children do not have such a sense of the temporally extended nature of the self (Moore & Lemmon, 2001b).

One important source of evidence comes from a modification of the classic marked face procedure for assessing self-recognition in mirrors (see Povinelli, 2001; Povinelli, Landau, & Perilloux, 1996). Povinelli and his colleagues (1996) videotaped young children playing a game with an experimenter. The children knew they were being videotaped. They were shown the videocamera and they were told that after the game they would get to watch themselves on TV. During the game, the experimenter surreptitiously marked the children's heads with a bright sticker. After a few minutes during which the videotape was rewound, the children sat down in front of a TV to watch what had happened just a few minutes earlier. They then watched the scene as the experiment placed the sticker on their heads. Spontaneous reactions to the marking event were observed and then a number of prompt questions were asked, including "who is that?," "what is that (pointing to the sticker on the TV)?," and "where is that sticker really?" If the children made no attempt to retrieve the sticker from their own heads, they were then shown a mirror and given the opportunity to find the sticker while looking in the mirror. Povinelli and colleagues reported that most children under 3.5 years failed to locate the sticker during the replay of the video but were able to find it when looking in the mirror. Moreover, it was not just that they failed to find the sticker during the video replay, they appeared to treat the image in the video as in some sense disconnected from their current selves. For example, although they could recognize themselves in the video, they were more likely to use third person language, such as their name, for the self.

The evidence from this delayed self-recognition task is consistent with work from other areas of self-understanding in showing that although children develop an objective sense of self normally by the end of the second year, they do not acquire a sense of self as being an individual with a connected personal past until about 3.5–4 years. For example, this is also the time during which children start to show clear evidence of autobiographical memory (see chapters in Moore & Lemmon, 2001b). Our suggestion is that future-oriented decisions in a future-oriented decision-making task must also require a sense that the self is connected in time, but here the understanding of the temporal extension of the self must include the future rather than the past.

To examine the link between future-oriented decision-making and the TES, we (Lemmon & Moore, 2001) tested children between 3.5 and 4.5 years on our future-oriented decision-making task and Povinelli's delayed self-recognition task. Whereas, the delayed self-recognition task assesses children's understanding that the self extends from past to present, the future-oriented decision-making task can be thought to test in part for the ability to conceive of the self as extended from the present into the future. The future-oriented decision-making task we used involved only choices involving self with the key choice being between one sticker available immediately and two stickers available later. We modeled the delayed self-recognition task after Povinelli et al. (1996), as described earlier. Children were given a 1 minute opportunity to touch the sticker spontaneously after watching the marking event on the TV and then, if they were not successful, they were prompted. This allowed a tripartite scoring system to increase variability in the self-recognition measure, with children retrieving the sticker spontaneously scored as 2, children retrieving the sticker after prompting scored as 1, and children not retrieving the sticker scored as 0.

The results from two separate experiments showed appropriate variability during the age ranges tested. Furthermore, performance on the delayed self-recognition task was significantly positively correlated with the tendency to make future-oriented decisions even with age in months controlled. That is, children who were able to locate the sticker on their heads when watching the delayed video also tended to opt for the larger delayed reward in the decision-making task. This result is consistent with the idea that at about 4 years of age children are developing a sense of self that spans past, present, and future. Success on the delayed self-recognition reveals the understanding of the connection between the past and the present, whereas future orientation reflects in part an understanding of the connection between the present and the future.

Conclusion

In this brief review of our work using the future-oriented decision-making task, we have covered evidence that the tendency to make future-oriented decisions is related developmentally to three aspects of social-cognitive development during the period from 3 to 4 years of age. Children who more often opt to delay in situations where either the self or the self and someone else will benefit in the future also perform better on standard ToM tasks measuring the ability to represent others' mental states even when they conflict with reality. Children who make future-oriented choices both for themselves alone and for others as well as the self are also better able to inhibit their actions in situations where there is a strong perceptual pull toward a maladaptive response. Finally children who make future-oriented decisions for themselves are also able to understand the temporal connectedness of past and present states of the self.

These results are consistent with the idea that future-oriented decision-making requires the ability to represent conflicting mental states, to inhibit prepotent responses to salient information and to conceive of the self as extended in time. It must be noted, however, that all of the studies we have reviewed here used a correlational design, so it is obviously not possible to draw strong inferences about causal relations among them. Indeed there has been considerable debate in the literature about these social-cognitive abilities may relate to each other casually. For example, it has been argued by some that EF changes underlie changes in ToM whereas others have argued for the reverse (see Moses and Tahiroglu, Chapter 9, this volume). The various abilities we have measured all show significant developmental change from about

3.5 to 4.5 years, but we cannot say whether change in one or more of these abilities enables future-oriented decision-making.

Another possible interpretation is that all of these abilities depend on more general changes in representational ability. The most likely candidate here is the ability to hold in mind more than one perspective on a situation and thereby consider the possible relations between these perspectives. The ToM achievements at 4 years of age have been suggested to require the ability to represent the same object or event is two conflicting ways (Flavell, 1988; Perner, 1991). Thus, to understand false belief, the child has to represent the situation from the point of view of the other person as well as the child's own current perspective. The notion of false belief rests on recognizing the relation between these two perspectives, to be able to say in effect that "although I know there are pencils in the box, he will think there are Smarties in the box." Similarly, the development of the TES has been linked to this more general change in representational ability. Povinelli (2001) has argued that the TES rests on the ability to represent simultaneously the self from two different points in time. Once children can simultaneously think of the self now and the self in the past or in the future, they can consider such self states in relation to each other and thus construct a sense of self that has temporal continuity. Even inhibition may depend on this representational ability. Inhibition of a prepotent response to salient information may be best achieved by being able to imagine simultaneously an alternative source of information that can serve to organize an alternative response. This idea is most simply illustrated in the case of conflict inhibition where a response to less salient information is required in the face of a prepotent response to more salient perceptual information. In such cases, inhibition may be achieved by being able to hold in mind simultaneously the possible responses to both the more salient perceptual information and the less salient imagined information and then choosing the response on the basis of the latter. Even inhibition in nonconflict situations such as the gift delay task described earlier may be best achieved by enabling an alternative response such as thinking about some other piece of information and thereby distracting one's attention from the pull of the attractive stimulus (cf., Mischel, 1974; Mischel & Ebbesen, 1970).

At present, we cannot say exactly how these various facets of social-cognitive development—ToM, EF, and the TES—fit together to allow future-oriented decision-making. Nevertheless, it does appear that all of them are involved. For now, we prefer to take the position that this period in development sees the development of a suite of interconnected social-cognitive abilities that together make possible the uniquely human ability to imagine the future and organize current action in relation to that imagined future.

ACKNOWLEDGMENTS

The research reviewed in this chapter was made possible through support from the Social Sciences and Humanities Research Council of Canada. I thank the collaborators who worked with me on the various projects described in this chapter: John Barresi, Karen Lemmon, Shannon Macgillivray, Shana Nichols, and Carol Thompson. Thanks also to Bryan Sokol for the excellent feedback on an earlier draft of the chapter.

REFERENCES

Astington, J. (2003). Sometimes necessary, never sufficient: False belief understanding and social competence. In B. Repacholi & V. Slaughter (Eds.), *Individual differences in theory of mind: Implications for typical and atypical development* (pp. 13–38). Hove, East Sussex, UK: Psychology Press.

Astington, J., & Baird, J. (2004). *Why language matter for theory of mind.* New York: Oxford University Press.

Byrne, R., & Whiten, A. (1988). *Machiavellian intelligence. Social expertise and the evolution of intellect in monkeys, apes, and humans.* Oxford: Oxford University Press.

Carpendale, J., & Lewis, C. (2004). Constructing an understanding of mind: The development of children's social understanding within social interaction. *Behavioral and Brain Sciences, 27,* 79–151.

Cassidy, K., Cosetti, M., Jones, R., Kelton, E., Rafal, V., Richman, L., et al. (2005). Preschool children's understanding of conflicting desires. *Journal of Cognition and Development, 6,* 427–454.

Dunn, J. (1995). Children as psychologists: The later correlates of individual differences in understanding of emotions and other minds. *Cognition and Emotion, 9,* 187–201.

Dunn, L., & Dunn, L. (1997). *Manual for the Peabody Picture Vocabulary Test-III.* Circle Pines, MN: American Guidance Service.

Eslinger, P. J., & Damasio, A. R. (1985). Severe disturbance of higher cognition after bilateral frontal lobe ablation: Patient EVR. *Neurology, 35,* 1731–1741.

Flavell, J. H. (1988). The development of children's knowledge about the mind: From cognitive connections to mental representations. In J. Astington, P. Harris, & D. Olson (Eds.), *Developing theories of mind* (pp. 244–267). New York: Cambridge University Press.

Gopnik, A., & Slaughter, V. (1991). Young children's understanding of changes in their mental states. *Child Development, 62,* 98–110.

Harlow, J. M. (1868). Recovery from the passage of an iron bar through the head. *Publications of the Massachusetts Medical Society, 3,* 1–21.

Hughes, C., & Dunn, J. (1997). "Pretend you didn't know": Preschoolers talk about mental states in pretend play. *Cognitive Development, 12,* 381–403.

Humphrey, N. (1976). The social function of intellect. In P. Bateson & R. Hinde (Eds.), *Growing points in ethology.* Cambridge: Cambridge University Press.

Jacques, S., & Zelazo, P. D. (2005). *Language and the development of cognitive flexibility: Implications for theory of mind* (pp. 144–162). New York: Oxford University Press.

Jenkins, J. M., & Astington, J. W. (2000). Theory of mind and social behavior: Causal models tested in a longitudinal study. *Merrill-Palmer Quarterly, 46,* 203–220.

Kochanska, G., Murray, K., Jacques, T., Koenig, A., & Vandegeest, K. (1996). Inhibitory control in young children and its role in emerging internalization. *Child Development, 67,* 490–507.

Lemmon, K., & Moore, C. (2001). Binding the self in time. In C. Moore & K. Lemmon, (Eds.), *The self in time. Developmental issues* (pp. 163–179). Mahwah, NJ: Lawrence Erlbaum Associates.

Lemmon, K., & Moore, C. (2007). The development of prudence in the face of varying future rewards. *Developmental Science, 10,* 502–511.

Lewis, M., & Ramsay, D. (2004). Development of self-recognition, personal pronoun use, and pretend play during the 2nd year. *Child Development, 75,* 1821–1831.

Mischel, W. (1974). Processes in delay of gratification. In L. Berkowitz (Ed.), *Advances in Experimental Social Psychology* (pp. 249–292). New York: Academic Press.

Mischel, W., & Ebbesen, E. B. (1970). Attention in delay of gratification. *Journal of Personality and Social Psychology, 16,* 329–337.

Moore, C. (2006). *The development of commonsense psychology.* Mahwah, NJ: Lawrence Erlbaum Associates.

Moore, C. (2007). Understanding self and other in the second year. In C. A. Brownell & C. B. Kopp (Eds.), *Transitions in early socioemotional development: The toddler years* (pp. 43–65). New York: Guilford Press.

Moore, C., Barresi, J., & Thompson, C. (1998). The cognitive basis of prosocial behavior. *Social Development, 7,* 198–218.

Moore, C., Jarrold, C., Russell, J., Lumb, A., Sapp, F., & MacCallum, F. (1995). Conflicting desire and the child's theory of mind. *Cognitive Development, 10,* 467–482.

Moore, C., & Lemmon, K. (2001a). The nature and utility of the temporally extended self. In C. Moore & K. Lemmon (Eds.), *The self in time. Developmental issues* (pp. 1–13). Mahwah, NJ: Lawrence Erlbaum Associates.

Moore, C., & Lemmon, K. (2001b). *The self in time. Developmental issues.* Mahwah, NJ: Lawrence Erlbaum Associates.

Moore, C., & Macgillivray, S. (2004). Altruism, prudence, and theory of mind in preschoolers. *New directions for child and adolescent development, 103,* 51–62.

Moore, C., Mealiea, J., Garon, N., & Povinelli, D. J. (2007). The development of the bodily self. *Infancy, 11,* 157–174.

Nelson, K. (2001). Language and the self: From the "Experiencing I" to the "Continuing Me." In C. Moore & K. Lemmon (Eds.), *The self in time. Developmental perspectives* (pp. 15–33). Mahwah, NJ: Lawrence Erlbaum Associates.

Nielsen, M., Dissanayake, C., & Kashima, Y. (2003). A longitudinal investigation of self-other discrimination and the emergence of minor self-recognition. *Infant Behavior and Development, 26,* 213–226.

Perner, J. (1991). *Understanding the representational mind*. Cambridge, MA: MIT Press.

Povinelli, D. J. (2001). The self: Elevated in consciousness and extended in time. In C. Moore & K. Lemmon (Eds.), *The self in time: Developmental perspectives* (pp. 75–95). Mahwah, NJ: Lawrence Erlbaum Associates.

Povinelli, D. P., Landau, K., & Perilloux, H. (1996). Self-recognition in young children using delayed versus live feedback: Evidence of a developmental asynchrony. *Child Development, 67*, 1540–1554.

Premack, D., & Woodruff, G. (1978). Does the chimpanzee have a theory of mind? *Behavioral and Brain Sciences, 1*, 515–525.

Repacholi, B. M., & Gopnik, A. (1997). Early reasoning about desires: Evidence from 14- and 18-month-olds. *Developmental Psychology, 33*, 12–21.

Russell, J., Mauthner, N., Sharpe, S., & Tidswell, T. (1991). The "windows" task as a measure of strategic deception in preschoolers and autistic subjects. *British Journal of Developmental Psychology, 9*, 331–350.

Suddendorf, T., & Corballis, M. C. (1997). Mental time travel and the evolution of the human mind. *Genetic, Social and General Psychology Monographs, 123*, 133–167.

Swayze, V. W., II (1995). Frontal leukotomy and related psychosurgical procedures in the era before antipsychotics (1935–1954): A historical overview. *American Journal of Psychiatry, 152*, 505–515.

Thompson, C., Barresi, J., & Moore, C. (1997). The development of future-oriented prudence and altruism in preschoolers. *Cognitive Development, 12*, 199–212.

Wellman, H. (1990). *The child's theory of mind*. Cambridge, MA: MIT Press.

Wheeler, M. A., Stuss, D. T., & Tulving, E. (1997). Toward a theory of episodic memory: The frontal lobes and autonoetic consciousness. *Psychological Bulletin, 121*, 331–354.

Whiten, A. (1991). *Natural theories of mind*. Oxford, England: Blackwell Publishing.

Wimmer, H., & Perner, J. (1983). Beliefs about beliefs: Representation and constraining function of wrong beliefs in young children's understanding of deception. *Cognition, 13*, 103–128.

PART III

Self-Regulation in Social Contexts: Parents, Peers, and Individual Differences

ARLENE R. YOUNG, DAGMAR BERNSTEIN, AND GRACE IAROCCI

P revious parts of this volume have emphasized the dynamic interconnection between the development of executive functions, social understanding, and the social contexts in which this development occurs. Our shared theoretical position is that executive functions and social understanding are interdependent aspects of development firmly grounded in social interaction. Hammond, Bibok, and Carpendale's introduction captures this nicely when they state that "executive functions are above all else, descriptions of the behavior of person within their sociocultural and sociohistorical contexts" (Theoretical Perspectives on Self and Social Regulation, p. 1). This final part of the book provides some flesh to these theoretical bones by focusing specifically on both the sociocultural contexts in which executive functions and social understanding arise (e.g., relationships within families, peers, and communities) and on the importance of very early individual differences.

Longitudinal methodologies and research involving atypically developing children provide unique opportunities to identify individual child characteristics that play a significant role in the development of executive functions. This in no way diminishes the role of social interaction; however, as genetic or neurocognitive predispositions are expressed within the social context in which a child develops. The subtle interplay between these factors is often difficult to capture in typically developing individuals or contexts. Hala, Pexman, Climie, Rostad, and Glenwright take the position that the child's environment, including the social context, has a reciprocal influence on the development of executive functions. They highlight ways in which aspects of the social world such as collaboration on a problem with peers or exposure to ambiguous social interaction with parents (comprehending verbal irony and learning two languages) may facilitate this development, and present theoretical and empirical evidence to support their claims. Hala et al. contend that the bidirectional relationship between executive functioning and social interaction goes beyond the notion of "scaffolding" by a more skillful partner and explain this reciprocal relationship in terms of Piaget's notion of equilibration (Piaget, 1995). In particular, social interaction can create cognitive conflict (disequilibriation) challenging existent executive functioning abilities such that they must expand to facilitate increased social understanding with the child's cognition shifting through "accommodation." This bidirectional process requires psychological distancing on the part of a child whereby they must step back and view their actions (i.e., a separation or "distance" between self and world is necessary). Similarly, the chapter by Flynn focuses on the individual characteristics of children including mental-state understanding and executive functioning that contribute to their potential scaffolding role with their peers in a collaborative learning situation. Flynn argues that effective tutoring demands an ability to disengage from one's own activity to focus on the activities of someone else.

Giesbrecht, Müller, and Miller present a view congruent with the arguments put forward in chapters by Hala et al. as well as Flynn and expand further on the concept of psychological distancing. They propose that the nature of parent–child relationships has implications for the development of psychological distancing in children (and therefore for their self-regulation). Giesbrecht et al. contend that constraining relationships typified by power assertive parenting, place few cognitive demands on children, and limit opportunities to expand and restructure thinking. In contrast, collaborative relationships are characterized by inductive parenting that encourages, supports, and challenges children in their emotional regulation and scaffolds their cognitive development. By broadening the focus to incorporate parenting practices in the facilitation of psychological distancing, these authors raise an array of issues for further research including whether qualitative differences in parenting behaviors or the context in which these behaviors occur have differential impacts on a child's development of self-regulation.

Perez and Gauvain also highlight the importance of parent–child interaction in the development of executive functions involved in planning. They stress the dynamic reciprocity between emotional, social, and cognitive development, and contend that parents collaboratively supply their children with both guidance and practice in emotional regulation (an important aspect of emerging executive functioning). Parenting practices, such as parent–child discourse, modeling of emotion, reactions to children's displays of emotion, and teaching about emotion are posited to be particularly influential in this regard. They expand this discussion by underscoring the importance of including individual child characteristics into this developmental model. For example, they propose that children with emotional difficulties may have fewer or less optimal opportunities to learn or to engage in planning during social interactions with parents than children who do not have these difficulties.

Chapters by Landry and Smith and by Hughes and Ensor incorporate individual differences into longitudinal research on predictors of self-regulation, executive function, and social functioning in both typical and at risk children. This impressive body of research, spanning from infancy to adolescence, underscores the importance of examining both individual differences and environmental factors over the course of development. Hughes and Ensor provide a nuanced account of how child characteristics at one point in development (individual differences in false belief understanding) and environmental events (harsh parenting) can influence child characteristics later in development (problem behaviors). Similarly, Landry and Smith provide support for the role of early executive functioning skills in promoting later self-regulation including the understanding of emotion and coordinating behavior with peers. Consistent with the findings cited by Giesbrecht et al., maternal parenting behaviors such as maintaining attentional focus and verbal scaffolding were associated with the children's development of self-regulation and executive functions, while restrictive, overly directive behaviors were viewed as hindering development (high maternal directiveness was associated with a range of negative child outcomes). The longitudinal research approach featured in some of the chapters in this part reveal an essential proviso, however, in that sensitive parenting requires adaptation as children develop. What is optimal at one age may not be at another. Likewise, as argued by Hughes and Ensor, certain child characteristics may help buffer the effects of parenting behaviors that are otherwise known to be detrimental for children. These authors call for more careful examination of the integration of early social, cognitive, and executive processing skills to establish optimal developmental trajectories and better answer theoretical questions.

Insights from the field of developmental psychopathology may be particularly useful in our quest to consider "executive functions as the outcome or consequence of a developing system jointly composed of individuals and their environments" (Martin & Failows, p. 35). Within the developmental psychopathology field great strides have been made in both the conceptualization and the empirical study of individual attributes, environments, and their transactions, largely due to the emphasis on the atypical nature of both the individual's psychological processes and the environments within which they develop. We highlight a few points inspired by developmental psychopathology research that we believe may propel executive function and social interaction studies forward.

Social activity in many situations is not a means to an end but an end in itself, and the products of this activity are coconstructed by two or more individuals with unique thoughts, feelings, and previous experiences. The implication is that human interactions (particularly when they entail social goals) are both expressions of underlying psychological processes and coconstructed experiences of subjective (self-other) reflections. Thus, the same objective event (or environmental conditions) may be interpreted quite differently even among genetically similar siblings (Plomin & Daniels, 1987; Plomin, Asbury, & Dunn, 2001). A more differentiated conceptualization of social interaction as it relates to executive functions may be useful to focus on process variables, including the unique experiences of the individual in specific relationships (e.g., sibling, parent–child, and peers) and social phenomena (e.g., social comparison) that affect the individual's experience of those relationships (McGuire, 2001).

Social interaction and executive functions are universal aspects of all children's development yet specific in how they would be expressed in particular contexts. We need to move beyond the parent–child (or other) dyad and develop integrative research paradigms that can capture the diverse family environments, communities, and the broader cultural contexts in which children develop. The study of the interplay between executive functions and contextual demands would provide an understanding of the essential components of the interplay that are necessary for development in all contexts as well as the diversity of strategies employed in different familial, community, and cultural contexts. Specifically, the focus on beliefs and practices of parents and other relevant agents of social mediation will identify components that are particularly useful or meaningful within a particular sociocultural context.

The study of social interaction and executive function is potentially informative about the long-term social and emotional outcomes of both typically and atypically developing children. Therefore, it is helpful to begin to qualify the relations between these two constructs in terms of what is essential, sufficient, and optimal at different periods in development, in particular types of social interaction (e.g., parent–child and peer relations) and within specific ecologies (e.g., home and school). Iarocci, Yager, and Elfers (2007) provide the example of social competence as both a developmental phenomenon that can be measured over the course of a child's development (i.e., ontogenesis) and a characteristic of a particular social encounter where the time scale is in the order of seconds/minutes (i.e., microgenesis). Accordingly, continuities and discontinuities in the development of social competence are expected as children are better able to coordinate abilities and take advantage of resources with increasing age but they may be less competent at certain developmental stages or in specific social contexts. With any individual child there is likely to be variation in social competence overtime and across contexts. However, within the general population, some children will show more consistently adaptive or maladaptive social behavior in various social situations and over the course of their development.

Together, chapters in the last part of this book direct us toward the challenge of attending to both the individual and the social context in our investigations of these crucial aspects of development. By highlighting the complex and dynamic interplay between social interaction, individual differences, and executive functions, this final part provides a bridge linking these essential aspects of development and a strong foundation for further exploration.

REFERENCES

Iarocci, G., Yager, J., & Elfers, T. (2007). What gene-environment interactions can tell us about social competence in typical and atypical populations. *Brain and Cognition, 65*, 112–127.

Martin, J., & Failows, L. (2010). Executive function: Theoretical concerns. In B. Sokol, U. Muller, J. Carpendale, A. Young & G. Iarocci (Eds.), Self and Social Regulation: Social Interaction and the Development of Social Understanding and Executive Functions (pp. 35–55). New York: Oxford University Press.

McGuire, S. (2001). Nonshared environment research: What is it and where is it going? *Marriage & Family Review, 33*(1), 31.

Piaget, J. (1995). *Sociological studies.* New York: Routledge.

Plomin, R., Asbury, K., & Dunn, J. (2001). Why are children in the same family so different? Nonshared environment a decade later. *Canadian Journal of Psychiatry, 46*(3), 225–233.

Plomin, R., & Daniels, D. (1987). Why are children in the same family so different from one another? *Behavioural and Brain Sciences, 10*(1), 1–16.

12

A Bidirectional View of Executive Function and Social Interaction

SUZANNE HALA, PENNY PEXMAN, EMMA CLIMIE,
KRISTIN ROSTAD, AND MELANIE GLENWRIGHT

> I think that, in addition to developmental factors—heredity or the maturation of the nervous system, external physical experience, the social milieu, language, and so forth—equilibration … plays a major role: the fact that the subject tries to give the maximum degree of coherence to his ideas and to resolve contradictions … The theory isn't perfect yet.
>
> FROM CONVERSATIONS WITH PIAGET, BRINGUIER (1980, P. 62)

In fitting with the overall goal of this volume, in this chapter we address the question of the nature of the relation between social interaction and executive functions (EF). As pointed out by Moses and Tahiroglu (chapter 9, this volume) as well as others, the relation may be highly complex, not uniform, and, not a one-way direction of influence. It is this latter point, that, in fact, the relation between the growth of EF abilities and emerging social understanding may well be discovered to be bidirectional in nature that we take as our guiding theme. As this volume attests, there is already a substantial body of research that points to a strong relation between EF development and the development of social understanding (e.g., Carlson & Moses, 2001; Carlson, Moses, & Breton, 2002; Carlson, Moses, & Hix, 1998; Hala, Hug, & Henderson, 2003; Hala & Russell, 2001; Hughes, 1998b; Zelazo, Carter, Reznick, & Frye, 1997.)

EF is an "umbrella term" that covers a somewhat diverse collection of cognitive functions associated with the prefrontal cortex. In recent years, researchers have been working toward identifying precisely those dimensions of EF that are most highly related to developing social understanding. Taken together, the picture that is emerging is that those executive measures that require a degree of inhibitory control as well as working memory demands (labeled "conflict tasks" by Carlson and her colleagues; e.g., Carlson et al., 2002) are consistently found to be the executive measures most strongly correlated with social understanding measures such as theory of mind (ToM) assessments (Carlson et al., 2002; Hala et al., 2003).

As Moses and Tahiroglu (Chapter 9, this volume) point out it is the exact nature of that relation that has yet to be well defined. Certainly, it seems reasonable to suggest that increases in EF abilities allow for the emergence of more sophisticated social understanding. One type of evidence offering support for this view comes from those few longitudinal studies that have been carried out so far (Brophy, Talor, & Hughes, 2002; Carlson, Mandell, & Williams, 2004; Hughes, Cutting, & Dunn, 2001). In general, these researchers have found that EF ability at an earlier age is a predictor of later ToM development, but that the reverse does not hold. Recent cross-cultural research, however, has found that more advanced EF ability does not guarantee more advanced ToMunderstanding (Sabbagh, Xu, Carlson, Moses, & Lee, 2006). Though much more longitudinal as well as cross-cultural research is needed to provide additional support for the possibility that executive abilities provide a crucial foundation for more sophisticated social understanding, what evidence there is suggests this to be the case. Nonetheless, even if we can safely conclude that EF abilities provide essential support for many aspects of social understanding, a crucial question remains only partially answered in the existing literature. How does EFing itself develop?

EF abilities are generally accepted to reside primarily in the prefrontal cortex (Pennington & Ozonoff, 1996; Roberts & Pennington, 1996; Welsh, Pennington, & Groisser, 1991). The early childhood years—the developmental period most studied with reference to the relation of EF to social understanding—are also the years during which an intense period of development of synaptic density and myelination occurs (Huttenlocher, 1990; Johnson, 2005; Thompson et al., 2000.). Indeed measures used to assess aspects of prefrontal functioning, for example, planning and working memory, approach adult levels by adolescence (Luciana, 2003; Luciana & Nelson, 1998; Nelson & Luciana, 2001). Although the development of the prefrontal cortex is so protracted, enormous advances are found in the preschool years—precisely the years corresponding to significant advances in performance of behavioral measures of EF (Carlson et al., 2002). As such, obviously biological maturation plays a role in supporting the development of EF abilities.

Nevertheless, biological maturation is insufficient, on its own, to account for the advances in EF found in the childhood years. Brain development, ergo executive development, does not exist in an environmental vacuum, either physically or socially. There is significant evidence that brain development itself is experience dependent (see Nelson, de Haan, & Thomas, 2006; Westermann et al., 2007). Although much of the research is based on animal models, some researchers of human development have found evidence that social experience may be related to alterations in brain functioning (e.g., Beers & De Bellis, 2002; Fishbein, 2001).

There are also numerous studies that indicate that differences in environment may well be related to differences in development of EF. For example, Sabbagh et al. (2006) found that children in China who spoke Cantonese performed at a higher level than their Western English-speaking counterparts in North America on measures of EF. These authors posit that something about the environment of the Chinese children may foster this cognitive development, be it the structure of the language or differences in socialization practices.

What we take from this type of evidence is that the environment, social and otherwise, has a reciprocal impact on the development of executive abilities. This impact could be obstructing, as in the case, for example, of the maltreated children in the Beers and De Bellis (2002) study. Alternatively, the effect could be facilitating, as in the case of the Chinese children in the Sabbagh et al. (2006) study. For the purposes of our chapter, we focus on the potential ways in which the social world might positively facilitate both the development and the expression of EF abilities.

Although there are, no doubt, numerous ways in which EF development and social interactions could be intertwined, we will limit ourselves to an illustration of two promising avenues of exploration. The first is the role that collaboration on a problem might play in facilitating executive processes. Here we will use the example of collaboration on a strategic deception task, the windows task, developed by Russell and his colleagues (Russell, Mauthner, Sharpe, & Tidswell, 1991). The second is the idea that exposure to the somewhat ambiguous nature of social interactions may force the child to exercise more executive control, resulting in advances in various aspects of EF. To illustrate, we will draw from two recent research literatures—children's understanding of sarcasm and, in a somewhat different vein, children's ability to grapple with acquiring more than one language. For the former, we provide an example by way of new research from our laboratory.

Collaboration and Executive Function

We turn now to an illustration of the role that collaboration may play in fostering increased executive control. The development of strategic deception in young children arguably can be considered a marker of the ability to understand that other people can be led into believing something that is not true. As such, deceptive ability is considered one of the hallmarks of having a "theory of mind," or more specifically in this case, understanding that beliefs may be false. The research regarding the emergence of deceptive ability is mixed. Some researchers conclude that at 3 years of age children are not yet capable of deception (Peskin, 1992; Ruffman, Olson, Ash, & Keenan, 1993; Russell, Jarrold, & Potel, 1994; Russell et al., 1991; Sodian, Taylor, Harris, & Perner, 1991). In contrast, other researchers find ample evidence for deception at this tender age (Chandler, Fritz, & Hala, 1989; Hala & Chandler, 1996; Hala, Chandler, & Fritz, 1991; Polak & Harris, 1999). In addition, the naturalistic observation work of Judy Dunn and her colleagues (Dunn, 1991, 1994) as well as Newton, Reddy, and Bull (2000) points to an even earlier onset of 2 years of age when children are observed in naturalistic settings, especially with their siblings.

One potential reason for the differences between these discrepant groups of research findings has been linked to the executive demands of some of the strategic deception tasks, most notably the windows task and other similar tasks that pit the child's interests against an opponent's (Carlson et al., 1998; Hala & Russell, 2001). In the windows task (Russell et al., 1991), children sit across a table from an opponent. On the table between them are two opaque boxes with transparent "windows" cut into the side facing the child. One box is baited with a treat. Children are told that if the opponent finds the treat then the opponent will keep the treat but that if the opponent fails to find the treat then the treat is awarded to the child. Children are instructed to point to the box they want the opponent to open. This task is notoriously difficult for 3-year-old children who typically point to the baited box, even after repeated failures resulting in the negative feedback of surrendering the treat to the opponent. As pointed out by Hala and Russell, however, the windows task is not only a test of strategic deception, but a test of executive control as well. In executive terms, to succeed on the windows task children must (1) inhibit the prepotent response to point to where the treat is and (2) remember the rule that any treats found by the opponent are lost to the child.

In a series of experiments, Hala and Russell (2001) manipulated the weight of the executive demands found in the standard version of the windows task. More specifically, these researchers introduced experimental procedures designed to reduce the inhibitory demands of the task. To accomplish this, they provided participants with various artificial media to indicate the box for the opponent to open. In the standard version of the task, children are required to point with their own extended finger to the chosen box. In the reduced inhibitory control versions, children indicated their choice using either a "pointer" or by placing a cardboard star on top of the chosen box.

All the artificial media conditions were effective in producing higher levels of success in 3-year-old children. In an earlier related study, Carlson et al. (1998) found comparable results using a strategic deception task with opaque boxes rather than "windows" boxes. These researchers concluded that use of artificial media enabled children to distance themselves from the prepotent response of veridical pointing, which in turn allowed children to be more reflective about their strategies.

It is certainly impressive that reduction of inhibitory demands through the use of "mechanical means" allows for better performance on a task that could be argued to be obstensively social. Nevertheless, Hala and Russell (2001) asked an additional question—whether a less "mechanical" manipulation would also facilitate performance. Specifically, is there a role of social collaboration in allowing for greater executive control in the windows task? In order to answer this question empirically, these researchers introduced a manipulation in which children were told that they were on a "team" with the principal experimenter—the "ally condition." The teamwork consisted of the child telling the collaborating experimenter which box to point to when the opponent returned to the room. Then, when the opponent was brought back in, it was the experimenter who simply followed the child's instructions. This manipulation resulted in performance that was far superior to the standard version of the task, in which the child points to the box in the presence of the opponent. To ensure that children were not performing better for the reason that they felt greater impunity from blame because they themselves were not seen to be the agent of the deception, Hala and Russell included a condition wherein, without any supporting rationale, children were instructed to first indicate to the experimenter which box the opponent was to open, but, as in the ally condition, it was the experimenter who carried out the actual pointing in the presence of the opponent. In contrast to the ally condition, this latter condition produced performance that was no better than in the standard version.

In a subsequent study, Hala and Russell (2001) went on to further rule out the possibility that the success of the ally condition was not due to a reduction of social apprehension, but instead that it indeed was the collaborative aspect that was facilitating strategic performance. After all, having the experimenter simply take up the role of a pointer without any explanation may have been confusing to the children in the previous study. In this second study, Hala and Russell included a new condition as well as the ally condition (described earlier) and the standard version of the windows task. In the new condition, children were instructed that they were on a team with the experimenter, as in the ally condition, but that they would be the ones to both select the box as well as point to the selected box when the opponent returned. In this way, any potential social apprehension that may have been experienced by children in standard versions of the task should be kept intact. The results from this second study indicated that children adopted the appropriate strategy of indicating the empty box irrespective of the opponent's presence.

Hala and Russell (2001) interpret the success of the ally manipulations as being the result of a type of cognitive "distancing" that is achieved when the child is nudged into adopting a third-person perspective. Specifically, these authors suggest that having children act on behalf of a collaborating second agent may help push the child to interpret the pointing as a more publicly committed act. Taking this more public stance subsequently results in a kind of psychological distancing, wherein the child is afforded a separation from the immediate goal of obtaining the treat for themselves. That is, by encouraging the child to view the action from a third person's point of view, and not just the perspective of the child in direct opposition with a competitor, the ally condition allows the child to exercise greater inhibitory control—enough to inhibit pointing to the desired treat (see also Prencipe & Zelazo, 2005). This interpretation is entirely in keeping with the tone of the current volume. Specifically, stated in social context terms, the success of the child in misdirecting the opponent is rooted in the child's ability to muster the necessary inhibitory control as a consequence of the partnership with the second agent.

We are not claiming that, in this case, social understanding (i.e., understanding deception and, as a corollary, false belief understanding) is a direct consequence of the social interaction. Instead, we suggest that there is a very complex interrelation between EF and social interaction that results in increased social understanding. We propose, as do others, that the relation is bidirectional, with EF development not only influencing, but being influenced by, social interactions. To be clear, we are not talking about a notion of "scaffolding," wherein a more advanced partner assists the child to reach their potential level of social understanding, though a Vygotskian scholar may certainly argue this point. Rather, we are suggesting that social interactions might place significant challenges on current executive abilities, which subsequently "stretch" to facilitate increased social understanding.

To elaborate, many social interactions are ambiguous in nature. We cannot always be certain what another person means, or predict how they will act. Intentions can be difficult to infer from verbal and nonverbal behaviors in social exchanges. This ambiguity may, in Piagetian terms (Piaget, 1977), provide the very sort of cognitive conflict that throws a child into disequilibration (for fuller discussions, see Chapman & McBride, 1992; Doise & Mugny, 1984; Perret-Clermont, 1980). In attempting to strive toward regaining equilibration, the child may have to exercise increased executive control, a development supported by a complex interaction of experience and experience-expectant brain development.

Verbal Irony Comprehension and Executive Function

One type of social interaction that is ambiguous, and thus may challenge children's EF skills, is conversation that involves verbal irony. Verbal irony is pervasive in everyday communication. It is present in conversations between friends and strangers (Gibbs, 2000), on television programs for children and for adults (Dews & Winner, 1997), and in computer-mediated conversations (Hancock & Dunham, 2001). In its most conventional form verbal irony is commonly referred to as *sarcasm* and involves saying something positive to mean something negative, as in *"you look gorgeous today,"* said to someone who looks disheveled. We will refer to this type of remark as ironic criticism.

It is believed that speakers go to the trouble of using irony, and in so doing risk possible misunderstanding, because irony serves a number of important communicative functions. In particular, irony allows the speaker to mute their critical or complimentary intent (Dews, Kaplan, & Winner, 1995; Pexman & Olineck, 2002a). Irony also allows the speaker to mock or tease someone (Kreuz, Long, & Church, 1991; Pexman & Zvaigzne, 2004) and to be humorous (e.g., Colston & Keller, 1998; Colston & O'Brien, 2000; Kreuz et al., 1991; Pexman & Olineck, 2002b; Roberts & Kreuz, 1994). In these and other ways irony provides an opportunity for significant interactional payoff. Yet the incongruity inherent in irony, between the speaker's tone and the speaker's words, may pose an interpretive challenge for children (e.g., Morton, Trehub, & Zelazo, 2003).

In order to appreciate verbal irony, a listener must detect the discrepancy between the speaker's beliefs and the literal sense of the speaker's utterance. The listener must infer that the speaker does not intend their statement to be taken literally; instead, the speaker's intent is to mock the literal sense of their statement (and anyone who would make such a remark) and make salient the difference between their belief and the belief conveyed by the literal sense of the remark. "Irony involves an interpretive relation between the speaker's thought and attributed thoughts or utterances" (Sperber & Wilson, 1995, p. 231). The perceiver must grasp the speaker's attitude and the relationship of that attitude toward the statement. Winner and Leekam (1991; also Dews & Winner, 1997; Sullivan, Winner, & Hopfield, 1995) argued that in order to understand irony the listener must recognize what the speaker actually believes, and also what the speaker wants the listener to believe.

As such, irony comprehension is a complex cognitive task and one that seems likely to depend on EF abilities. There is, in fact, considerable evidence for a connection between EF abilities and irony comprehension. In neuropsychological research irony comprehension has been linked to frontal lobe function. Shamay, Tomer, and Aharon-Peretz (2002) reported that adult patients with frontal lobe lesions were impaired in their ability to interpret ironic remarks. Similarly, McDonald and Pearce (1996) reported that adult patients with frontal lobe damage from traumatic brain injury showed deficits in understanding sarcastic irony. When Shamay-Tsoory, Tomer, and Aharon-Peretz (2005) examined comprehension of ironic criticisms by adult patients with focal lesions they found that patients with right ventromedial prefrontal cortex lesions had particularly profound deficits in irony comprehension. Given what we know about the importance of the frontal lobes to EF abilities, it seems reasonable to make the inference that EF abilities are important to irony comprehension (McDonald, 2000).

In line with the strong relation between executive dysfunction and understanding irony we might well expect a corollary relation between the development of executive control and emerging understanding of irony in children. If this is the case, then, certainly, increased executive ability would facilitate increased understanding of the ambiguous social interaction of verbal irony. In keeping with the aim of this chapter, we propose that exposure to this nonliteral form of language may, in turn, facilitate development of increased EF.

When parents use verbal irony in conversation with or around children, they present children with a situation where the literal meaning of their utterance is incongruent with their intended meaning. In order to reconcile this incongruity the child will need to make complex mental state inferences and in doing so could make use of some of the cues and constraints that facilitate detection of irony. Certainly, there are intonational styles and facial expressions that can signal a speaker's ironic intent (Winner, 1988). In addition, when a speaker's statement is outEF of keeping with the preceding events and remarks this can be taken as a strong cue to irony (e.g., Colston, Gerrig, & Goldvarg, 2002; Ivanko & Pexman, 2003). Ironic remarks, and the cues that accompany them, present children with the potential for cognitive conflict. As children struggle to make sense of these remarks, this cognitive conflict could provide the impetus for them to expand their understanding of language to include the possibility of nonliteral interpretation.

There is research to suggest that many children begin to comprehend irony around 6 years of age (e.g., Ackerman, 1982, 1983, 1986; Demorest, Meyer, Phelps, Gardner, & Winner, 1984; Dews et al., 1996; Hancock, Dunham, & Purdy, 2000; Harris & Pexman, 2003; Winner et al., 1987), at least in the sense that they recognize a discrepancy between the speaker's belief and the speaker's statement for counterfactual irony. Comprehension continues to improve, and expands to include more complex forms of irony, throughout middle childhood (Pexman, Glenwright, Krol, & James, 2005).

It seems likely that when parents use verbal irony in their own speech, they provide children with opportunities to practice interpreting ironic remarks.

Exposure to verbal irony could provide children with instances upon which they can base their emerging concept of ironic language. As a result, parents who use verbal irony with some frequency may have children who are relatively proficient at interpreting such remarks. This possibility was tested in two experiments conducted at our university by Penny Pexman, Melanie Glenwright, Andrea Krol, and Tammy James. The children in these experiments were middle school aged (7- to 10-year-olds in the first experiment, 9- to 10-year-olds in the second), and as such they were beginning to develop appreciation for verbal irony. We asked the parents of these children to answer questions about their own tendencies to use verbal irony. We also measured their children's appreciation for verbal irony: the children's impressions of speaker belief (detecting that the speaker holds a belief that is opposite to the literal meaning of their statement) and speaker attitude (speaker intent to be mean in the case of an ironic criticism).

The parents' tendencies to use sarcastic irony were captured by their responses on a self-report survey. The questions on the survey comprised two factors, which we here call *General* and *Risky*. The questions on the *General* factor asked about parents' global tendencies with respect to sarcastic speech (e.g., *how sarcastic are you?*) and also about their tendencies to use sarcasm in typical circumstances (e.g., *what is the likelihood that you would use sarcasm with your best friend? What is the likelihood that you would use sarcasm when criticizing someone?*). The questions on the *Risky* factor asked about parents' tendencies to use sarcasm in situations of low inferability; situations where a sarcastic remark could easily be misinterpreted (e.g., *what is the likelihood that you would use sarcasm with someone you just met?*). The risk for misunderstanding is high between new acquaintances, and many people will only use irony when they are certain it will be understood as intended, as per Kreuz's (1996) *heuristic of inferability*. For a participant to say there is a likelihood that they would use irony in those risky circumstances suggests that they value the sarcastic speech form even when it is risky and are probably sarcastic even when inferability is low.

The children in the experiments participated in an interpretation task that involved a series of short puppet shows. At the end of each show one puppet made a remark to the other, and these remarks included ironic criticisms and literal criticisms. After every puppet show, each child was asked questions in order to assess their appreciation of ironic remarks. These included (1) a speaker belief question: Participants were asked whether the speaker meant what he or she said in order to assess whether the children interpreted the speaker's statement as a positive or negative evaluation. For example, "When Kate said 'This cake is wonderful', did Kate think Lucy made a good cake or a bad cake?" (2) A speaker attitude question: The second question referred to the Nice/Mean Scale and children were asked to rate the speaker's attitude for their final remark (e.g., "When Kate said '*This cake is wonderful*', show me how nice or mean she was trying to be") by pointing to one of the faces on a 6-point mean/nice face scale.

In Experiment 1 the children were 7- to 10-year-olds and in their responses to the speaker belief and speaker attitude questions these children tended to be much more accurate for literal criticisms than for ironic criticisms. These accuracy differences were not surprising, and simply reflect the fact that children in this age range are not yet proficient at irony comprehension. Our real interest was in whether variability in these irony appreciation measures was explained by parents' self-reported speech tendencies. As such, we examined relationships between the children's accuracy on the irony appreciation measures and parents' self-ratings on the Parental Survey dimensions. There were, indeed, some significant relationships. For instance, parents' scores on the *Risky* dimension were significantly correlated with children's speaker belief accuracy for ironic criticisms, suggesting parents with higher sarcasm use tend to have children who are more accurate in their interpretation of speaker belief. In this experiment, parents' self-ratings were not correlated with children's interpretations of speaker attitude.

In the second experiment, the children were 9- and 10-year-olds and one of our goals was to test the validity of the parents' responses to the *General* and *Risky* dimensions of the Parental Survey. To accomplish this, parents in the second experiment were also given two production items to complete. For each item a situation was described, and parents were asked to select (from a list which included both literal and ironic remarks) the statement they would most likely make in that situation. The first production item asked parents to imagine a situation with their best friend, and responses on this item were found to be related to responses on the *General* dimension of the Parental Survey. The second production item asked parents to imagine a situation involving a new acquaintance, and responses on this item were found to be related to responses on the *Risky* dimension of the Parental Survey. These relationships suggested that there was some validity to the Parental Survey dimensions.

In this second experiment, children tended to show equivalent speaker belief accuracy for literal criticisms and for ironic criticisms. In this way, their appreciation for speaker belief seemed to be more sophisticated than that demonstrated by the children in the first experiment. When we again evaluated relationships between children's responses on irony appreciation measures and the parents' self-ratings on the Parental Survey dimensions it was perhaps not surprising, then, that there were no significant correlations with children's speaker belief accuracy difference values. The children's speaker attitude assessments, however, were related to parents' scores on the *General Parental Survey* dimension, the *Risky* Parental Survey dimension, and the "new acquaintance" production item. The nature of these relationships was that children who tended to perceive ironic criticisms as less mean than literal criticisms tended to have parents who chose the ironic statement on the production item and also tended to have parents who rated themselves as likely to use sarcasm in general and in risky contexts.

Taken together, these two experiments establish that children whose parents reported an inclination to use sarcasm had stronger appreciation for ironic remarks. One striking aspect of this relationship is the fact that the children's irony comprehension was assessed without their parents' involvement, and for novel ironic remarks, the precise wording of which the children could not possibly have encountered at home. It is possible, of course, that children whose parents reported an inclination to use sarcasm had stronger appreciation for ironic remarks because those children were more familiar with the general form of ironic interaction. It is also possible, however, that the critical mechanism for this relationship may not be that parents' speech gives children specific examples of nonliteral language. Instead, parents' speech may challenge children's comprehension abilities in ways that facilitate EF development. Consistent with our proposal, it is entirely possible that, while EF development no doubt assists in children's understanding of the ambiguous nature of sarcastic irony, parental use of sarcasm in turn may facilitate EF development in children.

We end our chapter with a final example of how children's need to struggle with the ambiguities of socially provided information may be useful in helping to advance their executive abilities—the case of children learning more than one language.

Bilingualism and Executive Function Development

Language use is a social construction. Historically, there have existed two contrasting views about the cognitive implications of children acquiring more than one language. One view would have it that children should first be allowed to gain a significant foothold in their first language before being made to acquire a second. Those who subscribe to this view would argue that very young children who are struggling to learn language at all will be terribly confused if they are expected to understand that a single thing can be termed more than one label, depending on the language spoken. Conversely, there are those that suggest that, rather than be a hindrance, exposure to dual labeling might actually facilitate not only the development of bilingualism, but may have broader reaching advantages for cognitive development in general. It is this second camp where we hang our hats.

Indeed, researchers in recent years have consistently found a positive relationship between bilingualism and cognitive abilities (e.g., Bialystok, 1999; Diaz, Padilla, & Weathersby, 1991). More specifically for the purposes of this volume, Bialystok and her colleagues have found a strong bilingual advantage (e.g., Bialystok & Martin, 2004), with bilingual children outperforming their monolingual counterparts on tasks measuring EF capabilities.

In keeping with the claims made earlier in this chapter, and in line with Bialystok's view, we propose that it is precisely the need to manage two competing languages that could account for the increased executive ability found in bilingual populations (Bialystok, Craik, Klein, & Viswanathan, 2004). Bialystok's (2001) suggestion is that development of inhibitory control is facilitated in bilingual children because, in a bilingual individual, both languages remain active during processing and intrusions from one language while another is in use must be minimized by inhibiting the nonrelevant language. Early on, when children are first acquiring the two languages, intrusions of the nonrelevant language are common. As children become more versatile in both languages they are able to exercise increased inhibition of the nonrelevant language. The possible superior development of EF in bilingual children can also be viewed in a slightly different way. Specifically, children learning two languages must be able to grasp that a single object can be represented in more than one way. If a child has an initial label for an object, then according to the mutual exclusivity hypothesis put forward by Markman and others (for review see Markman, 1991), it will be very difficult for the child to accept a novel word for the same object. Children who are in the process of acquiring two languages must overcome this difficulty on a daily, if not hourly, basis. Hearing the novel (alternative language) label applied to an object for which the child already has a known label may induce some cognitive conflict as the child struggles to grasp the dual label. Once again, this cognitive conflict, and the resulting disequilibration, would push the child toward further executive control. In understanding the nature of two languages children must be able to code switch, that is, switch from using one language to using the other, taking into account their listener's language. Consequently, the dimension of EF that we could expect most likely to be enhanced by bilingual language acquisition is cognitive flexibility (Diaz et al., 1991).

A prominent researcher in this area, Ellen Bialystok and her colleagues (1999; Bialystok & Martin, 2004) have examined the relation of bilingualism and preschool children's scores on a well-known measure of cognitive flexibility, the Dimensional Change Card Sort (DCCS) task developed by Zelazo and his colleagues (Zelazo, Frye, & Rapus, 1996). In this task, children are presented with cards that vary along two dimensions, such as color and shape. Children are asked, first, to sort the cards on the basis of one of these dimensions, for example by their shape. After a number of trials under the shape sorting rule, children are told that the rules of the game have changed and that they now must play the color game and sort on the basis of color. The challenge, of course, is that children must be able to switch from their previously learned response to a new one that is in opposition to the first. In Bialystok's research, bilingual children routinely outperform monolingual children, demonstrating greater ease in the postswitch phase than their monolingual counterparts. Bialystok (1999) posits that bilingual language users gain a superior level of control over their attention that allows them to selectively attend to specific aspects of a situation without being misled by incorrect information. As a result, they are able to focus on the relevant aspects of the situation (i.e., the language of the person to whom they are speaking) and ignore inappropriate portions (i.e., their own alternative language). This language control, or code switching ability, would seem to be indicative of underlying cognitive flexibility.

Summary

In this chapter, we have attempted to illustrate the complexity of the relation between social understanding and EF development. In doing so we limited ourselves to a few examples of programs of research that allow for exploration of this relation. Certainly, this list is far from exhaustive. What we hope we have accomplished is to demonstrate that there is an advantage in thinking of EF and social understanding developing, as it were, in tandem, offering support for each other. In addition, we have tried to highlight how Piaget's notion of equilibration may provide a useful framework for studying how social interaction might work to facilitate cognitive growth. Specifically, we proposed that the ambiguity inherent in many social interactions may push the developing child into disequilibration, resulting in the child striving to regain equilibration, which in turn results in a shift in the child's thinking, or in Piaget's term, accommodation.

We end as we began, with a quote from Bringuier's Conversations with Piaget (1980):

> **BRINGUIER**: Why "equilibration" and not simply "equilibrium"?
> **PIAGET**: Because it's a process, not a balance of forces. (p. 44)

ACKNOWLEDGMENT

This chapter was supported by a Canada Natural Sciences and Engineering Research Grant awarded to S. Hala and by a Canada Social Sciences and Humanities Research Grant awarded to P. Pexman.

REFERENCES

Ackerman, B. P. (1982). Contextual integration and utterance interpretation: The ability of children and adults to interpret sarcastic utterances. *Child Development, 53,* 1075–1083.

Ackerman, B. P. (1983). Form and function in children's understanding of ironic utterances. *Journal of Experimental Child Psychology, 35,* 487–508.

Ackerman, B. P. (1986). Children's sensitivity to comprehension failure in interpreting a nonliteral use of an utterance. *Child Development, 57,* 485–497.

Beers, S. R., & DeBellis, M. D. (2002). Neuropsychological function in children with maltreatment-related posttraumatic stress disorder. *American Journal of Psychiatry, 159,* 483–486.

Bialystok, E. (1999). Cognitive complexity and attentional control in the bilingual mind. *Child Development, 70*(3), 636–644.

Bialystok, E. (2001). *Bilingualism in development. Language, literacy, & cognition.* Cambridge: Cambridge University Press.

Bialystok, E., Craik, R., Klein, R., & Viswanathan, M. (2004). Bilingualism, aging, and cognitive control: Evidence from the simon task. *Psychology and Aging, 19*(2), 290–303.

Bialystok, E., & Martin, M. (2004). Attention and inhibition in bilingual children: Evidence from the dimensional change card sort task. *Developmental Science, 7*(3), 325–339.

Bialystok, E., & Miller, B. (1999). The problem of age in second-language acquisition: Influences from language, structure, and task. *Bilingualism: Language and Cognition, 2*(2), 127–145.

Bringuier, J. (1980). *Conversations with Jean Piaget.* Chicago: University of Chicago Press.

Brophy, M., Taylor, E., & Hughes, C. (2002). To go or not to go: Inhibitory control in "hard to manage" children. *Infant and Child Development, 11,* 125–140.

Carlson, S., Mandell, D., & Williams, L. (2004). Executive function and theory of mind: Stability and prediction from ages 2 to 3. *Developmental Psychology, 40*(6), 1105–1122.

Carlson, S., & Moses, L. (2001). Individual differences in inhibitory control and children's theory of mind. *Child Development, 72*(4), 1032–1053.

Carlson, S., Moses, L., & Breton, C. (2002). How specific is the relation between executive function and theory of mind? Contributions of inhibitory control and working memory. *Infant and Child Development, 11,* 73–92.

Carlson, S., Moses, L., & Hix H. R. (1998). The role of inhibitory control in young children's difficulties with deception and false belief. *Child Development, 69*, 672–691.

Chandler, M. J., Fritz, A. S., & Hala, S. M. (1989). Small-scale deceit: Deception as a marker of 2-, 3- and 4-year olds' early theory of mind. *Child Development, 60,* 1263–1277.

Chapman, M., & McBride, M. L. (1992). The education of reason: Cognitive conflict and its role in intellectual development. In C. U. Shantz & W. W. Hartup (Eds.), *Conflict in Child and Adolescent Development* (pp. 36–69). Cambridge: Cambridge University Press.

Colston, H. L. (2002). Contrast and assimilation in verbal irony. *Journal of Pragmatics, 34,* 111–142.

Colston, H. L., & Keller, S. B. (1998). You'll never believe this: Irony and hyperbole in expressing surprise. *Journal of Psycholinguistic Research, 27,* 499–513.

Colston, H. L., & O'Brien, J. E. (2000). Contrast of kind versus contrast of magnitude: The pragmatic accomplishments of irony and hyperbole. *Discourse Processes, 30,* 179–199.

Demorest, A., Meyer, C., Phelps, E., Gardner, H., & Winner, E. (1984). Words speak louder than actions: Understanding deliberately false remarks. *Child Development, 55,* 1527–1534.

Dews, S., Kaplan, J., & Winner, E. (1995). Why not say it directly? The social functions of irony. *Discourse Processes, 19,* 347–367.

Dews, S., & Winner, E. (1995). Muting the meaning: A social function of irony. *Metaphor and Symbolic Activity, 10,* 3–19.

Dews, S., & Winner, E. (1997). Attributing meaning to deliberately false utterances: The case of irony. In C. Mandell & A. McCabe (Eds.), *The problem of meaning: Behavioral and cognitive perspectives* (pp. 377–414). Hillsdale NJ: Elsevier.

Dews, S., Winner, E., Kaplan, J., Rosenblatt, E., Hunt, M., Lim, K., et al. (1996). Children's understanding of the meaning and functions of verbal irony. *Child Development, 67,* 3071–3085.

Diaz, R., Padilla, K., & Weathersby, E. (1991). The effects of bilingualism on preschoolers' private speech. *Early Childhood Research Quarterly, 6,* 377–393.

Doise, W., & Mugny, G. (1984). *The social development of intellect.* Oxford, UK: Pergamon Press.

Dunn, J. (1991). Understanding others: Evidence from naturalistic studies of children. In A. Whiten (Ed.) *Natural theories of mind: Evolution, development and simulation of everyday mindreading* (pp. 51–61). Oxford: Blackwell.

Dunn, J. (1994). Changing minds and changing relationships. In C. Lewis & P. Mitchell (Eds.) *Origins of an understanding of mind* (pp. 297–310). Hove: Erlbaum.

Fishbein, D. (2001). The importance of neurobiological research to the prevention of psychopathology. *Prevention Science, 1,* 89–106.

Gerrig, R. J., & Goldvarg, Y. (2000). Additive effects in the perception of sarcasm: Situational disparity and echoic mention. *Metaphor and Symbol, 15,* 197–208.

Gibbs, R. W., Jr. (2000). Irony in talk among friends. *Metaphor and Symbolic Activity, 15,* 5–27.

Hala, S., & Chandler, M. J. (1996). The role of strategic planning in accessing false-belief understanding. *Child Development, 67,* 2948–2966.

Hala, S., Hug, S., & Henderson, A. (2003). Executive function and false-belief understanding in preschool children: Two tasks are harder than one. *Journal of Cognition and Development, 4* (3), 275–298.

Hala, S., & Russell, J. (2001). Executive control within strategic deception: A window on early cognitive development. *Journal of Experimental Child Psychology, 80,* 112–141.

Hala, S. M., Chandler, M. J., & Fritz, A. S. (1991). Fledgling theories of mind: Deception as a marker of three-year-olds' understanding of false belief. *Child Development, 62,* 83–97.

Hughes, C. (1998a). Finding your marbles: Does preschoolers' strategic behavior predict later understanding of mind? *Developmental Psychology, 34,* 1326–1339.

Hughes, C. (1998b). Executive function in preschoolers: Links with theory of mind and verbal ability. *British Journal of Developmental Psychology, 16,* 233–253.

Hughes, C., Cutting, A., & Dunn, J. (2001). Acting nasty in the face of failure? Longitudinal observations of "hard to manage" children playing a rigged competitive game with a friend. *Journal of Abnormal Child Psychology, 29,* 403–416.

Hancock, J. T., & Dunham, P. J. (2001). *Irony use in face-to-face and computer-mediated conversations.* Poster presented at the 42nd Annual Meeting of the Psychonomic Society, Orlando, FL.

Hancock, J. T., Dunham, P. J., & Purdy, K. (2000). Children's comprehension of critical and complimentary forms of verbal irony. *Journal of Cognition and Development, 1,* 227–248.

Harris, M., & Pexman, P. M. (2003). Children's perceptions of the social functions of verbal irony. *Discourse Processes, 36,* 147–165.

Huttenlocher, P. R. (1990). Morphometric study of human cerebral cortex development. *Neuropsyhologia, 28,* 515–527.

Ivanko, S. L., & Pexman, P. M. (2003). Context incongruity and irony processing. *Discourse Processes, 35,* 241–279.

Johnson, M. H. (2005). Developmental cognitive neuroscience: An introduction (2nd ed.). Malden, MA: Blackwell Publishing.

Jorgenson, J., Miller, G., & Sperber, D. (1984). Test of the mention theory of irony. *Journal of Experimental Psychology: General, 11,* 112–120.

Katz, A. N., & Lee, C. J. (1993). The role of authorial intent in determining irony and metaphor. *Metaphor and Symbolic Activity, 8,* 257–279.

Keenan, T. R., & Quigley, K. (1999). Do young children use echoic information in their comprehension of sarcastic speech? A test of echoic mention theory. *British Journal of Developmental Psychology, 17,* 83–96.

Kreuz, R. J. (1996). The use of verbal irony: Cues and constraints. In J. S. Mio & A. N. Katz (Eds.), *Metaphor: Implications and applications* (pp. 23–38). Mahwah, NJ: Lawrence Erlbaum Associates.

Kreuz, R. J., Long, D. L., & Church, M. B. (1991). On being ironic: Pragmatic and mnemonic implications. *Metaphor and Symbolic Activity, 6,* 149–162.

Luciana, M. (2003). The neural and functional development of human prefrontal cortex. In M. de Haan & M.H. Johnson (Eds.), *The Cognitive Neuroscience of Development*. (pp. 157–179). Hove, UK: Psychology Press.

Luciana, M., & Nelson, C. A. (1998). The functional emergence of prefrontally-guided working memory systems in four- to eight-year-old children. *Neuropsychologia, 36*, 273–293.

Markman, E. M. (1991). The whole object, taxonomic, and mutual exclusivity assumptions as initial constraints on word meanings. In J. P. Byrnes & S. A. Gelman (Eds.), *Perspectives on language and cognition: Interrelations in development* (pp. 72–106). Cambridge: Cambridge University Press.

McDonald, S. (2000). Neuropsychological studies of sarcasm. *Metaphor and Symbol, 15*, 85–98.

McDonald, S., & Pearce, S. (1996). Clinical insights into pragmatic theory: Frontal lobe deficits and sarcasm. *Brain and Language, 53*, 81–104.

Morton, J. B., Trehub, S. E., & Zelazo, P. D. (2003). Sources of inflexibility in 6-year-olds' understanding of emotion in speech. *Child Development, 74*, 1857–1868.

Nelson, C. A., de Haan, M., & Thomas, K. M. (2006). *The role of experience and the developing brain*. Hoboken, NJ: Wiley & Sons.

Nelson, C. A., & Luciana, M. (2001). *Handbook of developmental cognitive neuroscience*. Cambridge, MA: The MIT Press.

Newton, P., Reddy, V., & Bull, R. (2000). Children's everyday deception and performance on false-belief tasks. *British Journal of Developmental Psychology, 18*, 297–317.

Pennington, B., & Ozonoff, S. (1996). Annotation: Executive functions and developmental psychopathologies. *Journal of Child Psychology and Psychiatry, 37*, 51–87.

Perret-Clermont, A. N. (1980). *Social interaction and cognitive development in children*. New York: Academic Press.

Peskin, J. (1992). Ruse and representation: On children's ability to conceal their intentions. *Developmental Psychology, 28*, 84–89.

Pexman, P. M., Glenwright, M., Krol, A., & James, T. (2005). An acquired taste: Children's perceptions of humor and teasing in verbal irony. *Discourse Processes, 40*, 259–288.

Pexman, P. M., & Olineck, K. M. (2002a). Does sarcasm always sting? Investigating the impact of ironic insults and ironic compliments. *Discourse Processes, 33*, 199–217.

Pexman, P. M., & Olineck, K. M. (2002b). Understanding irony: How do stereotypes cue speaker intent? *Journal of Language and Social Psychology, 21*, 245–274.

Pexman, P. M., & Zvaigzne, M. T. (2004). Does irony go better with friends? *Metaphor and Symbol, 19*, 143–163.

Piaget, J. (1977). *The development of thought. Equilibration of cognitive structures*. New York: Viking Press.

Polak, A., & Harris, P.L. (1999). Deception by young children following noncompliance. *Developmental Psychology, 35*, 561–568.

Prencipe, A., & Zelazo, P. D. (2005). Development of affective decision making for self and other: Evidence for the integration of first- and third-person perspectives. *Psychological Science, 16,* 501–505.

Roberts, R. J., Jr., & Pennington, B. F. (1996). An interactive framework for examining prefrontal cognitive processes. *Developmental Neuropsychology, 12,* 105–126.

Roberts, R. M., & Kreuz, R. J. (1994). Why do people use figurative language? *Psychological Science, 5,* 159–163.

Ruffman, T., Olson, D. R., Ash, T., & Keenan, T. (1993). Do young children understand deception in the same way as adults? *Developmental Psychology, 29,* 74–87.

Russell, J., Jarrold, C., & Potel, D. (1994). What makes strategic deception difficult for children—The deception or the strategy? *British Journal of Developmental Psychology, 12,* 301–314.

Russell, J., Mauthner, N., Sharpe, S., & Tidswell, T. (1991). The "windows task" as a measure of strategic deception in pre-schoolers and autistic participants. *British Journal of Developmental Psychology, 9,* 331–349.

Sabbagh, M., Xu, F., Carlson, S., Moses, L., & Lee, K. (2006). The development of executive functioning and theory of mind: A comparison of Chinese and U.S. preschoolers. *Psychological Science, 17*(1), 74–81.

Shamay, S. G., Tomer, R., & Aharon-Peretz, J. (2002). Deficit in understanding sarcasm in patients with prefrontal lesion is related to impaired empathetic ability. *Brain and Cognition, 48,* 558–563.

Shamay-Tsoory, S. G., Tomer, R., & Aharon-Peretz, J. (2005). The neuroanatomical basis of understanding sarcasm and its relationship to social cognition. *Neuropsychology, 19,* 288–300.

Sodian, B., Taylor, C., Harris, P. L., & Perner, J. (1991). Early deception and the child's theory of mind: False trails and genuine markers. *Child Development, 62,* 561–582.

Sperber, D., & Wilson, D. (1995). *Relevance: Communication and cognition* (2nd ed.). Cambridge, MA: Blackwell Publishing.

Sullivan, K., Winner, E., & Hopfield, N. (1995). How children tell a lie from a joke: The role of second-order mental state attributions. *British Journal of Developmental Psychology, 13,* 191–204.

Thompson, P. M., Giedd, J. N., Woods, R. P., MacDonald, D., Evans, A. C., & Toga, A. W. (2000). Growth patterns in the developing brain detected by using continuum mechanical tensor maps. *Nature, 404,* 190–193.

Welsh, M., Pennington, P., & Groisser, D. (1991). A normative-developmental study of executive function: A window on prefrontal function in children. *Developmental Neuropsychology, 7,* 131–149.

Westermann, G., Mareschal, D., Johnson, M. H., Sirois, S., Spratling, M. W., & Thomas, M. S. C. (2007). Neoconstructivism. *Developmental Science, 10,* 75–83.

Winner, E. (1988). *The point of words: Children's understanding of metaphor and irony.* Cambridge, MA: Harvard University Press.

Winner, E., & Leekam, S. (1991). Distinguishing irony from deception: Understanding the speaker's second-order intention. *British Journal of Developmental Psychology, 9,* 257–270.

Winner, E., Windmueller, G., Rosenblatt, E., Bosco, L., Best, E., & Gardner, H. (1987). Making sense of literal and nonliteral falsehood. *Metaphor and Symbolic Activity, 2*, 13–32.

Zelazo, P.D., Carter, A., Reznick, J.S., & Frye, D. (1997). Early development of executive function: A problem solving framework. *Review of General Psychology, 1*, 1–29.

Zelazo, P. D., Frye, D., & Rapus, T. (1996). An age-related dissociation between knowing rules and using them. *Cognitive Development, 11*, 37–63.

13

Underpinning Collaborative Learning

EMMA FLYNN

The benefits of young children's collaborative learning have been illustrated across a range of expertise, including skill acquisition (Azmitia, 1988), conceptual change (Howe, Rodgers, & Tolmie, 1990), communication skills (Brown, Anderson, Schillcock, & Yule, 1984), and meta-cognitive abilities (Brown & Palincsar, 1989), as well as in a range of domains, including mathematics (Phelps & Damon, 1989), literacy (Brown & Campione, 1990), and science (Howe, Tolmie, & Rodgers, 1992). This chapter investigates the development of, and relations between, children's collaborative abilities and other cognitive skills, most notably mental state understanding and executive functioning (EF). This includes first-order theory of mind, which develops at around 4 years of age, and is the appreciation of one's own and other people's mental states and once in place allows the prediction of behavior. Later, at about 7 years, typically developing children develop second-order theory of mind; that is, the ability to be able to embed and contrast the mental states of more than one person, for example, "I know that you know ... ." In this chapter, the role mental state understanding plays in children's collaboration at different ages is explored. EF is an umbrella term used to refer to a set of cognitive processes that regulate an individual's ability to organize thoughts and activities, prioritize tasks, manage time efficiently, and make decisions. Significant improvements occur in EF skills during both the preschool and early school years, and it is these developments and their relation to the development of collaborative skills that are a point of focus.

This chapter aims to draw parallels between children's mental state understanding, EF, and collaborative learning. Such an endeavor has important associations with Vygotsky's *Zone of Proximal Development* (Vygotsky, 1978), that is, the gap between what a child achieves alone and what s/he can achieve with the guidance of a more capable other. Such a definition leaves unanswered the processes involved in this transition and how these processes are underpinned by the characteristics of the learner and tutor. One possible example of the nature of the interaction is scaffolding (Wood, Bruner, & Ross, 1976). During scaffolding a more knowledgeable other facilitates the learner's interest, helps him/her to remain on task, points out critical features, demonstrates the task, and helps to overcome frustrations. The management of frustration is a critical issue, so that no learner is left to tackle too much complexity or left with too little involvement with the task. Wood and Wood (1996) focused on the issue of task control, suggesting that the most effective tutors were those who gradually handed responsibility for a task to the learner. They believed that the best method to provide support for this hand-over of responsibility was contingent tutoring—providing more support when tutees get into difficulty and less help when they succeed. These rules seem obvious, but Wood, Wood, and Middleton (1978) found that adults trained to teach contingently do not have full adherence to these principles.

Wood and Wood (1996) and Wood, Wood, Ainsworth, and O'Malley (1995) suggested that to be a contingent tutor one needs a number of important skills. First, an effective tutor will diagnose and respond to a learner's needs, and in order to do this the beliefs, knowledge, and needs of the learner must be analyzed and represented. Such representation requires second-order theory of mind, as it requires an appreciation of the learner's current knowledge in relation to the tutor's own knowledge and the future knowledge of the learner. From such a hypothesis we can predict that there should be a significant difference in the tutoring skills of children who do have and those who do not have recursive mental state understanding. Second, effective tutoring demands an ability to disengage from one's own activity to focus on the activities of someone else and to provide verbal instructions in place of task actions. Similarly, planning what and when to teach is critical to contingent tutoring. Flexibility, inhibitory control, and planning are all elements of EF. Therefore, children with better EF skills should be better tutors. The importance of regulation in relations to one's own and other's actions during peer tutoring has also been the focus of interest by other researchers (Rogoff, 1990; Tudge & Rogoff, 1989; Webb, 1991).

In the first half of the chapter a review of the development of children's collaborative skills, from early interactions in infancy to peer tutoring in school-age children is presented. Children's collaborative behavior is examined across different tasks, drawing parallels between the development of collaborative skills and the development of skills in the areas of intersubjectivity, planning, communication, and inhibition. It is argued that mastery of these skills underpins the ability to successfully engage in complex collaborative activity. The second half of the chapter presents a study that directly investigates the relations between children's peer tutoring and their second-order theory of mind, planning, referential communication, and recall skills. Initially, the study establishes the interrelations of the children's performance on the battery of cognitive tests, irrespective of peer-tutoring skills. The subsequent analysis assesses children's abilities to teach a same-age peer in a construction task, and the relation of this ability to the skills tested in the cognitive battery (second-order theory of mind, planning, referential communication, intelligence, and recall skills). The chapter concludes by focusing on the multidimensional, bidirectional nature of the relations between collaborative learning and the development of other important cognitive skills.

Although the effectiveness of collaborative learning has been shown across different skills and within different domains, work that has investigated peer collaboration has tended to focus on the conditions under which peer interaction leads to successful learning gains (e.g., differences in knowledge, ability or expertise between members of the dyad; opportunities for discussion or conflict). There has been relatively little work focusing on the ontogenesis of collaboration. Such a lack of research is surprising given the emphasis on social interaction in some of the seminal theories of child development. For social constructivism, social interaction is the key to development (Vygotsky, 1981). Vygotskian theory argues that it is impossible to understand individual cognition in isolation from the cultural context. Interaction with a more able other introduces children to social structures and tools that have developed over time, and which enable individual development. A child learns first by interaction on the social plane, and then internalizes this knowledge onto the psychological plane. Similarly, although social influences on development are not central to Piagetian research, Piaget stated that cognitive development depends on social contexts, as well as the physical environment. "Social life is a necessary condition for the development of logic. We thus believe that social life transforms the individual's very nature" (Piaget, 1928/1995, p. 120). Neo-Piagetian researchers developed this strand of thought, focusing on the effects of cognitive conflict in social learning situations. When a child has his views challenged by another child, who holds an alternative perspective, the children in the dyad are forced to compare their differing viewpoints, resulting in each child decentring from their own beliefs, leading to a deeper understanding of the problem (Doise & Mugny, 1984).

We now know when qualitatively different collaborative skills develop (Wood et al., 1995), how the composition of learning dyads affects learning outcomes (Verba & Winnykamen, 1992), and the effect of task structure on learning gains (Glachan & Light, 1982). Yet, research has not always supported the benefits of collaborative learning. Gauvain and Rogoff (1989) found that some children who worked together on an errand-planning task performed no better than children who worked alone, when later carrying out the task independently. One way to investigate this disparity is to examine the processes within different collaborative situations. Different events may be taking place in alternative situations, with these events having a profound effect on the quality of the interaction. Unpacking the different events and processes in collaborative learning situations allows the mechanisms that underlie the differences to be extrapolated. Do the different outcomes of collaborative learning situations relate to the style of interaction that occurs within them? And if so, are these different styles related to the different cognitive skills that children bring to the situation? The resultant learning outcome may not be the only variable of interest, for example, the nature of different tasks may demand different processes for successful collaboration. Therefore, research examining collaborative learning needs to investigate, not only the effects of collaboration on individual learning gains, but also the effect of an individual's skills on the processes within a collaborative interaction. By investigating the skills brought to an interaction and the processes within the interaction at a micro-level one can begin to understand what elements produce the outcomes. If the skills that facilitate effective collaboration can be pinpointed, then strategies can be used to encourage the use and development of these behaviors.

The Development of Collaborative Skills

Before presenting an overview of the development of collaborative skills, it is essential to present a definition of collaboration. At the simplest level tutoring occurs when a more expert individual assists a less knowledgeable individual to master a skill, while collaboration involves cooperation among equals. Yet such a definition relies heavily on the initial, task-based skills of the participants. Indeed, Verba and Winnykamen (1992) found that intellectual progress can be made in pairs of children in which the general abilities of the children differ, and also in pairs where the domain expertise differ, but the *nature* of the interaction of these pairs are different. When a high ability child is the domain expert, the interaction becomes one of tutoring, while if the high ability child is the novice with a low general ability domain expert, the interaction shows more elements of collaboration. Therefore, the distinctions between collaboration and tutoring, needs to be fluid, reliant not only on the initial knowledge of the participants, but also taking into account the cognitive and social skills that children bring to the learning environment, with consideration also given to how this changes over time. Therefore, this section contains a review of the development of children's collaborative learning, whether collaboration or tutoring. It outlines the qualitative shifts that occur in collaborative learning abilities over time, and draws parallels between these shifts, and shifts in other cognitive skills, such as mental state understanding and EF skills.

From the first days of life babies engage in sophisticated social behavior including taking-turns and imitation (Meltzoff & Moore, 1989; Schaffer, Collis, & Parsons, 1977; Trevarthen, 1977). From a Vygotskian and Piagetian viewpoint these interactions are not only positive for, but essential to, cognitive growth. Of course, this behavior is not necessarily intentional on the part of the infants, yet Trevarthen (Trevarthen, 1977, 1979; Trevarthen & Hubley, 1978) holds that by 8 or 9 months infants have achieved secondary intersubjectivity. Having passed through the primary stage, where they have recognized that the world is shared with others, they move on to create joint activity by focusing on other objects (see also Tomasello, 1995). Care-givers make use of this joint attention to increase infants' knowledge of the world, building on the interactive situation. Working within a Vygotskian framework as outlined at the beginning, we can see the beginnings of collaborative learning from the first days of life.

Whilst most research into collaborative learning has been carried out with school-aged children, some studies have examined such interactions with younger age groups. Verba (1994) observed the interaction styles of three young age-groups (13- to 17-month-olds, 18-month-olds to 2-year-olds, and 2- to 4-year-olds) in their usual day-care settings. The children were provided with a variety of different play objects such as containers, beads, and blocks, and were left to engage in spontaneous play. Verba describes three modes of socio-cognitive functioning, namely observation-elaboration, coconstruction, and guided activity. *Observation-elaboration* involves one child observing another child and then suggesting an idea for action. The suggestion results in both children carrying out the proposal simultaneously, giving each child an opportunity to view similar actions to his/her own actions being undertaken by another child. All the age groups showed similar patterns of observation-elaboration, but older children were more capable of complex coordination between their actions. *Coconstruction* occurs when a child starts to take part in another child's activity. Such an interaction provides the necessary framework for mutual adjustment. Meanings are shared by inferential processes, and some understanding of intentions is achieved by smiling, gesturing, and vocalizing. Patterns of coconstruction were similar across the age ranges; however, older children had longer and more involved instances of this behavior. Finally, *guided activity* occurred when one child acted as more knowledgeable and assisted another child to reach a goal. This style of interaction is a rudimentary form of tutoring, and appeared in the younger age group, though it was usually in the form of an explicit prompt or an action facilitation, which contrasts with more subtle forms of tutoring that have been observed in older children (Cooper, 1980). Verba argues that these three modes of interaction form a continuum from the individual to the social pole, with the learner moving from controlling his or her own actions to being guided by a more knowledgeable other.

Brownell and Carriger (1990, 1991) examined young children's action coordination in a problem-solving task, therefore examining collaboration when the task had an explicit goal. The task required one child to manipulate a spring-loaded handle to make some toys accessible, while another child had to retrieve the toys. Twelve-month-old children found the task impossible, 18-month-olds were able to successfully remove the toys, but this was unreliable and appeared to be mostly an "accidental" success. Only by 24 months were children able to coordinate their actions effectively and also reliably. Warneken, Chen, and Tomasello (2006) found that there was a significant improvement in children's coordination with an adult partner between the ages of 18 and 24 months. At 24 months children are adept cooperators, while at 18 months, although not initially successful, children showed that they had the potential to coordinate, as they were able to succeed at the tasks over the repeated trials. Therefore, Warneken et al. (2006) found that children can coordinate their actions earlier than suggested by Brownell and Carriger (1990, 1991). Yet, this distinction may lie in the characteristics of the partner. For Warneken et al. the children worked with a skilful adult, while in Brownell and Carriger (1990, 1991) children worked with a same-aged peer. This difference in partner may have facilitated the earlier appearance of coordinated behavior, as adults tend to be more predictable in their behavior and remain on task for longer (Ellis & Rogoff, 1982; Radziszewska & Rogoff, 1988; Rogoff, 1990).

The studies described so far provide evidence of early social cognition that enables young children to coordinate their actions with those of others. Formal assessments of theory of mind have demonstrated mental state understanding skills, in relation to conflicting desires, in children as young as 18 months (Repacholi & Gopnik, 1997; but see Carlson, Mandell, and Williams (2004) for a failure to replicate; see also Carpendale and Lewis, 2006, p. 76). Verba (1994), Warneken et al. (2006), and Brownell and Carriger (1990, 1991) extend this effort by showing differences between age groups with socio-cognitive skills being put into practice. Developments in other cognitive skills may also explain the improvements in children's collaborative activities between the ages of 13 months and 4 years. For example, coordinating one's actions with those of another person to reach a goal requires that one steps back from one's own activity and focuses on another person's activity. Improvements in EF would explain some elements of this controlled behavior. Evidence has shown significant changes in EF skills between the ages of 13 months and 4 years, in abilities including anti-imitation (Luria hand-game: Flynn, 2007; Flynn, O'Malley, & Wood, 2004; Hughes, 1998b), inhibitory control (day/night test: Gerstadt, Hong, & Diamond, 1994; whispering task: Kochanska, Murray, Jacques, Koenig, & Vandegeest, 1996), working memory (backward digit span: Davis & Pratt, 1996), and flexibility (bear/dragon task: Flynn, 2007; Reed, Pien, & Rothbart, 1984).

Ashley and Tomasello (1998) investigated the collaborative skills of slightly older children, 2- to 4-year-olds, when working with a same-aged peer. The collaborative problem solving of pairs of children aged 24, 30, 36, and 42 months was investigated in a physical task that required children to coordinate their actions in order to obtain a reward. Once each of the partners became proficient at the task, they were paired with a naïve partner and given the opportunity to teach the task to the new partner. The 24-month-old children failed to learn how to gain the reward, even when given adult assistance. The 30- and 36-month-olds rarely needed adult intervention to succeed, but they were slow to master the task and rarely coordinated their actions. The 30-month-olds often recognized that a new partner had not encountered the problem previously, but they seldom tutored their naïve partners. In contrast, the 36-month-olds were more successful than the younger groups as they made more adjustments for their new partners. The behavior of the 42-month-olds was qualitatively different to all the other groups. This was characterized by a comparatively high number of both coordinated attempted solutions and specific communicative directives. They were also the only age group who demonstrated the task to the naïve peers. These differences resulted in success being achieved in approximately half the time that it took the younger children to complete the task.

Ashley and Tomasello (1998) proposed that the better performance of the older children was due to their more sophisticated perspective-taking skills. In particular, they argued that the behavioral and linguistic performance of children in the study was consistent with changes in mental state understanding found in the theory of mind literature. Ashley and Tomasello (1998) go further and suggest that the developmental changes seen in the children's collaborative abilities cannot be explained in terms of linguistic competence, as the two most sophisticated types of communicative attempts were not beyond the capabilities of the younger children. Demonstrations do not require complex linguistic skills, and specific directives, such as "push it up," are not too complex for children aged 2 ½– 3 years. Therefore, the overall findings support the theoretical analyses by Tomasello, Kruger, and Ratner (1993), who argued that changes in children's abilities to engage in reasoning about others' mental states predict developmental changes in effective collaborative learning. Tomasello et al. describe an initial phase of collaboration that is largely carried out by the process of imitation. Here, children copy the actions of others and by doing this can achieve task success, but this may not involve any real sense of intentionality. The second phase is that of observation. Children know that another individual can achieve a goal more successfully than they can, and so they observe that individual's behavior in order to learn from it. The final phase involves true collaboration where both children understand that they need to coordinate their actions and their perspectives in order to obtain success.

In particular, Tomasello et al. (1993) argued that true collaborative learning, where children do not simply divide up a task between them, but engage in coconstruction of a shared goal, is likely only to emerge at around 6 or 7 years. Part of the argument made by Tomasello et al. hinges on their analysis of children's developing theories of mind. They argue that teaching involves intentions. Although children's understanding of concepts such as false belief develop much earlier, they argue that it is not until 6 or 7 years that children begin to engage in more complex second-order reasoning involving embedded mental states (e.g., John thinks that Mary thinks that ... ; Perner, 1988; Perner & Wimmer, 1985). Effective tutors need to appreciate that an attempt to instruct has failed, because a learner has misunderstood the attempt to teach, "she doesn't know that I want her to do X." Contingent tutoring dictates a modification in the tutoring strategy in relation to the tutor's and learner's mental states. As Tomasello et al. argue, these are the kind of skills upon which collaborative learning relies, where each partner's acts toward the other are simulated and interpreted recursively and at the same time in an integrated manner. They point to other evidence showing that such engagement in reflective and recursive dialogues emerges at around 6 or 7 years (Kruger & Tomasello, 1986). Similarly, Strauss and Ziv (2004) support such a stance arguing that tutoring or teaching represents an important form of collaborative learning, which requires an intentional stance, as "the essence of teaching is the intention to induce learning in others" (Strauss & Ziv, 2004, p. 451).

An alternative perspective has argued that humans have evolved a unique, complex, and specialized set of cognitive resources specifically adapted to teach (Csibra & Gergely, 2006; Gergely & Csibra, 2005). Csibra and Gergely (2006) argue that human infants are born with a "pedagogical stance," a specialized cognitive resource that enables them to learn from infant-directed teaching and also to communicate relevant information to conspecifics, that is, an innate ability to teach. This theory differs to that of Tomasello, Carpenter, Call, Behne, and Moll (2005), who propose that there are two basic prerequisites for joint collaborative activities, an understanding of intentional actions of others and a motivation to share the psychological states of others. Gergely and Csibra argue that without a third prerequisite, the ability to communicate relevant information, joint activities could not be realized. They suggest there are three minimum requirements for pedagogical knowledge transmission: ostension, reference, and relevance. Ostension refers to communicative signals that convey the act of knowledge manifestation, as opposed to knowledge use. In other words, teachers need to signal that they are teaching, and learners need to recognize that. Sperber and Wilson (1986) argue that speakers provide ostensive-communicative cues, such as meaningful eye contact, meaningful looks to parts of objects, pointing, facial expressions, as well as verbal hints, to a listener to emphasize that the contents of the speaker's utterance is relevant to the learner. Referential communication refers to connected communication, overcoming ambiguity between the learner and the teacher about the task at hand. A teacher needs to provide guidance as to exactly which elements of the environment or her behavior she is referring to. The third principle is relevance. In order to provide new and relevant knowledge, a teacher has to be able to understand what the learner does not know. This is difficult in most cases. Csibra and Gergely argue that the relevance principle means a teacher does not have to monitor or model the learner's knowledge state. Instead, she represents her own knowledge state in order to reason about what might be the next relevant step for the learner, in other words, modeling her own knowledge provides a good enough source for the next steps in instruction. So, teaching requires a certain amount of meta-cognitive access to one's own knowledge but not to the knowledge of others.

The proposal that deliberate or intentional teaching (i.e., pedagogy in Csibra and Gergely's terms) is a form of "natural cognition" is also put forward by Strauss and colleagues (Strauss, Ziv, & Stein, 2002). They argue that teaching is ubiquitous, despite its complexity as a skilled form of communication and despite the absence of formal (or informal) training in teaching. Strauss et al. (2002) carried out a study with 3- and 5-year-olds, which showed that whilst 3-year-olds had some basic understanding of teaching, that it requires a "knowledge gap" between, at least, two people, they did not seem to realize that it is the teacher's beliefs about the learner's knowledge that determines whether a teacher will teach or not. In contrast, 5-year-olds' understanding of teaching was more sophisticated, and they were able to correctly predict teaching actions based on the beliefs of the teacher.

Wood et al. (1995) investigated the peer-tutoring ability of preschool and school-aged children. Their results provided evidence, which supported the predictions made by Tomasello et al. (1993). Three-, five-, and seven-year-old dyads participated in a block-building task in which one child, who had previously been taught to construct the model, had to teach another child, who was naïve to the task. Wood et al. (1995) showed that it was not until around

7 years that children showed evidence of systematic contingent instruction, which is where the tutoring child's instructional steps were appropriate to the previous performance of the learner. If the last action by the learner was correct, then a contingent tutor will provide less support at the next step, whereas failure results in a higher level of support. As might be expected, the rate of contingency increased with age. Three-year-olds presented little evidence of contingent teaching, whereas 5-year-olds displayed more contingency. In the 7-year-old group, the rate of contingent teaching was high. Wood et al. (1995) argued that contingent instruction relies upon exactly the kind of recursive or second-order reasoning discussed by Tomasello et al. (1993).

Overall the results of these studies suggest that young children of about 3 years teach mostly through demonstrations of how to complete the task successfully. This style of teaching means that learners need to draw on their extensive imitative skills (McGuigan, Whiten, Flynn, & Horner, 2007; Whiten, Flynn, Brown, & Lee, 2006). By 5 years children are able to provide verbal instructions that allow a learner to understand the task (Ashley & Tomasello, 1998; Maynard, 2002; Wood et al., 1995). While at 7 years children are able to adapt their tutoring to the needs of the learner, which is contingent tutoring (Wood & Wood, 1996; Wood et al., 1995).

The behavior of the learners in Wood et al., (1995)'s study also displayed interesting age differences. All three age groups (3-, 5-, and 7-year-olds) were able to learn the task, but it took the youngest children much longer, and they had many more periods of trial and error learning, seeming to learn mainly from a laborious process with many mistakes. Five-year-olds' learning was based mainly on observation, rather than being related to the degree of contingency displayed by their tutor. The 7-year-olds, in contrast, were able to take advantage of the tutoring they received in order to learn how to carry out the task successfully.

Wood et al. (1995) argued that age-related changes in children's peer-tutoring ability could also be consistent with developments in children's EF abilities. There are robust associations between performance on theory of mind tasks and tasks that require flexibility in planning, self-regulation, and inhibition of prepotent responses (Carlson & Moses, 2001; Carlson et al., 2004; Flynn, 2007; Flynn et al., 2004; Hughes, 1998a, 1998b). Wood et al. (1995) argue that effective peer tutoring requires EF skills, as well as mental state understanding; that is, effective teaching involves being able to step back from the task and make space for the learner to act. It also involves being able to hold an instructional goal in mind whilst evaluating the responses of the learner and being able to adjust future instructions in flexible ways contingent upon the learner's performance. EF shows significant changes in the first 10 years of life, as explained earlier, which have been closely associated with developments in the prefrontal cortex. It seems sensible to assume that improvements in EF should have an effect on children's social interactions, especially in tutoring situations in which actions need to be planned, and executed in a controlled manner. Therefore, the complex link between mental state understanding, EF, and collaborative learning needs to be explored in detail.

Thus, as stated at the introduction, it appears that collaborative learning is in fact an umbrella term for a progression of intersocial activities, which rely more and more heavily on complex cognitive skills. When one considers the changes which occur between the ages of 1½ and 7 years, it would be surprising if children did not take advantage of their developing skills to improve their interactions with others. For example, the frontal lobe develops during early childhood leading to an increase in the ability to regulate one's behavior (Bunge, Dudukovic, Thomason, Vaidya, & Gabrieli, 2002; Durston et al., 2002). Similarly the enculturation of children into formal schooling is likely to bring new skills, such as the ability to follow formal rules. By the age of 7 years, when children appear to be able to collaborate effectively, they have an exemplary cognitive toolkit of skills at their disposal to facilitate this activity. An investigation of the nature of collaboration with a view to unpacking some of the constituent skills will enable us to propose some of these likely "tools."

The following section describes a study that provides direct evidence for the putative links between developments in second-order theory of mind, planning, and effective peer tutoring. Effective tutoring is a demanding activity and involves more than recursive reasoning about a tutees' mental states. Effective tutors need to communicate their instructions unambiguously and also to select from a complex array of information that which should be the focus of attention for both the tutee and the tutor. Thus, the following study addressed the relation between peer tutoring and referential communication and recall skills too.

Underpinning Peer Tutoring

The following study (Flynn, Ding, & O'Malley, 1997) investigated the connection between second-order theory of mind and peer tutoring, but also considered whether developments in planning (a measure of EF), communication or recall provided an alternative account for effective peer tutoring. Planning was chosen above other aspects of EF as we believed it to be a critical aspect of tutoring, for it is essential for effective tutoring to plan one's future actions in light of the past and current state of affairs. Of course, other aspects of EF are essential for effective peer tutoring, such as working memory, inhibitory control, and flexibility, yet we felt that a measure of planning would encompass these skills.

The study was carried out in two parts. First, a sample of 6- and 7-year-old children was tested on a battery of tasks which measured planning, referential communication, recall skills, as well as second-order false belief understanding.[1] Two false belief understanding tasks were presented, one was taken from Perner and Wimmer (1985) and the other was adapted from Sullivan, Zaitchik, and Tager-Flusberg (1994). Children were said to have passed these tasks if they answered all the memory and test questions correctly and provided a justification for a character's behavior that related to the child's recursive understanding of mental states. Children were given a score of zero (failing both tasks), one point (passing only one of the two tasks), or two points (passing both tasks).

A combinatorial problem (adapted from a task used by English, 1992) was used as a test of planning ability. The task required children to employ effective planning and self-monitoring to succeed. The participants were required to dress cardboard figures of monsters in different combinations of clothing. The task was to dress as many monsters as possible in outfits that differed from each other in at least one feature (see Figure 13.1 in which four different outfits could be created). The level of difficulty of the trials ranged from four different outfits to 18 combinations made from three different colored ties, three different colored shorts, and two different colored hats. More monsters and clothes were presented than were needed on each trial, so that children's regulation at completion of the task could be monitored. Children who were monitoring their behavior would stop dressing the monster after they had completed all the possible outfits, whereas repetition of outfits showed a

FIGURE 13.1. An example of the clothes combination and monsters provided for the first trial of the planning task.

lack of monitoring. Children were given a score for goal attainment, that is how many different outfits the children were able to make, and whether they recognized that they had achieved their goal or not. A separate score was also given for strategy use, that is, whether a child used a strategy, such as exhausting the combinations relating to one particular item of clothing, while completing the task.

The referential communication task was taken from Lloyd, Camaioni, and Ercolani (1995) and examined both speaking and listening skills. An identical set of cards was given to a child and an experimenter, who were separated by a screen. Each set of cards contained pictures of the same item, but each card differed by two or three factors including color, shape, and additional features (see Figure 13.2). In the speaking condition, children had to provide a description of one of the cards, so that it was possible for the experimenter to select the correct card from the array. If an ambiguous description was provided the experimenter followed a fixed protocol designed to allow a child to give the correct description. For the listening condition, children were presented with either an ambiguous or unambiguous description. When presented with an ambiguous description, children were coded according to whether they were able to recognize the ambiguous message. A separate score was given for speaking and listening skills.

FIGURE 13.2. An example of one of the sets of cards provided to either the child or the experimenter in the initial trial in the referential communication task.

In the narrative retelling task children had to recall a story that had been read to them. Each recall was transcribed and then coded for the number of core elements of the story (elements without which the story would not make sense) and detail elements (elements present in the story but not necessarily essential to the plot). Children were then given separate scores for the number of core and detail elements.

For the second part of the study two subsamples from the original sample were selected to participate: a group who had passed both tests of second-order theory of mind and a group who had failed both these tests. From these subgroups tutors were selected, half of whom had passed both tests (henceforth referred to as "2nd OToM" tutors) and half of whom had failed both tests (henceforth referred to as "non-2nd OToM" tutors). All learners within the dyads had failed both second-order false belief understanding tests. Each dyad was matched for gender and school class, so that the dyads were single sex (9 male and 12 female dyads) and all the children knew the partner with whom they had been paired.

The peer-tutoring task was The Tower of Nottingham, a construction task made from wooden blocks (Figure 13.3) created by Wood et al. (1976) and used by Wood et al. (1995). Children had to select four blocks of similar sizes and make a complete peg from two of these blocks, which each contained half of the peg. The whole peg could then be inserted into a hole in the other two blocks to make a complete layer. These layers could then be placed one on top of another to create a wooden pyramid. This was a novel task for the children as they would not have come across the task previously.

Initially, the children who were designated as tutors were trained on the Tower of Nottingham using a computerized system, which provided contingent instructions via a computer image of a person on a screen. Contingent instructions are the definition of effective tutoring, as they require a tutor to give the most efficient form of instruction to his/her tutee's needs. Contingent instructions follow two simple rules: if a tutee is failing on a task provide more

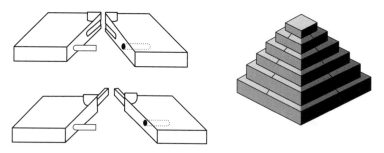

FIGURE 13.3. The Tower of Nottingham, a wooden block construction task made from 21 pieces and requiring a minimum of 20 moves to complete.

assistance, and if a tutee is succeeding on a task provide less assistance. All the tutors were successful on the 20-move task, making between 20 and 23 total moves during the training. Once the tutor had learnt to complete the task, the tutee was brought into the room. The experimenter then instructed the tutor that she/he was to help her/his friend to complete the puzzle; instructions like show, teach, and tell were avoided, so as not to influence the following interaction. Children were then allowed to complete the task as they wished, with intervention only occurring when children were off-task at which point the experimenter offered general encouragement.

The interaction between the tutor and the tutee was coded for every instruction given by a tutor, and every success or failure of a tutee. The tutor's instructions were categorized into five levels, these ranged from those with the highest level of intervention, that is pure demonstrations of an appropriate action, to those with the least lowest level of intervention, that is general encouragement. The different levels of intervention can be seen in Table 13.1. Comparisons of the tutee's successes and failures on the task and the level of instructions given by the tutor allowed a rate of contingency to be created for each tutor, as well as a rate for each level of instruction. For example, a contingent tutor would offer less help after a tutee's success, but more help after a failure. Finally, in order to be sure that the tutees had actually learnt how to complete the task a posttest was presented in which the tutees had to complete the Tower of Nottingham with no assistance. No tutee had difficulty completing the Tower of Nottingham during the posttest.

The analysis of the study was threefold. First, the initial stage of the study allowed the relations between second-order false belief understanding, referential communication, planning, and recall to be investigated. Second, the tutors' performance on the battery of cognitive task was examined in relation to their performance in the peer-tutoring task. Finally, the tutees were also tested on the battery of cognitive tests, and their performance on these tests was compared to their performance during the tutoring session.

TABLE 13.1. Levels of Instruction Used to Code for Contingency.

Level 1	General encouragement	"Carry on!", "You've made a pair."
Level 2	Specific verbal information	"Get a bigger one," "Twist them round."
Level 3	Selection	Pointing at or handing over material, as well as verbal cues.
Level 4	Orientation	Lining up blocks so they need only a minor action for success.
Level 5	Demonstration	Successful construction performed by the tutor.

RELATIONS BETWEEN THE COGNITIVE SKILLS

Children who pass tests of second-order false belief understanding performed better in tests of planning, referential communication, and narrative summarization than those who fail such tests. When all these variables were considered together, the strongest predictors of second-order theory of mind status were measures of planning (goal attainment) and referential communication (listening). Children who pass the theory of mind tests tended to be better planners and better at recognizing ambiguous referents than those who fail these tests. These results support previous research that has shown relations between theory of mind and EF (Carlson et al., 2004; Carlson & Moses, 2001; Flynn, 2007; Flynn et al., 2004; Hughes, 1998a, 1998b). As well as showing support for such associations, the results also extend this research to demonstrate that the relation exists beyond first-order theory of mind, the most common focus of study in mental state understanding research, and also beyond the working memory and/or inhibitory control elements of EF, which have again been the main focus of attention. Indeed the results show a relation between second-order theory of mind and planning. Previous work has found a lack of relations between planning and theory of mind (Carlson, Moses, & Claxton, 2004), but this is related to first-order theory of mind. The current study shows that more sophisticated mental state understanding does relate to planning.

The results also implicate certain pragmatic aspects of linguistic functioning, which are the recognition and clarification of ambiguous utterances, in the development of abilities to engage in more complex reasoning about mental states. The tasks used in this study certainly relate to comprehending and producing appropriate linguistic markers for co-reference. However, they also involve the need to go beyond the information given and consider what the speaker might have *meant* or what the listener needs to *know*. In this respect, referential communication almost by definition involves understanding something about another's mental state. Again, it is this very skill that is required in providing appropriate contributions or relevant instructions in collaborative learning and peer-tutoring situations. Such a link offers an exciting opportunity for examining the relations between referential communication and forms of collaborative interactions, such as collaborative learning or collaborative play.

EFFECTIVE TUTORING AND COGNITIVE SKILLS

In line with the claims of Wood et al. (1995) and Tomasello et al. (1993), it was predicted that tutors who passed tests of second-order false belief reasoning would be more contingent in their tutoring than those who failed. This was found to be the case, 2nd OToM tutors were significantly more contingent in peer tutoring, than their same-aged non-2nd OToM counterparts; with 2nd OToM tutors being, on average, over twice as likely to provide a contingent instruction than their same-age non-2nd OToM peers. It was not the case that the 2nd OToM tutors were simply more able at the task as there was no difference in the behavior of the two types of tutor at the training phase. A closer examination of the tutoring sessions revealed that the contrast between the two types of tutors' techniques was not due to a difference at a specific level of instruction. For example, it was not the case that non-2nd OToM tutors provided more demonstrations than 2nd OToM tutors, or that 2nd OToM tutors provided more verbal instructions, as there was no significant difference in the rate of use of any level of instruction for the two groups of tutors. Therefore, the difference in tutoring was related to the manner in which the different levels of instructions were used rather than the rate of use of any individual level of instruction.

Importantly, a hierarchical regression showed that when all of the cognitive skills were entered in order to try to predict contingent tutoring the only variable that actually accounted for any of the variance (21%) was second-order false belief understanding. Since some of the measures of planning ability (goal-attainment scores) and communication (listening scores) had been found to be predictors of theory of mind status, a second regression analysis was carried out, but with theory of mind measures not entered. Such an analysis could establish if the theory of mind variable accounted for variance that was shared by other variables. Again, the regression found that none of the other variables, communication, planning or recall, predicted rate of contingency in the peer-tutoring session. Therefore, the current findings secure the relation between second-order theory of mind and peer tutoring, showing that the association exists above and beyond the development of other cognitive skills, namely planning, referential communication, and recall.

Specific features of the children's performance in the peer-tutoring session, beyond contingency, were related to their scores in tests of communication and planning. Children with good listening scores in tests of referential communication were less likely to simply demonstrate the task for learners and more likely to provide verbal instructions. The tutor's listening scores were also positively correlated with the rate of verbal instructions given in the peer-tutoring phase. Scores in tests of planning were also related to tutoring ability. Children with higher scores in terms of problem-solving strategy gave more instructions in the tutoring session. This suggests that children with good planning strategy skills were more likely to give more instructions during the peer-tutoring session.

PEER TUTORING AND LEARNER'S SKILLS

Since peer tutoring involves a dyadic interaction it is appropriate to take account of the learner's characteristics and the potential effect of these characteristics on a tutoring session. Such a perspective was advocated by LeBlanc and Bearison (2004), who investigated the dynamics of the process of change in both learners and tutors in a tutoring situation. For example, tutors may perform better in a peer-tutoring context when paired with more capable learners than equally competent tutors paired with poorly performing learners. Correlations between learners' scores on the profiled tests and measures of their tutor's performance showed that learners with higher goal attainment scores on the planning task received more contingent tutoring and were also given fewer demonstrations by their tutors. Therefore, a learner's planning skills, in terms of their ability to attain a goal, affects the rate of contingent tutoring that they receive.

It was surprising to us that there was no direct link between EF and peer-tutoring skills. There are a number of possible explanations for this. First, EF is an umbrella term for a set of skills and perhaps planning was not the most appropriate skill needed in peer tutoring either in general, or in this particular task, the Tower of Nottingham. However, we feel that this is an unlikely explanation as an extensive task analysis into the skills necessary for effective tutoring, and predictions by other researchers (Wood et al., 1995) suggested that planning would be a key factor. Similarly, the measure of planning tapped into the factor's key features, including development and implementation of strategies, recognition of strategy errors, recovery from errors, and goal completion. Second, other EF skills not profiled here may have played a greater role in peer tutoring. Again, this seems unlikely as planning is a higher-level EF skill, and it is argued that other EF skills feed into planning ability (Miyake, Friedman, Emerson, Witzki, & Howerter, 2000). Therefore, any relation between peer tutoring and other EF skills should have come through in an association between peer tutoring and planning. Finally, EF may have an indirect affect on peer tutoring, mediated by mental state understanding. EF skills, such as planning affect the development or implementation of second-order theory of mind, and in turn mental state understanding skills have a direct affect on peer tutoring. Further we believe contingent tutoring, as outlined by Wood and Wood (1996), offers the most effective form of tutoring if the goal is for the learners to be independently successful on the task. The Tower of Nottingham was a complex task, requiring effective planning skills when tutored by a same-aged peer, yet this direct relation was not apparent. Further work is needed to examine whether the same results are produced at different ages and with different tasks, in terms of both the peer-tutoring tasks, and the tests of theory of mind and EF.

Conclusion

In summary, these findings lend strong support to the predictions made by Wood et al. (1995) and are in line with Tomasello et al. (1993, 2005)'s analysis of the development of collaborative learning. Children with more sophisticated recursive mental state understanding provided a higher rate of effective peer tutoring than same-age peers with less sophisticated mental state understanding. Further, the results found that this association was robust, and was not underpinned by other important cognitive skills namely planning, referential communication, and recall. Both the referential communication and planning skills of the tutor had an impact on the style of tutoring a learner received, but these skills were not directly related to the rate of contingency. Although this study was primarily concerned with the cognitive skills that the tutor brought to the peer-tutoring session, the skills of the learner also affected the manner in which the tutor taught. Future work could extrapolate the role of the learner's skills by comparing learners with differing levels of mental state understanding.

Although providing strong support for Tomasello et al.'s predictions, the results are also in line with the theoretical stance of Csibra and Gergely, that is, children are born with an innate pedagogical stance. The work presented in the first half of this chapter illustrated that not only do individuals benefit from a "teaching" environment from an early age, but that young children *can* teach (Ashley & Tomasello, 1998; Verba, 1994). Yet it appears that it is only at about 4 years, as children develop first-order mental state understanding skills, that children can conceptualize a collaboration or tutoring interaction in relation to the knowledge skills of the individuals involved. Further, the present study, along with Wood et al. (1995), shows that young children can provide tutoring, although whether instances of contingent behavior in young children are intentional rather than chance is moot. But it is only once children have developed second-order theory of mind, providing a multilevel platform for the reflection of one's own and other's mental states at time points in the past, present, and future, that children are able to provide a level of support appropriate to the needs of a learner.

Two important final points must be noted. First, although the association between second-order theory of mind and effective peer tutoring was found to exist beyond the influence of other cognitive skills (planning, referential communication, and recall) it is extremely unlikely that the development of effective peer tutoring is wholly unrelated to skills other than mental state understanding. Effective peer tutoring is a sophisticated ability reliant on a number of skills in a child's repertoire, and considering only one of these skills to be important is naïve. Of course some skills may be more influential than others, and this influence may change over time, but it is critical to view effective tutoring as multidimensional.

Second, the relation between mental state understanding and effective peer tutoring must not be viewed as unidirectional. Theory and evidence suggests that more sophisticated mental state understanding leads to more effective peer tutoring (Strauss et al., 2002; Tomasello et al., 1993). Yet the alternative is also true; more sophisticated interactions will lead to more complex mental state understanding, as well as more refined skills in other areas such as EF. For example, children who have more contact with adults, even those outside their immediate family, show an earlier understanding of mind (Lewis, Freeman, Kyriadidou, Maridaki-Kassotaki, & Berridge, 1996). The frequency with which a child is placed in a social interaction that requires effective communication, controlled actions, better understanding of the minds of others, the better developed these skills will become.

Therefore the development of, and relations between, collaborative skills and cognitive skills should not be viewed as unidirectional and discrete, instead the relation is multidimensional. Unpacking the association between the development of collaborative skills and cognitive skills is a complex undertaking, but long-term microgenetic studies may provide a solution. In such studies, the same children's collaborative and cognitive skills are repeatedly measured at discrete intervals during the period of change. Such analyses would attempt to draw parallels between changes in children's collaborative skills and changes in cognition. Such long-term microgenetic studies of cognitive change have already been undertaken in the areas of mental state understanding (Flynn, 2006; Flynn et al., 2004) and EF (Flynn, 2007; Flynn et al., 2004). This work now needs to be extended to the ontogenesis of collaborative skills.

NOTE

1. A subset of 71 children were also tested for their nonverbal general intelligence using the Colored Progressive Matrices (Raven, 1965). Bivariate correlations found that nonverbal intelligence did not correlate with any of the other profiled variables. Therefore it was not included in any further analysis.

REFERENCES

Ashley, J., & Tomasello, M. (1998). Cooperative problem-solving and teaching in pre-schoolers. *Social Development, 7*(2), 143–163.

Azmitia, M. (1988). Peer interaction and problem solving: When are two heads better than one? *Child Development, 59,* 87–96.

Brown, A., & Campione, J. (1990). Communities of learning and thinking, or a context by any other name. In D. Kuhn (Ed.), *Developmental perspectives on teaching and learning thinking skills: Contributions to human development* (pp. 108–126). Basel: Karger.

Brown, A., & Palincsar, A. (1989). Guided cooperative learning and individual knowledge acquisition. In L. B. Resnick (Ed.), *Knowing, learning and instruction: Essays in honour of Robert Glaser* (pp. 393–451). Hillsdale, NJ: Lawrence Erlbaum Associates.

Brown, G., Anderson, A., Shillcock, R., & Yule, G. (1984). *Teaching talk: Strategies for production and assessment.* Cambridge: Cambridge University Press.

Brownell, C., & Carriger, M. (1990). Changes in cooperation and self-other differentiation during the second year. *Child Development* 61, 1164–1147.

Brownell, C. & Carriger, M. (1991). Collaborations among toddler peers: Individual contributions to social contexts. In L. Resnick, J. Levine & S. Teasley (Eds.) *Perspectives on socially shared cognition* (pp. 365–393), American Psychological Association.

Bunge, S. A., Dudukovic, N. M., Thomason, M. E., Vaidya, C. J., & Gabrieli, J. D. E. (2002). Immature frontal lobe in contributions to cognitive control in children: Evidence from fMRI. *Neuron, 33,* 301–311.

Carlson, S., Mandell, D., & Williams, L. (2004). Executive function and theory of mind: Stability and prediction from ages 2 to 3, *Developmental Psychology, 40,* 1105–1122.

Carlson, S., & Moses, L. (2001). Individual differences in inhibitory control and children's theory of mind. *Child Development, 72,* 1032–1053.

Carlson, S. M., Moses, L. J., & Claxton, L. J. (2004). Individual differences in executive functioning and theory of mind: An investigation of inhibitory control and planning ability. *Journal of Experimental Child Psychology, 87,* 299–319.

Carpendale, J., & Lewis, C. (2006). *How children develop social understanding.* Oxford: Blackwell Publishing.

Cooper, C. R. (1980). Development of collaborative problem solving among pre-school children. *Developmental Psychology, 16*(5), 433–440.

Csibra, G., & Gergely, G. (2006). Social learning and social cognition: The case for pedagogy. In M. H. Johnson & Y. Munakata (Eds.), *Processes of change in brain and cognitive development. Attention and performance XXI* (pp. 249–274). Oxford: Oxford University Press.

Davis HL, Pratt C. 1996. The development of children's theory of mind: The working memory explanation. *Australian Journal of Psychology, 47,* 25–31.

Doise, W., & Mugny, G. (1984). *The social development of the intellect.* Cambridge: Cambridge University Press.

Durston, S., Thomas, K., Yang, Y., Ulug, A., Zimmerman, R., & Casey, B. J. (2002). A neural basis for the development of inhibitory control. *Developmental Science, 5,* F9–F16.

Ellis, S., & Rogoff, B. (1982). The strategies and efficacy of child vs. adult teachers. *Child Development, 53,* 730–735.

English, L. (1992). Children's use of domain-specific knowledge and domain-general strategies in novel problem solving. *British Journal of Educational Psychology, 62,* 203–216.

Flynn, E. (2006). A microgenetic investigation of stability and continuity in theory of mind development. *British Journal of Developmental Psychology, 24,* 631–654.

Flynn, E. (2007). The role of inhibitory control in false belief understanding. *Infant and Child Development, 16,* 53–59.

Flynn, E., Ding, S., & O'Malley, C. (1997). The development of peer tutoring skills. *Proceedings of the B.P.S. Developmental Psychology Section Annual Conference, 6*(2), 87.

Flynn, E., O'Malley, C., & Wood, D. (2004). A longitudinal, microgenetic study of the emergence of false belief understanding and inhibition skills, *Developmental Science, 7,* 103–115.

Gauvain, M., & Rogoff, B. (1989). Collaborative problem solving and children's planning skills. *Developmental Psychology, 25,* 139–151.

Gergely, G., & Csibra, G. (2005). Sylvia's recipe: Human culture, imitation, and pedagogy. In S. Levenson & N. Enfield (Eds.), *Roots of human sociality: Culture, cognition and human interaction.* (pp. 229–255) Oxford: Berg Publishers.

Gerstadt, C.L., Hong, Y.J., & Diamond, A. (1994). The relationship between cognition and action: performance of children 3 1/2–7 years old on a Stroop-like day-night test. *Cognition, 53,* 129–153.

Glachan, M., & Light, P. (1982). Peer interaction and learning: Can two wrongs make a right? In G. Butterworth & P. Light (Eds.), *Social cognition: Studies in the development of understanding* (pp 238–262). Chicago: University of Chicago Press.

Howe, C., Rodgers, C., & Tolmie, A. (1990). Physics in the primary school: Peer interaction and the understanding of floating and sinking. *European Journal of Psychology of Education, 5,* 459–475.

Howe, C., Tolmie, A., & Rodgers, C. (1992). The acquisition of conceptual knowledge in science by primary school children: Group interaction and the understanding of motion down an inclined plane. *British Journal of Developmental Psychology, 10,* 113–130.

Hughes, C. (1998a). Executive function in preschoolers: Links with theory of mind and verbal ability. *British Journal of Developmental Psychology, 16,* 233–253.

Hughes, C. (1998b). Finding your marbles: Does pre-schoolers' strategic behaviour predict later understanding of mind? *Developmental Psychology, 34,* 1326–1339.

Kochanska, G., Murray, K., Jacques, T., Koenig, A., & Vandegeest, K. (1996). Inhibitory control in young children and its role in emerging internalisation. *Child Development, 67,* 490–507.

Kruger, A., & Tomasello, M. (1986). Transactive discussions with peers and adults. *Developmental Psychology, 22,* 681–685.

LeBlanc, G., & Bearison, D. (2004). Teaching and learning as a bi-directional activity: Investigating dyadic interactions between child teachers and child learners. *Cognitive Development, 19,* 499–515.

Lewis, C., Freeman, N., Kyriadidou, C., Maridaki-Kassotaki, K., & Berridge, D. (1996). Social influences on false belief access. *Child Development, 67,* 2930–2947.

Lloyd, P., Camaioni, L., & Ercolani, P. (1995). Assessing referential communication skills in the primary school years: A comparative study. *British Journal of Developmental Psychology, 13,* 13–29.

Maynard, A. E. (2002). Cultural teaching: The development of teaching skills in Maya sibling interactions. *Child Development, 73,* 969–982.

McGuigan, N., Whiten, A., Flynn, E., & Horner, V. (2007). Imitation of causally-opaque versus causally-transparent tool use by 3- and 5-year-old children. *Cognitive Development, 22,* 353–364.

Meltzoff, A. N., & Moore, M. K. (1989). Imitation in newborn infants: Exploring the range of gestures imitated and the underlying mechanisms. *Developmental Psychology, 25,* 954–962.

Miyake, A., Friedman, N. P., Emerson, M. J., Witzki, A. H., & Howerter, A. (2000). The unity and diversity of executive functions and their contributions to complex "frontal lobe" tasks: A latent variable analysis. *Cognitive Psychology, 41,* 49–100.

Perner, J. (1988). Higher order beliefs and intentions in children's understanding of social interaction. In J. Astington, P. Harris, & D. Olson (Eds.), *Developing theories of mind* (pp. 271–294). Cambridge: Cambridge University Press.

Perner, J., & Wimmer, H. (1985). "John thinks that Mary thinks that"—Attribution of 2nd order beliefs by 5-year-old to 10-year-old children. *Journal of Experimental Child Psychology, 39*(3), 437–471.

Phelps, E., & Damon, W. (1989). Problem solving with equals: Peer collaboration as a context for learning mathematics and spatial concepts. *Journal of Educational Psychology, 81,* 639–646.

Piaget, J. (1928/1995). Genetic logic and sociology. In J. Piaget (Ed.), *Sociological studies.* (pp 184–214) New York: Routledge.

Radziszewska, B., & Rogoff, B. (1988). Influence of adult and peer collaborators on children's planning skills. *Developmental Psychology, 24,* 840–848.

Reed, M., Pien, D., & Rothbart, M.K. (1984). Inhibitory self-control in preschool children. *Merrill-Palmer Quarterly, 30,* 131–148.

Repacholi, B., & Gopnik, A. (1997). Early understanding of desires: Evidence from 14 and 18-month-olds. *Developmental Psychology, 33,* 12–21.

Rogoff, B. (1990). *Apprenticeship in thinking: cognitive development in social context.* New York,: Oxford University Press.

Schaffer, H. R., Collis, G. M., & Parsons, G. (1977). Vocal interchange and visual regard in verbal and pre-verbal children. In H. R. Schaffer (Ed.), *Studies in mother-infant interaction* (pp. 291–324). London: Academic Press.

Sperber, D., & Wilson, D. (1986). *Relevance: Communication and cognition.* Oxford: Blackwell Publishing.

Strauss, S. & Ziv, M. (2004). Teaching: ontogenesis, culture, and education. *Cognitive Development, 19,* 451–456.

Strauss, S., Ziv, M. & Stein, A. (2002). Teaching as a natural cognition and its relations to preschoolers' developing theory of mind. *Cognitive Development, 17*(3–4), 1473–1487.

Sullivan, K., Zaitchik, D., & Tager-Flusberg, H. (1994). Preschoolers can attribute 2nd-order beliefs. *Developmental Psychology, 30*(3), 395–402.

Tomasello, M. (1995). Joint attention as social cognition. In C. Moore & P. J. Dunham (Eds.), *Joint attention. Its origin and role in development* (pp. 103–130). Hillsdale, NJ: Lawrence Erlbaum Associates.

Tomasello, M., Carpenter, M., Call, J., Behne, T., & Moll, H. (2005). Understanding and sharing intentions: The origins of cultural cognition. *Behavioral and Brain Sciences, 28,* 675–691.

Tomasello, M., Kruger, A., & Ratner, H. (1993). Cultural learning. *Behavioral and Brain Sciences, 16,* 495–552.

Trevarthen, C. (1977). Descriptive analysis of infant communicative behavior. In H. R. Schaffer (Ed.), *Studies in mother-infant interaction* (pp. 227–270). London: Academic Press.

Trevarthen, C. (1979). Communication and cooperation in early infancy: A description of primary intersubjectivity. In M. Bullowa (Ed.), *Before speech. The beginning of interpersonal communication* (pp. 321–347). Cambridge: Cambridge University Press.

Trevarthen, C., & Hubley, P. (1978). Secondary intersubjectivity: Confidence, confiding and acts of meaning in the first year. In A. Lock (Ed.), *Action, gesture and symbol* (pp. 183–226). London: Academic Press.

Tudge, J. and Rogoff, B. (1989) Peer Influences on Cognitive Development: Piagetian and Vygotskian Perspectives. In M. Bornstein and J. Bruner (Eds.), *Interaction in Human Development* (pp. 17–40), Hillsdale, NJ: Lawrence Erlbaum Associates.

Verba, M. (1994). The beginnings of collaboration in peer interaction. *Human Development, 37,* 125–139.

Verba, M., & Winnykamen, F. (1992). Expert-novice interactions: Influence of partner status. *European Journal of Psychology of Education, 7*(1), 61–71.

Vygotsky, L. S. (1978). *Mind in society: The development of higher mental processes,* ed. and trans. M. Cole, V. John-Steiner, S. Scribner & E. Souberman. Harvard University Press (original work published 1930–1935).

Vygotsky, L. S. (1981). The genesis of higher mental functions. In J. V. Wersch (Ed. and Trans.), *The concept of activity in soviet psychology.* (pp. 147–188) Armonk: M. E. Sharpe.

Warneken, F., Chen, F., & Tomasello, M. (2006). Cooperative activities in young children and chimpanzees. *Child Development, 77*(3), 640–663.

Webb, N. M. (1991) Task related verbal interaction and mathematics learning in small groups. *Journal for Research in Mathematics Education,* 22 (5), 366–389.

Whiten, A., Flynn, E., Brown, K., & Lee, K. (2006). Imitation of hierarchical structure in actions by young children. *Developmental Science, 9,* 575–583.

Wood, D., Bruner, J., & Ross, G. (1976). The role of tutoring in problem solving. *Journal of Child Psychology and Psychiatry, 17,* 89–100.

Wood, D., & Wood, H. (1996). Commentary: Contingency in tutoring and learning. *Learning and Instruction, 6*(4), 391–397.

Wood, D., Wood, H., Ainsworth, S., & O'Malley, C. (1995). On becoming a tutor: Toward an ontogenetic model. *Cognition and Instruction, 13*(4), 565–581.

Wood, D. J., Wood, H. A., & Middleton, D. J. (1978). An experimental evaluation of four face-to-face teaching strategies. *International Journal of Behavioral Development, 1,* 131–147.

14

Psychological Distancing in the Development of Executive Function and Emotion Regulation

GERALD F. GIESBRECHT, ULRICH MÜLLER, AND MICHAEL R. MILLER

T he concept of psychological distancing has a venerable history in developmental psychology and can be traced back to the writings of Baldwin (1906; see Müller & Runions, 2003), Werner (1915, 1926; Werner & Kaplan, 1963), Piaget (1936/1963, 1937/1954), and Vygotsky (Vygotsky & Luria, 1994). At the outset, it should be noted that the term "psychological distancing" is also used in the field of social psychology. However, social psychologists use this term to refer to the phenomenon that individuals perceive themselves as less similar to others with undesirable characteristics—sometimes referred to as "defensive distancing" (Schimel, Pyszczynski, Greenberg, O'Mahen, & Arndt, 2000)—whereas developmental psychologists use the term to refer to the process whereby children create a psychological "space" between themselves and their actions and their immediate spatial-temporal surrounding. Put differently, psychological distancing, within developmental psychology, captures the phenomenon that human beings can step back and withhold an immediate response, survey the environment, and reflect on the course of action instead of being dominated by immediate stimulation.

The distancing construct may be viewed as a "spatial metaphor representing the mental separation of the self from the ongoing present" (Sigel, Stinson, & Kim, 1993, p. 214). This notion is nicely captured in the following remarks by Gehlen (1988):

The things in our world thus have the essentially human character of *acquired neutrality*. This is not the indifference toward anything that does not appeal directly to instincts, as is the case in the environments of the higher animals. In contrast, the things around us are thoroughly known and "worked through," but remain "undecided" for the most part, available for interaction at any time. This is how man masters the overwhelming barrage of impressions, this is how he obtains relief: He *actively "checkmates" the forcefulness of the world's impressions, making the world potentially available at any time.* (pp. 162–163, emphasis in original)

In this chapter, we focus on the role that psychological distancing plays in the development of self-regulation. Our purpose in taking this approach is to highlight linkages between cognitive aspects of self-regulation (hereafter referred to as executive function [EF]) and emotional aspects of self-regulation (hereafter referred to as emotion regulation). We begin by summarizing some classical views of psychological distancing and how they inform our understanding of self-regulation. We then examine the role of EF in the development of psychological distancing and especially how such development facilitates emotion regulation. Drawing on Sigel's contemporary theory of psychological distancing, the final section examines how social interaction may facilitate psychological distancing and the development of EF and emotion regulation.

Psychological Distancing in Development

The concept of psychological distancing has been used as a descriptive device to highlight an important aspect of development in many classical theories of development, most notably those of Piaget and Vygotsky. In Piaget's theory, distancing (or what he calls decentration) is closely tied to the idea that any form of knowledge results from the interaction of the child (subject) and the world (object), and that at the beginning of development, subject and object are relatively undifferentiated. For him, intelligence originates and perpetuates itself, as he claims, "neither with knowledge of the self nor of things as such but with knowledge of their interaction, and it is by orienting itself simultaneously toward the two poles of that interaction that intelligence organizes the world by organizing itself" (Piaget, 1937/1954, pp. 354–355). In the course of their interactions with the world, children develop more complex coordinations between action schemes and representational schemes. More complex coordinations constitute higher-order control structures that lead to the progressive distancing between the child and the world and result in increasingly successful ways of regulating interactions with the world.

Whereas Piaget emphasized the importance of the coordinatory or operative aspect of intelligence in psychological distancing, Vygotsky emphasized the role of signs, or more specifically, speech (i.e., the figurative aspect of intelligence; see Amin & Valsiner, 2004). For Vygotsky, psychological distance is achieved through semiotic mediation (i.e., language) and play. Functionally, both facilitate the "emancipation from situational constraints" that derives from its "demands on the child to act against immediate impulse" (Vygotsky, 1933/1978, p. 99). Speech and play transform the child's relation to the world (Child → World) by creating a representational "space" that is psychologically removed from the immediate perceptual field:

> The child is much more easily able to ignore the vector that focuses attention on the goal itself, and to execute a number of complex preliminary acts, using for this purpose a comparatively long chain of auxiliary instrumental methods. The child proves able to include independently, in the process of solution of the task, objects which lie neither within the near nor the peripheral visual field. By creating through words a certain intention, the child achieves a much broader range of activity, applying as tools not only those objects that lie near at hand, but searching for and preparing such articles as can be useful in the solution of its task and planning its future actions. (Vygotsky & Luria, 1994, p. 110)

In play, the relation between perception and activity loses its determining force: "In play thought is separated from objects and action arises from ideas rather than from things: a piece of wood begins to be a doll and a stick becomes a horse" (Vygotsky, 1933/1978, p. 97). At the same time, speech and play transform the child's relation to him- or herself and his or her own behavior (Child → Self) with the same consequence: "With the aid of speech the child for the first time proves able to the mastering of its own behaviour, relating to itself as to another being, regarding itself as an object. Speech helps the child to master this object through the preliminary organization and planning of its own acts of behaviour" (Vygotsky & Luria, 1994, p. 111).

In summary, Piaget and Vygotsky both suggest that the development of controlled and self-regulated action is closely tied to severing of ties between stimulation and action—to a process of distancing between child and world. For both, this process leads to increasingly more complex and adaptive interactions with the social and physical world, as well as to increasing self-awareness and self-regulation of the psychological world. In the next section, we suggest several processes that might support psychological distancing in the development of emotional self-regulation.

EXECUTIVE FUNCTION AS A MECHANISM FOR
EMOTION REGULATION

Until recently, little attention has been given to the nature of the relation between EF and emotion regulation (contrast this with the spate of work on the relation between EF and social understanding—see Moses & Tahiroglu, Chapter 9, this volume). Broadly defined, emotion regulation refers to the intrinsic and extrinsic processes responsible for monitoring, evaluating, and modifying emotional reactions in keeping with the individual's goals or social convention (Thompson, 1994). In contrast, EF refers to a set of psychological processes involved in the conscious control of thought and action (Zelazo & Müller, 2002).

Although we maintain that these constructs are separable, we suggest that the overlap between them is as interesting as their distinction. There are also substantive theoretical and empirical reasons to believe that emotion regulation and EF may rely on shared resources. For example, on a neurological level, distinctions between cognition and emotion are not clearly demarcated in the brain (Lewis & Todd, 2007). Further, from the perspective of EF, there is evidence to suggest that the conscious control of action and thought may proceed through relatively "hot" processes (i.e., personally significant or emotional) or relatively "cool" processes (i.e., little personal significance or relatively cognitive) (Hongwanishkul, Happaney, Lee, & Zelazo, 2005; Zelazo & Müller, 2002).

Cunningham and Zelazo (2007) have recently proposed that emotion regulation depends critically on EF and that the two constructs are isomorphic when the goal of EF is the regulation of emotion (Zelazo & Cunningham, 2007). Although we note that the relation between emotion regulation and EF is likely reciprocal, and that EF also depends to some extent on emotion regulation, we believe that examining the commonalities between cognitive and emotional regulation deepens our understanding of the development of emotion regulation. In this section, we consider how different components of EF contribute to psychological distancing, which in turn facilitates emotion regulation. In the final section, we consider how social processes (i.e., parenting practices) influence the development of self-regulatory abilities.

Despite its importance, the meaning of EF has remained elusive (Lehto, Juujärvi, Kooistra, & Pulkkinen, 2003). A major controversy revolves around whether EF is unitary (i.e., a homogenous function that does not include component processes or subfunctions) or multifaceted (i.e., a heterogeneous function that involves several component processes and subfunctions; see Hughes & Graham, 2002). Factor-analytic studies support the view that EF is multifaceted (e.g., Huizinga, Dolan, & van der Molen, 2006; Lehto et al., 2003; Levin et al., 1991; Miyake et al., 2000; Ozonoff, 1997), composed of interrelated functions of shifting, inhibitory control, and updating. We examine each of these in turn for their potential significance for emotion regulation.

Shifting

The ability to shift focus from one aspect of a problem to another or to shift perspectives is a fundamental requirement for emotion regulation. Attentional flexibility (i.e., shifting focus from one element to the next), for example, aids emotion regulation by ensuring that problem-solving efforts do not become fixated on one aspect of the problem to the exclusion of other relevant aspects (Fernandez-Duque, Baird, & Posner, 2000). Likewise, representational flexibility (i.e., shifting from one perspective or set of rules to another) is a core requirement of success on various self-regulatory tasks (Müller, Zelazo, & Imrisek, 2005). For example, instructing a child to represent a desirable object in abstract terms lengthens waiting times in a delay of gratification task (Mischel, Shoda, & Rodriguez, 1989). Shifting abilities generate psychological distance because they create alternatives to the representation of a problem. At the same time, shifting abilities may "cool" the problem space. For example, consider a situation in which a child becomes angry at not being allowed to play with the family's TV remote control. Regulating anger in this situation is likely to pivot around the child's ability to shift focus from the desired object to another object or activity. Continued focus on the forbidden remote control is likely to increase anger while shifting focus to another object or activity is likely to decrease anger. Shifting is one mechanism for generating the requisite psychological distance to regulate emotion.

Developmentally, shifting abilities are among the first evidence of nascent emotion regulation. Kopp (1982; see also Kopp, 2002), for example, suggests that shifts in visual attention observed in neonates are a rudimentary precursor to emotion regulation. The ability to break the bonds of obligatory attention is perhaps also the earliest example of psychological distancing. By exerting an influence over the kinds of stimulation they attend to, infants not only control their emotional arousal, they also begin to experience the possibility of modulating their emotional experience. This flexibility is a setting condition for emotion regulation because it creates a psychological space in which infants may exercise control over the experience and expression of emotion through manipulating the psychological distance between stimulation and response (Gross & Thompson, 2007).

Empirical evidence supporting the link between shifting and emotion regulation is found across infancy and childhood. Not only do emotional and attentional control covary in young infants (Fox & Calkins, 2003; Morales, Mundy, Crowson, Neal, & Delgado, 2005) but also research by Rothbart as well as by Eisenberg (e.g., Eisenberg, Shepard, Fabes, Murphy, & Guthrie, 1998; Eisenberg, Smith, Sadovsky, & Spinrad, 2004; Rueda, Posner, & Rothbart, 2005) has supported the role of attentional control (i.e., the ability to voluntarily focus or shift attention as needed) in the regulation of reactive temperamental tendencies (a notion akin to emotion regulation). Furthermore, Simonds, Kieras, Rueda, and Rothbart (2007) found that executive attention abilities were related to the ability to substitute a smile for feelings of disappointment in a mistaken gift task.

Although the role of emotion in human adaptation is not well understood, one of its functions is to prepare the body to respond very rapidly through a "quick-and-dirty" appraisal of situational significance (LeDoux, 1995). The efficiency of this rapid appraisal and activation system requires that certain features of the situation are selected for attention while others are ignored (Öhman, 2002). Emotion regulation may function as a mechanism to decouple attention from those aspects of the problem that are phylogenetically prepotent to allow for reappraisal through slower limbic and cortical pathways (Lewis & Todd, 2007). Although quick responses have obvious survival value, more reflective aspects of evaluative processing allows a person to view stimuli vis-à-vis a wider range of contexts and considerations (Cunningham & Zelazo, 2007). In summary, attentional and representational flexibility appear to facilitate the development and exercise of emotion regulation by interposing potentially available but previously ignored information between individuals and their actions.

Response Inhibition

Closely related to shifting, response inhibition refers to the ability to suppress a dominant response in favor of a nondominant response. Everyday examples of response inhibition might include the ability of a child to wait until his mother is off the telephone to tell her about an invitation he received to attend a birthday party or the ability to resist the urge to have a cookie before dinner. According to Baumeister and colleagues (e.g., Baumeister, Bratslavsky, Muravan, & Tice, 1998; Tice & Bratslavsky, 2000), the function of self-regulation is to effect a substitution or reversal of an appetitive or natural tendency for another response or to withhold a response altogether. In the context of emotion regulation, response inhibition may be involved in the suppression of emotional expression (Butler & Gross, 2004), the forgoing of an immediate positive feeling in order to preserve action toward a self-regulatory goal

(Schmeichel & Baumeister, 2004), or the substitution of one emotional expression for another (Campos, Mumme, Kermoian, & Campos, 1994), to name but a few examples.

Earlier, we suggested that emotions bias action by providing quick-and-dirty appraisals leading to phylogenetically endowed adaptations to common problems of life. By this account, emotion itself is a prepotent response to the (internal or external) stimulus in the sense that it entails a response to immediately perceived information—as opposed to information that is currently not perceived but merely represented. One important contribution of response inhibition, therefore, is the building up of "defenses" to the forcefulness of emotion. In this sense, emotion regulation supports the ability to resist the urge to act in a predefined (emotional) manner.

Response inhibition is perhaps the most basic mechanism for emotion regulation because it generates a temporal "space" in which other self-regulatory mechanisms may operate. Lewis and Todd (2007), for example, argue that phylogenetically later brain systems (especially the prefrontal cortex) exert self-regulatory influence through temporal distancing between a stimulus and response:

> If all we had was a brain stem, the perception of motion would immediately lead to freezing behaviour. If we were stuck at the level of the limbic system, we would use stored meanings to automatically assign preference and value to certain stimuli and certain outcomes; our actions would be slowed down enough for "meaning" to intervene. Luckily, with the possession of a prefrontal cortex, we can slow down action almost indefinitely, allowing higher cognitive processes to compare and discard many possible plans or strategies in favour of what is likely to be most beneficial in the long run. (pp. 409–410)

Temporal distancing is a psychological tool for disrupting the forcefulness of stimulus qualities, thereby allowing processes such as shifting and updating to operate between stimulation and response. The higher psychological functions emancipate, to use Vygotsky's (1933/1978) term, the young child from the immediate urge to act on the current perception. Moore's research (Chapter 11, this volume) with future-oriented decision-making, a form of psychological distancing, supports the notion that response inhibition is linked developmentally to psychological distancing.

Several studies have directly assessed the relation between response inhibition and emotion regulation. Hoeksma, Oosterlaan, and Schipper (2004), for example, found a correlation of 0.41 between response inhibition (measured using a stop signal paradigm—a type of go/nogo task in which a stop signal is presented after the target signal) and modulation of anger (measured in vivo over a 4-day period). Likewise, a number of studies that compared response inhibition to children's ability to regulate emotion after receiving a disappointing gift have shown that response inhibition is related to the ability to display positive emotion after receiving a disappointing gift (Kieras, Tobin, Graziano, & Rothbart, 2005), as well as the ability to suppress negative displays of emotion even after controlling for general cognitive abilities (i.e., language) (Carlson & Wang, 2007; Liebermann, Giesbrecht, & Müller, 2007).

In summary, response inhibition appears to be important for adaptive emotion regulation. However, emotion regulation requires more than the inhibition of a prepotent and unwanted emotional response; in addition it requires the activation of a more appropriate response (which, in turn, may involve shifting and updating). Psychological distancing achieved through response inhibition is, therefore, only one ingredient of the regulatory processes that shape the emotional response.

Updating

The updating function refers to monitoring and coding incoming information for relevance to the task at hand and then appropriately revising the items held in working memory by replacing old, no longer relevant information with newer, more relevant information (Miyake et al., 2000; Morris & Jones, 1990). Within both self-regulation (Bandura, 1991) and EF (Welsh & Pennington, 1988) literatures, updating is sometimes referred to as *self-monitoring*, and has at least two meanings, both of which are related to the concept of feedback: updating appraisals and discrepancy signaling. In the first instance, updating appraisals provides important feedback concerning the need for and quality of regulatory efforts. How and when to modify emotion depends critically on various factors (i.e., the surgency and strength of the initial emotion, alternate viewpoints that can be constructed, secondary emotions that may arise as a result of the initial emotion, etc.) that must be taken into account. Since emotions are, in part, constituted by appraisals of situations, updating of appraisals is likely a primary mechanism of emotion regulation. Updating and monitoring of working memory representations provides moment-by-moment information concerning the need to initiate, maintain, or terminate regulatory attempts. This process creates psychological distance because its function requires bringing implicit emotional appraisals to consciousness where they can be manipulated.

The second meaning of updating in the self-regulation literature is to signal whether there is a discrepancy between a standard or goal for a certain class of action and current functioning. This aspect of self-monitoring is clearly exemplified by cybernetic models of self-regulation, such as a test-operate-test-exit (TOTE) system (Miller, Galanter, & Pribram, 1960, as cited in Carver & Scheier, 1990). In the initial "test" phase, a person compares his or her current emotional state, for example, to a desired emotional state. If a discrepancy is noted, the "operate" phase is initiated through regulatory actions intended to move the system toward the desired end state. Progress toward the goal is monitored by further "test" phases. This process continues until the initial discrepancy has been resolved and the TOTE process is terminated. Becoming aware of and addressing discrepancies between current behavior and situational demands creates psychological distance. The importance of discrepancies for emotion regulation is that they "function as *instigators*, *activators*, and *organizers* of mental operations" (Sigel et al., 1993, p. 215, emphasis in original).

Although updating and monitoring of working-memory representations has clear links with self-regulation across many domains (Febbraro & Clum, 1998; Gottman & McFall, 1972; McClure, Botvinick, Yeung, Greene, & Cohen, 2007; Paris & Newman, 1990; Stevens, Quittner, Zuckerman, & Moore, 2002; Tomarken & Kirschenbaum, 1982; Towse, Lewis, & Knowles, 2007; Williams, Donovan, & Dodge, 2000), little attention has been given to the role this mechanism may play in regulating emotion (for a theoretical treatment of self-monitoring and ER, see Carver & Scheier, 1982, 1990, 1998). One study that did examine this relation (Liebermann et al., 2007) found that parent reports of updating/working memory and emotion regulation were related ($r = 0.43$, $p < 0.01$), but these findings were not replicated in performance-based measures of updating/working memory and emotion regulation.

In summary, aspects of cognitive self-regulation also appear to facilitate emotional control. One of the means by which EF may support emotion regulation is by creating psychological distance between individuals and their emotional behaviors. This is consistent with the writings of Piaget and Vygotsky, both of whom suggest that the development of controlled and self-regulated action is closely tied to the severing of the ties between stimulation and action. That is, to a process of distancing between child and world. In the next section, we consider the effect of parenting on distancing and how this influences the development of emotion regulation.

Social Interaction as a Context for Psychological Distancing

Given the prominence that the concept of distancing received in classical theories of development, it is somewhat surprising that it is hardly discussed in contemporary theories of development. One exception is the work of Irving Sigel, to which we now turn. Based on the work of Werner, Vygotsky, and Piaget, Sigel (e.g., 1970, 2002) proposed a model of psychological distancing that emphasizes the importance of social interaction in the development of cognitive competence.

Sigel's work applies the theories of Vygotsky and Piaget by specifying how social interaction generates the context in which self-regulatory abilities are formed. For example, Piaget's discussion of morality attaches a great deal of significance to the distinction between relationships of cooperation and constraint (Wright, 1982) because development, according to Piaget (1932/1965), "is facilitated by relationships of cooperation and mutual respect and hindered by relationships of constraint and unilateral respect" (Carpendale & Lewis, 2004, p. 93). The important point, for our purpose, is that relationships of cooperation and mutual respect play an essential role in the development of knowledge because they "constitute the most favourable condition for counteracting individual centrations on certain aspects of the issue at hand" (Carpendale & Müller, 2004). It follows, therefore, that the nature of parent–child relationships should impinge on the development of psychological distancing.

Sigel's distancing model emphasizes the manner in which parents construct the linguistic environment to activate synthesis and organization of representational schemes. In particular, Sigel focuses on the discursive practices of parents, which he views as a primary source of intellectual stimulation (Sigel et al., 1993). For example, parents create psychological distance for children by drawing their attention to aspects of the problem they had not considered before. Parents might use an interrogative approach to facilitate distancing, by asking, for example, "how do you think your friend felt when you walked out on her like that?". In Sigel's model, these "distancing strategies function to create temporal and/or spatial, and/or psychological distance between self and object (Sigel et al., 1993, p. 214) by placing a "cognitive demand on the child to separate the self mentally from the ongoing present" (Sigel, Stinson, & Flaughter, 1991, p. 126). Crucially, this process of parent–child engagement serves not only as a social scaffold to the development of psychological distance and the exercise of self-regulation, but also it creates a laboratory in which children experiment with various regulatory solutions.

According to Sigel's distancing model, individual differences in children's cognitive self-regulation are related to individual differences in distancing strategies employed by parents (Sigel et al., 1991). Parents who demand obedience and force their children to adopt their perspective, for example, place few cognitive demands on their children and, therefore, create limited opportunities for their children to restructure their own thinking. This point, in particular, has received strong support in Sigel's empirical studies (e.g., Sigel et al., 1993) as well as in those of others (e.g., Dornbusch et al., 1987).

In this final section, we examine how parenting practices contribute to the development of psychological distancing and thereby facilitate the development of EF and emotion regulation. In our view, self-regulation in young children is the product of an ongoing partnership between children and their caregivers.[1] We view this partnership as bidirectional—that is, children evoke social interactions to regulate their emotions (e.g., social referencing, use cues to request specific assistance, and initiate plans that require a caregiver's assistance—see Kopp, 1989), and caregivers actively socialize self-regulation (e.g., through direct teaching, scaffolding, limit-setting, and monitoring). Here, we focus on the manner in which parent-directed social interaction facilitates emotion regulation through a process of psychological distancing.

Inductive discipline, an approach that emphasizes reasoning and parent–child collaboration, has strong links to the development of emotion regulation (Krevans & Gibbs, 1996). Parenting practices characterized by inductive control (e.g., taking a reasoning approach, reminding about rules, and explaining the impact of behavior on others) and behavioral control (e.g., setting limits, monitoring, and making maturity demands) seem to be effective in promoting internalization of rules and development of self-regulatory behaviors (Kerr, Lopez, Olson, & Sameroff, 2004; Paulussen-Hoogeboom, Stams, Hermanns, & Peetsma, 2007). For example, parents who openly discuss feelings to explain the varying consequences of behavior tend to have children with more advanced empathy than parents who do not use this approach (Ensor & Hughes, 2005).

Parents who use an inductive approach also structure their interactions in a manner that models the use of distancing strategies. These models provide both a social scaffold for current self-regulatory functioning and a template for future development (Grolnick & Farkas, 2002). As children gain facility in the process of psychological distancing, they then begin to evoke it for themselves. For example, Houck and LeCuyer-Maus (2004) found that clear limit-setting and displays of disapproval when limits were not followed had a salutary effect on self-regulation. They speculate that parents help their children develop self-regulatory abilities by making them aware of standards, rules, and goals. When these expectations are modeled in a warm and respectful relationship, the result is a process of reflection that creates psychological distance between the child and his or her behavior. Similarly, a longitudinal study by Gottman, Katz, and Hooven (1996) found that parents who "coach" their children through emotionally stressful situations had children who demonstrated better self-regulation and social skills than children of parents who did not use such an approach.

With regard to emotion regulation more specifically, we argue that by simultaneously supporting and challenging children to regulate their emotions, parents actively scaffold the cognitive abilities that support emotion regulation (Landry, Miller-Loncar, Smith, & Swank, 2002). Through scaffolding, parents structure the salient emotional elements of distressful events so that their children can remain attentive and organize their self-regulatory strategies accordingly (Landry et al., 2002). In other words, the interactions between child and parent are formative in the development of psychological distancing needed for emotion regulation. Further, psychological distancing facilitated by parents provides the child with opportunities to consider new information and action possibilities that would otherwise remain outside the child's purview of consideration. For example, a child who is distressed due to a disagreement with another child may initially focus only on his own distress, to the exclusion of the other child's feelings. Parents who help their children create psychological distance from their own distress (e.g., by considering the feelings of the other child) not only broaden the range of considerations that children bring to their understanding of distress, but they also assist them in reframing the distressful situation so that it is less negative (Morris, Silk, Steinberg, Myers, & Robinson, 2007). For example, when parents engage their children in a supportive dialogue about the discrepancy between a social rule and the child's current behavior, they provide scaffolding for the exercise of shifting and updating processes. Parents who use an inductive approach are also likely to anticipate a child's future behavior and draw the child's attention to the possible consequences, leading to preparatory self-reflection that supports the development of inhibitory control.

Paradoxically, by drawing attention to children's emotions and behaviors, parents assist children in creating psychological distance between themselves and their actions. Inductive parenting not only structures interactions in such a manner that psychological distancing becomes more likely, it also facilitates the development of underlying abilities (i.e., shifting, updating, and response inhibition) that are required for emotion regulation.

However, parents who use power-assertive strategies to secure compliance from their children may undermine their child's ability to develop emotion regulatory skills. Parental control characterized by power assertive, negative, intrusive, hostile, or overcontrolling behavior has been associated with externalizing problems (Calkins & Howse, 2004; Rothbaum & Weisz, 1994), higher rates of child defiance (Crockenberg & Litman, 1990; Power & Chapieski, 1986), and emotional dysregulation (Morrell & Murray, 2003). Moreover, a recent meta-analysis on parenting and self-regulation found that parents who are insensitive to and excessively control their children's behavior have children who display fewer self-regulatory behaviors compared to the children of parents who directly attempt to instruct and encourage their children's behavior (Karreman, van Tuijl, van Aken, & Dekovic, 2006).

The psychological distancing hypothesis is particularly useful for understanding the differential affects of power assertive and inductive parenting. The primary distinction lies in the parental influence on the attentional focus of the child. In an inductive approach, emotional support and dialogue generated by the parent allow the child to focus on dealing with the problem. Power-assertive parents, however, tend to focus the child's attention on the interpersonal "space" between parent and child rather than the self-regulatory "space" between a child and her or his behavior. Power-assertive parenting practices tend to draw the child's attention to the power differential between parent and child (Barber, 1996), to the heightened arousal experienced in such encounters (Hoffman, 2000), or to the relational withdrawal that may result from a parent's disapproval (Aunola & Nurmi, 2005; Barber, 1996). Because their attention is focused on the dynamics of interaction—as opposed to the problem at hand—these children become emotionally enmeshed with their parents in the problem, with little opportunity to create psychological separation from either the problem itself or the intense interpersonal exchange. The result is a loss of opportunities for psychological distancing or for practicing the underlying processes of shifting, updating, or inhibiting that are necessary for emotion regulation.

Interestingly, Baumrind (e.g., 1967) and Steinberg and colleagues (e.g., Steinberg, Elmen, & Mounts, 1989) found that children of power-assertive parents (i.e., authoritarian parents) demonstrated competence in certain domains (e.g., academic achievement) and conformed well to conventional dictates (e.g., they showed low levels of deviant behavior), but they lacked the *self-confidence* and *initiative* needed for self-regulation. Not surprisingly, didactic-controlling parenting strategies have also been shown to generate weaker forms of psychological distancing and produce fewer cognitive demands (Sigel et al., 1991). The result is that children experience little cognitive disequilibrium and, thus, have little opportunity to develop a sense of agency with regard to their own self-regulatory ability. In addition, parental intrusiveness (i.e., taking responsibility for emotion regulation) weakens children's own motivation to take responsibility for dealing with their own distress (Grolnick & Farkas, 2002). From a psychological distancing perspective, power-assertive strategies fail to provide a context in which children are expected and supported in developing the requisite skills to regulate their own emotions and behavior.

In summary, inductive parenting strategies have a salutary effect on emotion regulation because they structure the problem-solving context in a manner that broadens the child's focus of attention and affords the use of cognitive abilities that support emotion regulation. Power-assertive parenting strategies, however, may facilitate compliance and achievement (under certain circumstances) but they fail to structure the problem context in a manner that allows children to engage the self-regulation problem. Furthermore, power-assertive parenting in essence takes control of the situation by imposing a solution (i.e., a demand for rule compliance) and thus fails to engage the child's own nascent self-regulatory capacity. In short, the active ingredient in parenting that leads to self-regulation is a process of psychological distancing.

Conclusion

In this chapter, we have examined the role of psychological distancing in emotion regulation. We have proposed that key aspects of EF create psychological distance and facilitate the development of emotional control. Furthermore, we have shown how parenting practices facilitate psychological distancing and provide a context in which children develop the cognitive and emotional abilities related to emotion regulation.

In closing, we raise several questions that derive from our application of the concept of psychological distancing to emotion regulation. First, although psychological distancing has been understood primarily in cognitive terms, to what extent might psychological distancing also facilitate emotional forms of distancing? Understanding the ways in which emotional distance may contribute to emotion regulation would make a valuable contribution to self-regulation research. Do children, for example, require different kinds of psychological distance when the problem at hand is highly emotional, as opposed to problems that are primarily intellectual or behavioral? When parents give their children a "time out," does the physical and temporal "space" provide a form of psychological distancing that helps children restructure their emotions? Are children in the throws of emotional turmoil capable of engaging the cognitive demands placed on them by parental distancing behaviors, or is some amount of emotional distance a setting condition for self-regulatory cognition? We speculate that children in the midst of a temper tantrum may benefit from the psychological distance generated by a parent's structuring of the environmental response (e.g., time out) but lack openness to engage the cognitive demands related to self-regulation (e.g., reasoning).

Another issue raised by our analysis concerns the question of whether there is some "optimum" amount of psychological distance. The research seems clear that inadequate psychological distance is detrimental to self-regulatory effort, but is too much distance deleterious? In delay of gratification tasks, for example, fixating on the reward is strongly related to termination of the waiting period (Mischel et al., 1989). Being able to see the reward seems to enhance its salience and immediacy, making psychological distancing difficult (Mischel & Rodriguez, 1993). Waiting times tend to decrease when the rewards are not visible. However, when children are performing mundane or boring tasks, they tend to wait longer when they regularly glance at the reward (Mischel & Rodriguez, 1993). In other words, when it comes to self-imposed waiting, too much and too little psychological distance both appear to impair self-regulation.

In addition to testing hypotheses derived from our application of the concept of psychological distancing to emotion regulation, future research might usefully explore whether different aspects of EF facilitate different aspects of emotion regulation. Overall, however, we hope that our chapter illustrates how the concept of psychological distancing can illuminate critical aspects of emotion regulation, including the interplay between cognitive and emotional aspects of self-regulation, and the facilitative effects of social interaction on development.

NOTE

1 Our focus on parental practices is not meant to downplay the effects of peer interactions on the development of self-regulation (see, e.g., Denham, von Salisch, Olthof, Kochanoff, & Caverly, 2002).

REFERENCES

Amin, T. G., & Valsiner, J. (2004). Coordinating operative and figurative knowledge: Piaget, Vygotsky, and beyond. In J. I. M. Carpendale & U. Müller (Eds.), *Social interaction and the development of knowledge* (pp. 87–109). Mahwah, NJ: Lawrence Erlbaum Associates.

Aunola, K., & Nurmi, J. E. (2005). The role of parenting styles in children's problem behaviour. *Child Development, 76*, 1144–1159.

Baldwin, J. M. (1906). *Thought and things, Vol. 1: Functional logic.* New York: The Macmillan Company.

Bandura, A. (1991). Social cognitive theory of self-regulation. *Organizational Behaviour and Human Decision Processes, 50*, 248–287.

Barber, B. K. (1996). Parental psychological control: Revisiting a neglected construct. *Child Development, 67*, 3296–3319.

Baumeister, R. F., Bratslavsky, E., Muraven, M., & Tice, D. M. (1998). Ego depletion: Is the active self a limited resource? *Journal of Personality and Social Psychology, 74*, 1252–1265.

Baumrind, D. (1967). Child care practices anteceding three patterns of preschool behavior. *Genetic Psychology Monographs, 75*, 43–88.

Butler, E. A., & Gross, J. J. (2004). Hiding feelings in social contexts: Out of sight is not out of mind. In P. Philippot & R. S. Feldman (Eds.), *The regulation of emotion* (pp. 101–126). Mahwah, NJ: Lawrence Erlbaum Associates.

Calkins, S. D., & Howse, R. B. (2004). Individual differences in self-regulation: Implications for childhood adjustment. In P. Philippot & R. S. Feldman (Eds.), *The regulation of emotion* (pp. 307–332). Mahwah, NJ: Lawrence Erlbaum Associates.

Campos, J. J., Mumme, D. L., Kermoian, R., & Campos, R. G. (1994). A functionalist perspective on the nature of emotion. In N. A. Fox (Ed.), *The development of emotion regulation: Biological and behavioral considerations. Monographs of the Society for Research in Child Development, 59*(2–3, Serial No. 240).

Carlson, S. M., & Wang, T. S. (2007). Inhibitory control and emotion regulation in preschool children. *Cognitive Development, 22,* 489–510.

Carpendale, J. I., & Lewis, C. (2004). Constructing an understanding of mind: The development of children's social understanding within social interaction. *Behavioral and Brain Sciences, 27,* 79–151.

Carpendale, J. I., & Müller, U. (2004). Social interaction and the development of rationality and morality: An introduction. In J. I. Carpendale & U. Müller (Eds.), *Social interaction and the development of knowledge* (pp. 1–18). Mahwah, NJ: Lawrence Erlbaum Associates.

Carver, C. S., & Scheier, M. F. (1982). Control theory: A useful conceptual framework for personality-social, clinical, and health psychology. *Psychological Bulletin, 92,* 111–135.

Carver, C. S., & Scheier, M. F. (1990). Principles of self-regulation: Action and emotion. In E. T. Higgins & R. M. Sorrentino (Eds.), *Handbook of motivation and cognition: Foundations of social behaviour* (Vol. 2, pp. 3–52). New York: The Guilford Press.

Carver, C. S., & Scheier, M. F. (1998). *On the self-regulation of behavior.* Cambridge, UK: Cambridge University Press.

Crockenberg, S., & Litman, C. (1990). Autonomy as competence in 2-year-olds: Maternal correlates of child defiance, compliance, and self-assertion. *Developmental Psychology, 26,* 961–971.

Cunningham, W. A., & Zelazo, P. D. (2007). Attitudes and evaluations: A social cognitive neuroscience perspective. *Trends in Cognitive Sciences, 11,* 97–104.

Denham, S., von Salisch, M., Olthof, T., Kochanoff, A., & Caverly, S. (2002). Emotional and social development in childhood. In P. K. Smith & C. H. Hart (Eds.), *Blackwell handbook of childhood social development* (pp. 308–328). Malden, MA: Blackwell Publishing.

Dornbusch, S. M., Ritter, P. L., Leiderman, P. H., & Roberts, D. F. (1987). The relation of parenting style to adolescent school performance. *Child Development, 58,* 1244–1257.

Eisenberg, N., Shepard, S. A., Fabes, R. A., Murphy, B. C., & Guthrie, I. K. (1998). Shyness and children's emotionality, regulation, and coping: Contemporaneous, longitudinal, and across-context relations. *Child Development, 69,* 767–790.

Eisenberg, N., Smith, C. L., Sadovsky, A., & Spinrad, T. L. (2004). Effortful control: Relations with emotion regulation, adjustment, and socialization in childhood. In R. F. Baumeister & K. D. Vohs (Eds.), *Handbook of self-regulation: Research, theory, and applications* (pp. 259–283). New York: The Guilford Press.

Ensor, R., & Hughes, C. (2005). More than talk: Relations between emotion understanding and positive behaviour in toddlers. *British Journal of Developmental Psychology, 23*, 343–363.

Febbraro, G. A. R., & Clum, G. A. (1998). Meta-analytic investigation of the effectiveness of self-regulatory components in the treatment of adult problem behaviors. *Clinical Psychology Review, 18*, 143–161.

Fernandez-Duque, D., Baird, J. A., & Posner, M. I. (2000). Executive attention and metacognitive regulation. *Consciousness & Cognition, 9*, 288–307.

Fox, N. A., & Calkins, S. D. (2003). The development of self-control of emotion: Intrinsic and extrinsic influences. *Motivation and Emotion, 27*, 7–26.

Gehlen, A. (1988). *Man, his nature and place in the world.* New York: Columbia University Press. (Original work published 1940)

Gottman, J. M., Katz, L. F., & Hooven, C. (1996). Parental meta-emotion and the emotional life of families: Theoretical models and preliminary data. *Journal of Family Psychology, 10*, 243–268.

Gottman, J. M., & McFall, R. M. (1972). Self-monitoring effects in a program for potential high school dropouts: A time series analysis. *Journal of Consulting and Clinical Psychology, 39*, 273–281.

Grolnick, W. S., & Farkas, M. (2002). Parenting and the development of children's self-regulation. In M. H. Bornstein (Ed.), *Handbook of parenting, V.5: Practical issues in parenting* (pp. 89–110). Mahwah, NJ: Lawrence Erlbaum Associates.

Gross, J. J., & Thompson, R. A. (2007). Emotion regulation: Conceptual foundations. In J. J. Gross (Ed.), *Handbook of emotion regulation* (pp. 3–24). New York: The Guilford Press.

Hoeksma, J. B., Oosterlaan, J., & Schipper, E. M. (2004). Emotion regulation and the dynamics of feelings: A conceptual and methodological framework. *Child Development, 75*, 354–360.

Hoffman, M. L. (2000). *Empathy and moral development: Implications for caring and justice.* Cambridge, UK: Cambridge University Press.

Hongwanishkul, D., Happaney, K. R., Lee, W. S., & Zelazo, P. D. (2005). Assessment of hot and cool executive function in young children: Age related changes and individual differences. *Developmental Neuropsychology, 28*, 617–644.

Houck, G. M., & LeCuyer-Maus, E. A. (2004). Maternal limit setting during toddlerhood, delay of gratification, and behavior problems at age five. *Infant Mental Health Journal, 25*, 28–46.

Hughes, C., & Graham, A. (2002). Measuring executive functions in childhood: Problems and solutions? *Child and Adolescent Mental Health, 7*, 131–142.

Huizinga, M., Dolan, C. V., & van der Molen, M. W. (2006). Age-related change in executive function: Developmental trends and a latent variable analysis. *Neuropsychologia, 44*, 2017–2036.

Karreman, A., van Tuijl, C., van Aken, M. A., & Dekovic, M. (2006). Parenting and self-regulation in preschoolers: A meta-analysis. *Infant and Child Development, 15*, 561–579.

Kerr, D. C., Lopez, N. L., Olson, S. L., & Sameroff, A. J. (2004). Parental discipline and externalizing behavior problems in early childhood: The roles of moral regulation and child gender. *Journal of Abnormal Child Psychology, 32*, 369–383.

Kieras, J. E., Tobin, R. E., Graziano, W. G., & Rothbart, M. K. (2005). You can't always get what you want: Effortful control and children's responses to undesirable gifts. *Psychological Science, 16*, 391–396.

Kopp, C. B. (1982). Antecedents of self-regulation: A developmental perspective. *Developmental Psychology, 18*, 199–214.

Kopp, C. B. (1989). Regulation of distress and negative emotions: A developmental view. *Developmental Psychology, 25*, 343–354.

Kopp, C. B. (2002). Commentary: The codevelopments of attention and emotion regulation. *Infancy, 3*, 199–208.

Krevans, J., & Gibbs, J. C. (1996). Parents' use of inductive discipline: Relations to children's empathy and prosocial behavior. *Child Development, 67*, 3263–3277.

Landry, S. H., Miller-Loncar, C. L., Smith, K. E., & Swank, P. R. (2002). The role of early parenting in children's development of executive processes. *Developmental Neuropsychology, 21*, 15–41.

LeDoux, J. E. (1995). Emotion: Clues from the brain. *Annual Review of Psychology, 46*, 209–235.

Lehto, J. E., Juujärvi, P., Kooistra, L., & Pulkkinen, L. (2003). Dimensions of executive functioning: Evidence from children. *The British Journal of Developmental Psychology, 21*, 59–80.

Levin, H. S., Culhane, K. A., Hartmann, J., Evankovich, K., Mattson, S. J., Harward, H., et al. (1991). Developmental changes in performance on tests of purported frontal lobe functioning. *Developmental Neuropsychology, 7*, 377–395.

Lewis, M., & Todd, R. (2007). The self-regulating brain: Cortical-subcortical feedback and the development of intelligent action. *Cognitive Development, 22*, 406–430.

Liebermann, D., Giesbrecht, G. F., & Müller, U. (2007). Cognitive and emotional aspects of self-regulation in preschoolers. *Cognitive Development, 22*, 511–529.

McClure, S. M., Botvinick, M. M., Yeung, N., Greene, J. D., & Cohen, J. D. (2007). Conflict monitoring in cognition-emotion competition. In J. J. Gross (Ed.), *Handbook of emotion regulation* (pp. 204–228). New York: The Guilford Press.

Miller, G. A., Galanter, E., & Pribram, K. H. (1960). *Plans and the structure of behavior.* New York: Henry Holt and Company.

Mischel, W., & Rodriguez, M. L. (1993). Psychological distance in self-imposed delay of gratification. In R. R. Cocking & K. A. Renninger (Eds.), *The development and meaning of psychological distance* (pp. 109–121). Hillside, NJ: Lawrence Erlbaum Associates.

Mischel, W., Shoda, Y., & Rodriguez, M. L. (1989). Delay of gratification in children. *Science, 244*, 933–938.

Miyake, A., Freidman, N. P., Emerson, M. J., Witzki, A. H., Howerter, A., & Wager, T. D. (2000). The unity and diversity of executive functions and their contributions to complex "Frontal Lobe" tasks: A latent variable analysis. *Cognitive Psychology, 41*, 49–100.

Morales, M., Mundy, P., Crowson, M. M., Neal, A. R., & Delgado, C. E. (2005). Individual differences in infant attention skills, joint attention, and emotion regulation behaviour. *International Journal of Behavioral Development, 29*, 259–263.

Morrell, J., & Murray, L. (2003). Parenting and the development of conduct disorder and hyperactive symptoms in childhood: A prospective longitudinal study from 2 months to 8 years. *Journal of Child Psychology and Psychiatry, 44*, 489–508.

Morris, A. S., Silk, J. S., Steinberg, L., Myers, S. S., & Robinson, L. R. (2007). The role of the family context in the development of emotion regulation. *Social Development, 16*, 361–388.

Morris, N., & Jones, D. M. (1990). Memory updating in working memory: The role of the central executive. *British Journal of Psychology, 81*, 111–121.

Müller, U., & Runions, K. (2003). The origins of understanding self and other: James Mark Baldwin's theory. *Developmental Review, 23*, 29–54.

Müller, U., Zelazo, P.D., & Imrisek, S. (2005). Executive function and children's understanding of false belief: How specific is the relation? *Cognitive Development, 20*, 173–189.

Öhman, A. (2002). Automaticity and the amygdala: Nonconscious responses to emotional faces. *Current Directions in Psychological Science, 11*, 62–66.

Ozonoff, S. (1997). Components of executive function in autism and other disorders. In J. Russell (Ed.), *Autism as an executive disorder* (pp. 179–211). New York: Oxford University Press.

Paris, S. G., & Newman, R. S. (1990). Developmental aspects of self-regulated learning. *Educational Psychologist, 25*, 87–102.

Paulussen-Hoogeboom, M. C., Stams, G. J., Hermanns, J. M., & Peetsma, T. T. (2007). Child negative emotionality and parenting from infancy to preschool: A meta-analytic review. *Developmental Psychology, 43*, 438–453.

Piaget, J. (1954). *The construction of reality in the child.* New York: Basic Books. (Original work published 1937)

Piaget, J. (1963). *The origins of intelligence in children.* New York: Norton. (Original work published 1936)

Piaget, J. (1965). *The moral judgment of the child.* New York: The Free Press. (Original work published 1932)

Power, T. G., & Chapieski, M. L. (1986). Childrearing and impulse control in toddlers: A naturalistic investigation. *Developmental Psychology, 22*, 271–275.

Rothbaum, F., & Weisz, J. R. (1994). Parental caregiving and child externalizing behavior in nonclinical samples: A meta-analysis. *Psychological Bulletin, 116*, 55–74.

Rueda, M. R., Posner, M. I., & Rothbart, M. K. (2005). The development of executive attention: Contributions to the emergence of self-regulation. *Developmental Neuropsychology, 28*, 573–594.

Schimel, J., Pyszczynski, T., Greenberg, J., O'Mahen, H., & Arndt, J. (2000). Running from the shadow: Psychological distancing from others to deny characteristics people fear in themselves. *Journal of Personality and Social Psychology, 78,* 446–462.

Schmeichel, B. J., & Baumeister, R. F. (2004). Self-regulatory strength. In R. F. Baumeister & K. D. Vohs (Eds.), *Handbook of self-regulation: Research, theory, and applications* (pp. 84–98). New York: The Guilford Press.

Sigel, I. E. (1970). The Distancing hypothesis: A causal hypothesis for the acquisition of representational thought. In M. R. Jones (Ed.), *Miami symposium on the prediction of behavior, 1968: Effects of early experience* (pp. 99–118). Coral Gables, FL: University of Miami Press.

Sigel, I. E. (2002). The psychological distancing model: A study of the socialization of cognition. *Culture and Psychology, 8,* 189–214.

Sigel, I. E., Stinson, E. T., & Flaughter, J. (1991). Socialization of representational competence in the family: The distancing paradigm. In L. Okagaki & R. J. Sternberg (Eds.), *Directors of development: Influences on the development of children's thinking* (pp. 121–144). Hillsdale, NJ: Lawrence Erlbaum Associates.

Sigel, I. E., Stinson, E. T., & Kim, M. (1993). Socialization of cognition: The distancing model. In R. Wozniak & K.W. Fischer (Eds.), *Development in context: Acting and thinking in specific environments* (pp. 211–224). Hillsdale, NJ: Lawrence Erlbaum Associates.

Simonds, J., Kieras, J. E., Rueda, M. R., & Rothbart, M. K. (2007). Effortful control, executive attention, and emotional regulation in 7–10-year-old children. *Cognitive Development, 22,* 474–488.

Steinberg, L., Elmen, J. D., & Mounts, N. S. (1989). Authoritative parenting, psychosocial maturity, and academic success among adolescents. *Child Development, 60,* 1424–1436.

Stevens, J., Quittner, A. L., Zuckerman, J. B., & Moore, S. (2002). Behavioral inhibition, self-regulation of motivation, and working memory in children with attention deficit hyperactivity disorder. *Developmental Neuropsychology, 21,* 117–140.

Tomarken, A. J., & Kirschenbaum, D. S. (1982). Self-regulatory failure: Accentuate the positive? *Journal of Personality and Social Psychology, 43,* 584–597.

Thompson, R. A. (1994). Emotion regulation: A theme in search of definition. In N. A. Fox (Ed.), *The development of emotion regulation: Biological and behavioral considerations. Monographs of the Society for Research in Child Development,* 59(2–3 Serial No. 240), 25–52.

Tice, D. M., & Bratslavsky, E. (2000). Giving in to feel good: The place of emotion regulation in the context of general self-control. *Psychological Inquiry, 11,* 149–159.

Towse, J. N., Lewis, C., & Knowles, M. (2007). When knowledge is not enough: The phenomenon of goal neglect in preschool children. *Journal of Experimental Child Psychology, 96,* 320–332.

Vygotsky, L., & Luria, A. (1994). Tool and symbol in child development. In R. van der Veer & J. Valsiner (Eds.), *The Vygotsky reader* (pp. 99–174). Oxford, England: Blackwell Publishing.

Vygotsky, L. S. (1978). *Mind in society: The development of higher psychological processes.* Cambridge, MA: Harvard University Press.

Welsh, M. C., & Pennington, B. F. (1988). Assessing frontal lobe functioning in children: Views from developmental psychology. *Developmental Neuropsychology, 4,* 199–230.

Werner, H. (1915). Begriffspsychologische Untersuchungen [Investigations into the psychology of concepts]. *Archiv für systematische Philosophie, 21,* 162–172.

Werner, H. (1926). *Einführung in die Entwicklungspsychologie* [Introduction into developmental psychology]. Leipzig: Barth.

Werner, H., & Kaplan, B. (1963). *Symbol formation.* New York: Wiley.

Williams, K. J., Donovan, J. J., & Dodge, T. L. (2000). Self-regulation of performance: Goal establishment and goal revision processes in athletes. *Human Performance, 13,* 159–180.

Wright, D. (1982). Piaget's theory of moral development. In S. Modgil & C. Modgil (Eds.), *Jean Piaget: Consensus and controversy* (pp. 207–217). New York: Holt, Rinehart and Winston.

Zelazo, P. D., & Cunningham, W. A. (2007). Executive function: Mechanisms underlying emotion regulation. In J. J. Gross (Ed.), *Handbook of emotion regulation* (pp. 135–158). New York: The Guilford Press.

Zelazo, P. D., & Müller, U. (2002). Executive functioning in typical and atypical children. In U. Goswami (Ed.), *Blackwell handbook of childhood cognitive development* (pp. 445–469). Oxford, England: Blackwell Publishing.

15

Emotional Contributions to the Development of Executive Functions in the Family Context

SUSAN M. PEREZ AND MARY GAUVAIN

This chapter discusses the development of executive functions in the social context of the family with particular attention to the contributions made by children's emotional development to this process. Executive mental functions control cognitive activity and include selective attention, intentional memory, behavioral inhibition, and planning. Changes in the frontal cortex from early childhood to late adolescence regulate the development of executive functions (Diamond, 2002). The protracted course of this development opens these capabilities to myriad influences, including social experience. We are particularly interested in how social interactions in the family setting, including the broader cultural values, beliefs, and practices that help organize these interactions, and children's emotional competence are related to the development of executive functions.

Emotional competence, including emotional expression, understanding, and regulation, is pertinent to cognitive activity and its development, including the development of executive functions. Over the course of development, but especially in early childhood, the skills required for both executive functions and emotional competence are mutually influential. For example, children's ability to engage in selective attention or to plan may influence opportunities to develop an understanding of their own and others' emotions and to practice effective emotion regulation skills, such as behavioral inhibition. However, children's emotional competence may contribute to the ability to use executive functions, for instance, by regulating arousal levels that can interfere with intentional and conscious control of mental activity (Keenan, 2002; Rothbart & Posner, 2001).

To examine how the development of executive functions in the family context is related to children's emotional competence, this chapter uses the theoretical and empirical foundation provided by a sociocultural approach to cognitive development in which social interactions between children and more skilled partners are seen as critical to intellectual growth (Vygotsky, 1978). In this perspective, cognitive development is guided by the opportunities children have to participate in cognitive activity with more skilled partners. The family setting is not the only social setting that contributes to cognitive development, even in the early years. However, the sustained nature of the family, differences among family members in age and experience, and the relational and emotional bonds of family members make this setting an important social context for the development of complex cognitive skills. In addition, by concentrating on the contributions of children's developing emotional competence to the development of planning skills in the family setting, this chapter attempts to broaden the sociocultural approach by specifying some of the links between social, cognitive, and emotional processes in the development of complex cognitive skills. Although social, cognitive, and emotional development are ordinarily conceptualized and examined in research as separate facets of child adjustment, in children's everyday experience these aspects of development inform and influence one another.

This chapter focuses on the development of executive functions involved in planning. Planning, which involves the determination, organization, and implementation of future-oriented behaviors (Rogoff, Gauvain, & Gardner, 1987), is crucial to the ability to engage in and carry out complex cognitive activities—the very types of activities children are increasingly expected to participate in with development. Planning is not an entirely cognitive act; both social and emotional processes are critical to the development and effective utilization of planning skills. Social experience is intricately involved in planning in several ways. The need to plan often arises when people try to coordinate actions with others. Social considerations also occur when a planner must anticipate or account for the actions of others relevant to the task being planned, considerations that rely on some understanding of intentionality and of the mind itself (Tomasello, Carpenter, Call, Behne, & Moll, 2005). Finally, research has demonstrated that more experienced planners support the development of planning through modeling, instruction, and collaborative activity (Gauvain, 2001).

Planning competence also relies on emotional processes. Effective planning entails reflecting on the activity being planned and formulating strategies for future actions, both of which require that children be able to suspend or inhibit action and delay gratification. Research indicates that individual differences in a tendency toward high emotional arousal as well as skill at emotion regulation are associated with children's planning performance on laboratory tasks. For example, children who have higher rates of emotional intensity display less effective planning strategies and ability to remain on task; children who display better emotion regulation or coping skills display better planning skills, regardless of their level of emotional intensity (Perez, 2004). An important question stemming from these observations concerns the role of social partners, especially parents, in helping children learn how to regulate emotional processes that may interfere with or be used to enhance performance on complex cognitive activities, particularly activities that rely on executive functioning.

While considering the influence of parent–child interactions on the development of planning skills, this chapter recognizes the embeddedness of such interactions within the emotional climate of the family (Saarni, 1999) and the larger cultural values, beliefs, and practices that help constitute these interactions (Bronfenbrenner & Morris, 2006; Bugental & Grusec, 2006). With regard to family emotional climate, opportunities to develop planning skills may be influenced by the concurrent and historical socioemotional experience the interactive partners have with each other (Dix, 1991; Gauvain & DeMent, 1991; Gauvain & Perez, 2008). This influence may be positive or negative depending on the emotional ties parents and children have and how the demands of the planning situation activate the cognitive and emotional capabilities of the child and the parent. With regard to the broader cultural context, variations in cultural values, beliefs, and practices as they are expressed in family interactions may provide different types of opportunities for participating in activities that allow children to practice planning and observe the planning of others. This view is consistent with research that has established that the family plays a critical role in the development of emotional competence (e.g., Denham, 1998; Eisenberg, Cumberland, & Spinrad, 1998; Gottman, Katz, & Hooven, 1996; Saarni, 1999) and that socialization goals and practices with regard to child emotion are influenced by cultural values and beliefs (Halberstadt et al., 2006; Saarni, Campos, Camras, & Witherington, 2006; Tsai, Knutson, & Fung, 2006).

We extend these ideas to the process of cognitive socialization, specifically in relation to the development of executive functions, as it occurs in the family setting. Through their socialization efforts, parents may provide children with both guidance and practice as to how to regulate emotions that are important to learning about and practicing executive skills. For example, a mother may encourage her child to learn to regulate his emotions, such as anger and frustration, or even excitement, while solving a mathematics problem to minimize the potential interference of emotional arousal on learning and performance or as a means of communicating culturally valued or accepted ways of learning in this domain. In contrast, the parent may encourage enthusiasm and heightened states of arousal in other forms of knowledge acquisition and expression, such as music or physical skills. Because parents are arbiters of both the family and the culture, considering the relation of cognitive development to emotional competence within the family context may provide insight into the cultural nature of human development (Rogoff, 2003). The next section discusses the socialization of cognitive development, followed by a brief review of theory and research relevant to understanding the contribution of children's emotional development to the development of planning in the family context.

Cognitive Development in the Context of Family Socialization

Children need to develop the knowledge and skills that will enable them to function as mature and contributing members of their community. To reach this goal, cognitive development must be tailored to the types of problems and demands that children encounter in their everyday lives. Cross-generational processes of knowledge transmission, or socialization practices, help children learn this information via the many experiences they have every day (Gauvain & Perez, 2007). These experiences include social interaction with more experienced members of the community, opportunities to learn about and use material and symbolic cultural tools that support intelligent action, and participation in organized patterns of activity that are devised and valued by the culture. Adults and other more experienced partners play instrumental roles in this process by defining and modeling behaviors for children and by assisting children as they engage in activities that draw on thinking skills. Children play active and directive roles in that their capabilities, interests, and needs set the stage and establish the boundaries for development in social context.

Characteristics of the human species ensure that children have substantial opportunity to learn the knowledge and skills needed in the setting in which they live. The immaturity of the human organism at birth and the protracted rate of physical and intellectual maturation necessitate a long period of dependency by children on more mature members of the species (Bjorklund & Pelligrini, 2002). This long period of growth provides children with protection and nurturance along with many opportunities for learning—opportunities that largely occur in social situations. The family and kin system are integral to this process. Interactions among family members often include information about culturally valued skills and practices. Moreover, these interactions involve people who are in relationships with one another. Consequently, they provide children with repeated opportunities for learning, which are especially valuable for learning complex cognitive skills, such as those involved in executive functioning. Also important is the fact that these relationships involve emotional ties, which facilitate motivational and other arousal states important to learning. Finally, these relationships involve people of varying developmental status, which increases the likelihood that processes important to learning in social context, such as modeling, scaffolding, and guided participation, may occur and yield beneficial outcomes. Thus, the complexity inherent to the family and kin group provides children with a vast and motivating set of learning opportunities that span the years of childhood (Gauvain & Perez, 2007).

Much of the research on family and kin influences on cognitive development, especially research conducted in Western and industrialized societies, has concentrated on parent–child interaction. In general, this research shows that the parent–child relationship is a particularly important context for the development of a wide swath of cognitive skills (Gauvain, 2001). This research has demonstrated that parents influence children's emerging cognitive skills through the behaviors they encourage and model, and through the experiences they provide for their children (Gauvain & Perez, 2007). The methods of cognitive socialization used by parents are vast. Parents introduce ideas and ways of thinking to children through the use of explanation and guidance, and by their participation alongside children in activities as they learn about and practice new skills (Rogoff, 2003). They also help children understand and solve problems by breaking problems down into manageable subgoals (Saxe, 1991), arranging opportunities for children to develop skills through play, lessons, and other activities both inside and outside the home, and making technology and other learning tools available (Gauvain & Perez, 2005). The psychological dynamics of these interactions are influenced by many factors, including characteristics of the participants. Parental characteristics that influence cognitive socialization include the parent's personality, beliefs, emotional expressiveness and responsiveness, exercise of control, and expectations about child behavior. Contributions of children that are influential include temperament and emotionality, cognitive and social skills, and developmental status. Some characteristics of parents and children that regulate cognitive interactions are not independent. Family members are related biologically (Plomin, 1990), and parents and children share an interactional history (Gauvain & DeMent, 1991). In addition, the family is embedded in a larger social and cultural system that may influence the nature and extent of parent–child interactions that are relevant to cognitive development (Bronfenbrenner & Morris, 2006).

Although opportunities for cognitive development often emerge spontaneously in parent–child interaction, such experiences do not always occur nor necessarily lead to positive outcomes. Gauvain and Perez (2008) observed that mothers of chronically noncompliant preschoolers expressed more disapproval and were more directive toward their children during joint cognitive activity than mothers of compliant children and that noncompliant children were less involved in the task than more compliant children were. Similarly, Winsler, Diaz, McCarthy, Atencio, and Chabay (1999) observed mother–child interaction involving children rated by teachers as having behavior problems and children identified as not having these problems. Although there were no group differences in children's behavior during the interaction, mothers of children identified as having behavior problems used more behavior regulation and negative control, and less praise in comparison to mothers with children without behavioral problems. These patterns suggest that mothers who have experienced difficulty with their children are more concerned with managing behavior than with promoting learning during cognitive interaction.

Before discussing relations between the development of emotions and executive functions in the context of the family, we provide an overview of emotional, cognitive, and socioemotional development. This overview describes the major developmental changes in these areas in early infancy, infancy, toddlerhood, and early and middle childhood, and will serve as background for the remainder of the chapter.

The Development of Emotional Competence in Relation to Cognitive and Social Development

Children's emotional competence, that is, their expression, understanding, and regulation of emotion undergoes enormous change from early infancy to middle childhood (Lewis, Haviland-Jones, & Barrett, 2008). These changes, which coincide with changes in cognitive capabilities and social functioning, are summarized in Table 15.1 in relation to the developmental periods from early infancy to middle childhood. The changes that occur in each of these important areas of development are described in detail in many sources (see Eisenberg, Damon, & Lerner, 2006; Kuhn, Siegler, Damon, & Lerner, 2006), therefore our purpose is not to summarize them in detail. Rather, we aim to draw attention to the patterns and coherence of capabilities across these areas within different developmental periods. The following sections briefly summarize the coincident and mutually influential areas of emotional development in the areas of expression, understanding, and regulation, and cognitive and social development.

TABLE 15.1. Overview of the Development of Emotional Competence, Cognition, and Socioemotional Functioning Through Middle Childhood.

	Emotional Development	Cognitive Development	Socioemotional Development
Early Infancy (0–3 months)	Expression 　Express basic emotions Understanding 　Discriminate between own and other's cry Regulation 　Limited self-soothing behaviors (turning away, sucking)	Basic reflexes; Interest in faces and in sounds with different intonations; Increased ability to adapt reflexes to environmental conditions, see objects clearly and track them from side to side, attend selectively, recognize sights and sounds	Vicarious response to other infant's cry; Imitate adult expression; Parental response to distress; Caregiver-supported emotion regulation; Mutual gaze and face-to-face play increase
Infancy (3–24 months)	Expression 　Emergence of social smile; Increased variability in basic emotions (laughter, fear, frustration, wariness, anger) Understanding 　Begin use of emotion words to refer to own and others' emotional responses Regulation 　Rudimentary emotion-regulation (distraction, movement away from distressing stimuli); Rudimentary forms of behavioral inhibition	Increased auditory and visual skills; Increased attention regulation and visual anticipation; Increased sensitivity to object features, causal relations, conceptual groupings, and tools to support action; Increased memory for familiar stimuli; Increased ability to communicate, use imitative learning, and engage in goal-directed behavior; Rudimentary planning, e.g., moving one object out of the way to grasp another object; Emergence of sense of self	Begin to match emotion expression of others; Understanding of other's emotional expression; Participate in joint attention to people and objects; Use social referencing; Stranger distress and separation anxiety; Display more genuine smile with caregiver; Caregiver-supported emotion regulation; Display of positive emotions encouraged
Toddlerhood (24–36 months)	Expression 　Emergence of secondary emotions (embarrassment, shame, pride, guilt) Understanding 　Label emotional expressions and begin to understand causes and consequences of emotions Regulation 　Behavioral inhibition and emotional self-regulation improve	Language and symbolic skills develop; Increased use of language to direct attention, regulate behaviors, and interact with others; Autobiographical memory appears; Increased display of goal-directed actions, anticipatory skills, and planning behaviors	Emergence of empathy and prosocial behavior; Socialization of emotion expression (Display Rules); Caregiver-supported emotion regulation and coaching; Use of emotion language in the family; Responsive to other people's moods

	Emotional Competence	Cognitive Development	Social/Emotional

Early Childhood (3–5 years)	Expression
	  Decrease in negativity but not in overall intensity of emotional expression; Begin to use emotional dissemblance
	Understanding
	  Increased understanding and use of display rules; Ability to identify emotion eliciting situations
	Regulation
	  Begin to use behavioral emotion regulation strategies (help seeking)
		Increased knowledge base, memory span, and use of mental operations to solve problems; Improved language and communication skills; Improved attention, problem-solving and planning skills; Begin perspective-taking; Use scripts to organize and convey knowledge; Increased awareness of the mind (content, functions); Beginning of executive functioning (awareness of task difficulty, role of effort, and child knowledge in performance)	Begin to understand social regulatory aspects of emotion; Begin to understand reasons for the use of display rules; Able to express emotions effectively and appropriately, e.g., more frequent expression of positive than negative emotions; Able to regulate emotions effectively that are related to social competence; Able to recognize emotions in others from expressive body movements

Middle Childhood (6–10 years)	Expression
	  Improved ability to mask emotions
	Understanding
	  Increased knowledge of the simultaneous experience of multiple emotions
	Regulation
	  Increased use of cognitive emotion regulation strategies and ability to match strategies to the situation
		Able to conserve, take the perspective of others, and reason deductively; Continued improvements in attention, problem-solving, planning, categorizing, and decision-making skills along with their strategic use; Able to distinguish between controllable and uncontrollable events	Decreased reliance on social support for emotion regulation; Use of display rules as a social strategy; Increased understanding that people can experience different emotions about the same event

Note: Information drawn from several sources (see Denham, 1998; Hetherington, Parke, Gauvain, & Locke, 2006; Saarni, 1999; Saarni et al., 2006).

EMOTIONAL EXPRESSION

Emotional expression is central to social interactions and has implications for children's development of socioemotional competence. The extent to which a child is emotionally expressive and responsive is associated with others' perception of that child as a good social partner (Denham, 1998). It appears that infants have an innate capacity to express basic or primary emotions, that is, emotions that can be inferred from facial expressions and do not require self-reflection. Infants display startle, disgust, distress, and reflex smiles in the first weeks of life, and between 3 and 7 months of age begin to display emotions such as anger, interest, surprise, and sadness reliably (Camras, Malatesta, & Izard, 1991). Emotional expression is related to children's increasing perceptual abilities and sensitivity to social information. For instance, infants display what appears to be a precursor of empathy as evidenced by distress in response to another infant's cry. Furthermore, infants are able to discriminate between their own and another infant's cry in that the distress response is not present for recordings of their own cry (Scharfe, 2000). Emotional expression has also been referred to as the first language between children and caregivers, and may contribute to social interactions and the development of attachment relationships in the first few months of life (Denham, 1998; Maccoby, 1994).

Over time, along with the advancement of language and cognitive skills, patterns of emotional expression shift and become more dependent on situational factors. For instance, children display a social smile and display more genuine smiles with caregivers than they do with unfamiliar adults. The facial expression of negative emotion also decreases in the toddler and preschool period as children develop language skills and begin to engage in more verbal expression of emotion. However, the overall intensity of emotional expression is not decreased.

In early and middle childhood, as children are developing skill in perspective taking, children also gradually develop the understanding that emotional expression has social consequences and that their inner experience of emotion does not need to correspond to their outer expressions. As a result, the implementation of self-presentation or emotional dissemblance strategies, that is, the separation of emotional experience from emotional display, emerges. During the preschool years, children demonstrate attempts at masking emotion in disappointing situations or exaggerating emotional expression during pretend play. However, children at this age are not yet able to verbalize this as an explicit strategy (Denham, 1998). By age 5–6, children begin to report planful use of emotional expression and rely on emotional dissemblance as a way to avoid hurting another's feelings or punishment. With development, this tendency expands and is increasingly complex. By age 8 children report the use of emotional dissemblance to protect self-esteem or cope with feelings. By age 9–10 they report the use of emotional dissemblance to regulate interactions with others and adhere to cultural conventions or social standards regarding the appropriate expression of emotions in given contexts and circumstances (Saarni, 1999). These examples illustrate the close connections between the development of emotional expression and cognitive and socioemotional development.

EMOTIONAL UNDERSTANDING

Emotional understanding involves awareness of one's own emotional experience, the ability to discern emotion in others, and knowledge regarding the causes and consequences of emotion as well as the appropriateness of emotional expression in different contexts. Such understanding supports children's attempts to deal with and communicate about emotions they experience and in negotiating their way through social transactions and emotionally arousing situations (Saarni, 1999). Emotional understanding plays a role in reading social situations and social partners accurately, noticing when affective signals are needed, and knowing what affective messages to send and how to send them in a given situational context and is thus important in being able to sustain positive social interactions (Garner & Estep, 2001; Halberstadt, Denham, & Dunsmore, 2001; Saarni, 1999). Knowledge and understanding of emotion undergo many changes with the development of language, cognitive skills, and self-understanding.

Awareness of one's own emotional experience is the most basic of the emotional competence skills (Saarni, 1999) and requires that children have a developed sense of self as distinct from others, which emerges in the middle of the first year (Harter, 1998). Awareness of other's emotions also develops in the first year (as early as 10–12 months) and is evidenced by *social referencing* in which children attend to and make decisions based on other's emotional reactions to novel or potentially fear-provoking events (Feinman, 1982; Repacholi, 1998). By age 2, with the emergence of language skills, children begin to use emotion labels to refer to their own and other's emotions. According to Harris (2000), preschool children are increasingly able to discern other's emotional expressions accurately as well as the causal incidents related to the emotion. With advancements in their understanding of the mind, children also begin to appreciate the connection between desires or expectations and emotion. For instance, children understand that if they receive something they want, then they feel a positive emotion such as happiness or if they do not receive something expected, they may feel a negative emotion such as sadness or disappointment (Terwogt & Stegge, 1998). In middle childhood, at about age 7, children's understanding of the causes and consequences of emotion becomes more complex as children realize that the same situation can elicit different emotions in different people depending on the perspective of the individual and that one can experience multiple emotions at the same time (Saarni, 1999). Other aspects of emotional understanding that continue into middle and later childhood include knowledge about the consequences of emotional expression, such as knowledge of the effect that one's emotional expression can have on others or the situation, knowledge of display rules, and knowledge of emotion regulation or coping strategies.

EMOTION REGULATION

Emotion regulation as a construct varies across studies in its definition and how it is operationalized (Cole, Martin, & Dennis, 2004). On a general level, emotion regulation refers to the processes involved in coping with positive and negative emotions. It consists of both intrinsic and extrinsic processes responsible for monitoring, evaluating, and modifying the dynamic features of emotional experience, including the intensive and temporal features, in order to accomplish one's goals (Kopp, 1989; Thompson, 1994). Emotion regulation is one of the most important of the emotional competence skills in that it plays a central role in the pursuit and accomplishment of individual goals. Specifically, emotion regulation is important for facilitating performance on tasks requiring inhibition, sustained attention, or replacement of current for long-term goals (Thompson, 1994). It is associated with children's social competence (Eisenberg & Fabes, 1999) and relies on the development of cognitive skills.

Kopp (1989) outlined several developmental trends in the development of emotion regulation. Early in life, children are extremely reliant on caregivers to assist in the regulation of emotion, but they are capable of some rudimentary forms of emotion regulation. The first attempts in the first days of life include reflexive and simple behaviors such as head turning and sucking. Between 3 and 9 months infants develop more motor maturity, improved attention processes and vision, and can begin to engage in more effective self-distraction and self-soothing physical behaviors (e.g., thumb sucking, gaze aversion). Toward the end of the first year with the development of cognitive skills including anticipation and intentionality as well as increased physical capability, children anticipate that caregivers will respond to and aid with emotional distress. They also begin to rely on social cues via social referencing as a means of interpreting various emotional or novel experiences. In the toddler period (age 2–3) children develop an increased sense of agency and have greater awareness of the causes of emotional distress and can thus begin to engage in what Kopp (1997) refers to as planful emotion regulation with the support of the caregiver. Also, with the development of language, children can begin to regulate emotion by stating their feelings to others, and they can receive verbal feedback and coaching about their emotional expression and emotion regulation.

Children's repertoire of emotional regulation skills continues to become more sophisticated in preschool and early childhood as they advance cognitively. Children have available to them internal coping strategies, such as cognitive restructuring, as well as external or behavioral strategies, such as emotion dissemblance or problem-focused coping (Saarni, 1999). Children also transition from a reliance on others (e.g., help seeking) to more solitary emotion regulation strategies (Brenner & Salovey, 1997). Research has demonstrated both stability and change in children's emotion regulation skills from preschool into middle and later childhood with children maintaining their relative standing among the group with respect to their emotional functioning as assessed by emotional intensity and emotion regulation skills (Losoya, Eisenberg, & Fabes, 1998; Murphy, Eisenberg, Fabes, Shepard, & Guthrie, 1999). By age 10, children are able to generate more coping alternatives and show an overall increase in cognitive emotion regulation strategies, particularly in situations in which they have minimal control (Saarni, 1999). Thus, emotion regulation skills undergo many changes from early infancy through later childhood with a shift from reliance on others to more solitary efforts as well as from behavioral strategies to cognitive strategies.

As the summary above indicates, emotional, cognitive. and social development are interrelated across development. We recognize that identifying causal or even facilitative links among these areas either within or across developmental periods is, for the most part, difficult. Although this difficulty may be due in some measure to empirical limitations, it is likely that these areas of functioning belie clear connections of this sort because, over development, they are in continuous and dynamic transactions with each other. This is not to say that causal relations do not exist; some may. For example, the absence or severely limited range of a particular capability in one area may interfere with further development in other areas. Such a pattern may describe the increasingly pervasive effects of autism as children advance in years. However, for children within normal range, the presence of a capability, even in rudimentary form, may be sufficient for a child to enter into a transaction that can then facilitate further development of this and related capabilities. For example, an infant with very limited self-soothing skills may display a behavior, perhaps accidentally, that communicates to the caregiver the need to be soothed by another. This behavior may then set in motion the social process described as caregiver-supported emotion regulation, which may, in turn, bootstrap the early development of other emotional or cognitive capabilities, such as the social smile or more advanced attention skills. In brief, given the complex interrelations of these areas of psychological development, we are not prepared to suggest causal links but, rather, have examined these developmentally related changes as a unit, albeit a unit in which the exact interconnections are presently unknown. With this information as background, we now turn to the relations between the development of planning skills and emotional competence in the context of parent–child interaction.

The Development of Executive Function and Planning Skills in the Family Context

Executive function includes effortful, higher-order psychological processes involved in the conscious control of thought and action, goal-directed responses, and self-regulatory ability, such as attentional flexibility, inhibitory control (e.g., ability to redirect a strong habitual response), and decision-making. Planning is an important aspect of executive function (Hughes & Graham, 2002; Zelazo & Müller, 2002), and the development of planning skills is critical for mature social and cognitive activity. Although infants can engage in rudimentary planning, it is in the preschool years that children begin to understand what a plan is, when a plan is needed, and how to devise a simple plan in advance of action (Haith, Benson, Roberts, & Pennington, 1994). Over middle childhood, planning competence increases; children can plan several steps in advance and suspend action to monitor and evaluate a plan as it is being implemented (see Friedman & Scholnick, 1997). Planning skills increase in importance throughout childhood in that they help children manage school-related demands and balance various activities, such as homework assignments, family and chore responsibilities, and recreational activities that require children to behave in planful ways (Blair, 2002; Kopp, 1997).

Although much of the research on planning has concentrated on how children plan on their own, particularly in the laboratory, planning outside the laboratory often involves coordinating actions with others. Research that has examined planning in social context has demonstrated that children can develop planning skills through participation in planning activities with adults. In these situations, adults help children develop planning skills by assuming some of the more difficult components of planning and by modeling planning behaviors for children (Gauvain, 2001). Opportunities for children to learn about planning in social context are particularly likely to emerge when children are allowed or encouraged to share responsibility for planning. When children are not collaboratively involved in planning, for instance when adults divide responsibility for planning among the participants or utilize children in instrumental ways to carry out an adult's plan, children learn less about planning (Gauvain & Rogoff, 1989). Thus, while adult instruction may help improve children's planning skills, it appears essential that the child participate actively in the process for this learning to occur.

To support children's participation in and learning about planning in social context, adults need to understand the task at hand and have some conception of what they can do to help a child on the basis of their interaction with and observation of the child. Some of the information important to the interaction and its outcomes may extend beyond the immediate task experience. For instance, research has demonstrated that, for varying reasons (e.g., child behavior and compliance problems, child temperament, and task difficulty), parental instruction and guidance varies in sensitivity to children's presenting capabilities and needs (Gauvain & Perez, 2008; Gauvain & Fagot, 1995; Rogoff, Ellis, & Gardner, 1984; Winsler et al., 1999). When sensitive cognitive support does not occur, fewer cognitive gains for children emerge as seen in poorer performance on follow-up tests in comparison to children who receive more sensitive instruction.

Better understanding of variations in children's opportunities to learn and develop skills in social context is needed. Such research will improve understanding of the social nature of cognitive development, especially in areas like executive functions, and may provide insight into patterns of individual and cultural variability in cognitive development. For instance, we know that the development of planning in social context relies on the ways in which the more skilled partner and the child participate in cognitive activity, with some patterns of participation being more beneficial than others. We also know that there is variation in adult–child planning patterns. Specifically, not all adults support children's experience during joint planning in ways that benefit learning. Variation in parental support can stem from many sources, including the parent's skill at planning or cognitive assistance, parental stress, and parenting style. In an analysis of the family interaction data from the Family Socialization and Developmental Competence Project (Baumrind, 1973), Gauvain and Huard (1999) found that children with directive or authoritarian parents initiated fewer planning discussions in middle childhood and adolescence than did children whose parents used other parenting styles. Despite high levels of maturity demands in directive households, the accompanying low level of warmth and responsiveness in these families may not encourage the development of children's planning skills. This observation is consistent with research that shows that directive parenting does not foster autonomy in children and further specifies this relation in terms of cognitive components that may underlie autonomy.

It has been increasingly recognized that the effects of cognitive and emotional processes are reciprocal and work together to shape developmental outcomes (Keenan, 2002; Thompson, 1994). Learning, which is a primary facet of development, is a process that involves cognitive components, ranging from basic skills to higher-order metacognitive skills, and emotional components, especially components involved in focusing attention on important elements of the environment, prioritization of activity, and maintaining motivation (Blair, 2002; Brown, Bransford, Ferrara, & Campione, 1983; Lemerise & Arsenio, 2000). To elaborate on this point our discussion turns to ways in which emotional development may influence or contribute to opportunities to develop planning skills in the context of parent–child interaction.

The Development of Emotional Competence in the Family Context: Relations with the Development of Planning Skills

Emotions are a significant component of social interactions in that they serve as an important source of information to the person experiencing the emotion and to those with whom the individual is communicating (Halberstadt et al., 2001). Thus, mature functioning, particularly in social contexts, is contingent upon emotional competence. This view is consistent with the functionalist approach to emotional development, which serves as the theoretical basis of this discussion. The functionalist approach emphasizes the practical importance of emotions in managing relations between the individual and the environment. This approach considers emotions as dynamic processes within social interactions that can create and facilitate social relationships and that can also be created in the course of social interactions (see Saarni et al., 2006). In other words, emotions are purposeful in that they involve the individual's attempt or readiness to establish, maintain, or in some way alter the relations between the individual and the environment, particularly on matters or with individuals of significance to the person. Emotions are seen as closely linked to action, specifically in terms of preparation for and performance of actions in relation to events or people in the environment that are significant to the individual. Thus, emotions are functional; they affect the way in which the person and environment, including people in the environment, relate to each other. As such, emotions are an inherent part of social interaction as well as implicated in planning as people anticipate, prepare for, and navigate their way through social experiences.

Both research and theory have focused on the socialization of children's emotion within the family context. This research indicates that parenting practices, such as parent–child discourse, modeling of emotion, reactions to children's displays of emotion, and teaching about emotion, influence children's development of emotional competence (e.g., Denham, 1998; Halberstadt & Eaton, 2002; Harris, 2000; Parke, 1994; Saarni, 1999). Theory helps us to understand what processes may underlie these associations. Models of parenting posited by Dix (1991) highlight the importance of emotion in examining what he terms *parental competence.* Dix suggests that parenting is itself an emotional experience and that emotions guide parenting behaviors and influence the strategies that parents use to understand and control emotions in themselves and in their children. Another approach, proposed by Gottman et al. (1996), discusses parental meta-emotional philosophy, which consists of parents' organized sets of feelings and thoughts about their own and their children's emotions along with how the parents' emotions are expressed in their parenting behaviors and, thereby, influence children's emotional experience and expression. Gottman et al. consider meta-emotion philosophy to refer to the executive functions of emotions and, thus, as parallel to the executive functions of cognition. In their research, Gottman et al. have identified different meta-emotion philosophies in parents, including an emotion-coaching philosophy in which parents have a high sense of awareness of emotion; a reactive-instructional philosophy in which the child's expression of emotion presents opportunities to the parent to teach the child about emotion; a cognitive form of emotion coaching in which children are taught explicitly about emotion (e.g., labeling an emotion, discussion of goals and strategies for dealing with the situation that led to the emotion); and a dismissing meta-emotion philosophy in which parents have a low sense of awareness about emotion, a tendency to deny or ignore negative emotion, endorse the view that negative emotions need to be changed as quickly as possible, and a low level of emotion coaching (e.g., conveying to children that emotions are not very important). These patterns have different relations to the development of emotional competence in children and their relations are both indirect, through more general parenting practices and temperamental differences in children, and direct, through the coaching of emotion regulation and the development of emotion regulation abilities.

Another conception is presented by Eisenberg et al. (1998), who suggest that the development of understanding, experience, expression, and regulation of emotion in children is subject to parental socialization via parents' beliefs about emotions (e.g., negative emotions are bad and should be controlled). This approach explicitly allows for cultural and other forms of variation in emotion socialization because goals and practices may vary with culture-specific situational contexts, child characteristics (e.g., sex, age, temperament), and even the specific emotion of concern (e.g., sadness vs. anger).

Although little is understood about how socialization goals and practices regarding emotion may vary by culture and context, observations of cultural variation in socialization practices related to emotional control have been reported by psychologists and anthropologists (e.g., Mead, 1963; Whiting & Child, 1953; Whiting & Edwards, 1988). Such observations suggest that cultural value systems include ideas about the extent and type of emotional expressions that are appropriate and that more experienced cultural members are involved in inculcating these values and their associated behaviors to children. Much of the research identifying cultural differences in the expression and experience of emotions has concentrated on the emotional experience of adults (e.g., Kitayama & Marcus, 1994; Matsumoto, 1993; Wierzbicka, 1999). This research has implications for developmental study, however. For instance, affect valuation theory as posited by Tsai et al. (2006) examines the balance between and individual's sense of ideal affect, that is, the affective states the person values and would ideally like to feel, something that is likely to be shaped by cultural factors; and actual affect, that is, the affective states that the person actually feels, something likely to be influenced by temperament. Their findings have indicated that people do identify and distinguish ideal and actual affect in themselves, and that cultural differences lead to variations in this understanding. For example, people from individualistic cultures, such as European Americans, tend to value high-arousal positive affect, such as excitement, to a greater extent than do those from collectivistic cultures, such as Hong Kong Chinese, who tend to value low-arousal positive affect, such as a state-of-calm. Although the research discussed earlier (Kitayama & Marcus, 1994; Matsumoto, 1993; Tsai et al., 2006; Wierzbicka, 1999) was conducted with adults, it is reasonable to assert that such values regarding certain types of emotions, along with the identification of discrepancies between ideal and actual affect as defined in a particular cultural context, may lead to variation in socialization goals for children's emotion development.

Recent research by Halberstadt, Dunsmore, and colleagues (e.g., Dunsmore & Karn, 2004; Halberstadt et al., 2006; Dunsmore, Her, Halberstadt, & Perez-Rivera, 2009) suggests that one way in which culture may play a role in the socialization of emotion is via parental beliefs about emotion. Their findings have indicated that parental beliefs about emotion along the dimensions of whether emotions are valuable, dangerous, or controllable, and whether parents need to guide children's emotions are related to mothers' own emotional expressiveness, reactions to children's displays of emotion, and discussion of emotion.

Parental beliefs about emotions and mother's emotional expressiveness are, in turn, related to various child outcomes including aspects of emotional competence such as the recognition of emotion in others and emotion regulation skills.

More research regarding cultural values, beliefs, and practices with regard to the socialization of emotion is needed. The theory and research discussed here suggest that the broad socialization goal that children become competent members of the culture in which they live pertains to both cognitive and emotional areas of development. This assertion coincides with our claim that cognitive and emotional development cannot be examined meaningfully apart from the cultural context and social transactions that shape and guide such development. We now explore ways in which three areas of emotional competence, expression, understanding, and regulation, may be related or contribute to the development of planning skills in social context.

THE RELATION OF EMOTIONAL COMPETENCE WITH THE DEVELOPMENT OF PLANNING SKILLS

Both normative developmental changes and individual differences in children's emotional functioning may contribute to children's opportunities to develop planning skills in the family context. Variation in children's ability to display emotion appropriately in social contexts, tendencies toward overarousal or the experience of negative emotion, and emotion regulation skills may influence children's ability to engage in complex cognitive activities like planning and their opportunities to develop these skills during social interaction with more skilled partners. Research has demonstrated that children with a tendency toward overarousal and the experience of negative emotion are perceived to demonstrate poor social competence by teachers and peers (e.g., Eisenberg et al., 1995). Individuals with a tendency toward expressing negative emotions, such as anger, frustration, or sadness, tend to be less effective at processing information (Cummings & Davies, 1995). Evidence from neuroscience suggests that negative emotion results in a deactivation of the frontal areas of the brain associated with higher-order cognitive functioning as well as the ability to regulate attention and behavior (Davis, Bruce, & Gunnar, 2002), and children prone to negative emotionality do display deficits in their ability to focus attention (Fox & Calkins, 2003; Keenan, 2002).

Variation in the development of emotion regulation may also be important to consider. Research has suggested that emotion regulation strategies can be differentiated according to more and less adaptive strategies, particularly with regard to social functioning (Eisenberg et al., 1995). Saarni (1999) suggests that problem-solving strategies, support-seeking strategies, distraction, and cognitive reframing tend to be more adaptive emotion regulation methods in comparison to avoidance strategies (e.g., withdrawing from others), internalizing strategies (e.g., covering up anxious feelings), or externalizing strategies (e.g., venting, blaming) as evidenced by more effective social and emotional functioning.

There are also individual differences in a set of skills referred to as executive control, which underlie processes of both emotion regulation and higher-order cognitive functioning (Eisenberg, Smith, Sadovsky, & Spinrad, 2004). Executive control processes include attentional regulation and response inhibition or inhibitory control, which aid in the control of emotional expression and intensity (Fox & Calkins, 2003). These control processes also enable the pursuit of short- and long-term goals. Attention regulation and inhibitory control are considered to be dimensions of temperament and individual differences in each of these control processes can be identified as early as the first year (Davis et al., 2002; Rothbart, Ahadi, Hershey, & Fisher, 2001; Rothbart & Posner, 2001). Attention is important to the regulation of emotion in that the ability to focus on alternative stimuli, as in distraction strategies, may help modulate emotional reactivity (Kopp, 1989). Inhibitory control involves the ability to withhold a response, interrupt a process that has already begun, avoid interference with ongoing activity, or delay a response, skills central to the ability to regulate emotional arousal and engage in adaptive coping skills (Tamm, Menon, & Reiss, 2002). These forms of regulation have implications for cognitive development in general, and specifically for the development of planning skills. Deficits in inhibitory control have been associated with poorer performance on planning tasks in early childhood (Brophy, Taylor, & Hughes, 2002).

The research reviewed here suggests that variation in emotional competence may play a significant role in children's opportunities to develop planning skills in social context. For instance, children skilled at socially appropriate emotional expression may be more effective at soliciting and receiving help in learning contexts because they display more success in social interaction in general (Halberstadt et al., 2001). Findings from our research (Perez, 2004; Perez & Gauvain, 2009) indicated that children who expressed more frustration during a planning task had mothers who focused more on regulating children's behavior rather than learning goals and also displayed more negative affect themselves. Thus, emotional expression may not only play an important role in maintaining general social interaction, but may also contribute to what children can gain from interactions in which teaching and learning are the goals.

Our research (Perez, 2004; Perez & Gauvain, 2005; Perez & Gauvain, 2009) has also demonstrated that children high in emotional intensity and negative emotionality, when working on a planning task independently, demonstrated less effective planning in terms of their overall engagement in the task and the types of strategies used to complete the task. In addition, mothers of children high in emotional intensity and negative emotionality issued more directives to children and displayed more negative affect while working on a joint planning task. These relations were found despite a lack of relations between children's emotional intensity and child performance on the task during mother–child interaction. Perhaps mothers, who anticipate interactions with their children to be difficult due to children's high emotional arousal, are more directive and controlling of their children's behavior during instruction as a means of managing the interaction and enabling completion of the planning task, even in the absence of difficult behaviors from children in the immediate task context. However, mothers who do not anticipate such difficulty may approach the task with the child in a way that promotes learning versus behavior management.

Finally, our research indicated that children who display deficits in attention focusing and inhibitory control planned less effectively on their own and when working with their mother. We also found that children who reported using less adaptive emotion regulation skills, such as avoidance and externalizing behavior, were less engaged in planning when they worked on their own and with mother. Mothers of these children provided more instruction aimed at regulating the child's behavior versus instruction that promoted learning. Some forms of emotion regulation appeared to moderate the relation between children's emotional intensity and children's and mother's behaviors during planning, however. Children who reported using more adaptive emotion regulation skills, such as cognitive restructuring and distraction, were more engaged in the task and received more learning promotion instruction from mothers regardless of the child's level of emotional intensity (Perez & Gauvain, 2005).

Together, these findings indicate the relevance of examining emotional contributions to children's opportunities to develop planning skills in social context. They also suggest that the cognitive requirements of planning interact with emotional competence in ways that can interfere with children's ability to devise and execute a plan, whether children plan alone or with a parent. We expect that parental support for the development of other executive functioning skills might follow a similar course. The demands of planning that appeared to exacerbate the interactions of parents and children with emotional difficulties, such as attentional and inhibitory control and other forms of voluntary regulation, are also present in situations that entail other metacognitive or executive skills. This claim does not imply that social support for the development of executive functions is more important than the neural changes associated with this development. Rather, as Nelson, Thomas, and De

Haan (2006) stress, changes in the prefrontal cortex are informed by and interact with other brain regions and with experience. Our aim is to direct attention to one important set of developmental experiences, interactions with parents, and how these experiences may relate in a systematic and interrelated way to the development of emotional competence and executive functions.

Concluding Comments

The research and theory reviewed in this chapter suggest that children's emotional competence and skill at using executive functions, such as planning, develop in social context with the guidance of more skilled partners who support children's development via culturally influenced socialization goals. Our primary goal was to draw attention to the mutual influences of emotional and cognitive development across childhood in the area of executive functions as well as underscore the contributions made in the social context of the family to this developmental process. Specifically, children's emotional competence appears to contribute to the pattern of social interactions children have with others, especially familiar and emotionally connected others like parents, as well as children's ability to engage in and learn about complex cognitive skills in social context. To support this claim we described research, including our own findings, which focused on how children who differed in emotional competence interacted with others during joint cognitive activity that involved planning. Children with emotional difficulties, especially children with less adaptive regulatory capabilities, planned less well alone and appeared to benefit less from planning with mother than did children without emotional difficulties or children with such difficulties but who had more adaptive regulatory skills available. The observation that children with emotional difficulties may not experience or benefit from planning with a more experienced partner to the same degree as children without these difficulties is particularly troubling when paired with our observations that these children had difficulty planning on their own, and were, therefore, in need of adult assistance. However, the fact that children with emotional difficulties who had more adaptive regulatory skills fared better cognitively during planning interactions raises interesting issues. The repercussions of these parent–child interactions are important to consider.

Theory regarding the consequences that may emerge from varying patterns of parent–child interactions during joint cognitive activity as related to children's cognitive and emotional development will depend, in part, on how observed patterns are interpreted. On the one hand, it may be that adult instruction that focuses on behavior regulation and directives is less than optimal and because this may be a form of instruction that children with emotional difficulties are more likely to experience, especially in the years when executive skills are developing, children with emotional difficulties may have fewer social opportunities to develop and practice these skills. On the other hand, it may be that for mothers and children who share a history of problematic interactions related to child emotional competence, interaction during joint cognitive activity provides further evidence, especially for the mother, of the child's difficulties on tasks such as these. Thus, it may be that the behavior regulation and directives observed when mothers collaborate on a cognitive task with children demonstrating emotional difficulties provide increased structure for the child's learning and, thereby, minimize the impact of children's emotional difficulties on these experiences. This, in turn, may help children's performance and opportunities to learn from these interactions. This interpretation is consistent with Vygotsky's (1978) notion of the zone of proximal development, which suggests that more skilled partners will use an instructional approach that addresses the child's learning needs. Perhaps, in these cases, rather than directive or controlling behavior reflecting a less than optimal form of instruction, it represents an adaptive instructional strategy for scaffolding the cognitive development of children experiencing difficulty that is related to their individual differences in emotional regulation. In other words, child emotionality may function to adjust the scaffolding an adult provides for learning during joint activity.

There are two points to make about the nature and long-range consequences implied in these patterns. First, these patterns illustrate the functionalist view of emotions, that is, as purposeful, dynamic processes that are closely linked to action, particularly in relation to events or people in the environment that are significant to the individual. Second, if experience in the social context is a critical component of cognitive development, as sociocultural theory contends, then there are two long-range possibilities. Children with emotional difficulties may experience a cumulative toll in terms of the development of planning skills, and perhaps other executive functions, as a result of the types of interactional difficulties that emerge. That is, children with emotional difficulties may have fewer or at least different opportunities to learn about and practice planning during social interaction with parents than children who do not have such difficulties. These difficulties may have carry over effects when children enter school, and both the expectation by teachers of planning skills and the possibility that teachers may compare same age children on this dimension may cascade into a new set of difficulties for these children in that social setting. Second, children, over time, may improve in the skills with which they struggle as a result of difficulties in emotional functioning precisely because more skilled partners provide sensitive instruction on the basis of children's needs.

These partners may also help by modeling ways to approach or structure a task that may, in turn, influence how children with emotional difficulties learn to regulate the overarousal that may accompany a new learning situation. Thus, perhaps one way to improve children's learning opportunities in social context may be to provide tasks with clearly defined goals. In other words, explicit structuring of cognitive activities may reduce the learning demands that can undermine the success of children with emotional difficulties. This suggestion is akin to Saxe's (1991) observation that adults can support children's learning by dividing the task into manageable subgoals. However, it extends this idea into the realm of metacognitive or executive functioning as a means of helping children regulate emotional factors that interfere with learning about or implementing executive skills. In conclusion, more research on the integration of emotional development and executive functioning is needed. We hope that our discussion will influence this research by encouraging consideration of the important role of the social context, especially the family, in the development and refinement of these mutually influential capabilities that, together, make significant contributions to children's psychological development and well-being.

REFERENCES

Baumrind, D. (1973). The development of instrumental competence through socialization. In A. Pick (Ed.), *Minnesota symposium on child psychology* (Vol. 7, pp. 3–46). Minneapolis, MN: University of Minnesota Press.

Bjorklund, D. F., & Pelligrini, A. D. (2000). Child development and evolutionary psychology. *Child Development, 71,* 1687–1708.

Blair, C. (2002). School readiness: Integrating cognition and emotion in a neurobiological conceptualization of children's functioning at school entry. *American Psychologist, 57,* 111–127.

Brenner, E. M., & Salovey, P. (1997). Emotion regulation during childhood: Developmental, interpersonal, and individual considerations. In P. Salovey & D. J. Sluyter (Eds.), *Emotional development and emotional intelligence: Educational implications* (pp. 168–195). New York: Basic Books.

Bronfenbrenner, U., & Morris, P. A. (2006). The bioecological model of human development. In W. Damon & R. M. Lerner (Eds.), *Handbook of child psychology: Theoretical models of human development* (6th ed., Vol. 1, pp. 793–828). New York: Wiley.

Brophy, M., Taylor, E., & Hughes, C. (2002). To go or not to go: Inhibitory control in "hard to manage" children. *Infant & Child Development, 11,* 125–140.

Brown, A. L., Bransford, J. D., Ferrara, R. A., & Campione, J. C. (1983). Learning, remembering, and understanding. In J. H. Flavell & E. M. Markman (Eds.), *Handbook of child psychology* (Vol. 3, pp. 515–629). New York: Wiley.

Bugental, D. B., & Grusec, J. E. (2006). Socialization processes. In W. Damon & R. M. Lerner (Series Eds.) and N. Eisenberg (Vol. Ed.), *Handbook of child psychology: Social, emotional, and personality development* (6th ed., Vol. 3, pp. 366–428). New York: Wiley.

Camras, L. A., Malatesta, C., & Izard, C. E. (1991). The development of facial expressions in infancy. In R. S. Feldman & B. Rimé (Eds.), *Fundamentals of nonverbal behavior* (pp. 73–105). New York: Cambridge University Press.

Cole, P. M., Martin, S. E., & Dennis, T. A. (2004). Emotion regulation as a scientific construct: Methodological challenges and directions for child development research. *Child Development, 75*, 317–333.

Cummings, E. M., & Davies, P. T. (1995). The impact of parents on their children: An emotional security perspective. *Annals of Child Development, 10*, 167–208.

Davis, E. P., Bruce, J., & Gunnar, M. R. (2002). The anterior attention network: Associations with temperament and neuroendocrine activity in 6-year-old children. *Developmental Psychobiology, 40*, 43–56.

Denham, S. A. (1998). *Emotional development in young children.* New York: The Guilford Press.

Diamond, A. (2002). Normal development of prefrontal cortex from birth to young adulthood: Cognitive functions, anatomy, and biochemistry. In D. Stuss & R. Knight (Eds.), *Principles of frontal lobe function* (pp. 466–503). New York: Oxford University Press.

Dix, T. (1991). The affective organization of parenting: Adaptive and maladaptive processes. *Psychological Bulletin, 110*, 3–25.

Dunsmore, J. C., Her, P., Halberstadt, A. G., & Perez-Rivera, M. B. (2009). Parents' beliefs about emotions and children's recognition of parents' emotions. *Journal of Nonverbal Behavior, 33*, 121–140.

Dunsmore, J. C., & Karn, M. A. (2004). The influence of peer relationships and maternal socialization on kindergartners' developing emotion knowledge. *Early Education and Development, 15*, 39–56.

Eisenberg, N., Cumberland, A., & Spinrad, T. L. (1998). Parental socialization of emotion. *Psychological Inquiry, 9*, 241–273.

Eisenberg, N. Damon, W., & Lerner, R. M. (Eds.). (2006). *Handbook of child psychology: Vol. 3, Social, emotional, and personality development (6th ed.).* Hoboken, NJ: John Wiley & Sons Inc.

Eisenberg, N., & Fabes, R. A. (1999). Emotion, emotion-related regulation, and quality of socio-emotional functioning. In L. Balter & C. Tamis-LeMonda (Eds.), *Child psychology: A handbook of contemporary issues* (pp. 318–335). Philadelphia, PA: Psychology Press.

Eisenberg, N., Fabes, R. A., Murphy, B., Maszk, P., Smith, M., & Karbon, M. (1995). The role of emotionality and regulation in children's social functioning: A longitudinal study. *Child Development, 66*, 1360–1384.

Eisenberg, N., Smith, C. L., Sadovsky, A., & Spinrad, T. L. (2004). Effortful control: Relations with emotion regulation, adjustment, and socialization in childhood. In

R. F. Baumeister & K. D. Vohs (Eds.), *Handbook of self-regulation: Research, theory, and applications* (pp. 259–282). New York: The Guilford Press.

Feinman, S. (1982). *Social referencing and the social construction of reality in infancy.* New York: Plenum Press.

Fox, N. A., & Calkins, S. D. (2003). The development of self-control of emotion: Intrinsic and extrinsic influences. *Motivation and Emotion, 27,* 7–26.

Friedman, S. L., & Scholnick, E. K. (1997). *The developmental psychology of planning.* Mahwah, NJ: Lawrence Erlbaum Associates.

Garner, P. W., & Estep, K. M. (2001). Emotional competence, emotion socialization, and young children's peer-related social competence. *Early Education and Development, 12,* 29–48.

Gauvain, M. (2001). *The social context of cognitive development.* New York: The Guilford Press.

Gauvain, M., & DeMent, T. (1991). The role of shared social history in parent-child cognitive activity. *The Quarterly Newsletter of the Laboratory of Comparative Human Cognition, 13,* 58–66.

Gauvain, M., & Fagot, B. (1995). Child temperament as a mediator of mother-toddler problem solving. *Social Development, 4,* 257–276.

Gauvain, M., & Huard, R. D. (1999). Family interaction, parenting style and the development of planning: A longitudinal analysis using archival data. *Journal of Family Psychology, 13,* 1–18.

Gauvain, M., & Perez, S. M. (2005). Parent-child participation in planning children's activities outside of school in European- and Latino-American families. *Child Development, 76,* 371–383.

Gauvain, M., & Perez, S. M. (2007). The socialization of cognition. In J. E. Grusec & P. D. Hastings (Eds.), *Handbook of Socialization: Theory and research* (pp. 588–613). New York: The Guilford Press.

Gauvain, M., & Perez, S. M. (2008). Mother-child planning and child compliance. *Child Development, 79,* 761–775.

Gauvain, M., & Rogoff, B. (1989). Collaborative problem solving and children's planning skills. *Developmental Psychology, 25,* 139–151.

Gottman, J. M., Katz, L. F., & Hooven, C. (1996). Parental meta-emotion philosophy and the emotional life of families: Theoretical models and preliminary data. *Journal of Family Psychology, 10,* 243–268.

Haith, M. M., Benson, J. B., Roberts, R. J. J., & Pennington, B. F. (Eds.). (1994). *The development of future-oriented processes.* Chicago, IL: University of Chicago Press.

Halberstadt, A. G., Beale, K., Parker, A., Stelter, R., Craig, A., & Bryant, A. (2006, August). *Parents' beliefs about children's emotion: A questionnaire.* Paper presented at the Annual Conference of the International Society for Research on Emotions, Atlanta, GA.

Halberstadt, A. G., Denham, S. A., & Dunsmore, J. C. (2001). Affective social competence. *Social Development, 10,* 79–119.

Halberstadt, A. G., & Eaton, K. L. (2002). A meta-analysis of family expressiveness and children's emotion expressiveness and understanding. *Marriage & Family Review, 34*, 35–62.

Harris, P. L. (2000). Understanding emotion. In M. Lewis & J. M. Haviland-Jones (Eds.), *Handbook of emotions* (2nd ed., pp. 281–292). New York: The Guilford Press.

Harter, S. (1998). The development of self-representations. In W. Damon & N. Eisenberg (Eds.), *Handbook of child psychology: Social, emotional, and personality development* (5th ed., Vol. 3, pp. 553–617). Hoboken, NJ: John Wiley & Sons Inc.

Hetherington, E. M., Parke, R. D., Gauvain, M., & Locke, V. O. (2006). *Child psychology: A contemporary viewpoint.* New York: McGraw Hill.

Hughes, C., & Graham, A. (2002). Measuring executive functions in childhood: Problems and solutions? *Child and Adolescent Mental Health, 7*, 131–142.

Keenan, T. (2002). Negative affect predicts performance on an object permanence task. *Developmental Science, 5*, 65–71.

Kitayama, S., & Marcus, H. R. (1994). *Emotion and culture: Empirical studies of mutual influence.* Washington, DC: American Psychological Association.

Kopp, C. B. (1997). Young children: Emotion management, instrumental control, and plans. In S. L. Friedman & E. K. Scholnick (Eds.), *The developmental psychology of planning: Why, how, and when do we plan?* (pp. 103–124). Mahwah, NJ: Lawrence Erlbaum Associates.

Kopp, C. B. (1989). Regulation of distress and negative emotions: A developmental view. *Developmental Psychology, 25*, 343–354.

Kuhn, D., Siegler, R. S., Damon, W., & Lerner, R. M. (Eds.). (2006). *Handbook of child psychology: Vol 2, Cognition, perception, and language* (6th ed.). Hoboken, NJ: John Wiley & Sons Inc.

Lemerise, E. A., & Arsenio, W. F. (2000). An integrated model of emotion processes and cognition in social information processing. *Child Development, 71*, 107–118.

Lewis, M., Haviland-Jones, J. M., & Barrett, L. F. (2008). *Handbook of emotions, 3rd ed.* New York: The Guilford Press.

Losoya, S., Eisenberg, N., & Fabes, R. A. (1998). Developmental issues in the study of coping. *International Journal of Behavioral Development, 22*, 287–313.

Maccoby, E. E. (1994). The role of parents in the socialization of children: An historical overview. In R. D. Parke, P. A. Ornstein, J. J. Rieser, & C. Zahn-Waxler (Eds.), *A century of developmental psychology* (pp. 589–615). Washington, DC: American Psychological Association.

Matsumoto, D. (1993). Ethnic differences in affect intensity, emotion judgments, display rule attitudes, and self-reported emotional expression in an American sample. *Motivation and Emotion, 17*, 107–123.

Mead, M. (1963). Socialization and acculturation. *Current Anthropology, 4*, 184–188.

Murphy, B. C., Eisenberg, N., Fabes, R. A., Shepard, S., & Guthrie, I. K. (1999). Consistency and change in children's emotionality and regulation: A longitudinal study. *Merrill-Palmer Quarterly, 45*, 413–444.

Nelson, C. A., Thomas, K. M., & De Haan, M. (2006). Neural bases of cognitive development. In W. Damon & R. M. Lerner (Series Eds.) and D. Kuhn & R. S. Siegler (Vol. Eds.), *Handbook of child psychology: Cognition, perception, and language* (6th ed., Vol. 2, pp. 3–57). New York: Wiley.

Parke, R. D. (1994). Progress, paradigms, and unresolved problems: A commentary on recent advances in our understanding of children's emotions. *Merrill-Palmer Quarterly, 40*, 157–169.

Perez, S. M. (2004). Relations among child emotionality, mother-child planning, and children's academic adjustment and achievement in the first grade (Doctoral dissertation, University of California, Riverside, 2004). *Dissertaion Abstracts International, 65*, 2128.

Perez, S. M., & Gauvain, M. (2005). The role of child emotionality in child behavior and maternal instruction on planning tasks. *Social Development, 14*, 250–272.

Perez, S. M., & Gauvain, M. (2009). Mother-child planning, child emotional functioning, and children's transition to first grade. *Child Development, 80*, 776–791.

Plomin, R. (1990). *Nature and nurture: An introduction to behavioral genetics.* Belmont, CA: Brooks/Cole.

Repacholi, B. M. (1998). Infants' use of attentional cues to identify the referent of another person's emotional expression. *Developmental Psychology, 34*, 1017–1025.

Rogoff, B. (2003). *The cultural nature of human development.* New York: Oxford University Press.

Rogoff, B., Ellis, S., & Gardner, W. (1984). Adjustment of adult-child instruction according to child's age and task. *Developmental Psychology, 20*, 193–199.

Rogoff, B., Gauvain, M., & Gardner, W. (1987). The development of children's skill in adjusting plans to circumstances. In S. L. Friedman, E. K. Scholnick, & R. R. Cocking (Eds.), *Blueprints for thinking: The role of planning in psychological development* (pp. 303–320). New York: Cambridge University Press.

Rothbart, M. K., Ahadi, S. A., Hershey, K. L., & Fisher, P. (2001). Investigations of temperament at three to seven years: The children's behavior questionnaire. *Child Development, 72*, 1394–1408.

Rothbart, M. K., & Posner, M. I. (2001). Mechanism and variation in the development of attentional networks. In C. A. Nelson & M. Luciana (Eds.), *Handbook of developmental cognitive neuroscience* (pp. 353–363). Cambridge, MA: MIT Press.

Saarni, C. (1999). *The development of emotional competence.* New York: The Guilford Press.

Saarni, C., Campos, J. J., Camras, L. A., & Witherington, D. (2006). Emotional development: Action, communication, and understanding. In W. Damon & R. M. Lerner (Series Eds.) and N. Eisenberg (Vol. Ed.), *Handbook of child psychology: Social, emotional, and personality development* (6th ed., Vol. 3, pp. 226–299). New York: Wiley.

Saxe, G. B. (1991). *Culture and cognitive development: Studies in mathematical understanding.* Hillsdale, NJ: Lawrence Erlbaum Associates.

Scharfe, E. (2000). Development of emotional expression, understanding, and regulation in infants and young children. In R. Bar-On & J. D. A. Parker (Eds.), *The handbook of emotional intelligence: Theory, development, assessment, and application at home, school, and in the workplace* (pp. 244–262). San Francisco, CA: Jossey-Bass.

Tamm, L., Menon, V., & Reiss, A. L. (2002). Maturation of brain function associated with response inhibition. *Journal of the American Academy of Child and Adolescent Psychiatry, 41*, 1231–1238.

Thompson, R. A. (1994). Emotion regulation: A theme in search of definition. *Monographs of the Society for Research in Child Development, 59*, 25–52, 250–283.

Terwogt, M. M., & Stegge, H. (1998). Children's perspective on the emotional process. In A. Campbell & S. Muncer (Eds.), *The social child* (pp. 249–269). England: Psychology Press.

Tomasello, M., Carpenter, M., Call, J., Behne, T., & Moll, H. (2005). Understanding and sharing intentions: The origins of cultural cognition. *Behavioral and Brain Sciences, 28*, 675–735.

Tsai, J. L., Knuston, B., & Fung, H. H. (2006). Cultural variation in affect valuation. *Journal of Personality and Social Psychology, 90*, 288–307.

Vygotsky, L. S. (1978). *Mind in society: The development of higher psychological processes.* Cambridge, MA: Harvard University Press.

Whiting, J., & Child, I. (1953). *Child training and personality: A cross-cultural study.* New York: Yale University Press.

Whiting, B. B., & Edwards, C. P. (1988). *Children of different worlds: The formation of social behavior.* Cambridge, MA: Harvard University Press.

Wierzbicka, A. (1999). *Emotions across languages and cultures: Diversity and universals.* Paris: Cambridge University Press.

Winsler, A., Diaz, R. M., McCarthy, E. M., Atencio, D. J., & Chabay, L. A. (1999). Mother-child interaction, private speech, and task performance in preschool children with behavior problems. *Journal of Child Psychology, Psychiatry, and Allied Disciplines, 40*, 891–904.

Zelazo, P. D., & Müller, U. (2002). Executive function in typical and atypical development. In U. Goswami (Ed.), *Blackwell handbook of childhood cognitive development* (pp. 445–469). Malden, MA: Blackwell Publishing.

16

Early Social and Cognitive Precursors and Parental Support for Self-Regulation and Executive Function: Relations from Early Childhood into Adolescence

SUSAN H. LANDRY AND KAREN E. SMITH

Important goals for school-age children include the ability to (a) develop strategies for solving problems, (b) show flexibility in modifying those strategies on the basis of feedback they receive, (c) inhibit inappropriate behaviors, and (d) apply these strategies to a range of problem-solving situations. These skills often are referred to as executive functions (EFs) and are also considered important under the rubric of self-regulation. In spite of the importance of these school-age goals, little is known about what influences their attainment. In this chapter, we will first examine the evidence for a range of skills in early childhood to be considered important developmental precursors for school-age self-regulation (SR) and EF. Throughout the chapter these two abilities will be referred to as SR/EF skills. These include cognitive, language, and social skills in the toddler and preschool period including early search skills, independent goal-directed play and social competence during interactions with caregivers.

The second objective is to demonstrate the importance of caregivers' early scaffolding in providing the support that is necessary for children to ultimately accomplish SR/EF skills. In our research, early parent interactive behaviors have been examined for their relation to these later school-age goals on the basis of Vygotsky (1978) and other theoretical frameworks (Bruner, 1972) for understanding the origins of children's later independent cognitive and social functioning. Finally, the third objective is to highlight, with measures of a range of EF and social interactive skills, the importance of examining early and later EF skills for understanding social competence, self-regulation, and complex problem solving in early adolescence. As the field is now debating whether social interaction plays a role in the development of self-regulation, and if so, what aspects of social interaction are important, we will describe findings that support a link between these two skills. Our research also has been able to systematically address whether relations between EF and social-emotional skills, and knowledge are similar for typically and atypically developing children, this important question will be targeted in this chapter.

In this chapter, we will address our three objectives with data from a longitudinal research program involving 360 children and their parents recruited in infancy and followed through early adolescence. In relation to our first objective, we have identified a set of early childhood developmental precursors for later SR/EF skills. To address Objective 2, we will describe how this longitudinal study reveals that some early parenting behaviors (e.g., provision of high structure) have direct influences on later independent functioning whereas others (e.g., maintaining attentional focus, verbal scaffolding) have an indirect influence by directly supporting early developmental precursor skills such as language, social competence, and nonverbal problem solving. Finally, as the children in this study now have been followed into early adolescence, we are able to examine and describe interrelations between early SR/EF skills with later social and cognitive competence.

The original sample consisted of 224 very low birthweight (VLBW) children placed into two risk groups on the basis of the severity of medical complications during the neonatal period (Low Risk—LR = 130; High Risk—HR = 94) and one comparison group of children born at term (n = 136). Parents of all children who met eligibility criteria at birth at three large hospitals (county, state, and university) across the 18 month recruitment period were approached for participation. Infants born at term were recruited from pediatric clinics at the same three hospitals to ensure similar socioeconomic status (SES) and ethnic background. Of those parents who declined participation (11%), demographic and medical characteristics are comparable to those who enrolled in the study. Sample strengths are inclusion of families from three ethnicities, families from lower economic levels representative of the VLBW population, and demographic comparability across groups. Evaluations were conducted when the child was 6 months and at 1, 2, 3, 4, 6, 8, 10, and 12 years of age and included standardized assessments of skills (e.g., cognitive, language) and observation of mother-child interactions. Beginning at 3 years of age, executive processing skills were assessed using traditional approaches (e.g., search series tasks, Tower of London [TOL]) and observation of independent goal-directed play skills. Beginning at 8 years of age, observations of peer interactions and skill in a social problem-solving task with a novel adult were conducted. For all analyses, we examined whether relations varied for those born term versus preterm.

Self-Regulation and Executive Functioning: Definitions and Developmental Course

DEFINITIONS ACROSS DISCIPLINES

In the neuropsychological literature, the skills outlined earlier are termed EFs; in the cognitive literature, they are labeled executive processes; and in the developmental literature, these skills often are grouped under the rubric self-regulation. Although different terminology is used, all three disciplines emphasize the need for the child to interact independently with their world without a high degree of structure and support from others. Within the *neuropsychology* literature, EF skills are the behaviors required for effective problem solving and social competence (Lezak, 1982). EFs help operationalize the child's ability to profit from and comprehend social experiences (Rourke & Fuerst, 1991). Some researchers emphasize behaviors under a rubric referred as "microlevel components" such as working memory and response inhibition, while others examine more "macrolevel skills" such as self-regulation, planning, and problem solving (Senn, Espy, & Kaufman, 2004). Developmental neuropsychologists suggest that the rudiments of EF skills are present early and have an extended developmental course (Diamond, 1988; Welsh & Pennington, 1988). Behaviors such as goal-directedness and behavior planning, which are described as important early markers for SR by developmentalists (Kopp, 1982), are hypothesized to be the early developmental origins of later EF abilities (Welsh & Pennington, 1988).

Cognitive psychologists have typically referred to a similar set of skills as executive processes. These researchers have emphasized the importance of a child independently developing a strategy, being flexible in modifying that strategy, inhibiting inappropriate behaviors (Posner, 1978), and creating strategies that can be applied to a wide range of novel and/or challenging problem-solving situations. In addition, Flavell (1971) and Brown and DeLoache (1978) describe the importance of planning and self-monitoring for fostering increases in children's cognitive competencies.

Developmental psychologists label as SR children's ability to inhibit motor and verbal behaviors, increase in their compliance and flexibility, initiate social interactions, actively explore their environment, and independently carry out goals (Block & Block, 1980; Kopp, 1982; Mischel & Patterson, 1979;

Wertsch, 1979). SR begins in early infancy with the ability to respond to maternal requests, and it is evident in later childhood with the ability to inhibit responses in the presence of attractive stimuli (Vaughn, Kopp, & Krakow, 1984). The interrelations among developing social competencies and cognitive abilities, as these relate to SR/EF skills, have also been strongly emphasized by research in this field (Kopp, 1982; Perlmutter, Behrend, Kuo, & Muller, 1989), although precise relations have not been fully documented. SR skills are present across early childhood with behaviors such as goal-directedness and planning during play, the ability to respond to maternal requests and initiate social interactions, inhibit responses in the presence of attractive stimuli and learn to understand others' perspectives (Zelazo, Carter, Reznick, & Frye, 1997).

DEVELOPMENTAL COURSE OF SELF-REGULATION AND EXECUTIVE FUNCTION SKILLS

Across the first 2 years of life, children's ability to solve problems and carry out goals depends on their parents providing structure for the regulation of their behavior (Wertsch, 1979). Over time, children become increasingly more capable of assuming control over regulation of their own behavior, including identifying goals and strategies to carry out these goals, in both social and nonsocial situations. A number of changes in children's development of these skills which occur from 3 through 8 years of age make this an important period for the examination of SR/EF skills (Denckla, 1996). In general, children are learning a broad range of cognitive processes required to monitor, control, and plan thought and action. Areas frequently studied involve inhibitory control (Carlson & Moses, 2001; Hughes, 1998; Leslie & Polizzi, 1998), flexible rule following (Zelazo et al., 1997), and working memory, including the ability to hold information in memory that is used to make a correct response (Keenan, 2000).

Specifically, across 3 and 4 years of age, children are beginning to use overt speech to regulate their behavior and, ultimately, internalization of speech is a critical milestone in the development of SR (Luria, 1973; Vygotsky, 1978). Further development of language skills, including the ability to think beyond the "here-and-now", may be critical to the development of self-control (Denckla, 1996). With the support of this, children also are beginning to develop cognitive skills that allow them to take another's perspective, process information in a more efficient manner, and hold mental representations of desired goals (Gottman, Gonso, & Rasmussen, 1975). Zelazo et al. (1997) also emphasize the need for children to learn to evaluate the results of their problem-solving approach with dramatic changes occurring in executive processing from toddler through later school-age years. Barkley (1997) describes how they become progressively more internalized across this age period.

From 5 to 8 years of age, children continue to develop the use of internal speech to assist them with SR (Hartig & Kanfer, 1973), and also to develop greater competence in information processing, working memory, and selective attention (Welsh, Pennington, & Grosier, 1991; White, 1970). Across these ages, development of social skills includes learning to assert independence and autonomy without eliciting negative interactions (Kuzcynski, Kochanska, Radke-Yarrow, & Girnius-Brown, 1987).

SR/EF skills continue to develop across school-ages years. However, as this is a time when more complex skills are emerging rather than being well consolidated, it is critical to examine this progression over a developmental period when these skills are evolving. Studies have documented, with cross-sectional samples, that children's performance on neuropsychological measures of EFs (e.g., word fluency, TOL) show change from early school age into adolescence (Levin et al., 1991; Weyandt, & Willis, 1994). However, it has been theorized that rather than there being a single continuous progression, separate sets of skills probably emerge at different points in development (Barkley, 1996). These then interact with each other to progressively organize into more competent EFs by adolescence. Across the school-age period, children develop greater capacity for emotional regulation, frustration tolerance, and concern for others (Weyandt & Willis, 1994), SR skills that are critically important for establishing and maintaining successful social relationships in and outside of the family. However, during these years there is considerable variability in skill development. For example, we have seen that some children in the school-age years are engaging peers in a cooperative manner to reach a common goal, while others are incapable of initiating a group effort and attempt to solve the problem independently rather than cooperatively.

Entry into adolescence begins a period where SR/EF skills increase in complexity, are multidimensional, and vary depending on the social context (e.g., parent vs. peers) (Steinberg et al., 2006). Young adolescents are expected to show independent control over behavior, negotiate social relations with others, and process and act on multiple pieces of information when solving problems (Taylor, Klein, Minich, & Hack, 2000; Taylor, Minich, Bangert, Filipek, & Hack, 2004). Early in adolescence there are strong increases in emotions (e.g., anxiety, anger, passion) and motivations including drives for reward and novelty related to pubertal changes (Steinberg et al., 2006). Strong increases in these areas place new challenges on an individual's SR including the ability to be more internalized in terms of planning, monitoring, evaluating, and reflecting. However, self-regulatory skills develop much more slowly requiring much of the adolescent period until they approximate adult levels (Steinberg, 2005).

Adolescence is a time when one should be able to express knowledge of how to accomplish goals indicating more sophisticated metacognitive skills regarding strategy use. Support for the importance of adolescents' ability to take into account how they and others are thinking was found to predict their ability to regulate their behavior in the face of risk (Connor-Smith, Compas, Wadsworth, Thomsen, & Saltzman, 2000), and to understand the role of masking feelings in conflicts with others (Cooke, 2004). Cognitive flexibility becomes more complex across adolescence as evidenced by more sophisticated deductive reasoning (Klaczynski, 2001), skills in how to maintain friendships, (Keller, Edelstein, Schmid, Fang, & Fang, 1998), shaping their own experiences (Steinberg et al., 2006), and use of effective coping strategies (Connor-Smith et al., 2000). For example, understanding how choices can impact friendships and the ability to consider others' perspectives in making such choices are challenges for adolescents. Across adolescence, the ability to carry out effective negotiations during conflict should increase, in part, as a result of adolescents' increasing need for autonomy.

Measurement of Self-Regulation and Executive Function Skills across Development

In our approach to examining the development of SR/EF skills, it was important to consider the developmental period and the type of demands (e.g., cognitive vs. social) placed on the child. Because standardized assessment approaches fall short in capturing the integration of reasoning and EF skills related to everyday functioning, we thought it important to also include contextually relevant observational measures. Outlined below are the measurement approaches used in our research and ages administered.

MEASURES OF COGNITIVE SKILLS

Preschool Ages—3, 4, 6 Years

Across the preschool period, measures of cognitive flexibility included examination of *independent goal-directed play* and *delayed search tasks* (Kopp, 1982; Welsh & Pennington, 1988). The delayed search tasks require a child to hold a mental representation of an object which has been previously hidden, develop an efficient plan with which to achieve the goal of finding the hidden object, and exercise flexibility in their planning when the task demands shift (Diamond, 1988). The skills assessed by the delayed search task are similar to those assessed in independent goal-directed play, since children need to set goals and sequence their behaviors in a planned and organized way to achieve their goals. For example, a child attempting to complete a puzzle may find that a piece does not fit. The child must reorganize his/her problem-solving plan (e.g., try a new piece or try to fit the puzzle piece elsewhere) in response to this dilemma. Both object oriented and pretend play skills were captured. As described in more detail later in this chapter, early search skills appear to be important as a foundation for later executive processing skills as demonstrated by relations between scores on early search tasks with competence on more complex executive tasks such as TOL.

Elementary and Adolescent Ages—8, 10, 12, 13 years

Across elementary school and into early adolescence, typical measures of EF were used including the ability to sustain attention and/or inhibit behavioral responding were measured by the *Continuous Performance Task (CPT)* and the *TOL* to measure planning and implementation of strategies to meet a specific goal. In planning, children need to remember a set of basic rules and behavioral regulation is required because of the need to shift strategies on the basis of examiner feedback. Children who have difficulty with EF skills may perseverate on a particular strategy rather than flexibly shift to a new approach or not follow the appropriate rules.

Two additional measures included at the 13 year assessment, involved children's ability to develop strategies for solving a problem without structure or information to guide their planning (e.g., deductive reasoning), *20 Questions*, and the ability to understand reasons for modulating emotional expressions, the *Real and Deceptive Emotion Task* (Dennis, Barnes, Wilkinson, & Humphreys, 1998). In the 20 Question task we were able to examine for developmental differences in the strategies used to determine the target picture with the least number of questions. For example, constraint seeking questions were those that referred to two or more pictures and eliminated several alternatives (e.g., is it a living thing), whereas, hypothesis seeking questions simply named one particular picture (e.g., is it the hammer). A greater use in constraint seeking questions predicts concept formation and planning/strategy skills (Landry, Smith, Swank, &

Miller-Loncar, 2000). The real and deceptive emotion task is considered to involve metacognitive skills as it requires the consideration of another's thought process to understand reasons for masking feelings with different facial expressions. This skill is thought to develop across early adolescence (Dennis et al., 1998) and is quantified through children listening to short narratives of hypothetical characters that involve a mismatch between feelings and facial expressions and responding to questions regarding knowledge of why emotional concealment is important.

MEASURES OF SOCIAL SKILLS

As children develop, they are involved in ever-widening social situations beginning with caregivers and proceeding to involvement with peers and others within the community. In our research we have examined children's social competence in three social situations. These include interactions with their mothers, social problem solving with peers, and social problem solving with a novel adult.

Interactions with Mothers

Two aspects of SR in a social context that were used included *initiating* and *responding* in an interaction with mother (i.e., 3 through 10 years of age). Due to the presence of a social partner, these skills require setting goals and responding flexibly to feedback (e.g., Rourke & Fuerst, 1991). Social initiating places high demands on a child to independently determine a social goal and use a sequenced set of behaviors (e.g., eye gaze, gestures, verbalizations) to carry out this goal. While responsiveness appears to have more structure because of a social partners' specific request, this behavior requires the ability to control impulses (e.g., when a mother requests a child to stop a behavior). It also requires flexibility in social problem solving, since competence in social responsiveness requires children to negotiate with social partners when requested behaviors do not fit with the children's goals (Landry, Smith, & Swank, 2006).

A second mother-child task used at 13 years of age, conflict resolution, was on the basis of the protocol by Rueter and Conger (1998) where adolescents and their mothers complete a checklist to rate level of conflict for various topics (e.g., homework). The examiner determines the four most conflictual topics and asks the pair to resolve each of them by answering four questions. The interaction is videotaped and coded for maternal and adolescent behaviors.

Multiple adolescent behaviors are coded using rating scales ranging from 1 (not at all characteristic) to 5 (very characteristic).

Interactions with Peers

Children's competence when *solving problems with peers* was evaluated during two, 15 min sessions with the target child and two peers beginning at the 8 year time point (Hebert-Myers, Guttentag, Swank, Smith, & Landry, 2006). The two tasks included building a structure together with blocks and role playing in a pretend scenario (e.g., veterinarian game) using a modification of a task by Newcomb, Brady, and Hartup (1979). Specific task instructions have been previously published but included the directive for the peers to decide as a group what to build and/or who would play what role and to remember to play together. Specific interactive behaviors were coded using a time sampling procedure (e.g., comments, comply/ noncomply with peer requests) and global ratings were used to capture behaviors that reflected more dispositional characteristics (e.g., social connectedness, frustration tolerance) (see Hebert et al., 2006). On the basis of a principle-axes factor analysis with a Promax oblique rotation, four factors were identified: social connectedness, frustration tolerance/flexibility, compliance to requests, and noncompliance with requests. These factors were then used in analyses.

Interactions with a Novel Adult

In the middle school-age years (i.e., 8, 10, 12 years), an additional social problem-solving task, *Monopoly game task*, was developed that placed demands on understanding that another person may have different knowledge or intentions. As playing board games is a naturally occurring activity for children in this age range, we developed this approach using the board game, Monopoly Jr. to better assure an ecologically sensitive measurement approach. Specifically, it measured school-aged children's ability to understand when a person needed information about the rules of a game and the quality of the information provided. A competency score from this task, incorporating children's ability to take initiative, respond to cues, and alter strategies given feedback from the social partner was expected to quantify a complex set of EF skills. Children were expected to be more competent in this activity if they maintained awareness that they had knowledge that needed to be shared to play, were able to read the nonverbal signals of their adult partner, and appreciate that their partner needed information when appearing confused or hesitant.

Objective 1: Developmental Precursors of School-Age Self-Regulation and Executive Functioning Skills

THE IMPORTANCE OF THE INFANT AND TODDLER PERIOD

Children's developing independent play, social communication and responsiveness, language, and early search skills all are thought to contribute to the development of later SR/EF skills. During social interactions, infants and young children learn to attend to their caretaker while signaling their interests. These interactions promote flexibility in goal formulation, since children who are more competent in this context will learn how to act upon objects in an organized way and develop the awareness that they can share another's interest in objects and toys. Thus, the set of abilities that develops through joint play activities may be direct precursors to the abilities required for SR/EF development.

Infants' ability to explore their environment motorically (i.e., early neuromotor skills) also may provide early cognitive experiences which are needed for later strategy development and goal formulation (Thelan & Smith, 1995). Research has shown that children who have limited early exploratory experiences, compared to mental-age-matched, nonmotorically impaired children, have specific problems with independently forming goals and sequencing their behavior to carry out these goals (Landry, Robinson, Copeland, & Garner, 1993). Furthermore, across 3–8 years of age, children's rate of development of SR/EF skills (e.g., goal-directed activities) may continue to be influenced by their ongoing development of motor skills, including motor planning and coordination.

Early mental and linguistic skills may affect the development of EF skills by facilitating verbal mediation of strategies for inhibiting behaviors and solving novel problems. In toddlers, significant relations have been found between performance on measures of language and self-control during delayed gratification tasks (Vaughn et al., 1984), suggesting a link between general language abilities and the ability to use verbal mediation. One would expect that some of the same behaviors in earlier interactions with parents lay the foundation for dealing with same age peers, who do not accommodate children's own needs in the way that parents might.

THE IMPORTANCE OF THE EARLY CHILDHOOD PERIOD

There are a number of early skills that children across 3–8 years of age may need to achieve to develop later social, behavioral, and learning competences (Mischel & Mischel, 1983; Rourke & Fuerst, 1991). For example, children's early ability to cooperate with parents' requests and restrictions in social interactions, and their skill in controlling their behavior (e.g., in delayed search tasks), may have direct links to their later ability to control impulses when asked by adults or peers to focus their attention on an activity. These same skills may also indicate flexibility in using feedback to shift strategies, which can lead in later years to effective use of feedback from peers in social and academic interactions. Similarly, children's ability in the preschool years to establish goals in social initiating and independent play may be an early expression of the kinds of goal-directed behaviors later necessary for successful entry into peer interactions, as well as success in mastering academic concepts.

Our research supports these hypotheses as reported in a number of studies that have used structural equation modeling approaches. For example, when examining the importance of social behaviors in the context of mother-child interactions and early cognitive/language skills for understanding later social initiative taking and independent goal-directed behavior, we found strong support for the role of these two areas of early development on aspects of SR/EF functioning at 4 years of age. In this model we examined these early social and cognitive precursor skills across both the toddler and early preschool period in relation to SR/EF skills just before entrance into kindergarten (Landry et al., 2000). The model demonstrates that children's early social responsiveness had direct influences on their later ability to take initiative in social situations, but not on their independent goal-directed play in nonsocial situations. In contrast, measures of cognitive and language skills influenced goal-directed play but not social initiative. While these social and cognitive skills in the toddler period were important predictors, their influence on later SR/EF skills occurred through their influence on these same precursor skills in the preschool period. The model demonstrated that at 2 and 3 years of age, children developed basic social and cognitive skills that assisted in their development of internal regulation of their cognitive and social behaviors at later ages.

EARLY SOCIAL SKILLS AS PRECURSORS FOR SCHOOL-AGE SELF-REGULATION AND EXECUTIVE FUNCTIONING

Another model, illustrated in Figure 16.1, documented that two early social skills, responding and initiating, in mother-child interactions at 3 years

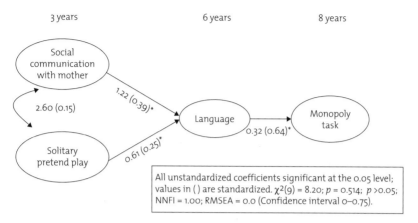

FIGURE 16.1. The influence of children's social communication skills with mother and solitary pretend play skills at 3 years on 8-year Monopoly game skills that is mediated by 6-year language skills.

influenced social problem solving including perspective taking at 8 years of age (i.e., Monopoly task). Higher social skills in the mother-child interactions reflected a child's ability to follow a sequence of the conversation, pick up on contextual cues, and activate their language and gestural skills to organize a response to their mothers' requests, or initiate an interaction. The early influence of social interactive skills on the Monopoly game skills occurred indirectly through a direct influence on early school-age language skills (Assel, Swank, Landry, & Smith, 2006) (CE: delete ref and add Landry, Smith, & Swank, 2009). As described previously, the Monopoly task required children to teach a novice adult the game. A higher score on this task required skills similar to those in the mother-child interaction, although more complex. Thus, the child needed to take the novice partner's perspective and provide information about the game rules while maintaining the flow of the game. Support for the skills on the Monopoly task placing demands on EFs is demonstrated by its moderate correlation with a traditional EF measure, the TOL, $r = 0.36$. These results, consistent with the previously described model, demonstrate that children's ability to interact and communicate in early childhood with a caregiver is an important foundational skill for their later ability to keep another's perspective in mind to share information with the other person.

Early social interactions were expected to be important for later social problem solving because they support children's ability to take turns, read the cues of another person, and know when to offer information. Interactions with caregivers during early childhood also provide a context for children to learn to use their language skills so that they are more competent in later social problem-solving situations. As revealed in the model, a second developmental precursor for the Monopoly task was early pretend play. Again, the influence of pretend play on skills in this SR/EF task occurred through a direct influence on language skills. These results support other research linking pretend play with language skills (McCune-Nicolich, 1981) and language with perspective taking (Garfield, Peterson, & Perry, 2001), but previous work has not examined the interrelations across these three skills within the same study. Experiences in early pretend play allow children to learn to represent, or symbolize, characteristics of the real world including understanding social situations. Harris and Kavanaugh (1993) describe how children's skill with pretend play precedes their ability to understand the mind (e.g., others may have different beliefs, information).

EARLY LANGUAGE AND NONVERBAL PROBLEM SOLVING WITH SCHOOL-AGE SELF-REGULATION AND EXECUTIVE FUNCTIONING

In a third model the importance of early language for later EF skills again was highlighted (Landry, Miller-Loncar, Smith, & Swank, 2002). In a structural model, language during the preschool period was found to influence search retrieval skills at 6 years. While nonverbal problem-solving skills were another important precursor to EF skills, these did not influence search skills but rather, independent goal-directed play. Although early auditory and visual memory skills were included in the model, these did not predict either of the later EF skills. The differential influence of language on the two EF skills examined in this model may be related, in part, to the task demands. The link between language and search skills was thought to occur because children with more complex language may be more likely to develop internal, or self-directed, speech that promotes the ability to use self-questioning strategies to understand the task rules and develop plans for solving this task as well as potentially inhibit impulsive responses (Barkley, 1997; Berk, 1986). The lack of a link between earlier language and later independent goal-directed play may be due to the decreased requirement in the play task for the use of rule-based strategies and higher demands on complex manipulation of play materials to achieve a higher score. It is interesting that in the first model described, 3 year language was an important influence on 4 year goal-directed play. One important difference in the models that may explain this inconsistency is that nonverbal skills were not examined in the first study. With nonverbal skills in the model, the influence of language on goal-directed play may be suppressed by its shared variance with nonverbal skills.

Relations for Children Varying in Biological Risk

The models also were tested to determine whether the relations examined differed for children born term versus preterm. Although skill levels differed for the children on the basis of the severity of neonatal risk, and thus risk for developmental problems, the pattern and strength of relations among the skills studied were found to be similar. The consistency of this finding provides support for the hypothesis that the developmental processes explaining inter-relations among these skill areas are similar for different types of children, particularly for those that vary in their birth histories.

Objective 2: Early Caregiving Environments Support Self-Regulation and Executive Functioning Skills

Parenting is recognized as an important influence on the development of SR/EF skills, particularly the quality of parent-child interactions (Landry et al., 2000; Wertsch, 1979). Theories of socialization suggest that children first learn to regulate their behavior when interacting with caregivers and then generalize these skills to interactions with others in terms of SR and problem solving (e.g., Feldman & Klein, 2003; Kochanska & Murray, 2000; Kuczynski & Kochanska, 1995). In the preschool period, this includes the ability to initiate conversation, use language to communicate needs, and to successfully cooperate with requests made by caregivers (Landry, Smith, Swank, Assel, & Vellet, 2001). A child's ability to take the lead in social interactions with caregivers also is thought to contribute to an internal knowledge base that fosters competence in shared activities with a social partner other than the parent. Through the process of repeated experiences in interactions which promote responsiveness to parental requests (e.g., learning how to cooperate and follow directions), children are expected to internalize rules that later govern social behavior (Grusec & Goodnow, 1994) and begin to learn about differences between themselves and others (Kohut, 1971; Winnicott, 1971). However, Feldman and Klein (2003) note that support for this notion requires linking early social behavior with caregivers to later social competency with others. Such links have been shown in relation to impulse and behavioral control (e.g., Kochanska, 2002), but less frequently related to competencies in shared activities with others.

PARENT RESPONSIVENESS BEHAVIORS

In our investigation of the influence of early parenting on SR/EF skills we have focused on responsiveness behaviors described in the literature to be important for the development of a range of children's behaviors including SR/EF (e.g., Bornstein & Tamis-LeMonda, 1989; Landry et al., 2006; Parpal & Maccoby, 1985). Parental responsiveness included behaviors that supported the immature cognitive, attentional, and organizational skills of young children (e.g., maintaining rather than redirecting children's attention). Focus also was given to behaviors consistently shown to be important for promoting children's autonomy and independence (e.g., contingently responding to children's signals). As quality of language input has been reported to help children organize their behavior and internalize problem-solving strategies, characteristics of parents' language input also were examined. Finally, emotional support and the absence of negativity, behaviors consistently reported to promote cooperation in young children, were a fourth aspect of our parenting framework. Behaviors included in each of these aspects of parenting have been studied in relation to SR/EF skills and recently, through factor analyses, we have documented that these behaviors comprise four discrete but overlapping aspects of responsiveness (Landry et al., 2006). Another aspect of parenting that we have examined is the extent to which a mother provides high degrees of directiveness of her child's behavior.

Maintaining Attention and High Directiveness

Two aspects of maternal responsiveness that were the focus of our longitudinal research included the extent to which caregivers attempted to maintain versus redirect their children's attention and provision of low versus high directiveness. Maintaining is described in our research and others (e.g., Landry, Smith, Miller-Loncar, & Swank, 1998; Tomasello & Farrar, 1986) as an important scaffolding behavior because it supports the young child's immature attentional abilities and provides the message that the child's interests are important. In contrast, redirecting places greater demands on attention and cognitive skills and is frequently reported to make it more difficult for young children to organize a response (Landry, 1995). Although consistency in maintaining attention appears important, the role of directiveness is more complex and requires a mother to adjust this behavior from higher levels during the infancy and toddler period to lower levels in the preschool years.

EARLY CHILDHOOD AND SCHOOL-AGE YEARS Returning to the models described under Objective 1, in addition to the examination of the relation of early child precursors with SR/EF skills, the role of maintaining and directiveness was examined for their influence on children's SR/EF skills. In the case of maintaining, mothers' use of this behavior during the toddler period indirectly influenced initiative taking and goal-directed play skills through support of toddler and preschool age language and social responsiveness skills (Landry et al., 2000). There also was an influence of consistency in mothers' maintaining across the two early developmental periods that supported preschool language development, and in turn, goal-directed play.

This same model demonstrated evidence for the need for directiveness to change across time. The need for adjustment was found in the positive influence of early directiveness on children's early social responsive skills that, in turn, promoted children's later competence in taking social initiative (Landry et al., 2000). However, consistency in this behavior across these two early developmental periods predicted less optimal initiating skills prior to entry into kindergarten. That is, higher levels of directiveness that continued into the preschool period predicted lower levels in social initiating. While toddlers appear to be supported socially by greater maternal structure in interactions, when they become capable of taking more responsibility in interactions, mothers needed to decrease the level of structure to allow this early initiative taking to develop optimally. As high levels of maternal directiveness in the preschool period also negatively influenced skill in goal-directed play, the role of decreased directiveness for the effective development of SR/EF skills appears to cut across both social and cognitive domains.

ADOLESCENT AGE Our findings also show that early parenting can hinder SR/EF competence by early adolescence. In a recent examination of EF skills into early adolescence (i.e., deductive reasoning), high levels of early directiveness across early childhood negatively predicted this EF skill by negatively influencing attention skills across the school-age years. This model, illustrated in Figure 16.2, demonstrated support for the long term, negative impact of high levels of directiveness that persisted through the toddler period on 13 year deductive reasoning skills as measured by the 20 Questions game. When level and growth in attention skills across middle childhood were included in the model, the negative influence of high directiveness on later reasoning was found to occur through its negative impact on level of attention skills across 8, 10, and 12 years. This is consistent with our publications showing the negative influence of early high directiveness on a range of child outcomes; slower growth in daily livings skills (Dieterich, Hebert, Landry, Swank, & Smith, 2004), and language, and play (Herbert, Swank, Smith, & Landry, 2004).

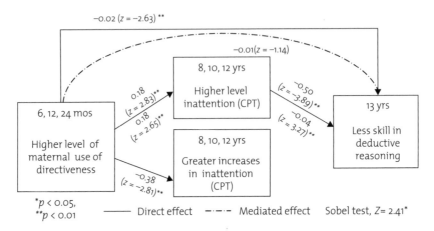

FIGURE 16.2. The influence of maternal directiveness experienced in the first 2 years of life on adolescent deductive reasoning skills that is mediated by attention skills across middle childhood.

Another aspect of parenting that involves negative control or high degrees of direction, the extent to which mothers restricted children's exploration, was coded in the mother-child interactions and entered into the model. The model demonstrated that highly restrictive parenting across early childhood ("Don't put that in your mouth."; "Stop playing with that.") hindered language development across 3 through 8 years of age that, in turn, predicted lower levels of listening and enjoyment at 13 years when discussing conflicts with their mothers. Other adolescent researchers have described how high levels of restrictiveness and rigidity in parenting can interfere with effective adolescent development (Allen, Hauser, Bell, & O'Connor, 1994; Steinberg, 2001). What also is important about this finding is that negative parenting in the early childhood period had a strong influence on development as far removed as early adolescence.

Use of Rich Language Input

The role of rich language input from caregivers is consistently shown to support children's cognitive and language development (e.g., Akhtar, Dunham, & Dunham, 1991; Huttonlocher, Haight, Bryk, Seltzer, & Lyons, 1991; Weizman & Snow, 2001). During observations of mother-child interactions, we have coded mothers' use of labels for actions and objects as well more complex language input (i.e., verbal scaffolding) that makes connections between objects and actions, and objects and objects. This would include, for example, helping children understand where objects belong, how they function, and how a current experience links with a past experience (Smith, Landry, & Swank, 2000). While the relation of this form of caregivers' language input to children's cognitive and language outcomes is often examined, its role in supporting SR/EF skills has received much less attention.

EARLY CHILDHOOD AND SCHOOL AGE In the third model described under Objective 1, the role of maternal use of rich language (i.e., verbal scaffolding) in promoting search task skills and goal-directed play at 6 years was evaluated (Landry et al., 2002). While verbal scaffolding was included in the model at both 3 and 4 years of age, this input only at the earlier age was found to be important in understanding the 6 year EF skills. As we have found before, this influence was indirect and occurred through a direct influence on the children's language and nonverbal problem-solving skills at 4 years. Findings from these models highlight the important role early maternal behaviors play in facilitating the development of basic verbal and nonverbal skills that, in turn, are important foundation skills for understanding later SR/EF abilities.

ADOLESCENT AGE The quality of maternal language input also predicted the quality of dyadic discussions between early adolescents and their mothers and this model is illustrated in Figure 16.3. In conflict resolution, the extent to which a mother and adolescent worked together to discuss problems was positively influenced by rich language children received across 3, 4, and 6 years of age. Inclusion of children's skill in the Monopoly task across middle childhood partially mediated this influence. These results suggest that as children hear language that gives them information about how objects function and how one experience links with another, they are able to not only develop a range of vocabulary, but also to use it in ways that help them work with others in problem-solving situations. As the Monopoly and conflict resolution tasks place demands on children to take another's perspective, the link between early language input and better skills in perspective taking support research of others examining even more specific types of language input to the development of theory of mind (ToM). For example, researchers have questioned whether young children who hear words that describe hidden properties such as emotions and beliefs facilitate their understanding of what others think and know (e.g., Peterson & Slaughter, 2003; Ruffman, Slade, & Crowe, 2002). This has been described as "mindedness talk" (Meins et al, 2003). While our observational system did not specifically code for this type of language input, it captured it along with a range of other types of verbal scaffolding.

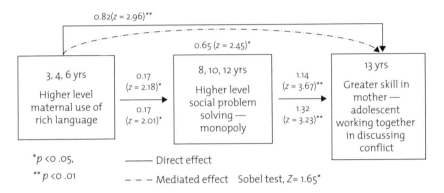

FIGURE 16.3. The influence of early maternal rich language input on adolescent conflict resolution skills mediated by level of Monopoly game skills across middle childhood.

Warmth and Contingent Responsiveness

Maternal behaviors from the attachment framework (Ainsworth, Blehar, Waters, & Wall, 1978; Londerville & Main, 1981), warmth and contingent responsiveness, also appear to play an important role in understanding individual differences in the development of SR/EF skills in our research. The children whose caregivers conveyed a sense of enjoyment in their activities and sensitivity to their interests and needs (i.e., warmth) as well as received contingent responses to their signals were expected to have better outcomes. Better outcomes were expected to occur, in part, because these maternal behaviors supported the children's development of a sense of trust in their caregivers (Grusec & Goodnow, 1994). This trust builds when these parenting behaviors are consistently at high levels across early childhood because children are receiving the message that their signals are important and acknowledged. This, in turn, promotes a willingness to cooperate and engage in positive ways with caregivers. It is through this greater positive engagement that then promotes greater growth in social and cognitive skills. Thus, in our research we expected a relation between these two aspects of responsive caregiving and aspects of children's SR/EF skills (e.g., social initiating).

EARLY CHILDHOOD AND SCHOOL AGE In a previous report we found that mothers with higher levels of warm sensitivity had children with faster growth in their responsiveness to maternal requests and in their ability to initiate interactions with their caregiver (Landry et al., 1998). A similar finding was apparent for higher levels of contingent responsiveness. These results suggest that warm sensitivity along with responses that are contingent on children's signals promotes children's ability to learn they can take a more active role in social interactions. By taking more initiative in social interactions, children learn how to regulate their behavior and gain feedback about their behavior from others which, over time, is expected to build a better understanding of how to work with others. In a separate model, early maternal warmth was found to support children's language development that, in turn, predicted higher quality in children's social responsiveness (Steelman, Assel, Swank, Smith, & Landry, 2002). However, the amount of warmth children experienced in early childhood also had a direct relation to social skills at early school age emphasizing the far-reaching influence of this aspect of early responsive caregiving.

ADOLESCENT AGE When we examined maternal contingent responsiveness across 3, 4, and 6 years of age to children's ability to problem solve effectively with peers at 13 years of age, a strong positive relation was found. Similar to other structural models, this occurred indirectly through a direct relation of this maternal behavior on children's competence in the Monopoly task across 8, 10, and 12 years of age. Theorists hypothesize that contingent responsiveness promotes social behaviors such as SR because, similar to warm caregiving, children receive the message that their engagement in interactions with their caregiver is valued. Also, this form of parenting supports children's immature social skills so that they receive more positive feedback about their effort to participate and thus are more likely to remain engaged. Repeated experiences involving contingent responsiveness may establish a foundation on which children are more likely to develop complex social interaction skills.

Relations for Children Varying in Biological Risk

In our research, we are beginning to examine the extent to which variability in biological risk (i.e., born at term vs. very low birthweight) may mediate the relation between early maternal behaviors and early adolescent outcomes. Because of the difficulty children born at very low birthweight have in shifting attention at early ages (Landry, Leslie, Fletcher, & Francis, 1985), the extent to which mothers maintained their young children's attentional focus was expected to show different relations for those born VLBW versus term. In this model, higher levels of early maintaining predicted 13 year conflict resolution skills, but only for those born at VLBW.

At earlier ages we documented that highly negative behaviors including restrictiveness had a particularly strong negative relation with growth in cognitive and social skills for those born at VLBW because of their greater vulnerability to parenting that did not support their needs (Landry, Smith, Miller-Loncar, & Swank, 1997). When we examined the relation of this form of negative parenting on SR/EF skills in adolescence, mothers' use of restrictions across early childhood predicted poorer skills on the Monopoly task but again, this was only found for children born premature.

Objective 3: Links Between Early Social Interactions and Executive Function Skills for Early Adolescent Social and Cognitive Competence

There are multiple conceptual models in the literature linking EF, language skills, perspective taking, SR and social competence across child and adolescent development. For example, in Barkley's framework (1997) explaining the development of attention deficit disorder, early skills such as goal-directed action and response inhibition are hypothesized to be important early links to children's later competency in SR and attention control. Research demonstrates links between impairments in self-regulation, planning, and flexibility in problem solving with attention and learning problems, and also emphasizes the importance of bridging the literature between these problems and constructs of SR/EF skills (e.g., Barkley, 1997; Denckla, 1996; Welsh, et al., 1991).

In contrast, other researchers have emphasized the importance of skills developed in early social interactions (e.g., ability to learn to respond, use of language, awareness/knowledge of social cues, and caregiver scaffolding) as establishing a foundation for later development of SR/EF skills (e.g., Astington & Pelletier, 2005; Bandura; 1986; NICHD Early Childcare Research Network, 2005; Zelazo, 1999). Related to this, the focus of some investigations has been on understanding the role early EF skills, self-regulation, and language play in children's development of perspective taking and ToM (Astington, 2001; Astington & Pelletier, 2005; Carlson, Mandell, & Williams, 2004; de Villiers & de Villiers, 2003; Hughes, 1998; Ruffman et al., 2002). Research from this framework has demonstrated that some early indices of ToM are eye gaze, establishing shared attention, and reading others' intentions and their development is linked to children's early word use (Baldwin, 1994; Tomasello & Farrar, 1986). The role of language (de Villiers & de Villiers, 2003) and the role of early EF skills (Carlson et al., 2004) have both been described as important foundation skills for perspective taking and ToM.

Through our longitudinal research, structural models provide support for the early role of EF skills in promoting later SR including understanding of emotion and coordinating behaviors with peers. However, we also have found support for the role of early social skills and language in promoting perspective taking skills in the Monopoly task that places demands on the development of goals described earlier.

EARLY EXECUTIVE FUNCTIONING ESTABLISHING A FOUNDATION FOR ADOLESCENT SELF-REGULATION

In multiple models, we find strong support for the influence of early executive processing skills (i.e., search series task, independent goal-directed play) for later SR in adolescence. However, because we had measures of EF in middle childhood, the question of the role of EF skills during this developmental period was examined to determine if it was a mediator between the early skills and adolescent self-regulation.

The top graph in Figure 16.4 illustrates the results of a latent growth curve model that included early EF skills across 3, 4, and 6 years of age as measured by independent goal-directed play in predicting positive peer engagement in early adolescence. When including the 8, 10, and 12 year measure of EF, TOL, the model demonstrated that EF skills during middle childhood completely mediated this relation. Thus, while early goal-directed play skills significantly predicted adolescent self-regulation, to understand the mechanism by which these early skills influence later SR it is important to consider how they establish a foundation for more complex EF skills that, in turn, support later self-regulation.

For adolescents to work effectively with peers and others, they need to develop a complex understanding of emotions. For example, adolescents need to be aware that sometimes a facial expression may mask an internal emotion for a person to be socially appropriate. Thus, differentiating real versus deceptive emotions is described as critical for responding appropriately to the changing social cues in peer interactions. As we had evidence to support the importance of early EF skills for later self-regulation, we also were interested in whether similar relations could be found for knowledge of emotions. The findings of the latent growth curve model shown in the bottom graph of Figure 16.4 add to our understanding of why the early and later EF skills are important for social outcomes. In this model, early skills on a search task directly influenced competency on the TOL during middle childhood as well as adolescents' ability to recognize situations where internal feelings would be different from those displayed through facial expression (i.e., knowledge of emotions) as on the basis of the Deceptive Emotion task. Again, although the early skills predicted adolescents' emotion knowledge, this relation was mediated through its influence on TOL skills in middle childhood.

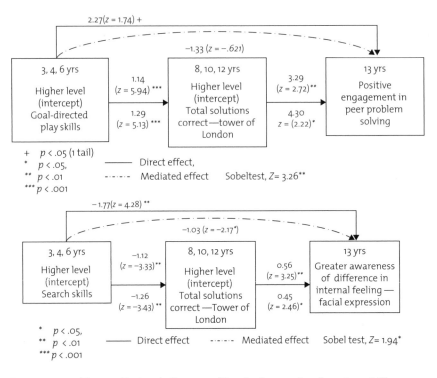

FIGURE 16.4. The mediating influence of level of executive function skills across middle childhood on the relation between: (1) level of goal-directed play across early childhood and positive peer engagement in adolescence (top graph) and (2) level of search skills across early childhood and adolescents' understanding of reasons for modulating expression of emotions (bottom graph).

EARLY SOCIAL SKILLS ESTABLISHING A FOUNDATION FOR ADOLESCENT SELF-REGULATION

Although the above models demonstrate strong support for the importance of early EF in promoting aspects of SR in adolescence, we also have evidence that early social skills play a role in supporting the development of later EFs. Using latent growth curve analyses, children's verbal responsiveness in toy-centered interactions with their mothers, measured at 3, 4, and 6 years, predicted children's skill in the Monopoly task across 8, 10, and 12 years and this is illustrated in Figure 16.5. Higher levels of verbal responsiveness reflected the child's ability to follow the sequence of the joint play activity, pick up on contextual cues, activate their language skills, and organize a response to their mothers' requests. A higher score on the game task required similar, but more complex, skills. The Monopoly task required the child to keep the goal in mind

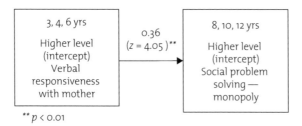

FIGURE 16.5. The influence of children's verbal responsiveness with mother across early childhood on Monopoly game skills across middle childhood.

that different rules needed to be explained as needed, and to do this the novice partner's perspective had to be appreciated. Thus, this task also requires language skills as well as perspective taking.

Further evidence for the importance of language and early awareness of rules for responding in social interactions was found in a separate model where early social communication skills and pretend play predicted the Monopoly task but this prediction was mediated by 6 year language skills. The importance of pretend play for the understanding of later executive processing and perspective taking has been described by others (Harris & Kavanaugh, 1993; Wolf, Rygh, & Altshuler, 1984). In our play measure, goal-directed behaviors were evident in children's selection of play materials and how they sequenced their behaviors to achieve goals. The act of role playing during their pretend play may show links to the Monopoly task as role playing allows a child to begin to understand that the different members of a scenario might have different needs and perspectives.

ROLE OF EARLY EXECUTIVE PROCESSING, ATTENTION, AND LANGUAGE FOR ADOLESCENT EXECUTIVE FUNCTIONING

Early Executive Processing and Attention

We also have found significant models consistent with Barkley's framework (1997) that place emphasis on control of attention for understanding effective problem solving. In one model, deductive reasoning during adolescence was considered a form of cognitive flexibility and thus, a measure of later EF (Levin et al., 1991). Goal-directed play involving objects across 3, 4, and 6 years of age was examined as an early precursor of adolescent deductive reasoning in a latent growth curve model that included the attention measure from the CPT across middle childhood as a potential mediator. Early play predicted later deductive reasoning through its influence on attention skills that developed across middle childhood. This suggests that as children are able to develop and carry out play goals, they are building the capacity to focus and sustain attention in ways that promote better attention skills in later childhood. Play has been described by developmental psychologists as being of great importance in promoting cognitive development and ultimately appears to lead children to the development of skills necessary for more complex problem solving (Bruner, 1972). In this case, play appears to be promoting control of attention that, in turn, supports the young adolescent to use their attention and sequencing skills to more efficiently demonstrate deductive reasoning skills.

Language Skills

Language development also is described as being important for SR/EF, however, less is known about the pattern of influence across developmental periods. Previously we have mapped out the importance of language development across 2 and 3 years of age in predicting SR/EF skills prior to entry into Kindergarten (Landry et al., 2000). The importance of early language on later more complex EF skills across middle childhood was examined in relation to deductive reasoning in early adolescence through a latent growth curve model. Deductive reasoning again was measured by the 20 questions task. The findings showed that language during early childhood was important in understanding later reasoning skills. However, its impact occurred, in part, through its influence on EF skills, TOL, during middle childhood. Interestingly, unlike demands placed on the use of language for success on the deductive reasoning task, competency on the Tower of Language does not require using overt language. The findings support the notion that children are likely using internal language to solve the TOL problems and, together, their language and nonverbal problem-solving skills explain variability in competency in the deductive reasoning task.

Summary

The importance of early cognition and social interactions for the development of SR/EF skills is supported in our research as is the critical role language plays in this developmental process. There is some evidence of domain specific links with early cognitive skills being important for later cognitive

EF skills and early social skills establishing a foundation for later social competence and social problem solving. The findings described throughout the chapter highlight how skills developing in infancy and early childhood (e.g., social initiative, search tasks) are providing a foundation for SR/EF skills in middle childhood and early adolescence. SR/EF skills in the middle childhood period, in turn, support those developing in early adolescence. Parenting behaviors, specifically those that provide support for children's changing developmental needs also are important for understanding what promotes SR/EF skills. While there are key parenting behaviors that support growth in SR/EP skill development (e.g., maintaining attentional focus, verbal input), there are also parenting behaviors that interfere with, or hinder their development (e.g., high directiveness). Finally, the importance of longitudinal designs for revealing information about these developmental processes is clearly shown in our models. In addition, it is through longitudinal designs that researchers can further clarify the many remaining theoretical issues including identification of precursors for later SR and EF as well as developmental periods where the support of parenting behaviors for these constructs is most critical.

ACKNOWLEDGMENT

This research was supported in part by NIH HD25128.

REFERENCES

Ainsworth, M., Blehar, M., Waters, E., & Wall, S. (1978). *Patterns of attachment: A psychological study of the Strange Situation*. Hillsdale, NJ: Lawrence Erlbaum Associates.

Akhtar, N., Dunham, F., & Dunham, P. (1991). Directive interactions and early vocabulary development: The role of joint attentional focus. *Journal of Child Language, 18*, 41–49.

Allen, J., Hauser, S. T., Bell, K. L., & O'Connor, T. G. (1994). Longitudinal assessment of autonomy and relatedness in adolescent-family interactions as predictors of adolescent ego development and self-esteem. *Child Development, 65*, 179–194.

Astington, J. W. (2001). The future of theory-of-mind research: Understanding motivational states, the role of language, and real-world consequences. *Child Development, 72*(3), 685–687.

Astington, J. W., & Pelletier, J. (2005). Theory of mind, language, and learning in the early years: Developmental origins of school readiness. In B. D. Homer & C. Tamis-LeMonda (Eds.), *The development of social cognition and communication* (pp. 205–231). Hillsdale, NJ: Lawrence Erlbaum Associates.

Baldwin, D. A. (1994). Understanding the link between joint attention and language acquisition. In C. Moore & P. Dunham (Eds.), *Joint attention: Its origins and role in development* (pp. 131–158). Hillsdale, NJ: Lawrence Erlbaum Associates.

Bandura, A. (1986). *Social foundations of thought and action.* Engelwood Cliffs, NJ: Prentice-Hall.

Barkley, R. A. (1996). Linkages between attention and executive functions. In G. R. Lyons & N. A. Krasnegor (Eds.), *Attention, memory, and executive function* (pp. 307–325). Baltimore, MD: Paul H. Brookes.

Barkley, R. A. (1997). Behavioral inhibition, sustained attention, and executive functions: Constructing a unifying theory of ADHD. *Psychological Bulletin, 121,* 65–74.

Berk, L. E. (1986). Relationship of elementary school children's private speech to behavioral accompaniment to task, attention, and task performance. *Developmental Psychology, 22,* 671–680.

Block, J. H., & Block, J. (1980). The role of ego-control and ego-resiliency in the organization of behavior. In W. A. Collins (Ed.), *Minnesota symposia on child psychology* (pp. 39–101). Hillsdale, NJ: Lawrence Erlbaum Associates.

Bornstein, M., & Tamis-LeMonda, C. S. (1989). Maternal responsiveness and cognitive development in children. In M. H. Bornstein (Ed.), *Maternal responsiveness: Characteristics and consequences* (pp. 49–61). San Francisco, CA: Jossey-Bass.

Brown, A. L., & DeLoache, J. S. (1978). Skills, plans, and self-regulation. In R. S. Siegler (Ed.), *Children's thinking: What develops* (pp. 3–35). Hillsdale, NJ: Lawrence Erlbaum Associates.

Bruner, J. S. (1972). Nature and use of immaturity. *American Psychologist, 27,* 687–708.

Carlson, S. M., Mandell, D. J., & Williams, L. (2004). Executive function and theory of mind: Stability and Prediction form ages 2 to 3. *Developmental Psychology, 40,* 1105–1122.

Carlson, S. M., & Moses, L. J. (2001). Individual differences in inhibitory control and children's theory of mind. *Child Development, 72,* 1032–1053.

Connor-Smith, J. K., Compas, B. E., Wadsworth, M. E., Thomsen, A. H., & Saltzman, H. (2000). Response to stress in adolescence: Measurement of coping and involuntary stress response. *Journal of Consulting and Clinical Psychology, 68,* 976–992.

Cooke, R. W. I. (2004). Health, lifestyle, and quality of life for young adults born very preterm.

Archives of Disease in Childhood, 89, 201–206.

Denckla, M. B. (1996). A theory and model of executive function: A neuropsychological perspective. In G. R. Lyon & N. A. Krasnegor (Eds.), *Attention, memory, and executive function* (pp. 263–277). Baltimore, MD: Paul H. Brookes.

Dennis, M., Barnes, M. A., Wilkinson, M., & Humphreys, R. P. (1998). How children with head injury represent real and deceptive emotion in short narratives. *Brain and Language, 61,* 450–483.

Villier de s, J. G., & de Villiers, P. A. (2003). Language for thought: Coming to understand false beliefs. In D. Gentner & S. Goldin-Meadow (Eds.), *Language in mind: Advances in the study of language and cognition* (pp. 332–384). Cambridge, MA: MIT Press.

Diamond, A. (1988). Differences between adult and infant cognition: Is the crucial variable presence or absence of language? In L. Weiskrantz (Ed.), *Thought without language* p. 337–370). New York: Oxford University Press.

Dieterich, S. E., Hebert, H., Landry, S. H., Swank, P. R., & Smith, K. E. (2004). Maternal and child characteristics that influence the growth of daily living skills from infancy to school age in preterm and term children. *Early Education and Development, 15,* 283–304.

Feldman, R., & Klein, P. S. (2003). Toddlers' self-regulated compliance to mothers, caregivers, and fathers: Implications for theories of socialization. *Developmental Psychology, 39*(4), 680–692.

Flavell, J. H. (1971). First discussant's comments. What is memory development the development of? *Human Development, 14,* 272–278.

Garfield, J., Peterson, C., & Perry, T. (2001). Social cognition, language acquisition and the theory of mind. *Mind and Language, 16*(9), 494–541.

Gottman, J., Gonso, J., & Rasmussen, B. (1975). Social interaction, social competence, and friendship in children. *Child Development, 45,* 709–718.

Grusec, J. E., & Goodnow, J. J. (1994). Impact of parental discipline methods on the child's internalization of values: A reconceptualization of current points of view. *Developmental Psychology, 30,* 1–19.

Harris, P. L., & Kavanaugh, R. D. (1993). Young children's understanding of pretense. *Monographs of the Society for Research in Child Development, 58* (1, Serial No. 231), 1–231.

Hartig, M., & Kanfer, F. H. (1973). The role of verbal self-instructions in children's resistance to temptation. *Journal of Personality and Social Psychology, 25,* 259–267.

Herbert, H., Swank, P. R., Smith, K. E., & Landry, S. H. (2004). Maternal support for play and language across early development. *Early Education and Development, 15,* 93–113.

Hebert-Myers, H., Guttentag, C., Swank, P. R., Smith, K. E., & Landry, S. H. (2006). The importance of language, social, and behavioral skills across early and later childhood as predictors of social competence with peers. *Applied Developmental Science, 10,* 174–187.

Hughes, C. (1998). Finding your marbles: Does preschoolers' strategic behavior predict later understanding of mind? *Developmental Psychology, 34,* 1326–1339.

Huttonlocher, J., Haight, W., Bryk, A., Seltzer, M., & Lyons, T. (1991). Early vocabulary growth: Relation to language input and gender. *Developmental Psychology, 27,* 236–248.

Keller, M., Edelstein, W., Schmid, C., Fang, F., & Fang, G. (1998). *Developmental Psychology, 34,* 731–741.

Keenan, T. (2000). Mind, memory, and metacognition: The role of memory span in children's developing understanding of the mind. In J. W. Astington (Ed.), *Minds in the making. Essays in honor of David R. Olson* (pp. 233–249). Oxford, UK: Blackwell Publishing.

Klaczynski, P. A. (2001). Analytic and heuristic processing influences on adolescent reasoning and decision-making. *Child Development, 72,* 844–861.

Kochanska, G. (2002). Committed compliance, moral self, and internalization: A mediational model. *Developmental Psychology. 38*(3), 339–351.

Kochanska, G., & Murray, K. T. (2000). Mother-child mutually responsive orientation and conscience development: From toddler to early school age. *Child Development, 71*, 417–431.

Kohut, H. (1971). *The analysis of the self.* New York: International Universities Press.

Kopp, C. B. (1982). Antecedents of self-regulation: A developmental perspective. *Developmental Psychology, 18*(2) 199–214.

Kuczynski, L., & Kochanska, G. (1995). Function and content of maternal demands: Developmental significance of early demands for competent action. *Child Development, 66*, 616–628.

Kuczynski, L., Kochanska, G., Radke-Yarrow, M., & Girnius-Brown, O. (1987). A developmental interpretation of young children's noncompliance. *Developmental Psychology, 23*, 799-806.

Landry, S. H. (1995). The development of joint attention in preterm infants. Effects of maternal attention-directing behaviors. In C. Moore & P. Dunham (Eds.), *Joint attention: Origins and role in development* (pp. 223–250). Hillsdale, NJ: Lawrence Erlbaum Associates.

Landry, S. H., Leslie, N., Fletcher, J. M., & Francis, D. J. (1985). Effects of intraventricular hemorrhage on visual attention in very premature infants. *Infant Behavior and Development, 8*, 309–322.

Landry, S. H., Miller-Loncar, C. L., Smith, K. E., & Swank, P. R. (2002). The role of parenting in children's development of executive processes. *Developmental Neuropsychology, 21*(1), 15–41.

Landry, S. H., Robinson, S. S., Copeland, D., & Garner, P. W. (1993). Goal-directed behavior and perception of self-competence in children with Spina Bifida. *Journal of Pediatric Psychology, 18*, 389–396.

Landry, S. H., Smith, K. E., Miller-Loncar, C. L., & Swank, P. R. (1997): Predicting cognitive-linguistic and social growth curves from early maternal behaviors in children at varying degrees of biologic risk. *Developmental Psychology, 33* (6), 1–14.

Landry, S. H., Smith, K. E., Miller-Loncar, C. L., & Swank, P. R. (1998): The relation of change in maternal interactive styles with infants' developing social competence across the first three years of life. *Child Development, 69* (1), 105–123.

Landry, S. H., Smith, K. E, & Swank, P. R. (2006). Responsive parenting: Establishing early foundations for social, communication, and independent problem solving. *Developmental Psychology, 42*(4), 627–642.

Landry, S.H., Smith, K.E., & Swank, P.R. (2009). New directions in evaluating social problem solving in childhood: Early precursors and links to adolescent social competence. *New Directions for Child and Adolescent Development, 123*, 51–68.

Landry, S. H., Smith, K. E., Swank, P. R., Assel, M. A., & Vellet, S. (2001). Does early responsive parenting have a special importance for children's development or is consistency across early childhood necessary? *Developmental Psychology, 37*(3), 387–403.

Landry, S. H., Smith, K. E., Swank, P. R., & Miller-Loncar, C. L. (2000). Early maternal and child influences on children's later independent cognitive and social functioning. *Child Development, 71*, 358–375.

Leslie, A. M., & Polizzi, P. (1998). Inhibitory processing in the false belief task: Two conjectures. *Developmental Science, 1*, 247–253.

Levin, H. S., Culhane, K. A., Hartmann, J., Evankovich, K., Mattson, A. J., Harward, H., et al. (1991). Developmental changes in performance on tests of purported frontal lobe functioning. *Developmental Neuropsychology, 7*, 377–395.

Lezak, M. D. (1982). The problem of assessing executive functions. *International Journal of Psychology, 17*, 281–297.

Londerville, S., & Main, M. (1981). Security of attachment, compliance, and maternal training methods in the second year of life. *Developmental Psychology, 17*, 289–299.

Luria, A. R. (1973). *The working brain.* New York: Basic Books.

McCune-Nicolich, L. (1981). Toward symbolic functioning: Structure of early pretend games and potential parallels with language. *Child Development, 52*(3), 785–797.

Meins, E., Fernyhough, C., Wainwright, R., Clark-Carter, D., Gupta, M. D., Fradley, E., et al. (2003). Pathways to understanding mind: Construct validity and predictive validity of maternal mind-mindedness. *Child Development, 74*(4), 1194–1211.

Mischel, H. N., & Mischel, W. (1983). The development of children's knowledge of self-control strategies. *Child Development, 54*, 603–619.

Mischel, W., & Patterson, C. J. (1979). Effective plans for self-control in children. In W. A. Collins (Ed.), *Minnesota symposia on child psychology* (Vol 11, pp. 199–230). Hillsdale, NJ: Lawrence Erlbaum Associates.

Newcomb, A. F., Brady, J. E., & Hartup, W. W. (1979). Friendship and incentive condition as determinants of children's task-oriented social behavior. *Child Development, 50*, 878–881.

NICHD Early Childcare Research Network. (2005). Predicting individual differences in attention, memory, and planning in first graders from experiences at home, child care, and school. *Developmental Psychology, 41*, 99–114.

Parpal, M., & Maccoby, E. E. (1985). Maternal responsiveness and subsequent child compliance. *Child Development, 56*, 1326–1334.

Perlmutter, M., Behrend, S. D., Kuo, F., & Muller, A. (1989). Social influences on children's problem solving. *Developmental Psychology, 25*, 744–754.

Peterson, C., & Slaughter, V. (2003). Opening windows into the mind: Mothers' preferences for mental state explanations and children's theory of mind. *Cognitive Development, 18*, 399–429.

Posner, M. I. (1978). *Chronometric explorations of mind.* Hillsdale, NJ: Lawrence Erlbaum Associates.

Rueter, M. A., & Conger, R. D. (1998). Reciprocal influences between parenting and adolescent problem-solving behavior. *Developmental Psychology, 34*, 1470–1482.

Rourke, B. P., & Fuerst, D. R. (1991). *Learning disabilities and psychosocial functioning: A neuropsychological perspective.* New York: The Guilford Press.

Ruffman, T., Slade, L., & Crowe, E. (2002). The relation between children's and mothers' mental state language and theory-of-mind understanding. *Child Development, 73*(3), 734–751.

Senn, T. E., Espy, K. A., & Kaufman, P. M. (2004). Using path analysis to understand executive function organization in preschool children. *Developmental Neuropsychology, 26*, 445–464.

Smith, K. E., Landry, S. H., & Swank, P. R., (2000). Does the content of mothers' verbal stimulation explain differences in children's development of verbal and nonverbal cognitive skills? *Journal of School Psychology, 38* (1), 27–49.

Steelman, L. M., Assel, M. A., Swank, P. R., Smith, K. E., Landry, S. H. (2002). Early maternal warm responsiveness as a predictor of child social skills: Direct and indirect paths of influence over time. *Journal of Applied Developmental Psychology, 23*, 135–156.

Steinberg, L. (2001). We know some things: Parent-adolescent relations in retrospect and prospect. *Journal of Research on Adolescence, 11*, 1–20.

Steinberg, L. (2005). *Adolescence.* (7th ed.) New York: McGraw-Hill.

Steinberg, L., Dahl, R., Keating, D., Kupfer, D. J., Masten, A. S., & Pine, D. (2006). The study of developmental psychopathology in adolescence: Integrating affective neuroscience with the study of context. In D. Cicchetti & D. Cohen (Eds.), *Developmental psychopathology* (2nd ed., pp. 710–741). Hoboken, NJ: Worldcat.

Taylor, H. G., Klein, N., Minich, N., & Hack, M. (2000). Middle-school-age outcomes in children with very low birthweight. *Child Development, 71*, 1495–1511.

Taylor, H. G., Minich, N., Bangert, B., Filipek, P. A., & Hack, M. (2004). Long-term neuropsychological outcomes of very low birth weight: Associations with early risks for periventricular brain insults. *Journal of International Neuropsychological Society, 10*, 987–1004.

Thelan, E., & Smith, L. B. (1995). A dynamic systems approach to the development of cognition and action. Cambridge, MA: MIT Press.

Tomasello, M., & Farrar, J. (1986). Joint attention and early language. *Child Development, 57*, 1454–1463.

Vaughn, B. E., Kopp, C. B., & Krakow, J. B. (1984). The emergence and consolidation of self-control from eighteen to thirty months of age: Normative trends and individual differences. *Child Development, 55*, 990–1004.

Vygotsky, L. S. (1978). *Mind and society.* Cambridge, MA: Harvard University Press.

Weizman, Z. O., & Snow, C. E. (2001). Lexical input as related to children's vocabulary acquisition: Effects of sophisticated exposure and support for meaning. *Developmental Psychology, 37*, 265–279.

Welsh, M. C., & Pennington, B. F. (1988). Assessing frontal lobe functioning in children: Views from developmental psychology. *Developmental Neuropsychology, 4*, 199–230.

Welsh, M. C., Pennington, B. F., & Grosier, D. B. (1991). A normative developmental study of executive function: A window on the prefrontal function in children. *Developmental Neuropsychology, 7*, 131–149.

Wertsch, J. V. (1979). From social interaction to higher psychological processes. *Human Development, 22,* 1–22.

Weyandt, L. L., & Willis, W. G. (1994). Executive functions in school-aged children: Potential efficacy of tasks in discriminating clinical groups. *Developmental Neuropsychology, 10,* 27–38.

White, S. H. (1970). Some general outlines of the matrix of developmental changes between five and seven. *Bulletin of the Orton Society, 20,* 41–57.

Winnicott, D. W. (1971). *Playing and reality.* New York: Basic Books.

Wolf, D. P., Rygh, J., & Altshuler, J. (1984). Agency and experience: Actions and states in play narratives. In I. Bretherton (Ed.), *Symbolic play: The development of social understanding* (pp. 195–217). New York: Academic Press.

Zelazo, P. D. (1999). Language, levels of consciousness, and the development of intentional action. In P. D. Zelazo, J. W. Astington, & D. R. Olson (Eds.), *Developing theories of intention: Social understanding and self-control* (pp. 95–117). Mahwah, NJ: Lawrence Erlbaum Associates.

Zelazo, P. D., Carter, A., Reznick, J. S., & Frye, D. (1997). Early development of executive function: A problem-solving framework. *Review of General Psychology, 1,* 198–226.

17

Do Early Social Cognition and Executive Function Predict Individual Differences in Preschoolers' Prosocial and Antisocial Behavior?

CLAIRE HUGHES AND ROSIE ENSOR

Young children's social cognition, defined here as the understanding of mind and emotion, and their executive functions (EF) (i.e., the processes underlying flexible goal-directed actions) have been intensively researched over the past 20 years. Despite the rapid progress made within these fields, relatively few studies have examined the real-life significance of developmental changes or individual differences in either domain. These omissions are striking, given the fundamental importance of each domain for human social interaction: deficits in social cognition are, for example, thought to underpin the profound social impairments in childhood autism (e.g., U. Frith & C. Frith, 2001); likewise, damage to this brain to the prefrontal cortex (a key neural substrate for EFs) has long been associated with major disturbance of behavioral and social functions (e.g., Eslinger, Biddle, & Grattan, 1997). This chapter aims to redress this neglect, and presents findings from recent longitudinal research on how individual differences in social cognition and EF help explain and predict individual differences in children's social behaviors, both positive and negative. To this end, the chapter is divided into four sections.

In the first section of this chapter we briefly summarize evidence that suggests an age-related differentiation of children's understanding of mind versus emotion, as well as evidence for close functional ties between both developmental changes and individual differences in children's understanding of mind and their EF skills. The second and third sections of this chapter focus on relations between individual differences in social cognition/EF and behavior in the toddler and preschool years. We begin each section with an outline of key findings from previous studies. Next we summarize findings from an ongoing longitudinal investigation that has, we think, several noteworthy strengths. These include the involvement of an "at risk" sample (with a high proportion of children from disadvantaged families); the use of novel cognitive measures; and the inclusion of multi-method, multi-informant aggregate indices for both prosocial and antisocial behavior. The findings we present demonstrate independent and interacting relations between early social cognition and later behavior. To refine our account of these relationships we next describe age-related shifts and present evidence for mediation effects. The fourth and final section of this chapter provides an integrative perspective; here, the guiding question concerns the extent to which specific cognitive skills show common or distinct patterns of influence on positive versus negative social behaviors.

Social Cognition: Divisions and Associations with Executive Function

DIVISIONS: DIFFERENTIATING BETWEEN UNDERSTANDING OF MIND AND EMOTION

Although the term "social cognition" encompasses a broad set of skills including, for example, children's understanding of both cognitive and emotional states, research in this field has relied heavily on a narrow set of tasks (in particular, tests of children's understanding of mistaken or "false" belief). Observational research has shown that although most children do not pass standard false-belief tasks until the age of 4 (Wellman, Cross, & Watson, 2001), from as early as 2 years children show some grasp of others' beliefs in their everyday social interactions: they engage in deception and trickery (Newton, Reddy, & Bull, 2000) and blame others for their own transgressions (Dunn, 1988; Wilson, Smith, & Ross, 2003). Rather than being simple behavioral routines to achieve desired and avoid undesired outcomes, such behaviors appear to reflect young children's deliberate attempts to create false beliefs in others (Newton et al., 2000). Since naturalistic observations suggest that young children have some understanding of false beliefs, their poor performance on formal tests may reflect the significant peripheral linguistic and information-processing task-demands (Bloom & German, 2000; Leslie & Polizzi, 1998; Siegal & Beattie, 1991). In support of this view, 3-year-olds appear more likely to succeed on false-belief tasks that have improved ecological validity (Cassidy, 1998; Chandler, Fritz, & Hala, 1989; Hala & Chandler, 1996; Hala,

Chandler, & Fritz, 1991; Wimmer & Perner, 1983) or that are administered using nonverbal paradigms (e.g., Carlson, Wong, Lemke, & Cosser, 2005).

Research into young children's early-appearing understanding of belief suggests a close entwinement with their knowledge of feelings: displays of deception or trickery are often most evident within emotionally charged interactions (Dunn, 1991), while children often evoke cognitions such as memories of past events to explain current (negative) emotions (Lagattuta & Wellman, 2001). Both 2- and 3-year-olds commonly succeed simple tests of emotion understanding (Denham, 1986), suggesting that emotion understanding tasks may offer a fruitful way of broadening assessments social cognition. Nevertheless, the exact relationship between children's understanding of belief and emotion has yet to be established. Indeed, there is experimental evidence to suggest that children's understanding of emotion and belief are distinct domains (Cutting & Dunn, 1999) with differential sequelae (Dunn, 1995). What is now needed is longitudinal research to assess whether these competing perspectives can be reconciled within a developmental framework. Below we briefly summarize findings from our recent work that suggest that children's understanding of mind and emotion are initially functionally interdependent, but become increasingly differentiated during development.

We used factor analyses to explore the relationship between children's performances at ages 2, 3, and 4 on theory of mind (ToM) and emotion understanding tasks. At age 2, ToM and emotion understanding task scores loaded onto a single factor that accounted for 51% of the variance; in contrast, at ages 3 and 4 the task scores yielded two distinct factors for ToM and emotion understanding that together accounted for 57% of the variance at age 3 and 62% of the variance at age 4. These results were unchanged when effects of verbal ability were controlled. A direct comparison of the strength between ToM and emotion understanding also supported this model of progressive differentiation; calculation using Fischer's r to z transforms showed that this correlation was significantly stronger at age 2 ($r = 0.55$, $p < 0.01$) than at age 4 ($r = 0.35$, $p < 0.01$; $z = 1.98$, $p < 0.05$).

ASSOCIATIONS BETWEEN THEORY OF MIND AND EXECUTIVE FUNCTION

Although at first glance quite distinct, several lines of evidence from studies of preschoolers suggest that the constructs of ToM and EF are in fact closely related. As detailed elsewhere (Hughes & Ensor, 2008), this evidence includes the following: parallel age-related improvements; robust correlations between individual differences in ToM and EF that are independent of covarying effects of verbal ability and apply equally to preschoolers in distinct cultural communities; longitudinal predictive associations between early EF and later ToM (but not vice-versa); micro-genetic findings that improvements in false-belief comprehension follow improvements in inhibitory control; changes in performance on ToM tasks when the need to resist a prepotent response is changed; and improvements in performance on tests of both ToM and EF following training.

A robust association between individual differences in ToM and EF has recently been reported for 2-year-olds (Hughes & Ensor, 2005). The similarity between the findings from this study and those from previous studies of preschoolers suggests that the mechanisms underpinning individual differences in ToM and EF are developmentally stable. To examine this proposal directly, we conducted a longitudinal follow-up study, assessing individual differences in ToM and EF in this sample at two further time-points (ages 3 and 4). Cross-lagged analyses demonstrated reciprocal predictive relations between ToM and EF at these time-points that remained significant when covarying effects of individual differences in verbal ability and family background were taken into account (Hughes & Ensor, 2007b). At a practical level, this close reciprocal relation is important as it indicates that each domain may show closely overlapping relationships with either prosocial or antisocial behavior; it is therefore imperative to examine these relationships in tandem.

Social Cognition and Prosocial Behaviors

Prosocial behaviors are actions (such as sharing, comforting and helping) that benefit others. Beyond their positive consequences for children's social partners, prosocial behaviors also bring significant developmental benefits to the children themselves. Children who are characterized by prosocial proclivity typically enjoy frequent positive interactions with their peers (Farver & Branstetter, 1994; Howes & Matheson, 1992) and siblings (Dunn & Munn, 1986) that afford a context for social and emotional growth (Newcomb & Bagwell, 1998).

Young children display striking individual differences in prosocial behaviors, perhaps reflecting individual differences in social cognition: the "cognitive act of imagining oneself in another's place" (Hoffman, 1982, p. 284) may, for example, be a prerequisite for prosocial behaviors. Consistent with this claim, an early meta-analysis (Underwood & Moore, 1982) found a modest but significant relationship between perspective-taking skills and children's prosocial overtures. However, little subsequent research has addressed the potential significance of individual differences in social cognition in the toddler years.

EARLY SOCIAL COGNITION AS A PREDICTOR OF PROSOCIAL BEHAVIOR: INDEPENDENT AND INTERACTING EFFECTS

One of the first studies of the relationship between early social cognition and prosocial behavior reported a significant positive correlation between emotion understanding and 2-year-olds' prosocial responses to others' emotions (Denham, 1986); a second later study (Ensor & Hughes, 2005) showed that this correlation was independent from covarying effects of verbal ability. Extending these findings with a larger and more representative sample, our own recent work has revealed a significant predictive relationship between age-2 emotion understanding and age-4 prosocial behavior (rated by both mothers and teachers); this relationship remained significant when effects of age, verbal ability and, notably, initial levels of prosocial behaviors were all taken into account (Ensor & Hughes, submitted). In other words, early emotion understanding appears to be a distinct and robust independent predictor of children's prosocial behavior at the start of school.

Beyond a simple independent effect it seems likely that the influence of social cognition upon prosocial behavior will also show an interplay with the effects of family function; however this proposal has yet to be examined directly. As a first step toward addressing this gap we examined whether the relation between social cognition and prosocial behavior is moderated by individual differences in the "mutuality" of mother-child relationships. To achieve an operational definition of mutuality we indexed four co-occurring behaviors as follows: (1) caregiver responsiveness to child, (2) child responsiveness to caregiver, (3) dyadic reciprocity, and (4) dyadic cooperation. Each of these indices was coded from 30-min videos of mother-child interaction during a "tidy up" paradigm, conducted in a university playroom (see Figure 17.1 for a storyboard example of mother-child interaction).

In Frames 1 and 2 of Figure 17.1 the mother suggests to her child that they should tidy and the child agrees. The child makes an additional suggestion and the mother agrees (Frames 2 and 3); these are examples of cooperation. Frame 5 shows the child throwing the baby doll into the box. As the mother comments on the bump the baby doll received, the child looks up and the mother and child make eye contact (Frames 6 and 7); this is an example of reciprocity. Frame 8 shows the child following the mother's suggestion and kissing the baby; this is an example of child responsiveness. The mother then names the next toy to be placed in the box and the child agrees (Frame 9—this is another example of cooperation and child responsiveness). Frame 10 shows the child suggesting taking a toy apart and Frame 11 shows the mother responding; this is an example of mother responsiveness. Frame 12 shows the mother and child placing the toy in the box.

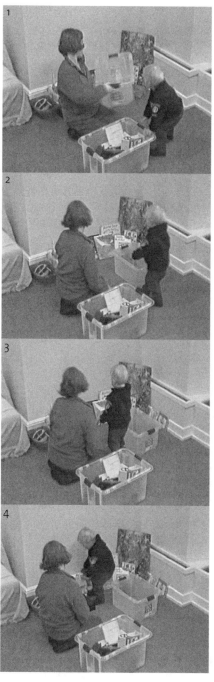

Mother : *Now I think we should put the baby away as well, because although we didn't play with the baby, I think the baby lives in this box. Can you put the baby in this box for me?*

Child: *Yeah, and the cot.*

Mother : *And the cot, yeah, I think it probably all goes in.*

FIGURE 17.1. Mother/child responsiveness and dyadic reciprocity/cooperation.

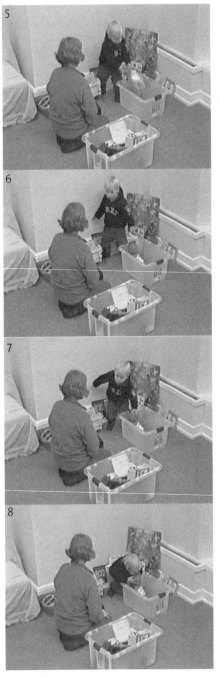

Mother: *Oh poor baby. Banged his head. Are you going to give it a kiss better?*

Figure 17.1. (*Continued*)

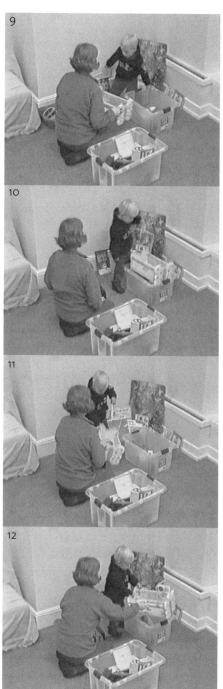

9

Mother : *And this bed?*
Child: *Yeah.*

10

Child: *Take to bits mummy, take to bits.*

11

Mother : *Yes, I don't think all the bits come apart. Do you think this comes out? Not sure? I think we'll leave this one all together because I don't know how it all breaks up.*

12

FIGURE 17.1. (*Continued*)

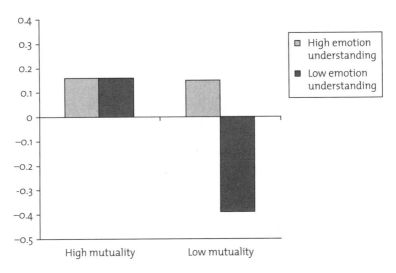

FIGURE 17.2. Mother-child mutuality moderates associations between age-2 emotion understanding and age-2 and age-4 prosocial behavior.

Caregivers who respond to the desires of their children promote a context in which children respond to their parents' needs (Maccoby & Martin, 1983); such reciprocal family interactions may result in children adopting a general set of prosocial values (Kochanska, 1997; Maccoby, 1992). This effect is likely to attenuate associations between social cognition and prosocial behaviors. In support of this hypothesis, our results indicated that mutuality moderated the influence of age-2 emotion understanding upon age-4 prosocial behavior, such that only the dual disadvantage of limited emotion understanding *and* low levels of mutuality predicted children's reduced levels of prosocial behaviors (Ensor & Hughes, submitted). This result is illustrated in Figure 17.2. Mutuality appeared to mask associations between emotion understanding and prosocial behavior, by compensating for less advanced emotion understanding (see the second bar of Figure 17.2). Equally, 2-year-olds' emotion understanding seemed to provide a buffer against the effect of low mutuality (see the third bar of Figure 17.3).

AGE-RELATED SHIFTS IN THE RELATIONSHIP BETWEEN SOCIAL COGNITION AND PROSOCIAL BEHAVIOR

Two strands of research indicate that, despite their considerable overlap, emotion understanding and false-belief comprehension may, by the preschool years, be quite separate skills. First, seemingly strong and reciprocal relations

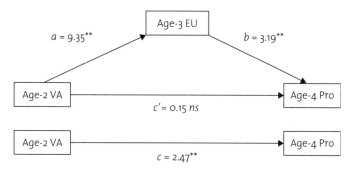

Key: VA = Verbal Ability; EU = Emotion Understanding; Pro = Prosocial

FIGURE 17.3 Age-3 emotion understanding mediates the association between age-2 verbal ability and age-4 prosocial behavior.

between emotion and false-belief comprehension have been found to be greatly attenuated once covarying effects of age, verbal ability, and family background were taken into account (Cutting & Dunn, 1999). Second, emotional but not cognitive perspective-taking has been found to show a robust association with prosocial behavior (Denham, 1986; Iannotti, 1985). Our earlier reported factor analytic findings support this distinction in preschoolers, but indicate that younger children may show a less differentiated understanding of cognitive versus emotional states.

Relations between emotion understanding, false-belief comprehension, and prosocial behavior may reflect underlying effects of linguistic competence (e.g., Cassidy, Werner, Rourke, Zubernis, & Balaraman, 2003). Dunn and Cutting (1999), for example, found that good performance on tasks tapping ToM, emotion understanding and verbal ability were all related to increased occurrence of children's cooperative play with friends and, importantly, that it was not possible to tease apart the relative contribution of each domain. Other researchers (e.g., Cassidy et al., 2003) have demonstrated that the associations between ToM abilities and children's prosocial behaviors diminish when verbal mental age is taken into account. With regard to the association between emotion knowledge and social skills, studies of different age-groups have produced contrasting findings. In particular, this association appears independent of verbal ability for school-aged children (Mostow, Izard, Fine, & Trentacosta, 2002) but not for preschoolers (Cassidy et al., 2003).

Here, we ask whether the posited progressive differentiation of verbal ability, emotion understanding, and false-belief comprehension is reflected in age-related shifts in the correlates of prosocial behavior? Specifically, we examined the correlations between individual differences in prosocial behavior and in children's understanding of emotion versus false belief at ages 3- and 4-years. At age 3 the relationships between these measures were modest and overlapped with associations with verbal ability suggesting that, in terms of prosocial behavior, children's early emotion comprehension, false-belief understanding, and verbal ability were enmeshed. In contrast, individual differences in prosocial behavior at age 4 showed significantly stronger correlations with emotion understanding at ages 3 and 4 than with false-belief comprehension at either age. These results were unchanged when effects of verbal ability were controlled. In sum, beyond the age of 3, individual differences in children's emotion understanding and false-belief comprehension appear to cleave in their relations with prosocial behavior.

Interestingly, cross-lagged regression analyses indicated that children's emotion understanding promoted prosocial behavior. We found no evidence in favor of the alternative interpretation, namely that children's emotion comprehension is heightened through their prosocial acts. Instead, age-3 emotion understanding predicted age-4 prosocial behavior even when effects of age-3 prosocial behavior were taken into account. Taken together these findings suggest that children who were skilled in emotional perspective-taking were more likely to engage in prosocial behaviors; however emotion comprehension was not improved through engagement in prosocial acts.

SOCIAL COGNITION MEDIATES RELATIONS BETWEEN VERBAL ABILITY AND PROSOCIAL BEHAVIOR

Longitudinal studies of school-aged children have demonstrated that emotion knowledge mediates associations between verbal mental age and children's social competence (e.g., Mostow et al., 2002). Likewise, Ensor and Hughes (submitted) reported that toddlers' emotion understanding mediated concurrent associations between individual differences in verbal ability and in prosocial behavior. In our recent work we also observed that association between early individual differences in verbal ability and in prosocial behavior could be explained in terms of an underlying relation between emotion understanding and prosocial behavior (Ensor et al., submitted; Ensor & Hughes, submitted). To test this proposal we used a bootstrapping method (Preacher & Hayes, 2004), in which our independent variable was age-2 verbal ability, our dependent variable was age-4 prosocial behavior, our posited mediator was age-3 emotion understanding, and our covariate was age-2 prosocial behavior. The results from this analysis are illustrated in Figure 17.3 and indicate that age-3 emotion understanding fully mediated the relationship between age-2 verbal ability and the change in prosocial behavior from ages 2 to 4.

Social Cognition and Problem Behaviors

The number of children with diagnosed disruptive behavioral disorders (e.g., attention-deficit hyperactivity disorder [ADHD], conduct disorder, and oppositional defiant disorder) has increased dramatically in recent years (Robison, Sclar, Skaer, & Galin, 1999). These disorders are linked with numerous negative long-term outcomes, including: school failure, substance abuse, criminal activity, and incarceration (Fergusson & Horwood, 1998; Fergusson & Lynskey, 1998; Mannuzza, Klein, Bessler, Malloy, & LaPadula, 1993; Mannuzza et al., 1991). Children with early-onset problem behaviors are especially likely to show a life-course persistent prognosis (Moffitt, 1990), and so targeting early-onset cases maximizes the potential gains of intervention programs.

Previous studies have shown that preschoolers with elevated problem behaviors demonstrate clear deficits in EF (e.g., Hughes & Dunn, 2000; Hughes, Dunn, & White, 1998; Moffitt, 1993; Pennington & Bennetto, 1993; Seguin, Boulerice, Harden, Tremblay, & Pihl, 1999). Evidence for an association between poor understanding of mind and problem behaviors is more mixed, at least for studies of school-aged children. For example, while children with conduct disorder are reported to show a theory of "nasty minds" (Happé & Frith, 1996), children with ADHD show no clear impairments in social cognition (Charman, Carroll, & Sturge, 2001; Perner, Kain, & Barchfield, 2002) and "ring-leader" bullies show intact or even superior understanding of mind (Sutton, Smith, & Swettenham, 1999a, 1999b). However, very few studies have examined the relationship between social cognition and problem behaviors in younger children.

EARLY SOCIAL COGNITION AS A PREDICTOR OF PROBLEM BEHAVIORS: INDEPENDENT AND INTERACTING EFFECTS

In one of the first studies of the relationship between social cognition and problem behaviors in very young children, individual differences in ToM skills at age 2 were found to show strong and specific associations with concurrent problem behaviors, as indexed by multi-informant, multi-measure, and multi-setting ratings (Hughes & Ensor, 2006). More recently we have extended this investigation to assess *predictive* relations, again using an aggregate index of problem behavior (that also included teacher ratings). Our analyses showed that age-2 ToM skills predicted age-4 problem behaviors, even when age-2 problem behaviors, family social disadvantage, harsh parenting, child age, verbal ability, and EF were all taken into account (Hughes & Ensor, 2007a). These striking findings suggest that early deficits in social cognition contribute to both concurrent and later problem behaviors, and predict increases in problem behaviors between the ages of 2- and 4-years.

Family factors are also known to contribute to individual differences in behavioral problems. The influence of distal family factors such as social disadvantage is thought to be mediated by negative parental attributes (e.g., Conger, Patterson, & Ge, 1995; Morrell & Murray, 2003; Webster-Stratton, 1990). Relatively few studies have, however, examined family and child influences upon problem behaviors in tandem.

In our present study we found that, at age 2, ToM skills and harsh parenting showed interacting associations with the following: (1) concurrent problem behaviors (Hughes & Ensor, 2006), (2) age-4 problem behaviors (Hughes & Ensor, 2007a), and (3) the change in problem behaviors between 2 and 4 years (Hughes & Ensor, 2007a). As illustrated in Figure 17.1, mean levels of problem behaviors were low for all children exposed to low levels of harsh parenting (regardless of ToM skills. For children exposed to medium levels of harsh parenting, raised problem behaviors were only found for children with poor ToM. For children exposed to high levels of harsh parenting, raised problem behaviors were found for children with poor to medium ToM, but not for children with good ToM. One plausible interpretation of this finding is that early ToM skills provide a buffer against the impact of harsh parenting. That is, the problems predicted by Patterson's (1981) model of "coercive cycles of violence" may be reduced when children have sufficient ToM skills to recognize and anticipate others' feelings and intentions; this interpretation highlights the real-life importance of individual differences in fledgling ToM skills. These findings are likely to be of considerable practical value, not least for identifying children who are especially likely to require support.

AGE-RELATED SHIFTS IN THE RELATIONSHIP BETWEEN SOCIAL COGNITION AND PROBLEM BEHAVIORS

Very few studies have examined individual differences in behavioral problems in relation to social cognition and EF in tandem; as a result, the independence of associations between deficits in social cognition and EF or problem behaviors remains in question. The findings of the two relevant studies here appear, at first glance at least, contradictory. As described earlier, individual differences in ToM but not EF at age 2 showed strong independent associations with problem behaviors, both concurrently (Hughes & Ensor, 2006) and at age-4 (Hughes & Ensor, 2007a). In contrast, a study of hard-to manage preschoolers observed playing with peers demonstrated robust and distinct associations between individual differences in EF (rather than ToM) and in angry, unsympathetic, and antisocial behaviors (Hughes et al., 2000).

How can these apparently paradoxical findings be reconciled? One possible explanation is that individual differences in problem behaviors show distinct cognitive correlates in toddler-hood and in the preschool years. This proposal is in line with recent theoretical accounts (based on studies of autism) that suggest that very early intuitive mentalizing has greater social salience than later explicit false-belief reasoning (e.g., C. Frith & U. Frith, 1999; Tager-Flusberg, 2001). In addition, tests of EF for very young children (e.g., Hughes & Ensor, 2005) are as yet in their infancy; it is therefore possible that the verbal demands of these tasks present a more significant constraint upon performance at age 2 than at older ages. To test this proposal we examined whether there was an age-related increase in the specificity of relations between EF and problem behaviors. We found that, in contrast with the findings at age 2, by age 4 the correlation between individual differences in EF and in behavioral problems remained significant even when individual differences in family disadvantage and related child characteristics (social cognition and verbal ability) were taken into account (Hughes & Ensor, 2008).

The developmental increase in the salience of EF for behavioral problems may reflect marked increases in children's self-regulatory capacities between the ages of 2 and 4 (e.g., Kopp, 1982; Zelazo & Jacques, 1997), such that by the start of school children are expected to regulate their expression of negative emotions (e.g., anger, distress) and of behavioral impulses (e.g., to run into the road, or to touch attractive but prohibited objects). Entry into the school system is a peak period for the diagnosis of externalizing problems (Mesman, Bongers, & Koot, 2001), and it seems likely that the need to comply with the more structured school environment makes the problems of children with poor self-regulatory skills more evident. That said, the results of our cross-lagged regression analyses indicated bidirectional associations between EF and problem behaviors at ages 3 and 4 (Hughes & Ensor, 2008). Thus, emerging EFs appeared to facilitate children's ability to regulate their behavior in everyday social situations; conversely, problem behaviors seemed to constrain children's developing EF skills, perhaps because of reduced participation in the kind of social interactions (e.g., collaborative, goal-directed activities) that foster the development of EF skills.

SOCIAL COGNITION MEDIATES RELATIONS BETWEEN
VERBAL ABILITY AND PROBLEM BEHAVIORS

In his early and seminal work on early EF, Luria (1966) proposed that a key function of language skills was to enable self-regulatory behavior. In support of this proposal, later studies (e.g., Berk, 1999; Winsler, Diaz, McCarthy, Atencio, & Chabay, 1999) have shown that children frequently display "private speech" when engaged in problem-solving or other goal-directed activities. We tested whether EF mediates the association between early verbal deficits and later problem behavior using Preacher and Hayes' (submitted) SPSS macros. Age-3 EF fully mediated the relationship between age-2 verbal deficits and both age-4 problem behaviors and the change in problem behaviors between the ages of 2 and 4 (Hughes & Ensor, 2008). These results support the view that the influence of verbal deficits on problem behavior reflects their impact on children's abilities to use language as a tool for self-regulation.

Similarities and Contrasts in Cognitive Predictors of Prosocial and Problem Behaviors

Thus far in this chapter we have presented findings that support the real-life significance of individual differences in both social cognition and EF for young children's everyday interactions with others, both positive and negative. In this section we aim to provide an integrative perspective on these findings, by considering the similarities and contrasts in the cognitive predictors of individual differences in prosocial and problem behaviors. We also discuss implications for the relationship between prosocial and problem behaviors, and outline ways in which the analyses reported here might be extended in future research.

COMMON PATTERNS OF INFLUENCE ON PROSOCIAL
AND PROBLEM BEHAVIORS

Our findings regarding the importance of individual differences in social cognition and/or EF for children's prosocial versus problem behaviors suggest several common conclusions. First, for each outcome, our findings highlight the importance of very early individual differences. Good emotion understanding at age 2 predicted both concurrent and later prosocial behaviors (and an increase in prosocial behaviors between 2 and 4). The consistency of the relationship between early emotion understanding and prosocial behavior at concurrent and later time-points supports and extends the findings from previous studies (e.g., Denham, 1986) and highlights the social impact of early individual differences in emotion understanding. Even more striking was the robust and independent relationship between poor understanding of mind at age 2 and both concurrent and later problem behaviors (as well as increases in problem behaviors between time-points); interestingly this relationship became less specific over time, such that individual differences in verbal ability at ages 3 and 4 fully accounted for the relationship between children's understanding of mind and individual differences in problem behaviors. The particularly prominent role played by individual differences in 2-year-olds' understanding of mind supports theoretical distinctions made (e.g., Hughes et al., 2005; Tager-Flusberg, 2001) between early intuitive mentalizing (affected in autism, and of profound social impact) and later, more explicit reasoning about false beliefs (affected by individual differences in children's social environments, and relatively modest in its unique impact on social relationships).

A second common conclusion across outcomes (prosocial vs. problem behaviors) was that family processes moderated the effects of early individual differences in social cognition. Specifically, as illustrated in Figures 17.2 and 17.4, exposure to a "dual disadvantage" of poor social cognition coupled with harsh or less mutual parent-child interactions was associated with both reduced prosocial behaviors and elevated problem behaviors. These findings are consistent with the consensus view from studies of individual differences in risk and resilience: individual risk factors have a cumulative impact, such that the number of risk factors (or the chronicity of exposure to risk factors) is more important than the specific nature of individual risk factors (Rutter et al., 1975; Sameroff, Seifer, Zax, & Barocas, 1987; Sanson, Oberklaid, Pedlow, & Prior, 1991). At a practical level, the finding that it is dual disadvantage that is associated with poor outcomes has direct implications for both identifying children most in need of support and for applying multi-pronged interventions to maximize the likelihood of intercepting negative developmental trajectories.

A third common conclusion from our longitudinal findings was that the nature and specificity of predictive relationships between cognitive performance and everyday behavior is developmentally sensitive. Specifically, the impact of emotion understanding and EF on behavioral outcomes initially showed considerable overlap with effects of verbal ability, but became increasingly differentiated; by age 4 emotion understanding and EF both showed relations with outcome measures that were independent of effects of verbal ability. Equally, within social cognition, individual differences in children's understanding of mind and emotion were initially closely entwined but

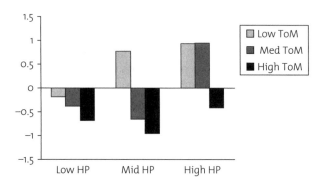

FIGURE 17.4. Harsh parenting moderates associations between age-2 theory of mind and age-2 and age-4 problem behavior.

became progressively differentiated; both from each other and in terms of their contrasting significance for individual differences in children's prosocial behaviors.

The fourth and final common conclusion from our findings was that the predictive relationships between age-2 verbal ability and age-4 behavioral measures were fully mediated by individual differences in either emotion understanding or EF at age 3. Thus very early individual differences in verbal ability have a largely indirect effect upon later individual differences in prosocial or problem behaviors; indicating that the mechanisms underpinning this predictive relationship are relatively complex. For example, rather than supporting a simple view of "good things go together," our findings indicate that it is how children *use* their early language skills (e.g., to engage in conversations about emotions and their causes, or to monitor and guide their goal-directed activities) that really matters for the success of their everyday social interactions.

IMPLICATIONS FOR THE RELATIONSHIP BETWEEN PROSOCIAL AND PROBLEM BEHAVIORS

Are problem and prosocial behaviors opposite ends of a continuum? In favor of this view, the absence of prosocial behavior in childhood predicts disruptive behavior (Hamalainen & Pulkkinen, 1996), and children with disruptive behaviors are less likely than other children to be prosocial (Hastings, Zahn-Waxler, Robinson, Usher, & Bridges, 2000; Hughes et al., 2000; Vinnick & Erickson, 1992). Supporting evidence was also found in the present study in that our two outcome measures showed significant inverse relations, both concurrently and across-time, suggesting that prosocial children typically showed low rates of problem behaviors (see also Hay & Pawlby, 2003). However, there is also evidence for a distinction between prosocial and problem behaviors; in that some children with behavioral problems appear to be as prosocial as other children (Del'Homme, Sinclair, & Kasari, 1994; Zahn-Waxler, Cole, Welsh, & Fox, 1995), suggesting that individual differences in problem versus prosocial behaviors may lie along orthogonal dimensions. Here again our findings provide some evidence for this proposal. Specifically, insofar as individual differences in prosocial and problem behaviors represent opposite ends of a single scale, common patterns of associations with social cognition and EF are predicted. However, our findings demonstrate the independence of relations between behavioral outcomes and specific cognitive domains. For example, individual differences in prosocial behaviors showed significantly stronger associations with individual differences in emotion understanding than in false-belief comprehension. In contrast, when effects of verbal ability were controlled, individual differences in problem behaviors were unrelated to individual differences in emotion understanding, but were significantly associated with both early understanding of mind and later EF. These findings suggest that problem and prosocial behavior do not share common cognitive underpinnings. What then explains the inverse association between these behavioral outcomes? One possible explanation is that children's displays of problem behaviors lead to reduced opportunities for positive social interactions that afford opportunities for prosocial behaviors. Conversely, prosocial behaviors elicit positive responses from others such that the frequency of conflict is minimized.

IMPLICATIONS FOR FUTURE RESEARCH

We hope the findings presented in this chapter will encourage others to bridge the gulf that exists between research focused on early cognitive development and investigations of individual differences in children's prosocial and/or problem behaviors. Our findings highlight the potential importance of early milestones in social cognition and EF for children's successful interactions with others, and indicate a number of interesting mechanisms that underpin individual differences in children's social behavior. These include independent and interacting effects of cognitive and family influences on behavior, as well as indirect pathways of influence, especially with regard to the influence of very early individual differences in verbal ability on later behavior. Of course, further work is needed; both to refine our understanding of this influence by adopting more fine-grained measures of specific prosocial and problem behaviors and to establish whether this influence extends beyond preschool into the early school years. It may also be worthwhile to go back as well as forward, by adopting new paradigms for investigating social cognition in infancy to explore the very early origins of individual differences in children's social behavior.

ACKNOWLEDGMENTS

This work was supported by a grant to the first author by The Health Foundation (543\1808). We thank the families who are participating in this ongoing study.

REFERENCES

Berk, L. (1999). Children's private speech: An overview of theory and the status of research. In P. Lloyd & C. Fernyhough (Eds.), *Lev Vygotsky: Critical assessments: Thought and language* (Vol. II, pp. 33–70). Florence, KY: Taylor & Frances/ Routledge.

Bloom, P., & German, T. (2000). Two reasons to abandon the false belief task as a test of theory of mind. *Cognition, 77*, B25–B31.

Carlson, S., Wong, A., Lemke, M., & Cosser, C. (2005). Gesture as a window on children's beginning understanding of false belief. *Child Development, 76*, 73–86.

Cassidy, K. (1998). Preschoolers' use of desires to solve theory of mind problems in a pretense context. *Developmental Psychology, 34*, 503–511.

Cassidy, K., Werner, R., Rourke, M., Zubernis, L., & Balaraman, G. (2003). The relationship between psychological understanding and positive social behaviors. *Social Development, 12*, 198–221.

Chandler, M., Fritz, A., & Hala, S. (1989). Small-scale deceit: Deception as a marker of two-, three-, and four-year-olds' early theories of mind. *Child Development, 60*, 1263–1277.

Charman, A., Carroll, F., & Sturge, C. (2001). Theory of mind, executive function and social competence in boys with ADHD. *Emotional and Behavioural Difficulties, 6*, 31–49.

Conger, R., Patterson, G., & Ge, X. (1995). It takes two to replicate: A mediational model for the impact of parents' stress on adolescent adjustment. *Child Development, 66*, 80–97.

Cutting, A., & Dunn, J. (1999). Theory of mind, emotion understanding, language, and family background: Individual differences and interrelations. *Child Development, 70*, 853–865.

Del'Homme, M., Sinclair, E., & Kasari, C. (1994). Preschool children with behavioral problems: Observation in instructional and free play contexts. *Behavioral Disorders, 19*, 221–232.

Denham, S. (1986). Social cognition, prosocial behavior, and emotion in preschoolers: Contextual validation. *Child Development, 57,* 194–201.

Dunn, J. (1988). *The beginnings of social understanding* (1st ed.). Cambridge, MA: Harvard University Press.

Dunn, J. (1991). Young children's understanding of other people: Evidence from observations within the family. In D. Frye & C. Moore (Eds.), *Children's theories of mind* (pp. 97–114). Hillsdale, NJ: Lawrence Erlbaum Associates.

Dunn, J. (1995). Children as psychologists: The later correlates of individual differences in understanding of emotions and other minds. *Cognition and Emotion, 9,* 187–201.

Dunn, J., & Cutting, A. (1999). Understanding others, and individual differences in friendship interactions in young children. *Social Development, 8,* 201–219.

Dunn, J., & Munn, P. (1986). Siblings and the development of prosocial behaviour. *International Journal of Behavioral Development, 9,* 265–284.

Ensor, R., & Hughes, C. (2005). More than talk: Relations between emotion understanding and positive behaviour in toddlers. *British Journal of Developmental Psychology, 23,* 343–363.

Ensor, R., & Hughes, C. (submitted). Mother-Child mutuality moderates relations between early emotion understanding and preschoolers' prosocial behaviour. "You feel sad?" Emotion understanding mediates effects of verbal ability and mother-child mutuality on prosocial behaviors: Findings from 2-to 4-years.

Eslinger, P., Biddle, K., & Grattan, L. (1997). Cognitive and social development in children with prefrontal cortex lesions. In G. R. Lyon & N. A. Krasnegor (Eds.), *Attention, memory and executive function* (pp. 295–335). *Baltimore, MD: Paul H. Brookes Publishing.*

Farver, J., & Branstetter, W. (1994). Preschoolers' prosocial responses to their peers' distress. *Developmental Psychology, 30,* 334–341.

Fergusson, D., & Horwood, L. (1998). Early conduct problems and later life opportunities. *Journal of Child Psychology and Psychiatry, 39,* 1097–1108.

Fergusson, D., & Lynskey, M. (1998). Conduct problems in childhood and psychosocial outcomes in young adulthood: A prospective study. *Journal of Emotional and Behavioural Disorders, 6,* 2–18.

Frith, C., & Frith, U. (1999). Interacting minds—a biological basis. *Science, 286,* 1692–1695.

Frith, U., & Frith, C. (2001). The biological basis of social interaction. *Current Directions in Psychological Science, 10,* 151–155.

Hala, S., & Chandler, M. (1996). The role of strategic planning in accessing false-belief understanding. *Child Development, 67,* 2948–2966.

Hala, S., Chandler, M., & Fritz, A. (1991). Fledgling theories of mind: Deception as a marker of three-year-olds' understanding of false belief. *Child Development, 62,* 83–97.

Hamalainen, M., & Pulkkinen, L. (1996). Problem behavior as a precursor of male criminality. *Development and Psychopathology, 8,* 443–455.

Happé, F., & Frith, U. (1996). Theory of mind and social impairment in children with conduct disorder. *British Journal of Developmental Psychology, 14*, 385–398.

Hastings, P., Zahn-Waxler, C., Robinson, J., Usher, B., & Bridges, D. (2000). The development of concern for others in children with behavior problems. *Developmental Psychology, 36*, 531–546.

Hay, D., & Pawlby, S. (2003). Prosocial development in relation to children's and mother's psychological problems. *Child Development, 74*, 1314–1327.

Hoffman, M. (1982). Development of prosocial motivation: Empathy and guilt. In N. Eisenberg (Ed.), *The development of prosocial behavior* (pp. 281–313). New York: Academic Press.

Howes, C., & Matheson, C. (1992). Sequences in the development of competent play with peers: Social and social pretend play. *Developmental Psychology, 28*, 961–974.

Hughes, C., & Dunn, J. (2000). Hedonism or empathy?: Hard-to-manage children's moral awareness, and links with cognitive and maternal characteristics. *British Journal of Developmental Psychology, 18*, 227–245.

Hughes, C., Dunn, J., & White, A. (1998). Trick or treat? Uneven understanding of mind and emotion and executive function among "hard to manage" preschoolers. *Journal of Child Psychology and Psychiatry, 39*, 981–994.

Hughes, C., & Ensor, R. (2005). Theory of mind and executive function in 2-year-olds: A family affair? *Developmental Neuropsychology, 28*, 645–668.

Hughes, C., & Ensor, R. (2006). Behavioural problems in two-year-olds: Links with individual differences in theory of mind, executive function and negative parenting. *Journal of Child Psychology and Psychiatry, 47*, 488–497.

Hughes, C., & Ensor, R. (2008). Does executive function matter for preschoolers' problem behaviors? *Journal of Abnormal Child Psychology, 36*, 1–14.

Hughes, C., & Ensor, R. (2007a). Positive and protective: Effects of early theory of mind on preschool problem behaviours. *Journal of Child Psychology and Psychiatry, 48*, 1025–1032.

Hughes, C., & Ensor, R. (2007b). Executive Function and Theory of Mind: Predictive relations from ages 2- to 4-years. *Developmental Psychology, 43*, 1447–1459.

Hughes, C., Jaffee, S., Happé, F., Taylor, A., Caspi, A., & Moffitt, T. (2005). Origins of individual differences in theory of mind: From nature to nurture? *Child Development, 76*, 356–370.

Hughes, C., White, A., Sharpen, J., & Dunn, J. (2000). Antisocial, angry and unsympathetic: "Hard to manage" preschoolers' peer problems, and possible social and cognitive influences. *Journal of Child Psychology and Psychiatry, 41*, 169–179.

Iannotti, R. (1985). Naturalistic and structured assessments of prosocial behavior in preschool children: The influence of empathy and perspective taking. *Developmental Psychology, 21*, 46–55.

Kochanska, G. (1997). Mutually responsive orientation between mothers and their young children: Implications for early socialisation. *Child Development, 68*, 94–112.

Kopp, C. (1982). Antecedents of self-regulation: A developmental perspective. *Developmental Psychology, 18*, 199–214.

Lagattuta, K., & Wellman, H. (2001). Thinking about the past: Early knowledge about links between prior experience, thinking and emotion. *Child Development, 72,* 82–102.

Leslie, A., & Polizzi, P. (1998). Inhibitory processing in the false-belief task: Two conjectures. *Developmental Science, 1,* 247–254.

Luria, A. R. (1966). *Higher cortical functions in man* (1st ed.). New York: Basic Books.

Maccoby, E. (1992). The role of parents in the socialization of children: An historical overview. *Developmental Psychology, 28,* 1006–1017.

Maccoby, E., & Martin, J. (1983). Socialisation in the context of the family: Parent-child interaction. In P. Mussen (Ed.), *Carmichael's manual of child psychology* (pp. 1–102) New York: Wiley.

Mannuzza, S., Klein, R. G., Bessler, A., Malloy, P., & LaPadula, M. (1993). Adult outcome of hyperactive boys: Educational achievement, occupational rank, and psychiatric status. *Archives of General Psychiatry, 50,* 565–576.

Mannuzza, S., Klein, R. G., Bonagura, N., Malloy, P., Giampino, T. L., & Addalli, K. A. (1991). Hyperactive boys almost grown up. V. Replication of psychiatric status. *Archives of General Psychiatry, 48,* 77–83.

Mesman, J., Bongers, I., & Koot, H. (2001). Preschool developmental pathways to preadolescent internalizing and externalizing problems. *Journal of Child Psychology and Psychiatry, 42,* 679–689.

Moffitt, T. (1990). Juvenile delinquency and attention deficit disorder: Boys' developmental trajectories from age 3 to age 15. *Child Development, 61,* 893–910.

Moffitt, T. (1993). The neuropsychology of conduct disorder. *Development & Psychopathology, 5,* 135–152.

Morrell, J., & Murray, L. (2003). Parenting and the development of conduct disorder and hyperactive symptoms in childhood: A prospective longitudinal study from 2 months to 8 years. *Journal of Child Psychology and Psychiatry, 44,* 489–508.

Mostow, A., Izard, C., Fine, S., & Trentacosta, C. (2002). Modeling emotional, cognitive, and behavioral predictors of peer acceptance. *Child Development, 73,* 1775–1787.

Newcomb, A., & Bagwell, C. (1998). The developmental significance of children's friendship relations. In W. Bukowski, A. Newcomb, & W. Hartup (Eds.), *The company they keep: Friendship in childhood and adolescence* (pp. 289–321). Cambridge, UK: Cambridge University Press.

Newton, P., Reddy, V., & Bull, R. (2000). Children's everyday deception and performance on false-belief tasks. *British Journal of Developmental Psychology, 18,* 297–317.

Patterson, G. R. (1981). *Coercive family process.* Eugene, OR: Castalia Press.

Pennington, B., & Bennetto, L. (1993). Main effects or transactions in the neuropsychology of conduct disorder. A commentary on the neuropsychology of conduct disorder. *Development and Psychopathology, 5,* 153–164.

Perner, J., Kain, W., & Barchfield, P. (2002). Executive control and higher-order theory of mind in children at risk of ADHD. *Infant and Child Development, Special Issue on Executive Functions and Development, 11,* 141–158.

Preacher, K., & Hayes, A. (2004). Asymptotic and resampling strategies for assessing and comparing indirect effects in simple and multiple mediator models. SPSS and SAS procedures for estimating indirect effects in simple mediation models. *Behavior Research Methods, Instruments & Computers, 36*, 717–731.

Robison, L. M., Sclar, D. A., Skaer, T. L., & Galin, R. S. (1999). National trends in the prevalence of attention-deficit/hyperactivity disorder and the prescribing of methylphenidate among school-age children. *Clinical Pediatrics, 38*, 209–217.

Rutter, M., Yule, B., Quinton, D., Rowlands, O., Yule, W., & Berger, W. (1975). Attainment and adjustment in two geographical areas, 3: Some factors accounting for area differences. *British Journal of Psychiatry, 126*, 520–533.

Sameroff, A., Seifer, R., Zax, M., & Barocas, R. (1987). Early indicators of developmental risk: Rochester longitudinal study. *Schizophrenia Bulletin, 13*, 383–394.

Sanson, A., Oberklaid, F., Pedlow, R., & Prior, M. (1991). Risk indicators: Assessment of infancy predictors of pre-school behavioural maladjustment. *Journal of Child Psychology and Psychiatry, 32*, 609–626.

Seguin, J. R., Boulerice, B., Harden, P. W., Tremblay, R. E., & Pihl, R. O. (1999). Executive functions and physical aggression after controlling for attention deficit hyperactivity disorder, general memory and IQ. *Journal of Child Psychology and Psychiatry, 40*, 1197–1208.

Siegal, M., & Beattie, K. (1991). Where to look first for children's knowledge of false beliefs. *Cognition, 38*, 1–12.

Sutton, J., Smith, P., & Swettenham, J. (1999a). Bullying and "theory of mind: A critique of the 'social skills deficit'" view of anti-social behaviour. *Social Development, 8*, 117–127.

Sutton, J., Smith, P., & Swettenham, J. (1999b). Social cognition and bullying: Social inadequacy or skilled manipulation? *British Journal of Developmental Psychology, 17*, 435–450.

Tager-Flusberg, H. (2001). A re-examination of the theory of mind hypothesis of autism. In J. Burack, T. Charman, N. Yirmiya, & P. Zelazo (Eds.), *The development of autism: Perspectives from theory and research* (pp. 173–194). Mahwah, NJ: Lawrence Erlbaum Associates.

Underwood, B., & Moore, B. (1982). Perspective-taking and altruism. *Psychological Bulletin, 91*, 143–173.

Vinnick, L., & Erickson, M. (1992). Relationships among accumulated lifetime life events, prosocial skills, and behavior problems in elementary school children. *Journal of Child and Family Studies, 1*, 141–154.

Webster-Stratton, C. (1990). Long-term follow-up of families with young conduct problem children: From preschool to grade school. *Journal of Clinical Child Psychology, 19*, 144–149.

Wellman, H., Cross, D., & Watson, J. (2001). Meta-analysis of theory of mind development: The truth about false belief. *Child Development, 72*, 655–684.

Wilson, A., Smith, M., & Ross, H. (2003). The nature and effects of young children's lies. *Social Development, 12*, 21–45.

Wimmer, H., & Perner, J. (1983). Beliefs about beliefs: representation and constraining function of wrong beliefs in young children's understanding of deception. *Cognition, 13*, 103–128.

Winsler, A., Diaz, R. M., McCarthy, E. M., Atencio, D. J., & Chabay, L. A. (1999). Mother-child interaction, private speech, and task performance in preschool children with behaviour problems. *Journal of Child Psychology and Psychiatry, 40*, 891–904.

Zahn-Waxler, C., Cole, P., Welsh, J., & Fox, N. (1995). Psychophysiological correlates of empathy and prosocial behaviors in preschool children with behavior problems. *Development and Psychopathology, 7*, 27–48.

Zelazo, P., & Jacques, S. (1997). Children's rule use: Representation, reflection and cognitive control. In R. Vasta (Ed.), *Annals of child development: A research annual* (Vol. 12, pp. 119–176). Bristol, PA: Jessica Kingsley Publishers.

INDEX